ISBN 978-0-265-97101-7
PIBN 10917452

BIENNIAL REPORT

OF THE

SUPERINTENDENT

OF

Public Instruction,

OF

NORTH CAROLINA,

FOR THE

SCHOLASTIC YEARS 1896-'97 AND 1897-'98.

RALEIGH:
GUY V. BARNES, PRINTER TO COUNCIL OF STATE.
1898.

29188

STATE OF NORTH CAROLINA,
DEPARTMENT OF PUBLIC INSTRUCTION.

RALEIGH, N. C., Dec. 1, 1898.

To His Excellency, DANIEL L. RUSSELL,
Governor of North Carolina.

DEAR SIR: In accordance with Section 2540 of the Code, I have the honor to submit my Biennial Report for the scholastic years 1896–'97, and 1897–'98.

In this report will be found recommendations such as seem to me, after careful thought and consideration, best for the advancement of the cause of public education in our State.

Very respectfully,
C. H. MEBANE,
Superintendent Public Instruction.

INTRODUCTION.

It has been my purpose in this, my first Biennial Report, not only to give information to the General Assembly as to the condition of our public schools, and to recommend further legislation needed, as my predecessors have done; but in addition to this I have attempted to secure valuable historical information pertaining to public schools, city schools, private schools, academies and colleges.

I wish to express my gratitude and appreciation to the various friends who have so generously aided me in this work.

C. H. MEBANE,
Superintendent Public Instruction.

RECOMMENDATIONS TO THE GENERAL ASSEMBLY OF NORTH CAROLINA.

STATE BOARD OF EXAMINERS.

The present State Board of Examiners is composed of the Superintendent of Public Instruction, *ex-officio* Chairman; Prof. W. L. Poteat, of Wake Forest College; Prof. L. L. Hobbs, Guilford College, and Prof. M. C. S. Noble, of the University.

This Board should be kept, and its powers increased instead of being diminished. The present Board has prepared an outline Course of Study for our Public School Teachers. Eight thousand copies were publiehed and distributed throughout the different counties in the State. This will prove to be a stimulus to the teachers, and much self-improvement and study witl follow as a result.

Examinations for all teachers in public schools should be prepared by this State Board of Examiners.

I advise that we have a uniform examination for the entire State prepared by this Board twice each year, instructions sent ont with the questions as to grading. Then let these certificates granted under these uniform examinations be good for one year in any county in the State, by making it the duty of the Supervisor to endorse every such certificate presented to him by teachers from any other county, unless he has information that such teacher or teachers are morally disqualified in any way; then he shall refuse to endorse such certificates. In cases where it can be shown that the applicant could not, for any cause, take either of the uniform examinations, then let the County Supervisor give examination and certificate, good for his county alone.

This Board should also prepare the Course of Study for the Colored Normal Schools of the State, and arrange a systematic course of work to be done in the County Institutes for teachers, of both races, in the public schools.

No school supplies, such as charts, maps, globes, blackboards and desks, should be allowed to be sold for use of public schools by any school-supply house, or their agents, unless such goods and prices are recommended by the State Board of Examiners as a body sitting for transaction of business.

One of the most sacred duties the Legislature has to perform is to enact a law which will stop the squandering of the public school fund for school supplies.

How many thousand dollars of the poor, helpless children's money have been squandered nnder the head of "School Supplies."

The Committeemen, I take it for granted, do not mean to waste the money of the children, as they often do, but they are simply deceived and led into contracts by shrewd agents. These Committeemen, I feel sure, are surprised at their own actions, after they sit down and reflect for a few moments. Then let this State Board of Examiners be the means of protection to the Committeemen as well as for the children.

At present there is no compensation for the members of this Board except their hotel and railroad fare. It would be well to allow a reasonable compensation to all the members, except the Superintendent of Public Instruction, if these additional duties that I have recommended are added.

COUNTY BOARD OF EDUCATION.

I advise that the County Board of Education be required to publish an itemized statement annually of the receipts and disbursements of the School Fund. The public have a perfect right to know how and for what every cent of the public school fund is spent. The reports for years in the office of Superintendent Public Instruction show that thousands and thousands of dollars have been spent in the columns marked "Paid for other Purposes."

If every one of these "purposes" were published in the counties, I think it would cause the fund to be spent more wisely and more carefully than it has been in some instances in the past.

The County Board of Education should be required to keep posted in every public school-house a list of the text books adopted to be used in the schools. The name of each book should be given and the price to be paid for it by the children.

This should be done as a matter of convenience to teachers and the children. It should be done especially as a matter of protection to parents in the purchase of books for their children. We heard of book dealers charging parents more for the books than the contract price. This could not be done if the teachers had the list published on stiff pasteboard and hung up in each school-house, because the parents as well as teachers and children would know just what the price of each book is, and could not be imposed upon by the dealer or any one else as to prices of books.

According to Sec. 770 of the Code, the County Treasurer is ex-officio the County Treasurer of the County Board of Education, and the commission of this treasurer of the school fund is fixed by County Commissioners.

Or, in other words, the treasurer who serves the Board of Education has his commission of the school fund fixed by a board who have nothing to do with the school fund. This commission on the school fund should be fixed by the County Board of Education.

I recommend that the treasurer of the school fund be elected by the County Board of Education, and that he be a man separate and apart from the County Treasurer, who handles the general fund of the county.

The County Board of Education is responsible for the school fund, and should have authority over the man who handles this fund more than they now have.

This treasurer of the school fund must be a bonded officer, of course.

The main reason why we should have a treasurer of the school fund, is that in some counties the Sheriff is County Treasurer as well as Sheriff, and often the school fund is mixed up with the county fund. This mixture occurs even where there are County Treasurers.

And again, if any fund in the county is to be borrowed, or needed for something else in the county, we find that the school fund is used first, last and all the time for these emergencies. Let us have a separate officer for this school fund. Let the County Commissioners build their bridges and their roads, but let us shut them out from our public school fund.

Some of the connty treasurers in North Carolina will oppose this plan because it means a decrease in their salaries. Some members of the Legislature will not vote for it because the county politicians will oppose, but I am for it because I believe it is the right thing to do. I believe it will save money for the schools. I know we would have less trouble in getting reports from the counties.

I now have letters from Treasurers of counties from which no report of the school fund was made last year, and none this year; and why? Because they say their predecessors mixed the school fund with other funds; that some of the school fund was used or borrowed for this purpose or for that purpose.

We have only to look over the records in the office here to see how this loose management of the school fund has gone on for twenty years.

In the name of the school children of North Carolina, I ask that we have this fund kept separate and distinct. Let us see to it that when the school year closes that the Superintendent of Public Instruction will have a report of the school fund from ninety-six counties.

Give us this separate treasurer of the school fund for the County Board of Education, and we will have no more of this borrowing and mixing of the most sacred public money that any county has.

AS TO SUPERVISORS.

Elsewhere I have recommended additional powers and duties in reference to the apportionment of the school fund and the employment of teachers.

I wish now to make some recommendations as to the qualification and election of the Supervisors.

In the first place, no man should be eligible to the office of County Supervisor unless he is a graduate from some college, or if not a graduate, he shall, at least, first be required to take the examinatian for life certificate, and if not competent to pass this examination he shall not be eligible to this important office.

We have some well educated, well qualified Supervisors; men who have done faithful work and are prepared for this work; some men who are making themselves felt among their teachers and the people of their counties, but we have not ninety-six such men, and this is what we want and must have.

I know that there is at least one good, strong school man to be found in every county in the State. In most of our counties there are numerous strong school men. Has North Carolina ever had ninety-six of these strongest school men for County Superintendents, or County Examiners, or for County Supervisors? If not, then why not?

In numerous cases, of course, the best men for the places would not accept them, because of the worry and small compensation.

In numerous cases the best men for these places have never had an opportunity to fill the positions.

Why have not the men best qualified to fill these positions been elected in every county in North Carolina ever since we had the office of County Superintendent, of County Examiner, and of County Supervisor? I am sorry to tell those of you why, who do not already know, but I will do it. Politics was the cause, and is the cause to-day.

The public schools have been in the galling grasp of the court-house politicians for twenty years in some of the counties.

The County Supervisor owes his election, both directly and indirectly, to the county officers. These are the masters he is supposed to serve; these are the men to whom he must render an account of his stewardship.

Away with such. Let us break away from this court-house ring business.

Let the Supervisor render his account to the teachers, to the children and to the parents. Yea, let him render his account to all the people of his county, not in the interest of half dozen men about the court-house, but in the interest and progress of public education of his entire county, regardless of any political party or power.

To this end I recommend that we elect the County Supervisor by the teachers and educators of the county. Let each first-grade certificate public school teacher have a vote, each life certificate teacher and each teacher in the county who is a graduate of a State chartered college.

This will be an inducement for the public school teachers to work and study to rise from a second grade to the first grade.

The college men and private school teachers would be a check on the Supervisor to keep him from manipulating to secure his own election, as he might possibly do if his election depended entirely upon public school teachers.

The college men and private school teachers would thus be brought into active touch with the public schools—would have an interest in the public schools. This interest and sympathy is sadly needed, and can never be secured under our present management. In fact, at present we do not even have the respect of some private school men. Why? Because school men have not been respected in the management of our public schools, as they should have been in many instances. I believe this method of electing the

Supervisor would release the schools from political influence so far as the Supervisor is concerned.

I believe in this way a man would be elected for *his educational power and influence*, instead of for *his political power*, as is often the case under the present law.

AS TO SCHOOL COMMITTEEMEN.

Elsewhere I have advised that we have separate committees—one for the white schools and one for the colored schools.

No man should be eligible to the office of School Committee unless he can write his name, is qualified to do ordinary business, and is known to be in favor of public education. Where colored men who are qualified cannot be found to serve as Committeemen, then in such townships white men should be appointed to manage the colored schools.

The committee should not be allowed to divide the school of any one year into two terms, as is now done in some places.

We have heard of schools where the Committee employed one teacher two months in the summer, and another teacher for two months, for the same children, in the winter.

How can children ever make any progress, and schools be of any value to a community, when we have such management on the part of School Committeemen?

The best teacher in the whole State could accomplish very little in two months, and then go back after a lapse of six months and teach two months or six weeks more. If the best teacher could accomplish very little by dividing the term, what can we expect from the average public school teacher, when one is employed six weeks in summer, and another, who teaches almost entirely different, is employed for two months during the winter season?

Above all, men should be selected who know something of the value of a good teacher to a community; men who will secure the services of the very best teachers, without any regard to whose sons or daughters such teachers may be; without any regard to what church such teachers may belong, and last, but by no means least, without any regard to *what political party* the teacher may be in sympathy with.

The provision in Section 2553, which says "that not more than three members of the said School Committee shall belong to any one political party," should be repealed.

This provision was intended to keep partisan politics out of the management of the schools in the townships, but I find in some instances it has kept good school men from serving on the Committees.

Let us have the very best men of the townships, whether they be Democrats, Republicans or Populists.

I want, in the name of the public school teachers, in the name of the children, and in the cause of public education, to demand that we have the very best men that can be secured for School Committeemen in every county in this entire State.

TOWNSHIP SYSTEM.

I advise that we hold to the Township System, and that the unity of the township be more and more emphasized.

I think we should have an amendment in regard to the Township Committee. Instead of having five men, as we now have, who have charge of all the public schools of the township, I think it better to have six men—three white men for the white schools and three colored men for the colored schools of the township. Let it be the duty of the County Supervisor to meet the six Committeemen in joint session and apportion the township fund to the two races, with a view to having the same length of term as far as practicable for both races of the township. The County Supervisor should be the presiding officer at these joint meetings of the Township Committee. An appeal from this joint committee's action to the County Board of Education should be provided for.

It should be the duty of the County Supervisor also to meet one day with each of these three Township Committeemen and assist them in employing teachers and apportioning the money to their respective schools of the township.

This means three days' service from the County Supervisor to each township. If the County Supervisor is the wise, prudent man he should be; if he knows the teachers of his county, and knows their qualifications and ability as teachers as he should know them; if he knows the people of his county and knows their peculiar needs and conditions as he should know them; then, indeed, these three days' expense, which means about $6 for a whole township, will prove the greatest blessing to the public schools of any fund ever spent for so much territory.

Too much power, some may say, to give to the Supervisor. The Supervisor *must* be a man of power, and must know how to use his power in order to advance in this great work.

We must do all we can to avoid race prejudice. The mixed Committees cause trouble and dissatisfaction, and, in my opinion, always would, if retained. The very instinct of our Anglo-Saxon race is against the idea of a colored man, either directly or indirectly, having authority over them. We must remove all the objections we possibly can in operating our public schools.

We have two distinct races and must have two distinct systems of public schools, as far as possible, without injury to the general system of the State.

The *most important reason why* we should hold to the Township System is that we may have local taxation.

In our rural districts, if we wish to increase our school fund by special tax we must do it by the township, as no territory less than this can vote a special tax, except incorporated towns and cities by special acts of the Legislature.

In 1897 eleven townships voted a special tax upon themselves.

This number, we hope, is only a beginning of a brighter day for the public schools of the rural districts in our State. We trust that others, seeing the good work in these townships, may go and do likewise.

DUTIES OF TOWNSHIP COMMITTEE.

The duties are somewhat burdensome to the Committee. I would advise that the Committee be empowered to employ one of their number, at a reasonable compensation, to take the census of the school children, in order that a complete and accurate census may be taken each year.

We find one advantage in regard to the Township Committee that I will mention. There are many others, but lack of space will not permit me to mention them:

The worthy Township Committeeman realizes the importance and the responsibility of his office more than the small District Committeeman. He knows and feels he is responsible for the progress of eight or ten schools, or in other words, for the progress of all the public school children of his township. When he comes to employ teachers, he lays aside personal favors and the thought of any such. He wants teachers who are best prepared for the work, without any thought of whose son or daughter he or she may be, without any special concern of where the teacher comes from, but the chief concern is what can the applicants do in the school-room; what will be the effect of the teacher's influence in the community for the cause of education and morality.

I would not be considered as casting any reflection upon the worthy committeeman of the small district system. We had some good, worthy men, of course, but often men did not realize the importance of their position, and would employ teachers as a matter of personal favor.

We have heard of Township Committeemen who use their power and office for personal gain and personal favor, but such men may be, and should be hastily, removed from office. The trouble is with the *officer* and *not* with the *office.*

COLORED NORMAL SCHOOLS.

The results that I see from our Colored Normal Schools are not satisfactory to me. I find that a great deal of the work done is not thorough and is not practical. I find that the pupils have a smattering of many subjects, and do not know thoroughly and well any one subject. I find great haste to get away from arithmetic, geography, spelling and English grammar, in order to study Latin, algebra and other higher studies, for which the most of the colored teachers will never have any practical use, none whatever, especially those who teach the public schools.

I would not for one moment find any objection to the higher studies if the lower studies are mastered first.

If I understand the object of these so-called Normal Schools, they are intended to teach the pupils the studies required in our public schools, that the pupils *shall know these subjects* and *know how to impart this knowledge* to their pupils.

I have advised, under the recommendations as to State Board of Examiners, that this Board prepare the course of study for these schools.

I advise also that this Board, instead of the State Board of Education, have the general management of these schools; that this Board be given the power to appoint the Local Board of Managers.

It will be the part of wisdom to do this because the State Board of Examiners is composed of school men, of educators, whereas the State Board of education has only one school man, the Superintendent of Public Instruction, on it, and he is helpless as an educator, in some cases.

Teachers and members of the Local Board are more likely to be selected by the State Board of Education, who do not and will not serve the best interest of education, than would be if these persons were appointed by a Board of school men, by a board of educators.

I further advise that the seven Colored Normal Schools be reduced to three, located, perhaps, one at Elizabeth City, one at Fayetteville and one at Winston.

Why have three schools instead of seven? Do I mean to save dollars and cents by this?

In one sense of the word I mean to save money. In that we could show results.

Let the money we spend in the seven schools be spent in three schools.

Let us have the very best brain and talent to be had among the colored teachers. I do not care where they come from. If we have the men in North Carolina, why, of course, let us use them; if not, let us go North, South, East or West until we find the men. The men can be found; no trouble about this.

Some will say it will never do, because we cannot reach so many of the colored people as we now do.

I admit that we might not reach so large a number of pupils, but we would do something for those we reach.

I would rather be able to send out one good, strong, well-trained teacher to a whole county, than to send to this same county twenty-four poorly-trained, weak teachers, "who know not, and know not that they know not."

This one well-trained, wide-awake teacher can and will organize the teachers of his county. He will have them pursuing a course of study similar to what he has had. He will give inspiration to others to go to the Normal. In a few years we will have a class of teachers of power and ability, and in this way my saving of money would come in, because *we are now spending the money and are not producing a class of strong teachers.*

STATE NORMAL COLLEGE, GREENSBORO, N. C.

This will not be a popular thing to do, because it means the loss of positions of some of the present teachers. It means the loss of the money that is spent in some of the towns that now have these schools.

I advise these changes as to these Normal Schools, without fear or favor, because I believe they will be an advantage to the progress of education among the colored people.

These recommendations were submitted to Dr. J. L. M. Curry, General Agent Peabody Fund. I quote from his letter:

"Your thoughts on Normal Schools I have read with much satisfaction. They are almost identical with what I said in my last address to the North Carolina Legislature. Normal Schools are frequently only so in name, and hence are deceptive and injurious. Three real Normal Schools for the training of colored teachers, properly located and supported, with *competent* and *faithful* instructors, would accomplish a vast good.

"We need to get rid of incompetence in both white and colored schools, to divorce from politics and mere local selfishness, and give children the benefit of men and women who know how and what to teach.

"All reforms meet with opposition.

"I trust you will not be deterred from doing right by 'fear, favor or affection.' Be assured of my readiness to co-operate with you and others in all wise efforts to improve the whole system of education."

AS TO TEXT-BOOKS.

There is perhaps no one subject of more vital interest in connection with public schools to the great mass of our common people than the subject of text-books.

How may we secure text-books for all the children who are, or should be, in our public schools?

How may we secure the best books for the least money?

In order that the members of the General Assembly may

have some information on this subject, and in order that they may see how the books are adopted in the various States of the Union, I sent a letter to each Superintendent of Public Instruction, and give, in the following list of States, what method is used in the respective States named, also give the opinion of the various Superintendents as to what they think is the best plan of adopting books.

There is diversity of opinion as to the best plan. Different conditions in the different States will readily show that a plan may be good for one State that will not work well in another State.

The Superintendent of Missouri seems to realize something of the difficulty of this great question.

In answer to the question as to what is the best plan of adoption, he says: "Please ask me something easy." Several of the Superintendents did not express an opinion at all.

The books cost the children of this State too much money, and why? What is the remedy? How may we furnish as good books as we now have, or better, for less money, to the parents of the poor children?

Why mention parents of the poor children any more than parents of means? In North Carolina there are many children who are kept away from school because they have not the books, and their parents are to poor to buy them.

I am aware that the inferior text-book, like a cheap piece of machinery, or an incompetent teacher, is dear at any price.

There are, of course, different things which enter into the manufacture of text-books. The times demand the *most education possible* in the *least time possible.* The arrangement and selection of material is of very great importance.

Our books must contain what is necessary for information, or discipline, and that which is unnecessary must be omitted.

The subjects must have the various points arranged in

their logical order, in order that these subjects may be instructive and at the same time entertaining to the young mind.

So we conclude that the text-book writer must be a thinker, a specialist and not a mere compiler.

But in my opinion the cost of books is not so much the expense of the literary work and mechanical make-up of the book as the cost of putting the books on the market.

The adoption of the text-books in North Carolina in June, 1896, cost the various text-book companies thousands of dollars.

Who pays all this enormous expense in the end? The parents of the children, of course. Those who use the books foot the bill.

Why not do away with all this expense of adoption and give the children the benefit of all these thousands of dollars in reduction of prices on text-books.

Can it be done? I believe it can.

I advise that the text-books be adopted by the State Board of Examiners, which is composed of educators, of school men.

The law should provide that the maximum price paid should not exceed seventy-five per cent. of the published list wholesale price.

If this Board could adopt the books for the whole State, we ought to secure the books at sixty per cent. of wholesale price, or perhaps even fifty per cent., because there would be no expense of thousands of dollars for agents, which expense, as was mentioned, comes out of the parents' pockets in the end, and this deduction of the thousands could be taken from the prices our parents pay at present for the books of their children.

In all the mercantile business, and other business of which I have heard anything, the amount of goods bought has a great deal to do with the price to be paid by the purchaser. For example, the merchant that buys a carload of bacon gets a great reduction of price in comparison with the merchant that buys only a few hundred pounds.

Applying this method of business to the purchase of books, it is reasonable to expect better terms as to cost of books from any publishing house, if said house can make sale for ninety-six counties instead of a county here and there.

But if the General Assembly does not think it the part of wisdom to put the adoption of text-books in the hands of the State Board of Examiners, and prefers the adoption by local boards instead, then, in this case, I advise that the local boards be given all the protection and aid possible in this important duty.

I publish, in connection with this subject, the law of the State of Ohio, which seems to me would be the best plan, if we are to continue local adoption. Certain changes can be made in the different sections to suit the conditions of our State.

For instance, in Section 2, instead of having a Commission composed of the Governor, Secretary of State, etc., I would put the State Board of Examiners. Other changes in other sections could be easily made to suit our needs in this State.

It will be seen from reading this law that each Board of Education shall determine, by a majority vote of all members elect, which of the books so filed shall be used in the schools under its control.

Each Board also has power to make necessary provisions and arrangements to place the books within easy reach of the pupils. Ten per cent. may be added to the cost of the price to pay for handling the books. Under this law it will also be observed that the Boards pay for all the books, and the proceeds of the sale of the books are repaid into the contingent fund. There is also a provision for free text-books if the electors so direct.

It is reported that thirty-eight leading companies have

sold books under this law to the different Boards in the State. This law, at least, does not crowd out the book companies.

OHIO TEXT-BOOK LAW.

SECTION 1. *Be it enacted by the General Assembly of the State of Ohio,* That any publisher or publishers of school books in the United States desiring to offer school books for use by pupils in the common schools of Ohio as hereinbefore provided, shall, before such books may be lawfully adopted and purchased by any school board in this State, file in the office of the state commissioner of common schools a copy of each book proposed to be so offered, together with the published list wholesale price thereof, and no revised edition of any such book shall be used in the common schools until a copy of such revised editlon shall have been filed in the office of the said commissioner, together with the published list wholesale price thereof. The said commissioner shall carefully preserve in his office all such copies of books and the prices thereof so filed.

SEC. 2. Whenever and so often as any book and the price thereof shall be so filed in the commissioner's office as provided in Section 1, a commission consisting of the governor, the secretary of state and the state commissioner of common schools, shall immediately fix the maximum price at which such books may be sold to or purchased by boards of education as hereinafter provided, which maximum price so fixed on any book shall not exceed seventy-five per cent. of the published list wholesale price thereof, and the state commissioner of common schools shall immediately notify the publisher of such book so filed of the maximum price so fixed. If the publisher so notified shall notify the commissioner in writing that he accepts the price so fixed, and shall agree in writing to furnish such book during a period of five years at the price so fixed, such written acceptance and agreement shall entitle said publisher to offer said book so filed for sale to said board of education for use by the pupils under the terms of this act.

SEC. 3. The said commissioner shall, during the first half of the month of June, 1896, and during the first half of the month of June in each year thereafter, furnish to each board of education the names and addresses of all publishers who shall have, during the year ending on the first day of said month of June in each year, agreed in writing to furnish their publications upon the terms provided in this act. And it shall not be lawful for any board of education to adopt or cause to be used in the common schools any book whose publisher shall not have complied, as to said book, with the provisions of this act.

SEC. 4. If any publisher who shall have agreed in writing to furnish books as provided in this act, shall fail or refuse to furnish such books adopted as herein provided to any board of education or its authorized agent upon the terms as herein provided, it shall be the duty of said board at once to notify the said commission of such failure or refusal, and the commission shall at once cause an investigation of such charge to be made, and if the same is found to be true the commissioner shall at once notify said publisher, and each board of education in the state, that said book shall not hereafter be adopted and purchased by boards of education; and said publisher shall forfeit and pay to the state of Ohio five hundred dollars for each failure, to be recovered in the name of the state, in an action to be brought by the attorney-general, in the court of common pleas of Franklin county, or in any other proper court or in any other place where service can be mande, and the amount, when collected, shall be paid into the state treasury to the credit of the common school fund of the state.

SEC. 5. Each board of education, on receiving the statements above mentioned from said commissioners, shall, on the third Monday in August thereafter, meet, and at such meeting, or at an adjourned meeting within two weeks after said Monday, determine, by a majority vote of all members elected, the studies to be pursued, and which of said text-books so filed shall be used in the schools under its control, but no text-books so adopted shall be changed, nor any part thereof altered or revised, nor shall any other text-book be substituted therefor for five years after the date of the selection and adoption thereof without the consent of three-fourths of all the members elected, given at a regular meeting; and each board of education shall cause it to be ascertained, and at regular meetings in April and August shall determine, which, and the number of each, of said books the schools under its charge shall require, until the next regular meetings in April and August, and shall cause an order to be drawn for the amount in favor of the clerk of the board of education, payable out of the contingent fund; and said clerk shall at once order said books so agreed upon by the board, of the publisher, and the publisher, on receipt of such order, shall ship such books to said clerk without delay, and the clerk shall forthwith examine such books, and if found right and in accordance with said order, remit the amount to said publisher, and the board of education shall pay all charges for the transportation of such books out of the school contingent fund; but if said boards of education can, at any time, secure of the publishers books at a price less than said maximum price, it shall be his duty to do so, and may, without unnecessary delay, make effort to secure such lower price before adopting any particular text-books. Each board of education shall have power to, and shall make all necessary provisions and arrangements to place the books so purchased within easy reach of and accessible to all the pupils in their district, and for that purpose may make such contracts and take such security as they may deem necessary, for the custody, care and sale of such books and accounting for the proceeds; but not to exceed ten per cent of the cost price shall be paid therefor, and said books shall be sold to the pupils of school age in the district at the price paid the publisher, and not to exceed ten per cent. therefor added, and the proceeds of such sale shall be paid into the contingent fund of such district, and whoever receives said books from the board of education for sale as aforesaid to the pupils, and fails to account honestly and fully for the same, or for the proceeds, to the board of education when required, shall be guilty of embezzlement and punished accordingly. Provided, however, boards of education may contract with local retail dealers to furnish said books at prices above specified, the said board being still responsible to the publishers for all books purchased by the said board of education, and when pupils remove from any district, and have text-books of the kind adopted in such district, and not being of the kind adopted in the district of which they remove, and wish to dispose of the same, the board of the district from which they remove, when requested, shall purchase the same at the fair value thereof, and re-sell the same as other books; and nothing in this act shall prevent the board of education from furnishing free books to pupils as provided by law. That for the purpose of carrying into effect the foregoing provisions of this act, and paying the expenses incident thereto, there be and is hereby appropriated out of any m ney in the state treasury, to the credit of the general revenue fund, not otherwise appropriated, the sum of five hundred dollars, to be disbursed and paid on the allowance and order of said commissioner.

SEC. 6. This act shall take effect and be in force on and after May 5, 1896.

Passed April 22, 1896.

In order that the members of the General Assembly may know something of the result of the only State, California, which owns its own plant, and prints its own books, I give figures showing the amount of money spent by the State and the prices of text-books to the children.

In 1885 the sum of $20,000 was appropriated for compiling a series of text-books for the common schools. One hundred and fifty thousand dollars was set aside for establishing a plant, purchasing material and payment of salaries. In 1887, $165,000 was added for the purpose last mentioned.

Other appropriations have been made from time to time to carry on the work.

According to figures compiled by Secretary of State of California, $405,000 has been appropriated for printing text-books.

It has been said that the State Board expects in eight years to pay, not only for the books published, but also for the plant.

But of course the books will need revision, the plant will wear out, and the number of books sold does not reach their expectation.

These things will greatly hinder the financial success on the part of the State.

From an examination of the list of books it will be seen that the prices to be paid by the children are not on the side of economy so far as the parents and purchasers are concerned.

CALIFORNIA.

TEXT-BOOKS.	RETAIL PRICE.
Revised First Reader	$ .20
Revised Second Reader	.35
Revised Third Reader	.50
Revised Fourth Reader	.60
Speller	.30
Primary Number Lessons	.25
Advanced Arithmetic	.50
Lessons in Language	.30
Revised English Grammar	.55
U. S. History	.80
Elementary Geography	.60
Advanced Geography	1.20
Physiology	.60
Civil Government	.55
English Grammar (old edition)	.50

From all the information I have gathered on this subject, State publication seems to be the most expensive plan of adopting text-books.

The objections we hear to State adoption are that it shuts out competition and results often in inferior books, but I think these objections would be removed if the plan first proposed were adopted and the Board have the authority to select from the latest and best books, and at the same time secure the books at seventy-five per cent. of wholesale list price or less.

It is my duty to advise on this subject, as well as on all others pertaining to the interest of the public schools, and I have done so without fear or favor.

Personally, I would much prefer to have nothing whatever to do with the text-books, because some of my precessors, who were honorable, honest men, were severely criticised on account of the duty they were called upon to perform in connection with the adoption of books.

I have not given a recommendation for any books or school supplies to any person or persons since I have been in the office of Superintendent of Public Instruction, but have observed the strictest impartiality towards agents, and have tried to be courteous and pleasant to all who have called upon me.

LIST OF STATES.

ALABAMA.

Have no adoption, except three counties that have uniformity. Books selected by County Boards.

Do you have uniformity? No.

What do you think the most satisfactory and economical plan of adopting books for the Common Schools? Let the teachers of County Boards select the books for the county.

ARKANSAS.

List of books is named by the State Superintendent. The Directors are limited to this list in making their adoption. Time, three years.

What do you think the most satisfactory and economical plan of adopting books for Common Schools? The Directors of each school district shall adopt the text-books.

CALIFORNIA.

The text-books are published by the State. The State owns its own plant, and publishes its own plant.

COLORADA.

Books are adopted by Local Boards.

CONNECTICUT.

Text-books are selected by Local Boards. State Board

of Education has authority by law to prescribe text-books, but never does so.

Do you have State uniformity? No.

What do you think the most satisfactory and econamical plan of adopting books for the Common Schools? The most economical way of obtaining books is probably the State system. The effect must be extended over ten years to realize any saving to the State.

DELAWARE.

All books are ordered by the Local School Boards, through the Trustees of the State School Fund. Time, five years.

Do you have State uniformity? Yes.

What do you think the most satisfactory and economical plan of adopting books for the Common Schools? Our plan.

FLORIDA.

Each County School Board adopts books for its county, Time, five years.

Do you have State uniformity? We have only county uniformity.

What do you think the most satisfactory and economical plan of adopting books for Common Schools? We are satisfied with our county adoption. We have never tried any other plan. State uniformity, properly guarded and honestly done, it strikes me, ought to be good.

GEORGIA.

Each County Board of Education selects books to be used in the county. No free books.

Do you have State uniformity? No.

What do you think the most satisfactory and economical plan of adopting books for the Common Schools? Allow County Boards to buy them direct from publishers and supply them to the people at cost.

ILLINOIS

Each District Board makes the selection for its district. No change can be made oftener than four years- Free of cost to indigent pupils.

Do you have State uniformity? No.

What do you think the most satisfactory and economical plan of adopting books for the Common Schools? Free text-books purchased by the Boards for the use of the pupils.

INDIANA.

Books are adopted by a Board of School Book Commissioners for five years. Free text-books to indigent pupils.

Do you have State uniformity? Yes.

What do you think the most satisfactory and economical plan of adopting books for the Common Schools? Our plan has been very satisfactory.

IOWA.

By County Board of Education.

IDAHO.

Adopted by a Commission appointed by the Governor. Furnished free to all.

Do you have State uniformity? Yes.

What do you think the most satisfactory and economical plan of adopting books for Common Schools? I would suggest that County Superintendent supply them direct to the districts.

KANSAS.

Books are adopted by the State Text-Book Commission for five years.

Do you have State uniformity? Yes.

What do you think the most satisfactory and economical plan of adopting books for Common Schools? State uniformity and State ownership.

KENTUCKY.

County Board of Examiners adopt books. Publishers

whose books are adopted are required to give bond, in a measure, guaranteeing prices. Term of adoption five years. Each county is required to furnish indigent children $100 worth of books on certificate of the County Superintendent that such is necessary.

Do you have State uniformity? State uniformity is not required by law, though the same books are largely used throughout the State.

What do you think the most satisfactory and economical plan of adopting books for Common Schools? State uniformity, giving the State Board of Education or some other central body power to contract, thus opening up a market that encourages competition.

LOUISIANA.

Books are selected by the State Board of Education once in four years, a uniform series being provided. The Board reserves the right to make changes or additions to the list.

Do you have State uniformity? Yes.

What do you think the most satisfactory and economical plan of adopting books for Common Schools? The plan followed in this and many other States seem to me the best of all, though it is not without disadvantage.

MAINE.

Books are adopted by the Boards of each town free to all the children. Time, five years.

Do you have State uniformity? No.

MASSACHUSETTS.

Each Local School Committee selects its own books, which are furnished free to the children. They remain the property of the towns and cities, however.

Do you have State uniformity? No.

What do you think the most satisfactory and economical plan of adopting books for the Common Schools? We like our plan very much.

MICHIGAN.

Books are adopted by Local Boards for five years.

Do you have State uniformity? Not yet; bill passed for that purpose last winter.

What do you think the most satisfactory and economical plan of adopting books for Common Schools? Free text-books.

MONTANA.

Books are adopted by a Commission composed of Superintendent of Public Instruction, the President of the University, the President of the Agricultural College, and three public school teachers actively engaged in public school work. Time, six years.

Do you have State uniformity? Yes.

What do you think the most satisfactory and economical plan for adopting books for the Common Schools? Our law gives complete satisfaction. The commission plan is undoubtedly the best, provided that the members thereof are modern, up-to-date school men, who are incorruptible.

MINNESOTA.

By the Local Boards, for not less than three years and not more than five years.

Do you have State uniformity? No.

What do you think the most satisfactory and economical plan of adopting books for Common Schools? We are well satisfied with the workings of our law, but think it should now be made compulsory on all districts.

MISSOURI.

School Book Commission composed of State Auditor, Attorney General, Superintendent of Public Instruction, President of State Normal School at Kirksville, and one practical public school teacher appointed by the Governor. Time, five years.

Do you have State uniformity? Yes.

What do you think the most satisfactory and economical plan of adopting books for Common Schools? Please ask me something easy.

NEW MEXICO.

Books are adopted by the Territorial Board of Education for four years.

Do you have State uniformity? Yes.

What do you think the most satisfactory and economical plan of adopting books for Common Schools? Adoption by State Board of Education.

NEBRASKA.

Independent Districts each selects its own books from three to five years. Schools are furnished free text-books. School Boards usually handle the books.

Do you have State uniformity? No.

What do you think the most satisfactory and economical plan of adopting books for Common Schools? We think Nebraska has the best text-book law. We buy books in the market of the United States and get as good prices as are made anywhere.

NEVADA.

Has State adoption by State Board of Education every four years. Expect to save from forty to fifty per cent. by having books distributed from the Superintendent of Public Instruction's office.

Do you have State uniformity? Yes.

What do you think the most satisfactory and economical plan of adopting books for the Common Schools? Our system.

NEW HAMPSHIRE.

Local option as to adoption of books. Books are free. Bought by School Board from publishers.

Do you have State uniformity? No.

NEW JERSEY.

Books are adopted by Local Boards and the County Superintendent.

Do you have State uniformity? No.

What do you think the most satisfactory and economical plan of adopting books for the Common Schools? I believe our system the best for our schools. Competition among publishers keeps the price of books down to a minimum. Conditions in our schools vary so that books suitable in one district are not as suitable as others in another district.

NEW YORK.

Books are adopted by Local Boards.

Do you have State uniformity? No.

OHIO.

Books must be endorsed and a maximum price fixed by the Commission, consisting of Governor, Secretary of State and State Commissioner of Schools, before they can be adopted by County or District Board of Education.

OREGON.

Every six years the selecting of school books is made by a vote of the County Superintendents and the State Board of Examiners, composed of nine members.

Do you have State uniformity? Yes.

What do you think the most satisfactory and economical plan of adopting books for Common Schools? There are some objections to our mode, but may be impossible to get a system against which no objection will be raised. I think the main objection is the board of adoption is too large.

RHODE ISLAND.

Adopted by Local Boards. Free of cost to the pupils Bought and distributed by the Boards.

SOUTH CAROLINA.

State adoption by State Board of Education. Time not

less than five years; may be as long as the State Board wishes. Last adoption was for seven years.

Do you have State uniformity? Partially so; to all intent and purposes, yes. It is a great saving to the people.

What do you think the most satisfactory and economical plan of adopting books for the Common Schools? Single list by the State Board, allowing the books in use to be worked out gradually, all new books to be the listed books.

TENNESSEE.

The County Superintendent suggests changes, and the Directors adopt or do not adopt, as they prefer. There is no compulsion as to adoption.

Do you have State uniformity? No.

What do you think the most satisfactory and economical plan of adopting books for Common Schools? Having intelligent Directors, it is best to leave the matter to them. In this State there are three Directors for each district.

TEXAS.

Books adopted by State Text-book Board, composed of State Board of Education, Superintendent of Public Instructions, President Sam Houston Normal Institute, and Atttorney General, for five years.

Do you have State uniformity? Will go into effect September 1, 1898.

What do you think the most satisfactory and economical plan of adopting books for the Common Schools? Free schools carry with them the idea of free books. I believe if the State furnishes free tuition, some plan of free books should be adopted.

UTAH.

Books are adopted by Local Boards for five years.

Do you have State uniformity? Yes.

What do you think the most satisfactory and economical plan of adopting books for Common Schools? Our experience has been confined to the method now in use, and it seems fairly satisfactory.

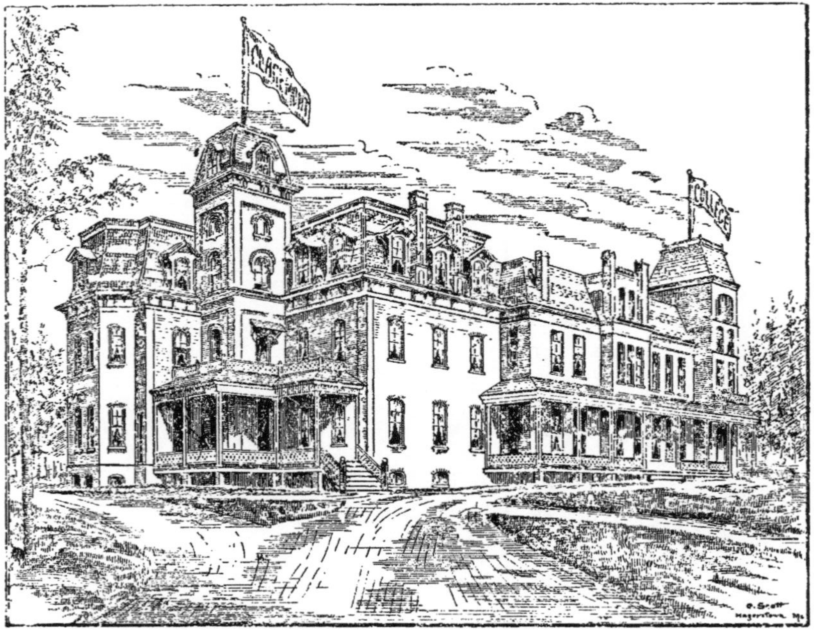

CLAREMONT COLLEGE, HICKORY, N. C.

VERMONT.

Each town selects the books. Change as the Board desires.

Do you have State uniformity? No.

What do you think the most satisfactory and economical plan of adopting books for Common Schools? Our present system. The Town School Board of each town selects, purchases and distributes. There is not uniformity in our towns even, because some books are better adapted to certain schools than others.

STATE OF WASHINGTON.

Books are adopted by the State Board of Education for five years.

Do you have State uniformity? Yes.

What do you think the most satisfactory and economical plan of adopting books for the Common Schools? The present plan, unless the State go into the business itself.

WEST VIRGINIA.

A part of the list is adopted by State contract and the rest by the County School Boards.

Do you have State uniformity? Partially.

What do you think the most satisfactory and economical plan of adopting books for the Common Schools? State contract by a State Commission.

WISCONSIN.

Books are adopted by the Local Boards.

Do you have State uniformity? No.

What do you think the most satisfactory and economical plan of adopting books for the Common Schools? Our law works quite satisfactory.

$400,000 MORE FOR PUBLIC SCHOOLS ATTAINABLE.

I sent out a letter of enquiry to the different States, in order to find how the various railroads are taxed, and what part of this tax is given to the public schools of the respective States. One special point I wished to know was, in what States were taxes laid on gross earnings.

From reading the list of States it will be seen that fourteen States tax the railroads on gross earnings, or gross receipts.

In North Carolina we do not receive any taxes at all from the gross receipts or gross earnings. We have a sweeping statute on this subject. It starts out as if wonderful results would be sure to follow. It is found in Chapter 168, Section 40, Laws of 1897, and reads thus: "Every railroad, steamboat or canal company incorporated under the laws of this State, doing business in this State, shall pay to the State a tax on the corporation equal to the sum of one per centum upon the gross receipts of said company. The said tax shall be paid semi-annually, upon the first days of July and January; and for the purposes of ascertaining the amount of the same, it shall be the duty of the treasurer of said company to render the Treasurer of the State, under oath or affirmation, a statement of the amount of gross receipts of said company during the preceding six months, and if such company shall refuse or fail, for a period of thirty days after such tax becomes due, to make returns or to pay the same, the amount thereof, as near as can be ascertained by the State Treasurer, with an addition of ten per centum thereto, shall be collected for the use of the State."

This reads well, and one might think was putting into the State Treasury from the railroads alone more than one hundred thousand dollars—which it would do, if it were not for that wise (?) proviso: "No railroad or canal company shall be liable to this tax if its property is taxed." This no doubt was prepared by some learned lawyer, who was the representative of the companies intended to be taxed. The proviso knocks the bottom out, so that we may paraphrase the whole section thus: "Every railroad, steamboat or canal company incorporated under the laws of the State shall be taxed one per centum upon the gross receipts of said companies, provided they are not taxed at all."

I advise the General Assembly to impose a tax upon the gross receipts of the railroads in North Carolina for the benefit of the public schools. It can be done. It ought to be done. We find taxes upon gross earnings in fourteen States. Why not have it in North Carolina?

The gross earnings of the railroads in this State are more than eleven million dollars. Suppose we had a law like Minnesota, taxing the roads 3 per cent. on gross earnings? What a handsome sum of more than three hundred thousand dollars to give instruction and intelligence to the great army of poor boys and girls now groping in darkness, and who must, under present conditions of our educational facilities, grow into manhood and womanhood burdened with all the disadvantages of the ignorant.

If the insurance, telegraph and the telephone companies are taxed on gross earnings in our State, and I am informed they are, then why not the railroads pay a similar tax?

We reasonably conclude that the natural increase in railroad business for the next year or so will be equal to and even greater than the last year. A tax of 3 per cent. on gross earnings next year would amount to about three hundred and sixty thousand dollars. In addition to this, let us have the same tax on gross earnings of telephone companies, telegraph companies, express companies, insurance companies, and then we will have a school fund from these sources of about four hundred thousand dollars. Think of having four hundred thousand dollars added to the school fund by the General Assembly of 1899. Remember, this tax would be annually.

Most every one will admit that in order to increase the

school terms, and in order to secure better and more efficient teachers, we must have an increase of school fund.

The General Assembly cannot do much more than it has done in the past, so far as general taxes on property are concerned, on account of constitutional limitations. This is the only way, so far as the General Assembly is concerned, to lift our schools out of the mire and put us on our feet. The source from which this tax would come would be one well able to bear it, in my opinion. The earnings of the companies, that is, the freights, fares, &c., come from the people.

I do not believe in making an individual or company bear a larger per cent. of any publilc expense just simply because such person or persons have the means. This is not what I mean, but I mean that after the railroads and companies referred to have paid their officers reasonable salaries and their stockholders reasonable income on their investment, then, as there have been large sums of money given as a bonus to stockholders or officers, it is evident that a part of this money should go back to the people from whence it comes, for the elevation and enlightenment of such people.

That which is of very great importance is that the railroads and corporations will have no way of evading this law. No injunction can be taken to stop this tax, if imposed by the General Assembly. As soon as the Railroad Commission reduces passenger or freight rates, then an injunction is issued an once, but if the General Assembly will have the courage to impose this tax, then Judge Simonton nor any other Federal Judge can have anything whatever to do with the case.

I leave the matter with the General Assembly. Here you have an opportunity to help the cause of public education. Will you do it? We shall see.

GEORGIA.

Four roads pay one-half of one percentum on net earnings. Income from this source last year was $3,356,044.

VIRGINIA.

Roads pay one percentum on net earnings. Amount derived from this source in 1898 was $6,371.41.

ALABAMA.

The only tax levied on railroad earnings is that of $12,500 per annum for the purpose of paying the Railroad Commissioners and their clerks, etc., and this is on the basis of gross earuings; percentage varies each year.

MARYLAND.

No tax applied to the School Fund.

MASSACHUSETTS.

Railroad stocks are taxed according to value of shares; none to the Public School Fund.

PENNSYLVANIA.

A tax of eight mills is levied on the gross earnings of railroads. Total amount derived unknown. About $6,070 of the tax goes to the School Fund.

MICHIGAN.

Tax on gross earnings not exceeding $2,000 per mile, two and one-half per cent. Exceeding $4,000, but not exceeding $6,000, four per cent. Exceeding $6,000, but not exceeding $8,000, four and one-half per cent. Exceeding $8,000, five per cent. Total amount received from this source, $985,150.49.

MAINE.

Tax on gross receipts not exceeding $1,500 per mile, is one-fourth of one per cent. Exceeding $1,500, but not exceeding $2,250, one-half of one per cent., and so on, increasing at the rate of one-quarter of one per cent. for each $750 of the average gross receipts per mile or fractional part thereof. Provided, that in no case the tax exceed three and one-fourth per cent. Provided, that in case the roads are operated exclusively for the transportation of freight, the tax shall not exceed one and three-fourth per cent. Total receipts about $173,000.

MINNESOTA.

Tax of three per cent. imposed on gross receipts. Total amount received from this source about $1,000,000. One mill State tax goes to free schools of the districts for forty days in the year.

OREGON.

Railroad stock assessed by the counties through which they pass. Three mills is the school tax.

VERMONT.

Roads are given the option to pay at the rate of two and one-half per cent. on gross earnings, if situated wholly in the State; if the option is not taken they are assessed on an appraisal of the property. Nearly all roads pay on gross earnings. Receipts from this source last year $112,910.96. None directly to the School Fund.

TEXAS.

Imposes an occupation tax of one per cent. on gross passenger earnings, and two and one-half per cent. on gross earnings of sleeping-car companies originating and ending in the State. Receipts last year $46,962.32. About one-fourth goes to the Public School Fund.

RHODE ISLAND.

Railroad stock not taxed on earnings. Express, Telegraph and Telephone Companies pay one per cent. on gross receipts, which money goes into the General Fund.

SOUTH CAROLINA.

Railroad stock not taxed on earnings; pay the same rate as do citizens, and three mills goes to School Fund.

TENNESSEE.

Not taxed on earnings. State tax, three mills; school tax, one and one-half mills.

NEW YORK.

Street Railway Companies pay a tax of one per cent. on gross earnings. Railroad Companies pay a tax of one-half of one per cent. on gross earnings. A dividend tax is also levied. All appropriations for public schools are made from General Fund, and vary each year.

OHIO.

Railroads pay a tax of one-half of one per cent. on gross earnings. Receipts from this source unknown.

LOUISIANA.

Tax on valuation. State tax for public schools one and one-fourth mills.

ILLINOIS.

Under Revenue Law no such tax is levied. Under original grant of lands to the Illinois Central Railroad by the State it was required that the railroad should forever pay to the State into the State Treasury seven per cent. on its gross earnings. Receipts from this sourcs $600,000 per annum.

MARYLAND.

Eight-tenths of one per cent. on the first one thousand dollars per mile of gross earnings, or on the total earnings if they are less than one thousand dollars per mile, and one and one-half per cent. on all gross earnings above one thousand dollars per mile, and when the earnings exceed two thousand dollars per mile two per cent. on all earnings above that sum. Total receipts from this source $177,000.

MISSOURI.

Railroad stocks are not assessed on their earnings, but on their tangible property.

NEBRASKA.

None on earnings. Pay tax same as resident property holders.

NEVADA.

None on earnings. Property assessed five cents on $100 of all taxable property goes to Public School Fund.

NEW HAMPSHIRE.

None to School Fund. Towns may appropriate their share to support their schools.

NEW JERSEY.

No tax on earnings, but on valuation of property. None to the School Fund.

WISCONSIN.

Four percentum of the gross earnings of all railroads, except those operated on pile and pontoon, or pontoon bridges, whose gross earnings equal or exceed three thousand dollars per annum of operated road. Three and one-half percentum of the gross earnings of all railroads, except those operated on pile or pontoon, or pontoon bridges, whose gross earnings equal or exceed $2,500 per annum, and less than $3,000 per mile per annum of operated road. Three percentum of the gross earnings of all railroads, except those operated on pile or pontoon, or pontoon bridges, whose gross earnings equal or exceed $2,000, and are less than $2,500 per mile per annum of operated road. Five dollars per mile of all operated railroads, whose gross earnings equal $1,500 per mile per annum and are less than $2,000 per mile per annum of operated road, and in addition two and one-half percentum of all gross earnings in excess of $1,500 per mile per annum, and under $2,000 per mile per annum.

Five dollars per mile of operated road by all companies whose gross earnings are less than $1,500 per mile per annum. Two percentum of the gross earnings of all railroads which are operated on pile and pontoon, or pontoon bridges, which gross earnings shall be returned as to such parts as are within the State.

CALIFORNIA.

Paid into the State Treasury and distributed according to mileage among the counties. Assessed by State Board of Equalization. Per cent. to School Fund varies in the different counties.

COLORADO.

No tax on earnings.

CONNECTICUT.

The State assesses tax one per cent. on market value of stocks and bonds on railroad stock out of the general revenues of State $2.25 to each person for the support of the schools.

DELAWARE.

No tax on earnings.

FLORIDA.

Railroads are not taxed on earnings. School tax is one mill. In addition an average of five mills is assessed by counties for school purposes.

IOWA.

None on their earnings. Assessed in every county just as other property. The taxes go to the different departments of government. About sixty per cent. of all taxes is spent for schools.

KANSAS.

Earnings are not assessed, only the actual property.

AS TO LOCAL TAXATION.

The General Assembly has done about all that can be done to increase the public school Fund on account of constitutional limitations. There is one way, however, that it can aid the Public Schools, and that way is pointed out elsewhere under the head of "$400,000 Attainable."

As I see it, there are only two ways to increase the Public School Fund—the one mentioned under the subject above referred to by taxation on gross earnings of railroads and corporations, the other by local taxation.

According to Chapter 421, Laws of 1897, an election was held on Tuesday after the second Monday in August, 1897.

As a result of this election eleven townships voted the special tax provided for in this chapter.

There is a provision, or an alternative in this law, that in case an amount is raised by voluntary subscription an equal amount shall be paid by the State Treasurer.

Under this provision there was $8,596.63 raised and duplicated by the State.

There seems to have been some considerable misunderstanding as to the condition upon which the State would duplicate funds.

I understand, and have stated so hundreds of times, that this provision meant that the money raised by private subscriptions and duplicated by the State should be subject to the order of the Committee for the Township for the benefit of all the Public Schools, just as the tax would have been if voted by the people.

I have reason to believe, in some instances, that my instructions as to the use of the funds raised in this way were not carried out.

The following circular letter was sent out all over the State:

OFFICE OF SUPERINTENDENT OF PUBLIC INSTRUCTION,
RALEIGH, N. C., February 28, 1898.

DEAR SIR :—A township becomes a special School District when a donation is put into the hands of the County Treasurer for the benefit of all the Public Schools, white and colored, in said township, and this donation is supplemented by the State. The funds thus raised by donation and by the supplement given on the part of the State becomes a special fund for this township.

This fund is subject to the order of the Township Committee, and for the benefit of all the public schools in the township, just as the money appo tioned to the township by County Board of Education is for the benefit of all the schools in the township.

No one or two schools in a township can expect to receive aid from the State. No territory less than a township need apply for aid.

This is a great opportunity for small townships, or townships where the number of schools is small.

Suppose a township only has five schools, and raises by donation five hundred dollars and the State gives five hundred dollars. Here we have a special fund of one thousand dollars, which will give to each school $200.

These donations will be duplicated at any time between January 31st and June 30th of a school year, provided that no township can receive more than $500 in any one year.

Very truly, C. H. MEBANE,
Superintendent of Public Instruction.

The results are not satisfactory for two reasons:

First, The law is not plain, so that there can be no doubt as to how the money is to be used that is raised by private subscription and duplicated by the State.

Second, The schools that need help most do not receive aid.

There are hundreds and hundreds of individual public schools that *could* raise from $25 to $50, and having it doubled by the State many dark corners would soon begin to see the light, and the State would encourage the cause of public education and the cause of local taxation where it is most needed.

I advise that the provision be amended so that the maximum amount of subscription to be duplicated by the State be $50, and the minimum be $15 to every Public School in the township. This minimum doubled would give the school $30 or one month's school.

What wonderful results would follow within a few years if each school had the opportunity to raise $15, $25 or $50, and have these amounts doubled by the State. This, indeed, will be a way to help those who are helping themselves.

Again, I recommend that the time for holding the election be changed to that of the regular election in order to save the expense of holding the election.

Even persons who are friendly to the cause of education will not go to an election for schools alone.

We hear some say, politics will crowd out the school question. I say I *want the school question to crowd out some of our politics*, at least to crowd out enough that men going before our people will *not dare to misrepresent the cause of education for political gain.*

The election for schools in 1897 cost between $12,000 and $15,000, and yet there are men who seek office in high positions, and go around over the State asserting that it cost $65,000.

By local tax the strong help the weak. Local tax is one way by which the *brotherhood of man* is forcibly brought before the public. Men are brought to realize an interest in the rising generation. The man of means and the poor man have a common interest in the instruction of the young. It does away with the false idea that has been prevalent in the minds of many that the children of the man of means are better than the poor man's children.

Look at our cities and towns where local tax has been the means of opening the schools alike to the poor and those of means. Here we find the children of the wealthiest men in the towns entering the same threshold with the children of the poorest men. Their little feet tread the same pathway of instruction, their little hearts are warmed around the same hearthstone, which is radiant with a glow of love and truth emanating from the soul of the faithful, conscientious teacher. Here they are taught to respect, honor and love each other. Here they learn to have an interest in each other which otherwise would be unknown. And last, but by no means least, the parents are drawn towards each other through their children, and we find unity of interest in the minds and hearts, not only of the children, but also in the minds and hearts of parents.

We do not expect to have the same kind of schools in the rural districts as in the towns—we do not need the same, but we do need the increase in school fund, the increase in length of term. *We do need more of the common interest in each other on the part of parents and teachers.* We do need the money which a farmer now and then spends to send his children off to have even primary teaching done. Let the money these farmers spend for education be spent in the way of local tax, which will benefit not only his own children, but his neighbors' children.

We hear farmers justly complain as to the society of their community; that they have no society which is interesting or elevating for their children. How soon all this would be changed if all the children in these rural districts had the opportunity and the advantage of a six or eight months good school. Soon we would have social circles, elevating and refining, and we would hear no more of leaving the country home in order to have the advantage of schools, and in order to have society of the refined and cultured.

We want our parents in the country to take a broader view of this subject than many of them have had. *We want more common interest in the future happiness and welfare of the children.*

We want it to be a thing of the past when a young man or a young woman who has secured an education is regarded as a person far above or apart from the masses of our young people. We want no great gulf between a college man and the man of the community.

The more money men put into anything the more interest they have in that thing. I think *we usually pay enough school tax to ease our consciences*, and *not enough to cause us any concern as to how it is spent and what results follow the expenditure.*

I believe there are men to-day who pay $3 public school tax and never give any special thought or consideration as to what the public schools are doing, whereas if they were paying $12 tax for this cause they would see to it that results were seen and felt from the expenditure.

One reason, then, why we should have *special tax for schools is to create special interest for schools.*

AS TO SCHOOL ATTENDANCE.

I am slow to advise a compulsory attendance of our public schools under our present conditions, and especially when I remember the character of work done in some of our public schools, but when I call to mind that in many cases the children are kept from schools by careless, indifferent parents, and sometimes by lazy parents, who compel them to work in cotton mills, while their fathers sit around the stores, talk politics, and discuss the ways and means of preserving the government; when I think of these cases I am compelled to conclude that the State ought to come to the rescue of these helpless children

Cases have come under my own personal observation, where children were put in the cotton mill at seven or eight years of age, and kept there until they were twenty-one years of age. I recall some young men and women whom I met a few years ago. They could neither read nor write because they had been kept in the cotton mill from seven years of age. Think of it, white boys and girls being bound down by their parents and not even able to read and write when twenty-one years old in this day and generation, and yet it is true in our own State.

In the rural districts also we often find boys roaming over the fields, idling away their time, when the Public School Fund is being spent for their benefit.

I advise that the General Assembly give us some mild form of compulsory attendance to begin with.

CIVIL GOVERNMENT.

I advise that we add Civil Government to our list of subjects to be taught in our Public Schools.

It is singular, but nevertheless true, that so large a per cent. of our more intelligent people are so poorly informed upon matters pertaining to our government, both the National and the State Government.

We want our children to be patriotic, to love our government, and one of the ways to do this is to teach them what our government is, and how our laws are made.

Our children should know the duties required of the various State officers; how laws are enacted, repealed or amended.

Our children should know the duties of the President of the United States, and of the different Cabinet officers. They should be taught the duties of both Houses of Congress, and the various departments of our government.

While we may not in many cases have regular classes studying this subject, yet the teachers should be well informed on this subject, and should give oral lessons at least once a week to the entire school, and even in this way our children may acquire a good general knowledge of our government.

THOUGHTS BY THE WAY.

I began my work on the 13th day of January, 1897. I was very kindly received by my predecessor, Hon. John C. Scarborough, who gave me a general insight into the records and duties of the office of Superintendent of Public Instruction.

My entire time has been given to the work, and not only my time, but my whole interest of mind, heart and soul has been thrown into the work.

I have no doubt made some mistakes, but these mistakes were of the head and not of the heart.

I have tried to win and merit the support and co-operation of our leading educators in the public school work, and it gives me very great pleasure to say, with becoming modesty, that I believe I have had not only their support in the public school work, but that which I appreciate even more—their respect and confidence.

OFFICIAL STANDING OF THIS OFFICE.

I have endeavored to bring this office and its duties into closer touch with our people than ever before.

This office has been regarded by many of our people as a kind of sinecure. Some people seem to think the object of the office was merely to satisfy the requirement of our Constitution by which the office was established; that the Superintendent has merely to furnish some blanks for records of schools and the preparation of some few statistics.

In this connection I wish to express my sincere appreciation for the assistance given me by the press of our State. The papers of all political parties have kindly printed official circulars sent out from this office from time to time, and in this way I have been enabled to reach the masses of our people as I otherwise could not possibly have done.

It is very gratifying to all the friends of public education to know that this office and its duties are more widely known to-day than ever before, not only to the general public, but even to our children.

RELATION OF THE OFFICE TO PARTY POLITICS.

It has been one of my special objects to remove the office and its duties as far as possible from partisan politics. To

GLIMPSE IN CAMPUS—UNIVERSITY OF NORTH CAROLINA.

this end I have taken no active part in any political campaigns. In this particular I have differed from some of my predecessors.

I have long felt that one of the most important things to be done in connection with our public educational work was to remove it as far as possible from partisan politics. I have pled for this to be done from the very beginning; when the county school officers were selected I asked that the men best qualified for the position be selected.

I have practiced what I preached on this subject, and expect to continue to do so as long as I am in this office.

I hope that the time is not far away when all the people of North Carolina will see to it that the Superintendent of Public Instruction, whoever he may be, will not only not be expected to take an active part in political campaigns, but that public opinion may be so strong against such actions that he will not dare to do so.

RELATION OF THIS OFFICE TO PRIVATE SCHOOLS AND DENOMINATIONAL COLLEGES.

I have endeavored to create a closer sympathy and common interest on the part of these schools and colleges.

I have recognized and appreciated what these schools and colleges are doing for the cause of education within our State.

I have striven to emphasize the fact that good public schools, well filled public schools, *will mean well filled academies and colleges.*

I have tried to have all of our schools—the State, the denominational colleges, and the private schools—to realize more than ever that there is one subject, one work, upon which we can unite our forces, and that is the work and progress of our public schools.

An index to this common interest will be found in the

expressions from the faculties and heads of the various institutions published elsewhere in this Report.

In order that my Report may show what educational work was done and is being done by these institutions, I have given space to them at an approximated cost, per page, by the State Printer.

AS TO SUPERVISION.

The most important thing the General Assembly of 1899 has to do is to legislate to increase the School Fund. I have tried to show how this may be done elsewhere.

The next act, in importance, is to legislate so that we may have a wise expenditure of this fund.

One great hindrance to the cause of public education in North Carolina for years past, and even now, is that we do not have the funds wisely spent in so many instances.

Where a farmer has a house to build he not only employs carpenters, but he employs one carpenter to supervise the work, to see that each man does his work well, to see that he keeps at his work and earns the wages he receives.

We even have our Road Supervisors. *We are not willing that earth and stones shall be handled without supervision.*

We must have supervision to lay stone and to place earth on our highways, we must have supervision to build our bridges, lest some harm may perchance come to the traveler. This is all right, but how strange, it seems to me, that laborers, men and women who fashion and mould the character of our future citizenship; men and women whose work, whether good or bad, will last when houses and bridges are crumbled into dust; men and women whose work will last throughout eternity itself; yet we are not only willing for these laborers to work without supervision, but in many counties our County Boards of Education actually refuse to send out the Supervisor *to even take a peep* at the work that is being done in the public schools. What excuse do we hear for such action on the part of the County Board of Education? They say it is needless expense—better let the schools of the county have the benefit of the money than to have the Supervisor out among the schools.

If the Supervisor is the man he should be, we cannot measure his worth to the cause of education by a few dollars and cents expended for sending him out among the schools. He will bring order and system out of confusion and chaos in many places, where the teachers are young and inexperienced. He will create interest, where there is no interest, in the public schools. He will make peace where there is turmoil and confusion. He will infuse life and inspiration into the schools which have become dry and monotonous.

He will be so full of zeal and enthusiasm for the work that every community into which he goes will feel the effects of his visit, not only in the school-room, but the life and noble ambition for higher and better things pointed out by him will be caught up by the children and carried into their homes, and the parents thus interested—and by and by the whole community—will be aroused on the subject of schools.

If we have not Supervisors who can do these things then let us secure them. There are such men in every county in North Carolina.

It gives me pleasure to say we have some Supervisors who are doing, and have done, the very things mentioned by me here. Others would do much greater things than they are, but their hands are tied by County Boards of Education.

I add below the resolutions passed by the Teachers' Assembly of North Carolina at its last meeting, in June, 1898, at Asheville.

I will not discuss these resolutions here, as a committee provided for in the resolutions will present the merits of the plan proposed.

Resolved, That in the opinion of the North Carolina Teachers' Assembly the supervision of the public schools would be greatly improved and the general cause of public education would be promoted if the State, should adopt a plan to secure about ten District State Supervisors, in addition to the ninety-six County Supervisors. The State Supervisors, under the advice of the State Superintendent of Public Instruction, should each have general oversight of the educational work in about ten counties, advising with County Supervisors, instructing teachers in Institutes, and arousing proper educational sentiment among the people.

Resolved further, That the Teachers' Assembly send a committee of nine to the General Assembly of North Carolina to petition the Legislature to make this improvement in the supervision of the public schools.

Resolved, That it is the sense of the North Carolina Teachers' Assembly that the State should bear all of the traveling expenses of the State Superintendent of Public Instruction necessary to a proper oversight and visitation of our schools.

DR. BATTLE'S WORK.

I have been very fortunate to secure the valuable services of Dr. Kemp P. Battle, of the University of North Carolina, to write a history or sketches of the old extinct schools in the counties of North Carolina. I congratulate the State upon having a man so well prepared to write our educational history as is Dr. Battle.

This work alone of Dr. Battle will make my Report of great value to the State and to all friends of education.

FINALLY.

I wish to remind the members of the General Assembly that the children of North Carolina, whose future power and influence as citizens, as men and women in society—these have no lobbyist to elbow you around, no one to whisper in your ear how great you are, how you may make a great name for yourself.

They have no one here to flatter you, to entertain you.

But could you fully realize that to-day, throughout the length and breadth of North Carolina, there are thousands of anxious, longing young minds and hearts crying for mental food, yearning for that which will brighten and make happy their lives, then you would listen, then you would come to their rescue, then would the empty praise and flattering words of the lobbyist be as "sounding brass and tinkling cymbal," in comparison to the still small voices of these little ones around your own fireside and those of your neighbors' hearthstones.

I have tried to be faithful to these little ones, I have tried to point out ways and means by which you may help them. I can close the two years' work with a clear conscience that I have done, though only a mite it be, what I could for the advancement of the education of *all our people*, the rich and the poor alike.

I now leave the subject with you. What may be accomplished within the next two years will largely depend upon you. I trust you may act wisely and prudently in all legislation pertaining to the cause of Public Education.

I am yours for service,

C. H. MEBANE,
Supt. Public Instruction.

LETTERS FROM COUNTY SUPERVISORS.

The following letter was sent to each of the County Supervisors. I publish, following this, the letters received in reply:

TO THE SUPERVISOR:

Will you please write me a short letter for publication in my forthcoming Biennial Report, touching upon the following points:

As to your teachers association, as to institute work, and as to general condition of public schools, and the subject of public education in your county. I hope to have a letter from each Supervisor at AN EARLY DATE. Please attend to this at once.

Very truly, C. H. MEBANE,
Superintendent Public Instruction.

NOVEMBER 10, 1898.

HON. C. H. MEBANE, State Superintendent, Raleigh, N. C.

DEAR SIR:—In compliance with your request, I beg leave to say that the Teachers' Association of Cherokee County was organized the first of this year with a large number of teachers present. The teachers were very much encouraged over the prospects of being benefited by their association. Believing this was what they had needed for quite a time, almost every teacher has attended these meetings since the organization. Many teachers have become more enthusiastic in their work by coming in contact with others of more experience and broader views.

The institute work, conducted by the supervisor, I think has been productive of causing some teachers to make their teaching professional. The work done in these was of such character as the teachers could make it applicable to the needs and wants of their schools.

In some of the townships we have had large educational gatherings, what we styled an "educational rally." Three or four schools would assemble together with appropriate exercises by each, thereby causing the people of the entire community to be present. The importance of better schools, better attendance, better equipments and the importance of education was brought before the people.

By means of the above-mentioned efforts the condition of the public schools have been greatly augmented.

While our public schools are not what they ought to be—as we would like to have them be—yet the people are in sympathy with them, and are manifesting some interest to make them better.

Very respectfully, your obedient servant,

J. M. LOVINGOOD,
Supervisor of Cherokee County.

WINDSOR, N. C., November 1, 189?.

HON. C. H. MEBANE, State Superintendent, Raleigh, N. C.

MY DEAR SIR:—We have held no institute work the present year. We find that our teachers, in considerable numbers, are taking educational publications, which contain very mnch the same matter usually exhibited in institute work; also, that the necessary expense and board upon the attendance of same would be an extra tax upon our teachers, many of whom fail to get a school at all, and others having but a short term and small salary. Reasons of this character influenced our School Board in declining to order an institute.

We have a Teachers' Association in the county. We were among the first counties of the State to organize them some six or eight years ago, and have kept them in unbroken existence ever since. We hold from two to three meetings annually—think two enough. The character of these meetings have been of marked interest, and have unquestionably exerted much good among our people. We have as few by-laws as possible. Every white teacher in the county, whether of a public or private school, is a reconigzed member, thereby retaining a much larger membership than if left to voluntary joining. For several past years our meetings were largely attended, not only by the teachers, but by the masses of our citizens. Our chiefest effort is to get the county people present at these educational rallies; thereby bringing them into a stronger and more interested sympathy with the education of their children. We look upon this feature of our meetings as being most productive of good. Hence we emphasize it.

Our present, as well as former State Superintendents, have honored us with their presence, with very entertaining and profitable talks and councils; and they can testify to the apparent good work these meetings are doing, and from our own observation and experience we would heartily advise the establishment and persistency of these educational meetings in all the counties of the State.

We flatter ourselves that, taken altogether, Bertie County can boast of as intelligent and efficient set of teachers as any county in the State. While they are not all up to as high grade in school studies as is usually desired, yet they possess as fair an average preparation for county school work as we deem ordinarily necessary. They are selected much for their moral as well as intellectual work. Our chief effort is to have efficiency for good, honest work, with special care as to their capacity for control or government over their children.

The general impression throughout the county is, that the attention, training and results of school work is largely on the up-grade.

Some features of our present new school law, we fear, are not going to work well.

After a years' experience and observation, we are beginning to very much question the reduction of number of school committeemen. We think we could give best of reasons why the old system in this particular should be re-established; also as to the present place of distributing the money. We find it very unequal, hence unsatisfactory. We feel sure at our next session of the General Assembly these matters will be well considered, and all defects, if any, duly corrected. We have reason to believe, at the proper time, we could make suggestions as to these things. As to the visitation work of the County Supervisor, we find a good, and believe, proper place to notify the teachers a few days ahead of the day of visitation at the school, and advise that the neighbors and patrons be requested to be out at the hour; then having teacher, children and parents together, we have the better opportunity to talk to them and thereby create, if possible, a deeper interest and closer sympathy between teachers and parents; result, better attendance and more interest in the educational growth of the children of such communities.

We have on our statute books such a thing as "Arbor Day" in our school work, the same to be appointed and proclaimed by the Governor and State Superintendent. In the absence of any like notice of the same, it will be the purpose of the Supervisor of this county to appoint the Friday before Christmas of the present year, as such a day in each school-house community, at which time the teacher will be requested to provide some public exercises by the children for half the day; and the other half to be used in fixing up, in any needed way, the school-house ground (assisted by the patrons), such as trimming up or cutting away such as should be thus; and planting out new trees, such as ornamental and fruit trees, principally the latter. Of fruit trees we shall suggest: Walnut, hickory, chestnut, pecan, persimmon, locust and others, such as will always be of benefit and pleasure to the children during the fall and winter months. We believe in making our little school centres attractive places in any community.

Trusting that in every conceivable way new life and energy may continue to be enthused in this most important work, and that blessings of approval may rest upon the heads that guide it, from State Superintendent to the humblest committeeman, I am sir,

Your obedient servant,

R. W. ASKEW,
Supervisor of Bertie County.

MARSHVILLE, N. C., October 18, 1898.

MR. MEBANE.

DEAR SIR:—Union County Teachers' Association was organized in the fall of 1897. Most of the teachers took hold at once, and have worked earnestly. It has an enrollment of eighty, an average attendance of sixty. It meets once a month. The teachers discuss methods of teaching, discipline, and other live questions relating to the profession; also, the different branches are reviewed. Through the Association teachers are being aroused and the people are being reached.

The institute was held in July. It was under the management of the County Supervisor, who secured, free of cost, all the high school teachers of the county to assist him. Each one was assigned a certain branch to discuss before the institute, and to answer all questions relating to it and to the method of teaching it. All teachers of the county were required to attend. The great majority were glad of this opportunity that they might better prepare themselves for their work. That the institute held this summer did great good is questioned by no one. It was a school in which the students worked hard and learned much.

Union County is now improving rapidly in education. Our county is so small that we send only one man to the Lower House of the General Assembly, still we now have eight flourishing high schools. Statistics show that education is increasing. The public schools are doing more good than ever before in the history of the county. Parents are becoming interested. Teachers are working hard. The present school law has given an impetus to education. The system of committee works nicely—much better than the old one. One more step and we will be all right: let us have compulsory education.

Yours sincerely,

PLUMMER STEWART,
Supervisor of Union County.

MARS HILL, N. C., October 25, 1898.

HON. C. H. MEBANE, Superintendent Public Instruction, Raleigh, N. C.

DEAR SIR :—We have a Teacher's Association in Madson county, composed at present of about thirty-five teachers. Our meetings have developed quite an interest in the Teachers work, and I trust that much good will result from the organization. It has been a very difficult matter to arouse inspiration in many of the teachers sufficient to induce them to take the proper interest in these meetings. My predecessor, as Superintendent, made many faithful efforts, but to meet with final failure, the average teacher preferring to rest on his own resources, rather than come in touch with the onward movement of the more progressive element. In order to overcome this spirit of indifference I have used every effort available to inspire them to a more meritorious course of action in their profession. Indeed I have found it necessary to so arrange matters in countersigning vouchers on certain days as to almost compel some of them to attend. I am glad, however, to say that there is much improvement and promise for the better in this much-needed work.

INSTITUTE WORK.

From July 1, 1897, to July 1, 1898, there were five Institutes held in the county, conducted by myself as County Supervisor, assisted by some of best and most efficient teaching force in the county. The object of this work has been to bring before the teachers better methods of giving instructions to the pupils. I think this department of our work has been of great interest and very good results. We are able in the Institutes to come in contact with nearly all of the teachers—a much larger per cent than in the associations. The number who attended the Institutes durthe year mentioned was sixty-six. It is generally found expedient to have certain hours set apart for examinations, which brings some teachers in who would otherwise remain out. The effect of this work is not confined to teachers alone, but reaches out into the community and gives a healthy inspiration to education among the people, and now and then we are able to induce a school committeeman to attend, aud thus get him enthused in his line of work.

While we have, no doubt, in Institutes, fallen below true standard work, I nevertheless feel that we have never failed to arouse, both in teachers and citizens, a higher spirit of education in our public school work.

It is with no little pride that I feel able to say that there has been a forward move in our public schools all over the county

Perhaps one of the healthiest indications of the above statement is found in the fact that public sentiment has been awakened along this line. People have been eager to talk about the public schools. Until public sentiment was diverted by the war question, or more recently by politics, the uppermost question in the minds of our people seemed to be the public schools. Our teachers are fast passing from the non-professional to the professional, and hence the teachers' work is rising to a higher plane.

The Supervisor in his visits to the schools has constantly kept before the teachers, the pupils and the public the claims of the State on these schools. Teachers have been urged to make every effort to enroll every scholar in their respective districts, and then so stimulate them and their parents as to secure a regular attendance. To this request they have, as a rule, been faithful. When boys and girls have been absent the reason of such absence has been inquired for, and hence our average attendance has been made better. Whether we shall ever be able to get the children all in and keep them in school without a compulsory law, is a question for the future to decide. It is, no doubt, the fond hope of the true friend of popular education in our dear old State, that political fanaticisim may not be allowed to lay its blighting hand on the progress now being made in our public schools, merely to further the ends of some political party.

The highest type of patriotism is that which stands with a drawn sword in order to protect our public school system from any who would cripple it, even for a time, for mercenary motives.

W. P. JERVIS,
Supervisor of Madison County.

PITTSBORO, N. C., October 27, 1898.

HON. C. H. MEBANE, Raleigh, N. C.

DEAR SIR:—Our schools were a little longer this past year; the attendance was better, and I think there was more interest and better work done than usual.

I think a proper system of grading schools gives the most uniform advantages. I recommend separate committees for the supervision of white and colored schools.

May is the wrong time to take the census, if the money is apportioned the following January; too far apart, and districts change too much. Better take census in November.

Truly, R. B. LINEBERRY,
Supervisor of Chatham County.

BEE LOG, N. C., October 20, 1898.

SUPERINTENDENT MEBANE:—I have only been Superintendent of Schools for Yancey County since about the middle of July. My predecessor, Will Peterson, upon whose resignation I succeeded, did most all of our Institute work, and very ably, giving certificates to only worthy teachers, and putting our school system upon a sound basis.

Since I have been Superintendent a Teachers' Association has been organized, to meet monthly, and all teachers are requested to attend the meetings, or be deprived of teaching next year.

With this understanding in view, we have the presence of nearly all our teachers at every meeting. We meet at various places in the county in order to let the people know just what we are doing.

Much enthusiasm is manifested in the interest of education in our county.

We now have five high schools in good progress, and two colleges in erection.

Yancey, although in the mountains, seldom heard from, is no longer going to be in the dark, but will in a few years rival her surroundings.

We are determinate, resolute and untiring in our work, and it is our motto: "Not to be outdone by our equals."

Very truly, W. M. McINTOSH,
Supervisor of Yancey County.

WATAUGA COUNTY, N. C., October 24, 1898.

HON. C. H. MEBANE:

We have no Teacher's Association in this county, neither have we had any Institute work done in several years. Our public schools are lagging in interest. Our teachers are of a very good grade, but our citizenship is seemingly uninterested on the subject of public education. I have just taken hold as County Supervisor, and think it impracticable to organize a Teachers' Association now, for this year, as many of the teachers are just closing their schools. I hope, however, to organize an association early next year, which, I think, will inspire our teachers with more enthusiasm.

Respectfully, L. H. MICHAEL,
Supervisor of Watauga County.

CLIFTON, N. C., October 26, 1898.

HON. C. H. MEBANE, Raleigh, N. C.

DEAR SIR:—I am sorry to say we have no Teachers' Association in our county. We organized one two years ago, but the teachers took so little interest that we had to abandon it.

We had a Teachers' Institute during the past summer, conducted by President Chas. D. McIver, and enrolled thirty-eight teachers, and every one who attended seemed well pleased with the work done, and went away, I am sure, determiued to do better work in the future than in the past.

Our public schools seem to be looking up considerably, but they are not what they ought or what they could be, by any means.

There seems to be a greater interest manifested in education than ever before, and I am confident the people will vote the special school tax in some of the townships in this county next year.

Yours truly, J. W. JONES,
Supervisor of Ashe County.

AYDEN, N. C., October 31, 1898.

C. H. MEBANE, Superintendent Public Instruction, Raleigh, N. C.:

I have not been able, so far, to organize a Teachers' Association. I think a lively Teachers' Association would do much good, but owing to the large territory of our county, I find it very difficult to get the teachers together.

Prof. J. Y. Joyner held an Institute of a week. The time was divided between the whites and colored, giving three days to the whites and two to the colored. We had fifty-nine white teachers and forty-five colored, in regular attendance. While the time was entirely too short, I am sure much good was accomplished.

I find the general condition of the public schools to be gradually improving, and I hope that my personal visits and direct contact with the schools will raise them to a higher standard. I feel safe in saying that a little encouragement to the teachers and pupils will lead them into higher ideas of life and increase the spirit of education. I hope to do much on this line during the fall and winter term of our schools.

I find the greatest difficulty to be indifference among the people. I am trying to awake the people to an interest in the public schools, and during my visits to the schools I shall try to reach the public by lectures at night in different neighborhoods where I can get a hearing; I hope in this way to overcome indifference and secure a larger attendance. I am fully satisfied that the public ear must be reached and the people educated in public school work.

J. R. TINGLE,
Supervisor of Pitt County.

OFFICE OF COUNTY SUPERVISOR,
WHITEVILLE, N. C.

HON. C. H. MEBANE. Raleigh.

DEAR SIR:—At first the teachers manifested a good deal of interest in their associations, but it seems to have all died out, for neither white nor colored have met since last June.

There has not been an Institute held in this county in three years. The Board of which I have the honor to be Secretary, believe it to be a waste of the children's money to have Institutes.

The general condition of the public schools has greatly improved during the past year The subject of popular education is taking on new life in old Columbus.

I had issued, from July 1 to November 1 last year, only thirteen certificates; for same time this year I have issued forty. Bogue Township the last school year made an average of seventy nine days to each school for the white race. Whiteville made an average of sixty-two days to each school for the white race. Bug Hill Township and Waccamaw stood at the foot of the list in the day schools. Waccamaw returned 161 children, enrolled only 48; average attendance, 28.

Your friend, W. H. SELLERS
Supervisor of Columbus County.

OCTOBER 14, 1898.

HON. C. H. MEBANE, State Superintendent Public Instruction, Raleigh, N. C.

DEAR SIR:—In answer to your request, I will say that no appropriation for an Institute has been made by the Board of Education for this county, and therefore none has been held.

Some teachers have advocated a voluntary Association, but no steps have been taken towards organizing it as yet. I am of the opinion that this would be a move in the right direction, if we could get our teachers to meet often enough. The plan would work no expense on the county, and might be a great help to teachers, especially the inexperienced.

The schools in this county are in fairly good condition, but the interest is not taken in matters of education that ought to be. In some sections we find a good many who should be in school that never attend.

In order to ascertain the needs of the schools and to improve the educational interests as much as possible, the Board of Education has directed the Supervisor to visit every school in the county.

Very truly yours, H. S. AVERITT,
Supervisor of Cumberland County.

NASHVILLE, N. C., October 18, 1898.

HON. C. H. MEBANE, Superintendent Public Instruction, Raleigh, N. C.

DEAR SIR :—In reply to yours of recent date, I have to say we have no Teachers' Association in this county yet. Hope to have one soon. No Institute held this year. The general condition of our schools is growing better. Teachers grade better, both white and colored. Houses much improved. The people generally becoming more interested The subject of education getting more attention. The school committee discharging their duty. Colored committeemen for colored schools recommended. Most respectfully your obedient servant,

L. M CONYERS,
Supervisor of Nash County.

ROCKINGHAM, N. C., October 15, 1898.

HON. C. H. MEBANE, Raleigh, N. C.

DEAR SIR :—We have no Teachers' Association. Have had no Teachers' Institute for several years. I have not visited schools. The law requires the "Supervisor to visit schools under the direction of the Board of Education." I am not able to find the needs of the schools nor conditions, as the Board of Education has not directed me to visit schools.

There is no doubt in my mind that public schools could be very much improved and made more popular if schools were visited and the claims of public schools properly presented to the people. I would, with pleasure, visit schools if directed by Board of Education.

Yours very respectfully, M. N. McIVER,
Supervisor of Richmond County.

OFFICE COUNTY SUPERVISOR,
LAKE COMFORT, HYDE COUNTY, N. C., October 15, 1898.

HON. C. H. MEBANE, Raleigh, N. C.

DEAR SIR:—In reply to your circular I would say, that we have no Teachers' Association or any Institute work done, but our schools are in a fair condition, and the interest in public education increasing.

The length of school term has been increased at least one-third in the district that carried the special school tax.

Very truly, H. L. McGOWAN,
Supervisor of Hyde County.

MT. PLEASANT, N. C., October 19, 1898.

HON. C. H. MEBANE, State Superintendent
Public Instruction, Raleigh, N. C.

DEAR SIR:—Replying to your circular which I had the honor to receive a few days ago, I have to say:

1. That the effort made last year to organize a Teachers' Association in this county met with failure. On one or more occasions heretofore similar attempts had been made, with apparent success at the beginning, but for some reason the teachers lost interest and the Association ceased to exist. Since then the teachers have not manifested much interest in forming an Association.

2. Two Institutes, one for white, the other for colored teachers, were held August 22-26, both dates included, in Concord. Prof. J. Y. Joyner, of the State Normal and Industrial College, Greensboro, conducted the Institute for the white teachers. He was assisted by Prof. T. A. Sharpe, formerly Superintendent of the Goldsboro Graded School.

The Institute was attended by seventy (70) teachers, thirty-one males and thirty-nine (39) females. Dr. C. D. McIver, President of the State Normal and Industrial College, delivered a public address on the 26th. Much interest was taken in the work by the teachers, and much good was no doubt accomplished.

The Institute for colored teachers was conducted by Rev. F. T. Logan, Principal of the Concord Graded School. He was assisted by President Jas. B. Dudley, of the State (Col.) Agricultural and Mechanical College, Greensboro, and Prof. W. M. Provinder, of the State Normal School, for colored teachers, at Salisbury. The County Supervisor also gave the institute one hour each day, instructing the teachers on such subjects as was thought would add to their efficiency as teachers. The Institute was attended by twenty-six teachers, seven males and nineteen females (which was one less than were examined during the year). The interest manifested by the colored teachers was all that could be desired. I think the Institute will prove to be of much benefit to the colored schools. President Dudley and Prof. Provinder delivered public addresses to the colored people on the 26th.

3. The public schools at this date have not opened for the winter term. The schools last winter were, as a general thing, well taught. The committees and people seemed to be pleased with the work done. Some of the houses are not such as to secure the best results, but that difficulty is gradually being overcome by paying more attention to the proper construction of new houses when occasion requires. Furniture, maps, globes, etc , are needed, but with the present school fund it has not been thought good policy to encourage the purchasing of such supplies. The chief want of many of the schools, other than money, is efficient teachers, such as will be fully competent to use maps, globes, charts, etc. If it be deemed well, then to make the outlay.

4. I think the interest in education is growing. The people more generally are coming to the point of seeing that the prosperity of a country depends upon the general intelligence of the people; that to raise North Carolina in the scale of prosperity the children must be educated, but in this field there is much work to do.

Very respectfully, H. T. J. LUDWIG,
Supervisor of Cabarrus County.

EAST BEND, N. C., October 28, 1898.

HON. C. H. MEBANE, Superintendent Public Instruction, Raleigh, N. C.

DEAR SIR:—We are trying by every possible means to raise the standard of education in Yadkin. We expect, through our Teachers' Association, white and colored, to secure a much higher grade of teachers and an increase in their salaries of at least twenty per cent. above last year.

Our County Institute, which opened the 19th and closed the 28th of July, was pronounced, by honest persons of all classes, a success. Prof. Foust, of Goldsboro, N. C., showed himself the proper man in the proper place, and by his gentle and unassuming conduct before the ninety-seven teachers who were in attendance, won for himself the esteem of them all.

In conclusion, I will say, without the least thought of sycophancy, the outlook for a higher standard of education in old Yadkin was never so hopeful as under our new system and with our present State Superintendent as our literary leader.

Truly yours,

J. H. PATTERSON,
Supervisor of Yadkin County.

WANCHESE, N. C., October 29, 1898.

HON C. H. MEBANE, Superintendent Public Instruction, Raleigh N C.

DEAR SIR:—The necessity of traveling by sail-boat (and hence the uncertainty) has prevented us from having a Teachers' Association. There has been no Institute held in the county.

Our people are aiding the publ c schools by employing, where practicable, the regular academies to do the public school work. There is a growing sentiment in favor of public primary and academic schools for the masses. Yours very truly,

L. BASNIGHT,
Supervisor of Dare County.

SHELBY, N. C., November 1, 1898.

HON. C. H. MEBANE, Superintendent Public Instruction, Raleigh, N. C.

DEAR SIR :—Cleveland county has two Associations for the teachers; one for the white teachers and the other for the colored teachers. The white Association is divided into two divisions, one the western division, the other the eastern division. Each of these Associations are well organized and are planning to do much practical educational work this winter.

We held two Institutes last July, one for the white teachers and the other for the colored teachers. Both of these Institutes were very largely attended, much interest being manifested by the public generally, and the teachers much better prepared for the work of the school-room.

All our public schools are improving rapidly in every respect. The teachers are well prepared for their work. The school rooms are being well equipped and public sentiment is more healthful.

J. A. ANTHONY,
Supervisor of Cleveland County.

STONY KNOLL, N. C., October 30, 1898.

HON. C. H. MEBANE, Raleigh, N. C.

SIR :—We have no Teachers' Association in this county now, and for what the Board of Education thought good reasons, we had no Teachers' Institute this year, although the county has not been backward in Institute work.

The condition of the public schools is good, in fact, I believe better than ever. The prevalence of measles in most all parts of the county last winter reduced the average attendance to a considerable extent. Our citizens are taking greater interest in schools than ever before. By voting a special school tax Mount Airy gets ten months school this year. The school is in a very flourishing condition, with able teachers and large attendance. It is, perhaps, one of the best schools of its kind in the State. The academies at Siloam, Pilot Mountain and others in the county are in successful operation and well patronized.

Yours truly, JOHN W. WILLIAMS,
Supervisor of Surry County.

CHARLOTTE, N. C., October 22, 1898.

HON. C. H. MEBANE.

DEAR SIR:—I am sorry to say that the Teacher's Association of this county is not what it should be by any means. I believe, however, that

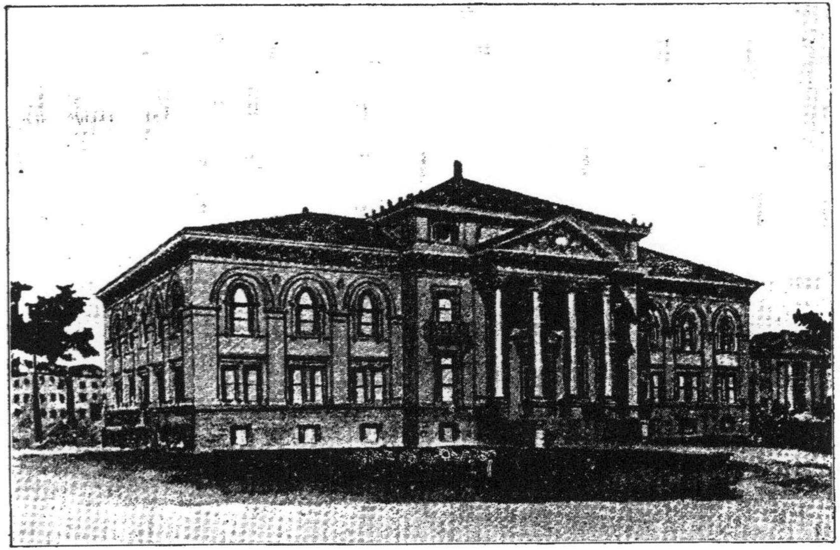

ALUMNUS HALL BUILDING, CHAPEL HILL, N. C.

some of the causes which have militated against it will be removed, and that, for the next year, it will be far more efficient and enthusiastic.

By order of our County Board of Education we had the Institutes during the month of July—one for each race. Both of these were well attended and highly appreciated by the teachers.

Prof. F. H. Curtier conducted the Institute for the white race. He was assisted by Prof. J. G. Baird, of the Charlotte Military Institute, and Profs. Coon and Bivens of the Graded Schools of the city. In addition to the regular work of the Institute, we had lectures by several prominent educators of the State. Among this number were Dr. Henry Louis Smith, of Davidson College; Dr. McIver, of the State Normal School, Greensboro; Dr. E. W. Sykes, of Wake For st College, and Hon. C. H. Mebane, State Superintendent of Public Instruction.

We had in attendance 104 teachers, and many friends of education in this and other States.

The colored Institute was conducted by Prof. G. E. Davis, of Biddle University, assisted by Prof. Baird and others. There were 129 teachers in attendance, and the work of Prof. Davis and his assistants was very practicable and helpful. Each Institute continued one week. Besides the regular free schools of the county, we have thirteen high schools in which our boys and girls are prepared for the higher colleges. All of these high schools are doing excellent work, and I am glad to say they are largely attended. The educational interests of this county are steadily improving, and I can see an increased desire on the part of our boys and girls for a liberal education. May this sentiment prevail all over our beloved old State.

Respectfully, R. B. HUNTER,
Supervisor of Mecklenburg County.

HERTFORD, N. C., October 22, 1898.

HON. C. H. MEBANE.

MY DEAR SIR :—I will say this county has not paid out any money for Institute work, because, I think, if the County Supervisor is careful to grant license to teach to none except those who are competent to teach, the money paid out for such purposes can be better expended in the employment of teachers—that is to say, in extension of the school term.. I am of the opinion that nothing is so essential to the good of our public schools as an extended school term. We have so little money to pay the expenses of our schools, that I deem it waste to use it for any other purpose than the employment of teachers. I am hoping that this winter's school term will be longer than that of last winter. I regard our public schools as the only reliable means by which the masses of our people are to be educated, and I hope to see the time when our people shall esteem the public school as the most priceless institution of our State. The status of the public school in each of the several States is a sure index of the value placed upon education by the several peoples thereof. Where-ever the public school does not exist, there education in its crudest form will be found. Yours very truly, etc.,

FRANCIS PICARD,
Superintendent of Perquimans County.

QUEEN, N. C., October 25, 1898.

C. H. MEBANE, Superintendent Public Instruction, Raleigh, N. C.

SIR:—Some of the public schools in Montgomery county are not as good as I thought they were before I began visiting them. In some of the schools where I have gone a very large per cent. of the books used are old and out of date. Some of the people say that they would buy the books needed if they could get them, while others don't seem to realize the need of having any books except Webster's old speller, etc. This is the case in some of our districts but not in all of them. We have some well conducted schools.

We have had no Teacher's Institute for several years, neither have we any Teachers' Association. There was a Teachers' Association organized a few years ago, but it soon died for want of interest.

In some townships the committee have decided to pay no teacher more than $20.00 per month. Many of our first grade teachers have to teach for that amount or not teach at all. I heard a school committeeman, who is a farmer, remark some time ago that he was not willing for any one to make more than he could.

We certainly need and must have a Teachers' Association, whether we have any other organization or not.

Most truly, GEO. L. REYNOLDS,
Supervisor of Montgomery County.

ELIZABETH CITY, N. C., October 13, 1898.

HON. C. H. MEBANE, Raleigh, N. C.

DEAR SIR:—We have no Teachers' Association here at present, but I expect to organize one shortly. As to Institute work, we have had none conducted here for some years, but we intend to do better in future.

I can say but little regarding the general condition of the public schools, because I have not visited them. I am reliably informed, however, that the condition of the school-houses in the county is for the most part good. With few exceptions the school-houses are comparatively new, having been built and furnished within recent years. And still the good work goes on. We continue to build new houses every year. Since I have been in office an appropriation of $412 50 has been made for a new house in one of our townships.

I believe we have one of the best schools in the State here at Elizabeth City. The building is a commodious brick structure, and six teachers are employed. The school is divided into five grades, under the direction of a superintendent, and bookkeeping and stenography will be taught during the present term.

As to the rural districts, more money is needed in order to secure high grade teachers at a liberal salary, and to lengthen the usual four months term. Very respectfully, GASTON POOL,
Supervisor of Pasquotank County.

GLEN AYRE, N. C., October 31, 1898.

PROF. C. H. MEBANE, Raleigh, N. C.

DEAR SIR:—The teachers of Mitchell county, N. C., met at Bakersville, July, 1897, and organized a Teachers' Associaton. The Association prospered during August and the following autumn. It was a good educational help for the teachers of Mitchell. It should have been kept up; but for the distance the teachers had to go, and the inclemency of the weather in this mountain section of country, the Association closed.

There has not been an Association organized this year. I think Teacher's Associations are a great help for the cause of education.

We had a very interesting Institute July, 1897. We did not have an Institute in Mitchell this summer.

The public schools of Mitchell are progressing. Better teaching is being done each year. We have better school-houses and more thorough teachers than formerly. The text-books are superior to those used some years ago. With these improvements in teachers, houses and books, the public schools are advancing.

Public education in Mitchell county is doing, and has done, a vast amount of good for our people, because the education of our people depends almost entirely on public schools.

There are not many young men and young women who are receiving, or have received, an academic education, and a very small number, indeed, who have gone to college. Those who have attended academies and colleges received their rudimentary instruction in public schools. If it were not for the public schools of our country, nine-tenths of the children would not receive any instruction. I am very thankful that we have a free school system in North Carolina. May our free schools become better, be prosperous and do good for the time to come, is my sincere desire. Very truly, AUGUSTUS MASTERS,
Supervisor of Mitchell County.

WENTWORTH, N. C., November 7, 1898.

HON. C. H. MEBANE, Superintendent Public Instruction, Raleigh, N. C.

DEAR SIR:—Your circular requesting a brief letter as to Teachers' Association, etc., to hand.

1. I have not organized a Teachers' Association in this county. My predecessor organized one for each race, but little or no interest was taken in it, and good results were not visible.

The time when work in these associations would be most helpful for teachers, is while the schools are in session. Unfortunately for us, our school term begins in October and closes in March, embracing the coldest period of the year. During the winter season travel in this county is difficult on account of the almost impassable condition of our roads.

These things, in connection with the small salaries usually paid our teachers, make the attendance at the meetings of a Teachers' Association such a burden to our teachers that I have not yet asked them to organize.

2. INSTITUTES.—I secured the services of Prof. Frank H. Curtiss and conducted an Institute of one week for each race.

I have never seen as much interest manifested in an Institute anywhere as we had here. The teachers expressed themselves as greatly benefited, and would gladly have remained twice as long as they did.

I really think it better to put our best efforts in an Institute of a week or ten days each year and have a wide-awake, lively, helpful meeting, than to try to have several less helpful and interesting meetings and call it an Association.

I think I may say without egotism or flattery that the public school teachers, white and colored, of Rockingham county, are decidedly above the average in the State in point of intelligence, skill and social standing.

3. THE GENERAL CONDITION OF PUBLIC SCHOOLS.—An increase in usefulness and interest is manifest in our schools.

Committeemen are seeking to secure better skill on the part of teachers in most of the schools. In some instances committeemen appear to have contracted ideas and make mistakes in the selection of teachers. It will require time to overcome this hindrance.

Sentiment in favor of *local taxation* is increasing. I hope in my next annual report to make advance in this direction.

NEEDS.—Larger and more regular attendance on the part of pupils.
Greater interest on the part of parents.
More money.

Very respectfully,
E. P. ELLINGTON,
Supervisor of Rockingham County.

OFFICE SUPERVISOR OF COUNTY SCHOOLS,
ASHEVILLE, N. C., October 15, 1898.

HON. CHAS. H. MEBANE, State Superintendent, Raleigh, N. C.

MY DEAR SIR:—I have the honor to give you the following information about the progress of education in the county of Buncombe:

1. TEACHERS' ASSOCIATION.—The teachers of the county meet monthly at Asheville, at the close of each school month. A program of three or four live, up-to-date topics is printed and distributed to all teachers two weeks before the meeting. General discussion is had on every topic after the leader has closed his remarks. An average attendance of seventy-five of the 120 teachers in the county has been made so far, besides most of the teachers in Asheville public and private schools.

2. TRAINING SCHOOLS.—During the past summer, the Board of Education provided five training schools, of one month each, at as many parts of the county, four for white teachers and one for negro teachers. One hundred and ten teachers attended these schools, and at the close of the

schools the regular county examination was held, covering three days, and the papers were graded by a competent committee, and certificates issued on this basis. Teachers express great satisfaction at the work done in these schools, and have petitioned for a two months term next year. The public schools are in fine condition, with well equipped teachers, and a longer attendance than ever before. The term this year will average five months. There is a great and growing enthusiasm on the part of the people for public education. The township's system is generally acceptable to all classes.

Nearly all the schools have raised from $5.00 to $20.00 to buy books for the foundation of a public school library. Many new school-houses are being erected throughout the county, after plans furnished by the County Board of Education. An effort is being made to seat all public school-houses with the best patent double desks This movement is likely to be carried to a successful issue in January, 1899.

I have the honor to be, my dear sir, very respectfully,

Your obedient servant, DAVID L. ELLIS,
Supervisor of Buncombe County.

Buncombe County has—

1. Three Colleges, with a total enrollment of five hundred students.

2. Seven High Schools and Academies, with an enrollment of nine hundred students.

3. A system of Graded Schools, with thirty teachers, instructing 2,000 white and 1,500 colored children.

4. A system of free Kindergarten Schools.

5. Five denominational schools, at which are taught the handcraft best suited to industrial pursuits in life.

6. One of the oldest and most enthusiastic Teachers' Associations in the State, with an average attendance of one hundred teachers monthly.

7. Five Training Schools for teachers, of two months session every year, each, officered by five trained in tructors.

8. One hundred and twenty-five public schools, enrolling 10,000 pupils.

9. Raised nearly $75,000 for public schools this year.

10. Not endorsed a certificate this year, but required a rigid examination for license to teach in her schools.

11. One of the most intelligent and progressive Boards of Education, and several of the most liberal and business-like School Committees in the State.

12. Raised this year (1898) money enough to place a working library in nearly every public school in the county.

13. The whole time of the Supervisor given to the work of the public schools.

14. Arranged to place the best patent double desks into all the school houses in 1898.

For any information about the educational interests of Asheville and Buncombe county, Address D. L. ELLIS,
Sec'y and Supervisor, Asheville, N. C.

LETTERS OF SUPERINTENDENT OF PUBLIC INSTRUCTION.

NOTE.—I publish here some of the most important official letters sent out from the office of Superintendent of Public Instruction during the last two years. This is done that the public may know the official advice and council of the present Superintendent as to whether it has been wise or otherwise.

OFFICE OF
SUPERINTENDENT OF PUBLIC INSTRUCTION,
RALEIGH, April, 1897.

To the Friends of Public Education:

I wish to explain one or two important changes in the School Law as enacted by the last General Assembly of North Carolina.

First—The township is to be the unit of our Public School System. The public schools in the township are under the control and management of the five School Committeemen. These men have large discretion as to establishing schools in their townships. As a matter of fact, under the old law, in many instances, there are three huts, not school-houses, each receiving about $75.00 per year. Under the new law it is possible to have, instead of three cabins, *one good school-house* near the centre of the territory covered by the three cabins, and have $225 for this school. Instead of having three $15 teachers we may have one good $50 man or woman, that may do more for the school children in four months than under the old system was done in two or three years.

Who would not rather send his children two, or even three miles to a school that is a school than to have a poor school on the corner of his farm? I am aware that some are very much opposed to the township system on account of school-houses being near them, and on account of work or money spent on some of these houses. I hope these persons will take a liberal view of this matter, lay aside personal preference and join in hearty co-operation for the greatest good to the greatest number. When we unite the small schools into one good, strong school, with one energetic, live teacher, then, and not until then, may we expect to have public schools of such force and character that will be felt in our State.

Second—The election, to be held "on Tuesday after the second Monday in August," is worthy of your careful consideration. This election is to be held in every township. The County Commissioners at their June meeting are to give notice of this election in every county in North Carolina.

Any township that votes to tax itself $500 for public schools will receive $500 from the State Board of Education. Friends, do not become alarmed when you hear the word tax. I am aware that our country people do have a hard time to pay their taxes, but consider how little would be the tax of each one in a township in order to raise $1,500, and then have this supplemented by the State with $500, making $2,000 in addition to what school fund you now have. Suppose where we now have twelve schools in a township we make only eight strong schools; each one would receive from the $2,000 $250; add this $250 to your regular school fund; if we can put three of the $75 schools together, then we would have $250 plus $225, which is $475 for each school. Now, my friends, do not say that all this looks very well on paper, but it cannot be done in our State.

I tell you it can be done, and when we have $475 for our public schools in our State, then we will have a right to demand professional teachers in our public schools.

What right have we to talk about professional teachers in our public schools, with only $75 or $100 a year to pay such teachers?

Third—I would like to remove, if possible, the idea that some of our people have in regard to teachers' salaries. I have heard School Committeemen compare the time of a school teacher with that of the wood-chopper, the ditcher and the ordinary laborer. I have not aught to say against any man who does this kind of work; it is honorable and right, but what I want to call your attention to is that a man's education is his investment. Let us see what an ordinary education costs. In time, it costs six years—two years preparatory, and four years in college.

We will say that the cost of the preparatory education is $300, of the college four years, at $250 each, making a cost of $1,300.

The six years' time spent in school would be worth at least six hundred dollars. Thus we see the total cost of an ordinary education in time and money is about $1,900. These figures mean strict economy on the part of the student. The interest on this education is 3c. per day at 6 per cent. interest. Now what farmer or business man would invest $1,900 and compare his income with the 25-cent wood-chopper or the ordinary laborer, who has invested neither time nor money?

C. H. MEBANE,
State Superintendent Public Instruction.

OFFICE OF
SUPERINTENDENT OF PUBLIC INSTRUCTION,
RALEIGH, April 10, 1898.

To the Members of the County Board of Education and the Members of the Respective School Committees:

GENTLEMEN:—You are aware that it is the custom in many of the School Districts, under the old law, to leave over a part of the School Fund from the winter school and have said fund taught out during the summer months. You are also aware that the apportionment of school funds was made last January, and that there can be no apportionment of school funds until January, 1898, which apportionment will be made under the new law and upon a different basis.

In view of these facts, as stated above, I, as State Superintendent of Public Instruction, advise you to allow the funds that were left over for a summer school to be taught out as usual. You will have no trouble to ascertain from the records what schools have such fund.

It is my earnest desire that as little friction as possible may be created in changing from the old system to the township system.

Let changes be made with care and deliberation. There are in many localities too many small districts, and in many instances it will be the part of wisdom to erect one good school-house and have one good school, where now there are two or three poor school-houses and two or three poor schools.

Gentlemen, the responsibilities that you have assumed are great, and the work is worthy of your greatest care and concern.

The success or failure of the new law is largely in your hands. Will you, like men, rise up and meet the duties that devolve upon you? I trust that you will. Remember that not only your children, and not only your neighbor's children are to be benefited, but your work is to have its effect upon the future generations of our great State.

Yours truly, C. H. MEBANE.

OFFICE OF
SUPERINTENDENT OF PUBLIC INSTRUCTION,
RALEIGH, N. C., June 1, 1897.

At a meeting of the State Board of Education on May 28, 1897, the following resolution was adopted:

"That in case the general State fund shall not be sufficient to meet the payment of the $50,000 appropriated by the Public School Law of 1897, the Board of Education authorizes a loan from the School Fund to the general State fund sufficient to meet such appropriation, or so much of it as may be called for."

There is now no longer any doubt as to the Local Taxation Act as passed by the last General Assembly. We want the united force of the press in North Carolina in the interest of public education. We are becoming more and more a reading people. A larger part of the masses of the people read the newspapers to-day than ever before.

We want the united force of the pulpit, of the teachers, and of all the true men and women in our State, to arouse the masses of the people on the subject of education, and on the importance of the election to take place on Tuesday after the second Monday in August. We want a campaign for education. The opposition to be overcome is great. The work to be done is immense.

If there are friends of education who cannot go out among the people, and yet want to do something for the cause, they can help by giving money to meet the expenses of those who are willing to go and proclaim the doctrine of universal education.

We hope to be able to effect an organization at the Teachers' Assembly, whereby we may have some man in every county in the State.

We are in the fight to accomplish something. We have had considerable space devoted to us to show our ignorance, etc., but our zeal rises with the opposition.

Yours very truly, C. H. MEBANE,
Sup't Public Instruction for N. C.

OFFICE OF
SUPERINTENDENT OF PUBLIC INSTRUCTION,
RALEIGH, N. C., July 19, 1897.

To the County Supervisor of Public Schools.

DEAR SIR:—The reorganization of the Public School

System of North Carolina, according to the Act of the General Assembly, is now complete.

The working force of the system consists of the State Board of Education, the State Superintendent of Public Instruction, the County Board of Education, the County Supervisor, the Township Committee and the teachers. We must work together. We must make a success of our efforts to educate the masses in North Carolina. As head of the system for the State, I shall expect much of you. The first object before us is to carry the local taxation election August 10, "for schools." We have a great opportunity here and great responsibility. Local taxation is the only hope of building up our Public School system; it is only hope of educating the poor children.

If we would have twenty-six weeks school instead of twelve weeks, if we would make North Carolina one of the most intelligent States instead of one of the most illiterate, we must get the people to vote for local taxation.

Therefore, I come to you with the request that you personally do all you can to carry the coming election "for Schools;" that you send out speakers, workers and literature, if possible; that you officially prepare a letter for the School Committee of your county, urging them to work for local taxation in their respective townships. Organize the county thoroughly. Show the people what little the tax will amount to and what great things it will do for them.

Go to the office of the Register of Deeds and make a table of one or two townships and show to the public how little will be the burden each one will have to bear, and how great things will follow for the schools of the townships that vote for local tax.

Yours very truly,

C. H. MEBANE,

Supt. Public Instruction for N. C.

OFFICE OF
SUPERINTENDENT OF PUBLIC INSTRUCTION.

August 24, 1897.

HOW SHALL WE IMPROVE THE ATTENDANCE OF OUR PUBLIC SCHOOLS?

I come to you with this important question and ask you to give it your careful consideration. This is a question that should interest all the friends of popular education.

The first remedy I shall suggest, is, to have better schools. How are we to have better schools?. Secure better teachers.

Our schools are largely what our teachers make them. So long as we have teachers that have only just enough interest in their work to secure the money at the end of the school, just so long we may expect to have a poor attendance of the children.

If the teachers are not interested in the schools we need not expect for the children to be interested, and if the teachers and children are not interested, the parents will not likely take much interest.

Let us then have teachers who are interested in school work themselves, and who will strive to create an interest in both the children and the parents of the community in which they teach.

Let our teachers go out among some of the indifferent parents and strive to show them what they can and will do for their children.

When their children come, be sure that something is done for them. *Our parents ought not to be such strangers to our schools*, and especially to our school teachers. Let our teachers have some entertainments occasionally that will improve and at the same time interest the children. Invite especially those parents who are known to take little interest or concern in the school. We have known cases of this kind where the most indifferent and even an opponent of the school has been won over to be its most ardent friend and supporter.

Above all things, I would suggest that our teachers use *common sense, tact* and *judgment.* Often a great deal of harm is done by some young Solon who goes out into a community of good, honest, but uneducated people. He goes out with some new-fangled idea that he has read about, or with some fine-spun theory, and he speaks of Pedagogy, Psychology, using high-sounding phrases of which the people and the children have no conception as to their meaning. Some one may say these last few lines are a reflection upon our teachers. I deny it—*I have seen and heard just such teachers.*

The cry was made during the late campaign for local taxation that our children do not attend what schools we now have—why spend any more money, when what we now have is not used and appreciated by those who need it most.

I am in favor of *better schools, better teachers, more earnest, honest effort* to make them worthy to be attended by our children, and then if, after we have good schools, the people will not send their children, *I shall be in favor of compulsory education.*

Yours truly, C. H. MEBANE,
Superintendent of Public Instruction.

OFFICE OF
SUPERINTENDENT OF PUBLIC INSTRUCTION,
RALEIGH, August 27, 1897.

To the County Supervisor:

I wish to call the attention of you and your County Board of Education to Section 2555 of the School Law of 1897.

I find that the printer omitted a very important part of this Section, as follows:

"No order given by a School Committee of any District (Township) for maps, charts, globes, or other school apparatus, shall be valid unless the same be indorsed by the Chairman of the Board of Commissioners (which now means

Chairman County Board of Education) and approved by the County Board of Education."

I call upon you in the name of the children of your county to put a stop to the squandering of the School Fund, if it has been in your county. Beware of vouchers that are presented to you for school supplies. These words, "school supplies," on some of these vouchers I have seen, simply mean $37.50 for a school chart.

Now, can you expect for people to be willing to pay taxes to support public schools when the money is squandered this way?

If I lived in a county where I had to pay taxes, to be wasted in this way, when an election came to vote on school taxes, I would take the stump and canvass the county against schools, until we could find men that had sense enough to know how to spend the money.

Yours truly, C. H. MEBANE,
Superintendent Public Instruction.

OFFICE OF
SUPERINTENDENT OF PUBLIC INSTRUCTION,
RALEIGH, N. C., Nov. 20, 1897.

To the Teachers:

DEAR FRIENDS:—I have sent to your County Supervisor a constitution for a Teachers' Association in your county. I send this letter to you and ask your co-operation in this great work.

It is of vital importance to public education for our teachers to be organized; to have united action for advancement among our teachers. No teacher is so wise but that he may learn something by coming in touch with his fellow-teachers. Those of you who are better prepared to teach, and who have had better opportunities than others, should meet with the others who are not so well prepared, and who have not had such favorable opportunities.

Come together in the Teachers' Association for mutual benefit, as well as for the cause of public education in general.

Why shall not our teachers be organized? The business men, bankers and merchants are organized.

We have our Dental Association, our Medical Association, our Press Association, our Pharmaceutical Association, and others too numerous to mention.

All these organizations mean something, and have force and effect, each one in its own special work. Why may not the teachers come together and have some force and power, not only in the county where the Association is, but be felt in adjoining counties, and still, of more importance, be felt in the Legislature of our State, to secure whatever legislation is needed from time to time for the best interest and progress of the schools?

Our teachers, both public and private, do not make themselves felt as they should, as a class of men and women, in their respective counties. Too many of our teachers are indifferent as to what public sentiment is on the subject of popular education. Too often they sit in silence while the politicians around the court-house and the school committeemen squander the public money.

The County Association may not only create public sentiment in favor of popular education, but it may be the means of securing school men for school committeemen instead of men who will do the bidding of the court-house politician.

It may be the means of making the public school money the most sacred, which it should be, of any public money in the county.

It may make the schools, instead of a farce and a subject of ridicule, a power and a blessing to each community.

Will you not do some of these things? Do not sit down in silence, like some of our teachers did last summer; because certain men favored local tax they were, therefore, against it.

If you have not good school men in your county, no better way to start a move for the right kind of men than in your Association as a body of teachers.

You, as an association of teachers and workers for popular education, can make demands of your county officers, which will be granted, for the benefit of your schools.

I hope you will give this subject your careful consideration, and that I shall hear of action along this line in your county at an early day.

Yours very truly, C. H. MEBANE,
Superintendent of Public Instruction.

OFFICE OF
SUPERINTENDENT OF PUBLIC INSTRUCTION.
RALEIGH, N. C., October 12, 1897.

To the Members County Board of Education:

I wish to call your special attention to Sec. 2569 of the School Law, which is as follows:

"The County Supervisor shall be required to visit the public schools of his County, while in session, but under the direction of the County Board of Education, and shall inform himself of the condition and needs of the various schools within his jurisdiction."

My reason for sending this circular letter is, that in some counties, I learn that the County Board of Education has decided that the Supervisor shall not visit any of the schools.

This decision is contrary to the law, which says: "Supervisors shall be required to visit," etc.

The provision, "but under the direction of the County Board of Education," is a wise one. Under the old County Superintendent system, I heard of one County Superintendend who visited schools the greater part of the year. He would only visit one school a day, no matter how near by another school was. He managed to have some schools taught during the summer, and some during the autumn and winter, in his county, so that he could find visiting to be done the greater part of the year. Thus you see the

A CAMPUS VIEW—UNIVERSITY OF NORTH CAROLINA.

need of a check for such characters. It is the duty of the County Board of Education to see that no useless time is charged against the School Fund by the County Supervisor. The teachers and the people will soon let it be known whether the Supervisor is killing time or is giving life and insipiration to the schools and teachers.

If any County Board of Education in North Carolina has a Supervisor *who cannot* and *will not* give impetus and life to the schools by his *council*, *pluck*, *push* and *power*, by *coming in touch* with these schools at least once a year; I say if the County Board of Education has a man who cannot do this, *then such a man is not the man for Supervisor* for our public schools, and the best thing to do is to declare the office vacant and find a man *who can and will make himself heard and felt* in the county.

I feel sorry for the public school teachears and the children of any county, of whose Supervisor it can truthfully be said that his visiting and coming in touch with the schools of his county is a waste of the public money.

If the Snpervisor is not capable of discharging his whole duty the County Board of Education is responsible for it, and if he is capable of discharging his duty I beg you not to tie his hands, but send him out among the schools and among the people. We must just *pound* it into many of our people, how great is their responsibility to their own children and their neighbors' children—and our County Supervisors should do a large share of this *pounding*.

Let the Supervisor get the people out and have an Educational Rallay-day in every township, if possible, at least once a year. Let the teachers, parents and children all feel the power and influence of your Supervisor. When this is done then you will see a month or six weeks being added here and there to the public schools by private subscriptions, and this will finally lead to a foundation for the support of all the schools in the townships, namely, local tax.

Yours truly, C. H. MEBANE,
Superintendent of Public Instruction.

OFFICE OF
SUPERINTENDENT OF PUBLIC INSTRUCTION,
RALEIGH, N. C., October 4, 1897.

To the Committeemem:

I hope you have the census of your respective townships, and that you have assigned the children to their respective schools. If you have not the census you must take it accurately and have the reports in the hands of your County Supervisor not later than the first Monday in December. This will only give the Supervisor one month to get his report in shape for the County Board of Education on the first Monday in January, 1898, when the apportionment will be made strictly by the township, and so much per capita.

Where it is necessary to continue a school near a township line, the committees which control the territory from which the children will come to compose such school or schools, should get together and decide how many, and who, shall attend or be assigned to such schools. Make these reports plain, so that the County Board of Education may easily understand.

The law does not require that each school shall have sixty-five children assigned to it, no more and no less, for, on account of geographical reasons, in certain localities, impassable streams and creeks and sparsely settled areas, it will not be practicable to have as many as sixty-five children for each school, and for these reasons one school may have fewer than thirty children, but others have as many as seventy-five or one hundred, but the average in the whole township should not be less than sixty-five.

If possible, I would much prefer to have an average of seventy-five or eighty. This would be much better, as the greater the average the fewer the schools, and consequently the longer the school term.

You are required to meet on the second Monday in January and re-apportion the money that has been apportioned to your township by the County Board of Education.

I have taken considerable pains to prepare a Record Book for you. This book is arranged as simple as can be, and should be in the possession of each School Committee in North Carolina. You will find a colored page for your account with the County Board of Education, and twelve white pages following each colored one, for an itemized account with each school in your township.

You have more power and larger discretion as to the re-apportionment of the School Fund than was ever allowed to School Committeemen before by the laws of our State, and I trust you will use this power and discretion wisely. Remember that the success or failure of the township system is largely in your hands. Use your wisest judgment and do what you know is for the best interest of the public schools. Do not expect to please everybody, but dare to do your duty.

I would remind you that a good, live, energetic teacher is cheaper at $35 or $40 per month than a teacher who knows nothing of what progress and real teaching is, even at $15 per month. Pay your teachers more and demand more of them—then you will move forward.

Do not, I beg you, waste the School Fund for school supplies. It is amazing to see how many thousands of dollars of our puplic school money has been spent for supplies, and yet where are the equipped public school houses?

C. H. MEBANE,
Superintendent Public Instruction.

OFFICE OF
SUPERINTENDENT OF PUBLIC INSTRUCTION,
RALEIGH, October 26, 1897.

To the Supervisors:

I wish to call your attention to a very important matter, to-wit: The employing of assistants in our public schools.

No person should be allowed to teach as an assistant in a public school unless said person has a certificate from the County Supervisor.

My attention has been called to some instances where the principals were paid $40 or $50 per month of the public fund, with the understanding that the principal teachers were to furnish their assistants. The assistants selected in these cases referred to were some pupils taken from the school and not qualified for the work.

Away with the idea that anybody can teach the primary children! This is the most difficult work, and it is a gross injustice to allow the children to be imposed upon by being placed under the care of the person who can be secured by the principal for the least money.

A case was reported to me last spring where a principal drew $20 per month of public funds for an assistant teacher and hired his assistant for $10 or $12.

If this be true, such a man is not fit to be in any schoolroom.

It is your duty as Supervisor to see that the *little ones* are not neglected, and are not placed in charge of anyone except a competent teacher. See to it that every man and woman has a certificate before he or she teaches in a public school. Where an assistant is needed, let the committee make contract with assistant in the same manner as with the principal, then we will have *no unworthy principals making money on incompetent assistants*, as in the case mentioned above.

In some of our counties a certificate does not mean much, but be sure that the children shall have the benefit of what it does mean. Very truly,

C. H. MEBANE,
Superintendent Public Instruction.

OFFICE OF
SUPERINTENDENT OF PUBLIC INSTRUCTION,
RALEIGH, N. C., December 8, 1897.

To the Supervisor:

MY DEAR SIR:—There will be a meeting of principals

and teachers of High Schools in Raleigh, December 28th to 30th. Several of these men are Supervisors. I have, therefore, called for a meeting of the County Supervisors on the 30th of December, in the Hall of the House of Representatives. We can meet at such hour or hours that will not conflict with the High School meeting.

Will you not make some little sacrifice to attend this meeting? Reduced rates on the railroads at this time.

Good board can be had at the Branson House at $1.00 per day.

There are many things pertaining to the future progress of the public schools, concerning which we need each others' counsel and advice. We need united action on the part of Supervisors. *We want to strive* for the same great end throughout the State. We want to use the very best means possible to secure this great end.

We will have a programme arranged, as a basis, but we want each Supervisor to come, feeling that this is his meeting. Come and bring us your successes and failures in the school work. We want to be encouraged by your success, and want to help you make good the failures of the past. Above all, we want to get life and inspiration into our work.

The less money we have in any movement the greater need of energy and activity. We have very little money for our public schools—let us have very much action, and show to the public that we are in earnest and mean to do the very best we can, and then we will have more friends of public schools in the future than we have had in the past. Come, if you possibly can.

Let me hear whether you think you can attend this important meeting or not.

C. H. MEBANE,
Superintendent Public Instruction.

OFFICE OF
SUPERINTENDENT OF PUBLIC INSTRUCTION,
RALEIGH, N. C., January 14, 1898.

To Supervisors and Members of County Boards of Education.

DEAR SIRS:—I write you in regard to orders given during the school year 1896 and 1897 for public funds when there were no funds due the districts.

The committees had no authority to sign orders for money when there was none due the school for which they gave the order for school supplies, and the person or persons accepting these orders did so at his own risk.

The banks that bought such paper or orders did so upon their own responsibility. I feel sorry for the banks, but I feel more sorry for the children whose money is squandered.

Some counties in the State have been canvassed by agents who knew there was no money due the schools, and the committee knew they had no money to pay the extravagant orders they were giving.

It is a burning shame to see the hundreds of dollars of orders given for money when there was none, expecting to gobble up the money of the children for this fiscal year.

Do not spend one cent of the school money due from July 1, 1897, to June 30, 1898, to pay orders made by your predecessors in office.

If there was money due the districts for which the goods were bought at the time they were bought, and for the school year in which they were bought, then, of course, such orders must be paid, otherwise do not pay them.

Yours very truly,

C. H. MEBANE,
Superintendent Public Instruction.

OFFICE OF
SUPERINTENDENT OF PUBLIC INSTRUCTION,
RALEIGH, N. C., January 5, 1898.

To the Members of the County Board of Education and Supervisors:

DEAR SIRS:—I wish to urge you to have the teachers examined on the public days provided for by law. There are two special reasons why this should be done, viz.: economy and systematic work on the part of the Supervisor.

How will it save money?

I find under the present arrangement in some counties that very few teachers are examined on the public days, but teachers go to the Supervisors on any day in the week and any week in the year, and as a result the Supervisors will have almost as many days' service to be paid out of the public fund as he has examined teachers.

The teachers of every county should be examined on one of the four days provided for in the law, with perhaps rare exceptions.

We ought to have twenty-five or thirty teachers examined on each of the public days, and have only to pay for one day's service instead of fifteen or twenty days, for the same number of teachers examined at the present loose way of doing in some counties.

Where Supervisors cannot arrange to have separate rooms for whites and colored to carry on examinations for both races at the same time, then continue the examinations after the public days until all have an opportunity to be examined.

We want this money that is paid the Supervisor for examining one teacher one day and another teacher the next day, and so on, to pay him for supervising schools, for going out and coming in touch with the people, and putting life into the schools.

I am not censuring the Supervisor, but he is often annoyed

and hindered in his teaching or private business by being called upon to examine a teacher just at any time, and of course cannot give his time in this service for nothing, and in this way he must necessarily have a large number of days' service in comparison with the number of applicants examined.

It seems almost needless to say that a Supervisor cannot and will not have as carefully prepared examination just at any and all days as he will on special days provided for in the law. The Supervisor cannot do his duty unless he can work systematically, and the County Boards of Education are hereby urged to take every action possible to aid the Supervisor to do efficient, systematic work, and at the same time enable him to accomplish a great deal within a few days along the line of examinations.

In some counties the money spent for these every-day examinations would pay for sending the Supervisor to a great number of the schools of the county.

Yours truly,

C. H. MEBANE,

Superintendent Public Instruction.

OFFICE OF
SUPERINTENDENT OF PUBLIC INSTRUCTION,
RALEIGH, February 28, 1898.

To the Public:

A township becomes a special School District when a donation is put into the hands of the County Treasurer for the benefit of all the public schools, white and colored, in said township, and this donation is supplemented by the State. The funds thus raised by donation and by the supplement given on the part of the State becomes a special fund for this township.

This fund is subject to the order of the Township Committee, and for the benefit of all the public schools in the township, just as the money apportioned to the township by County Board of Education is for the benefit of all the schools in the township.

No one or two schools in a township can expect to receive aid from the State. No territory less than a township need apply for aid.

This is a great opportunity for small townships, or townships where the number of schools is small.

Suppose a township only has five schools, and raises by donation five hundred dollars, and the State gives five hundred dollars. Here we have a special fund of one thousand dollars, which will give to each school $200.

These donations will be duplicated at any time between January 31 and June 30 of a school year, provided that no one township can receive more than $500 in any one year.

Very truly, C. H. MEBANE,
Superintendent Public Instruction.

OFFCE OF
SUPERINTENDENT OF PUBLIC INSTRUCTION.
RALEIGH, N. C., February 27, 1898.

To the Supervisors:

I would like for you to make special effort among your people to have them to supplement the public schools by private subscriptions. There could be raised in many localities enough money to continue the schools from four to six weeks. Especially could this be done where teachers have made themselves felt, and created interest among the children for study.

How do parents decide whether their children are making progress in school or not? Do they examine into the work the children are doing? Not so; they judge by the interest the children take in their books at home. Therefore if this iterest has been created among the children, then there is hope of reaching the parents.

You cannot even hope to supplement all of your schools,

but select some localities in your county where you know there has been good work done and some interest created. Use your efforts with such people, and if you can get even two or three schools to supplement the pulblic school this year, it may prove an object lesson for those schools near by to follow next year.

This is worthy of some effort on your part. Of course I shall not expect the same results from the efforts of the various Supervisors.

But where a Supervisor has been going out among the people, making speeches for education, and stirring the people in the interest of schools, I have a right to expect some results from an effort of this kind.

I trust you will make this effort regardless of what the result may be.

Yours very truly, C. H. MEBANE,
Superintendent Public Instruction.

OFFICE OF
SUPERINTENDENT OF PUBLIC INSTRUCTION,
RALEIGH, N. C., February 5, 1898.

DEAR SIR:—I am anxious that the next biennial report that is sent out from this office shall show, not only what North Carolina is doing in the public schools and State institutions, but also shall show what our denominational colleges and high schools are doing—the academies, private schools, and in fact, want all the educational interests of the State to be represented in this report.

In order to do this a considerable extra expense will be incurred, and in order to meet this expense I have decided to offer space in this report at exactly what it will cost the State to print it.

We want a short, concise history of the various schools, academies, and colleges, and an outline of what has been done and is being done. Do not mention what you expect to do. I hope you will do greater things in the future, but want this report to show what is being done now.

Would be glad to have a cut of your building and faculty to publish.

The State Printer estimates the cost to be about $1.50 per page.

This is a very reasonable expense to the schools, and will do them a great deal of good as well as the State.

This report will be sent to every State in the United States, as well as distributed throughout North Carolina.

I expect to have a brief general history of the work done by the denominational colleges, and especially what the academies did for us as a State in early years.

I hope you will give this matter your careful consideration.

Let me hear from you as soon as possible, also designate how much space you will want.

Very truly yours,

C. H. MEBANE,

Superintendent Public Instruction.

OFFICE OF

SUPERINTENDENT OF PUBLIC INSTRUCTION,

RALEIGH, March 30, 1898.

To the County Supervisor:

You are hereby notified that the State Board of Examiners have prepared a set of questions for teachers who may wish to stand the examination for Life Certificate. These questions will be forwarded to you in due time for the examination to take place on the second Thursday in July.

You will notify the teachers of your county, through the press or otherwise. Be sure that it is generally known, so that all who wish may have an opportunity to take the examination.

You will conduct this examination at the court-house of

your county, or some convenient room nearby the court-house.

The questions are not to be seen by the teachers until the examination begins.

Examination papers are to be forwarded to this office and graded by the State Board of Examiners. A diploma will be issued to all successful applicants. This Diploma will have the signature of each member of the Board of Examiners and their seal upon it, and will entitle the holder thereof to teach anywhere in North Carolina without examination by the County Supervisor.

Questions on the following subjects have been prepared:

English Grammar, English Literature, History, Geography, Physical Geography, Arithmetic, Algebra, Physics, Physiology and Hygiene, Elementary Botany, Civil Government, and School Law.

The following books, in addition to those adopted in the various counties, are suggested as indicating the scope of the examination on the several subjects:

Whitney's Essentials of English Grammar.

Pancoast's Composition and Rhetoric.

Lockwood's Lessons in English.

Maury's Geography, Tarr's Physical Geography.

Sully's Psychology for Teachers.

White's Elements of Pedagogy.

Physics, Avery and Gage.

Bergen's Botany.

Martin's Human Body.

Hoping that you will give this important matter your prompt attention, I am,

Yours very truly,

C. H. MEBANE,

Superintendent Public Instruction.

OFFICE OF
SUPERINTENDENT OF PUBLIC INSTRUCTION,
RALEIGH, April 6, 1898.

To the County School Officers:

GENTLEMEN:—I have been informed that certain school officials have been offering their services as agents to handle school desks, school supplies, etc.

This is a dangerous business for a school officer, and this circular is sent out to show you what the law is on this subject:

AN ACT FOR THE PROTECTION OF EDUCATIONAL AND OTHER INSTITUTIONS.

The General Assembly of North Carolina do enact:

SECTION 1. That it shall be unlawful for any member of any board of directors, board of managers or board of trustees of any of the educational, charitable, elemosynary or penal institutions of the State, or any member of any board of education, or any county or district superintendent of schools, or examiner of teachers, or any school trustee of any school or other institution supported in whole or in part from any of the public funds of the State, or any officer, agent, manager, teacher or employee of any said boards, to have any pecuniary interest, either directly or indirectly, proximately or remotely, in supplying any goods, wares or merchandise of any nature or kind whatsoever to any of said institutions or schools.

SEC. 2. Nor shall any of said officers, agents, managers, teachers or employees of said institutions or schools or State or county officers act as agent for any manufacturer, merchant, dealer, publisher or author for any article of merchandise to be used by any of said institutions or school, nor shall they receive, directly or indirectly, any gift, emolument, reward for their influence in recommending or procuring the use of any manufactured article, goods, wares or merchandise of any nature or kind whatsoever for any of said institutions or schools.

SEC. 3. Any person violating the provision of this act shall be forthwith removed from his position in the public service, and shall, upon conviction, be deemed guilty of a misdemeanor, and fined not less than fifty ($50) dollars, nor more than five ($500) hundred dollars, and be imprisoned in the discretion of the court.

SEC. 4. This act shall be in force from and after its ratification.

Ratified the 9th day of March, A. D. 1897.

Yours truly,

C. H. MEBANE,

Superintendent Public Instruction.

OFFICE OF
SUPERINTENDENT OF PUBLIC INSTRUCTION,
RALEIGH, N. C., May 30, 1898.

To the County Supervisor:

There seems to be some misunderstanding among some of the Supervisors in regard to the census; but there should not be, for I informed each Supervisor last year that the census that was taken in November, or December, 1897, would be accepted at this office instead of the May census 1898. It was necessary to have the census last November or December in order for the apportionment to be made per capita to the townships, as the present law requires. There would necessarily be very little change as to school population from December, 1897, to May, 1898. Hence I will accept this census in your annual report, to be made to me the first of July of this year.

I wish to urge you to make out your annual report promptly the first of July and forward to this office, so that ample time may be had to arrange the statistics for the press, that the report may be published in due time.

It is a shame, but nevertheless true, that there are always some counties in the State which never get in their reports, and the Superintendents, for years, have had to go back to former years and fill in with old statistics. Do not allow this to occur this year. Such negligence on the part of any Supervisor is sufficient cause for his removal from office. Business is business. Let us have no negligence this year from any source in the State. These words are not intended for those who are prompt in their official duties, but to those who are negligent and careless.

What I have said is meant in kindness and for the best interest of this great work.

Let us work together and have a full and complete report of the schools.

Very truly,

C. H. MEBANE,
Superintendent Public Instruction.

OFFICE OF
SUPERINTENDENT OF PUBLIC INSTRUCTION.
RALEIGH, N. C., June, 1897.

To the County Commissioners:

DEAR SIRS:—I wish to call your special attention to section 2 of the Local Taxation Law as enacted by the last General Assembly of North Carolina.

The section is as follows: "On Tuesday after the second Monday in August, within the year 1897, the Board of County Commissioners of every county shall cause an election to be held in every School District (Township) in their respective counties upon the question of levying a special District (Township) tax for the Public Schools of said District (Township), and notice of this shall be given by the County Commissioners at their regular June meeting, and such notice shall be published in the county papers and posted on the school-houses of said Districts" (Township).

I trust that the County Commissioners will do their full duty in regard to this Local Taxation Law, and that all the friends of public schools and education will work up a sentiment for this important measure.

If we have public schools of such character and of such length of time as we should, I believe it must come by Local Taxation.

The general School Tax is now twenty cents on the hundred dollars, and I do not believe we can hope to go much beyond this as a general tax for schools from the State.

Some of the greatest school systems in our county have very little if any general State tax, but are run almost or entirely by the Local Taxation principle.

Yours very truly,

C. H. MEBANE,
State Superintendent Public Instruction.

OFFICE OF
SUPERINTENDENT OF PUBLIC INSTRUCTION,
RALEIGH, N. C., June 12, 1897.

To the Members of the Boards of Education of the Several Counties of North Carolina.

DEAR SIRS:—I have adopted White's Elements of Pedagogy, in compliance with Section 41, Chapter 199, Laws of 1889. (See School Law, page 42).

The publishers have signed a contract to furnish the book to the teachers at one dollar, post-paid.

All teachers to whom certificates are granted must be examined on White's Elements of Pedagogy.

Yours very truly,

C. H. MEBANE,
Sup't Public Instruction N. C.

OFFICE OF
SUPERINTENDENT OF PUBLIC INSTRUCTION.
RALEIGH, August 5, 1898.

To the Teachers and Friends of Public Schools:

I call upon you as patriotic citizens of North Carolina to go to the polls on next Tuesday and see that all may have an opportunity to vote "for schools" at your respective voting precincts.

If the County Commissioners of your county have not prepared and distributed ballots, as the law directs them, you can write ballots with the words "for schools" on paper, and these will do as well as the printed ballots.

Next Tuesday will be a memorable day in the educational history of our State. What shall the record be? Will yod help to make the record one over which you will have reason to rejoice? I trust you will do your duty on this important day.

Yours very truly,

C. H. MEBANE,
Superintendent Public Instruction.

MAIN BUILDING CHAPEL HILL SCHOOL, CHAPEL HILL N. C.

OFFICE OF
SUPERINTENDENT OF PUBLIC INSTRUCTION,
RALEIGH, N. C., September 13, 1898.

The following letter explains itself. It is to be hoped that our colleges and schools will take some interest in this matter. Let not North Carolina be behind the other States in honoring LaFayette. C. H. MEBANE,
Superintendent Public Instruction.

To the HON. C. H. MEBANE, *Superintendent of Schools of the State of North Carolina, Raleigh, North Carolina.*

DEAR SIR:—A Special Commission has been formed by the Commissioner General for the United States to the Paris Exposition for the purpose of securing, by popular contributions, funds to erect a suitable monument to General LaFayette, whose remains now lie in a practically unmarked grave in the petit Picpus Cemetery of Paris.

It is now planned that the monument be built in time for unveiling and dedication on United States Day, the Fourth of July, 1900, at the Paris Exposition—thus making the day a most conspicuous one, both for America and for France.

It is proposed that in the raising of the funds the schools of America be utilized as the agency for reaching the people and procuring the contributions, and to this end I urgently request that you ask as early as convenient, that the teachers and officers of your schools, colleges and universities—(public and parochial)—recognize October the 19th, (the date of the fall of Yorktown—to which LaFayette contributed so greatly), as "LaFayette Day," and that they devote a part of the day mentioned to a relation of the historic events pertaining to LaFayette and the early days of the Republic.

In the higher grades an appropriate program of exercises may be rendered, to which an admission fee should be charged, or where collections may be made, the proceeds to be turned over by the school to the LaFayette Memorial Commission for the purposes mentioned.

In the primary grades it is suggested that the children be requested to solicit from their parents or acquaintances a small amount—from one to ten cents—to be used for the same purpose.

In furtherance of the work, I take pleasure in appointing you a member of an honorary Advisory Committee, to consist of the Superintendents of Education in the various States and Territories, and bespeak your hearty co-operation, to the end that this beautiful and significant movement may reflect the greatest of credit upon the youth of our country, upon their patriotism and the gratitude of our people.

Very respectfully,

FERDINAND W. PECK,
Commissioner-General.

OFFICE OF
SUPERINTENDENT OF PUBLIC INSTRUCTION,
RALEIGH, August 18, 1898.

To the County Supervisor:

I have numerous enquiries recently in regard to combining the public schools with denominational schools, and therefore write you that you may have my opinion on this subject.

I think it best for the committee always to provide a public school lot and building.

The spirit of all our laws seems to be against combining Church and State in any way.

When the public school is combined with a denominational one the best interest of the public school can rarely, if ever, be secured.

We cannot have the support of all the people when the public school is united with the church school.

The public schools are for all the people, supported by all the people, and must serve all the people in enlightenment without any regard to denominations or churches.

The law provides for combining public schools with private, but I do not think that this, in any sense, means denominational or church schools.

Therefore, my instruction to you as County Supervisor, is that you do not combine public schools with denominational schools.

I am aware that these church schools have well-prepared teachers, but notwithstanding this, the primary object for which they are employed is to benefit the church that sends them out, and in every community we find some parents who will not send their children because the school is under other church influence than their own.

Let us not have any hindrance in the way of united support in the schools, which must have the support of all our people if they are ever what they should be.

Yours truly,

C. H. MEBANE,
Superintendent Public Instruction.

OFFICE OF
SUPERINTENDENT OF PUBLIC INSTRUCTION.
RALEIGH, N. C., October 26, 1898.

To the County Supervisor:

DEAR SIR:—I send you pamphlet of recommendations to the next General Assembly.

You will not find any politics in this pamphlet, but only matters pertaining to the improvement of our public schools.

I call your special attention to the subject on page 31, "$400,000 attainable;" also to the subject of "Local Taxation."

I send you two copies of the pamphlet. Please see that the candidates of the respective parties have their attention called to the subjects mentioned above. Let these candidates express themselves publicly on the subject of increasing the school funds, so the people may know who are going to remember the children of our State, and who are unconcerned in regard to this matter of supreme importance.

I ask you to bring this matter before the public of your county as a school man, as an educator, as a man whose chief concern is to move forward in the great work of public education, regardless of what political power is in authority.

Yours for progress in the work,

C. H. MEBANE,

Superintendent of Public Instruction.

[NOTE.—The following address was published and distributed according to a resolution adopted by the Teachers' Assembly of North Carolina.]

SUPERINTENDENT MEBANE'S ADDRESS,

DELIVERED BEFORE THE TEACHERS' ASSEMBLY AT MOREHEAD CITY, 1897.

First, I will make the assertion that we have a right to expect greater results from the efforts in the interest of our public schools, from the county supervisor, than we ever received from the county superintendent or the county examiner. Why do I say this? Upon what do I base my expectations? It is this: Because section 7 of the general school law as passed by the last General Assembly says that the county supervisor shall be a practical school teacher. What is a practical school teacher? He is a man whose business is that of teaching, a man whose profession is that of teaching. We want a school man and no other for county supervisor. A man who even taught two years ago, and has since engaged in other business as a profession, I shall not call him a practical teacher, but I shall declare such a man ineligible to the office of county supervisor. Yes, my friends, the law calls for a practical teacher to fill the important office of county supervisor, and we expect just such a man in every county in North Carolina. How was it under our former school laws? Who were our county superintendents? While we had some wide-awake, energetic school men for county superintendents, some men who made sacrifices for the schools, whose hearts were in this work; men by whose energies and perseverance the standard of scholarship was raised among their teachers, men who taught their teachers how to teach, men who gave life and inspiration to the schools over which they had control—while we had some such men as these, we also had very many lawyers, preachers, doctors, merchants and others who would secure the office of county superintendent to supplement their salaries or other business in which they were engaged. The trouble was not with the office but with the officers. Some of these men seemed to be more interested in their per diem, and number of days they could charge against the school fund, than they were in the progress of the schools of their counties. I sincerely hope we will not have county supervisors of this character. What can we expect of our public schools if they are to receive their life and inspiration from a man who devotes his efforts and energies to preaching the gospel? There is no class of men for whom I have a more profound respect than for the ministers of the gospel, but we do not want them for our county supervisors. What may we expect if this life and inspiration is to come from a lawyer who will only give a day of thought now and then to schools and education? What can we expect if this life and inspiration must come from a man engaged in general mercantile business, whose mind is absorbed in his business, or should be? Such a man as this to lead the educational forces of a county, and yet we have had just such men in many of our counties. If we have no school men, no educators, for these important offices, then it is a burning shame for the professional teacher. I, as the official head of the public school system, say we have the men. I say we have practical teachers to fill these important offices, and I say further that we must have school men in these offices.

Would the physician think of calling on a teacher to examine medical students for license? Would the lawyer of North Carolina call on a school teacher for legal advice? Would the merchant ask the advice and guidance of the teacher in his business transactions? These questions are simply absurd, and yet there is just as much sense in doing these things as there is in asking these men to do the work of education. The ministers, the lawyers, the doctors, and the merchants all have their places, and theirs is a noble work, or should be. But away with such men as educational leaders! We want men for supervisors whose hearts are in the school work, whose interest and chief concern are for the improvement of the public schools, a man who can and will come in close touch with the people, who will make special efforts to interest the parents of our State in the education of their children, and will show to these parents the importance of making use of the opportunities now offered in the schools, and thus largely increase the average attendance of our schools.

We want supervisors who will give life and inspiration to the public school teachers, who can and will guide and direct worthy young teachers who are striving to become more efficient workers in the schools, a man that can give practical common-sense instruction as to the government of schools and methods of teaching; a man who, when he visits the schools and finds poor management and poor teaching, will have the tact and judgment to make order and system out of confusion and choas. My friends, if you can have such men as these for County Supervisors; and we may and will have them if the County Boards of Education and the Clerks of our Courts and Registers of Deeds of the respective counties will only have the courage to do their whole duty.

Such men as I have been describing *will not be around seeking this important office*, but it is my honest desire to have *these boards seek the men.* Here are cases in which it is all important for the offices to seek the men.

Consider for one moment what it means for our public schools to have ninety-six men going in and out among our people in the great work of educating the masses. Ninety-six men who are able to reach the parents and the voters of the counties; ninety-six men of character and real worth, and not politicans, or narrow, selfish, one-sided men; ninety-six men in whom the people have confidence and for whom they have respect; ninety-six men who will have the courage to tell the people the whole truth as to our ignorance and our neglect of educating our thousauds of poor children; ninety-six men who will not spend their time rejoicing over the glorious things for the future, but men who will take up the work of to-day; men who will act in the living present and do something now to drive ignorance and superstition from our midst; do something now to feed the hungry minds of our thousands of precious boys and girls in North Carolina; ninety-six men to persuade and to show the parents their duty in regard to sending their children to school; ninety-six men to tell the parents that unless the attendance in our public schools is largely increased within the next two years that the State of North Carolina will compel them to send these children to school.

The last and perhaps most important of all is ninety-six men who will carry ninety-six townships in North Carolina for local taxation at the August election, and cause the State Superintendent to issue ninety-six warrants for $500 each, making the sum of $48,000 from the State; and even the same amount in the townships would make the sum of $96,000. We hope, however, in many townships these amounts will be $1,000, or even $1,500, thus making a grand total of $125,000 or $150,000 for the public schools.

EXPRESSIONS OF INTEREST FOR PUBLIC SCHOOLS.

I sent out a letter of enquiry to all the State schools, the denominational colleges, and the private schools, respectfully requesting an official expression of the faculties or the heads of these institutions and schools in regard to their attitude towards the public schools of our State.

I had a right to expect sympathy and encouraging words from every State institution, but a glance over the following list will show that my expectations were not realized. It is very gratifying to see the interest manifested in the cause of public education in the following list of expressions:

PRESIDENT'S OFFICE,
THE UNIVERSITY OF NORTH CAROLINA,
CHAPEL HILL, September 30, 1898.

Hon. Chas. H. Mebane, Raleigh, N. C.

MY DEAR SIR:—The Faculty of the University of North Carolina, recognizing that the supremest need of this State is an adequate system of public schools for the education of all the children of the State, is anxious and eager to bend all its energies to the accomplishment of that end. The University wishes to take its place in the vanguard of this movement, not alone because it is the chief public school of the State and the head of the public school system, but because it realizes that a large majority of the children of the State are dependent upon the public schools for all the training they will get in life. The first President of this University, Joseph Caldwell, was the first citizen of the State to reveal the value of the public school and to plead for its establishment. Archibald Murphy, a Professor here, was the first North Carolinian to draw up a rational system of public education and to seek to enact it into law. Calvin H. Wiley, a graduate of the University, first organized and equipped the system for its work. The Presidents of later years have, without exception, given time and thought to this great problem and have some right to claim a share in the great work done by yourself and your predecessors in awakening public conscience on this great question. Ignorance is slavery, and ignorant citizenship is in a condition of slavery to intelligence, and the time has come for thoughtful men of all classes, sects and parties, to unite in a determined effort to provide the proper school facilities for every child in the borders of the State. I beg to assure you that in all of your laudable efforts to bring about this end you will have the support of the students and authorities of this University. Very truly,

EDWIN A. ALDERMAN, *President.*

The Faculty of Trinity College, at the regular meeting, October 13, 1898, adopted the following expression in regard to the public schools:

Trinity College is committed by the action of the Board of Trustees to the development of the public schools of the State. With this action of the Board the members of the faculty are in full accord, and are ready to co-operate with others in any worthy plan or movement for increasing the efficiency of these schools.

W. H. PEGRAM, *Secretary.*

RESOLUTION ADOPTED BY THE TRUSTEES OF TRINITY COLLEGE IN REGARD TO OUR PUBLIC SCHOOLS.

WHEREAS, The Trustees of Trinity College are now, and ever have been, heartily in favor of free public schools, and also of higher education; therefore,

Resolved, That we pledge ourselves to renewed efforts to lengthen the term and so increase the number and efficiency of said free schools as that every child in the State shall have the opportunity of acquiring an education.

(Signed) W. J. MONTGOMERY.
W. R. ODELL.

PRESIDENS'S OFFICE,
WAKE FOREST COLLFGE.
WAKE FOREST, N. C.

Resolutions of the Faculty of Wake Forest College, passed October 21, 1898:

"In reply to the inquiry of the Superintendent of Public Instruction as to the attitude of the Faculty of Wake Forest College in regard to the public school system of North Carolina, we desire to express our conviction that, next to religion, a well organized system of public schools, with efficient teachers and at least four months sessions, is the greatest need of our State.

And we desire moreover to express our sympathy and promise our co-operation with every effort to improve and extend the system."

J. B. SHEARER,
PRESIDENT DAVIDSON COLLEGE.

DAVIDSON, N. C., October 6, 1898.

Hon. C. H. Mebane, Superintendent Public Instruction.

DEAR SIR:—The Faculty of Davidson College desire me to say to you on our behalf that we are much pleased with your earnest and judicious work in behalf of the public schools. We are gratified at the increasing efficiency of the public school system of North Carolina, and we trust that the day is not very far distant when yet larger facilities, better teachers, and longer terms of service shall be secured for popular education; and we hope for yet larger success for your administration of this important public trust.

With sincere respect and cordial sympathy, I subscribe myself, for myself and colleagues,

Yours sincerely,
J. B. SHEARER, D. D., *President.*

CATAWBA COLLEGE,
NEWTON, N. C.

Our abiding interest in the welfare of the children of North Carolina constrains us, the undersigned members of the Faculty of Catawba College, to declare our anxious concern for the cause of elementary education through the public schools of the State. We favor, for their additional length of term, elevation of standard and efficiency of operation, whatever additional legislation may be required. We favor terms of at least six months in the year, and the compulsory attendance of all the children in the State, between the ages of seven and fourteen years, who are not otherwise and equally well provided with advantages of education, with permission of attendance to the age of eighteen years.

To render the school fund adequate to this end, we favor additional taxation, if possible, or, at least, such legislation as shall reach a vast amount of the wealth of the State not now listed because not given in by the owners thereof, and, if need be, a curtailment of appropriations to institutions of higher education.

J. C. CLAPP,
President Catawba College.
J. A. FOIL,
Professor Math. and Nat. Science.
J. C. LEONARD,
Professor English and History.
J. B. LEONARD,
Tutor of Latin.

Catawba College, Sept. 11, 1898.

THE FREE SCHOOLS.

GUILFORD COLLEGE.

The need of education in our State is so great that any effort to give our children a better opportunity to become intelligent and useful citizens, should meet with hearty encouragement.

When we consider how large a per cent of the boys and girls, as at present situated, have no other source but the public or free school to which to look for an education, and how the perpetuation of popular government is imperiled by ignorance and its attendant evils, we shall surely make a more earnest appeal than we have hitherto done to the great body of our citizens to rise above partisan politics, and unite their efforts to secure better schools and for a longer time each year.

More funds should be appropriated to the public schools, and the full opportunity given to counties, in accordance with the present law, to add to the school funds by local taxation. Let any friend of the free schools who does not approve of local tax to improve and prolong them, propose a better plan to accomplish the desired end.

If our people could be induced to unite their efforts to secure good free schools for the boys and girls, and to take a patriotic pride in them, the result would soon be felt not only in the high schools and colleges and in education in general, but also in the various industrial interests of the State. Let us welcome discussion of the needs and conditions of our free schools, seek to get more money to be thus expended, and stir up in our people all over the State a deeper interest in education, and appeal to the best judgment in every community for necessary improvement and support of the free schools.

L. L. HOBBS, *President.*

CLAREMONT COLLEGE,
HICKORY, N. C., September 26, 1898.

To the Honorable Superintendent of Public Instruction:

We, the Faculty of Claremont College, recognize the public schools as the chief feeders of our college and of all other colleges in the State. As such they are markedly deficient in three particulars, viz: (1) Length of term. (2) Ability of teachers. (3) Adequateness of salaries. We think that "local taxation" is the best remedy in sight for (1) and (3), and, indirectly, for (2). We would respectfully recommend that the number of the public schools be sacrificed, if necessary, for their efficiency, and that the matter of local taxation be doubly emphasized before the people.

By order of the Faculty.

S. P. HATTON, *President.*

OAK RIDGE INSTITUTE.

OAK RIDGE, N. C., September 13, 1898.

Hon. C. H. Mebane, Raleigh, N. C.

DEAR SIR:—You desire an expression from Oak Ridge Institute as to our feeling and interest in the public school work. Permit us to say that we regard the work of the public schools as, by all odds, the most important educational work of the State. They reach more people than any other schools, and are, without question, the schools that our State should take the greatest interest in. We can never have an educated people until we have a first-class system of public schools. Two things have been lacking in the State of North Carolina, from the beginning—one is the thorough appreciation of the value of the public school by the people, and the other is a woeful lack of funds. If we had good school-houses our people would be more interested in the schools, and if we had a larger fund we could have better school-houses and better teachers. We have prepared hundreds of teachers for the public school work, and stand ever ready to lend a helping hand in anything pertaining to these schools.

Wishing you abundant success in everything that you undertake in the educational line that has for its purpose the good of the school, we are,

Very truly yours,

J. A. & M. H. HOLT.

WHITSETT INSTITUTE.
WHITSETT, GUILFORD COUNTY, N. C.,
November 3, 1898.

WHEREAS, The education of all the people of our great Commonwealth is a subject demanding our patriotic concern, and

WHEREAS, As workers in the field of the private schools we realize the need of each and every worthy means towards this great end; therefore be it

Resolved, That the Faculty of Whitsett Institute hereby expresses its heartiest good wishes and deepest concern in public education as offered in our free public schools, and trust that the day is not distant when they will be greatly improved as to length and amount of money appropriated for their use.

W. T. WHITSETT, *Chairman*.
J. HENRY JOYNER, *Secretary*.

THE BINGHAM SCHOOL.
MEBANE, N. C., September 26, 1898.

Hon. C. H. Mebane, Raleigh, N. C.

MY DEAR SIR:—Although I am the Principal of one of the private schools of the State, yet I am heartily in sympathy with the progress and success of the public school work. Sound and wisely administered government in the State depends to a great extent on an intelligent voting population, and I am in sympathy with every proper move for the education of the masses. I believe that our faculty of nine teachers join heartily with me in this view.

With great respect, I am

Truly yours,
PRESTON LEWIS GRAY.

PEABODY EDUCATION FUND AND PEABODY SCHOLARSHIPS IN PEABODY NORMAL AT NASHVILLE, TENN.

The following Circular of Information, giving rules and regulations concerning the Peabody scholarships, was distributed by Hon. J. L. M. Curry, LL. D., General Agent of the Peabody Education Fund, on February 25th, 1898, for the information of the State Superintendents of Education and applicants for the scholarships, to be awarded according rules in the circular. A similar circular was distributed during the year 1897.

I. The intent of the Peabody Board of Trust in establishing these scholarships in the Normal College is to affect public education in the South through a high grade of professionally educated teachers.

1. The realization of this intent implies, on the part of teachers, high moral aims; natural aptness to teach; an education of the liberal type; a knowledge of the history, theory, and art of education; and the pursuit of teaching as a vocation.

II. A Peabody scolarship is worth $100 a year and the student's railroad ticket from his home to Nashville and return by the most direct route, and is good for two years. The college year consists of eight months. beginning on the first Wednesday in October, and closing on the last Wednesday in May; and scholarship students receive from the President of the College $12.50 on the last days of each month of the college year.

1. No payment will be made except for time of actual attendance.

2. Scholarships will be withdrawn from students who allow bills for board to go unpaid.

3. Scholarships will be forfeited for partial or irregular attendance.

4. So far as possible, railroad tickets will be sent to students before leaving their homes; but students who do not receive tickets will be repaid their railroad fare within one month after entrance, and return tickets will be issued just previous to the close of the session in May. Students who leave the College before the close of the term will not be paid their return fare. Railroad tickets to Nashville will be furnished only twice on the same scholarship.

III. These scholarships are distributed to the several States by the General Agent, and their award to students is vested in him; but for convenience of administration this award is delegated to the State Superintendents in conjunction with the President of the College. The whole number of scholarships is now 200, distributed as follows:

Alabama, 15; Arkansas, 17; Florida, 8; Georgia, 18; Louisiana, 13; Mississippi, 15; North Carolina, 18; South Carolina, 14; Tennessee, 33; Texas, 20; Virginia, 18; West Virginia, 11.

1. No State can claim scholarships as a right. They are gifts from the Peabody Board of Trust; and, as such, the ratio of their distribution, as well as their amount, may be changed, or they may be withheld a together.

2. At the close of each college year the President will notify State Superintendents of the vacancies that are to be filled in their respective States for the ensuing college year, and send the names and standing of non-scholarship students who are deemed worthy of scholarship appointments. If the President's nominations are not acted on within two weeks after they are forwarded, his nominees will be enrolled as scholarship students.

3. If appointees do not report at the College promptly at the opening of the year, or do not render a satisfactory excuse for their absence, their places will be declared vacant.

IV. In the award of scholarships, precedence is to be given to students who have been in the College for *one or more years*, at their own expense, and have there given proof of their fitness for the vocation of teaching.

1. In case there are more vacancies than can be filled in the manner just stated, resort should be made to competitive examination.

2. When State Superintendents cannot conduct these competitive examinations in person, they should be careful to delegate this duty to competent hands.

3. Only two years of scholarship aid will be given to the same student.

V. For the purpose of securing to all applicants a uniform basis of competition, the questions for examination will be prepared by the President of the College, and sent to the State Superintendent for distribution to the examiners whom they may appoint.

1. The next competitive examination will be held on July 21 and 22, 1898.

2. These questions, with specific instructions for their use, should be sent to the examiners in sealed envelopes, which are not to be opened till the hour for examination has come.

3. Each competitor should be required to return the lists of printed questions to the examiners as soon as the answers have been written.

VI. The qualifications for becoming a competitor for a scholarship are as follows: The applicant must not be less than seventeen years of age, nor more than thirty; of irreproachable moral character; in good health; with no physical defects, eccentricities, or habits which would interfere with success in teaching; and must make a pledge of intent to teach for at least two years after graduation.

1. The task of the examiners will be simplified by making a preliminary examination, as suggested above. Good health is an indispensable qualification. Any candidate who has any chronic affection, such as weak lungs or weak eyes, should be rejected at once.

2. The use of tobacco in any form is a disqualification for a scholarship.

3. If it should appear that a candidate intends to use his scholarship chiefly as a means of securing an education, or of ultimately preparing himself for some profession other than teaching, he should not be allowed to compete.

4. Persons of sluggish or indolent temperament, of slovenly habits, or of vicious disposition should be rejected at once.

5. When a choice must be made between a young man and a young woman whose examination papers are of equal merit, the young man should be preferred. This is not intended to discriminate against young women, as such; but it is thought that young men will be more likely to continue the vocation of teaching.

6. As fitness for teaching involves other qualities besides scholarship, students will be excused from attendance when it becomes apparent that they have habits or elements of character incompatible with the teacher's office.

VII. The minimum literary qualifications required of all students matriculating for a degree are as follows:

A. English Studies.—1. English grammar. 2. English Composition. A short essay based on the prescribed reading of the year, will be required of the candidate. The books prescribed for examination in 1898 are: Goldsmith's *The Vicar of Wakefield*, Coleridge's *Ancient Mariner*, and Hawthorne's *The House of Seven Gables;* for 1899, Southey's *Life of Nelson*, Cooper's *Pioneer*, and Shelley's *Skylark*; for 1900, Scott's *Ivanhoe*, Burke's *Speech on Conciliation with America*, and Shakespeare's *As You Like It*.

(Most of these books are to be found well edited, with introductions, in Longman's series of English Classics.)

B. United States History.

C. Geography, complete.

D. Mathematics.—1. Arithmetic, complete. 2. Elementary Algebra, complete. 3. Geometry, two books (Wentworth's).

E. Latin.—*Beginner's Latin Book*, Collar's *Gate to Cæsar*, or equivalents.

1. In the main, the examinations should be written; but certain intellectual qualities can best be tested in the oral way.

2. The ability to think and reason is of more importance than mere attainment of facts and rules. General intelligence and brightness may offset some deficiencies in mere book learning.

3. Good breeding, politeness and a pleasant manner should be counted in a candidate's favor.

VIII. A scholarship is good for any two consecutive years—that is, for Freshman and Sophomore, for Sophomore and Junior, for Junior and Senior, or for Senior and Post Graduate.

1. When scholarship students reach the College, they will not be re-examined for admission.

2. As the number of scholarships is small, compared with the number of competitors, it will often happen that some of those who miss the prize are competent to enter the Freshman Class of the College. When persons of this class desire to enter the College, they will, on application, receive from their State Superintendent a Special Certificate, which will admit them to the College without further examination. This certificate has no money value.

3. Students who have gained admittance to the College have the privilege of being examined for advanced standing. See Schedule of Examinations.

4. The completion of the Sophomore Course entitles the student to the degree of Licentiate of Instruction (L.I.); of the Senior Course to the degree A.B., B.S., or B.L.; and of the Post Graduate Course to the degree of A.M., M.S., or M.L.

5. Every member of the College is required to pay an incidental fee of $10 a year.

IX. The pledge required of scholarship students shall be prescribed by the General Agent, and shall be uniform for all the States.

J. L. M. CURRY, *General Agent*,
February 25, 1898. Washington, D. C.

PEABODY EDUCATION FUND OF DR. J. L. M. CURRY:

1897—Jan.	25.	To check from Dr. J. L. M. Curry........	$	700 00
March	1.	To check from Dr. J. L. M. Curry........		2000 00
April	20.	To check from Dr. J. L. M. Curry........		900 00
May	22.	To check from Dr. J. L. M. Curry........		1400 00
July	20.	To check from Dr. J. L. M. Curry........		300 00
Oct.	23.	To check from Dr. J. L. M. Curry........		1400 00
Nov.	22.	To check from Dr. J. L. M. Curry........		950 00
Dec.	15.	To check from Dr. J. L. M. Curry........		950 00
1898—Jan.	25.	To check from Dr. J. L. M. Curry........		550 00
March	2.	To check from Dr. J. L. M. Curry........		850 00
May	21.	To check from Dr. J. L. M. Curry........		150 00
		Total..................................	$	10,150 00

PEABODY FUND DISBURSED, 1897 AND 1898:

1897—Feb.	1.	Durham Graded School, check to C. W. Toms, Durham, N. C..................	$	200 00
May	24.	Durham Graded School, check to C. W. Toms, Durham, N. C..................		100 00
		Total	$	300 00

1897—Feb.	16.	State Normal College, E. J. Forney, Greensboro, N. C.	$ 500 00
March	2.	State Normal College, E. J. Forney, Greensboro, N. C.	1,000 00
May	24.	State Normal College, E. J. Forney, Greensboro, N. C.	600 00
July	21.	State Normal College. E. J. Forney, Greensboro, N. C.	200 00
Dec.	8.	State Normal College, E J. Forney, Greensboro, N. C.	800 00
Nov.	22.	State Normal College, E. J. Forney, Greensboro, N. C.	650 00
1898—Feb.	5.	State Normal College, E. J. Forney, Greensboro, N. C.	750 00
March	12.	State Normal College, E. J. Forney, Greensboro, N. C.	650 00
June	29.	State Normal College, E. J. Forney, Greensboro, N. C.	150 00
		Total	$ 5,300 00
1897—Nov.	27.	High Point Graded School, Fred N. Tate, High Point, N. C.	$ 200 00
1898—March	12.	High Point Graded School, Fred N. Tate, High Point, N. C.	100 00
		Total	$ 300 00
1897—Dec.	8.	Washington Graded School, John H. Small	$ 200 00
1897—March	3.	Clinton Graded School, Treasurer	$ 200 00
May	24.	Clinton Graded School, Treasurer	100 00
		Total	$ 300 00
1897—March	3.	Colored Normal School, Goldsboro, N. C., H. L. Grant	$ 200 00
May	24.	Colored Normal School, Goldsboro. N. C., Jno. F. Dobson	90 00
		Total	$ 290 00
1897—March	3.	Colored Normal School, Winston, N. C., W. A. Blair	$ 200 00
May	24.	Colored Normal School, Winston, N. C., W. A. Blair	200 00
Nov.	22.	Colored Normal School, Winston, N. C., W. A. Blair	300 00
March	12.	Colored Normal School, Winston, N. C., W. A. Blair	100 00
		Total	$ 800 00

1897—March	3.	Colored Normal School, Fayetteville, N. C., A. H. Slocumb	$ 200 00
April	21.	Colored Normal School, Fayetteville, N. C., A. H. Slocumb	190 00
Dec.	15.	Colored Normal School, Fayetteville, N. C., F. P. Williston	300 00
		Total	$ 690 00
1897—May	24.	Colored Normal School, Salisbury, N. C., J. Rumple	$ 100 00
1897—March	3.	Colored Normal School, Elizabeth City, N. C., F. F. Cohoon	$ 200 00
April	21.	Colored Normal School, Elizabeth City, N. C., F. F. Cohoon	130 00
July	21.	Colored Normal School, Elizabeth City, N. C., C. E. Cramer	100 00
Dec.	15.	Colored Normal School, Elizabeth City, N. C., C. E. Cramer	300 00
May	24.	Colored Normal School, Elizabeth City, N. C., C. E. Cramer	210 00
		Total	$ 940 00
1897—April	21.	Colored Normal School, Plymouth, N. C., G. W. Horney	$ 290 00
Dec.	15.	Colored Normal School, Plymouth, N. C., F. M. Bunch	150 00
		Total	$ 440 00
1897—April	21.	Colored Normal School, Franklinton, N. C., B. W. Ballard	$ 290 00
Dec.	15.	Colored Normal School, Franklinton, N. C., T. H. Whitaker	200 00
		Total	$ 490 00

RECAPITULATION.

State Normal College	$ 5,300 00
Durham Graded School	300 00
High Point Graded School	300 00
Clinton Graded School	300 00
Washington Graded School	200 00
Colored Normal School, Winston, N. C.	800 00
Colored Normal School, Fayetteville, N. C.	690 00
Colored Normal School, Salisbury, N. C.	100 00
Colored Normal School, Elizabeth City, N. C.	940 00
Colorod Normal School, Plymouth, N. C.	440 00
Colored Normal School, Franklinton. N. C.	490 00
Colored Normal School, Goldsboro, N. C.	290 00
Total	$ 10,150 00

PEABODY SCHOLARSHIPS.

Under the rules and regulations North Carolina now has nineteen scholarships worth $100 per annum for two years and travelling expenses to and from Nashville.

The scholarships are filled by the State Superintendent under regulations made by the Instituion.

Examinations are prepared by the College authorities and sent to the State Superintendent.

The last two years the examinations have been conducted by the County Supervisors, and papers sent to the Supertendent for grading the work. The Superintendent has had the assistance of competent educators in grading the work done.

The Superintendent has no option to select students from different counties, but must be guided by scholarship as shown by the examinations, by the physical health of the applicants and their purpose to make teaching their regular profession. Thus the applicant's location as to county has nothing whatever to do with securing a scholarship.

The following is the list of those receiving appointment of scholarship at Nashville, Tenn., 1897:

Mr. W. M. Stancell, Jackson, N. C., October 1, 1897, for two years.

Miss Blanch Dupey, Davidson, N. C., October 1, 1897, for two years.

Miss Emma Conn, Raleigh, N. C., October 1, 1897, for two years.

Mr. J. V. Simms, Dillsboro, N. C., October 1, 1897, for two years.

The above persons were awarded the scholarships by competive examinations.

At the special request of Dr. Curry made to this office by President Payne, Miss Mary Hufham, of Henderson, was appointed as a scholarship student.

W. H. Payne, President of the Peabody Normal College, nominated the following non-scholarships in accordance with Article III, paragraph 2, of the Circular of Information:

Miss Kate Bagley, Littleton, N. C.
Mr. William G. Reeves, Lee, N. C.
Miss Sallie C. Smith, Scotland Neck, N. C.
Mr. Leander W. Trivitte, Net, N. C.

These persons were appointed as nominated by President Payne.

There were nine vacancies for Peabody scholarships for North Carolina at the end of the spring term, 1897, at Nashville Peabody Normal College.

President Payne nominated Wm. T. Graybeal and Joseph C. Wright as scholarship students to fill two of these vacancies. This was done by the President in accordance with Article III, paragraph 2, of the Circular of Information.

The following is a list of those to whom scholarships were awarded by competitive examination to fill the remaining seven vacancies:

Miss Eva Culbreth, Clinton, Sampson county, N. C.
Miss Stella M. Ray, Asheville, Buncombe county, N. C.
Miss Carrie Owen, Winton, Hertford county, N. C.
Miss Leila Thornton, Faison, Duplin county, N. C.
Mr. J. D. Everett, Robersonville, Martin county, N. C.
Mr. C. S. Kirkpatrick, Crabtree, Haywood county, N. C.
Mr. F. H. Lyon, Wilkesboro, Wilkes county, N. C.

These scholarships are good for two years; worth $100 per year and railroad fare to and from the college by the nearest route.

The Peabody Fund is given to the State by Dr. J. L. M. Curry, General Agent of the Fund.

The State Superintendent receives and disburses this fund according to the advice and direction of the General Agent.

Dr. Curry confers with the State Superintendent as to where and how the money shall be spent so as to accomplish the greatest good to the cause of education, and especially for the training of teachers.

The State Superintendent receives nothing from this Fund for his services and gives no bond.

The statement of receipts shows how much money has been received by me since I came into this office.

The statement of disbursements shows to what schools the money was paid, when paid, and how much to each one.

The vouchers are on file in this office for each item of disbursements.

North Carolina owes a debt of lasting gratitude to the memory of George Peabody. Though dead he speaks in our midst to-day.

There are young men and women in our State who call him blessed, who, without the aid received from the Peabody Fund, would have been compelled to grope in darkness, but because of this aid are a power and blessing to our State, who are letting their lights shine and giving intelligence and enlightenment to those about them.

I wish to express to Dr. Curry, the General Agent of this Fund, the thanks of a grateful people for what he has done for us in educational matters, not only in the generous and philanthropic spirit shown to us in the distribution of the Peabody Fund, but for his hearty interest shown in our legislation pertaining to education.

I, as Superintendent of Public Instruction, have had most pleasant business relations with him, and words of encouragement from time to time, for which I am personally very grateful.

We have done the best we could under the circumstances with the funds. I am not satisfied with the results altogether. Perhaps in some instances I expected to much.

APPORTIONMENT OF PUBLIC SCHOOL FUND BY THE STATE BOARD OF EDUCATION.

The State school fund is apportioned by the State Board of Education. It has been the custom of the State Board for several years to allow the fund to accumulate until it would amount to from eight to ten cents per capita of the school population. This fund is composed of interest on bonds, sale of public lands and swamp lands.

The amount of the fund varies, as some years very little land is sold, while other years the sales may be much larger.

The following apportionment was made August, 1897, giving to each county nine cents per capita of school population, according to Superintendent's report for the scholastic year 1895 and '96:

The amount of the bonds belonging to the State school fund is $145,250. Of this amount $143,250 is four per cent. bonds, and the remaining $2,000 is six per cent. bonds.

In the apportionment following, no part of the bonds were used, only the interest that had accumulated since the last apportionment by the former State Board of Education in 1894. In this apportionment there is also the money received from sale of public lands

There is now (November 14th) to the credit of the State school fund $5,331.01 in addition to the bonds mentioned above.

COUNTIES.	NO. CHILDREN.	TOTAL FOR COUNTY.
Alamance	8,093	$ 728 37
Alexander	3,722	334 98
Alleghany	2,819	253 71
Anson	7,908	711 72
Ashe	7,018	631 62
Beaufort	7,842	705 78
Bertie	7,879	709 11
Bladen	6,813	613 17
Brunswick	4,328	389 52

COUNTIES.	NO. CHILDREN.	TOTAL FOR COUNTY.
Buncombe	14,556	1,310 04
Burke	6,217	559 53
Cabarrus	7,490	674 10
Caldwell	5,420	487 89
Camden	1,854	166 86
Carteret	3,802	342 18
Caswell	4,902	441 18
Catawba (census of 1894)	7,632	686 88
Chatham	9,175	825 75
Cherokee	4,365	392 85
Chowan	3,045	273 75
Clay	1,715	154 35
Cleveland	9,659	869 31
Columbus	7,593	683 37
Craven	7,115	640 35
Cumberland	9,266	833 94
Currituck	2,204	198 36
Dare	1,494	134 46
Davidson	8,156	734 04
Davie	4,683	421 83
Duplin	7,542	678 78
Durham (census of 1894)	7,091	638 19
Edgecombe	8,617	775 53
Forsyth	11,881	979 29
Franklin	6,096	548 64
Gaston	8,650	778 50
Gates	3,972	357 48
Graham	1,473	132 57
Granville	7,525	677 25
Greene (census of 1894)	3,783	340 47
Guilford	10,870	978 30
Halifax	11,587	1,042 83
Harnett	5,708	513 72
Haywood	5,959	536 31
Henderson	5,427	488 43
Hertford	5,307	477 63
Hyde	3,375	303 75
Iredell	10,150	913 50
Jackson	4,210	378 90
Johnston	11,017	991 53
Jones	2,891	260 19
Lenoir	5,801	522 09
Lincoln	5,330	479 70
Macon	4,230	380 70
Madison	5,159	464 31

COUNTIES.	NO. CHILDREN.	TOTAL FOR COUNTY.
Martin (census of 1894)	5,763	518 67
McDowell	4,330	389 70
Mecklenburg	13,384	1,204 56
Mitchell	5,783	520 47
Montgomery	4,531	407 79
Moore	8,406	756 54
Nash	8,758	788 22
New Hanover	7,609	684 81
Northampton	7,878	709 02
Onslow	4,085	367 65
Orange	4,815	433 35
Pamlico	2,842	255 78
Pasquotank	4,354	391 86
Pender	4,940	444 60
Perquimans	3,556	320 04
Person	5,108	459 72
Pitt	10,582	952 38
Polk	2,426	218 34
Randolph	10,105	909 45
Richmond	9,725	875 25
Robeson	12,916	1,167 84
Rockingham	10,325	929 25
Rowan	9,488	853 92
Rutherford	8,796	791 64
Sampson	9,673	870 57
Stanly	4,963	446 67
Stokes	7,095	638 55
Surry	6,686	601 74
Swain (census of 1894)	2,222	199 98
Transylvania	2,375	213 75
Tyrrell	1,676	150 84
Union	9,740	876 60
Vance	5,470	492 30
Wake	17,724	1,595 16
Warren	6,980	628 20
Washington	3,626	326 34
Watauga	4,658	419 22
Wayne	10,605	954 45
Wilkes	9,988	898 92
Wilson	8,579	772 11
Yadkin	5,333	479 97
Yancey	4,279	385 11
	631,657	$ 56,849 13

SUMMARY OF STATISTICS.

SUMMARY OF RECEIPTS FOR 1897 AND 1898.

	1897.	1898.
General poll tax:	$305,647 93	$318,933 58
General property tax	416,183 00	441,526 92
General property tax, local acts	13,167 13	21,522 32
Fines, forfeitures and penalties	13,507 74	15,653 50
Liquor license	65,998 74	74,777 01
Auctioneers	....	70 80
Estrays	9 49	11 24
State Treasurer	....	56,849 13
Other sources	15,986 15	57,170 35
Total	$830,500 18	$986,514 85

SUMMARY OF DISBURSEMENTS 1897 AND 1898.

	1897.	1898.
Paid white teachers	$451,474 84	$412,455 43
Paid colored teachers	227,195 27	228,033 97
Paid houses and sites, white	30,663 63	41,823 34
Paid houses and sites, colored	16,507 61	12,177 28
Paid County Superintendents	149 07	21,283 08
Paid Institutes, whites	....	697 73
Paid Institutes, colored	....	234 74
Paid Treasurer commission	17,269 77	18,071 06
Paid milage per diem Board of Education	3,217 62	5,586 03
Paid expenses Board of Education	2,976 26	3,903 71
Paid city schools	34,490 76	37,075 51
Paid other purposes	46,292 90	49,501 18
Total	$830,237 73	$931,082 86

CENSUS SCHOOL CHILDREN FROM 6 TO 21 YEARS.

	WHITE.	COLORED.	TOTAL.
For 1897	412,143	211,519	623 662
For 1898	415,262	213,218	628,480

ENROLLMENT IN SCHOOLS.

	WHITE.	COLORED.	TOTAL.
For 1897	222,252	131,404	353,656
For 1898	261,223	138,152	399,375

PER CENTAGE OF SCHOOL CHILDREN ENROLLED IN SCHOOLS.

	WHITE.	COLORED.
For 1897	$53\frac{9}{10}$ per cent.	$62\frac{7}{10}$ per cent.
For 1897	$62\frac{9}{10}$ per cent.	$64\frac{7}{10}$ per cent.

AVERAGE ATTENDANCE ON SCHOOLS.

	WHITE.	COLORED.	TOTAL.
For 1897	110,677	58,548	169,225
For 1897	144,357	68.894	213,240

PER CENTAGE OF SCHOOL POPULATION IN AVERAGE ATTENDANCE ON SCHOOLS.

	WHITE.	COLORED.
For 1897	$26\frac{8}{10}$ per cent,	$27\frac{6}{10}$ per cent.
For 1898	$34\frac{7}{10}$ per cent.	$32\frac{3}{10}$ per cent.

PER CENT. OF ENROLLMENT IN AVERAGE ATTENDANCE ON SCHOOLS.

	WHITE.	COLORED.
For 1897	$54\frac{2}{10}$ per cent.	$44\frac{5}{10}$ per cent.
For 1898	$55\frac{2}{10}$ per cent.	$54\frac{9}{10}$ per cent.

AVERAGE LENGTH OF SCHOOL TERMS IN WEEKS OR DAYS.

	WHITE.	COLORED.
For 1897	$11\frac{3}{5}$ weeks or 58 days.	$10\frac{4}{5}$ weeks or 54 days.
For 1898	$14\frac{1}{5}$ weeks or 71 days.	$12\frac{4}{5}$ weeks or 64 days.

AVERAGE SALARY OF TEACHERS REPORTED.

For 1897—White males	$23 21
For 1897—White females	20 81
For 1897—Colored males	21 54
For 1897—Colored females	18 25
For 1898—White males	24 66
For 1898—White females	22 96
For 1898—Colored males	21 64
For 1898—Colored females	19 85

VALUE OF PUBLIC SCHOOL PROPERTY REPORTED.

For 1897—Whites	$644,309 75
For 1897—Colored	234,324 00
Total	$878,633 75
For 1898—Whites	$683,363 00
For 1898—Colored	246,851 00
Total	$930,214 00

NUMBER OF SCHOOL HOUSES REPORTED.

For 1897—White	4,369
For 1897—	2,037
Total	6,406

NUMBER OF PUBLIC SCHOOLS TAUGHT.

For 1897—White	4,369
For 1897—Colored	2,037
Total	6,406
For 1898—White	4,297
For 1898—Colored	2,042
Total	6,339

NUMBER OF SCHOOLS DISTRICTS REPORTED.

For 1887—White	5,247
For 1897—Colored	2,540
Total	7,787
For 1898—White	5,083
For 1898—Colored	2,404
Total	7,387

COMPARATIVE STATISTICS FROM 1884 TO 1898, INCLUSIVE.

Receipts for 1884	$ 580,311 60
Receipts for 1885	631,904 38
Receipts for 1886	670,671 79
Receipts for 1887	647,407 81
Receipts for 1888	670,944 73
Receipts for 1889 (8 months)	612,151 31
Receipts for 1890	721,756 38
Receipts for 1891	714,966 27
Receipts for 1892	775,449 63
Receipts for 1893	751,608 11
Receipts for 1894	777,079 29
Receipts for 1895	825,988 84
Receipts for 1896	824,238 08
Receipts for 1897	822,757 09
Receipts for 1898	988,409 11

CENSUS FROM 6 TO 21 YEARS.

	White.	*Colored.*	*Total.*
For 1884	321,561	193,843	515,404
For 1885	330,890	199,237	530,127

	White.	*Colored.*	*Total.*
For 1886	338 059	209,249	547,308
For 1887	353,481	212,789	566,270
For 1888	363,982	216,837	580,819
For 1889—Not taken.			
For 1890	370,144	216,524	586,668
For 1891	380,718	213,859	594,577
For 1892	386,560	211,696	588,256
For 1893	399,753	218.788	618,541
For 1894	389,709	212,191	601,900
For 1895	403,812	217,437	621,249
For 1896	420,809	223,376	634,185
For 1897	412,143	211,519	623,662
For 1898	415,262	213,218	628,480

ENROLLMENT.

	White.	*Colored.*	*Total.*
For 1884	170,925	113,391	284,316
For 1885	185,225	112,941	298,166
For 1886	188,036	117,562	305,598
For 1887	202,134	123,145	325,279
For 1888	211,498	125,884	337,372
For 1889..			
For 1890	205,844	116,689	322,533
For 1891	214,908	115,812	330,720
For 1892	215,919	119,441	335,358
For 1893	232,560	124,398	356,958
For 1894	235,486	323,899	359,385
For 1895	245,413	128,150	373,563
For 1896	231,059	117,551	348,616
For 1897	222,252	331,404	353,656
For 1898	261,223	138,152	399,375

AVERAGE ATTENDANCE.

	White.	*Colored.*	*Total.*
For 1884	106,316	66,679	172,995
For 1895	115,092	70,486	185,578
For 1886	117,121	68,585	185,706
For 1887	124,653	71,466	196,119
For 1888	133,427	75,230	208,657
For 1889			
For 1890	134,108	68,992	203,912
For 1891	120,747	71,016	201,863
For 1892	133,001	66,746	198,747
For 1893	142,362	74,417	216,779
For 1894	149,046	71,246	220,250
For 1895	136,954	70,461	207,415
For 1896	137,115	67,088	204,203
For 1897	110,677	58,548	169,225
For 1898	144,346	68,894	213,240 ✓

AVERAGE LENGTH OF SCHOOL TERMS.

For 1884	11.50	weeks for	whites and	11.75	for colored.
For 1885	12	"	"	11.75	"
For 1886	11.75	"	"	12	"
For 1887	12		"	12	"
For 1888	12.80	"	"	12.30	"
For 1889					
For 1890	11.85		"	11.81	"
For 1891	12.14		"	11.91	"
For 1892	12.66		"	12.15	"
For 1893	12.81		"	12	"
For 1894	12.85		"	12.12	"
For 1895	12.45		"	11.83	"
For 1896	12.42	"	"	11.75	"
For 1897	11.73	"	"	10.86	"
For 1898	14.06	"	"	12.79	"

AVERAGE SALARY OF TEACHERS.

For 1886	white	males,	$26 23;	females,	$23 77
For 1887	"	"	25 10;	"	23 30
For 1888	"	"	25 68;	"	22 82
For 1890	"	"	25 80;	"	22 95
For 1891	"	"	25 03;	"	23 11
For 1892	"	"	26 20;	"	25 72
For 1893	"	"	26 46;	"	23 37
For 1894	"	"	25 53;	"	23 08
For 1895	"	"	24 87:	"	22 39
For 1896	"	"	24 75;	"	21 64
For 1897	"	"	23 21;	"	20 81
For 1898	"	"	24 66;	"	22 96
For 1886	colored	males	24 69;	females,	20 36
For 1887	"	"	24 10;	"	19 60
For 1888	"	"	22 67;	"	20 45
For 1890	"	"	22 72;	"	20 36
For 1891	"	"	22 23;	"	18 45
For 1892	"	"	23 33;	"	20 14
For 1893	"	"	23 33;	"	21 28
For 1894	"	"	23 08;	"	19 27
For 1895	"	"	23 14;	"	20 91
For 1896	"	"	26 70;	"	20 96
For 1897	"	"	21 54;	"	18 25
For 1898	"	"	21 64;	"	19 85

VALUE OF PUBLIC SCHOOL PROPERTY

1888—For whites	$ 506,291 90
1888—For colored	230,218 68
Total in 1888	$ 735,510 58
1890—For whites	$ 612,303 51
1890—For colored	240,402 60
Total in 1890	$ 852,705 11
1891—For whites	$ 606,922 00
1891—For colored	241,152 00
Total in 1891	$ 848,074 00
1892—For whites	$ 636,525 00
1892—For colored	255,839 00
Total in 1892	$ 892,364 00
1893—For whites	$ 785,637 34
1893—For colored	269,147 60
Total in 1893	$1,054,784 94
1894—For whites	$ 817,148 08
1894—For colored	301,149 80
Total in 1894	$1,118,297 88
1895—For whites	$ 721,160 00
1895—For colored	372,074 50
Total in 1895	$1,093,234 50
1896—For whites	$ 654,925 75
1896—For colored	233,206 60
Total in 1896	$ 888,132 35
1897—For whites	$ 644,309 75
1897—For colored	234,324 00
Total in 1897	$ 878,632 73
1898—For whites	$ 683,363 00
1898—For colored	246,851 00
Total in 1898	$ 930,214 00

COMMONS HALL.—UNIVERSITY OF NORTH CAROLINA.

NUMBER OF PUBLIC SCHOOL HOUSES.

1888—For whites	3,779
1888—For colored	1,766
Total in 1888	5,543
1890—For whites	3,973
1890 - For colored	1,820
Total in 1890	5,793
1891—For whites	4,034
1891—For colored	1,779
Total in 1891	5,813
1892—For whites	4,168
1892—For colored	1,992
Total in 1892	6,160
1893—For whites	4,271
1893—For colored (five counties not reporting)	1,942
Total in 1893	6,213
1894—For whites	4,356
1894—For colored (three counties not reporting)	2,010
Total in 1894	3,366
1895—For whites	4,372
1895—For colored	2,213
Total for 1895	6,585
1896—For whites	4,875
1896—For colored	2,374
Total for 1896	7,249

NUMBER OF PUBLIC SCHOOLS TAUGHT.

1888—For whites	4,438
1888—For colored	2,317
Total in 1888	6,775

1890—For whites	4,508
1890—For colored	2,327
Total in 1890	6,835
1891—For whites	4,574
1891—For colored	2,260
Total in 1891	6 834
1892—For whites	4,603
1892—For colored	2,376
Total in 1892	6,979
1893—For whites	4,599
1893—For colored	2,219
Total in 1893	6,818
1894—For whites	4,811
1894—For colored	2,296
Total in 1894	7,107
1895—For whites	4,372
1895—For colored	2,213
Total for 1895	6,585
1896—For whites	4,897
1896—For colored	2374
Total in 1896	7,249
1897—For whites	4,368
1897—For colored	2,037
Total in 1897	6,406
1898—For whites	4,279
1898—For colored	2,042
Total in 1898	6,339

NUMBER OF DISTRICTS REPORTED.

1888—For whites	4,763
1888—For colored	2,031
Total in 1888	6,794

1890—For whites	4,893
1890—For colored	2,289
Total in 1890	7,182
1891—For whites	4,926
1891—For colored	2,302
Total in 1891	7,228
1892—For whites	5,168
1892—For colored	2,387
Total in 1892	7,555
1893—For whites (four counties not reporting)	4,937
1893—For colored " " " "	2,296
Total in 1893	7,233
1894—For whites (three counties not reporting)	5,123
1894—For colored " " " "	2,424
Total in 1894	7,547
1895—For whites	4,484
1895—For colored	2,290
Total in 1895	6,774
1896—For whites	5,157
1896—For colored	2,404
Total in 1896	7,560
1897—For whites	5,247
1897—For colored	2,540
Total in 1897	7,787
1898—For whites	5,083
1898—For colored	2,403
Total in 1898	7,487

TOWNSHIPS WITH SPECIAL DONATIONS.

The following is a list of counties and townships which raised the amounts named. These amounts were duplicated by the State, according to special act of the Legislature of 1897.

The total amount of donations raised is $8,596.63, which being duplicated by the State, makes an increase in the School Fund of these townships of $17,193.26.

SPECIAL FUND BY SUBSCRIPTION.

Greene county	Snow Hill township	$ 354 50
Greene county	District, No. 5	37 25
Haywood county	Township, No. 4	210 00
Haywood county	District, No 1	50 00
Jackson county	Webster township, No. 6	220 00
Jackson county	Cullowhee township, No. 9	35 00
Jackson county	Coney Fork township, No. 11	60 00
Jackson county	River township, No. 10	50 00
Rutherford county	Rutherfordton township, No. 1	500 00
Rutherford county	High Shoal township, No. 5	500 00
Rutherford county	Coal Spring township, No. 7	403 00
Rutherford county	Logan's Store township, No. 10	447 35
Mecklenburg county	Clear Creek township	250 00
Buncombe county	Avery's Creek township, No. 1	60 00
Buncombe county	Lower Hominy township, No. 2	163 20
Buncombe county	Upper Hominy township, No. 3	147 00
Buncombe county	Leicester township, No. 4	56 69
Buncombe county	Lime Stone township, No. 6	22 50
Buncombe county	Swannanoa township, No. 8	12 00
Buncombe county	Asheville township, No. 9	147 00
Buncombe county	Reem's Creek township, No. 10	30 00
Buncombe county	Ivey township, No. 12	500 00
Cleveland county	Township, No. 3	265 00
Cleveland county	District, No. 4	120 00
Cleveland county	District, No. 5	100 00
Cleveland county	District, No. 7	50 00
Cleveland county	District, No. 8	50 00
Surry county	Township, No. 6	50 00
Surry county	Township, No. 5	250 00
Yancey county	District, No. 10	125 00
Yancey county	Jack's Creek township, No. 6	122 40

Cleveland county	Township, No. 9	500 00
Forsyth county	Kernersville township	30 00
Forsyth county	Kernersville township	25 00
Forsyth county	Old Town township	25 00
Forsyth county	Middle Fork township	50 00
Forsyth county	Vienna township	32 00
Forsyth county	Vienna township	25 00
Pitt county	Farmville township	55 00
Watauga county	Beaver Dam township	92 00
Beaufort county	Washington District	500 00
Forsyth county	South Fork township	35 00
Forsyth county	Lewisville township	30 00
Greene county	Hookerton township, Dist. No. 3,	125 00
Buncombe county	Leicester township	80 00
Buncombe county	Swannanoa township	7 50
Buncombe county	Black Mountain township	12 50
Gaston county	District, No. 6	125 98
Mecklenburg county	Pineville township	208 26
Jackson county	District, No. 9	17 50
Cleveland county	District, No. 2	500 00
Cleveland county	District, No. 3	71 00
Cleveland county	District, No. 4	15 00
Cleveland county	District, No. 5	42 50
Cleveland county	District, No. 6	85 00
Cleveland county	District, No. 7	26 50
Cleveland county	District, No. 8	25 00
Cleveland county	District, No. 10	22 50
McDowell county	Crooked Creek township	31 00
Buncombe county	Asheville township, No. 9	100 00
Haywood county	District, No. 1	37 00
Greene county	District, No. 1	50 00
Madison county	District, No. 14	227 50
Total		$ 8,596 63

TOWNSHIPS VOTED LOCAL TAX.

The following is the list of townships that voted the special tax according to the Act of the Legislature of 1897. This is a small beginning, but we hope the number will increase until every township in the State will have its own special tax for schools:

SPECIAL TAX VOTED.

Bertie county	Woodville township	$ 356 97
Watauga county,	North Fork township	50 87
Jackson county.	Hamburg township	85 00
Mecklenburg county	Pineville township, Dis. No. 4	291 74
Davidson county	Yadkin College township	103 41
Surry county	Ararat township	114 28
Hyde county	Lake Landing township, Dis. No. 5	483 48
Surry county	Granite township	238 74
Surry county	Granite township	202 71
Surry county	Ararat township	94 73
Dare county	East Lake township	105 86
Macon county	Ellija township	132 28
Total		$2,260 07

NORMAL DEPARTMENT OF THE CULLOWHEE HIGH SCHOOL.

The Legislature of 1893 provided for the establishment of a Normal Department in the Cullowhee High School, located in Jackson county, by the enactment of the following statute, Chapter 120, (Private Laws of 1893) which the Legislature of 1896 amended to read as printed below:

AN ACT TO AMEND CHAPTER 170, PRIVATE LAWS 1891, AMENDING CHAPTER OF THE CULLOWHEE HIGH SCHOOL, AS AMENDED BY CHAPTER 59, PRIVATE LAWS OF 1895.

The General Assembly of North Carolina do enact:

SECTION 1. That section one, chapter one hundred and seventy, Private Laws of 1891, be amended by adding at the end of said section the following: "And there shall be established in connection with said High School a Normal Department to fit and train young men and women for the position of teachers in the public schools of the State, and the sum of fifteen hundred dollars is annnally appropriated for this purpose. Said Normal Department shall be under the supervision of the Superintendent of Public Instruction of the State and David Coward, John T. Wike, A. J. Long, Sr., Zebulon Watson and D. D. Davis, as a Board of Local Managers; and said Superintendent and Board of Local Managers shall have power to prescribe rules for the regulation and management of the same. Said Superintendent and Board of Local Managers shall also have power, upon being satisfied that said Normal Department is inefficient or unnecessary, to discontinue the same, and the appropriation herein provided for shall thereupon cease. The Principal of said High School, upon the completion of the prescribed course in the Normal Department, shall grant certificates which shall entitle the holders to teach in any of the schools of the State, subject to the general school laws of the State as to character, which certificates shall be good for three years, subject to examinations upon branches that may be subsequently added to the public school course: *Provided*, that all young men and young women who are preparing themselves for teachers shall pay no charges for tuition.

SEC. 2. That this act shall be in force from and after its ratification.

The following is the list of the Local Board of Managers: J. M. Cowder, David Coward, J. R. Long, A. J. Long, John T. Wike, J. H. Painter, A. C. Queen, H. C. Cannon and D. D. Davis.

REPORT OF ROBT. L. MADISON AND W. D. WIKE OF THE CULLOWHEE HIGH SCHOOL.

PAINTER, N. C., May 19, 1898.

To the Local Board of Managers of the Normal Department of Cullowhee High School.

GENTLEMEN:—We respectfully present herein our joint report of the work done in our Normal Department during the fall and spring terms of the session 1897–'98

The total enrollment for the session is seventy.

The course of study has been adhered to faithfully. This embraces the common school branches, and, in addition, algebra, physics, physical geography, English composition, civil government, theory and practice of teaching, principles of education, history of education, psychology, practice teaching, lectures and professional reading. The methods of teaching and the discipline of the institution, we believe, will be found in accord with the latest practical advancement.

The work of the past five years has been eminently satisfactory, judged in the light of results. And we point with pride to the educational improvement made in this section of the State, in which this department has played no small part. Our graduates have nearly every one attained conspicuous success, and we are unable to supply the demand for them as teachers in this county and those adjoining. Four of them are at present county surveyors, one was a county examiner, one is the head of a high school in Rockingham county, one taught a nine months' school in Jackson county last year and will teach at the same place ten months' this year at an increased salary, and thirty or forty others might be mentioned who have completed our course with credit, and are doing or have done superior and lasting work for the State.

Our present equipment, while small and limited, is good. The library is small but select, and should be increased at an early date by the addition of some of the best recent professional publications Also, the reading table should be provided with a few more of the most approved educational periodicals An appropriation to purchase needed apparatus for the class in physics should be made before the spring term, 1899.

The department is now in excellent condition, and the outlook is brighter than ever before. State Superintendent Mebane paid us a visit at the close of the session, and delivered before the school and its patrons and friends an address of great power, replete with practical suggestions and timely advice. The results of this speech will be widespread and long-continued.

In conclusion, we would give hearty expression of our gratitude to the officials in charge of the Normal Department for their kindness, helpfulness and encouragement to us and their faithful endeavors to promote every interest of the work.

Respectfully submitted, ROBT. L. MADISON,
Principal of Cullowhee High School.

W. D. WIKE,
Teacher in charge of Normal Department.

Approved by A. J. LONG, SR, J. H. PAINTER, } *Committee Appointed to Receive the Report.*

REPORT OF TREASURER, 1897 TO 1898.

J. D. Coward, Treasurer, in account with Cullowhee High School:

DR.

1897—Received from Z V. Watson, ex-Secretary.....$	4 09	
Oct. 15.—Auditor's warrant..........................	1,000 00	
1898—March 18.—Auditor's warrant................	1,000 00	
Total......................................		$2,004 09

CR.

By disbursements as per account filed with Superintendent Public Instruction.......................$	1,974 19	
1898—Sept. 2.—Balance on hand..................	29 90	
Total....................................		$2,004 09

GENERAL INFORMATION.

This institution is situated in the centre of Jackson county. It was established in 1888 and incorporated in 1891. More than one thousand students have attended since the opening, representing nine States and one territory. In the past six years there have been one hundred and two graduations. The present organization includes two literary societies and seven departments, as follows: Primary, Intermediate, Classical, State Normal, Commercial, Military and Fine Arts. The enrollment last session was 234.

SOME RESULTS.

POSITIONS OF A FEW GRADUATES AND UNDER-GRADUATES.

W. Galloway, attorney at law, Brevard, N. C.

Mrs. Lena Smith Wallace, assistant teacher Government Indian School, Reserve, Wis.

C. A. Wallace, primary teacher Government Indian School, Reserve, Wis.

W. D. Wike, teacher in charge Normal Department Cullowhee High School.

J. N. Wilson, ex-County Examiner Jackson county; law student University of North Carolina.

A. C. Wike, Normal student University of Georgia, 1897; Normal student Howard Payne College, Texas.

J. U. Gibbs, County Supervisor of Schools Swain county.

F. E. Alley, nominee for office Clerk Superior Court Jackson county.

J. N. Moody, County Supervisor Schools Graham county.

Mrs. Nancy Wilson Brown, primary teacher Cullowhee High School.

J. K. Henderson, ministerial student Wake Forest College.

H. A. Price, student Tusculum College, Tenn.

T. B. Davis, Principal of River Hill School, Jackson county.

J. Robt. Long, nominee for office Register of Deeds Jackson county.

A. G. Pless, Principal Glenville School, Jackson county.

M. Parker, nominee for office of Clerk of Superior Court Jackson county.

J. Parker Moore, nominee for office of Register Deeds Macon county.

S. B. Parris, Principal of Bryson City School, Swain county.

J. E. Triplett, Principal of Stoneville Collegiate Institute, Rockingham county.

J. H. Painter, County Supervisor of Schools Jackson county.

Judson Corn, County Supervisor of Schools Transylvania county.

Miss Nellie Smith, primary teacher Cullowhee High School, 1896-'97 and 1897-'98.

Miss Ida Smith, primary teacher Cullowhee High School, 1894-'95.

Mrs. Mary Robinson Sims, teacher of Dillsboro School, Jackson county.

W. T. Jenkins, nominee for office of Register of Deeds Swain county.

J. H. Clayton, traveling salesman for J. B. & E. C. Atkins, Atlanta, Ga.

J. C. Moss, private in U. S. Army, engaged at Santiago, July, 1898.

L. J. Zachary, merchant, Grange, Transylvania county.

Miss Lela Potts, postmaster, Sylva, N. C.

R. D. Sisk, attorney at law, Franklin, N. C.

W. H. Bryson, photographer, Vinita, Indian Territory.

N. A. Davis, salesman, Blackfoot, Idaho.

UNDERGRADUATES.

A. J. DeHart, Register of Deeds Swain county.

C. B. Wike, telegraph operator, Washington, D. C.

W. H. Hayes, nominee for office of Clerk of Superior Court Swain county.

W. H. Painter, conductor on Southern Railway—Asheville to Salisbury.

A. D. Raby, attorney at law, Robbinsville, N. C.

John M. Moore, Presbyterian minister, Vinita, Indian Territory.

John Green, ex-County Superintendent Jackson county.

Nine volunteers in the Spanish-American war, besides about eighty public school teachers in various counties.

NORMAL SCHOOLS FOR THE COLORED RACE.

STATE APPROPRIATION $14,000 PER ANNUM.

NAMES OF LOCAL BOARDS OF MANAGERS AND PRINCIPALS.

SALISBURY.—Sen. J. A. Ramsey, Capt. Chas. Price, Sen. S. A. Earnhardt, Dr. J. Rumple, Treasurer; Hon. Theo. F. Klu z, Rev. John O. Crosby, Principal.

WINSTON.—H. E. Fries, W. A. Blair, Treasurer; Rev. J. H. Clewell, Maj. J. T. Brown, J. J. Blair, D. D.; Lt. C. A. Reynolds, S. G. Atkins, Principal.

ELIZABETH CITY.—John Poleman, M. B. Culpepper, W. J. Griffin, C. E. Kramer, Treasurer; Prof S L. Sheep, Prof. P. W. Moore, Principal.

FRANKLINTON.—H. E Long, B. S. Mitchell, J. A. Hawkin, Jas. I. Moore, T. H. Whitaker, Treasurer; Prof. J. A. Savage, Principal.

PLYMOUTH.—L. N. C. Spruil, Stewart Jones, Capt. G. W. Horney, James Hassell, F. M. Bunch, Treasurer; Prof. J. W. McDonald, Principal.

FAYETTEVILLE.—S. R. Deal, Dr. N. P. Melchor, F. P. Williston, Treasurer; D. A. Bryant, G. A. P. Wilkerson. Secretary; L. E. Fairley, Principal.

GOLDSBORO.—Dr. J. D. Spincer, W. D. Herring, Treasurer; A. C. Davis, B. S. Stephens Rev, P. W. Russell, Principal.

REPORTS OF THE STATE NORMAL SCHOOL AT WINSTON.

WINSTON, N. C., June 7, 1897.

To the Local Board of Central State Normal School, Winston-Salem, N. C.

GENTLEMEN:—As Principal of the Normal School under your direction, I beg to submit the following brief statement concerning the work being done.

The Normal School here has been organized only two years. From the first we have undertaken to develop a course of instruction and practice work that would offer such normal preparation as is considered important for teachers in the public schools. This we have undertaken by doing three things especially, viz.:

1. Giving the students a thorough knowledge of the common school branches, including all the subjects usually taught in our public schools.

2. Acquainting them with the main facts of the science, art and history of education through both text-books and lectures, using Page's "Theory and Practice of Teaching," Parker's "Talks on Teaching," and White's "School Management" as text-books.

Our reference library on Pedagogics includes such widely used professional books as White's "Elements of Pedagogy," Spencer's "Education," Payne's "Lectures of Education," Baldwin's "Art of School Management," Parker's "Talks on Pedagogics," Swett's "Methods of Instruction," Partridge's "The Quincy Methods," Bain s "Education as a Science," "Quick's Educational Reformers," etc.

3. Illustrating before the normal classes the principles thus learned by actual contact with class room work—sometimes the students observing and sometimes teaching under criticism.

Our plan is to enlarge this course of professional training by lectures, accompanied by diagrams and blackboard outlines on the history of education with Quick's "Educational Reformers" as a basis. We have made it a point to make haste with all necessary deliberation by requiring our students to take a course so full and thorough as to guarantee the best preparation when they leave us.

Although the Normal School has been open only two years, we might easily have graduated a class from courses of study often so-called normal' if we had been satisfied to send them out poorly prepared to defend their diplomas.

But we think it better to lay the foundation well in our sub-normal department, and pass the students up regularly and successfully, than to rush them out with unsatisfactory preparation.

With the next school term there will pass regularly into the sub-normal department seventy-eight (78) pupils, and into the normal department proper twelve (12).

A number of these students have already taught and a large number of them are candidates for the teaching profession. The methods and means of doing this work for the State will be greatly improved with the opening of the next school year.

By the co-operative arrangement with the Slater Industrial Academy we shall have a stronger Faculty and superior accommodations in an up-to-date new building next session.

This arrangement has added one of the strongest teachers of the State to the Faculty, and thus furnished the Normal a larger instruction force than it would otherwise have. Besides, it has been determined that in the near future a model school, after the New England type, shall be opened under an expert to illustrate in the most modern and scientific way the latest and best methods of teaching.

In this way it is the purpose of the Board of Directors, we trust, to furnish the State in the Normal School here such facilities for the preparation of teachers and such results as will prove of ever-increasing value.

Your obedient servant,

S. G. ATKINS.

PRINCIPAL'S OFFICE,
STATE NORMAL SCHOOL.
WINSTON, N. C., August 29, 1898.

To the Local Board of Managers,
State Normal School, Winston, N. C.

GENTLEMAN :—I beg to submit to your honorable Board the following statement regarding the work of the State Normal School for the past school session :

The school is still in its period of development, having been established only three years ago, and our effor.s have necessarily been limited by the conditions which always obtain in the first years of the history of a school. We have been devoted during these three years mainly to the development of the course of instruction and to building up the classes according to the demands of the course of instruction. The class of 1899 will, therefore, be the first regular graduating class from the full course.

The attention of the Board is called to our courses of study as laid in the catalogue. It will be seen that the co-operation of the Normal School with the Slater Industrial Academy gives a decided advantage, in the fact that the Academic Department of the Academy furnishes the literary foundation requisite to a successful prosecution of the course in the Normal Training Department. This enables the institution to calculate upon purely professional training in the Normal Training Department, or Department of Pedagogy ; and thus put us in position to do the real normal work so much needed for the colored teachers of the State. This is a fact about the Normal School, as co-operating with the Slater Industrial Academy, to which we can well afford to call the attention of the State Board of Education and that of the public at large.

This co-operatton has done even more for us. In the course of training of the Slater Industrial Academy, besides the Academic Department, there are the Industrial Department, the Music Department and the Commercial Department. The Industrial Department furnishes training for men in carpentry, shoe-making and agriculture, and, for girls, in sewing, cooking and general domestic economy.

All of this we feel to be important in the preparation of teachers ; and in view of the thoroughness of the work done in all these departments, it is the opinion of your humble servant that your Board, as well as the State, is to be congratulated on an arrangement which offers such all-around training to those who are candidates for the responsible place of teacher in our public schools.

The growth of the school in numbers and in the public favor during the past three years has been steady, and the outlook for the next session is unusually bright. Several of the instructors in the Normal School are visiting different places in the State in order to invite the attention of the people of the State to the benefits which are offered by the State Normal School under your direction, and I am receiving letters from them daily which give assurance of a largely increased attendance of boarding pupils the next year. Others of the faculty have been, during this vacation, attending celebrated summer schools for teachers in New England.

There was enrolled in the Normal and Sub-Normal Departments of the school last year 95 males and 150 females, including the attendance upon the summer term.

The summer term of the school is held during one of the summer months, and is intended for only those who are actively connected with the work of teaching, or engaged in it.

It is earnestly hoped that the model school for observation and practice work may be brought up to the desired standard next year. This model school will exhibit the work of an expert teacher for the benefit of the members of our Normal Training Department.

It will doubtless be interesting to the Board to know that fifteen counties of the State were represented among our students during the the past session. The names of the counties are as follows: Forsyth, Davidson. Wilkes, Rockingham, Surry, Iredell, Durham, Wake, New Hanover, Craven, Wilson, Nash, Yadkin, Davie and Guilford.

In addition to the means of training referred to above, the members of the school have the benefit of a good library, literary societies, and the Y. M. C. A. and C. E. society, organized as a part of the work of the school.

The moral tone of the school is notably high. The teachers are all active christian workers, and their influence is telling, not only in the class room, but particularly upon the moral character of the pupils. The effort is to do more than produce scholars. Our main purpose is to make good men and women with substantial character, who will go out from the school prepared to lift the colored race up along the lines that make for permanent, progressive, christian citizenship.

The Board, I am sure, will be glad to know that the splendid new building, which we have been trying to erect for the past two years, has been completed and occupied. This building will furnish us unusual facilities for successful work, and it marks a new era in the history of the institution.

I should not fail to make special reference to the generosity of friends at home and in the North, and of both races, who have aided in erecting and furnishing the building. The interest which has been manifested by the members of this Board has been particularly gratifying. Without desiring to be invidious, I wish to mention especially Mr. H. E. Fries and Mr. W. A. Blair, as a fitting recognition of their unceasing labors in connection with the work of the school, and in view of their frequent contributions of financial aid to the school in its struggles. The time and labor which both of them have given to the building up of the school are not to be easily estimated. I desire also to express my personal thanks to Profs. J. J. Blair and John W. Woods for their co-operation and help in making out the course of study; and we must not forget the cordial sympathy of the State Superintendent of Public Instruction with our effort to bring the school up to a high standard of efficiency as a Normal School.

I am sure that the Board will join with me in acknowledging our gratitude to Superintendent Mebane.

Permit me, gentlemen of the Board, to call your attention to the importance of laying our needs and opportunities before the next Legislature. Normal education in North Carolina for the colored teachers has never been more than an experiment, and it is earnestly hoped that the next Legislature will change this condition of things. I am sure that it becomes our duty to help bring about this good result. In doing this we can only be true to the ideal which we have already been endeavoring to attain.

The report of the Treasurer will give you the condition of our finances. Thanking the Board for their uniform kindness and co operation, I am

Your obedient servant,

S. G. ATKINS.

RELATION OF THE SLATER INDUSTRIAL ACADEMY TO THE NORMAL SCHOOL, AS PROVIDED BY ACT OF THE LEGISLATURE OF 1895.

(See Public Laws of 1895, Chapter 393.)

Of the amount which goes to the Normal School at Winston under Act of the Legislature, 1895, as shown by the Public laws of 1895, chapter 393, $1,000 is appropriated for the benefit of the Slater Industrial Academy, on condition that the Academy should raise a like amount. The following quotation from the Act is in point:

"For the purpose of aiding the Slater Industrial School, located near said towns (Winston-Salem), and for securing for the use of the State the buildings erected and now used by the Slater Industrial School, the State Treasurer shall pay to the State Board of Education, out of any funds in the Treasury not otherwise appropriated, a sum equal in amount to the sum annually raised by the trustees and officers of the Slater Industrial School; provided, that the amount in any one year shall not exceed the sum of one thousand dollars."

Reference is made also to the report of Hon. John C. Scarborough, ex-Superintendent of Public Instruction, for 1894–'96. It will be seen that the Act gives the Slater Industrial Academy one thousand dollars on condition that it will raise one thousand dollars, and makes it an independent appropriation solely for the benefit of said institution, in order that the Normal School, established under the same Act, may profit by the one thousand dollars which the Slater Industrial Academy is required to raise to secure the appropriation therein made.

W. A. BLAIR, *Secretary and Treasurer.*

STATEMENT OF RECEIPTS AND EXPENDITURES FOR INSTRUCTION AND INCIDENTALS IN CONNECTION WITH THE STATE NORMAL SCHOOL AT WINSTON.

W. A. BLAIR, *Secretary and Treasurer,*

In account with Local Board of Directors.

DR.

	To State appropriation for Normal School	$ 1,852 00	
	To State appropriation for benefit of the Slater Industrial Academy, on condidition that it raise a like amount.....	1,000 00	
	To Peabody appropriation..............	400 00	
			$ 3,252 00

CR.

1898.	By disbursements as per account filed with the Superintendent Public Instruction................................	$ 3,200 00	
Aug. 29.	By balance on hand....................	52 00	
			$ 3,252 00

W. A. BLAIR, *Secretary and Treasurer.*

REPORTS OF THE STATE NORMAL SCHOOL AT GOLDSBORO.

STATE NORMAL SCHOOL,
FOR THE TRAINING OF COLORED TEACHERS,
GOLDSBORO, N. C., January, 1898.

Hon. C. H. Mebane, Raleigh, N. C.:

The school now enjoys, I think, the moral support of the entire community, which is inspiring both to the students and teachers.

Early in the session we organized a class in methods, which soon commended itself to the aspiring teachers of the community and section. Only a short time was necessary to enroll in this department of the Normal School more than twenty teachers of this and adjacent counties. They continued in regular attendance until the district schools opened last fall. Most of these, in fact all of them save two, are now engaged in teaching in this and neighboring counties.

We have now, and have had all along, a training class of some thirty others, who have never been examined to teach. In addition to the regular course in arithmetic, grammar, geography, history physiology, etc., which this class is pursuing, it receives weekly instruction and training in pedagogics. At the close of the session the Faculty hopes to be warranted in commending the members of this class as suitable candidates for certificates to teach.

In a few weeks the district schools will begin to close, and the mem-

bers of our class in methods are expected to return to the Normal. With the proper vigilance and interest put forth by the Faculty of our school there is no reason why the number enrolled in the class in methods should not be doubled after the schools in country districts close.

This, however, can the better be done by the addition of another, or rather by the increase of our teaching force to four, for the work of instructing and drilling the class in methods will require about all the time of the Principal, especially if the work be conducted as has been designed. And to continue the routine work of the school as mapped out, there must necessarily be at least three teachers, as there are twenty-four recitations to be heard daily.

I have respectfully recommended to the Local Board of Managers the appointment of an additional instructor. The instructors are anxious to effect the best results possible under existing circumstances. Doubtless the Local Board will expect good results from the session; and certainly the State Superintendent of Public Instruction is desirous to have the school accomplish all it possibly can to prepare proficient teachers for the public schools of the State, and thus assist in the development of useful and patriotic citizens.

The Normal School here is certainly located in a section of the State thickly settled by those for whom it was intended to directly benefit, and with the proper encouragement, and efficiently managed, it might easily become one of the most useful schools of its kind in the State. Already the attendance of the present session surpasses that of any former year; and permit me to remark by way of parenthesis, that the students enrolled are neither children nor "trashy," as has been stated by one. The age of the students range between twelve and forty years. Students unknown to the Faculty are required to present, upon application to enter the school, testimonials of good character. All must be twelve years of age or upwards, and pass a satisfactory examination in reading, writing, arithmetic and geography. Last week our daily attendance was nearly one hundred. Respectfully,

E. E. SMITH, *Superintendent.*

REPORT OF TREASURER.

H. L. GRANT, *Treasurer,*

In account with Goldsboro Colored Normal School.

1896.	DR.		
	To balance last report	$ 277 97	
Sept. 4.	To warrant	783 33	
1897.			
Jan. 4.	To warrant	783 33	
Mar. 3.	To check (Peabody Fund)	200 00	
			$ 2,044 63
1897.	CR.		
	By voucher	$ 1,800 00	
	By voucher	164 48	
	Amount turned over to J. F. Dobson, Secretary and Treasurer	80 15	
			$ 2,044 63

REPORT OF TREASURER.

W. D. HERRING, *Treasurer*,

In account with Goldsboro Normal School.

DR.

1897.			
Sept. 8.	Received of former Treasurer.........	$ 31 25	
Sept. 8.	Received of former Treasurer, cash...	138 90	
Oct. 25.	Received of Supt. Public Instruction..	500 00	
1898.			
Feb. 1.	Received of Supt. Public Instruction..	1,357 14	
			$ 2,027 29

CR.

	By disbursements as per account filed with Supt. Public Instruction.......	$ 1,288 77	
1898.			
June 11.	To balance on hand	738 52	
			$ 2,027 29

REPORTS OF THE STATE NORMAL SCHOOL AT SALISBURY.

STATE NORMAL SCHOOL,
SALISBURY, N. C., June 5, 1897.

To the Hon. C. H Mebane, Superintendent of Public Instruction of North Carolina, and the Directors of the Salisbury State Normal School.

DEAR SIRS:—I have the honor to submit the following report of the Salisbury State Normal School for the session beginning September 21, 1896, and ending May 6, 1897:

There were enrolled during the session 134 students, 58 males and 76 females, an increase of more than 19 per cent. over the enrollment of the previous session, notwithstanding the age for admission was raised from 12 for girls and 13 for boys to 14 for girls and 15 for boys.

Fifteen counties were represented, as follows:

Alamance 1, Buncombe 5, Cabarrus 5, Catawba 5, Davie 5, Davidson 7, Forsyth 2, Guilford 1, Gaston 2, Iredell 3, McDowell 2, Mecklenburg 3, New Hanover 1, Rowan 88, Union 2. Of those accredited to Rowan county, 56 give Salisbury as their postoffice address, and the remaining 32 give their addresses as follows: Gold Hill 1, Millbridge 3, Omega 4, Trading Ford 2, China Grove 1, Mountulla 2, Spencer 7, Woodleaf 2, Zeb 1, Watsonville 2, and Rockwell 2. It is more than probable that some of these students should be accredited to other counties, as some of the above named postoffices are near the county line. At all events, only 63 of the students are from Salisbury and vicinity, which includes Spencer.

During the session of 1895-'96 there were enrolled 112 students, 44 males and 68 females, representing 12 counties, as follows: Anson 2, Cabarrus 4, Catawba 2, Davidson 1, Davie 4, Forsyth 2, Gaston 2, Iredell 3, Mecklenburg 2, Rowan 87, Union 1, and South Carolina 1. Of the 87 from Rowan, 53 were from Salisbury and vicinity, including what is now called Spencer.

It will be seen from the above statistics of the last session that 46 students were non-residents of Rowan county, as against 25 during the previous session. It will also be seen that more than half the total enrollment are non-residents of Salisbury and vicinity. I write this to show that the school is not altogether local in its character. Of the 134, fifty-eight were new students. The average age was $17\frac{49}{64}$, and the average daily attendance was the largest within the history of the institution. There were five graduates. The deportment of the students was excellent, the general progress commendable, and the relation of faculty and students harmonious. Every student went home well pleased with his year's work, and with the hope of returning at the opening of the next session.

Respectfully,

J. O. CROSBY.

STATE NORMAL SCHOOL,
SALISBURY, N. C., June, 1898.

To the Hon. C. H. Mebane, Superintendent of Public Instruction of North Carolina, and the Directors of the Salisbury State Normal School.

SIRS:—The session of the State Normal at Salisbury, which closed on the 26th of April, 1898, was, in all respects, the most successful within the entire history of the institution. The total attendance was 162—fifty-nine males and 103 females, the average age being a little more than 18½ years. Not only was the enrollment larger, but the average daily attendance exceeded that of any former session. By reference to the accompanying list of names it will be seen that fifteen counties and four States were represented. The enrollment, which is the greatest ever recorded, would have reached even a greater number had it not been for the "smallpox scare" which led the city to adopt an ordinance in favor of compulsory vaccination. Some students, rather than be vaccinated, left the school, and others lived in daily dread both of the smallpox and the vaccination.

Just as the "scare" was over, and things began to assume their normal condition, a genuine case of smallpox broke out. This put an end to further additions to the enrollment, as the quarantine continued till the end of the session. The sohool, however, has sustained no permanent injury, as each student went to his home with the full determination to return to the State Normal early next session. But we do not rely upon the enrollment alone to measure the success of the school—the work in the class-room furnishes a truer index to the real standing of an institution, and the industry and moral tone of the students a better guage for measuring its rank. We, therefore, prefer to estimate our success or failure by these standards. For many years the State Normal School at Salisbury ranked first for its thoroughness and efficiency, and its graduates compared favorably with those from other schools of greater pretensions and longer standing.

It is a pleasure to know that those in authority are making every reasonable effort to bring the institution back to its former position ; but this takes time as well as labor, as only so much is possible within a given period. The withdrawal of the Peabody money cannot be otherwise regarded than as an unwarranted and unjust discrimination against an institution, which, in point of usefulness and opportunity, is second to no Normal School in the State, and whose local directors, Faculty, graduates and students merit better treatment. The action on the part of Dr. Curry has greatly hampered the school.

A fact that seems to have escaped general notice is, that the colored population of this section of the State is sparse and widely distributed, and yet the school with its meager facilities and cramped accommodations has sustained itself nobly ; and measured by its work, and the men and women it has sent forth, and even by its enrollment (which does not include small children) has many things of which it feels justly proud. Notwithstanding the apportionment to colored districts does not exceed forty to fifty dollars, our young men and women have managed, by hard labor and rigid economy, to save sufficient money each year to take a few months in school.

The deportment of the students has been excellent, and their activity in behalf of the school unprecedented. The institution has been greatly favored with lectures by distinguished persons, who have, from time to time, dropped in to visit us. These lectures have been of a high order and well received by the students and friends of the school. The members of the faculty have given weekly lectures on "Theory and Practice," "North Carolina History," "School Management," etc.

The Faculty themselves have endeavored to keep abreast of the times, and to this end have held frequent meetings to discuss methods of instruction, discipline, etc. At these meetings the Post Graduate and Senior classes were present.

The present needs of the school are many, but the most urgent ones are, a good building, improved apparatus and two additional teachers. With these a broader and more liberal policy can be inaugurated which will be very helpful to those who are to lead in educational affairs among the colored people of the section. The colored teacher, in order to be highly successful, must be accomplished, in some degree at least, in many useful things. In most committees the teacher is a cyclopedia of general information.

The prospects for the coming session are bright. We are under many obligations to yourself and the State Board of Education for the timely aid given the institution. But for this assistance the school would have suffered permanent harm.

Very respectfully, J. O. CROSBY, *Principal.*

REPORT OF TREASURER.

J. RUMPLE, *Treasurer*,

In account with Salisbury State Normal School.

DR.

1896.			
May 18.	To balance on hand..................	$ 66 49	
June 3.	To amound received from J. C. Scarborough..........................	60 00	
Sept. 9.	To amount received from J. C. Scarborough..........................	783 33	
1897.			
Jan. 5.	To amount received from J. C. Scarborough..........................	783 33	
April 15.	To amount received from C. H. Mebane	200 00	
May 26.	To amount received from C. H. Mebane, Peabody Fund	100 00	
			$ 1,993 15

CR.

By disbursements as per account filed with Superintendent of Public Instruction :

1897.			
May 26.	Total expenditures..................	$ 1,943 61	
	To balance..........................	49 54	
			$ 1,993 15

REPORT OF TREASURER.

J. RUMPLE, *Treasurer*,

In account with Salisbury Colored Normal School.

DR.

1897.			
Jan. 16.	To balance last report................	$ 49 54	
Sept. 22.	To warrant Supt. Mebane............	500 00	
Nov. 26	To warrant Supt. Mebane............	500 00	
1898.			
Jan. 31.	To warrant Supt. Mebane............	657 15	
Mar. 28.	To warrant Supt. Mebane............	200 00	
			$ 1,906 69

CR.

By disbursements as per account filed with Superintendent of Public Instruction :

1898.			
	May 30,............................	$ 1,861 43	
May 30.	To balance..........................	45 26	
			$ 1,906 69

BIENNIAL REPORT OF THE STATE NORMAL SCHOOL AT FAYETTEVILLE.

FAYETTEVILLE, N. C., August 17, 1898.

To the State Superintendent Public Instruction, Hon. C. H. Mebane, Raleigh, N. C.

As Assistant Principal of the above named school for 1896-'97, I beg leave to submit the following report for that interim:

The school opened September 6, 1896, with its usual encouraging prospects. The activity of Principal and teachers during the vacation in putting the claims and advantages of this school before the public did much to enhance the number of pupils at the opening.

The school has done much for the education of the sons and daughters of the people of this section, and, indeed, pupils from all parts of the State have taken advantage of the educational facilities here afforded.

At no period in the history of the school were the conditions and environments more conducive to a continuation of its usefulness than now.

Being the first Normal School founded in this State for the training of colored people, she enjoys a prestige, which constantly acts as a stimuli to both pupils and teachers, to keep her in the front rank among her Junior Normals.

Among those who have been trained here, are men in all the professions and useful occupations of life. Quite a large per cent. of her graduates have engaged in and distinguished themselves as teachers. Many who did not finish the course are rendering acceptable service as instructors in the county schools.

She enjoys the distinction of having been principalled by some of the ablest negro educators in the State, viz.: Harris, Smith, Chestnut, Williams, *et al.* These worthy Principals have usually been supported by able assistants—Hood, Council, Simpson, *et al.*

The school is divided into two departments—Normal and Preparatory Normal. Number of pupils in the Preparatory Normal, 60; number in the Normal Department, 83.

The Preparatory Normal is designed to fit pupils for the higher branches, by giving them a thorough rudimentary training.

During the last two weeks of the term a very successful Institute was conducted by the Principal and faculty. This was quite a stimulus to the teachers of the county. The Institute was addressed by some of the ablest educators of the State. Prof. M. C. S. Noble, Superintendent of the City Schools of Wilmington, took charge for a whole day.

Number of males enrolled in the Institute, 40; number of females enrolled, 77. Total enrollment in the Normal for the term, 153. Total enrollment in the Institute, 270. Enrollment of different students and teachers in both Normal and Institute, 205. Per cent. of daily attendance in Normal, 94; in the Institute, 985.

Duration of term, in weeks, 34.

Duration of Institute, two weeks.

Number of counties represented, 11.

Number graduated during the term, 10.

This school enjoys the sympathy and support of both races. The moral and intellectual influence it sheds upon the community evince the good results that emanate from it.

The school opened on the first Monday in September with the largest opening number in its annals. This number was augmented the entire term by fresh recruits, making the enrollment during the year the most numerically flattering of any previous year.

The school has a large area of operation, being located in a section of the State densely peopled by that race for whom it was founded. It is now in a measurably healthy condition.

This school, in common with other State Institutions, has had its usefulness impaired, at stated times in its history, by political bearings. This, in my opinion, has done more toward crippling the efforts of these Normal Schools than any other evil. The local political boss feels that they are public patronage; that he must control, and hence endeavors to secure his nominees for members of Local Boards, and thereby largely controls the appointment of teachers. You may readily see how a gateway is opened for the influx of incompetents.

The grand old man and statesman, in whose mind the idea of the founding of these schools originated, saw with prophetic eye and vision clear their imperative demand. Any failure on their part to meet the requirements of this demand is attributable, not to a want of clearness in the horizon of conception, but in our application of his idea to actual conditions. This, however, need not discourage us. "It is easier to plan than to execute."

We readily concede that our school, located here, has by no means reached the zenith of its usefulness, nor has it come up to the very sanguine expectations of some, but all things being considered, it is hard to see how more could have been accomplished under the circumstances.

Let the friends of education unite in helping us to secure local officers of these schools, who will not be actuated by partisan views or selfish motives in the selection of teachers. Let the State Board lend its influence in extirpation of the evil effects brought to bear upon our Normals by the little politicians who try to control them for selfish ends.

We are highly pleased with the very excellent service being rendered the State, in the cause of popular education, by our present Superintendent of Public Instruction, Hon. C. H. Mebane.

TEACHERS.

The school has four teachers, two males and two females. These are now men and women of unquestioned integrity and competency.

LOCAL BOARD OF MANAGERS.

These are, as a rule, men who are thoroughly imbued with the idea of giving to the youth of the State such liberal education as shall fit them for usefulness and good citizenship.

The school disseminates a good influence upon the community, very often evoking high praise from individuals of both races. "Do right" is our motto.

The school is divided into two departments—Normal and Preparatory Normal. The latter is designed to prepare the student for the Normal course, and give him a thorough rudimentary training.

SOCIETIES.

A Literary Society, which meets every Friday night, and a Band of Hope-Templars, are among the agencies designed for the literary and moral culture of the students.

Total enrollment during the term, 163. Number of males enrolled, 65; number females enrolled, 98. Per cent. of daily attendance, 96. Duration of session, in weeks, 36. Number having completed course this year, 8. Number looking forward to teaching, 75. Number in school having already taught, 25. Counties represented, 11. States, 2.

Very respectfully submitted,

PROF. L. E. FAIRLY, A. M., *Principal.*

REPORT OF TREASURER FOR 1897 AND 1898.

F. P. WILLISTON, *Treasurer,*

In account with Fayetteville Colored Normal School.

DR.

1897.			
Sept. 1.	By balance last report.	$ 37 58	
Sept. 1.	By State vouchers.....................	833 33	
Jan. 22.	By State vouchers..........	833 33	
Mar. 19.	By Peabody fund:.........	200 00	
Apr. 22.	By Peabody fund	190 00	
			$ 2,094 24

CR.

1897.			
May 14.	Total expenditures as per account filed with Supt. Public Instruction.......	$ 1,923 38	
	Balance on hand.....................	170 86	
			$ 2,094 24

DR.

1897.			
May 19.	By balance last report................	$ 170 86	
	By Peabody fund.....................	300 00	
1898.			
July 29.	By amount all other sources..........	1,857 14	
			$ 2,328 00

CR.

1898.			
May 29.	By disbursments as per account filed with Supt. Public Instruction.......	$ 2,046 50	
	Balance on hand.....................	281 50	
			$ 2,328 00

REPORTS OF THE STATE NORMAL SCHOOL AT ELIZABETH CITY.

ELIZABETH CITY, N. C., June 8, 1897.

Hon. C. H. Mebane, Supt. Public Instruction, Raleigh, N. C.

DEAR SIR:—I have the honor to submit for your consideration my sixth annnal report of the work which has been done in the State Colored Normal School, located at Elizabeth City, N. C., for the year 1896-'97.

The session was begun Monday, September 14th, 1896, and closed Friday, May 28th, 1897, making a session of nine months. During this time 162 pupils were enrolled, representing twenty (20) counties as follows: Pasquotank, Camden, Perquimans, Currituck, Chowan, Dare, Northampton, Washington, Pamlico, Martin, Wayne, Tyrrell, Gates, Jones, Onslow, Bertie, Pitt, Hyde, Norfolk, Va., and Southampton, Va.

Fifty-three (53) of the above number are public school teachers. Twenty (20) have first-grade certificates; twenty-six (26) have second-grade certificates, and seven (7) have third-grade certificates, while there are others as well qualified, who have never applied for a teachers' certificate.

The graduating class consisted of eleven (11) young men and women, who will contiuue to teach in the public schools of the State. A portion of the class will apply for first-grade life certificates.

Much of the work done consisted of real class-work in the common school branches, because the students were deficient in these branches. A student cannot be taught very well the methods of teaching arithmetic until he learns how to work arithmetic. Nevertheless, we accomplished some excellent professional work with the graduating class and with the members of the middle class. We have used White's Elements of Pedagogy for two years as a text-book in the Senior class. Page's Theory and Practice has been used in the Middle class. Simple lectures on the best and most effective methods of teaching have been made by the Principal. The "Practice work" has been done with the Preparatory class, and with the members of the Senior class teaching each other, while acting in turn, as student and teacher, respectively. We have pursued this course for the lack of funds, and because a large amount of academic work had to be done. The work for training teachers to teach in the public schools of the State has been greatly improved for the next year.

A one-year professional course has been added to the course of study, including a Training School for practice, both of which are hereto subjoined:

ONE-YEAR PROFESSIONAL COURSE.

The Professional Teachers' Course of study for one year comprises the following subjects:

1. Psychology, Pedagogy (Compayre's), School Management, Child Study (in connection with Psychology), History of Pedagogy and Solid Geometry.

2. Methods of teaching the Elementary English branches of study and Cæsar..

3. Observation and practice in the Training School, observation in the city public school, and the school law of North Carolina.

4. Students completing the Teachers' Course of study will be required to write a thesis evidencing some independent reasearch with reference to authorities substantiating the views set forth.

NOTE.—There will be occasional lectures.

TRAINING SCHOOL.

The training school will contain pupils in the Primary and Intermediate grades. The Primary grade is divided into first, second and third-reader grade. The Intermediate is the fourth-reader grade. Students in the Intermediate grade pursue some of the Preparatory class studies by which they are prepared to enter the Normal Department.

Each grade is limited as to number of pupils; first, for lack of accommodation; second, in order that the student teacher may gain skill in management before he assumes the responsibility of larger classes.

The work in the practice school is designed to prepare teachers for the public schools of the State. The teaching is to be done by students of the Senior and Professional classes, under the supervision of the Principal of the Normal School until money is available to employ a teacher for the Training School.

Our plans in this department are not perfect. As soon as we can have sufficient funds the course of study will be varied and improved, to the extent that we may educate and train teachers who will do most effective and efficient work in the public schools.

The chief object of the Training School is to afford the students of the Senior and Professional classes an opportunity to manifest their natural aptitude to teach and to apply the methods and principles learned in their other professional work.

We humbly but sincerely ask that you use your best influence with Dr. J. L. M. Curry for sufficient aid of the Peabody funds to run the school successfully.

Three assistant teachers are needed regularly in the Normal Department, and one teacher in the Training School.

Complete harmony prevailed in the school during the session. Our students are faithful, earnest and courteous in deportment. They are taught how to be virtuous, moral and upright ladies and gentlemen. We have but one rule—"Do right."

The daily average attendance was by far the largest in the history of the school.

The citizens manifested considerable interest in boarding the students and in the general welfare of the school.

The Commencement Exercises were more largely attended than ever before. It has been estimated that about eight or nine hundred people were present on Tuesday and Wednesday evenings of Commencement week. The annual address was delivered by Mr. J. E. Felton, of Winfall, N. C., a graduate of the class of '96. The Diplomas were presented in a most happy and graceful manner by Rev. C. S. Blackwell, of Elizabeth City.

I desire to thank the Local Board of Managers, under whose very wise and efficient management the school has steadily improved for six consecutive years in usefulness and power, for the great interest and untiring energy which they have manifested in the welfare of the school.

Faithfully submitted,

P. W. MOORE, *Principal.*

ELIZABETH CITY, N. C., June 27, 1898.

Hon. C. H. Mebane, Superintendent Public Instruction, Raleigh, N. C.

DEAR SIR:—Obeying legal requirements, I have the pleasure to offer herewith to you, and through you to the public, a brief report of the work which has been accomplished by the State Colored Normal School, located at this place, for the year ending May 27, 1898.

This institution having completed six years of its useful existence, resumed the task of the seventh session September 13, 1897, with an enrollment of sixty-three (63) pupils, who represented nine (9) separate counties and twenty (20) post-offices.

The Normal Department was in session thirty-six weeks, being a term of nine (9) months. For lack of funds the Model School Department was not formally opened until November 17. The Model School was in session six months and thirteen days.

The following account of the year's work, as compared with the results of former sessions, proves the session just closed to be the most successful one in the history of the school. The Normal Department maintains five separate classes, represented as follows:

Preparatory class	58
Junior class	64
Middle class	23
Senior class	34
Professional class	5

Total number of students in the Normal Department is one hundred and eighty-four (184), representing fifty-seven (57) post-offices, and twenty-one (21) counties. During the session of 1896–'97, we enrolled one hundred and sixty-two (162) pupils, representatives of twenty (20) counties and about forty (40) post-offices.

In the Normal Department we aim, first, to assist the student in laying a substantial foundation in all the common school branches of learning which is necessary to good teaching. In fact, it is essential that academic instruction be given before a knowledge of the history of pedagogy and the methods of teaching can be acquired and comprehended, but our students readily acquire this knowledge afterwards by theory, observation and practice in the Department of Pedagogy and the Model School.

The Model School is organized with four grades—first, second, third and fourth—which embrace the principles that are required to be taught in the rural schools. Not having teaching force, this school did not admit but thirty-five (35) pupils, which makes the total number, including both departments, two hundred and nineteen (219) pupils.

Thirty-nine normal pupils of the senior and professional classes devoted, on an average, one recitation period daily to observation and practice under efficient supervision in the Model School. The instructo of this school and the Principal, who is in charge of the Department of Pedagogy, demonstrated, as observation work, the most approved methods of teaching the common school branches from time to time. The class also had practice in organizing, classifying of pupils, and in school government, including lectures on the different phases of these topics.

All of this work throughout is planned and executed with reference to preparing teachers for the public schools of the State.

Twenty-three (23) of the students who attended the Normal during the session have first grade certificates. Forty (40) taught in the public schools a few months during the session.

We thank the following counties for patronage: Pasquotank, Hyde, Perquimans, Martin, Pitt, Washington, Dare, Bertie, Wayne, Gates, Jones, Onslow, Camden, Tyrrell, Craven, Northampton, Currituck, Chowan, Beaufort, Norfolk, (Va.,) and New Haven, (Conn.)

It is evident that the Elizabeth City State Normal School is doing as thorough and practical work as can reasonably be hoped under its present equipment. However, it shall be our constant aim to improve along every line year by year.

The general deportment of the students for the year, in school and before the public, was commendable, with few exceptions. We teach our students chiefly by example to be courteous, truthful, honest, orderly and to do and act right because it is right. They are also taught the necessity of honest labor. They are told that good education helps one to be more useful in the performance of any task, whether it be cutting wood or cooking a meal. But until better facilities are afforded us there can be but little accomplished along industrial lines.

A kind and gracious providence greatly favored us during the session. There was no serious sickness among us, and not one student was lost by death.

STUDENT TEACHERS.

Besides doing practice-teaching in the Model School, the following students, who have first-grade certificates, taught one recitation period per day for several weeks in the preparatory class, under the supervision of the Principal:

Miss H. S. Rayner (Bertie), Geography.

Miss Georgianna Harrell (Northampton), Grammar.

Miss M. E. Mebane (Chowan). Grammar.

Miss M. E. Brockett (Pasquotank), Spelling.

Miss M. E. Lewter (Bertie), Spelling.

Mr. I. Williams (Camden), Negro History.

Mr. W. W. Parker (Onslow), Arithmetic.

Mr. G. R. Whitfield (Pitt), Negro History.

Mr. J. F. Pierce (Bertie), Reading.

The teachers who were associated with me were faithful in the performance of the work assigned to them, and their influence upon the students was helpful.

The following gentlemen visited and addressed the Normal School:

The Superintendent of Public Instruction, Hon. C. H. Mebane, delivered an interesting, highly instructive and practical address to the school in a happy and pleasant style. He impressed the school as a Christian gentleman of broad culture. Mr. C. E. Kramer, Treasurer of the Normal, accompanied the Superintendent and made a practical address which was highly appreciated and enjoyed by the Faculty and students. Dr. Palemon John delighted the school by his presence and visit to each room by which he acquainted himself with the character of the work. His address was a literary treat. It greatly encouraged us. Hon. John C. Dancy, Collector of Customs, Wilmington, N. C., addressed the school on the subject, "Be True to Yourself;" Misses Waugh and Williams, of James City, "Morals and the Heart;" that scholar and Christian gentleman, Prof. T. H. Briggs, of the Faculty of the Atlantic and Collegiate Institute, subject, "How to Study a Poem;" Mrs. C. E. Cartwright, "Africa;" Rev. C. C. Somerville, "Which Way Out;" Rev. S. P. Smith, "Diligence and Its Reward;" Rev. Luke Pierce, "A Great Resolution." Among others whose addresses were beneficial are: Dr. John A. Savage, Principal of Franklinton Normal School; Rev. Davis, of Raleigh; Dr. Mabrey; Rev. Byrd, of Newbern; Rev. Russell, of Goldsboro; Rev. Bonard, of Wilmington; and Prof. Vick, of Wilson.

The closing exercises were on a higher order than formerly. They were well attended and much enjoyed by those who witnessed them. Prof. E. A. Johnson, of Raleigh, delivered the annual address, subject: "Self-Reliance." The annual sermon was preached by Rev. P. R. Anderson, of this city, and the address before the Normal School Lyceum was made by Mr. A. B. Rogers, of Columbia, N. C., member of the class of '97. There were no graduates. The course of study has been raised. Students are required to know more subject matter and be better qualified to teach. We are succeeding in convincing our students that short cuts in learning are detrimental to intellectual and moral developments, and that teaching should be a profession in the sense in which law and medicine are professions.

I wish herein to make acknowledgements of my gratitude to you for your manifest interest in the Normal School at this place, and in the educational uplift of the whole people of North Carolina.

It should be noted that the enrollment for the session is the largest in the existence of the school, and the results in qualifying teachers the best. This school is located within accessible reach of a large number of young men and women, who are gradually being induced to enter this Normal for training.

I cannot conclude this report without placing myself upon record in gratefulness to the Local Board of Managers, under whose helpful supervision and wise counsel I have worked during the past session for the respect and confidence shown to me by them.

Sincerely submitted,

P. W. MOORE, *Principal.*

REPORT OF TREASURER, 1896 TO 1898.

F. F. CAHOON, *Treasurer,*

In account with Elizabeth City Colored Normal School.

DR.

1896.			
Aug. 1.	To balance on hand	$ 289 14	
1897.			
	To Peabody Fund	330 00	
	To State appropriations	1,066 66	
June 1.	To Peabody Fund (Paid C. E. K.)	115 00	
			$ 1,800 80

CR.

1896-'97.			
	By disbursements as per account filed with Supt. Public Instruction	$ 1,789 75	
1896.			
July 6.	By balance on hand	11 05	
			$ 1,800 80

C. E. KRAMER, *Treasurer,*

In account with Elizabeth City Normal School.

DR.

1897.			
May 25.	To check Peabody Fund (C. H. Mebane)	$ 210 00	
Aug. 3.	To check Peabody Fund (C. H. Mebane)	100 00	
Oct. 25.	To State appropriation	500 00	
Dec. 16.	To check Peabody Fund (C. H. Mebane)	300 00	
Feb. 1.	To State appropriation	1,357 14	
Aug. 1.	Amount due from F. F. Cahoon	11 05	
			$ 2,478 19

CR.

1897-'98.			
	By disbursements as per account filed with Supt. Public Instruction	$ 1,899 79	
1898.			
Aug. 1.	Balance on hand	578 40	
			$ 2,478 19

A SHORT SKETCH OF THE PLYMOUTH STATE COLORED NORMAL SCHOOL.

Plymouth Normal School was established by an Act of the General Assembly of North Carolina, appropriating a small sum for that purpose. This institution, located at Plymouth, N. C., opened its first session on August 8th, 1881, under the supervison of Prof. Alexander Hicks, Jr. He died in the latter part of the second session, and was succeeded by Prof. H. Cheatham, (now Recorder of Deeds, Washington, D. C.) who acceptably filled the position of Principal for the next two sessions. He resigned to become Register of Deeds of Vance county, N. C. He was succeeded as Principal by Prof. J. W. Pope. The institution was rapidly losing its prestige, but in the autumn of 1886, the late Dr. H. C. Crosby was elected Principal. He at once completely reorganized the school, adopting new methods and awakening a great educational enthusiasm throughout this section. The school, under his superior management, took on new life, and for eleven years increased in popularity and usefulness, until it is now regarded as the beacon light of education in Eastern North Carolina. Under his control, not only was its enrollment increased from eighty-four (84) in 1886–'87 to one hundred and eighty-four (184), representing nineteen counties, but there was erected at a cost of several hundred dollars a beautiful two-story frame building, 25 feet by 60 feet, capable of accommodating two hundred and fifty (250) scholars. Nowhere else in North Carolina has there been constructed a building especially for a State Colored Normal School. This fact should be emphasized and credit given to whom credit is due, for this fact shows the interest the citizens of both races take in the Plymouth Normal. The General Assembly of 1887 appropriated an additional one thousand dollars, annnually, for its support. The lamented Dr. H. C. Crosby, having resigned, owing to ill health, in April 1897, the present Principal, Prof. John W. McDonald, was elected to fill the vacancy. That there is no better Colored Normal School in North Carolina than that located at Plymouth, N. C., is evidenced by its work. There have been two thousand and ninety-five (2,095) students matriculated during its seventeen sessions. Its graduates are among the best colored teachers in the State. It has in the past sixteen years sent out over *one hundred and fifty* young men and women to instruct the youth and bless the homes of the colored citizens of the State. Besides teachers it has sent out a score of preachers, three doctors, two lawyers, several government clerks, two postmasters, several merchants and seamstresses, and two mechanics, all of whom are a credit to the school. Prominent among the teachers are Profs. J. H. M. Butler, A. M., Greensboro A. and M. College; George T. Hill, Scotland Neck Training School; R. H. Riddick, Edenton Industrial High School; R. R. Cartright, J. C. Cordon and J. W. McDonald, (all teachers in the Plymouth State Normal); L. F. Sharp, Albemarle Training School; W. A. Taylor, Hertfort Academy, and others. Among ministers, Revs. M. W. D. Norman, A. M., ex-Dean of the Theological Department of Shaw University, Raleigh, N. C.; W. W. Ryan, Connecticut; A. S. Dunston, Z. W. White, North Carolina, and J. T. Askew, Pennsylvania. Among doctors, Drs. A. L. Winslow, Danville, Va., and J. S. Sessoms, Rendville, Ohio. Among lawyers, J. E. White, Esq., Chicago, and G. H. Walker, Esq, Portsmouth, Va.

This institution is indeed a fountain of life and light in its section—a truth accentuated by the annual increase of its attendance. Under the present management the increase in enrollment, regular actual attendance, interest manifested in study, are phenominal. Among the improvements this session the most important is the addition of a *sewing department* for girls. The students Sewing Club

LIBRARY—UNIVERSITY OF NORTH CAROLINA.

raised the major part of the money to purchase the sewing-machines. The opening of this department necessitated the use of another building, and an annex of some forty feet was generously given by our colored citizens. In the few months since this department has been added, some fifty dresses and other garments have been made, besides quilting, knitting, crocheting, etc. The work in vocal music, writing and drawing departments is excellent.

Plymouth Normal was established for the purpose of *training colored teachers in the common school branches;* and along this line we have labored faithfully, and endeavored to do our work as thoroughly as possible, but we have not failed to give special attention to *moral training* as well, for we believe now, as we always have, that the training of the heart is of more importance than that of the head. We believe in virture, truthfulness, honesty, industry and economy, for without these no home can be happy and no people prosperous. With this end in view, a number of lectures by the teachers and prominent white and colored clergymen have been delivered to the students this session. The Plymouth Normal is doing her share as best she can in purifying the moral atmosphere of the home. We are striving to brighten the prospects of the next genaration by properly training the teachers of the public schools, and emphasizing the importance of both *manual and moral training*.

REPORTS OF STATE NORMAL SCHOOL AT PLYMOUTH.

PLYMOUTH, N. C., June, 1897.

To the State Superintendent Public Instruction, Raleigh, N. C.

DEAR SIR.—I take pleasure in submitting, for your consideration, the following report:

The sixteenth session of the Plymouth State Normal opened September 7, 1896, and continued forty weeks, closing June 11, 1897.

We enrolled fifty-eight males and one hundred and fifteen females, making a total of one hundred and seventy-three, representing seventeen counties.

For January, February, March and April, the average attendance was over a hundred; for the entire session, it was about ninety.

The health of the students was good, their deportment commendable, and their advancement in study was all that might be expected.

Eight young men and one young woman finished the course of study and received diplomas.

Peace and harmony prevailed among the pupils from the opening to the close. There was no friction of any kind in the school. On the other hand, everything moved on like clock work. All things considered, I believe the last is the best session this school ever had.

For further information, we refer you to the catalogue of 1896–'97, all of which we most respectfully submit for you consideration.

H. C. CROSBY.

PLYMOUTH, N. C., June 11, 1898.

Hon. C. H. Mebane, State Superintendent Public Instruction, Raleigh, N. C.

DEAR SIR:—I have the pleasure to submit the following report of the Plymouth State Colored Normal School to your consideration:

The seventeenth session, just ended, opened August 30, 1897, continued forty weeks, and closed June 3, 1898. There were enrolled 205 pupils—72 males and 133 females. Thirteen counties were represented, as follows: Beaufort, 1; Bertie, 14; Camden, 3; Chowan, 2; Gates, 5; Halifax, 1; Hertford, 1; Martin, 23; Pitt, 2; Washington, 146; Baltimore, Md., 1; Brooklyn, N. Y., 2; Norfolk, Va., 4.

The average attendance was better than ever before. The course of study was adhered to and the most strenous efforts were put forth to teach more thoroughly than ever the branches prescribed. There were seven members of the Senior class, one of which completed the required course and received a certificate of graduation. He is above the average graduates of this school. Financial environments prevented the regular attendance of the others, hence they failed to complete the course. During the year White's Elements of Pedagogy was added to the course, otherwise the course remains unchanged from previous reports. Special lectures on moral and intellectual subjects were delivered weekly by the Principal and Assistants during the session. Not only have the colored people of the community shown a deeper interest in the school, but the whites have really manifested a magnanimous spirit. Never have they shown so much concern in the moral and educational welfare of the students as this session by their frequent visits and telling lectures to the school. The following white gentlemen delivered lectures to the school: Reverends F. T. Wooten, J. L. Cuninggim, D. W. Davis, Editor W. F. Ausbon and Hon. L. N. C. Spruill, Secretary of the Local Board. The following colored gentlemen, prominent in church and educational work, also delivered lectures: Revs. W. L. Clayton, S. P. Knight, of Edenton, N. C.; John A. Faulk, of Hertford, N. C.; C. C. Summerville; A. B. Easton, District Missionary, Rocky Mount, N. C.; Messrs. W. A. Taylor, of Hertford Academy; B. F. Haley, Edenton, N. C.; R. A. Lloyd, Williamston, N. C.; J. J. Jones, Henry Williams, medical students, and H. G. Wilson, law student of Shaw University, Raleigh, N. C.

These practical lectures have had telling effect, and much good was accomplished. Special attention was given this session to drawing, vocal music and composition work. Prizes were offered to stimulate interest in drawing and essay writing. The results of these "special efforts" were gratifying in every way.

During the session an Industrial Department was added, to the delight of both students and patrons. The moment the establishment of the department was assured the school took on new life. Applications from new students began to pour in. Never was an addition to a school hailed with greater joy. Not only did the enrollment far surpass any in the history of the school, but the actual regular attendance was unprecedented. The leisure hours of the female students, which had been fruitlessly wasted in previous sessions, were now utilized in sewing, and when called to the recitation rooms they were as cheerful and deeply interested in their studies as soldiers ever were when they charged under the strains of music. Even in the spring term the listless student was seldom seen. Early in the session clubs were organized to raise money to assist in purchasing machines. The willingness and eagerness of these young people, both sexes (for the brothers were glad to see the opportunity of their sisters to learn how to sew), would alone satisfy Dr. Curry for his liberal donation. The wisdom of this great man has been more than vindicated in this school. During the few months this dement has been opened some two hundred (200) different pieces have been made by the students. Besides crocheting, quilting, knitting, cutting, fitting, making chair tidies, etc., ninety per cent. of the dresses for the closing exercises were made by them. Several who had some knowledge before have gone home and commenced to take sewing for others. One student went to Brooklyn, N. Y., and obtained a situation in the Soldiers Home at a good salary. Never has the Peabody money been spent wiser in this school nor the results more gratifying. At an art exhibition, which the students gave to show their needle work, map drawing, writing, two white gentlemen, who examined the needle work, and the colored people generally, expressed astonishment at the results. The number of teachers sent out this session was larger, and the high character of their work won the commendation of the supervisors. It is estimated that twelve hundred pupils were under the instruction of the Plymouth Normal's students the past winter and spring. An "era of good feeling" and harmonious work characterized this school year. Every one apparently gave their heartiest support. The mouth of the "croaker" was closed. The unique closing exercises were a fitting climax to the year's work. Besides the regular exercises of public debate, annual oration and class exercises, an annual sermon was preached and memorial exercises in honor of the late Dr. Henry Clay Crosby, ex-Principal, added greatly to the occasion. Many distinguished friends from afar, and many white ladies and gentlemen, attended the exercises and expressed surprise at the work accomplished. Every one says they were the finest literary exercises ever held in this section of the State. A gentleman who had visited four of the State Normals says the work of this school was far above the others. From applications already coming in the prospects for next year are indeed bright. Great credit is due Mrs. E. J. Dance, Prof. R. R. Cartwright, Mrs. E. H. Corprew and Rev. J. C. Cordon, assistant teachers, for the success which has attended this session of the Plymouth Normal. They did all in their power to build the school up.

In conclusion, we tender our profound gratitude to Dr. J. L. M. Curry for his invaluable aid, Hon. C. H. Mebane, State Superintendent, for his instruction, the Local Board for their encouragement, our white friends for their advice, the patrons generally for their loyal support, and Hon. Wheeler Martin for the donation of a gold medal to the school. A Teachers' Institute was held during the last two weeks of the school for which there was no compensation. This has indeed been the best session of the Plymouth State Normal School.

For further particulars, see Catalogue for 1897-'98.

J. W. McDONALD, *Principal.*

REPORT OF TREASURER FOR 1896-'97.

GEORGE W. HORNEY, *Treasurer,*
In account with Plymouth Colored Normal School.

DR.

1896.			
June 6.	To balance on hand last report........	$ 266 26	
Oct. 14.	To State appropriation................	783 33	
1897.			
Jan. 6.	To State appropriation................	783 33	
April 24.	To C. H. Mebane, check Peabody Fund,	290 00	
			$ 2,122 92

CR.

1897.			
May 14.	By disbursements filed with Superintendent Public Instruction..........	$ 1,782 84	
May 24.	To balance paid (F. M. Bunch)........	340 08	
			$ 2,122 92

F. M. BUNCH, *Treasurer,*
In account with Plymouth Colored Normal School.

DR.

1897.			
May 24.	Balance on hand....................	$ 340 08	
Oct. 21.	State warrant........................	500 00	
Dec. 7.	State warrant........................	500 00	
Dec. 17.	Peabody Fund........................	150 00	
1898.			
Feb 2.	State warrant........................	357 15	
Feb. 5.	State warrant........................	500 00	
			$ 2,347 23

CR.

1898.			
Feb. 5.	By disbursements as per account filed with Supt. Public Instruction.......	$ 2,325 69	
Feb. 5.	Balance on hand.....................	21 54	
			$ 2,347 23

REPORTS OF THE STATE NORMAL SCHOOL AT FRANKLINTON.

FRANKLINTON, N. C., June 9, 1897.

Hon. C. H. Mebane, State Superintendent Public Instruction of North Carolina.

HONORED SIR:—I beg leave to submit our annual report, covering the academic year of 1896–'97.

Our term began October 5, 1896, and closed May 14, 1897, making a term of eight months.

There were enrolled 258 pupils from the following counties: Alamance, Cabarrus, Carteret, Craven, Bertie, Edgecombe, Franklin, Granville, Greene, Halifax, Harnett, Iredell, Jones, Nash, Johnston, Lenoir, Mecklenburg, Moore, Northampton, Orange, Robeson, Vance, Richmond, Wake, Warren, Wayne and Wilson.

We employed ten teachers during the year, and in the main they were competent and faithful.

The industrial feature of the school is made very prominent. The young men do all of the carpenter work and shoe-making. The young ladies are under proficient teachers, and are taught housekeeping, washing, cooking, etc., as well as their regular Normal studies.

The needs of my people are peculiar, and, to meet them, an industrial education is imperative.

Our teachers can do their best work when they can teach books and every day economies by precepts and examples.

The girls deserve great praise for the progress they have made in the art of home-making.

Our cottages are models of neatness. We have ample facilities for the accomplishment of great things here.

The discipline is good. No insubordination, no scandal. The sexes are kept apart, and live in separate buildings with their teachers.

The location is happy. We are in the midst of a large negro population, and this town is very healthy. The races live happily together in all their business relations. The entire white population is proud of this school and its work for the negro. All of our entertainments are largely attended by the best people of the city, both white and colored. The school is an honor to the State and the race.

Our plan has been to require all applicants for admission to our senior class to bring a teacher's first-grade certificate, as well as stand the examination here. Persons thus prepared can easily take the advanced studies, and, at the same time, do practice work in our model school. Our graduates will work in ungraded schools, and should be trained for that specific work. It is quite easy for one to accommodate himself to graded school work if such a position should come to him.

Our efforts are in the direction of bettering the country school. Accordingly, a regular district school is organized for the training of the senior class in actual teaching. The best teacher in the school is put at the head of this work.

During the year several gentlemen delivered lectures before the school and public on practical themes.

The commencement exercises were well attended by both races, and the citizens seemed to be pleased.

We graduated a class of ten. Several of our pupils are teaching in different counties in the State, and the reports sent up indicate great improvement on all lines in school work.

Our Local Board of Managers exercised a helpful oversight, and spared no pains to make our school a success.

We own over $10,000 of property, free from all incumbrance. The State has the use of all of it.

Believe me, kind sir, your most obedient servant,

JOHN A. SAVAGE.

FRANKLINTON, N. C., July 1, 1898.

Hon. C. H. Mebane, State Superintendent Public Instruction, Raleigh, N. C.

DEAR AND HONORED SIR :—I respectfully submit the report of the work done in the Colored State Normal School of the above named place for the year 1897-'98.

The term began October 4, 1897, and closed May 13, 1898, making a term of eight months.

There were enrolled during the term 268 pupils from 41 counties.

Ten teachers were employed last scholastic year.

While thr primary object of the school is to prepare teachers for the instruction of the youth, by thoroughly grounding them in the essentials of English, Mathematics, History, Hygiene, Physiology, Geography, Drawing and Music; a high standard of morality is held up and insisted upon, and encouragement is given to industry in all departments.

The location is everything that could be desired, being near the main line of the railroad. We are in the midst of a large negro population, and this is the only school of its kind in this Congressional District. The town is healthy as well as inexpensive to those who come to us from afar. The races live happily together in all of their business relations. The entire white population speak kindly of the work done here, and encourage us on all public occasions. All of our entertainments are largely attended by the best people of the city, both white and colored. The school is an honor to the State and the race.

During the year several lectures on practical subjects were given by prominent educators.

The last two weeks of the term a Normal Institute was held, and attended by teachers from all over the State. The departure was a happy one. In this Institute the most improved and successful methods of teaching were used by able and efficient instructors. The interest raised and fostered by this, our first Normal Institute, has encouraged us to devote two weeks, at the beginning, next term, to the same kind of Institute work. This is done that old teachers may have an opportunity to see and learn improved methods, and carry them with them in their winter's work.

The commencement exercises were well attended by both races, and the citizens seemed to be pleased. We graduated a class of five. The grade of the school is varied, and the requirements more than ever; hence, the few to graduate this year. The class will be larger and better after this.

The teachers have been faithful and are worthy of high commendation.

Several of our people are now teaching in different counties of the State, and the reports sent us up to date indicate great improvement on all lines in school work.

Our receipts from all sources have amounted to $6,000. We report no debt—the salaries have been too small.

Our Local Board of Managers exercised a helpful oversight, and spared no pains to make our school a success. They visited the school several times during the year.

We thank you personally for your interest in our behalf, and for the words of comfort and good cheer you brought us.

Very respectfully,

J. A. SAVAGE, *Principal.*

REPORT OF TREASURER, 1896-'97.

B. W. BALLARD, *Treasurer*,

In account with Franklinton Colored Normal School.

DR.

1896.			
June 30.	To balance on hand..................	$ 54 01	
Sept. 1.	To R. M. Furman (voucher)..........	783 33	
1897.			
Jan. 15.	To R. M. Furman (voucher)..........	783 33	
April 20.	To C. H. Mebane (Peabody Fund)....	290 00	
			$ 1,910 67

CR.

1896.			
June 30.	By disbursements as per account filed with Supt. Public Instruction........		$ 1,910 67

REPORT OF TREASURER, 1897-'98.

T. H. WHITAKER, *Treasurer*,

In account with Franklinton Colored Normal School.

DR.

1897.			
Aug. 25.	To State warrant (C. H. Mebane).....	$ 250 00	
Oct. 29.	To State warrant (C. H. Mebane).....	500 00	
Dec. 15.	To Peabody Fund (C. H Mebane).....	200 00	
1898.			
Jan. 31.	To State warrant (C. H. Mebane).....	1,107 14	
			$ 2,057 14

CR.

1898.			
June 30.	By disbursements as per account filed with Supt. Public Instruction.......	$ 1,759 32	
	Musical instrument...................	280 00	
June 30.	To balance	17 81	
			$ 2,057 13

STATE BOARD OF EXAMINERS.

The present State Board of Examiners is composed of the following persons:

C. H. Mebane, President, ex-officio; W. L. Poteat, M. C. S. Noble and L. L. Hobbs.

This Board prepared the first set of examination questions for life certificate during the spring of 1897. The list of questions for that year and for the year 1898 will be found in the following pages.

There were very few applicants the first year on account of lack of time to put the matter before our people. Only two were granted diplomas the first year, as follows:

R. C. Craven and A. M. Garwood.

The second year (which is the present, 1898) there was a great increase in number of applicants. The following is a list of those receiving diplomas this year:

C. N. Jervis, Mrs. N. W. P. Garden, O. E. Sams, E. P. Mendenhall and J. N. Bradly.

This Board also prepared a course of study for teachers in the Public Schools of North Carolina, published in this Report.

The following is the form of diploma issued by the State Board of Examiners:

State Board of Examiners

NORTH  CAROLINA.

has passed the examination prescribed by this Board, and in testimony thereof this

First Grade Life Certificate

is granted..................is therefore entitled, without further examination, to teach in the Public Schools of any County in the State, in accordance with the provisions of Chapter 108, Section 3, of the Laws of 1897.

...., *Supt. Public Instruction.*

Raleigh, N. C.,.... ......*189*....

State Board of Examiners.

LIFE CERTIFICATES.

The following law was enacted by the Legislature of 1897 in regard to life certificates:

"The State Board of School Examiners shall have power to grant first-grade life certificates, which may be used in any county in the State, and shall furnish to the public, through the several County Supervisors, at least one month before the regular annual county examination of teachers, full information as to the nature and character of the requirements for such first-grade life certificates; it shall annually prepare and furnish to the several County Supervisors a set of examination questions covering subjects required by law to be taught in the public schools of the State, which shall be submitted at the regular annual county examination of teachers in July to all applicants for a first-grade life certificate, under such rules and regulations as the State Board of School Examiners may prescribe. The State Board of School Examiners shall examine and grade the papers of all applicants for a first-grade life certificate, and shall issue said certificate to such applicants as are properly qualified and justly entitled thereto, and all examination papers of applicants to whom first-grade life certificates shall have been granted under this act shall be kept on file in the office of the State Superintendent of Public Instruction: *Provided*, that each applicant for a first-grade life certificate shall pay in advance to the County Supervisor the sum of five dollars, which shall be reported to the County Board of Education and paid into the general school fund of the county: *Provided further*, that every first-grade life certificate, to continue valid and operative, shall be renewed by the State Board of School Examiners every five years, and before such board shall renew said certificate it shall be accompanied with an affidavit of the teacher holding said certificate that he or she has been actually engaged in teaching school since receiving said certificate, or since its last renewal, and no charge shall be made for such renewal."

The following is the examination prepared by the State Board of Examiners for applicants for life certificates during the year 1897:

HISTORY EXAMINATION.

1. What nations settled North America, and where did each settle?

2. Give a brief account of the "French and Indian War."

3. Bound the United States, as recognized by Great Britain, and describe briefly the territorial growth of the country.

4. Tell something of the public acts of Thomas Jefferson.

5. What were the causes of the "War of 1812?"

6. What was the "Omnibus bill?" Tell something of its author.

7. Tell something of the early settlement of North Carolina.

8. Describe briefly any battle fought in North Carolina during the Revolution.

9. Give a short account of any one of the following battles: Bentonville, Seven Pines, Gettysburg, Fort Fisher and The Crater.

10. Name five important inventions made by Americans and give the name of the inventor.

PHYSICS EXAMINATION.

1. Define (*a*) energy, (*b*) matter, (*c*) tenacity.

2. Give the three laws of motion.

3. What is the difference between adhesion and cohesion? Illustrate.

4. What is meant by "specific gravity?" Tell how it is found.

5. Why do we make two openings in a barrel of vinegar when we wish to tap it?

6. Define (*a*) ohm, (*b*) volt.

7. What is the effect of heat upon most metals?

8. State and illustrate the difference between induction and conduction.

9. Define luminous, translucent and transparent bodies.

10. Define centrifugal force and give an illustration of it.

11. A cubic foot of water weighs 1,000 oz. What is the pressure upon the bottom of a tank which is ten feet square and eight feet high, when the tank is three-fourths full of water?

PHYSIOLOGY AND HYGIENE.

1. Define organ and tissue and give examples.

2. Tell how bones are nourished.

3. Explain the advantage of exercise.

4. Describe the structure and state the functions of the skin.

5. Explain how the body maintains a uniform temperature.

6. Define waste and repair.

7. How does food pass from the alimentary canal, where it is digested, to the tissues where it is used?

8. Explain the difference between arterial and venous blood.

9. Mention the chief ganglia of the brain and state their function.

10. Explain "short-sight" and "long-sight."

ALGEBRA EXAMINATION.

1. Explain why $-3x \div 2 = 6$.

2. When is $a^n + b^n$ divisible by $a + b$? $a^n - b^n$ divisible by $a + b$? $a^n - b^n$ divisible by $a - b$?

3. Factor in as many ways as possible $a^{12} - b^{12}$; $a^{10} - b^{10}$; Factor $a^2 - a - 42$; $a^2 + a - 12$; $a^2 - 10a + 24$; $a^2 + 12a + 35$; $x^4 + x^2$, $y^2 + y^4$.

4. $\frac{m^2 + n^2 + 2mn - c^2}{c^2 - m^2 - n^2 + 2mn} \div \frac{m + n + c}{n + c - m}$?

5. Divide 20 into two parts such that the sum of three times one part and five times the other part, may be 84.

6. A can do half as much work as B, B can do half as much as C, and together they can complete a piece of work in 24 days; in what time could each alone complete the work?

7. $x + 2y = 7$, and $x + y = 5$, find value of x and y.

8. $\frac{1}{x} + \frac{1}{y} = a$, $\frac{1}{x} + \frac{1}{z} = b$, $\frac{1}{y} + \frac{1}{z} = c$.

9 The sum of two numbers is twenty-four; their difference is eight; what are they?

10. Expand $(a + b)(a - b)(a^2 - b^2)(a^4 - b^4)$.

SCHOOL LAW.

1st. What are the principal duties of the State Superintendent Public Instruction?

2d. Name some of the duties of the State Board of Education.

3d. Who compose the State Board of Education?

4th. When and for what purpose was the State Board of Examiners established?

5th. How are the County Boards of education elected, and what are their duties?

6th. Who elects the County Supervisor, and what are his duties?

7th. Where does the school fund come from?

8th. Who adopts the text-books to be used in our public schools, and how often?

9th. How would a public school teacher proceed to obtain his salary?

10th. Give some of the duties of the School Committee.

ARITHMETIC EXAMINATION.

1st. If silk is worth \$3-4 a yard, how much can be bought for \$2-3?

If satin is worth \$2-5 a yard, how much can be bought for \$7-8?

In these two examples is the arithmetical thought identical? If so, explain. If not, explain. Under which one of the "Four Rules" is each of these examples classed? State the "Rule."

2d. Tell how you would explain to a class why "you divide by 2 to find one-half of a number," as for instance \$24.

3d. A can build a fence in six days, B in ten days, and C in twelve days. If they all work together, how long will it take them to finish the fence?

4th. At what per cent. must I mark goods so that I may fall 25 per cent. below the marked price and still make 25 per cent. on the original cost?

5th. I have two pieces of cloth, each 15 yards long; one is 25 per cent. longer than it should be, and the other 25 per cent. shorter than it should be. What would be the combined length of the two pieces if each was of the proper length?

6th. The commissioners of a certain county wish to build a court-house, to cost \$18,000. The cost of collecting this sum, together with several incidental expenses, will amount to \$1,644. The total cost must be raised by a tax on property valued at \$6,584,000. How much will I have to pay on a piece of property valued at \$987.63?

7th. An estate is divided among three persons, A, B and C, so that A has 5-8 of the whole, and B twice as much as C. It is found that B has 27 acres more than C. How large is the estate?

8th. Copper weighs 550 lb. and tin 462 lb. to the cubic foot. What is the weight of one cubic foot of the mixture containing 6 parts of copper and five parts of tin?

9th. A has \$8 and B \$7, with which they buy a boat for \$15. C gave \$10 for 1/3 interest in the boat, with the understanding that each of them shall own only 1/3 of the boat. How much of the \$10 received from C belongs to A and how much to B?

10th. Find the difference beween the bank discount and the true discount on \$987.56 due in one year, 6 months and 15 days, money being worth 6 per cent.

GEOGRAPHY EXAMINATION.

1st. Define mathematical, physical and political geography.

2d. How many motions has the earth, and what is the effect of each?

3d. Describe the great globe water-parting and name the principal rivers on either side of it.

4th. How does the climate of the eastern coast of North Carolina compare with that of western Europe?

5th. Name six of the largest cities in the world, and tell some facts of importance about each.

6th. Name and locate six places (cities, counties, or towns) in North Carolina named after foreign places, and locate these also.

7th. Name and locate five countries in Europe, tell some fact of importance about each, give their form of government, name and locate the capital of each.

8th. Describe the surface and drainage of Asia.

9th. Draw a map of North Carolina, locate and name the principal rivers, mountain ranges, capes and sounds. Locate Raleigh, Wilmington, Asheville, Charlotte, Winston, Greensboro, Goldsboro, Newbern, Durham, and tell one fact of either commercial or historical importance about each.

10th. Write a very short sketch (not more than 200 words) about your county.

QUESTIONS ON CIVIL GOVERNMENT.

1. (*a*) How many members in Congress, counting both branches? (*b*) How are Senators elected? (*c*) If a vacancy should occur, what would be done? (*d*) If there should be no election as provided by law what would be the result?

2. (*a*) How many Justices on the United States Supreme Court Bench? How are they chosen and what is the term of office? (*b*) Could Congress abolish the United States Supreme Court? (*c*) Could Congress increase the number of Justices? (*d*) What is a circuit justice?

3. (*a*) How is the President elected? (*b*) Give full account? (*c*) Is the vote of the Territories counted in election of the President? (*d*) The twenty-three smallest States have 57 votes in the House of Representatives, the ten largest States have 229 votes; if the House should have to elect a President in 1900 and these twenty-three States with 57 Representatives should vote solidly for a Republican, these ten States, with 229 votes, for a Democrat, and the remaining States should give their votes all for a Populist, who would be elected? (*e*) Suppose no President should be elected before the 4th of March, 1901, what would be done?

4. (*a*) How many members in each branch of the Legislature of this State? (*b*) How are they elected? (*c*) Can the Governor veto a bill passed by the Legislature? (*d*) What is the term of office of the members of the Legislature?

5. (*a*) How many Justices on North Carolina Supreme Court Bench? (*b*) Can the number be increased or diminished by the Legislature? (*c*) How are the Superior Court Judges chosen? (*d*) How are Solicitors chosen? (*e*) What is the salary of Judges? Are the Solicitors all paid the same?

ENGLISH LITERATURE.

1. The English: Their original home, their *migration* to the British Islands, their *religion*, their *language*, their relations to the *original* Britons.

2. The Normans: Their origin, their conquest of England, their influence on the English language and literature.

3. Elizabethan England: Give the various influences that were shaping the *rational life* and *literature* at this time.

4. Modern period: Give the various causes, *political*, *social*, *religious* and *literary* which brought about the *revival in literature* in the 18th century.

5. Brief biographical sketch of any one of the following: Shakespeare, Milton, Addison, Burns, Wordsworth, Scott, Tennyson.

QUESTIONS IN ELEMENTARY PSYCHOLOGY.

1. Define Psychology, and mention some phenomena belonging to this science.

2. Into how many classes may all psychical phenomena be divided?

3. Give an example under each of the above classes.

4. Point out the distinction between the terms subjective and objective. Which preceded, the objective or the subjective, Brooklyn bridge?

5. Define attention, and name one or more conditions which operate to secure attention. Comment upon the difference between the force or power of attention of a robust and a sickly child; upon food, ventilation, exercise, sleep, as they may be related to mental growth.

6. Define perception, and show how its cultivation may be promoted. Why is its cultivation in early life important? Mention some studies which are useful in the cultivation of perception. What effect will drawing have? Why?

7. Define memory, and show how the power of memory may be effected by perception, and by cultivation, and suggest some means by which its cultivation at school may be promoted.

8. Point out the difference between the will element and the emotional and cognitive elements in any psychical state.

9. Suggest one or more ways by which the power of right willing may be cultivated.

ENGLISH COMPOSITION.

1. Choice of words: Explain what is meant (1) by standard usage; (2) by good taste. Give two rules under each head, and illustrate by examples from your own experience.

2. Phraseology: Give three rules for placing of modifiers and illustrate by examples.

3. The sentence: (1) Explain what is meant by the *unity* of the *sentence.* (2) Give three rules to be observed in the *structure or organism* of the sentence. Illustrate, as far as you can, by examples under each head.

4. The paragraph: *Define the paragraph*, showing how it is related to the sentence. How is the beginning of a new paragraph indicated? Illustrate in the page you are now writing. Give *two general principles* to be observed in the use of the *paragraph as a whole.*

EXAMINATION ON BOTANY.

1. Describe the structure of a seed.

2. Describe root-hairs and state their function.

3. What changes take place during the germination of a seed?

4. What constitutes a fruit?

5. What are the parts and functions of a typical leaf?

6. Give some of the properties of protoplasm?

7. What food does the plant get from the soil and what from the air?

8. Name the parts of a typical flower and state the function of each part.

9. Mention some special contrivances for the dispersal of seeds.

10. Describe two ways in which stems increase in diameter.

ENGLISH GRAMMAR.

Thought is the property of him who can entertain it, and of him who can accurately place it.—*Emerson.*

Oh, when I am safe in my sylvan home,
I mock at the pride of Greece and Rome;
And when I am stretched beneath the pines,
Where the evening star so holy shines,
I laugh at the lore and pride of man,
At the sophist schools and the learned clan;
For what are they all in their high conceit,
When man in the bush with God they meet?—*Emerson.*

The first five questions refer to the paragraphs above:

1. Name the various kinds of clauses.

2. Classify the verbs as (*a*) transitive or intransitive, (*b*) regular or irregular, giving your reason for such classification.

3. Give two modifiers each for *mock*, *laugh* and *am stretched.*

4. State to what part of speech each of the following words belong: *Who, holy, all, their, for.*

5. Give all the case forms, both singular and plural, of *my, their, who, man, pride.*

6. (*a*) Give the plurals of *genus, son-in-law, goose-quill, pailful, fish, sky, motto, staff, flag-staff, axis.* (*b*) Give the feminine of *Sultan, hero, administrator, Paul, tiger.*

7. Write a sentence containing a participle used as a noun, and a sentence containing a participle used as an adjective.

8. Write sentences containing (*a*) a noun used as an adjective, (*b*) an adjective used as a noun, (*c*) a verb in the passive voice, (*d*) a verb in the imperative mode, (*e*) a noun used as an adverb.

9. What determines the person, number, gender and case of a relative pronoun?

10. Correct, if necessary, and give your reason for so doing: (*a*) May I lay down for an hour? (*b*) How could you set still and see the barrel bursted by those careless children? (*c*) There comes the butcher, baker and milkman. (*d*) No time, no money and no labor was spared. (*e*) Five dollars was offered for the book.

The following is the examination prepared by the State Board of Examiners for applicants for life certificates during the year 1898:

HISTORY EXAMINATION.

1. Write a short account of De Soto.

2. Define the "Monroe Doctrine" and tell who was Monroe.

3. What was the "Missouri Compromise?"

4. Give a short account of "The Battle of King's Mountain."

5. Give the cause and result of the "Mexican War."

6. Give a short account of the battle between the Virginia (Merrimac) and the Monitor, and tell the influence of that battle upon modern warfare.

7. Tell something of the discovery and settlement of Roanoke Island.

8. Locate and name three early permanent settlements in North Carolina.

9. Give a short account of the Battle of Moore's Creek.

10. Tell one or more facts about Wm. A. Graham, James C. Dobbin, Z. B. Vance, T. H. Benton, Thos. L. Clingman, Jos. E. Johnson, Gen. Wolfe.

ARITHMETIC.

1. Give the "Rule" for the division and addition of Decimal Fractions and give the reason for the "Rule" in each case.

2. A pole 60 feet high broke into two pieces, such that two-fifths of one piece equalled two-sevenths of the other. What was the length of each piece?

3. Three men bought a factory. A gave $20,000, B gave two-fifths more than A, and C gave 25 per cent. less than the total amount paid by both of the others. If a six per cent. dividend is declared on the capital stock, how much money should C receive?

4. A man's property is assessed at $6,741. His State tax is 41½ cents on a hundred dollars, his county tax is 22⅓ cents on a hundred dollars, his road tax is 2 cents on a hundred dollars, and his poll tax is $2. What is his whole tax?

5. At what per cent. above cost must I mark goods so as to fall 10 per cent. below the marked price and still make 12½ per cent.?

6. What are the proceeds of a note for $968, due in 90 days, with interest at 6 per cent., and discounted at a bank at the same rate of interest?

7. A note dated January 4, 1895, for $9,874.69, with interest at 6 per cent., had the following indorsements:

July 1, 1895, received $379.28.
February 18, 1896, received $458.74.

What was due on the note January 1, 1898?

8. Two men start from the same point. One travels 30 miles due north, and the other travels 40 miles due west in the same time, and then they both turn and travel towards each other at their former rates of speed. When they meet, how far will each have traveled from the common starting point?

9. A man bought hats for $1.25 each. He sold half of them at a profit of 33⅓ per cent. The remainder he sold at a loss of $50, and then found that he had lost 8⅓ per cent. on the whole transaction. How many hats did he buy?

10. How many cubic feet in a wall 2 feet thick and 6 feet high, built about a rectangular cellar whose interior dimensions, when the wall is completed, shall be 20 feet long and 16 feet wide?

CIVIL GOVERNMENT.

1. Name and define the three principal departments of our Government.

2. How is the President elected?

3. (a) How are Senators elected? (b) Members of the House?

4. If you had a bill drawn up in due form, explain how this could be made a law.

5. (a) Name some of the chief duties of the Government. (b) Of the Lieutenant Governor. (c) Secretary of State. (d) State Treasurer. (e) Attorney General. (f) Auditor. (g) Superintendent of Public Instruction.

6. (a) How many Justices on North Carolina Supreme Court Bench? (b) How are they chosen? (c) How are Superior Court Judges chosen?

7. How are Solicitors chosen, and what are some of their duties?

8. Explain how a case may pass from a Magistrate's Court to the Supreme Court of the State.

9. Explain how a bill is found by a Grand Jury and a case made out against a man for violating a law of the State.

PHYSIOLOGY AND HYGIENE.

1. Name the organs which lie in the thorax and those which lie in the abdomen.

2. Describe the articulation of the bones of the skull.

3. State the function of the red corpuscles of the blood.

4. Explain the coagulation of the blood.

5. Describe the structure of the heart.

6. Explain the movement of the air into and out of lungs in respiration.

7. State the function of the pancreatic juice.

8. Describe the structure and state the functions of the spinal cord.

9. Distinguish voice from speech.

10. Name the structures through which air vibrations pass to the auditory centre in the brain.

ENGLISH LITERATURE.

1. Show how the introduction of Christianity influenced the early literature of England.

2. King Alfred and his work in behalf of literature.

3. The influence of the Norman Conquest on English literature. Name four *cycles* or groups of poems that grew up under Norman influence.

4. Discuss at some length Shakespeare and his works, referring to such of the plays as you have read.

5. Addison; his life and his work as the originator of a new form of literature.

6. Tennyson, as the representative poet of the nineteenth century.

SCHOOL LAW.

1. Who compose the State Board of Education, and what are the duties of this Board?

2. When and for what purpose was the State Board created?

3. Explain why we have five months school in some counties, and only two and a half in others.

5. (a) How is the County Board of Education elected? (b) The County Supervisor? (c) The School Committee?

6. When and by whom are text books adopted for our public schools?

7. (a) Give the principal duties of County Supervisor. (b) Duties of the committees under the present law.

8. What are the sources of the public school fund?

9. How would a public school teacher proceed to obtain his salary?

PHYSICS EXAMINATION.

1. Define hardness and brittleness.

2. State the law of inertia.

3. With what momentum would a steamboat, weighing 12,000 tons, strike against a sunken rock if the steamboat were running at the rate of twelve miles an hour?

4. Define adhesion and capillarity.

5. Are any two plumb lines parallel? If they are, why? If not, why?

6. What is the pressure of the air on a piece of ground eight feet long and six feet wide?

7. What is the difference between noise and music?

8. What is a spectroscope?

9. Define evaporation.

10. What is the difference between static and dynamic electricity?

ENGLISH GRAMMAR.

1. "The whole cavalcade paused simultaneously when Jerusalem appeared in view; the greater number fell upon their knees, and laid their foreheads in the dust, whilst a profound silence, more impressive than the loudest exclamations, prevailed over all; even the Moslems gazed reverently on what was to them a holy city, and recalled to mind the pathetic appeal of their forefathers. 'Hast thou not a blessing for me, also, O my father?'"

2. "Having reached the house I found its rescued inmate safely lodged, and in serene possesssion of himself, beside a fire."

Questions 1—5 refer to the first selection, and No. 6 to the second.

1. Give all the dependent clauses and state how each one is used.

2. What are the modifiers of *paused*, *silence* and *appeal?*

3. (a) Write in separate columns the transitive and intransitive verbs. (b) Write in separate columns the regular and irregular verbs. (c) Give the principal parts of *all* of the irregular and *one* of the regular verbs.

4. State the voice of any two of the transitive verbs, and change the clauses in which they are used so that the verbs will be in the other voice.

5. (a) Give the rules for the capital letters in this selection. (b) What part of speech is *what*, and how is it used in this selection?

6. (a) Analyze the second selection. (b) Give the case of each noun and pronoun, and your reason for thinking so.

7. Correct the following, if needful, giving reason for each correction. (a) Who can this telegram be from? (b) My head feels badly this morning. (c) She is a girl of twelve years old. (d) It is I that you fear. (e) This has been a real cold day.

8. Write the plural of *fish*, *courtyard*, *German*, *Englishman*, *son-in-law*, *deer*, *spoonful*, *tooth-pick*, *daisy*, *gulf*, *sheaf*.

9. (a) Write the possessive form, singular number, of *James*, *mother-in-law*, *fox*. (b) The possessive, both singular and plural of *chair*, *child*, *chimney*, *who*, *ally*.

10. Write sentences containing, (a) A participle used as a noun. (b) A participle used as an adjective. (c) An infinitive phrase used adverbially. (d) An infinitive phrase used as an adjective. (e) A relative clause. (f) An adverbial clause. (g) A noun clause.

…them ap-
…laid their
…sive than
…gazed
…mind the
…ing for me,

…nate safely

second.

used.

…tive verbs.
…c Give

…other voice.
(b) What

each noun

…correction.
…this morn-
…at you fear.

…w, son-in-

…, mother-

…un. (b) A
…adverbially
…tive clause.

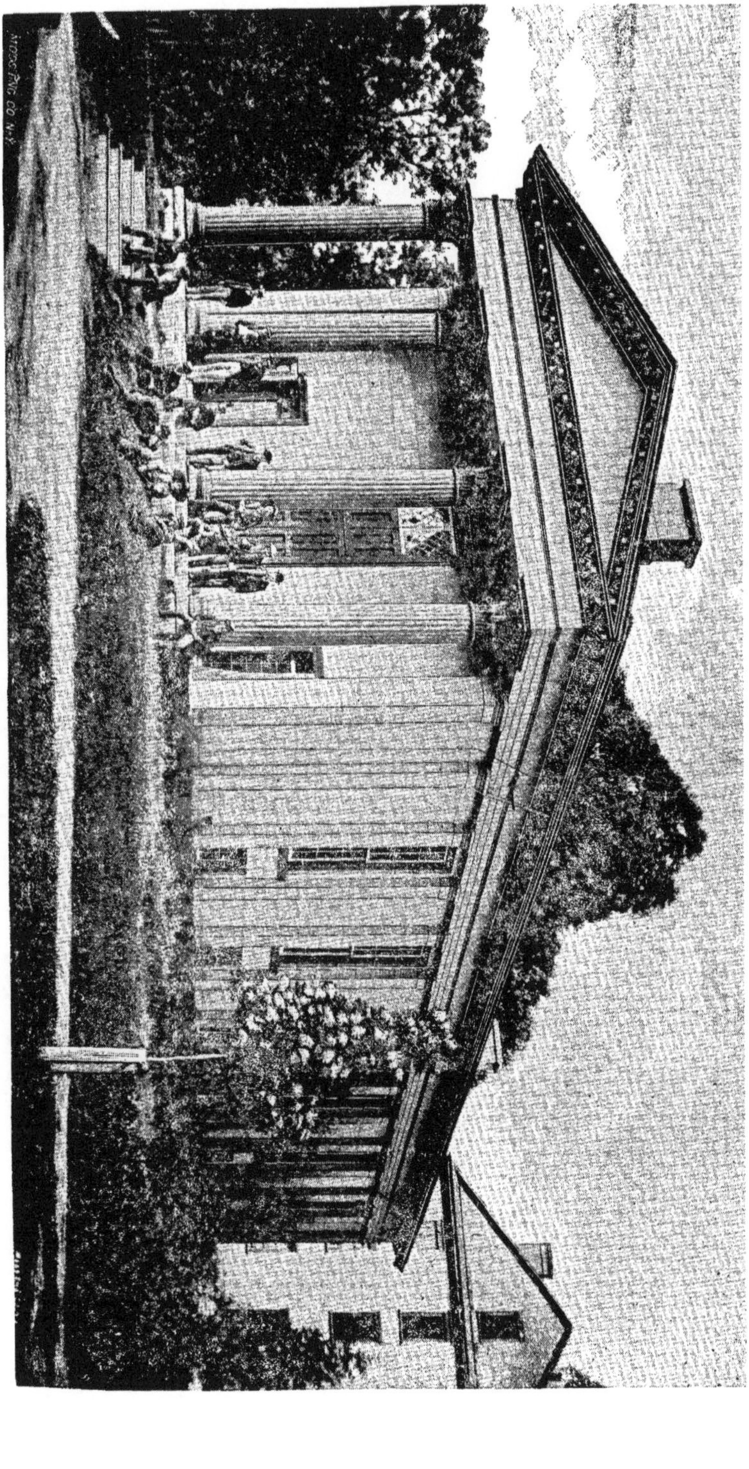

ALGEBRA.

1. If $\begin{array}{r} -2. \\ -9 \\ \hline \end{array}$ is an example in substraction, why do you change the sign of the subtrahend and add it to the minuend?

2. Factor in as many ways as possible a^6-b^6, $a^2+b^2+c^2-2ab-2ac+2bc$, c^4-y^4, $x^4+x^2y^2+y^4$.

3. $\frac{1}{x}+\frac{1}{y}=\frac{5}{6}$, $\frac{1}{2x}+\frac{1}{3y}=\frac{17}{36}$. Find value of x and y.

4. Find greatest common divisor of $2a^3+2a^2-4a$, $3a^4+6a^3-9a^2$, $4a^5-20a^4+16a^3$.

5. $\frac{1}{a}+\frac{1}{b}=1$, $\frac{1}{b}+\frac{1}{c}=\frac{3}{2}$, $\frac{1}{c}+\frac{1}{a}=2$. Find value of a, b and c.

6. If 1 be added to the numerator of a fraction its value is $\frac{1}{3}$, if 1 be added to the denominator its value is $\frac{1}{4}$. Find the fraction.

7. Find the square root of $4x^4-4x^3-3x^2+2x+1$.

8. Separate 29 into two parts, such that the larger divided by the smaller will give 3 as a quotient and 1 as a remainder.

9. Solve $\frac{4a-b}{2a-b}-\frac{a+b}{a-b}=1$.

10. Reduce to simplest form

$$\frac{\frac{a^2+b^2}{a^2-b^2}-\frac{a^2-b^2}{a^2+b^2}}{\frac{a+b}{a-b}-\frac{a-b}{a+b}}$$

BOTANY.

1. Desbribe the vegetative organs of a young seedling.
2. Explain the passage of soil water into the root-hairs.
3. Distinguish trees, shrubs and herbs.
4. Describe the structure of a bud.
5. Mention examples of the daily movement of leaves.
6. What is pollen? State three ways by which it reaches its destination.
7. State the characteristics of the fungi.
8. Tell how ferns reproduce themselves.
9. Explain the wilting of a cut stem.
10. Describe a cell.

PSYCHOLOGY.

1. Give a definition of the term psychology and explain the meaning of the words used in your definition.

2. Give the usual classification of the mental powers, state why such classification is made, what it means, what it does not mean, show their interdependence, and give examples of phenomena belonging to each class.

3. What constitutes the nervous system proper, and what is the relation of the activities of the mind to the nervous system?

4. Mention some facts which illustrate the connection of mind and body.

5. Explain and illustrate what is meant by consciousness.

6. Explain what is meant by presentative power, and distinguish the same from representative power. To which of these does memory belong?

7. Define and illustrate induction and deduction.

8. Give an example showing the operation of the will element in a mental activity.

GEOGRAPHY EXAMINATION.

1. Describe the surface of Asia and tell some of its striking features.

2. Describe the surface and drainage of North America and compare it with that of South America.

3. Give a brief outline of your plan of teaching Geography to a class of beginners.

4. Name five of the largest cities in the Uuited States and give some facts of importance in regard to each.

5. What city or town in North Carolina has bright prospects of growth because of its geographical advantages? Name those advantages.

6. Name five European cities, and give some facts of importance relating to each.

8. Define Latitude, Longitude, Tropic of Cancer, Tropic of Capricorn.

9. Name all the larger rivers flowing into the Atlantic Ocean, its gulfs and bays.

9. What is a river basin? In what river basin do you live? What river basins bound the one in which you live.

10. Draw a map of North Carolina, locate and name the sounds, capes, rivers, lakes and mountains.

COURSE OF STUDY

FOR

TEACHERS

IN THE

Public Schools of North Carolina,

BY

STATE BOARD OF EXAMINERS.

1898.

INTRODUCTION.

It is the purpose of the State Board of Examiners to help especially those teachers who are willing to help themselves.

Under the various subjects will be found helpful suggestions not only upon the work in the school-room, but also suggestions on private study for the teachers.

We feel sure that there are many honest, conscientious teachers, who are not satisfied with their present qualifications for their work, but are not sure just what to do or what course to pursue in order to make progress and to better prepare themselves for the school-room and its duties.

Owing to the multiplicity of books at this time, the average public-school teacher is at a loss to know what is best for him when he needs a book on any special subject.

The State Board of Examiners has suggested, under each subject, books that are among the best. It is not expected that the average teacher will purchase all of the books on any subject. If only one can be purchased, we think the first one named under a given subject should be selected.

We would like especially to impress upon the teachers the importance of making, if necessary, a sacrifice in order to have some good educational books. You should study the history and the science of education. You should become acquainted with some of the master minds in the teaching profession. Our successful lawyers study law. Our successful physicians study medicine. Our successful business men study business, and no less true is it that our successful teachers study teaching.

Let not any teacher throw aside this book, with the idea that it may do some good to teachers who are in the school-room for eight or ten months in the year, but for a teacher of three or four months work it will be of no service. The subjects were especially prepared with this in mind, that the terms are very short, and because the terms are short makes it all the more important for the teacher to be prepared for his work. The shorter the time to teach the children the better prepared should be the teacher in order for results to be what they should.

We call especial attention to the suggestions in the latter part of this pamphlet. These subjects are passed over lightly and sometimes totally disregarded by some teachers. The "Care of the Eyes," by Dr. Lewis, should receive careful study by our teachers.

These things are perhaps of more importance in the public schools than in private schools. To many children the standard or ideal of what is manly and womanly is gotten from the school-room.

We send this pamphlet out trusting it may be helpful to many of our teachers; that it may be the means of infusing life and inspiration in the hearts of some who may have become weary, discouraged and disheartened; that it may enable our teachers to more fully realize the importance of their work; and most important of all, that our teachers may realize that they *must study* and keep up with their profession, or fall out by the way and make room for those who are progressive.

C. H. MEBANE, *Pres. ex-officio;*
W. L. POTEAT,
M. C. S. NOBLE,
L. L. HOBBS, *Secretary,*
State Board of Examiners.

COURSE OF STUDY.

READING.

Every pupil in the public schools of our State studies reading. One half of the pupils in our country public schools never pass beyond the Third Reader, and therefore their teachers should make a special effort to teach primary reading in the very best way. Good reading means the ability to read not only for one's self, but for others. Reading for one's self is silent reading; reading for others is oral reading or "reading out aloud." In both cases the pupil must get thought from a printed page. Oral reading depends upon the reader's ability to not only get thought from the printed page, but to call plainly and distinctly the words that contain the thought thereon. All reading lessons should finally be "read out aloud" by the pupil for the teacher's correction and criticism. Many children come to school unable to pronounce correctly the simplest words used by them every day. "Some of them cannot speak their own names correctly; Smith may be Smif; Ethel, Effel; Robert, Wobbet, etc.* Care, then, should be taken, at the first, to teach beginners to correctly pronounce words in every-day use since they, in the main, constitute the words of the First Reader.

A spoken word is a combination of elementary sounds. A written word is a combination of letters, or letters and diphthongs, which stand for elementary sounds. He who can make the sound that a letter or diphthong stands for, and knows how to combine into a word the sounds they stand for, is able to call at sight that word without the teacher's help. When he has this power he has mastered the first great difficulty in reading. Until he knows words at sight, or knows "how to find them out" for himself, he is unable to get thought from the printed page.

The teacher's attention is called to the following usual methods of teaching reading:

1. Alphabetic.
2. Word.
3. Sentence.
4. Phonic.
5. A combination of any two or more of the above.

The alphabetic method consists of—

(*a*) Having the pupil learn the names of letters so that he may call them at sight.

(*b*) Having the pupil call the names of the letters in a word, after which the teacher pronounces the word for him.

(*c*) Having the pupil call the names of the letters in a word, and then pronounce by memory the word as it was at first pronounced for him by the teacher.

*Moses' Phonic Reader, Page 8.

THE ALPHABETIC METHOD.—Of course, the first time a pupil calls the names of a letter in a word the teacher must tell him " what they spell."

For instance, the pupil looks at the word "sit" and says "es-i-te,", then the teacher says "sit."

THE WORD METHOD is the alphabetic method, omitting the calling of the names of the letters. The teacher shows the word as a whole, and trains the pupil to know it at sight, without reference to the powers of the letters it contains.

"THE SENTENCE METHOD begins with sentences rather than with letters or words. The thought is expressed first orally, and then the printed or written expression is presented and taught."—*Raub.*

THE PHONIC METHOD.

By the phonic method pupils are taught the sounds of the letters and how to combine them into words, thus acquiring the ability to find out words for themselves without the aid of the teacher. The following indicates the order in which the different steps may be taken:

(*a*) Teach pupils to pronounce correctly simple monosyllabic words used by them in their daily conversation, especially those which are to be met with in the future lessons of the First Reader.

(*b*) Let the teacher pronounce slowly the elementary sounds in a word and then have the pupils tell the word thus pronounced.

(*c*) Pronounce a simple monosyllabic word for the pupils and have them give the elementary sounds in that word, *i. e.* have pupils to separate a word into its elementary sounds.

(*d*) Teach pupils the sound each letter stands for, and later on the sound each diphthong stands for.

(*e*) Have pupils look at each letter in a word, give the sound it stands for, and then combine into the correct word the sounds thus given.

The successive steps as above given constitute, in the main, the essential features of the phonic method. All who have given this method a fair trial are well pleased with it. A letter is intended to indicate to the reader that a certain sound is to be made, and the phonic method insists upon teaching the power of a letter.

Those who use the alphabetic method are finelly forced to resort to either the phonic method or the word method. For instance, suppose the words, fit, bed, fed, fuu, sun, have been spelled by the pupil and pronounced for him by the teacher, he is then sent to his seat and told to "study his lesson." In due time he is called up to recite. He points to the letters one by one calls their names, but fails to remember the word which a few minutes before was pronounced for him by the teacher, and hence comes to a standstill. At this point the theacher, to help him, either tells him the word at once, or pronounces the initial sound of the word, which is the sound represented by the initial letter. Suppose the word be "fit" and the pupil calls the names of the letters,—ef, i, te, and is yet unable to give the word. Now the teacher, resorting to phonics, gives for him the "f" sound as a hint, next she gives slowly and distinctly "f" sound followed by the sound of short i, and finally, if the pupil is yet unable to catch the word, she gives the "f" sound, short i sound, and "t" sound so clearly and distinctly that the word is at last caught by the pupil's ear. In other words, she emphasizes the second step of the phonic method. It is safe to say that the phonic method is the only one by which a pupil ever finds out for himself any new word, and then he becomes his own helper in reading.

No matter what other method a teacher may use with beginners, all agree that the sounds of the letters or phonics must be taught finally. For those who use either alphabetic, word, or sentence method, a plan for introducing the teaching of phonics is here given. It has been often tried with gratifying results.

The following list of words, or one similar to it, may be made from those to be found on the first twenty or twenty-five pages of the ordinary First Reader:

and, boy, cat, dog, fat, girl, hat, it, jump, kite, let, me, not, pig, run, see, top, up, very, was, yes.

In making a list of words the teacher should have reference to the alphabetical arrangement of the initial letter, should take a word for each letter as soon as found in a lesson, and in the case of words beginning with vowels, should take those beginning with short sounds only,—as and, every, it, ox, up.

As soon as a word has been learned and adopted as a list word, put it there and place the initial letter some distance to the right, show pupils that it is first in the word and stands for the first sound in the word. Train them to give this first sound by "starting to say" the word. Ask them to tell you some words beginning like it, as for instance, if the word be "and" you will get such words as apple, axe, ant, axle, etc. In this way the sound of short "a" or any other letter may be taught.

On page 5, Holmes' First Reader, the new words are cut, see, rat, I. When pupils reach this page, no matter by what method, place the three first in the list either upon the blackboard or upon stout paper. They may be written or printed, as the teacher prefers, but the sooner a pupil knows written letters, the sooner the teacher may do a much greater amount of teaching by using the blackboard. The words should be put in the list just where they ought to be after it shall have been completed. Follow the same plan with Lesson 3, page 6, at which time the list will be in this shape:

and	a
....	
cat	c
....	
dog	d
....	
man	m

Lesson 4, page 6, has the following words: I, a can, cup. I and a should be taught as words pronounced like their names as letters. From this point on pupils should be taught to utilize the knowledge gained as to the sound of letters in finding out other words. For instance, let pupils look at the list and tell which of the new words begins like the list word, cat. Pupils will point to the word can. The teacher should now write the list word just over the new word, thus: cat
can; after which she should ask pu-

pils to "begin to say" cat, and show that in beginning to say "ca'," they have really begun to say "can." In the same way use "and" of the list to get the sound of short "a," with which knowledge the pupils will be able to find out for themselves almost all of the new word can.

A SUGGESTED PLAN OF LESSON XXIII, HOLMES' FIRST READER.

First Step. Awaken interest in the lesson and thus lead pupils to wish to read it.

Means. Use picture which is very suggestive. The skilful teacher may, by well directed questions, lead the pupils to use the new words in sentences descriptive of the picture. These sentences may be like the following, and should, if possible, be written on the blackboard:

I see a *swan*.
A swan is a *bird*.
A swan can swim.
A swan can swim fast.
A swan can swim very fast.
A swan cannot walk very fast.
I see the neck of the swan.
I see the side of the neck.

Second Step. The above, or similar sentences having been written on the board, have pupils point out the new words in each.

Learning the new words. Write "sw" on the board, give the combined sound of the two letters, and have pupils repeat the sound after you.

Method. Next, give four pupils the sound that "an" has in "swan" and have them repeat it after you, and by again giving the sounds of "sw" and "an" more and more rapidly, pupils doing the same, lead them to give the correct pronunciation to the word.

"Swim" is easily taught after "swan" has been taught. It is merely a combination of the sw sound, short i, and the m sound.

The next word in the lesson is "bird," and is easily taught if the pupils have a fair knowledge of phonics. The "ir" sound has been learned in the word "girl" on page 8. The three sounds involved are the "b" sound, "ir" sound, and the "d" sound. And again, even if the pupils should be led by the teacher to give the sound of b, short i, r, and d, he would so nearly give the correct pronunciation of the word as to know how it should be pronounced and call it accordingly.

"Side" may be taught by telling pupils that "e" at the end of a word makes "i" say its own name.

"Very." Here we have a "v" sound at the beginning of a word. Show how to give its sound by placing the upper teeth upon the lower lip and causing breath to pass out of the mouth.

"Fast" and "neck" are regular save that ck in neck has the same sound that either c or k has by itself.

"Walk" may be utilized to show that "a" before "l" has the sound of "a" in the word all.

After the above has been rapidly developed before the class, Lesson XXIII may be assigned for the "next lesson," which may then well become a "recitation."

Pupils will have acquired much power for finding out new words for themselves when they have learned the short sounds of the vowels, the sounds of the consonants, that final "e" in words of one syllable lengthens the other vowel and makes it say its own name, that "a" before "l" has the "au" sound, and before "r" has the sound of "a" in "car".

"THE BLUE BACK SPELLER."

This book is yet used in many of our public schools. If it is used as its author intended it should be used; it is a great aid to the First and Second Reader pupils, in that it will drill them in the use of the powers or sounds of the letters in finding out a new word. Its author believed absolutely in the phonic method, and never for a moment thought that teachers would ever abuse the book by having their pupils call the letters in a word as a means of finding out the pronunciation of the word.

There is a phonic chart on the top of every page, and there is a seven-page preface devoted to a discussion of the sounds of the letters. On page 8 we read: "Each of the vowels has its regular *long and short sounds*, which are *most used*, and also certain occasional sounds," etc. Guided by this it would be well for the teacher to give careful drill, first in such words only as contain short-vowel sounds; next, those containing long-vowel sounds, and after that, those which contain vowels having the "occasional sounds," in the order here suggested: Nos. 4, 5, 12, 13, 14, 15 (omitting bar, far, tar, etc., unless the teacher should prefer to teach just here the sound of "ä" before "r"), 21 (omitting the first line and carp, scarp, etc., unless the teacher wishes to teach the sounds of "ar," "or," "ur") 36 and 37. After this have careful drill in the short sounds, teach the fact that as a rule "e" at the end of a word (monosyllable) lengthens the preceding vowel and makes it say its name, and drill in this by use of the following lessons:

Nos. 17, 18, 19, 20, 55, 61, after which, the regular long and short sounds now having been taught, begin at No. 21 and follow the order given in the book.

One of the very best books for primary teachers wishing to learn or teach the phonic method is Moses' Phonic Reader, published by Edwards & Broughton, Raleigh. Nearly every page contains valuable hints and suggestions for the teacher.

SPELLING.

Every person who writes spells some way or other, but every writer is not a correct speller.

One should not write a word unless he knows its meaning, therefore it would be well to see that the pupil knows the meaning of every word in the spelling lesson that you assign. Part of the spelling time might be well spent in "going over" with the class the words in next day's lesson and helping each child to master the meaning of the words. The written recitation is the best that can be used, but nothing works up more enthusiasm than an old time spelling class once or twice a week, and allowing the pupils to have "cutting down."

WRITING.

The teacher should rule the slates of all pupils who do not have copy-books. The slates should be ruled in conformity to the copy-book used in the school. The ruling should be done with the point of a sharp knife. Care should be taken not to bear too hard upon the knife while ruling.

Many teachers devote much time to their writing lessons and yet spoil it by imposing writing tasks for bad conduct or bad lessons. These tasks are not performed with care, and thus the good effects of the training in writing are lost.

TEACHING ENGLISH.

Language teaching should be made incidental with instruction in History, Geography' Botany, and especially with reading.

In all recitations, whatever be the subject, care should be exercised, in a kind, helpful way, over the spoken as well as the written language of pupils.

A clear and forceful reading of a sentence will often bring to light the relations of words, phrases and clauses not before seen by pupils; and it is not possible for teacher or pupil to give such reading without a perception of such relation. Good reading will aid deficient knowledge of language; and clear linguistic perception will facilitate good reading.

The tendency of our children is to adopt the incorrect forms of speech uttered in their hearing; and our schools should make intelligent and persistent effort to counteract this tendency, and to inspire pupils with a love for our mother tongue in its purity and simplicity. The teacher, therefore, has a two-fold object before him—to secure in pupils the habitual use of good English, and to inspire in them a love of our English Classics. Happily in this day of multiplied books, there are very valuable aids to teaching the English language to young pupils in some of the admirable books published for this purpose.

Less is said about formal Grammer than about language-learning, because formal Grammar is an inheritance which has come down to us from Greece and Rome and is not neccessary to the understanding of English; while language-learning concerns every child from the time the first words are spoken till the use of good English has become a fixed habit. The purpose sought in our schools in the teaching of English may be better gained by giving more time to Language Lessons and composition, and less to technical English Grammer.

The length of time our children are likely to remain in school cannot wisely be ignored by a teacher in adjusting subjects to be taught; and it is ever well to remember that a few things well learned will be much better than a smattering in many.

The following are given as example lessons in the beginning of this subject. The best plan will probably be to get the best text-book published, if possible, and follow it with such abreviation and variation as the needs of the people may clearly show.

If the length of time during which all the schools are operated were the same, and the text-books the same, a scheme might here be presented that would be very helpful to many teachers. The following outline of lessons is intended to be suggestive and thereby helpful.

LESSON ON THE SENTENCE.

The thought must precede its expression. The sentence is the expression of a thought. The proper method will require first the study of the thought, and second the study of the sentence.

Teacher. Children, you may write something on your slates about horses, dogs, birds, men.

You may write thus:

Horses run.

The pupils write:

Horses run.

Men walk.

Birds fly.

T. Which did you do first, think, or write?

Pupils. We thought.

T. What then do the words written tell?

P. They tell what we thought.

T. From this lesson I wish you to learn that words so put together as to express a thought, form a sentence.

Definition:

A sentence is the expression of a thought in words. Copy this and be able to repeat it to-morrow.

T. Do the words as thus arranged express a thought: Horses run.

P. They do.

T. What is a sentence?

P. A sentence is the expression of a thought in words.

T. What then may we call the expression, Horses run?

P. A sentence.

T. Men walk.

P. A sentence.

T. Birds fly?

P. A sentence.

Continue, if time allows, by other examples.

LESSON ON SUBJECT AND PREDICATE.

1. Apples are good.
2. The teacher rang the bell.
3. The boys brought water.
4. The school closed on Friday.

T. What may each of these four expressions be called?

P. A sentence.

T. About what is something said in the first?

P. Apples.

T. In the second?

P. Teacher.

T. In the third, in the fourth?

T. That part or word in a sentence which tells the person or thing about which something is said is called the subject of the sentence.

T. What is the subject of the first sentence?

P. Apples.

T. Of the second?

P. Teacher.

T. Of the third?

P. Boys.

T. Of the fourth?

P. School.

T. What is said in the first sentence about apples?

P. Are good.

T. What in the second about teacher?

P. Rang the bell—the teacher rang.

T. What in the third about boys?

P. Brought water.

T. What in the fourth about school?

P. Closed on Friday.

T. Copy the following definition:

What is said of the subject is called the predicate.

T. Class, what is the predicate of the first sentence? Of the second? Of the third? Of the fourth?

Other examples may be given and the pupils asked to name subject and predicate in each and give their reasons for so thinking.

LESSON ON THE NOUN.

T. Each pupil please name five things that may be seen in the schoolroom.

P. Chair.
Desk.
Stove.
Books.
Boys.

T. Each of these is the name of something, and so is called a name, or *noun*; the two words, noun and name, meaning the same thing.

T. Class, please to write five sentences using the names you have mentioned as subjects.

Pupils write:

The chair stands on four legs.

The desk is made of wood.

The stove is made of iron.

Books are read by the boys.

Boys like to play ball.

T. Name every noun in these five sentences.

The pupils name all but "legs," "wood," and "iron."

T. Does the word "legs" name anything?

Think!—"Legs" is the name of the four wooden posts on which the chair stands, as a man stands on his two legs. Also wood is the name of the material out of which the chair is made; and "iron," the name of the metal or material of which the stove is made. Therefore they are nouns.

Write the following definition on your slates:

A noun is the name of anything.

Write ten names of things not before used in this lesson:

Pupils write birds, horses, hog, chicken, duck, water, bread, fire, tree, axe.

T. Why do you think the word birds is a noun?

P. Because it is a name.

The same may be asked of every other of the ten words.

T. What is the definition of noun?

P. A noun is the name of anything

LESSON ON KINDS OF SENTENCES.

A sentence may make a statement, ask a question, give a command, or utter an exclamation.

Examples:

1. The boy went home.
2. Has the boy gone home?
3. Bring in some wood.
4. How glad I am to see you!

T. Each pupil please write four sentences of each of the four kinds here mentioned.

A sentence that declares is called declarative.

A sentence that asks a question is called interrogative.

A sentence that commands is called imperative.

A sentence that expresses an emotion is called exclamatory.

LESSON ON ERRORS.

The following expressions are correct. Drill the pupils on them, and call attention to the errors heard in the school or at home in relation to these expressions:

FACULTY CHAPEL HILL SCHOOL, CHAPEL HILL, N. C.

1. He doesn't know anything about it.
2. I don't know where my book is.
3. He does not recite well.
4. We do not wish to go.
5. We don't wish to go.
6. I wasn'st there.
7. I was not there.
8. It was I that broke that slate; it was not she.
9. It is they that need advice, and not we.
10. I don't like that kind of hats.

Teachers of English Language should carefully study the text-books adopted in their counties. Valuable aid may be obtained from W. D. Whitney's Essentials of English Grammar, and the same author's Language and Language Study, from Tarbell's Lessons in Language, and Hyde's Practical Lessons in the use of English.

See also Rev. A. H. Sayce's article on Grammar in Encyclopædia Brittannica, and the work of Mr. Sweet on Words, Logic and Grammar; also Richard Grant White's Everyday English, and Lounsbury's History of the English Language.

It is suggested that teachers may render great service to the communities in which they teach by leading in the formation of School Libraries. In some counties Literary Societies have been formed, and such deserve encouragement. These cannot be conducted satisfactorily without books. A school can do nothing better for a child than the implanting of such a thirst for knowledge as will lead to the formation of a habit of reading. Books are cheap, yet wisdom is needed in their selection.

The following list is suggested with the hope that it may prove helpful to those teachers throughout the State who are impressed with the importance of this kind of work.

Seek to form the nucleus of a Library in every community in which you teach.

No effort is made to indicate the importance of a book by the order in which it is named.

1. Grimm's Tales, selected, 2 vols., Ginn & Co.
2. Ruskin's King of the Golden River, Ginn & Co.
3. Robinson Crusoe, condensed, Ginn & Co.
4. Hans Andersen's Tales, first and second series.
5. Hawthorne's Wonder Book and Tanglewood Tales, Houghton, Mifflin & Co.
6. Beautiful Joe, the story of a dog.
7. Black Beauty, the story of a horse.
8. Kingsley's Water Babies, Ginn & Co.
9. Alice in Wonderland, Macmillan & Co.
10. Palgrave's Children's Treasury of Lyrical Poetry, Macmillan & Co.
11. Mrs. Gatty's Parables from Nature, Macmillan & Co.

12. Boyesen's Viking Tales, Scribners.
13. Miss Alcott's Little Women.
14. Miss Alcott's Old-fashioned Girl.
15. The Heart of Oak Books, edited by C. E. Norton.
16. Bunyan's Pilgrim's Progress.
17. Gulliver's Travels.
18. Church's Stories from Homer.
19. Fiske's History of the United States.
20. Dickens' Child's History of England.
21. The Boys of '76.
22. Scott's Novels.
23. Leatherstocking Stories, by Jas. Fennimore Cooper.
24. Self-Help, by Samuel Smiles.
25. Macaulay's Lays of Ancient Rome.
26. Tom Brown at Rugby.
27. The First and Second Jungle Book by Rudyard Kipling.

Harris. Uncle Remus, Songs and Sayings.
Andrews. Ten Boys. (Ginn & Co.)
Longfellow. Evangline. (Crowell)
Lubbock. Beauties of Nature. (Macmillan.)
Creasy. Fifteen Decisive Battles. (Crowell.)
George Eliot. Silas Marner. (Crowell.)
Scott. Lady of the Lake. (Crowell.)
Buckley. Fairy Land of Science. (Appleton.)
Osgood. Citizen Bird. (Macmillan.)
Osgood. Four Footed Americans. (Macmillan.)
Goldsmith. Vicar of Wakefield. (Crowell.)

ENGLISH LITERATURE.

The teacher should always be mindful of Matthew Arnold's maxim that "a single line of poetry, a single great thought, put to work in a pupil's mind, is worth any number of facts of literary history." With this end in view, the pupil should be given real literature as soon as possible. Mere selections are to be avoided, and the traditional "Reader," if retained, should be supplemented with unmutilated classics in prose and verse. Only under exceptional circumstances should pupils be given disjointed passages from the novelists or dramatists. It will be found helpful to give a small part of each day to reading aloud some short story or poem to the whole school. Drill in elocution, when directed to reading, rather than to speaking, is time well spent. Pupils should be especially encouraged to memorize passages of prose and verse suited to their age and progress.

The following course of supplementary reading is recommended:

First Reader Grade.—Golden-Rod Book No. 1 (University Publishing Co., 20c.); Scudder's Fables and Folk Stories, Part 1.

SECOND READER GRADE.—Golden-Rod Book No. 2 (25c.); Scudder's Fables and Folk Stories, Parts 2 and 3 (Houghton, Mifflin & Co., 15c. a part in paper, or all three parts in one volume, cloth, 40c).

THIRD READER GRADE.—Hans Andersen's Tales, first series (Ginn & Co., 25c.); Ruskin's King of the Golden River (Maynard's Classics, 10c.); Golden-Rod Book No. 3 (30c).

FOURTH READER GRADE.—Palgrave's Children's Treasury, (Macmillan Co, 50c); Dickens' Christmas Carol (Maynard's Classics, 10c.); Kingsley's Water Babies (Ginn & Co., 25c.); Selections from Irving's Sketch Book (Ginn & Co., 25c.); Robinson Crusoe (Maynard's Classics, 20c).

TEACHER'S COURSE.

The basis of the teacher's private study should be Pancoast's Introduction to English Literature, supplemented by Green's Short History of the English People. The following classics should be read in connection with the study of the periods they illustrate:

I. NORMAN-FRENCH PERIOD.—Tennyson's Harold, Shakespeare's King John, Scott's The Betrothed and Ivanhoe, Bulwer's Last of the Barons.

II. ELIZABETHAN PERIOD.—Shakespeare's Merchant of Venice, Julius Cæsar, and King Lear, Palgrave's Golden Treasury, (Part I), Scott's Kenilworth.

III. PURITAN PERIOD.—Scott's Woodstock, Milton's L'Allegro, Il Penseroso, Comus, and Paradise Lost (Books I and II), Bunyan's Pilgrim's Progress.

IV. EIGHTEENTH CENTURY.—Selections from Addison and Steele and Macaulay's Life of Addison (Allyn and Bacon's edition in one volume, 50c.); Macaulay's Life of Johnson (Maynard's Classics, 10c.); Goldsmith's Deserted Village (Maynard's Classics, 10c.); Pope's Rape of the Lock (Maynard's Classics, 10c); Palgrave's Golden Treasury (Part III), Burns' Tam O'Shanter and Cotter's Saturday Night (Maynard's Classics, 10c).

In fiction, Thackeray's Henry Esmond and The Virginians cover this period.

V. THE MODERN PERIOD.—Wordsworth (Selections in Maynard's Classics), Byron's Prisoner of Chillon (Maynard's Classics, 10c.); Scott's Marmion (Maynard's Classics, 10c.); Keats' St. Agnes' Eve (Maynard's Classics, 10c.); Tennyson's Enoch Arden, Locksley Hall, Crossing the Bar (the Astor edition of Tennyson may be had for 35c.); Dickens' David Copperfield, Old Curiosity Shop, and Oliver Twist; George Eliot's Silas Marner, Mill on the Floss, and Adam Bede; Thackeray's The Newcomes, Pendennis, and Vanity Fair.

The novels mentioned above may be had in the Astor edition at 35c. Shakespeare may be studied alone best in Hudson's edition (Ginn & Co., 40c. a play). Palgrave's Golden Treasury may be had in the school edition at 50c. (Macmillan Co.); the selections from Milton, one volume, with notes (Houghton, Mifflin & Co., 40c).

GEOGRAPHY.

In too many schools Geography is confined to the printed page of the text-book. The recitation consists of the teacher's asking the questions laid down at the end of each lesson, and requiring the pupil to give the correct answer. If the pupil succeeds he has "said his lesson," if not, he is "kept in at recess" or "must say it after school." Geography teaching of this kind has no connection with nature and develops in the pupil no profitable interest in a study which is of the greatest value, on account of the mental training and culture to be derived from it when properly taught. The average child comes to school possessing a knowledge of many facts and phenomena that are the basis of much geographical knowledge. He should be taught to so use these facts as to gain a knowledge of the great world far removed from his every-day life. It will be impossible to give at length in this manual a full discussion of the best methods of teaching geography. It is hoped that many may make an effort to bring their work to a higher standard each year. The work done by the class would be more permanent in its results if the teacher would make for review a short blackboard outline of what has been studied. Certainly after each continent has been studied, the teacher should, with the aid of the class, make a blackboard outline of the leading facts learned. This should be preserved and made the basis of frequent reviews. The following is by no means complete, but is offered by way of suggestion, as a brief

ANALYSIS OF NORTH AMERICA.

Position—
1. In? Hemisphere.
2. North (?) or South (?) of Equator.
3. In? Zones.

Boundaries—North, South, East, West:

Size—
1. Length and breadth (approximately).
2. Third in size.
3. ? are larger and ? smaller.

Form—
1. General Form—Triangular.
2. General direction of Arctic coast-line.
3. General direction of Atlantic coast-line.
4. General direction of Pacific coast-line.
5. Prominent projections, Peninsulars and Capes, on coast from Gulf of California northward to Point Barrow.
6. Prominent projections from Point Barrow to Gulf of Mexico.
7. Prominent indentations (Gulfs and Bays) from Point Barrow to Yucatan.

8. Prominent indentations on the Pacific coast.

Surface—

1. Atlantic Highlands.
2. Atlantic Slope.
3. Pacific Highlands.
4. Pacific Slope.
5. Great Central Plain.
6. Height of Land.

Atlantic Highlands—

1. Green Mountains.
2. Adirondacks.
3. White Mountains.
4. Alleghanies.
5. Blue Ridge Mountains.
6. Smoky Mountains.

Pacific Highlands—

1. Rocky Mountains.
2. Sierra Nevada.
3. Coast Range.
4. Sierra Madre.

Drainage—

1. Atlantic Slope—give six rivers.
2. Pacific Slope—give four rivers.
3. Northern Portion of Great Central Plain—give two rivers.
4. Southern Portion of Great Central Plain—give two rivers.

Lakes—

1. Fresh.
2. Salt.

Islands—Give larger ones only.

Climate—

1. With reference to distance from the Equator—Northern, Southern and Central portions.
2. As modified by elevations, winds, oceans currents.

Vegetation—

1. In extreme Northern portion.
2. In extreme Southern portion.
3. In intermediate portion.
4. Locate corn, cotton, wheat.

Minerals—

1. Gold.
2. Silver.
3. Copper.
4. Iron.
5. Lead.
6. Coal.

Inhabitants—
1. White.
2. Negro.
3. Indian.

Political Divisions—
1. British America.
2. Danish America.
3. United States.
4. Mexico.

In using this "Analysis" for a review, point to each topic and have pupils tell about it. Have pupils supply the proper word where the "?" occurs.

TEACHERS' COURSE.

Teachers should carefully study the books adopted for use in the schools in their county, and should endeavor to thoroughly acquaint themselves with the author's plans of teaching the subject.

The following books are especially helpful to those who wish to increase their knowledge and power of teaching Geography:

King's Methods and Aids in Geography.

Parker's How to Study Geography.

Maury's Physical Geography.

Geological Story Briefly Told. (Dana).

Frye's Child and Nature.

N. C. Edition of the Geography adopted in your county.

North Carolina and Her Resources. (Agr. Department, Raleigh).

Bulletin and all other publications of the Agricultural Department, Raleigh.

All publications of N. C. Geological Survey. (Prof. J. A. Holmes, Chapel Hill, N. C).

Any advertising matter published by Railroads of the State.

Railroad Commission Map of the State.

This list might be indefinitely extended, but it is thought better to recommend a few than too many for, etc.

HISTORY.

THE PURPOSE OF HISTORY TEACHING.

1. To increase our love of home and native land—to make our boys and girls true patriots.

2. To get a view of the great men of the past and be thereby stimulated to endeavor to become like them.

3. To learn wisdom by studying the lives of great men.

4. To learn how the blessings of liberty were secured, and how they must be preserved.

5. To strengthen the memory, cultivate the imagination, and to acquire such knowledge from the experience of others as will enable us to judge wisely, and act correctly at all times.

HOW AND WHEN TO INTRODUCE THE STUDY.

Children like stories and pictures; every teacher of history, therefore, should know how to tell a story and draw a map upon the blackboard. He must know how to draw as he talks, and how to fill in each detail on the map as he speaks of it to the class. The school terms in our State are so very short, and of such unequal lengths that it is impossible to say just what should be accomplished in each school. In the average school of three or four months term, it would be well to divide the whole number of pupils into three classes in history, as follows:

1. All who cannot read well enough to study a book or who will not get one.
2. Those who read well enough to study the primary history book.
3. Those who are prepared to study the larger book.

WHAT TO TEACH EACH CLASS.

First Class.

Teach orally stories of Columbus, the Indians, omitting cruelties, the Mound Builders, Americus Vespucius, the Cabots, Ponce de Leon, Balboa, De Soto, Magellan, Sir Humphrey Gilbert, Sir Walter Raleigh, Amadas and Barlowe, Roanoke Settlements, Drake, Pocahontas and John Smith.

Second Class.

This class should begin the use of the smaller history. Teach orally Plymouth Rock, Jamestown, Cartier, Champlain, Father Marquette, La Salle. Locate on the map all the places connected with the above. The fact that the class has or has not reached all of these topics as laid down in the text-book need not prevent you from teaching them orally. This oral instruction should be given carefully so as to emphasize these important and leading facts in American history. If your county is named after a person, your pupils should be taught something of his life, and every pupil should know after whom our State was named and something of his history.

Third Class.

This class should study the larger book. In studying the Revolution, reinforce the text-book by teaching carefully and thoroughly the battles of Moore's Creek, Alamance, Ramsour's Mill, King's Mountain, and Guilford Court House, and the Mecklenburg Declaration of Independence. The Stamp Act Disturbances on the Cape Fear should be taught by all means. When the anniversary of any of these important revolutionary events occurs during the school term it should be observed by the whole school and made the special lesson of the day.

SUGGESTIONS TO TEACHERS.

The amount of work assigned to each class should be made larger or smaller, as the interests of the pupils may demand.

First Class.

The most available help for teaching any of the subjects in this class is found in the opening chapters of any United States History. The instruction need not necessarily be given daily, and should be entirely oral or read to the children from some well-written history. If a pupil should become so much interested in the subject as to bring to school any old history book he might find at home, it may stimulate the others to let him read aloud certain passages selected by the teacher. Reading "The Story of Columbus" from first one history and then another will not tire the pupils, but will hold their interest. The same is true of stories descriptive of the Indians. These stories may be as many and as comprehedsive as desired, but the main points should finally be brought out in short sentences, written in reply to such questions as the following, written on the blackboard:

Where did Columbus live?
What was his occupation?
What did he think was the shape of the earth?
What country did he think he could reach by sailing westwardly?
In sailing westwardly what country did he reach?
What country did he think it was?

These questions are merely suggestive and should be added to. Those who know the answers and are unable to write the replies should be allowed to answer orally.

Second Class.

Follow the same general plan laid down for the first class, but make the work more comprehensive. Insist upon a grcat deal of written work in reply to questions on the blackboard. In this kind of work it is always best to let pupils give oral replies before they attempt to write them. Be sure to answer such questions as may be answered with a short sentence.

Third Class.

Continue plan used in the other classes. Throw light upon the text by reading occasionally to the class the same subject from another book. Make frequent use of "Topical Outline" and "Blackboard Form" as an aid in review lessons. Let these be written on the board and "questioned" about as they are built up before the pupils.

TEACHERS' COURSE.

Study the text-books adopted for use in the schools of the county.

Study also any history that you may get posession of, whether you regard it as trustworthy or impartial or not. The fairest student of history will read not only those books which he regards as impartial, but those also which are said to be partial, and thus make an honest investigation for the truth. In teaching United States History much attention must be given to the history of our own State. The following books are very helpful: Spencer's First Steps; Moore's History of North Carolina; Tales of the Cape Fear (Sprunt); A Colonial Officer and His Times (Waddell); Wiley's North Carolina Reader; Caruthers' Old North State; Wheeler's History of North Carolina; Colonial Records (Office Clerk of Court).

PEDAGOGICAL LIBRARY.

North Carolina Journal of Education.
The Essentials of Method, (DeGarmo).
Applied Psychology, (McLellan).
Elements of General Method, (McMurray).
Herbart and the Herbartians.
Practicai Lessons in Pedagogy, (Krohn).
Talks on Pedagogics, (Parker).
History of Education, (Painter).

A BRIEF COURSE IN CIVICS OUTLINED FOR THE PUBLIC SCHOOLS.

INTRODUCTORY.—A prominent educator spoke a great truth when he said, "The object of education is not to teach men to be great scholars, but *how to live*." The teacher has no grander opportunity to carry out this idea than in teaching civil government. The study of civil government, or Civics, is finding out how people live under government, and its object should be to teach boys and girls the *best* way of living. And would not our teaching be more effective if we should impress upon their minds that they become citizens, in the broader sense, as soon as they are born, and that they should strive to be good, patriotic citizens—beginning right *now*.

Pupils cannot too early be taught to be patriotic, but this is often done improperly. Patriotism does not consist—as many suppose—in bragging about one's country, nor in sneering at other nations or races. Patriots are those people who love their country and can tell *why* they love it. They can only tell *why* when they know something of its government. A man's opinion about his country isn't worth much, and will not be respected, unless it is based upon knowledge, for "knowledge is power." Patriots, then, are men who know the history of their country, how it is governed, how its laws are made. what rights are to be enjoyed, and what duties are to be performed. People who are without this knowledge are nearly always narrow-minded, prejudiced, unscrupulous, wavering, and ready to follow any popular craze that comes along.

The class of people above referred to is becoming a dangerous element in our country, and the only sure way of meeting the danger is to begin with the public schools, and there apply the remedy.

Let all the public school pupils in our country be instructed in the history of our government, its constitution, its laws, and the great princi-

FOOT NOTE.—The course in Civics was prepared by Prof. C. F. Tomlinson, Winston, at the request of the Superintendent of Public Instruction.

ples that guided its founders, and then there need be no fears for our future.

In preparing the following brief course in Civics the formost aim of the writer has been, not to stick strictly to the "pedagogic arrangement of the course," but to present something that is suitable for the public schools of North Carolina just as we find them *to-day*—a course that may be completed in three months' time, and one which every teacher holding a certificate should be able to teach successfully.

BOOKS.—The teacher should be supplied with "The American Citizen" by Dole (D. C. Heath & Co., Boston, $1.00); "Finger's Civics," (University Publishing Co., N. Y., 60 cents); "Civic Reader" (Maynard, Merrill & Co., N. Y., 60 cents), and a World's or Washington Post Almanac. The first mentioned book contains an excellent list of additional works—some of which may be desired. If the pupils can afford a book; Finger's Civics will be of most benefit to them, as it contains the State Constitution.

CLASSES.—A public school may be divided, for our purposes, into two classes—the one composed of younger pupils, the other of older In a school of 65 pupils probably 40 would rank in the former and 25 in the latter class. The outline given is intended to be followed only by the older pupils. But the younger ones (not including beginners) should not be left out entirely. Read them a chapter three times a week from that elegant, yet simple Civic Reader mentioned in the book list. Ask them questions on what is read, and they will know the book from cover to cover at the close of the term.

OUTLINE OF WORK.

Civil government is inseparably associated with history—therefore the historical feature of the study should receive all the consideration necessary to make the course complete. It will also stimulate interest and original research on the part of pupils.

THE VILLAGE.—Every village, every town or city, every couuty, has a history. Let the pupils, if they live in a village, find out all they can about its history. Who were some of its first inhabitants? Have any very prominent men lived in it? Has it grown fast? If not, are the reasons to be attributed to its location, its soil, its climate, or lack of the progressive spirit? All sorts of answers to such questions will be given by the pupils, but they will all help to get down to the real facts.

Do any officers live in the village? A Justice of the Peace? How did he become an officer? Who appointed or elected him? Does he get a good salary? What are his duties? Can he send a horse thief to the penitentiary? Can he send him to the county roads? Could he settle a dispute over a piece of land valued at $500?

Similar questions may be asked concerning any other officer that lives in or near the village. If the public school is in a larger town, or city, which has a Mayor, commissioners, policemen, tax collectors, school committee and numerous other officers, the duties, election, salaries, etc., of these men should be fully discussed. The topic might be concluded with a general debate on the question: "Resolved, that country life is preferable to town, or city life."

THE COUNTY.—This must be the starting point with many schools situated in thinly populated districts, for the people in such districts come in contact only with the officers of county government. A historical study of the county is first made - when formed, for whom named, county seat, for whom named, etc. Take Mecklenburg county for an example. It was named in honor of the wife of George III—Charlotte of Mecklenburg. We can easily see in a moment just where the name of county and county seat came from. And as it was Admiral Anson who brought Charlotte of Mecklenburg to England, it was quite natural that the county adjacent to Mecklenburg should be named for him—hence Anson county. These two counties being very large, it was thought best in 1842 to *unite* adjoining parts of each, and form a new county. The result was Union. These exercises may be made exceedingly interesting.

Next take up the county officers—their names, duties, salaries, when and how elected. Taxes will also be an interesting topic to discuss. Let the pupils find out the meaning of poll-tax, tax on personal and real property, what taxes are used for, why every citizen should pay tax, etc. They should know also that in North Carolina the rule is that the tax on $300 worth of property must always be the same as the poll-tax Give them simple problems like this: "What tax must a man pay on $750 worth of property, if poll-tax is $1.50? What will his total tax be?" Each pupil should know the rate of taxation in his own county, and how much is used for county, and how much for State purposes.

THE STATE.—A brief sketch of the history of the State—such as may be found in Superintendent Noble's Supplement to Mauray's Geography—should be read to the class, even if they have made North Carolina History a regular study previously.

Departments of State Government follow—Legislative, Judicial, Executive.

The pupils should know that the Legislature is divided into two bodies - House and Senate, the one composed of 120 members, the other of 50. The members of the two Houses are elected by the voters of the counties. Each county must be represented in the Legislature. The Legislature meets every two years in Raleigh—the capital. The Lieutenant-Governor presidee over the Senate, and the Speaker over the House. The duty of the Legislature is to make laws.

The Judicial Department finds out whether or not the laws made are just and constitutional. The Supreme Court Judges should be known, where they meet, how often, etc.

The Superior Courts, held in each county at stated times, are a branch of the Judicial Department of the State. There are twelve Superior Court Judges and a like number of judicial districts. The pupils ought to know the judge from their own district, and all the officers that are in any way connected with the Superior Court held in their county.

They should know the duties of the grand jury, solicitor, regular jury, etc., understand such terms as indictment, bail, evidence, testimony, the oath, cross-examination, and appeal. Also explain what the judge does when he "charges the grand jury."

The Executive Department sees that the laws of the State are executed, or enforced. The chief executive officer is the Governor. The names, duties, salaries, term of office, etc., of all the executive officers should be known. The Governor of North Carolina does not have as much power as governors of some States, because he cannot *veto* bills. The Governor has a Council of State to advise him on matters of public concern. This council is composed of the Secretary of State, the Auditor, the Treasurer and the State Superintendent of Public Instruction.

When the Executive Department is studied, a history of all the governors of the State excites interest and brings out valuable information. The study of the Judicial Department should cause inquiry concerning the State's greatest jurists and members of the bar.

When the Legislative Department is taken up each pupil should know who represents his county in the Legislature. Let the teacher add further topics under State government according to the time that can be devoted to the subject.

THE GENERAL GOVERNMENT.—Why do we say "General Government"? Because this government makes laws that affect people generally. It does not legislate for any particular section. It is for the protection of the people of all the States *united*.

The study of the General Government may be carried on in much the same manner as that of State government. It is divided into the same number of departments, with corresponding duties. Possibly the best way to study this topic is through the Constitution, which we take up later. All along, the teacher and pupils should note the points of similarity between State and General Government. For example, the term of a member of the Legisiature begins when he is elected, while the term of a congressman does not begin until the 4th of March following his election. By contrasting such facts, they will easily be remembered.

THE STATE CONSTITUTION.—The first Constitution of North Carolina was made at Halifax in December, 1776, by "representatives of the freemen of the State." This continued to be our fundamental law until 1835, when a convention held in the city of Raleigh adopted amendments which were ratified by the people. Subsequent amendments have been made from time. There are two ways of changing our State Constitution: (1.) By calling a convention. Two-thirds of all the members can make a change. (2.) By legislative enactment. Three-fifths of all the members of the legislature must first pass the constitutional change, then publish it, and then it must be passed by a two-thirds majority in the *next* legislature.

Under the old Constitution a man could not vote unless he had property in land, or paid a certain amount of taxes. The State officers were then elected by the Legislature. By amendments to the Constitution any freeman may now vote, and State officers are no longer elected by the Legislature, but by the people directly.

The present State Constitution may be divided into fourteen leading topics, viz: (1.) Declaration of rights. (2.) Legislative department. (3.) Executive department. (4.) Judicial department. (5.) Revenue and taxation (6.) Suffrage and eligibility to office. (7.) Municipal corporations. (8.) Other corporations. (9.) Education. (10.) Homesteads and exemptions. (11.) Punishments. (12.) Militia. (13.) Amendments—how made. (14.) Miscellaneous.

The best way to study the Constitution is to make an outline of each topic, copy on the blackboard, and require the pupils to fill in the answers. In this way they not only read the Constitution but make an analysis of it also.

Below is given an analysis of the ninth topic—Education. The teacher can easily outline the others in a similar manner, always guarding against too many details, for it is the Constitution as a whole that we wish to be familiar with. Details destroy its unity.

IX. Education.
- I. Why the State should educate.
- II. *Legislature *required* to provide
  - Free public school, for both races, for all children of State between ages of 6 and 21, said schools to be maintained at least four months in every year.
- III. *Legislature *may* provide for
  - 1. State University.
  - 2. Colleges of Agriculture, Mechanics, Mining, Normal Colleges, etc.
  - 3. Compulsory attendance in public schools.
- IV. Sources of support for public education.
- V. State Board of Education.
  - 1. Of whom composed.
  - 2. Powers.

CONSTITUTION OF UNITED STATES.—May be studied in a similar manner to that of the State. Pupils are often required to commit to memory the Preamble, but do they always get the full meaning out of it? If not, place on blackboard, as the first lesson on the Constitution, the following outline:

The Constitution of U. S. †

- I. Parties to the compact.
- II. Purposes.
  - 1
  - 2
  - 3
  - 4
  - 5
  - 6
    - 1
    - 2
- III. Things done.

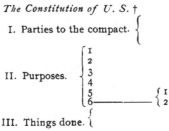

* These questions filled out to illustrate the method.
† Doles' American Citizen.

Ask the pupils to get *every answer* to the above from the Preamble. When they have done this they will not only know the Preamble, but also know *why* they *should* know it.

* * * * * * * * *

The outline may be continued after the following manner, always requiring that the answers be fitted in directly from the Constitution itself.

I. Parts of the General Government.

(*a*.) Law-making power, or Congress.

1. House of Representatives composed of 357 members (at present), apportioned to the various States according to population. The qualifications, election, term of office, salary, etc., of Representatives should be noticed. North Carolina has nine Congressmen from as many districts. The pupils should at least know the Congressman from their own district.

2. Senate—composed of 90 members, two from each State. Apply same questions given above to Senators.

(*b*.) Judicial or Law-Interpreting power.

1. Judges of Supreme Court.

2. Judges of Inferior Courts held in the State of North Carolina.

Numerous examples should be given of cases that come before the United States Courts at their sessions in different parts of the State.

(*c*.) Executive.

1. President—term, election, qualifications, duties, powers, etc.

2. Vice-President (same questions).

Duties of cabinet officers should be considered here also. The name of each cabinet officer should be known.

II. Powers granted to Congress.

III. Powers denied to Congress.

IV. Powers denied to the States.

All powers not granted to Congress nor denied to the States, *are reserved for the people of the States*.

The final work along this line should be a comparison of the Constitution of the State with the Federal Constitution—so far, at least, as is necessary to show that the one is a Constitution of limitations, while the other is one of grants; that the Constitution of the United States is the supreme law of the land only because the States have made it so, and that, therefore, the real supremacy in our government lies in the people, as members of sovereign States.

SUPPLEMENTARY—DUTIES OF CITIZENS.

Pupils may easily get the notion that the object of the study of Civics is to enable them to discover all the *rights* that are due them by the government. Unfortunately the average citizen knows too well how to get something *out* of the government, but too little about what his duties *toward* the government are.

Our government fulfills its mission, and helps the people, just in proportion as the people do their duty toward it. Because of the importance of this idea, a brief supplementary outline is added.

I. SOME DUTIES OF CITIZENS.

(1.) Voting.
(2.) Pay taxes.
(3.) Assume responsibility.
(4.) Work for education of all the people.
(5.) Make sacrifices for the good of all.
(6.) Obey the laws.
(7.) Respect authority.
(8.) Protect public property.
(9.) Serve the public for the public good.
(10.) Possess public spirit.

II. SOME ABUSES GOOD CITIZENS SHOULD SEEK TO REMEDY.

(1.) Government meddling with business.
(2.) Offensive partisanship.
(3.) Selfishness on part of those in power.
(4.) "Jobbery" and "patronage."
(5.) Government going into debt.
(6.) Allowing ignorant men to vote.
(7.) Lobbying.
(8.) Following popular crazes.

III. Finally let the pupils sum up the qualities that a person should possess to make him a good citizen. Their statements summarized will doubtless include the following:

A GOOD CITIZEN is one who is obedient, polite, orderly, clean, chivalrous, able to control himself, has a high sense of honor, knows how to use money, is thorough, truthful, respects authority, does not shirk responsibility, knows how to use power rightly, is conservative yet liberal, and is always hopeful that good will triumph over evil.

ARITHMETIC.

The teacher of arithmetic should ever have in mind the fact that the subject is of great practical value and that the pupil will have an immediate need for a knowledge of it in every walk of life. As necessary preparation for the teacher the following is suggested:

(1.) All possible arithmetical knowledge

(2.) An accurate knowledge of the relative value of problems and puzzles.

(3.) A clear conception of the aims of the author of the text-book used.

(4.) Such a knowledge of the uses of arithmetic as will enable him to know what subjects in the book should be either omitted or postponed until the more useful subjects have been mastered.

(5.) A knowledge of what problems are of greatest worth.

(6.) An accurate knowledge of the problems occurring in the business circles of the community where the school is located, and

(7.) To thoroughly understand that a "Rule" should be derived from experience in solving a problem, and that it shou'd not be first committed to memory and *then* used as a means of "finding the answer."

(8.) To know how to make charts that will hlep in the work, and not only to know *how* to make them but to actually make them and use them.

The following order of teaching the different subjects treated in the usual arithmetics is suggested as the best to be followed so as to impart the greatest amount of knowledge in the short time the pupils spend in our schools:

1. The four fundamental processes of addition, subtraction, multiplication and division.
2. Common fractions.
3. Decimal fractions.
4. United States currency.
5. Compound quantities.
6. Percentage.
7. Interest.
8. Analysis

In following the above order it will be necessary to skip much of the text in the book, but this may be done without injury to the class and then those subjects which have been postponed may be taken up after the more important subjects are thoroughly understood.

"THE FOUR FUNDAMENTAL RULES."

It will be impossible in this manual to present an extended discussion of the many excellent devices and methods employed by the best teachers of arithmetic.

Addition. A careful study of objects should precede the use of figures. After addition has been studied objectively, make a chart containing the following combinations:

2	1	7	5	1	6	1	2	4	6	3	3	8
3	5	2	4	1	3	9	5	1	4	1	3	1

4	2	4	8	6	5	4	7	2	5	7	2
2	1	3	2	1	3	4	1	2	5	3	6

6	5	2	6	4		6	7	5	4	3
6	8	9	7	8		5	8	9	7	9

4	8	5	8	7	3	9	7	8	9
9	8	7	6	9	8	9	7	9	6

This chart should be made on a large piece of manilla paper and

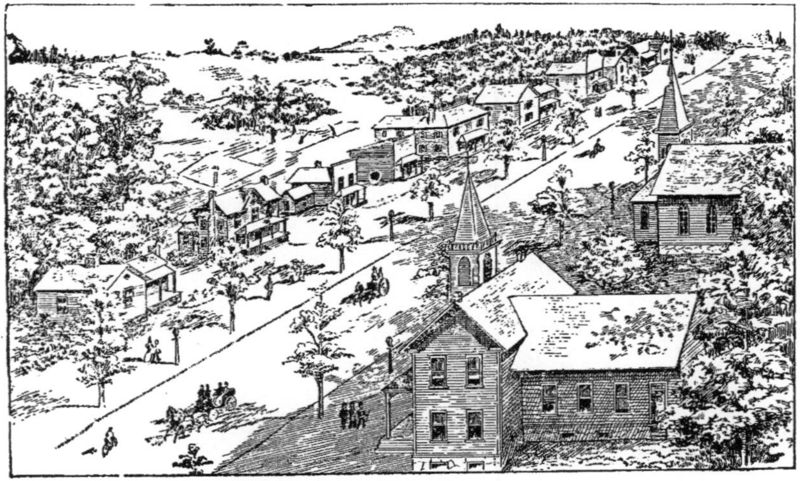

WHITSETT INSTITUTE, WHITSETT, N. C.

fastened to the wall and the children should be taught to know the sum of each group at sight as the teacher points to it.

Give a great many examples like these for slate work.

Give longer columns to the higher classes. There should be frequent drill in addition and children should never be allowed to "count on their fingers" Aim at accuracy first, and then rapidity.

In adding a column of figures like the ones here given do not let pupils say: "Two and six are eight, and eight and five are thirteen, and thirteen and four are seventeen, and seventeen and three are twenty, and twenty and eight are twenty-eight, and twenty-eight and seven are thirty-five." Insist upon their adding in this way: Two, eight, thirteen, seventeen, etc.

7
8
3
4
5
6
2
—

Sprague's Rapid Addition, price 10 cents, published by Ginn & Co., will help any teacher.

Substraction.—Three classes of problems occur.

1. I had 9 cents and spent 3 cents. How many did I then have? This problem involves the use of nine objects of the same kind and is readily understood by any child who knows that 9 cents is the sum of 6 cents and 3 cents.

2. I had 9 cents and John had 3 cents. How many cents did I have more than John? This problem involves the use of 12 objects of the same kind.

3. A farmer had 9 horses and 3 mules. How many more horses than mules did he have? This problem involves the use of 12 objects of different kinds. The first of the above should be taught thoroughly before the others are studied. The process of substraction is soon understood and mastered by the pupils. The process of "borrowing and carrying" is too often so very much explained as to become difficult to understand.

Multiplication.—Great care should be used in teaching the "thought" of multiplication. Very frequently teachers begin the subject by requiring the pupil to commit to memory a part or all the table by a certain time. Of course it must be finally committed to memory, but the "thought" should be taught first and then the process. We have here . . . . . . , three groups of two each or "three times two = six. Substitute × for "times" and we may write it $3\times2=6$. Make this plain by having pupils write on slates figures for .·. .·. = , :: :: ::= , as $2\times3=6$, $3\times4=12$.

Next require pupils to express with figures in the same way such examples as

.. .., .·. .·. .·. .·., :·: :·: :·: .

Give a great many examples in multplication, but be sure to have many short problems rather than a few long ones. Such an example as,

```
7897643
 298764
-------
31580572
47395858
```

etc., are too long and tedious for real profit.

A few short problems are far more valuable than one like the above.

Divison.—A few intelligent remarks by the teacher will make division very simple for those who know the multiplication table. Show the meaning of such expressions as 12÷3=4. Illustrate by drawing . . . . and dividing them into groups of three, as ... ... Show that the quotient 4 and the dividend 12 are equal, the one being four threes and the other being twelve ones. Long division should be taught, as every one does, just after short division. Remember that the operation is a difficult one to perform, and hence require pupils to go slowly.

Fractions.—The size of this manual will not admit of any extended outline of a treatment of fractions. They should be taught thoroughly rather than rapidly, and the addition, subtraction, multiplication, and division of fractions should be taught by means of objects. Each principle should be learned from objects. In fact, all arithmetic should be taught from objects, and in no other way.

Pupils should be required to explain each problem in correct English, and in a proper tone of voice. Insist upon neat work and plain figures. Occasionally give exercises in such multiplication as 9876
7435 and require the figures of the product to be written in straight columns. Dictate many long columns to advanced classes for addition and require neat work.

The "Four Fundamental Rules" are employed every day in business, and pupils should receive careful instruction in them. Time spent upon Greatest Common Factor, Least Common Multiple and Allegation is, practically, time lost.

PHYSIOLOGY AND HYGIENE.

Instruction in these subjects is prescribed by the school law, as are the text-books to be used. The study of the physiological effects of alcohol and narcotics is important, but it is a mistake and a perversion to subordinate the whole science of physiology to it. The best practical results for the pupil should be expected, not from exaggerated accounts and flaming pictures of abnormal conditions, but from a clear comprehension of the normal processes that go forward in the body. The text-book ought to be supplemented by demonstrations wherever possible. For example, the relations of the bones to one another, the different kinds of joints and levers, may be illustrated by a portion of the skeletons of other animals; so also the structure of the muscles, the internal organs, the heart, lungs, kidneys, etc., may be demonstrated upon specimens to be had by keeping an eye open for the opportunities which the kitchen offers.

TEACHER'S COURSE.

The teacher will find almost indispensable for his private study some such book as Martin's Human Body, Briefer Course (Henry Holt & Co., $1.20). Most valuable directions for practical demonstrations are given in the appendixes to a number of the chapters. If a more elaborate reference book is desired, Kirke's Handbook of Physiology (Blakiston, Son & Co., Philadelphia, 14th edition, $3), is recommended.

BOTANY.

The study of plants ought to begin early in the school life of the child. It occupies those two faculties which are the first to assert themselves in development—observation and memory—and the teacher cannot afford to violate the order of nature.

The material for the study is everywhere abundant, costs nothing, is easily handled and attractive, and, contrary to the common opinion, may be had all the year round. This is important, because without this material botany counts for nothing. There can be no profitable study of plants apart from the plants themselves Indeed, mere book knowledge is here not only worthless, but positively harmful. Instead of feeding, it dwarfs the very faculty for the sake of which botany stands in the school course. Accordingly, no lesson should be given without the material actually in hand to illustrate it, particularly in the case of pupils beginning to study.

The school law does not require instruction in botany, but the introduction of it into the course will not to any extent displace what is prescribed. On the contrary, it will give the teacher an opportunity to quicken the minds and enliven the energies of the whole school, so that when the brief lesson here suggested is over, the pupils will turn refreshed to their other work.

First, as to the time of the lesson. It need not occupy more than five minutes, say, three times a week, though the material in hand may warrant an extension beyond this limit. Let it be taken up whenever the circumstances of the day seem to call for it. An occasional excursion under the guidance of the teacher will be useful. It may fall at the midday recess or on Saturday, according to the distance to be covered.

The lesson itself will be conducted in a variety of ways by the alert teacher. The following suggestions are offered to indicate the kind of work which may be undertaken profitably and the general way in which it ought to be done. Turn the entire school for the time into one class. Let there be no text-book. Direct attention to the specimen in hand by questions, such as. What is it? Where does it grow? What is it good for, etc? Suppose the plant to be a mushroom gathered on the way to school. By questioning, guide the observation of the pupils to the chief features in the structure of the plant and give the names (the common names whenever possible) of these features. Cut the cap from the stem and lay it, gills down, on a piece of paper with some such statement as "We shall see to-morrow what will happen." The spores will be found to have fallen from the gills in radial ridges on the paper, when the cap is lifted carefully. There may follow comment on the number of the spores, their minute size, their dispersal by the wind, and their work in making new plants when they fall in the proper places. The spores from a mushroom which bears on the underside many tubes instead of gills may be collected in the same way. They will fall out of the tubes in little heaps. In a favorable season the pupils may be asked to bring as many different kinds of mushrooms to the school as they can find, with the suggestion that the situation in which they grow be noted. There may follow a lesson on moulds, specimens of which are to be found on decaying fruit, etc. In some two or three lessons the pupils have discovered the great group of the fungi. The same method may be pursued with a moss, a fern, and a number of flowering plants. Germinating beans and other seeds in wet sand, and noting the stages of their growth will be simple and profitable. There should be lessons on leaves, on buds, on the storage of food, on flowers and insects, and on fruits.

TEACHER'S COURSE.

The more thoroughly at home in the plant world the teacher is, the more effective will the instruction in botany be. But this work may be taken up on a much slighter basis of knowledge than would appear to be necessary, provided the preparation for the particular lesson is genuine and full. Sufficient preparation for the work here suggested may be made by the study of the following books: Bergen's Elements of Botany (Ginn & Co., $1.10) and Spalding's Introduction of Botany (D. C. Heath & Co., $1). These books supplement one another and may be mastered without a teacher. Goodale's little book Concerning a Few Common Plants (Heath's Guides for Science Teaching, 20c.) is strongly recommended. Wilson's Nature Study (Macmillan Co., 90c.) is a teacher's manual and abounds in helpful suggestions. Bailey's Lessons with Plants (Macmillan Co., $1.10) will prove itself an invaluable companion. Geddes' Chapters in Modern Botany (Scribner's Sons, $1.25), presents the wider aspects of the science and will give the teacher a rich fund of illustrative material. If a microscope is available, so much the better; but it is not absolutely necessary.

SCHOOL-ROOM SUGGESTIONS.

Have few rules and never make a rule unless you need it. A good teacher is seldom troubled with disorder.

On the first day of school—and every day of school—be in the room ready to receive the pupils. Organize at once and endeavor to give each pupil something to do as soon as possible. Do dot talk your pupils into disorder by telling what "nice boys and girls" you wish them to be, or by boasting that your last school was the best you ever had and that you don't see why your present one may not even surpass it. Stop talking and go to teaching.

The teacher should do all in his power to prevent disorder and to this end he should have scholarship;

Should carefully prepare each lesson, neglecting not even the lowest reading class;

Should try to learn more and more about teaching year by year;

Should know where the lesson begins and not lose time asking the question, "Where does the lesson begin to-day?"

Should remember that too much talk means too little teach;

Should not teach in a loud tone of voice;

Should not teach unless the pupils are quiet.

CARE OF SCHOOL-ROOM.

The school-room should be kept "neat and clean" at all times. The teacher who sweeps the floor will find volunteers among his pupils eager to do the sweeping, and when pupils undertake the care of the school-room less ink will be spilled, less paper thrown on the floor, and less mud brought in on the shoes. With little effort a wood box may be secured and the general appearance of the floor greatly improved by not having wood piled up near the stove.

Before leaving the school-room at the close of the day erase all work on the blackboard and put everything in readiness for the next day's work.

Too much cannot be said about the importance of keeping the school-room "neat and clean." Dirty floors and window panes indicate a careless teacher. The teacher who likes a neat, tidy school-room will find a way to keep it so. One who is willing to teach where the window panes are dirty, the floor unswept, and the walls unsightly, should not be employed to teach our youth.

RECESS.

Children should be under the teacher's supervision at recess. Many a serious quarrel has begun in play at recess and could have been prevented had the teacher been on the play-ground. When the recess signal is given pupils should not be allowed to rush from the school-room laughing and talking. The teacher should have the pupils rise and march from the building in as perfect order as possible. They should return to the school-room in the same manner after recess. Too often at recess, or when the school is dismissed, pupils are allowed to leave the room in noise and confusion. When they march from the room require them to form in line in the yard and wait until a signal from you before they "break ranks."

PUNISHMENTS.

The best teachers resort to punishments less and less the longer they teach. It savors of the brute when a teacher boasts of his having "conquered a boy" by the infliction of corporal punishment. All punishment, however, is not corporal punishment, and it is a fact that the best teachers must punish occasionally. It is impossible to state how and for what, punishment shall be inflicted. The teacher's desire should be not so much to find out a penalty for, but rather a preventive of, bad conduct.

The best preventive is tact. Tact is inborn, and yet it may be made more and more effective if the teacher strives to gain knowledge and skill by studying the ways of successful teachers and attending teachers' meetings of all kinds.

The following books are very helpful: Hughes' Mistakes in Teaching; Hughes' How to Keep Order.

THE SCHOOL MUSEUM.

As a means of stimulating and guiding the observing powers, the gathering of natural objects in the vicinity of the school is entitled to the first consideration: Let it be understood that anything, whether common or uncommon, will be acceptable, so that the collection will stand as a sort of epitome of the school district.

There are the different kinds of rocks and minerals, which should be reduced to approximately uniform size, say, three inches diameter; the different kinds of soil, which may be put in small bottles; mosses, lichens, ferns, and flowering plants, which may be dried and pressed and fastened to stiff paper of uniform size; likewise many forms of animal life and many specimens of the work of animals.

A few simple shelves will suffice to receive the material, which ought to be grouped "with the assistance" of the pupils; and here the teacher has an excellent opportunity of training the judgment, which is one of the chief advantages of nature study. Let each specimen be named, if possible, on a label, together with its locality and collector.

It will be necessary to select typical specimens from the number of duplicates brought in, though it is more important to have all the pupils represented in the museum than to save space on the shelves.

The primary object sought in such a museum is, not the possessions of the specimens, but the gathering of them by the pupils. The teacher will, therefore, feel no embarrassment because of his inadequate means either of displaying or of preserving them. He will seek to have each generation of pupils contribute to the collection, and so replace lost or deteriorated material, as well as enlarge the number of specimens.

THE CARE OF THE EYES OF SCHOOL CHILDREN.

RICHARD H. LEWIS, M. D, RALEIGH, N. C., IN NORTH CAROLINA JOURNAL OF EDUCATION.

Of all the special senses, that of sight is by far the most important to the welfare of the individual, and, in general estimation, to his happiness as well. The preservation, therefore, of this most precious sense in its perfection should receive thoughtful attention from all those who are in any way responsible for the care and management of their fellow beings. Inasmuch as the teacher has the immediate oversight and control of nearly the entire population for a large part of the time during the period of life when the eye is most liable to damage from preventable causes, which causes are incidental to the work done under his supervision, it is manifest that upon him, above all others, rests this responsibility. The object of this paper is to make as plain as may be possible, in dealing with a technical subject, how he can best form his duty in this respect. In order to have an intelligent appreciation of the best method of caring for an organ it is necessary to have some idea of its structure and workings, or functions, and so I shall lay the foundation for the practical part that is to follow, by giving, as simply as possible, the essential features of the eye as the organ of vision.

The eye is, roughly speaking, a globe, a trifle less, as a rule, than an inch in diameter, the walls of which are composed of three layers lying upon one another like those of an onion, and the cavity of which is filled with three perfectly transparent fluids or humors. The outermost of the three coats is called the sclerotic, from a Greek word meaning hard. It is white, opaque and very tough. It is the skeleton of the eye and preserves its shape, at the same time, by its strength and toughness, protecting from injury the extremely delicate structure it encloses. It is "the white of the eye." This white coat does not cover the entire ball, but in front there is an opening equal in area to about one-sixth of the whole surface. This opening is filled in with a transparent structure known as the cornea, which is set in the white coat very much like a watch crystal is set in its rim. The middle coat, the choroid, is composed chiefly of blood vessels for nourishing the other structures, and a kind of dark pigment, which is an element in the visual process. Intimately connected with the choroid, though an entirely different structure, is the iris (rainbow), the beautiful, many colored circular curtain, with a round opening near its center, the pupil, which hangs suspended from the junction of the sclerotic and cornea. The pupil, or window through which we see, varies in size according to the amount of light, automatically regulating the amount that falls upon the sensitive retina, which is the innermost and most important of the three coats. The retina is an extremely delicate and complex structure, and is *par excellence* the organ of vision. It may be compared to the telegraph instrument which is connected with the central office, the brain, by means of the fibres of the optic nerve, the conducting wires.

Of the three humors filling the hollow of the ball, the only one of practical interest to us in this connection is the crystalline. This is an extremely elastic semi-solid enclosed in a little sac or bag, the capsule. Of the shape of a double convex lens, it hangs suspended just behind the iris, touching it at the pupillary border. Surrounding the edge of the lens is a circular muscle, the ciliary, or muscle of accommodation, which regulates the amount of the convexity of the lens, thereby adjusting its focus of light from objects at different distances.

The eye is moved in different directions—up, down, out, in—by four recti, or straight muscles, and rotated on its axis by two oblique. Of these, only the internal recti, which converge the two eyes on near objects, as in reading, etc., are of special interest to us.

Optically considered, the eye is admirably illustrated by the camera of the photographer, with which many of my readers are doubtless familiar: the double convex lens which focuses the light from the object to be photographed, thereby making a distinct picture of it on the sensitive plate, just as the lens of the eye does upon the retina; the perforated disc, the iris; the sensitive plate, the retina; and the adjusting screw which regulates the focus, the muscle of accommodation. In the camera, when the ground-glass plate at the back, on which the operator brings out a clear and sharply defined image of the object to be photographed before he substitutes for it the plate covered with chemicals sensitive to light, is out of focus—too near to or too far from the lens—thereby blurring the image, he changes its position by turning the adjusting screw until the plate is precisely at the focus. In the eye, the distance between the lens and the retina is fixed, and the latter cannot be moved to and fro to find the focus, so another method must be employed. That method consists in a change in the convexity of the crystalline lens, which, owing to the optical fact that the more convex a lens the shorter its focus, and *vice versa*. accomplishes the same end by putting the focus exactly on the retina. This is done by the varying contractions and relaxations of the ciliary muscle which thus accommodates or adjusts the eye.

The essential difference between the two methods, as bearing on our subject, is that in the one case it is a mechanical process, while in the other it is a vital one. Brass and steel never get tired, but muscles always do, if overworked. And right here is the trouble in most weak eyes—the overstraining from one cause or another of this little muscle of accommodation. Let us see how it can be overstrained. In the normal eye, the retina is exactly at the focus of parallel rays of light, which is synonymous with rays of light from distant objects. So that when we look at distinct objects the muscles of accommodation and those of convergence, the internal straight muscles of the two eyes, are completely relaxed—at rest—just as the muscle of our body are when we are lying down—we see without effort. The nearer the object is brought to the eye the more divergent are the rays of light, the farther from the lens and, therefore, the farther behind the retina, whose position is fixed, is the focus, and the greater the effort required of the muscle of accommodation, to sufficiently increase the convexity of the lens and shorten the focus up to the retina and make a distinct picture of the object, until, finally, the limit of the muscle's power is reached, and we can no longer see clearly. The nearer, also, the object the greater the effort required of the muscles of convergence, which act *pari passu* with the muscles of accommodation, to keep both eyes fixed on the object, and they, too, are strained by too close an approximation of the object. Try reading a few minutes at the very nearest point you can see distinctly, and you will obtain a practical demonstration of eye strain. But all eyes are not normal. Some are too short—the far-sighted eye—and the focus for all rays is behind the retina, and even a distant vision requires an accommodation effort. Some are too long—the near-sighted eye—in which a clear image can be made on the retina only by bringing the object sufficiently near, by making the rays sufficiently divergent to put the focus on the retina. Then there are other eyes whose curvatures are irregular, in which lines at right angles to each other can never be brought to a focus on the retina at the same time. When the horizontal lines of the object, for example, are distinct the vertical are blurred, and when the eye is adjusted for the vertical, the horizontal become correspondingly indistinct. Consequently, such an eye can never, through any inherent power of its own, see clearly any object, eithter far or near. This error is called astigmatism, and is the most troublesome and annoying of all, being an extremely common cause of headache and other nervous symptoms.

From what has been said, it is clear that the muscle of accommodation is strained in the normal eye if the book is held too close ; that in the far-sighted eye this strain is still greater, because such an eye has to use a part of its adjusting power for distance, and therefore has less than the normal amount of power of adjustment for near objects in proportion to the degree of the error—the shortness of the eye from before backward ; that in the near sighted eye the muscles of covergence are strained, owing to the necessity for approximating the object too near; and the astigmatic eye, from the attempt of the little muscle, on all occasions, to do two things at the same time, or as nearly at the same time as possible. Operating under such unfavorable conditions, the astigmatic eye is easily fatigued by continuous work of any kind, as in sight-seeing, reading or sewing.

Having paved the way for an intelligent appreciation of it, we are now prepared for the statement that the main thing in the practical care of the eyes school children is to prevent too close an approximation of the book to the eye. It should be held at least ten inches from the eye. How is this to be done? By removing the causes of it. What are the causes ? (1) Insufficient light. Every one knows that in a dim light we must hold a small object closer to the eye than in a bright light. (2) Small or bad print. (3) Faulty arrangement of seats and desks—such a proportion between the heights of the two as to make the desk relatively too high, thereby pushing the book up under the child's nose, no matter how erect he may sit. Seats without proper backs, compelling the child, for want of support to rest himself by leaning on the desk. (4) Improper position in writing, which not only brings the paper too close to the eyes, but puts a further strain upon the external muscles, which direct and fix the eyes upon the object, by causing the writer to look obliquely instead of straight ahead and slightly downward—the natural direction. On this account, as well as because an erect position of the body is a necessity—not to mention other advantages—the vertical system of writing is to be highly commended. The above enumerated causes act upon all eyes, but with most effect upon defective eyes, which see with more or less difficulty, at best.

What is the effect of this strain upon the eyes? Whenever an organ is required to do an unusual amount of work, nature provides the extra power needed by sending more blood to it. So the over-strained eye is in a state of congestion, and often aches from the pressure of the blood. But the discomfort is not the greatest trouble. The nutrition of the eye is impaired by the irregularity in the circulation, the retina becomes irritable and sensitive, and often the other coats become softened and the ball being squeezed laterally by the excessive convergence, these coats gradually give way behind, and the ball becomes elongated.

It is in this way near-sightedness originates and is increased in degree. Children are not born near-sighted, but become so in the early years of their school life when their tissues, including, of course, those of the eye, are soft and plastic. Investigations on this line show that the proportion of near-sighted in some of the large schools, particularly in Germany, varies from 1 or 2 per cent. in the first grade, to 60 per cent. or more in the highest. The variation is not usually so great, but there is a marked increase as school life progresses. The darker the school houses the greater the percentage of near-sighted. The popular idea, that near-sighted eyes are strong eyes is an error; they are often weak, and not infrequently diseased—blindness occasionally being the final result in the worst forms.

Strain of any kind can be better borne by the strong and vigorous than by the feeble and delicate, and it should be kept in mind that anything that lowers the vital powers will react unfavorably upon the eye, as well as upon the other organs of the body. Nothing is more important to a proper performance of the vital processes than a full supply of oxygen, plenty of fresh air. Children suffer greatly in this respect in our over-crowded school-rooms heated by a close-stove. So, in caring for the eyes do not forget the proper ventilation of the school-room.

But most important of all to the eye is the proper lighting of the school-room. The aggregate amount of window space should not be less than 25 per cent. of the floor space; 33⅓ would be better. The windows should be high, reaching nearly to the ceiling, and located on the left side and behind, the wall in front of the pupils being always without openings—a dead wall.

In conclusion, I beg to suggest to all teachers the advisability of testing* both the sight and hearing of each pupil upon admission, assigning those with defective sight tn the seats nearest the windows, and those with defective hearing to the seats nearest the teacher. By doing this many a child would not only be enabled to do better work, but would also be saved the pain caused by unjust and undeserved reproaches.

---

*The State Board of Health has had it in mind to distribute test types with instructions to all our schools, but the appropriation has been too small to permit the expenditure necessary.

CARE OF THE TEETH.

THE N. C. STATE BOARD OF DENTAL EXAMINERS,
PRESIDENT'S OFFICE,
RALEIGH, N. C. March 4, 1898.

To Instructors in the Public Schools :

In consideration of the marked deterioration of the human teeth, so clearly demonstrated by the experience of all practitioners of dental surgery, the Dental Society of North Carolina has requested the Board of Dental Examiners to invite your attention to this most important subject, and to ask that you urge upon parents and pupils the great necessity for intelligent care of the teeth.

In obedience to this request we submit the following :

First. The premature loss of the teeth, and the disorders incident to decayed and broken teeth, are misfortunes of the gravest character, resulting not only in the disfiguration of the mouth and face, but absolutely destroying health.

Second. The critical period is from the third to the sixteenth year. The want of attention to the temporary, or shedding teeth, is fraught with great danger to the health of the child, and may be an incalculable injury to the permanent, or second set.

Third. At an early age children easily contract habits which may be difficult to correct ; particularly is this true of the habit of swallowing food without proper mastication, a condition which generally results from the inability to chew comfortably. Thus a mass of food is thrown into the stomach, unmasticated, and unmixed with saliva, in which condition it ferments, and half of its nutritive power is lost. Indigestion and chronic dyspepsia often result. Faulty nutrition, arising from the want of proper assimilation of food, prevents a healthy mental and physical growth and development.

Fourth. To prevent the decay and premature loss of teeth the simplest and most effective treatment is a thorough use of the brush, with a well prepared dentrifice, at least twice daily—in the morning, and at night before retiring. Those who cannot afford a dentrifice, prescribed by some competent dentist, will find English Precipitated Chalk answers well for the purpose indicated, at a trifling cost.

Fifth. Parents should direct and encourage their children to cleanse their mouths and dislodge all particles of food after each meal. Every child between two and three years of age should be placed under the charge of a competent dental surgeon, in order that even the decay of the temporary teeth may be treated, and irregularities may be prevented.

V. E. TURNER, D. D. S., President,
R. H. JONES, D. D. S., Secretary,
THOS. M. HUNTER, D. D. S.,
J. E. MATTHEWS, D. D. S.,
SID. P. HILLIARD, D. D. S.,
C. A. BLAND, D. D. S.,
Members of Examining Board.

I heartily endorse this letter and trust that our public school teachers will give this important subject the time and consideration it deserves.

C. H. MEBANE,
Supt. Public Instruction N. C.

The following circular was distributed throughout the State during the year 1897:

TO THE SCHOOL COMMITTEEMEN OF NORTH CAROLINA

PRINCIPAL POINTS OF THE PUBLIC SCHOOL LAW EXPLAINED.

To the School Committeemen of North Carolina:

For your guidance and direction in performing the duties of the important office you hold, I send you this circular of general information in regard to the school law.

Your services and your labor must be that of love and of patriotism, as there is no compensation provided for you. Upon you largely depends the success or failure of our public schools for the next two years.

FORMATION OF DISTRICTS.

The law requires the County Board of Education on the first Monday in July to divide the county into as many school districts as there are townships in each county. It does not require the township lines and the school district lines to be the same, but it does require that there shall be the same number of districts as there are townships.

SCHOOL NEAR TOWNSHIP LINE.

A school may be taught at or near a township line by the consent of the committees of the adjacent townships, subject to the approval of the County Board of Education. When children are transferred from one township to another, the *pro rata* share of the school money of the district from which they are transferred should be transferred also to the district into which they are received.

BALANCE ON LEDGER.

The chairman of each committee should obtain from the County Supervisor a statement of the balance on the school fund ledger due each school, white and colored, in his township, as the term of the old committee has expired, and the schools now pass under the entire control of the new committee, and the balance due each school will be disbursed by the new committee.

OLD CONTRACTS.

While the old committe had no power to enter into a contract with a teacher to extend beyond their term of office, yet several of the old committees have done so, and in such case the new committee should endorse and carry out, in good faith, all such contracts, provided they are reasonable and for the best interests of the schools, otherwise they need not regard such contracts, as they are not bound in law or morals so to do.

NEXT APPORTIONMENT, HOW MADE.

The next apportionment of school money will be made by the County Board of Education on the first Monday in January next, and each district's share will be on a *per capita* basis, as shown by the census report. To illustrate, if there are 10,000 children of school age in the county, and there are $10,000 of school money to be apportioned, and your district has 800 children, then your district will receive $800. The County Supervisor, on the first Monday in January, will mail you a statement of the amount of your apportionment. Your committee is then required to meet on the second Monday in January and apportion this money to the various schools, white and colored, in your district. The law requires that each committee shall have a book, and open an account with each school. In this book will be kept an account, not only of the amount received from the County Board of Education annually for that district, but also the amount apportioned by the committee to each school, the amount received from teachers from pay pupils, and the amount paid out for each school for teachers' salaries, for building and repairs, and for all other purposes.

NAME OF SCHOOL DISTRICTS.

The names of the districts of the various counties have been named and designated by the names of the townships of these counties.

The committee of each of these townships will number their schools as follows: School No. 1, white; school No. 2, white, and so on, until all the white schools are numbered in their districts. Then they will number the colored schools likewise, beginning with No. 1, colored; school No. 2, colored, and so on, until all the colored schools are numbered. We will suppose there are five white schools and three colored schools in a township. If there are $800 apportioned to this township, it is not divided among these schools equally, nor is it apportioned between them *per capita*, but to each school, white and colored, according to its grade; therefore, the committee is required to grade their schools and divide the money accordingly, so that each school in the district shall have approximately the same length of school term, as nearly as may be, each year. This is the *most delicate and careful work* that you will be called upon to do. Your powers here are broad and absolute, and upon your judgment and wisdom, in dividing this fund among your schools, depend the harmony among your schools and the success of the new system.

HOW SCHOOLS ARE GRADED.

By grading, the law does not have reference to the classes in the schools, but has reference only to the character of the schools, the qualifications and salaries of the teachers required. The grade of each school will depend largely upon three conditions, namely: 1st, The grade of advancement among the pupils attending that school; 2nd, The interest manifested by the patrons of the school in public education; and 3rd, The average attendance during the school term. Let us illustrate: If school No. 1, white, has a large average attendance, and there is educational interest in the community, and the children are advanced, their school, No. 1, white, should be so graded, and the apportionment to that school should be sufficiently large to warrant the employment of a suitable teacher at a good salary. If at school No. 2, white, no advanced pupils attend, all probably in the primary grades, little interest is taken in education in that community, and the average attendance is small, then school No. 2, white, should be so graded, and the apportionment so made that they will obtain a good primary teacher, at a salary commensurate with the grade of work required.

SALARIES OF TEACHERS AND LENGTH OF TERM.

The apportionment to the other schools, white and colored, in the township, will be made according to the conditions and requirements of those schools, as we have outlined above, but must be made with the purpose to give all the schools the same length of term, and consequently in apportioning the money the committee necessarily fixes the salary of the teacher for each school.

It will be observed, from the above explanation, that the money is no longer apportioned to the schools, white and colored, *per capita*, but to each according to the grade of the school and the qualifications of the teacher required therein. Two schools may have the same number of children in each district, but in one school the enrollment may be twice as large, the average attendance may be twice as large, they may be more regular in their attendance, and manifest more interest in education, and the pupils may be much higher advanced than in the other district, and to give to each of these schools the same amount of money as we have formerly been doing, is manifestly unjust, as I can show. Suppose each of these schools should receive $90 for their annual apportionment, and the advanced school should select a teacher suitable to the requirements of their school, at a salary of, say, $30 per month, then they would have a three months' school. The other school may require only a primary teacher at a salary of, say, $15 per month, consequently they would receive a six months' school. Here both schools had the same number of children in the district, and receive the same apportionment, but one had a three months' school and the other a six months' school. The new law disregards the number of children in the district in making the apportionment to a school, and considers only the average attendance, the grade of work required, the advancement of the pupils, etc., and gives all the schools the same length of time.

TAKING THE CENSUS.

The County Supervisor is required to mail to each committee, on the first Monday in May, each year, a blank report, on which they are to report the census of the school property and children, white and colored, in their township district, which report must be returned to the County Supervisor on or before the first Monday in June of each year. The census report taken by the old committee, this year, will not answer for the purpose of making the next apportionment in January, consequently it will be necessary for the new committee to take the census this fall for the January apportionment, blanks for which will be furnished the committees in due time.

AVERAGE OF SIXTY-FIVE PUPILS.

When this census is taken, if the committee finds that

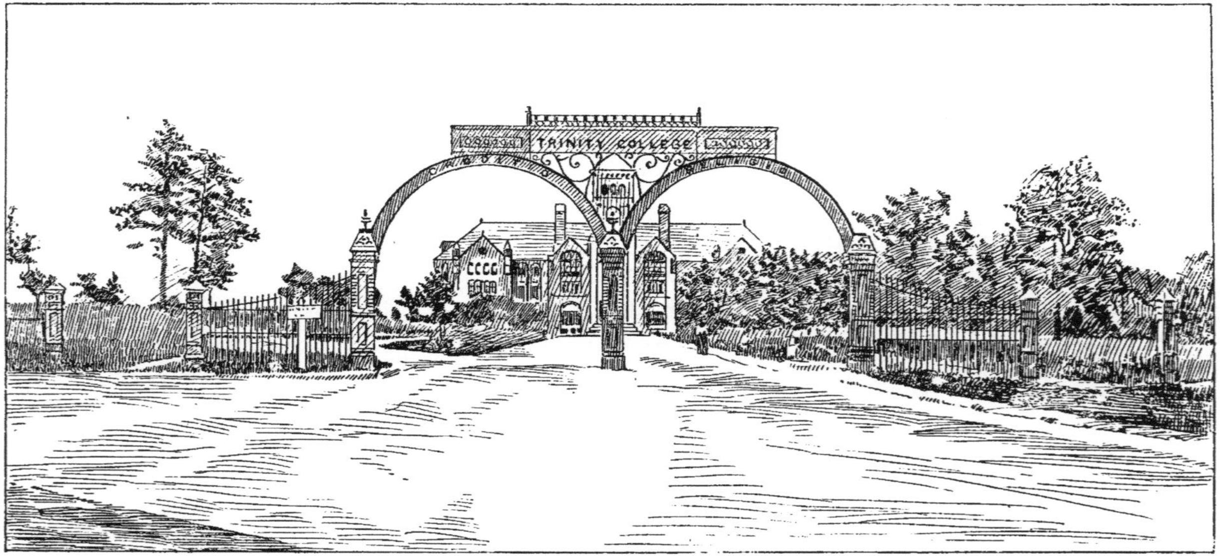

TRINITY COLLEGE, DURHAM, N. C.—FRONT ENTRANCE.

there are too many school-houses in the district, and the average is less than sixty-five pupils to the school, then it will be their duty to decrease the number of schools until the average is reached, or if they find they have the required average without interferring with any school, still, they should not hesitate to discontinue any school wherever it is possible to do so, and the children are not inconvenienced thereby. To illustrate: Suppose township A has five white schools and three colored schools, making a total of eight schools in that township; suppose the census shows that township A has 600 school children, then it appears that the average to the school is seventy-five pupils, and no change need be made either in the location or the number of the schools, unless by so doing the committee can better serve the school interests of their township. Suppose, on the other hand, that the census shows that township A has only 450 school children and eight schools, then it appears that the average to the school is only about fifty-six pupils, and in that case it will be necessary for the committee to discontinue some school in order that they will not fall under the required average.

The law does not require that each school shall have sixty-five children assigned to it, no more and no less, for, on account of geographical reasons, in certain localities, impassable streams and creeks, and sparsely settled areas, it will not be practicable to have as many as sixty-five children for each school, and for these reasons one school may have fewer than thirty children, but others may have as many as ninety or one hundred, but the average, in the whole school district, should be not less than sixty-five. Should it be possible in any township to have the general average as many as seventy-five or eighty, it would be better for their schools to do so, as the greater the average the fewer the schools, and consequently the longer the school term.

DIVIDING LINES BETWEEN THE SCHOOLS.

The committee of each township, on or before their January meeting, should fix the dividing lines between the various schools in their township so as to designate the school for the children in each locality to attend. These lines may be continued as they have been formerly, or they may be changed by the committee whenever by so doing they can better accommodate the children of the district. The boundary and description of each school should be recorded by the secretary in the committee book.

The committee need have no fear that the boundaries, as formerly established, have been too large, for they have been remarkably small, and the number of schools has been too large in many instances. I heard of one section where there are three small, weak schools, and the whole territory might be combined into one strong school, and no child in said territory would have to walk even two miles. Evils of this kind should be remedied at once.

SMALL ATTENDANCE.

While these facts are deplorable, yet the same conditions exist throughout the State. The census report for North Carolina shows that only 61 per cent. of the children of school age are enrolled in the public schools, and the average attendance is only 62 per cent. of the enrollment; consequietly there is little danger of making your districts too large, provided the children can reach the school-house without great inconvenience. When our districts are made larger and the number of our schools reduced (which can easily be done, as shown in the case referred to above), then will our schools have longer terms with the same money.

The respective County Supervisors and County Boards of Education will be ready, I feel sure, to co-operate with you, the committeemen, and will join in your efforts to enlighten the masses of your poor illiterate children in your respective counties.

C. H. MEBANE,
Superintendent Public Instruction.

LIST OF COUNTY SUPERVISORS AND MEMBERS OF THE COUNTY BOARDS OF EDUCATION—1898.

COUNTY.	SUPERVISOR.	POST-OFFICE.	COUNTY BOARD OF EDUCATION.	POST-OFFICE.
Alamance	P H Fleming	Graham	J W Holt	Burlington.
			[illegible]s W Vincent	P[illegible]t G[illegible]e.
			David H [illegible]n	Holman's Mill.
Alexander	A Frank [illegible]e	Hiddenite	J J Hendren	Vashti.
			A A Hill	[illegible]sville.
			J C Bell	Avilla.
Alleghany	Prof S W Brown	Sparta	S F [illegible]n	Ch[illegible]ery Lane.
			J T Evans	Piney Creek.
			H K Boyer	Sparta.
Anson	W D Redf[illegible]ern	Ansonville	W C Hardison	[illegible]ro.
			W F Crump	Polkton.
			L L Little	Ansonville.
Ashe	J W Jones	Clifton	D M [illegible]al	Graybeal.
			James B Woodie	Trausau.
			[illegible]ey Eller	Berlin.
Beaufort	Burton Stilley	Edwards	F B Guilford	Aurora.
			J[illegible]s L Winfield	Washington.
			W R Brinn	[illegible]e.
Bertie	R W Askew	Windsor	W A Capehart	Merry Hill.
			M J Rayner	Powellsville.
			[illegible]e P[illegible]e	W[illegible]r.
Bladen	D T Perry	Rosindale	Dr W K Anders	Gravelly Hill.
			C W Lyon	Lyon's Landing.
			Z G [illegible]n	Abbottsburg.
Brunswick	Isaac Jenrette	Iredell	E M Parker	Shallotte.
			J Johnson	Town [illegible]k.
			T J [illegible]tt	Southport.

LIST OF SUPERVISORS, ETC.—Continued.

COUNTY.	SUPERVISOR.	POST-OFFICE.	COUNTY BOARD OF EDUCATION.	POST-OFFICE.
Buncombe	D L Ellis	[illegible]ville	T B Long	Asheville.
			P H Folsom	[illegible]a.
			J H McDowell	Weaversville.
Burke	R L Patton	[illegible]n	J [illegible]hn A [illegible]	[illegible]n.
			S C [illegible]y	[illegible]n.
			J H Hoffman	[illegible]n.
Cabarrus	Prof H T J Ludwig	Mt Pl[illegible]t	Rev C B [illegible]r	[illegible]d.
			J M W [illegible]er	Harrisburg.
			A W [illegible]e	Mt P[illegible]ant.
Caldwell	Prof E B Phillips	[illegible]r	P G [illegible]e	[illegible]e Falls.
			M L Greer	King's Creek.
			J W [illegible]	[illegible]e.
Camden	C B Garrett	Shiloh	George H Riggs	South Mills.
			W G Ferebee	Gregory.
			S W [illegible]s	Shiloh.
Carteret	Joseph Pigott	Straits	W S [illegible]k	Beaufort.
			C N Mason	Harlowe.
			[illegible]h Daniels	[illegible]e.
Caswell	A E Henderson	Yanceyville	W G [illegible]n	Yanceyville.
			R L [illegible]ll	[illegible]e.
			J S Rasco	[illegible]s.
Catawba	J D [illegible]e	Conover	J H Hoyle	[illegible]n.
			J W [illegible]	Hickory.
			L H Shuford	[illegible]o.
Chatham	R B Lineberry	Pittsboro	Rev A T Edwards	M[illegible] Springs.
			Prof Alex [illegible]er	[illegible]k.
			Joseph A [illegible]n	Merry [illegible]s.

Cherokee	J M Lovingood	Marbee	J [illegible]mes [illegible]d	[illegible]y.
			J T J [illegible]s	[illegible]a.
			A K [illegible]y	Ranger.
Chowan	W F Watson	Edenton	M P [illegible]s	Edenton.
			A T [illegible]	[illegible]n.
			W B Felton	[illegible]k.
Clay	W J Winchester	Hayesville	George W Sande[illegible]on	Hayesville.
			[illegible]n A [illegible]s	Elf.
			George [illegible]	[illegible]e.
Cleveland	J A Anthony	Shelby	D S [illegible]e	King's [illegible]n.
			T D Falls	Fallston.
			H P [illegible]n	King's [illegible]n.
Columbus	W H Sellars	Whiteville	J D Maultsby	[illegible]e.
			C C [illegible]e	[illegible]nd.
			J W [illegible]n	Lake W[illegible]camaw.
Craven	John S Long	New Bern	[illegible]d H [illegible]s	New Berne.
			Sam W [illegible]n	N[illegible]w Berne.
			C E Palmer	New Berne.
Cumberland	H S [illegible]t	Stedman	John C Bain	[illegible]a.
			J T [illegible]ale	[illegible]lle.
			P N [illegible]r	[illegible]lle.
Currituck	F W [illegible]r	Moyock	J E C [illegible]ll	Shawboro.
			E D [illegible]n	Knott's [illegible]d.
			J F Summerell	Harbinger.
Dare	[illegible]uel Basnight	Wanchese	W C Pugh	[illegible]e.
			[illegible]n [illegible]e	[illegible]o.
			John W Ward	[illegible]
Davidson	[illegible]t S [illegible]n	Jime's	[illegible]e W [illegible]es	[illegible]n College.
			T H [illegible]r	Tryo Shop.
			R S [illegible], Jr	Jim's.
Davie	C M [illegible]ts	Advance	W R Ellis	[illegible]e.
			P M Bailey	[illegible]lle.
			D L [illegible]wery	[illegible]ty Line.

LIST OF SUPERVISORS, ETC.—Continued.

COUNTY.	SUPERVISOR.	POST-OFFICE.	COUNTY BOARD OF EDUCATION.	POST-OFFICE.
Duplin	[illegible] Millard	Kenansville	J C [illegible]	Teachey's.
			[illegible]	[illegible]nsville.
			R W [illegible]	[illegible]
Durham	[illegible] Massey	East Durham	[illegible] V [illegible]	Durham.
			R G Sussell	South [illegible]ell.
			[illegible] H Massey	[illegible]
Edgecombe	R M Davis	Tarboro	J H [illegible]	Tarboro.
			W T Mayo	[illegible]
			[illegible] Johnston	[illegible]
Forsyth	A P Davis	Salem	H [illegible]	Salem.
			W S Linville	[illegible]ville.
			[illegible] H [illegible]	[illegible]
Franklin	B S Mitchell	Youngsville	J F [illegible]	Y[illegible]ungsville.
			T D Farrar	[illegible]
			R L [illegible] (col)	Franklint[illegible]
Gaston	L M Hoffman	Dallas	F P [illegible]	Be[illegible]
			J R Connell	[illegible]
			Thomas [illegible]	[illegible]
Gates	J [illegible] Walton	Gatesville	L L [illegible]	[illegible]
			T W Costen	Sunbury.
			John S [illegible]	[illegible]
Graham	J N Moody	Robbinsville	O P [illegible]	Y[illegible]
			W C [illegible]	[illegible]ille.
			D A Taylor	Stecoah.
Granville	Alexander Baker	Oxford	G T Sikes	[illegible]
			Dr A J Dalby	[illegible]
			J A Fuller	[illegible]

Greene	Fred L Carr	Castoria	George W Sugg	Snow Hill.
			James S Smith	[redacted].
			[redacted] Taylor	Shine.
Guilford	Prof J R Wharton	Greensboro	J Allen Holt	[redacted].
			W T [redacted]	[redacted].
			J S Cox	[redacted].
Halifax	Col Aaron Prescott	Halifax	J M [redacted]	Halifax.
			J E [redacted]	[redacted].
			C P [redacted]	Dawson's [redacted].
Harnett	Rev J A Campbell	Poe's	B F Shaw	Lillington.
			[redacted]	[redacted].
			Duncan [redacted]	[redacted].
[redacted]	A J Garner	Peru	R A L Hyatt	[redacted].
			J R [redacted]	Platt's.
			J N [redacted]	[redacted].
[redacted]	R H Staton	Hendersonville	[redacted] Staton	Saluda.
			[redacted] P [redacted]	Pink [redacted]
			M S [redacted]	[redacted].
Hertford	P E Shaw	Winton	Solomon [redacted]	[redacted].
			[redacted] C [redacted]	[redacted].
			[redacted] C S [redacted]	[redacted].
[redacted]	H L McGowan	Lake Comfort	Zach [redacted]	[redacted]
			W B Swindell	Swan [redacted].
			T F Creele	[redacted].
Iredell	James A Butler	Statesville	J H Hill	Statesville.
			M W White	[redacted] [redacted].
			M K Steele	[redacted].
Jackson	J H Painter	Webster	H C [redacted]	Webster.
			A J [redacted], Sr	[redacted].
			[redacted] L [redacted]	[redacted].
Johnston	Prof Ira T Turlington	Smithfield	J A T Jones	Gulley Mills.
			P H C Dupree	[redacted].
			W F [redacted]	Pine [redacted].

LIST OF SUPERVISORS, ETC.—Continued.

COUNTY.	SUPERVISOR.	POST-OFFICE.	COUNTY BOARD OF EDUCATION.	POST-OFFICE.
Jones	W H [illegible]d	Trenton	R B [illegible]	Trenton.
			C D [illegible]y	Maysville.
			[illegible]	[illegible]r.
Lenoir	E A Simkins	Kinston	James W [illegible]y	Kinston.
			E [illegible]	Kinston.
			E A [illegible]s	Kinston.
Lincoln	J E Hoover	Hill's Cross-Roads	A [illegible]n	Lincolnton.
			[illegible]n H. Hoover	[illegible]
			[illegible]	[illegible]y.
Macon	J R [illegible]s	Franklin	M L Kelly	[illegible]n.
			J G Siler	[illegible]n.
			W J Evans	[illegible]s.
Madison	W P Jervis	Mars Hill	W B [illegible]d	[illegible]all.
			Ira [illegible]s	[illegible]e.
			C A [illegible]s	[illegible]d.
Martin	R J Peel	Jamesville	James A [illegible]y	Everett's.
			William T [illegible]n	[illegible]
			J P Butler	J[illegible]e.
McDowell	W F Wood	Marion	J S [illegible]y	Old [illegible]t.
			H A [illegible]e	[illegible]e.
			J L [illegible]n	Nebo.
Mecklenburg	R B Hunt[illegible]	Charlotte	W S [illegible]rr	[illegible]tte.
			J G [illegible]d	[illegible]te.
			S S [illegible]on	[illegible]e.
Mitchell	Augustus Masters	Glen Ayer	J S [illegible]n	[illegible]n Ayer.
			S J Bl[illegible]k	[illegible]e.
			[illegible]n M[illegible]st[illegible]s, Jr.	[illegible]d Hill.

Montgomery	Geo L Reynolds	Queen	H L Steed	Steed's.
			W T H Ewing	Sulpher Springs.
			T F Haywood	Mt Gilead.
Moore	Eugene M Cole	Carthage	W M Kivett	Carthage.
			J R [illegible]er	Spencer.
			T M Langly	Bensalem.
Nash	Maj L M Conyers	Nashville	M N Bissette	Glover.
			W T Taylor	Castalia.
			George W Coley	Rocky Mount.
New Hanover	M C S Noble	Wilmington	F W Foster	Wilmington.
			F J Dempsey	Wilmington.
			Jordon Nixon	Wilmington.
Northampton	Paul J Long	Jackson	B F Martin	[illegible]y.
			W E Harris	Seaboard.
			E B Lassiter	Potecasi.
Onslow	A W Cooper	Jacksonville	James B [illegible]ant	Sneed's Ferry.
			S L Gerock	Maysville.
			William [illegible]rell	Catharine Lake.
Orange	John Thompson	Cedar Grove	James H Monk	South Lowell.
			A R Holmes	Rock Springs.
			C H Burch	Chapel Hill.
Pamlico	D P Harris	Vandemere	J F Paul	[illegible]o.
			J F [illegible]ell	Bayboro.
			T J Sower	Merritt.
Pasquotank	Gaston Pool	Elizabeth City	John D Fulmer	Elizabeth City.
			N A Jones	Rosedale.
			John T Davis	Elisha.
Pender	T H W McIntire	Ivanhoe	John B Davis	Rocky Point.
			F P Flynn	Viola.
			T H W McIntire	Grit.
Perquimans	Francis Picard	Hertford	Elihu A [illegible]	Belvidere.
			Joshua Skinner	Winfree.
			Hezekiah Overton	Durant's Neck.

LIST OF SUPERVISORS, ETC.—Continued.

COUNTY.	SUPERVISOR.	POST-OFFICE.	COUNTY BOARD OF EDUCATION.	POST-OFFICE.
Person	G F Holloway	Roxboro	W D Merritt	Roxboro.
			J W Clayton	Woodsdale.
			John S [illegible]man	[illegible]h.
Pitt	J R Single	Ayden	Fernando Ward	Greenville.
			Jesse Cannon	Redalia.
			Albert Ward	Bethel.
Polk	S H Hudgins	Saluda	B F Wilson	Poplar Grove.
			J M Putman	Collinsville.
			John L Jackson	Walker's.
Randolph	N C English	Trinity	B F Blair	Progress.
			W H Watkins	Ramseur.
			J T Thornburg	Lassiter.
Richmond	M N McIver	Rockingham	Henry Fairly	Laurinburg.
			J D Yates	Rockingham.
			D M Jackson	Rockingham.
Robeson	W R Surles	Sterling	J P Price	Sterlings'.
			G B Patterson	Maxton.
			D M Hall	Rex.
Rockingham	E P Ellington	Wentworth	E N Anderson	Leaksville.
			P H Simpson	Simpson's Store.
			J [illegible] Jones	Reidsville.
Rowan	R G Kizer	Salisbury	Rev C H Rose	Zeb.
			P A Sloop	Vest.
			John K Goodman	Rowan.
Rutherford	C C Gettys	Duncan	N Scoggin	Rutherfordton.
			W P Watson	Sunshine.
			A F Morgan	Otter Creek.

Sampson	Street Brewer	Owensville	A R Herring	Taylor's Bridge.
			Willie J Faircloth	Chance.
			R A [illegible]gham	[illegible] Grove.
Stanly	J A S[illegible]ce	Albemarle	S H Hearne	Albemarle.
			J Hatchcock	Norwood.
			M F Whitley	Eferd's Mill.
Stokes	Prof M T Chilton	Danrion	D V Carroll	Mizpah.
			M V [illegible]e	J[illegible]el.
			James H Heytton	Sandy Ridge.
Surry	Jno Williams	Stony Knoll	John H Lowe	Westfield.
			J H T Callaway	Elkin.
			[illegible]m F Needham	Bliss.
Swain	J U [illegible]bs	Whittier	R L Davis	Bryson City.
			W H Owen	Ocona Lufty.
			John Burnette	Almond.
Transylvania	Judson Corn	Brevard.	Fitz Taylor	Brevard.
			J L Wicker	Brevard.
			Jesse R [illegible]en	Penrose.
Tyrrell	James L Norman	Columbia	J Warren Swain	Columbia.
			Allen Cahoon	Gum Neck.
			John H T[illegible]mas	Bay.
Union	Pl[illegible]mmer Stewart	Marshville	J Z Green	Marshville.
			J E Brown	Indian Trail.
			R N [illegible]	Zoar.
Vance	[illegible]Matics	Henderson	W H [illegible]ins	Henderson.
			B M [illegible]en	Kittrell.
			W M Henderson	Henderson.
Wake	H W [illegible]ris	Ballentine's Mills	J J Bagwell	Garner.
			J H Fleming	Raleigh.
			N F Roberts	Raleigh.
Warren	James R Rodwell	Warrenton	John [illegible]	Ridgeway.
			W E Davis	Creek.
			John P Williams	Warrenton.

LIST OF SUPERVISORS, ETC.—Continued.

COUNTY.	SUPERVISOR.	POST-OFFICE.	COUNTY BOARD OF EDUCATION.	POST-OFFICE.
Washington	W R Chessom	Mockey's Ferry	C B Latham	Monticello.
			P S Swain	Plymouth.
			H A [illegible]field	Creswell.
Watauga	L H Michael	Rutherwood	W H Farthing	Leander.
			L M Trinett	Boone.
			W H Norris	Boone.
Wayne	E T Atkins	Goldsboro	Col H C Davis	[illegible]o.
			W F English	Mount Olive.
			Barnes Aycock	Fremont.
Wilkes	James H Foote	Roaring River	B D Haynes	[illegible]k.
			W G Meadows	Moravan Falls.
			C H M Tulbert	Hunting Creek.
Wilson	James W Hayes	Elm City	[illegible] W [illegible]	[illegible]n.
			Nathan Bass	Black Creek.
			S H Vick	Wilson.
Yadkin	Rev J H Patterson	East Bend	A J [illegible]n, Jr	Marlea.
			A S Speea	Boonville.
			F B Benbow	East Bend.
Yancey	William McIntosh	Bee Log	John Hunter	Day Book.
			T W Rolland	Burnsville.
			James Smith	Micaville.

PROCEEDINGS OF THE MEETING OF SUPERVISORS IN THE HOUSE OF REPRESENTATIVES, RALEIGH, N. C., DECEMBER 30, 1897.

A WORD OF EXPLANATION.

This report is published by the Superintendent of Public Instruction, in accordiance with the Constitution of the Association of Supervisors.

I regreat that we cannot publish all the papers read before the Association and a full report of each general discussion.

The Secretary of the Association took down only a synopsis of the proceedings, not knowing at the time that we would publish the report.

I have written out, as best I could, from the Secretary's report, the general proceedings of the meeting.

I have copied a great deal from the report given in the *News and Observer.*

The Supervisors and I were very much gratified to see such a full and complete report of the meeting in the Raleigh press.

The Supervisors who were not at this meeting missed a great deal.

I feel sure that every one present went away more determined to make progress than when he came.

Inspiration and zeal were kindled here that will surely have its effect.

I appreciate most sincerely the sacrifice that was made by some of the Supervisors to attend this meeting. It speaks well for them and the cause they represent.

I wish to call *special attention* of *school officers* to Prof. Brewer's address on "Grading Schools in the Township."

I trust this meeting was only the beginning of what shall be at the future Annual Meeting.

This meeting was an experiment on my part, and I am well pleased with the result so far.

C. H. MEBANE,
Superintendent Public Intruction.

PROCEEDINGS.

Pursuant to the call of C. H. Mebane, Superintendent of Public Instruction, the County Supervisors assembled in the House of Representatives Thursday morning, December 30, 1897.

The Supervisors from the following counties were present, to-wit:

D. L. Ellis, Buncombe county.
J. D. Rowe, Catawba county
R. B. Lineberry, Chatham county.
Robt. S. Green, Jr., Davidson Co.
A. P. Davis, Forsyth county.
B. S. Mitchell, Franklin county.
Alex. Baker, Granville county.
Jas. A. Butler, Iredell county.
J. H. Painter, Jackson county.
Ira T. Turlington, Johnson county.
E. A. Simpkins, Lenoir county.
H. A. Grey, Mecklenburg county.
J. M. Deaton, Montgomery county.
E. M. Cole, Moore county.
M. C. S. Noble, New Hanover Co.
A. W. Cooper, Onslow county.
J. R. Tingle, Pitt county.
N. C. English, Randolph county.
M N. McIver, Richmond county.
W. R. Surls, Robeson county.
E P. Ellington, Rockingham Co.
Street Brewer, Sampson county.
A. M. Matics, Vance county.
H. W. Norris, Wake county.
J. R. Rodwell, Warren couty.
E. T. Atkinson, Wayne county.
Jas. W. Hayes, Wilson county.

H. W. Norris, of Wake county, called the meeting to order. Song, "Blest be the tie that binds," was sung.

Devotional exercises were conducted by Rev. E. C. Glenn, of Raleigh Central Methodist Church. The Scripture read was a portion of the Sermon on the Mount, followed by a beautiful and appropriate prayer.

Election of a presiding officer resulted in the unanimous choice, by acclamation, of Hon. C. H. Mebane, State Superintendent of Education.

Mr. Mebane, on accepting the chair, appointed J. R. Rodwell, of Warren County, as Secretary, and delivered a most excellent address on the object and importance of the meeting. He also took occasion in his address to pay a very high compliment to the press of the State for its effort in behalf of public education. He wanted it distictly understood that the object of the meeting was not to make a display of oratory, but to come together in a practical organization for practical and effectual work. He spoke in detail as follows:

I am very much encouraged to see you here. This meeting was called that we, as school officers and educators, might see each other face to face, that we may reason together for each other's good in the great work entrusted to us; that we may have the benefit of the wisdom and experience of each other in securing the best result under the present school law; that we may have unity of action for one great object, namely, the improvement and progress of our public schools.

I know you have the interest of the public schools at heart and want to make progress in your work, because you have made a sacrifice to attend this meeting in order that you may accomplish more in your work when you return home, and I sincerely hope that in this particular your expectations may be fully realized.

My sympathies go out to those who are with us in interest and good wishes, but are not able to be present in person.

It is a source of great pleasure to me, and I am sure of great encouragement to all of us here, to know that every single Supervisor has endorsed this meeting and expressed a desire to be present.

This meeting represents that interest upon which the future of North Carolina depends. The boys and girls of your respective counties of to-day are to be the men and women of to-morrow. What the future manhood and womanhood of our State shall be largely depends upon you, who are responsible to a large extent for what instruction the majority of the children will receive.

Would that I could, to some extent, impress upon you the greatness of your responsibility.

Would that you could more fully realize that the life and inspiration of the public schools of your respective counties must come from you.

Would that you could realize that you must make and create sentiment in favor of public education.

Would that I could make you more fully realize that the only way to make progress in our public school work is to keep everlastingly at it.

Would that I could make you realize that the most important and most responsible county office is that of Supervisor of the public schools.

What is our responsibility in this meeting? Great, you say.

Yes, it is even awful. Whose interest do we represent? Not that of any political party, not that of any party, but we represent the children of North Carolina. We are making history to-day. How long shall this history last? Shall this meeting and its results be like the morning cloud and the early dew, which soon passes away?

I sincerely hope that we shall sow seed here that shall spring up and bring the sunshine of intelligence into many homes that are now groping in ignorance, that we shall go out from this meeting full of inspiration and zeal for the great work of public education, and that the entire

TRINITY COLLEGE, DURHAM, N. C.—TECHNOLOGICAL BUILDING.

State may feel the effects of this meeting. Let no Supervisor hesitate to speak out in our general discussions. Let those whose names are not on the programme take no less interest in this meeting than those whose names appear on the programme.

We want to hear of the difficulties peculiar to any particular county. We want to hear of the success of any particular county.

In short, we want us all to feel that we are benefited and better prepared for our work by having attended this meeting.

The first subject on the programme, "Organization of Supervisors' Association" was taken up by H. W. Norris, of Wake.

On motion of D. L. Ellis, of Buncombe county, the Chair was requested to appoint a Committee on Organization.

The following committee was appointed: D. L. Ellis, of Buncombe; M. C. S. Noble, of New Hanover; H. A. Grey, of Mecklenburg.

At this point the Chairman read the following communication:

Governor and Mrs. Russell will be glad to receive the County Supervisors, principals, and teachers in the public, high and graded schools, and other friends of education in attendance upon the meeting of the Supervisors, at the Mansion this afternoon, from 5.30 to 6.30, and extend to them, through you, a cordial invitation to be present.

Sincerely yours,

J. E. ALEXANDER,
Private Secretary.

TO HON. C. H. MEBANE,
Superintendent Public Instruction.

Immediately after the reading of this invitation, D. L. Ellis, of Buncombe, offered the following resolution:

Resolved, That the Supervisors, now in session, most heartily acknowledge the receipt of an invitation to be received at the Mansion of the Governor of North Carolina this evening at 5.30 o'clock, and hereby tender our sincere thanks to Governor and Mrs. Russell, for this honor conferred upon our body.

President E. A. Alderman, of the State University, addressed the meeting on the "Training of Teachers." After some general thoughts on the great importance of public school education, Dr. Alderman said: The best way to establish in the minds of a community the great importance of public-school education, was a good school in that community in charge of a devoted, patient, and untiring teacher. The teacher is becoming a power. There was a time when the teacher—the school-master—was so distinctive in peculiarity of make-up that the Dickenses, the Washington Irvings and other writers caricatured him with glasses on his nose and with other funny school-master peculiarities, but now the school-teacher has an economic, a social, a business and a political function in life. He is a being reckoned with and consulted with. In North Carolina, not long ago, when it was found that there was some public school money in the Treasury, the idea was for somebody to come along and teach it out. The paramount idea was not to teach education into the children's minds, but teach the money out of the Treasury. This has all changed, or is changing. The teacher is, and ought to be, prepared to teach. They are being prepared and are preparing themselves.

If you want power you must prepare for it. The poorest teacher is the one that locks the door one evening and does not think about the school until the next morning. Thos. Arnold wanted his boy to drink from a running fountain and not from a stagnant pool. "He died learning," is on the tomb of Sir Richard Green. When the right kind of a teacher dies this would be an appropriate inscription, "He died learning."

Professional preparation is necessary. Books can be had in this day and time for mere songs.

The Superintendent of Public Instruction should prepare and suggest a little library of the very best books on the science, art and theory of teaching, for every teacher and Supervisor; they are available and cheap.

Character as well as culture is necessary. Culture without character, you say, is dangerous. Likewise, I would say, character without culture may be dangerous. Moral preparation is eminently necessary. Teachers, it is said, teach as they are taught, not as they are taught to teach. There is no room in the school-room for any but a good man or woman, pure and clean. That idea must dominate the school; there are great natural laws of morality, great natural truths that teach that a lie is a lie, natural moral truths that are written in the Bible, because they are truths. Study these laws, ye teachers, as a part of your great preparation.

The entire address of Dr. Alderman was practical as well as eloquent.

D. L. Ellis, of Buncombe; H. A. Grey, of Mecklenburg; A. M. Matics, of Vance, made short talks upon this subject.

Lieutenant-Gov. Reynolds was present and responded to a call from the Chairman to address the meeting. He responded most cheerfully and gave his hearty endorsement to all efforts that were for educational progress in the State.

"Grading Schools in the Townships" was discussed by Street Brewer, of Sampson County, as follows:

GRADING SCHOOLS OF THE TOWNSHIP.

MR PRESIDENT, LADIES AND GENTLEMEN:

By the request of our worthy State Superintendent of Public Instruction, I am before you to speak briefly on the snbject, "Grading Schools of the Towhship." Before entering upon my subject proper I wish to congratulate the assembled Supervisors, teachers and friends of education of North Carolina on some material and gratifying advances which our State has made within recent years. In the first place, let us rejoice in the fact that it is no longer necessary in North Carolina to discuss the question of popular education. This is now *res judicata*. As an original question it has been decided by the court of public opinion that it is best for organized society to educate, because it is cheaper to prevent crime than to punish the criminal, because the safety of a republic depends on the enlightenment of the voter, and because it is the duty of a government to instruct because it commands.

The common school is a rich inheritance from the fathers. This is all conquered territory—the fortified base of all future advance. It may be necessary to keep it fortified and repel occasional attacks, but it will never be necessary, in all human probability, to make the conquest again. In the second place, let us rejoice that the last General Assembly of our dear old State, though greatly divided and much confused over the election of United States Senator and the ninety-nine-year railroad lease, did not forget the educational interests of the State, but gave such aid to all our institutions of learning as was practicable under the then existing conditions. In all of which we have cause to rejoice, be thankful and take fresh courage. But the most signal advance, however, made during recent years, and the one in which all the friends of popular education should especially rejoice, is the "New School Law," passed at the last session of our State Legislature—the change from the little one-horse school district system to the "township system." It would be ungenerous, it would be unjust—it would be to a limited extent untrue—to say that a man's confidence in the "township system" is a measure of his intelligence as to school systems. But there is not, and there never has been, another question of school policy upon which the opinion of those qualified to judge was so unanimous as it is to day in opposition to the further existence of the little school district. The oldest American educational idea was that of Massachusetts, which looked to one elementary school in every town containing fifty householders, with a grammar-school where there were fifty more householders. A somewhat recent but more widely-spread idea was to have ordinary schools in every township, a higher school for each county, and a college or university for the State. The township was the unit of the whole school system. The little district, as we have had heretofore, was a territorial unit not only too narrow, but too variable to serve either as the basis for a wise distribution of school funds or for efficient supervision of the schools. Chance, caprice, sometimes the interests of a single family, or an insignificant village rivalry, sometimes, also, the prejudice or carelessness of a single man, would determine the fate of a locality in regard to its public school. The old district system has been tried; it was not liberty, but chaos. That it has proved a dismal failure no well-informed, unbiased mind will deny. But it is not my purpose in this paper to attempt to show all the benefits of the "township system," but recently inaugurated in our State. The first condition of progress is the recognition of settled issues. In wise minds debate precedes decision, but never follows it. Hence we conclude that the superior advantages of the "township system" is not a debateable question, at least in this assemblage. I have read of an old man who replied to a younger friend who attacked one of his beliefs, "Sir, my mind is weakened; I am no longer able to argue with you. But when my powers were as vigorous as yours are, I studied this question carefully, and I reached a conclusion which experience has made a conviction. I have no skill to defend it, but I have faith to trust it; I forgot the solution, but I am sure the answer is correct." Life results in little to those who have not something of this spirit. The algebra of human thought must have known qualities. The man who can never clear either side of his equation from X's will never advance. 'Tis true education abounds in problems. Its nature, its applications, its methods are matters of question in every detail. No two of you would give the same definition of education, unless you had committed some one's else to memory for use in an examination; and as an assemblage of Supervisors and teachers, you would be divided and subdivided if it was asked whether mental arithmetic should form a special recitation, whether spelling should be taught orally, or whether there should be a recess. And yet, well-read and thinking teachers know that some questions are settled; and therefore I hope every County Supervisor in North Carolina is in full sympathy with the "township system," and is using his very best efforts to make it a success; for, to be sure, fellow Supervisors, no one could intelligently expect to make any system a success unless he has studied it, has faith in it, and is fully in accord with it. I am heartily glad that there are no fine-spun theories connected with the subject which has been assigned me. No need of conception, perception, apperception, correlation of forces, nature stndy, etc., in "grading the schools of a township." My purpose is to tell you how we graded the schools of my county, what has already been accomplished, and the advantages I claim for the "grading system."

To my mind, there is no one feature of the present school law upon which its ultimate and sure success depends as much as it does upon the proper grading of the schools. In fact, it is the fulcrum on which the whole structure of the school law rests. Take away the grading of the schools, and it is robbed of all its benefits. In order to make a success of "grading," the whole matter needs to be judiciously managed, and the administration should be placed in the hands of intelligent friends of liberal public-school education. It is possible so to manage the new system that the new order of affairs shall contain all the faults of both district and township systems, and but few of the advantages of the latter. In such case failure must, of course, be the result. Great responsibility rests upon the Supervisor and the committee in this needful and delicate work. It is the duty of the County Supervisor to assist the committee in "grading the schools," and it is the duty of the County Board of Education to require the Supervisor to do the work and pay him for it Economy by the Board in preventing the Supervisor from doing this work will lose the county several thousand dollars each year. After my election as County Supervisor of Sampson county my first resolve was (as it has always been in the school-room) to heed the injunction Paul gave Timothy when he sent him out to preach, "Study to prove thyself a workman that needeth not to be ashamed." My county, like the other counties of the State, seemed averse to any change. I saw as Supervisor that there was much circumspection to be used, and really necessary to get all the information possible and to use to the very best advantage that modicum of common sense which I claim to have. I have been favored in having access very often to Senator George E. Butler, the author or prime mover of the new school law.

I procured the school statutes from several States which are working wholly or in part under the township system, but by comparison I found that our school law is different in most of its features from theirs, especially in the "grading system." We have the colored race—an important factor in our schools. Their interests must be jealously guarded and cared for, as well as the interest of the whites. Under the district system, when the colored schools were controlled entirely by colored committees, they were very extravagant in paying their teachers, therefore it requires a double discretion to grade satisfactorily. My first step was to have a conference meeting with the committees of the different townships throughout the county. I met them on separate days in each township and assisted them in grading the schools. We used the Superintendent's instructions, entitled "Principal Points of the School Law Explained." In "grading the schools" we took into consideration, 1st. The advancement of the pupils; 2d. The average attendance, and the inteeest manifested in education in the community; 3d. The number of pupils within the boundary of the school, and, lastly, the teacher suited for the school, and what he or she was really worth per month as a teacher. By thus "grading our schools" we have saved Sampson county the present school year over $2,500. The term of our schools is increased over three weeks for the white schools and four weeks for the colored schools. We made few changes in number and location of schools because we desired to obviate any radical changes, owing to the apparent opposition among the people to the new system; also realizing that they must be gradually brought into the "new order of things," and feeling that a mistake in the beginning might work an irreparable injury. Our prices paid teachers per month range from $35 down to $17 per month. The new law discontinued third-grade teachers and left only two grades of teachers, but this does not mean that there are only two grades of schools, for it will be observed by all the Supervisors that there are few schools in the county of the same grade or requirement for a teacher, consequently there are several grades of schools, with as many grades of salaries for teachers as there are grades of schools. Saving $2,500 a year to a county is not a small item for the first trial under the "new law." When the "grading plan" is rigidly applied, as we will be able to do in a few years, a much greater saving will be made. All my schools, 137 in number, are now in successful operation. The people know that each school will be of the same length as near as may be, and teachers and patrons are almost unanimous in their praise of the system, and it is daily growing in favor among both races of our people. I claim the following for the "grading plan": (*a*) Equal school privileges; (*b*) Impartial selection of teachers (*c*) Increased interest in and respect for the schools; (*d*) Higher education extended; (*e*) Economy of more wholesale and intelligent expenditure. The old district was manifestly and iniquitously unequal and unjust.

The grading system is advantageous to poor neighborhoods. Under the old plan, the money being apportioned per capita to the district, teachers and patrons of certain districts would succeed in getting every family attached to their district possible that they could use to advantage in building up their own private school, thus leaving a few poor families to shift for themselves as regarded school facilities. Fundamentally, the whole matter rests upon a simple principle, that every child of the State has an equal right to the education provided by the State. Grading the schools, and each school of equal length, is the panacea for the great disparity heretofore existing. I find selecting the teachers at the same time the schools are graded works admirably. It beats the old plan of the teachers canvassing each committeeman separately and getting Mr. Smith to say if Mr. Jones is willing he is willing. Then he goes and sees Jones and tells Jones Smith is willing for him to have the school. Now he has two of the committee secured, gets the school—is not really the choice of any of the committee and perhaps none of the patrons, and the school is practically a failure. In connection with the feature of the law that provides that all the schools shall be in session at one time, it prevents teachers from monopolizing two or three schools the same year, thus keeping as worthy, or perhaps worthier, teachers than themselves out of employment, and some of the schools taught at a season of the year when the children could not attend—all to accomodate some dear relative or other special favorite. "Grading the schools" also prevents dishonest and unprincipled committeemen from receiving bribes or a part of the teacher's salary, as has been sometimes done in the past under the old district system by both races. "Grading the schools" is a great advantage to the competent and true teacher. The two great requisites to a profession of teaching are discrimination in hiring and permanency of appointment. Both of these are promoted by the grading system. Instead of a multitude of ignorant and indifferent committeemen, unacquainted with other schools than their own, and hiring a teacher as they would stick an old hat into a broken window-pane, merely to stop a chink, choosing him instead of some other because he happens to chime in best with their whims—our schools are in charge of five efficient men, each school graded, which fixes the salary of the teacher. There is now no *cutting* of *prices*, as under the old system. The committee, with the Supervisor, can compare the work of the teachers and dismiss or promote, according to the work really done. The schools, instead of being a rope of sand, will have organic connection and form part of a system in which each will get help from all the rest. The wages of efficient teachers will rise, while the inefficient will be gradually dropped from the ranks. In short, the tendency under the "grading system" is toward the development of a profession of teaching where unprepared novices will have no foothold, and experts will command the respect and the salary their ability deserves. It is the fundamental principle on which economy of expenditure depends, that you must get what you pay for. One of the chief obstacles heretofore under the *old district* has been a lack of systematic and business like management. In one colored district in my county in which the average attendance was less than a dozen, the teacher received a salary of $35 per month. That school now, under the "grading system" is being taught at a salary of $18 per month, a saving of $17 per month in one school. From an economic point of view, the waste of the State school money under the old district system is both startling and ludicrous. One instance came to my attention a few years ago, where a young lady was teaching a public school with only two pupils, at a salary of $20 per month. She carried her crocheting, and one of the pupils her knitting, to the school-house, and the State paid for their household work. I could cite other cases equally as ridiculous, but the cases given show how the little public money we get from the State has been wasted by ignorant and prejudiced committeemen. I am sorry to learn that in some counties no attention at all has been given to the "grading of the schools." All the friction and disadvantages of the new system, with none of its benefits, will be the result in these counties where the schools are not graded, because the grading is the one feature of the new law, around which its success or failure depends. In those counties where they have not graded their schools the new law will not be a success, and I am afraid there will be a public sentiment for a change back to the old system. The reason of changing from thirty or more committeemen in a township, to only five, was to obtain wiser, better, more economic and judicious management, but all this change is a nullify if the schools are not graded. Again, how will the committe apportion the school money in January, if the schools are not graded? The new law says that it is not to be apportioned per capita, but according to the grade of the school. In conclusion, allow me to say, fellow-Supervisors, that the success or failure of the new school law depends, to a great extent, upon the County Supervisors of North Carolina. They can, by enlisting public sympathy, and trying to mould public opinion in favor of the new system, accomplish much good. It behooves us, therefore, to try, by all legitimate means, to create such favorable sentiment. Let us remember that "that towering over Presidents and State Governors, over Congress and State Legislatures, over Conventions and the vast machinery of party, public opinion stands out, in the United States, as the great source of power, the master of servants, who tremble before it." There have been autocrats whose will was law. There have been oligarchies whose decrees were unalterable. There have been assemblies whose edicts were undisputed. But no Roman Emperior, no Venetian Council, no French Convention, was ever so complete and so undisputed a sovereign as the power that rules the American people to-day. In former times the English people were accustomed to say, "lex is rex," and the same boast is sometimes made on this side of the Atlantic. But with us, at least, the assumption is unfounded. It is a well known fact that a law unsupported by public opinion is, in our Republic, a dead letter. Congress may enact it, the President may approve it, and the courts may affirm it, but unless public opinion sustain it no power known to a free public can enforce it. Let us try to get public opinion behind us, and you may be sure the average legislator is the last man to throw himself in the way of it. He would as soon place himself in front of an express train. We muat, therefore, *make* public opinion, which will support and endorse what we want. Let us learn a lesson from the past. What we have gained has been achieved, because in the course of time we have enlisted public opinion in our favor. And this will ever be the case. The success of all future effort will depend upon securing the support of this most inestimable of all moral and political forces.

Adjourned for dinner.

The afternron session was called to order by the Chairman at 3 o'clock.

D. L. Ellis, of Buncombe, discussed a plan for Supervising County Schools, as follows:

SUPERVISING COUNTY SCHOOLS.

BY D. L. ELLIS, SUPERVISOR BUNCOMBE COUNTY.

It will be admitted, no doubt, without argument, that the county schools ought to be supervised; and it is generally conceded that as now organized, administered, and sustained, it is impossible to give them any satisfactory supervision.

Indeed, the law creating this office and qualifying its executive officer, render it impossible properly to do the necessary work of supervising the schools, from the fact that it implies in its limitations that the Supervisor is not expected to devote his whole time and all his powers to this great and exceedingly important work. And let me say, that three hundred and sixty-five days are not enough time, each year, for any man to do the work required in supervising the schools in the smallest county in this State. How, then, shall any one of us hope to do this important business in eighty days—our school year?

At present we, as Supervisors, are acting mainly as clerks to the Boards of Education throughout the State. In some cases we are actually trying to teach and do the work of a Supervisor at the same time, stopping a day now and then, to run out to see about putting in stove flues or providing fuel for some school that has raised a complaint.

But is this supervision? Nay, verily.

Let me give my conception of supervision:

It is to have constant, personal contact and oversight of all the details of the school work that is being done by the teachers; to give that work its proper directions by suggestions, counsel and illustrative teaching, after a close inspection of methods already in use, and to look narrowly after the school-room management, the comfort and health of pupils; to shape public sentiment; to encourage the professional progress and growth of teachers—in a word, to grasp the whole situation, and legislate for each school to its best interests, by a perfect knowledge of its needs and remedies for the same.

Now all this is impossible for the average man to accomplish in eighty days.

The proposed plan of supervision is briefly this:

1. To subdivide the schools of the county into three groups, no two of which shall be in session at the same time, thus giving each section four months of school, subject to the proper inspection and supervision of the legal officer (Supervisor).

2. To require the Supervisor to give all his time to the schools, and pay him an annual salary for his services.

3. To raise the standard of teaching and the salary of teachers to the highest possible limit.

4. To require the Supervisor to be properly qualified by experience, training, and scholarship to discharge his duties efficiently.

5. To qualify and pay school committees for their work. But some one complains, "Oh, we can't do this; it is at variance with the law, the public sentiment, and we could not put such a plan into operation under the present educational system." I very readily and cheerfully grant that the plan is inoperative *now*; but are we working and planning for the *present* only. Not so, but the next two years, the next century, if you please

We are bound hand and foot at present, but I, for one, am not content to remain so bound.

Under the proposed plan, the same group of teachers could be employed in all the schools in the connty, thus making it possible to secure and pay the very best teaching talent obtainable anywhere. The skilled Supervisor, having four months to devote to twenty or thirty schools, could make his powers felt in the minutest workings of the system; he could easily gather his thirty teachers into weekly or monthly training classes, where a critical study of the science and art of education could be carried on. By an active public policy he could bring almost the entire mass of the people to a realizing sense of their duty toward the public school, and their enthusiastic support of the same.

Then, again, it is claimed, and with some show of reason, that the plan proposed could not succeed because the people would not send their children to school except in the fall of the year—that they are obliged to keep the children at home for work. Now, this is all stuff and nonsense. Who can blame any one from not patronizing the average public school as now conducted at inconvenient seasons? The schools do not *merit* patronage—that is why they are not crowded to the doors at every session. I have a few teachers in my county that teach from eight to thirteen months at different points in the county every year, in four months schools, and they always have about 80 per cent. or 90 per cent. of the school population in regular attendance. "The fault is not in our stars, dear Brutus, but in our" *teacher* and *school officials*—to change the quotation slightly.

The people will readily fall into the ranks under the proposed direction; and soon every school will be run eight or ten months by supplementing the public-school funds by private subscription, as is done in every progressive State in the Union.

It is clearly not sense or business to expect school committemen to spend ten or twenty days in the service of the schools during the year without some pay for their work. They are either a useless appendage, or else we have no idea of the fitness of things, if we expect them to do this work efficiently and properly without pay and without being duly fitted by special training for their duties.

I am firmly of the opinion that no one ought to be allowed to meddle with the school interests of the State or county without due preparation and certification for his duties, and that after such preparation, he should be paid a salary commensurate with his duties and labor.

The day has gone by when anybody can teach, when any lawyer, doctor, retired preacher, or the man who is out of a job, can act as Supervisor of schools. A good teacher is cheap at any price, a poor one dear at the smallest salary. It is an axiom that the article is always related in quality to its value in the market; so the price we pay our teachers is in proportion to their worth—small salaries, little teachers. You cannot catch real, live birds with chaff.

Let us, then, brother Supervisors, encourage one another in this great work upon which we are entering. Labor without ceasing for the upbuilding of every interest of your schools. Form a close copartnership with your school boards and committeemen, and outline a bold and rugged policy; place your ideal high and strive to raise it year by year. Let me beg of you not to be a "policy man," and try to secure your office for years to come by the effort to *please* everybody to the neglect of your sworn duty.

You will win both approval and criticism—the latter is your truest reward; for no man can succeed without opposition and criticism, often of the most violent type.

Remember that the thousands of children in your county look to you for their protection and guidance. You have taken a great responsibility upon yourself worthy to wear the badge of your office as Supervisor of a system of county schools in our grand old State of North Carolina!

J. D. Rowe, of Catawba, addressed the body on the subject of "Uniform Examinations." He treated his subject well and made some valuable suggestions.

An interesting general discussion was participated in by several.

A motion was made by D. L. Ellis, of Buncombe, to appoint a committee of five to take into consideration the question of uniform examinations, and to correspond with the various County Supervisors of the State, with power to act, if results can be obtained through this measure. The motion was adopted, and the following were appointed on this committee: D. L. Ellis, of Buncombe; E. P. Ellington, of Rockingham; Street Brewer, of Sampson; A. P. Davis of Forsyth; N. C. English, of Randolph.

"What may be done by combining some of our smaller schools," was discussed by H. A. Grey, of Mecklenburg. He was strongly in favor of concentration of schools at better salaries, rather than for more schools. There were already in his colony too many schools. His observations were thoroughly practical, and from his experience as Supervisor, which, at the request of some of those present, he took occasion to outline, in a very entertaining way. He gave his method of visiting the schools and of his present plans of bringing together two or more schools into one to the advantage of both teacher and pupil.

"What Supervisors may do to raise the standard of scholarship among our Public School teachers," was the subject of an able and most entertaining address by M. C. S. Noble, Supervisor of New Hanover county, and Superintendent of Wilmington Graded Schools.

Professor Noble emphasized the value of trained teachers, and said that the Supervisor ought to endeavor to get committees to employ such, even if by so doing the school term is shortened, for a good teacher can do more in one month than a poor teacher can do in two or three months. The value of a school taught by a scholar will assert itself, and then a longer term will be demanded.

Read the best educational books and jounals. Be men of scholarship yourself and strive to master the best methods of imparting instruction. Conduct monthly teachers' meetings and give outlines of model lessons.

After Professor Noble's address the meeting adjourned. The Supervisors, with their friends, some college men, high-school men and others, repaired to the Governor's Mansion. The receiving party was composed of the Governor and Mrs. Russell, the State officers, Private Secretary Alexander, Miss Belvin, Miss Bessie Belvin and Miss Ivey Hayes. The halls of the Mansion were never more brilliant, and formality never seemed less formal than on this pleasant occasion. Mrs. Russell knows just how to make the receipients of her generosity and goodness feel at home even on State occasions. The hour spent at the Mansion will long be remembered by each one present.

NIGHT SESSION.

The night session was called to order by the Chairman. "Moral Character as a Factor in Granting Certificates," was discussed by J. W. Bailey, editor of the *Biblical Recorder*, as follows:

MORAL CHARACTER AS A FACTOR IN GRANTING THE TEACHER'S CERTIFCATE.

CONDENSED BY J. W. BAILEY.

I congratulate you, Mr. Superintendent, that in the closing days of your first year as head of the Public School system of North Carolina, you have added the achievement of this meeting to your laurels. I congratulate you, Supervisors, upon the success of this meeting. It may no longer be said that our public school system is friendless; here are friends whose very presence is emphatic testimony to their zeal in the cause to which they have been called. If I mistake not, we have in your presence a token of the dawning of a better day for our public schools and a grander era for our noble Commonwealth.

You have heard to-day the discussion of some important phases of your work; you will hear others when I have taken my seat. But as I see it, the subject assigned me transcends all others. For though you have an infinite fund of money, and your schools run all the year round in reach of every child, and your teachers be learned as sages, our public school system will nevertheless be a curse upon us unless the teachers are men and women of moral character and make it their chiefest ambition to implant moral principles in their pupils.

Our State is a moral institution. North Carolina was not founded upon the theory that its voters should all be able to read and write; for it was founded in a day when this was undreamed of,—and though it is dreamed of now, it is yet only a dream—please God may it soon be realized. But our Commonwealth was founded upon the theory that her citiztns were, and ever should be, men of moral character, for it would have been the height of wild folly to deliberately entrust the destiny and the power of a great State into immoral hands. So, therefore, our State is a moral institution, in that its foundation rests upon the morality of the people of whom it consists and by whom it has its being. It is, moreover, a moral institution, in that its governing principle is a moral one—that of equal and exact justice to all men. For should you require of me a definition of morality, I would answer that morality is that principle, or system of principles, in a man that impels him to seek justice that is right, for all his fellow-men.

I can perceive how an absolute monarchy might sustain itself for a considerable time notwithstanding the immorality of its people; a king may rule by the terribleness of his sceptre. But even then the king must lay the foundation of his throne upon moral character, else in due season his sceptre will reap destruction. Trace any line of history you choose, and you will find one thesis writ large in letters of fire and blood, and that is, that no nation can endure except it be founded in moral character. When Israel forgot Sinai, God's own kingly line fell into servitude. Babylon with all her splendor, Persia with all her glory, Greece with all her culture, Rome with all her world-conquering power, and the empire of the mighty Napoleon, have passed like troubled dreams from the face of the earth, because deep down in their sources of life there were no springs of moral character, either for the people or for their rulers. If culture could preserve a nation, the sun of Greece had never set; if transcendent power were the essential of empire, Rome would still be mistress of the world; if mighty genius could make a nation, Napoleon had not died on St. Helena; if the favor of the Almighty could insure the preservation of a people, Miriam's harp had not been hanging on the willow tree all these centuries, Israel had not been scattered to the four winds of heaven. But it is not culture, it is not might, it is not genius, and it is not God's favor—it is, and is eternally, moral character in the nation, its rulers or its people, that make it strong to endure all the battering storms of political existence throughout all the trying tide of time.

True of monarchies, true of the past, a thousand-fold more essentially true is this thesis with respect to free countries in which the people rule, and of the present and of the future. And the truth comes home to us that North Carolina is a free country of self-governing citizens; the truth comes home to us that the sovereign of our Commonwealth is yonder citizen with ballot in hand. He is Cæsar, and if he fails, then has failed the last hope of free government. I say, in all soberness, that when our people depart from the principal of equal and exact justice to all men, which is the noblest expression of individual and national morality, government of the people, by the people and for the people is doomed to perish from the earth. Our nation is young yet; the testing crisis is in the future, and I am not so blinded with the achievments of our first century, nor so unmindful of present conditions, as not to believe that that future is near at hand, and to tremble at the prospect.

Shall the people of North Carolina be men and women of moral character? Shall our Commonwealth abide in the faith of the fathers; shall our State continue to do equal and exact justice by all men? Shall North Carolina endure a grand Commonwealth of noble freemen? I ask you, Supervisors, because the answer to the question rests not lightly upon those who have charge over the schools of the children to-day, the citizens who shall to-morrow stand with ballots in hand as makers and rulers of our State. I ask you, Supervisors, because you have charge over the schools from which the North Carolina of to-morrow shall march forth full grown. I ask you, Snpervisors, because the only hope of morality in thousands of our citizens-to-be rests in the moral character of the men and women to whom you shall grant certificates to teach in our public schools.

I am not unaware that there is some hope in the Sunday-schools, but I know that less than one-third of all the host of our six hundred thousand children are reached by these schools, and they inadequately. I do not underestimate the value of our Private Schools, but I must confront the fact that of all this rising host of citizens less than ten per cent. are reached by these institutions. I thank God for the great influence of the churchss which adorn our State, but I cannot be unmindful that our preachers preach to men and women, not to children, and that they do this for the most part only twelve times a year I take courage for the hope there is in thousands of our homes; but you know too well that there are thousands and tens of thousands of homes in which there is no ground for such hope—many in the cities and towns, many around the factories so rapidly increasing, and many out in the backwoods away from the railroads and the newspapers and the touch of the world. out yonder where the heart of North Carolina is.

I have shown to you the absolute essentiality of moral character to enduring government. I have shown to you that there is no hope of moral character in many of our future citizens save in the teachers in our public schools. I would to God that I could drive home to your hearts to-night this one conviction, that unless you withhold your certificates from charlatans, weaklings and scoundrels, unless you choose for teachers men and women of strong moral character, there is for many no hope at all, and the very foundations of our State are threatened. There is no way of obtaining teachers of moral characrer by examinations, but there is a way of selecting them by knowledge of men and it is your duty to use this knowledge in granting your certificates. If the president of the greatest university should stand a perfect examination before you, and you should know he was without moral character, in the name of all you hold sacred, you should refuse him your certificate. And as for the Supervisor who is moved in this matter by political motives, he is a traitor to his trust, to the children, to his State, and a shame upon his Creator.

You cannot teach the children morality out of text-books. I wouldn't give a peanut for a text-book of morality in the hands of an immoral teacher. All depends upon the teacher. One's character is determined by the environment of his childhood and youth. Heredity is powerful to assert, but environment declares and determines. As the physician can nurture the child out of the weakness which has been inherited, as the surgeon can straighten the twisted joint, even so the teacher can nurture the mind out of its weakness and cure the conscience of its immoral taint. If the teacher is true, all well; but if the teacher is weak or false, he can damn the children to a degradation of heart and conscience, which will be aggravated instead of alleviated by the learning they receive. Oh, it is a critical moment when a child begins school!

"God made men before he made books." The child in the school studies the teacher more than he studies arithmetic, language or geography. It is a thousand times more important that the child learn the right things of his teacher than that he learn anything from his books. I would rather have a million illiterate moral citizens to constitute the body politic of my State than one thousand immoral sages. It is character, not learning, that makes a nation strong and great. It is character that the child receives from the teacher; it is only learning that is gotten from the text-books.

Yours is the responsibility, Supervisors. If a man or woman of weak moral character is teaching in your county schools, it is your fault. If, by the influence of that teacher, the character of one child is injured instead of improved, the curse be upon you, for it was yours to prevent. You are the guardians of the children of North Carolina; you are the stewards of the State's most precious treasurer.

I am no dreamer, but I believe in visions. I have a vision of my North Carolina; it is not of her matchless resources—I am content to let them wait the inevitable fruition of time. It is not of her gracious rivers rolling their mighty waters unused, but not wasted, into the Atlantic. I am content with their beauty as they are. It is not of her mountains so rich in minaral wealth, so marvellons in their magesty. I am content that I may stand upon their heights sometimes and breathe the incense of heaven and worship God in the grandeur of his tabernacle. No, no, it is not of North Carolinia's material blessings: My vision is of her children to day, herself to-morrow. I hope to live to see the day when no longer shall her children cry for schools, when no longer shall her school-houses be closed forty weeks in the year, when no longer shall the minds of her children be sacrificed upon the altars of prejudice, politics and poverty; when we shall no longer be content with any but teschers of unquestionable moral character, and then I shall be content to depart without entering but having seen the era in which each rising sun that kisses our eastern waters shall grow brighter and each setting sun shall smile as it sinks to rest beyond Mitchell's lofty peak, beholding a race of men and women, "diviner but still human, solving the riddle old, shaping the age of gold," who serve each other as brothers, seeking the common good of all, equal and exact justice between man and man. I look upon the four months'

TRINITY COLLEGE, DURHAM, N. C.—EPWORTH HALL.

public schools, and a shadow seems to come over me; I look upon the teachers, and I yearn to tell them what destiny hangs upon them, I look upon you, Supervisors, and my tongue fails me to express my feelings. For my heart tells me that in these, and therefore in you, rests much of the hope of my vision. Please God, may it come true.

In the presence of the pyramids Napoleon inspired his men with rhe exclamation, "Soldiers, forty centuries look down upon you." We are in a presence more inspiring than they. Here the Father of his Country beholds us, and here the political redeemer of his Commonwealth—Vance—looks down upon us. Shall we not re-dedicate, re-consecrate ourselves to this cause, their cause, our cause, humanity's cause, God's cause, the uplifting our people by education.

The next subject, "General Course of Study for County Schools," was discussed in a very masterly way by P. P. Claxton, of the State Normal College. As a proof of the interest manifested in the splendid address of Prof. Claxton, the following resolution was adopted:

Resolved, That the Supervisors respectfully ask Prof. Claxton to formulate and publish, at his leisure, through the *Journal of Education*, the outline of the course of study discussed, for the benefit of our sceools.

Submitted by D. L. Ellis, of Buncombe.

"What Supervisors may do to secure needed legislation in 1899," was discussed by Charles D. McIver, President of the State Normal College. His address contains much that deserves careful thought and consideration. It is as follows:

"WHAT SUPERVISORS MAY DO TO SECURE NEEDED LEGISLATION,"

Was discussed by President C. D. McIver, of the State Normal College.

He took the ground that there was not a great deal of legislation needed, but that the local-tax election next year ought to be held on the same day as the regular election.

This, he said, would save expense and also insure more general public interest in the election and its results.

Without local taxation supplementing the State tax, no

system of schools has ever been satisfactory in this State or elsewhere.

He discussed township ownership of text-books and suggested it as a means of securing uniformity of books at a cheaper rate to the people, and as a means of securing a better attendance, as many parents keep their children away from school because they do not feel able to buy books.

The possibility of securing good school buildings by issuing bonds was suggested, as bonds are issued for railroads, new county houses, paved streets and other public improvements, where the expense of inaugurating them is too heavy to be borne by one generation.

The only two public improvements that go practically to every man's door are the public schools and public roads, and yet no bonds have ever been voted for them.

They are the most important permanent public improvements in any agricultural community.

He also advocated a mild form of compulsory education, by requiring that every boy who comes to his majority after 1905 must be able to read the Constitution of the State and of the United States, both of which he will swear to support, before he can vote. This would not deprive any man who is now unable to read of his vote, but would simply prevent recruits to the great army of illiterate voters after 1905, or such date as may be agreed upon.

In addition to the County Supervisors, it is necessary to have nine or ten District Supervisors, whose duty it shall be to stimulate educational thought and activity among the teachers and the people.

The State Superintendent is the only man employed for all of his time to act as a School Supervisor and educational leader.

Some one of the strongest representatives of public education ought to come in contact with each community every year. Such supervision and leadership cannot be secured by our system of County Supervisors, or the old system of County Superintendents. In order to secure the best service a man can give he must be employed all his time in one field and must be able to make his living in that field.

Supervisor Green, of Davidson, offered the following motion, which was adopted:

Motion, appoint a Legislative Committee of five, consisting of Hon. C. H. Mebane, Chairman; President C. D. McIver, Supt. M. C. S. Noble, Prof. N. C. English, and Prof. H. A. Grey: *Provided*, that any Supervisor shall have the privilege to submit suggestions as to what he conceives to be needed reforms and changes in our school law.

Made by D. L. Ellis and R. S. Green.

The following note of symyathy and interest was received from the Executive Committee of the Association of Academies:

To the Meeting of County Supervisors:

The Executive Committee of the Association of Academies of North Carolina sends hearty greetings to the County Supervisors, and assures them of the hearty sympathy of the Academies in the great work of public education.

W. T. WHITSETT,
Secretary and Treasurer.

Prof. Noble, in behalf of the Association of City Superintendents, assured the Supervisors of co-operation on the part of the city Superintendents to advance the cause of public education.

Prof. P. P. Claxtón spoke in the interest of the *North Carolina Journal of Education.*

After this, a motion prevailed adopting the *North Carolina Journal* as the organ of the Supervisors.

The columns of this journal are open to any Supervisor who has anything to say to promote the cause of education in North Carolina.

The Committee on Organization made a report, which was unanimously adopted.

The following is the Constitution adopted:

ORGANIZATION OF SUPERVISORS' ASSOCIATION.

CONSTITUTION.

We, the County Supervisors of Schools in North Carolina, do hereby organize ourselves into an Association, which shall be known as "The Association of County Supervisors of North Carolina Public Schools," and hereby adopt the following Constitution for our government and guidance:

ARTICLE I—OFFICERS.

The officers of this Association shall be: 1. A President, *ex-officio*, the State Superintendent; 2. A Vice-President, elected by the Association; 3. A Secretary, appointed by the President at opening of every session; 4. An Executive Committee of five, appointed by the Chair: *Provided*, that the Executive Committee shall be appointed annually, and shall be selected to represent as largely as possible the whole State; 5. A Programme Committee of five, appointed by the Chair.

ARTICLE II.—MEMBERSHIP.

The County Supervisors of the State and the members of County Boards of Education.

ARTICLE III—MEETINGS.

The Association shall hold one meeting annually, and the sessions shall be held at Raleigh, under the auspices of the Executive Committee, between the dates December 26-31, of such length as the aforesaid Executive Committee shall elect.

ARTICLE IV—DUTIES OF OFFICERS,

Section 1. President—The President shall preside at all meetings of the Association.

Sec. 2. Other Officers—All other officers shall discharge the duties that appertain to their offices.

Sec. 3. Programme for Annual Meetings—The Annual Programmes of the Association shall be published and distributed to the Supervisors sixty days before the stated meetings, by the State Superintendent.

ARTICLE V.—AMENDMENTS.

Amendments and By-Laws to this Constitution may be made by presenting them in writing and receiving the assent of two-thirds of the members present.

ARTICLE VI—QUORUM.

A quorum shall consist of twenty members assembled in regular session.

ARTICLE VII—MINUTES.

The Minutes of the Associatton shall be published by the State Superintendent and sent out to the County Supervisors.

D. L. ELLIS, Chairman,
M. C. S. NOBLE,
H. A. GREY,
Committee on Organization.

The following resolution of thanks was adopted:

Resolved, That the Association of Supervisors hereby express to the citizens of Raleigh their hearty appreciation of numerous courtesies shown to them; to the houses of public entertainment for low rates and hospitable cheer; to the State officers for the use of the Hall of Representatives; to the Railroad Commissioners for railroad maps; to our distinguished visitors, President Alderman and McIver; Prof. P. P. Claxton and Mr. J. W. Bailey, for their scholarly, admirable and timely addresses.

Submitted by D. L. Ellis, of Buncombe.

H. A. Grey, of Mecklenburg, was elected Vice-President.

After singing that patriotic song, "America," the Association adjourned.

C. H. MEBANE,
President.

J. R. RODWELL,
Secretary.

TABLE No. I.—1897.

School Fund Received by County Treasurer for the School Year Ending June 30, 1897.

COUNTIES.	State and County Poll Tax.	General Property Special Tax.	Special Property Tax. Local Acts.	Special Poll Tax. Local Acts.	Fines, Forfeitures and Penalties.	Liquor Licenses.	Estray.	State Treasurer.	Other Sources.	Total Receipts.	Balance on Hand Last Report.
Alamance	$ 4,860 00	$ 8,517 00	$	$	$ 319 75	$ 475 00	$ ..	...	$ 10 00	$ 14,181 75	$ 2,488 08
Alexander	2,230 00	1,715 00	....	.....	155 05	....	...	...	....	4,371 94	464 29
Alleghany	1,380 00	1,106 47	....	.....	44 98	....	...	...	....	2,537 45	1,587 75
Anson	2,305 65	3,536 41	....	.....	87 70	427 50	...	...	....	7,169 23	4,070 21
Ashe	3,598 50	2,289 39	....	.....	83 23	....	...	...	15 60	6,104 31	192 29
Beaufort	3,714 00	4,558 97	....	.....	31 30	1,480 00	...	...	234 61	10 018 88	6,174 53
Bertie	3 828 98	4,737 48	....	.....	258 98	2,097 50	...	...	134 49	11,057 43	5 347 03
Bladen	2,452 24	2,574 07	....	.....	57 06	....	1 74	...	521 11	5,606 22	1,872 26
Brunswick	2,101 50	2,207 81	....	.....	39 81	200 00	...	...	....	4,549 12	1 780 41
[illegible]	6 982 50	17,335 46	....	.....	249 79	....	...	...	....	24 567 75	10,084 16
Burke	2,770 50	3,054 24	....	.....	....	....	...	...	....	5,824 74	583 23
Cabarrus	3,900 00	5,854 50	....	.....	588 77	....	...	...	....	10,383 81	1,885 31
Caldwell	2,150 00	2,372 59	....	.....	93 51	....	...	...	....	4,616 10	161 21
Camden	909 48	1,489 40	....	.....	60 00	....	...	...	....	2 458 88	1,153 58
Carteret	1,451 41	1,152 33	....	.....	4 00	427 50	...	...	461 96	3,497 20	231 56
Caswell	4,822 00	....	....	.....	136 21	....	...	...	5 40	4,963 60	139 61
Catawba	8,450 00	4,450 00	....	.....	173 69	....	...	...	....	8,073 67	....
Chatham	3,787 50	4,918 15	....	.....	90 25	190 00	...	...	33 75	9,019 65	4 401 60
Cherokee	1,318 87	3,514 89	889 50	441 12	120 75	....	...	...	23 75	6,308 88	1,604 96
*Chowan	1,983 00	4,634 16	....	.....	26 35	641 25	...	...	5 75	7,284 76	....
Clay	....	1,456 72	....	.....	17 80	....	...	...	....	1,474 52	...
Cleveland	4,232 25	5,873 07	....	.....	525 49	300 00	...	...	29 00	10,959 81	2,946 52

Columbus	3,209 10	4,352 49			127 71	300 00			30 00	8,019 30	6,294 47
Craven	4,891 76	4,096 43			247 04	3,648 00				12,883 23	58 51
Cumberland	1,365 00	4,332 31			23 75				50 65	5,771 61	1,047 36
Currituck	1,633 23	1,505 18			42 55				30 00	3,210 96	
Dare	420 00	280 00			50 75	50 00			409 53	1,210 28	
Davidson	3,900 23	6,641 32			300 66	18 00				10,860 19	774 38
Davie	1,922 33	2,723 81			58 50				7 00	4,711 64	470 86
Duplin	3,157 80	3,709 59			48 46	95 00			1,317 16	3,328 01	1 728 54
Durham	3,393 94	17,496 81			166 33	2,310 00			71 25	23,438 33	427 69
Edgecombe	3,344 72	4,708 65			674 64	1,520 00			2,908 80	13 154 80	5,524 84
Forsyth	5,361 00	13,197 82			18 50	570 00				20,381 12	36 95
Franklin	3,957 42	4,112 07			160 40	1,520 00				9,729 89	2,842 47
Gaston	4,025 60	6,457 63			273 39					10,820 89	2,431 37
Gates	2,012 00	2,314 45			40 00	855 00			76 00	5.297 45	1,661 41
Graham	763 51	1,110 91			37 72					1,912 13	
[illegible]lle	3,796 00	5,001 12			122 75	650 00				9,569 87	2,077 55
[illegible]ne	2,371 68	3,304 31			221 65	760 00				6,657 64	2,318 53
Guilford	6,417 15	10,463 90			498 52	800 00			410 00	18,589 57	327 76
Halifax	2,234 28	6,625 42			22 12	3,277 50			90 00	12,249 32	6.345 10
Harnett	2,320 16	2,456 18			18 95	855 00				5,644 29	2,063 02
Haywood											
Henderson											
Hertford											
Hyde	1,695 75	1,677 77			39 47	443 33				3,856 32	3,291 48
Iredell	4,465 68	5,796 82			128 96	350 00			19 00	10.960 46	1,068 71
Jackson	2,437 14	2,687 15			78 25					5,202 54	
Johnston	6,360 12	6,622 66			133 65	1,900 00			386 65	15,403 08	4,914 90
Jones	1,487 70	1,841 93			25 00	444 60				3.799 23	
Lenoir	5,246 23	2,287 29			42 90				256 45	7,832 87	
Lincoln	2,639 10	3,232 80			64 25				332 82	6,268 97	881 52
Macon	2,307 27	1,848 70			27 74				124 00	4,307 71	
Madison	7,356 87				149 40	190 00			100 00	7,696 27	1 14
Martin	2,785 88	3,954 27			113 60	1,995 00			20 00	8,868 75	8,448 86

*Report for six months.

TABLE No I.—Continued.

Counties.	State and County Poll Tax.	General Property Special Tax.	Special Property Tax. Local Acts.	Special Poll Tax. Local Acts.	Fines, Forfeitures and Penalties.	Liquor Licenses.	Estray.	State Treasurer.	Other Sources.	Total Receipts.	Balance on Hand Last Report.
McDowell	......	......	......	......	......	......	...	...	......	......	......
Mecklenburg	8,584 92	18,408 87	......	......	904 07	3,211 00	...	...	371 50	31,480 36	6,821 86
Mitchell	......	......	......	......	......	......	...	...	......	......	......
Montgomery	2,191 48	2,136 90	......	83 70	104 14	......	...	...	......	4,516 23	2,160 01
Moore	4,114 00	5,194 00	......	......	378 17	......	6 00	...	......	9,692 17	700 00
Nash	3,421 00	5,711 13	......	......	416 46	1,356 06	...	...	86 00	10,989 65	......
New Hanover	2,996 82	12,352 22	......	......	158 70	11,058 00	...	...	511 52	27,057 16	3,153 42
Northampton	4,111 23	5,650 32	......	......	34 80	300 00	...	...	445 55	10,531 90	2,143 78
Onslow	2,392 78	2,840 02	......	......	88 90	437 00	...	...	......	5,759 70	3,300 36
Orange	1,700 00	4,552 99	......	......	271 33	......	...	...	10 00	6,514 32	......
Pamlico	1,161 00	1,476 56	......	......	5 81	......	...	...	......	2,643 37	2,112 99
Pasquotank	2,245 00	3,693 56	......	......	23 25	2,261 00	...	...	44 62	8,267 43	356 15
Pender	1,969 58	2,830 96	......	......	6 83	190 00	...	...	......	4,997 37	2,753 14
Perquimans	2,091 00	2,787 39	......	......	......	......	...	...	545 05	5,423 44	......
Person	1,380 40	4,894 09	......	......	......	......	...	...	......	6,274 49	......
Pitt	*11,415 93	......	......	......	343 30	3,074 00	...	...	66 45	14,901 69	1,225 64
Polk	926 00	2,617 00	......	......	38 75	90 00	...	...	......	3,066 75	50 00
Randolph	6,391 15	5,724 00	......	......	178 75	......	...	...	......	12,293 90	......
Richmond	3,885 97	5,381 29	......	......	293 35	522 50	...	...	......	10,083 11	6,134 99
Robeson	6,376 12	5,481 65	......	......	190 85	......	...	...	68 93	12,117 55	3,758 69
Rockingham	5,634 00	7,773 03	......	......	255 45	3,300 00	...	...	47 50	17,009 98	†1,669 04
Rowan	3,703 88	9,666 54	......	......	271 10	750 50	...	...	23 31	14,415 33	2,061 39
Rutherford	4,500 00	4,537 50	......	......	223 41	......	...	...	100 70	9,361 61	152 47

Sampson	4,275 00	3,270 13			41 04	760 00			478 85	8,825 02	1,813 22
Stanly	2,383 50	2,472 52			73 02					4,929 04	250 85
Stokes	3,633 72	3,179 54			159 00	600 00			5 00	7,577 26	
Surry	4,145 80	4,462 07			112 46				504 06	9,224 39	2,436 95
Swain	2,000 01	1,338 73			25 00					1,212 56	‡2,151 17
Transylvania	1,265 40	1,566 81			18 75					2,850 96	2,548 55
Tyrrell	1,051 15	882 71			5 06	9 00				1,947 92	1,963 22
Union	4,435 75	5,496 57			100 10	570 00			5 65	10,608 07	3,488 96
Vance	2,240 73	5,260 28			47 23	950 00	1 75		90 00	8,589 99	1,030 61
Wake	7,000 00	19,604 52	12,277 63		417 47	2,175 50			4 85	41,479 97	11,682 32
Warren	3,195 08	4,449 58			33 00	1,000 00				8,677 66	439 17
Washington	2,233 19	1,822 77			117 45	1,710 00			38 80	5,922 21	3,909 86
Watauga	2,361 23	2,047 29			65 00					4,473 52	909 80
Wayne	5,432 87	9,500 20			273 18	1,064 00			3,949 01	20,219 26	5,764 64
Wilkes	4,323 00	3,113 22			207 98	150 00				7,804 20	
Wilson	4,760 11	6,599 44			151 35	1,670 00			484 07	13,664 97	6,093 13
Yadkin	2,860 00	2,299 74			216 06					5,375 80	432 12
Yancey	352 12	923 96			35 28					1,311 36	1,196 81
Total	$ 305,647 93	$ 416,183 00	$ 13,167 13	$ 524 82	$ 13,507 85	$ 65,998 74	$ 9 49		$ 15,986 15	$ 822,757 09	$ 187,771 33

*General property tax included. †Overpaid by order Commissioners. ‡Due by Sheriff.

TABLE No. II—1897.

School Fund Disbursed by County Treasurer for School Year Ending June 30, 1897.

Counties.	Paid Teachers of White Schools.	Paid Teachers of Color'd Schools.	Paid for School Houses and sites (white).	Paid for School Houses and sites (colored).	Paid County Superintendents.	Paid Treasurers' Commissions.	Paid Mileage and per diem Board of Education.	Paid Expenses of Board of Education.	Paid to City Schools.	Paid for other Purposes.	Total Disbursements.
Alamance	$ 7,620 29	$ 2,984 08	$ 3,636 24	$ 305 13	$	$ 295 19	$ 89 67	$ 9 78	$	$ 213 97	$ 15,154 45
Alexander	3,475 90	331 75									3,807 65
Alleghany	2,448 57	281 96	205 87	57 02		30 00		12 00			3,035 42
Anson	3,153 23	2,880 46	532 93	490 82		151 26	45 00	1 00		459 29	7,714 62
Ashe	4,260 85	214 90	634 82			103 85	82 20				5,296 62
Beaufort	5,979 23	3,068 88	7 80	37 00		597 50	35 80			654 62	10,380 62
Bertie	5,017 92	5,294 85	398 29	221 50		282 25	15 50			664 61	11,844 44
Bladen	2,765 47	1,976 66	254 00	287 50		106 35	92 10	93 67		29 20	5,604 95
Brunswick	2,280 23	1,063 33	221 00	68 15		118 13	48 30			73 71	3,872 85
Buncombe	13,161 18	1,734 75	65 00	6 25		513 71			6,295 10	5,514 96	27,290 95
Burke	3,867 63	1,008 27				116 50				299 24	5,283 64
Cabarrus	5,591 31	2,134 46	169 98	96 02		215 82			2,800 00		11,007 59
Caldwell	3,764 96	627 45	251 58	65 97		94 20					4,804 16
Camden	1,851 72	964 71				74 93	33 30			458 16	3,382 82
Carteret	1,400 74	602 91				42 60	43 25			83 31	2,172 81
Caswell	2,317 82	2,618 16				105 52	112 06	5 00		233 68	5,392 24
Catawba	6,100 32	1,150 95	285 31	72 75		163 45				350 71	8,123 49
Chatham	5,499 72	3,384 60	264 70	627 43		154 29				509 57	10,440 31
Cherokee	5,101 85	213 50	30 00	121 07		121 07	9 00	9 00	51 33	641 00	6,176 89
*Chowan	2,261 86	2,208 70			33 00	102 81	13 20	77		623 20	5,243 54
Clay	1,372 39	37 35	20 45			29 33					1,459 52
Cleveland	9,557 16	2,443 04	538 18	104 80		215 93	19 00	13 24		20 81	12,950 16

Col[umbus?]	4 865 54	2,738 31	373 61	219 46		185 04	33 70			1,011 61	9,417 27
[Craven?]	5,288 68	5,067 46	172 86	560 33		225 50				185 50	11.500 33
Cumberland	3,316 98	2,218 61	28 00	54 00		136 26				161 96	6,815 81
Currituck	2,116 76	703 53	167 71	113 92		61 04					3,162 99
Dare	369 50		228 53	17 12		15 24					625 14
Davidson	7,762 06	1.790 39	696 48	106 55		232 69				1.046 40	11.634 57
Davie	3,270 87	1,213 38				99 36				293 86	5,067 57
[Duplin?]	4,730 68	2.379 98	316 81	253 99		155 96	19 70	92 19			7.949 21
Durham	8,985 61	6 252 98	373 51	109 20		561 66			3 758 30	2 984 91	23,886 17
Edgecombe	5,942 01	4 909 03	490 25	142 67		239 37	89 75		2,560 56	328 65	14,702 29
Forsyth	9,375 21	2 884 02		2,641 79		457 51			3,195 00		18.553 53
Franklin	4,914 84	4,177 77	377 83	94 20		194 60	58 00	85 00		92 00	9,994 24
Gaston	6,940 12	2,868 02	314 50	193 00		227 98	22 50	29 95		606 45	11 202 52
[Gates?]	2,155 25	2,143 59	130 43	78 97		95 24	22 60	35 48		220 34	4 881 81
Graham	1.409 95		442 69			37 49		6 00		16 00	1.912 13
[Granville?]	4,744 41	4.646 51	384 24	475 92		206 35	66 45				10.524 08
[Greene?]	2,799 00	2,241 40	285 59	131 47		113 95	240 48				5,811 89
Guilford	12.787 20	3,892 22	994 40	211 61		451 26		30 00			18 366 69
Halifax	5,091 72	7,246 66	1,346 14	1,500 55		327 82	768 60	132 94			17,726 13
Harnett	3 070 23	1,678 09	175 01	221 25		157 86	111 10	3 65		3 00	5,420 19
Haywood											
Henderson	5,845 91	1,039 84	363 10	79 12	22 00	100 00				105 10	7 554 97
Hertford											
Hyde	1,768 95	1,118 95	592 62			74 36	36 60	1 94		237 70	3,825 12
Iredell	6.862 17	3,798 83	198 74			202 00		48 00			10,069 74
Jackson	4,499 05	163 80	346 10	8 64	51 92	101 83	18 20			4 10	5,193 64
Johnston	10,888 36	2,551 78	934 57	378 99		306 80		400 00		1,288 52	16,749 02
Jones	859 26	997 18				43 03				295 08	2,194 55
Lenoir	2,809 54	2,102 17	333 89	127 88		300 43		55 16		122 40	
Lincoln	4,667 16	1,298 95	93 92	7 65		127 28	53 40	3 94		139 60	6 491 50
Macon	3,482 00	291 44	355 35	23 15		41 82					4,193 76
Madison	7,288 22	214 45				150 05					7,652 72
Martin	4,324 93	2.902 77	559 99	295 39		162 13				20 00	8.265 21

*For six months.

TABLE No. II—Continued.

Counties.	Paid Teachers of White Schools.	Paid Teachers of Color'd Schools.	Paid for School Houses and sites (white).	Paid for School Houses and sites (colored).	Paid County Superintendents	Paid Treasurers' Commissions.	Paid Mileage and per diem Board of Education.	Paid Expenses of Board of Education.	Paid to City Schools.	Paid for other Purposes.	Total Disbursements.
McDowell											
Mecklenburg	15,300 98	6,955 45	549 42	106 29		654 88	18 00		6,840 80	2,274 77	32,700 59
Mitchell											
Montgomery	3,695 69	1,247 57				102 61		89 06			5,134 93
Mre	5,252 22	2,685 84	104 05	231 64		186 34	26 40	31 31		85 55	8,585 35
Nash	6,970 63	5,062 34	209 08	250 00		212 60	20 70			854 99	13,580 34
New Hanover	10,606 00	7,393 00	652 51	420 56		466 56			1,800 00	2,467 61	23,806 24
Northampton	4,389 50	4,584 42	671 99	140 30		221 35	107 80			1,185 49	11,300 85
New	3,710 70	1,459 11	150 06	213 71		134 60	38 60	1 38		1,196 90	6,905 06
Orange	3,547 61	1,983 81	302 95	69 95		130 40	33 95	75 10		363 50	6,507 27
1 Mo	1,837 06	993 61	11 10	69 57		58 73	25 29				2,995 36
Pasquotank	3,352 38	2,503 80	1,229 36	25 90		157 33	19 30			768 64	8,056 71
Pender	2,201 93	2,186 48	275 52	374 13		100 76	53 23	58 57			5,250 62
Perquimans	2,477 13	1,819 08	122 22	77 98		126 94	14 70	30 00		617 09	5,285 14
Person	2,967 93	2,412 60	418 80	50 25		156 85		35 40		119 07	6,160 49
Pitt	7,308 36	5,517 75	65 00	215 00		310 83		44 70		2,390 98	5,852 62
Polk	2,039 99	558 68	15 35			56 52	101 85			10 50	2,782 89
Randolph	10,008 59	1,702 85				245 88	98 59			300 40	12,356 31
Richmond	4,435 12	4,697 12	1,144 79	939 73		227 50		168 48			11,602 74
Robeson	5,539 33	6,185 48	384 03	520 01		264 24	34 75	551 40			13,479 24
Rockingham	7,718 69	4,192 94	652 15	598 99		318 55		122 80	2,030 00	2,432 71	18,679 02
Rowan	11,019 87	3,518 47	530 06	194 23		312 07	163 30	4 50		173 10	15,915 60
Rutherford	6,826 95	1,488 50	122 49	111 38		172 23		62 37			8,783 92

Sampson	5,031 61	3,104 62	470 34	338 58		182 05	14 60	122 60			9,284 40
Stanly	4,405 27	600 00	205 31	10 00		104 77	10 65	7 60			5,343 60
Stokes	6,113 29	977 59				220 79	43 17				7,354 84
Surry	5,123 00	589 80	94 50			115 94	27 65				6,395 43
Swain	1,118 81	70 00				23 75					1,272 56
Transylvania	2,263 81	241 50	88 10	8 17		52 03					2,653 61
Tyrrell	1,572 97	495 56	72 47			45 24	21 95	14 45		129 75	2,352 59
Union	6,666 36	2,887 56	638 30	134 87	34 15	206 44	13 90	16 83		957 07	11,555 48
Vance	3,004 60	3,667 80	256 40	161 40		163 55	72 00			1,015 73	8,341 48
Wake	17,243 40	12,367 31	161 42	354 01		886 31			1,756 42	6,934 81	39,703 68
Warren	3,603 02	3,984 49	348 81	246 68		174 05	29 50			490 30	8,876 85
Washington	3,131 08	2,349 85	642 70	231 47		129 36	35 30	2 50		75 23	6,597 49
Watauga	4,488 47	226 78	103 20			96 73		14 00		3 80	4,932 98
Wayne	8,498 80	6,949 87	833 30	817 06		298 66	55 40	441 82	3,403 25	54 29	21,352 95
Wilkes	5,485 50	628 32	73 95			144 55	65 71			1,019 95	7,417 98
Wilson	7,201 37	6,165 12				273 03				284 85	13,924 37
Yadkin	4,125 84	599 96	342 50	14 14		101 93		13 48			5,197 85
Yancey	2,164 60	72 49	102 86			26 22	8 00				2,374 17
Total	$ 451,474 84	$ 227,195 27	$ 30,663 63	$ 16,507 61	$ 141 07	$ 17,269 77	$ 3,217 62	$ 2,976 26	$ 34,490 76	$ 46,292 90	$ 832,836 25

*Amount overpaid. †Due by Sheriff.

TABLE No. III.

Showing Number of Children Between Six and Twenty-one Years of Age. Number Enrolled, Average Attendance and Institute Statistics in the Several Counties of the State During the School Year Ending June 30, 1897.

COUNTIES.	CENSUS OF WHITE CHILDREN.			ENROLLMENT OF WHITE CHILDREN.			Average Attendance of White Children.	CENSUS OF COLORED CHILDREN.			ENROLLMENT OF COLORED CHILDREN.			Average Attendance of Colored Children.
	Male.	Female.	Total.	Male.	Female.	Total.		Male.	Female.	Total.	Male.	Female.	Total.	
Alamance	3,173	3,463	6,636	1,585	1,428	3,013	1,212	1,232	1,189	2,421	714	700	1,414	728
Alexander	1,741	1,766	3,507	1.267	1,036	2,303	28	196	203	399	125	137	257	18
Alleghany	1,362	1,274	2,636	924	821	1,745	30	128	110	238	36	30	66	12
Anson	2,026	1,842	3.868	1,048	906	1,954	1,411	1,997	1,938	3,915	962	1,006	1,968	1,205
Ashe	3,471	3,175	6,646	2,534	2,030	4.564	2,618	155	148	303	81	56	137	74
Beaufort	2.323	2,302	4,625	1,481	1,433	2,914	1,678	1,838	1,959	3,797	1,066	1,510	......	1,740
Bertie	1,662	1 530	3,192	875	797	1,672	1,017	2,456	2.355	4,811	1,316	1,413	2,719	1,670
Bladen	1,778	1,828	3,606	1,096	994	2,090	1,411	1,476	1,544	3,020	1,173	1,481	2,654	1.639
Brunswick	1,184	1,133	2,317	695	658	1.353	864	876	905	1,781	350	442	792	508
Buncombe	6.277	6,012	12,289	3,979	3,727	7,706	4,427	1,307	1,321	2 628	704	628	1,332	749
Burke	2,714	2,283	4,997	486	690	1,276	1,334	1,240	1.140	2,380	241	253	494	276
Cabarrus	2,852	2,839	5,691	1,315	1,154	2,469	1,596	1,006	949	1,955	472	430	902	515
Caldwell	2,424	2,389	4,813	1,195	1,106	2,301	2,259	402	373	775	197	185	382	18
Camden	540	552	1,092	350	376	726	460	377	375	752	225	218	443	266
Carteret	1,592	1,484	3,076	616	557	1,173	763	387	339	726	148	164	312	175
[illegible]ll	968	1,296	2 282	540	805	1,345	18	1,148	1,515	2,663	608	850	1,458	20
Catawba	3 362	3.143	6,505	2,054	1,805	3,859	2,550	638	648	1,286	377	337	714	......
Chatham	2,938	2 758	5,696	1,652	1,470	3,122	25	1,752	1,669	3,421	619	784	1,403	23
Cherokee	2,185	2,071	4 256	1,180	1,041	2,221	1,042	93	92	185	52	48	100	60

Chowan	761	671	1,432	560	447	1,007	581	1,085	908	1,943	490	739	1,229	679
Clay	869	805	1,674	...	...	...	...	21	29	50	...	...	...	...
Cleveland	3,726	3,552	7,278	2,594	2,368	4 962	...	1,017	1,003	2,020	678	668	1,346	...
Columbus	2,614	2,452	5,066	1,710	1,715	3,425	...	1,304	1,424	2,728	764	764	1,528	...
Craven	1,386	1,402	2,788	934	905	1,839	960	2,072	2,221	4,293	1,084	1,432	2,516	1,429
Cumberland	3,026	3,094	6,220	528	1,210	2,438	1,552	2,014	2,701	4,715	1,348	1,676	3,024	2,412
Currituck	788	686	1,474	500	413	913	...	371	367	738	219	226	445	2,267
Dare	668	664	1,312	597	494	1,091	862	81	73	154	75	62	137	114
Davidson	3,510	3,379	6,889	2,436	2,179	4,115	2,732	674	643	1,317	420	382	802	490
Davie	1,712	1,625	3,337	1,125	971	2,096	1,221	619	518	1,137	357	320	677	411
Duplin	2,332	2,159	4,491	1,479	1,407	2,886	1,710	1,527	1,667	3,194	804	1,062	1,866	1,182
Durham	2,434	2,472	4,906	973	869	1,842	2,030	1,434	1,478	2,912	566	652	1,218	2,408
Edgecombe	1,619	1,668	3,287	...	...	...	...	...	...	...	2,761	2,666	5,327	...
Forsyth	3,992	3,750	7,742	2,113	1,690	3,803	2,109	633	658	1,291	1,617	1,691	3,308	726
Franklin	2,227	2,057	4,334	1,073	1,059	2,132	1,191	1,945	1,852	3,797	1,343	1,523	2,866	1,740
Gaston	3,355	3,367	6,722	1,597	1,401	2,998	1,852	1,241	1,225	2,466	553	624	1,177	697
Gates	1,058	948	2,006	678	529	1,207	2,300	1,020	936	1,956	586	616	1,119	30
Graham	799	796	1,595	491	467	958	475	22	22	44	...	...	...	...
Granville	2,002	1,900	3,902	793	726	1,519	963	1,981	1,804	3,785	1,046	1,194	2,240	1,560
Greene	956	903	1,859	660	630	1,290	645	960	898	1,858	523	639	1,162	584
Guilford	3,951	3,742	7,693	2,733	2,400	5 133	3,139	1,949	1.988	3,937	1,014	1,140	2,154	1,236
Halifax	1,866	1,750	3,616	1,435	1,240	2,675	1,635	3,887	3,898	7,785	2,780	2,921	5,701	3,126
Harnett	1,981	1,824	3,805	868	796	1,664	1,048	920	959	1,879	433	538	971	601
Haywood	...	...	...	...	...	...	...	...	...	...	...	...	...	...
Henderson	...	...	4,495	...	...	...	...	...	...	691	...	...	...	...
Hertford	1,114	1,038	2,151	615	546	1,161	705	1,587	1,569	3,156	944	1,022	1,966	1,054
Hyde	988	875	1,863	564	406	970	676	746	762	1,508	428	467	895	685
Iredell	3,869	3,730	7,599	2,516	2,192	4,708	2,794	1,405	1,363	2,768	764	742	1,506	...
Jackson	1,978	1,900	3,878	1,094	1,034	2,128	1,120	113	112	225	54	51	105	57
Johnston	4,096	3,896	7,992	2,644	2,274	4,918	481	1,618	1,601	3,319	813	856	1,669	461
Jones	676	579	1,255	629	529	1,158	843	606	675	1,281	500	570	1,070	950
Lenoir	1,785	1,637	3,422	817	835	1,652	22	1,257	1,204	2,461	842	1,075	1,917	40
Lincoln	2,220	2,162	4,382	1,485	1,276	2,761	29	614	588	1,202	384	381	765	28
Macon	2,014	1,904	3,918	1,388	1,279	2,667	1,337	131	159	290	83	85	168	98

TABLE No. III—Continued.

Counties.	Census of White Children. Male.	Census of White Children. Female.	Census of White Children. Total.	Enrollment of White Children. Male.	Enrollment of White Children. Female.	Enrollment of White Children. Total.	Average Attendance of White Children.	Census of Colored Children. Male.	Census of Colored Children. Female.	Census of Colored Children. Total.	Enrollment of Colored Children. Male.	Enrollment of Colored Children. Female.	Enrollment of Colored Children. Total.	Average Attendance of Colored Children.
Madison	4,016	3,787	7,803	1,008	900	2,008	....	100	93	193	62	42	104	......
Martin	1,521	1,328	2,869	.....	.....	.....	.....	1,443	1,378	2,821	.....	.....	.....	......
McDowell	2.013	1,620	3,633	1,185	1,064	2,249	35	308	359	739	234	228	462	23
Mecklenburg	4,464	4,185	8,649	3,439	3,053	6,492	4,108	3,292	3,241	6,533	2,842	2,734	5,576	3,425
Mitchell	2,751	2,826	5,577	1,801	1,512	3,311	31	109	103	212	38	59	97	27
Montgomery	1,659	1,606	3,265	1,275	1,225	2.500	1,650	604	583	1,187	350	465	815	454
Moore	2,729	2 678	5,407	1,426	1,430	2,856	1,763	1,345	1,511	2,856	629	826	1,455	949
Nash	2,726	2,664	5,390	900	938	1,838	26	1,983	1,857	3,840	836	954	1,790	25
New Hanover	1,609	1,549	3,158	778	943	1,721	1,131	2,194	2,257	4,451	1,032	1,200	2,232	1,130
Northampton	1,485	1,347	2,832	800	798	1,598	1,027	2,223	2,218	4,441	800	798	1,586	1,301
Onslow	1,532	1,341	2,873	1,038	878	1,916	1,095	629	637	1,266	505	559	1,064	621
Orange	1,689	1,476	3,165	946	844	1 790	1,140	844	826	1,670	581	561	1,142	630
Pamlico	897	894	1,791	719	676	1,395	954	534	529	1,064	180	285	465	......
Pasquotank	1.214	1,121	2,335	608	560	1 168	751	1,140	1,209	2.349	503	511	1,014	588
Pender	1,165	1,109	2,274	621	551	1,172	803	1,255	1 314	2,569	631	740	1.371	859
Perquimans	964	879	1,843	588	533	1,121	697	924	862	1,786	611	618	1,229	698
Person	....	....	....	.....	.....	.....	.....	.....	.....	.....	....	.....	.....	.....
Pitt	2,673	2,607	5,280	.....	.....	.....	...	2,585	2,502	5,087	....	.....	.....	...
Polk	1,034	907	1,941	685	612	1,297	693	292	264	556	189	178	361	185
Randolph	4,436	4,230	8,666	2,989	2,714	5,703	4,102	707	657	1,364	437	421	858	549
Richmond	1,671	1,654	3,325	1,671	1,654	3,325	....	2,330	2,425	4,755	2,330	2,425	4,755	......

TRINITY COLLEGE, DURHAM, N. C.—WASHINGTON DUKE BUILDING.

Robeson	3,004	2,922	5,926	1,882	1,630	3,520	2,650	2,923	2,876	5,799	1,209	1,373	2,582	27
Croatans	....	....	....	....	....	....	....	834	776	1,610	473	384	867	43
Rockingham	3,417	3,193	6,610	1.834	1,571	3,405	1,821	1,986	2,046	4 032	1,055	1,095	2,150	1,115
Rowan	3,643	3,439	7,082	2,894	2,663	5.557	3,442	1.252	1,216	2,468	926	887	1,813	1,058
Rutherford	3,498	3,448	6,446	2,460	2,234	4 694	3.650	868	882	1,750	541	634	1.175	24
Sampson	2,930	2,861	5,791	1,789	1,692	3,481	2,236	1,790	1,807	3 697	894	1,200	2,094	1,325
Stanly	2,310	2,178	4,488	1,639	1.527	3,168	31	353	285	638	209	178	387	23
Stokes	3,101	2,777	5,878	1.781	1,494	3,275	27	642	647	1,289	304	289	593	19
Surry	3,589	3,194	6,783	2,125	1,885	4,010	2,209	614	547	1,161	250	208	458	302
Swain	1,287	1,205	2,492	....	....	....	....	39	25	64	....	....	....	....
Transylvania	1,118	1,093	2,211	....	....	2,025	1,415	117	131	248	....	....	235	200
Tyrrell	....	....	....	....	....	....	....	....	....	....	....	....	....	....
Union	3,587	3,197	6,784	2,782	2,266	5,048	3,034	1,526	1,423	2,949	1,009	1 182	2,191	1,263
Vance	1,137	1,167	2,304	389	511	900	320	1,779	1,672	3,451	784	785	1,569	863
Wake	4,809	4,688	9,497	3,113	2,981	6 094	3,842	4.301	4,523	8,824	3,418	3,506	6,924	4,092
Warren	1,015	940	1,955	413	427	840	....	2,606	2,616	5,224	1,178	1,374	2,552	....
Washington	905	846	1,751	608	524	1,132	665	902	900	1,802	479	534	1,013	536
Watauga	2,291	2.250	4,541	1,548	1,498	3 046	1,775	85	90	175	13	17	30	16
Wayne	3,085	2,762	5,487	1,458	1,329	2,787	1,651	2,417	2,309	4,726	955	1,116	2,071	1,011
Wilkes	4,422	4,288	8,670	2,600	2,354	4,954	26	499	520	1,019	244	296	540	18
Wilson	2,025	1,759	3,784	1,997	902	2,899	1,019	1,685	1,805	3,490	694	749	1,443	760
Yadkin	2,456	2,278	4,734	1,592	1 367	2,959	1,761	281	314	595	148	157	305	165
Yancey	1,972	2,268	4,240	951	766	1,717	796	60	73	133	17	18	35	21
Total	211,355	200,788	412,143	114,625	107,627	222,252	110,677	106,054	105,465	211,519	60,856	70,548	131,404	58,548

Number of Institutes—Mitchell, one white. Number teachers attending, male, 15; female, 14. Pitt, one colored. Sampson, one white. Number teachers attending, male, 12; female, 18. Colored, one. Number teachers attending, male, 20; female, 28.

TABLE No. IV.

Reports Showing the Number of Public School Districts, Number of School Houses, Number of Schools Taught, Value of Public School Property, Average Length of Terms in Weeks, and Average Monthly Salary of Teachers in the Several Counties in the State during the School Year Ending June 30, 1897.

COUNTIES.	NUMBER OF SCHOOL DISTRICTS		NUMBER OF SCHOOLS TAUGHT.		VALUE OF PUBLIC SCHOOL PROPERTY.		AVERAGE LENGTH OF TERM IN WEEKS.			AVERAGE SALARY OF TEACHERS PER MONTH.				NUMBER OF SCHOOL HOUSES.						
														WHITE.				COLORED.		
	White.	Colored.	White.	Colored.	White.	Colored.	White.	Colored.	City.	White Male.	White Female.	Colored Male.	Colored Female.	Numb'r.	Log.	Frame.	Brick	Numb'r.	Log.	Frame.
										$	$	$	$							
A[illegible]ce	65	28	59	27	$ 14,902 00	$ 3,275 0	15.44	16.03	....	30 00	25 24	25 70	22 00	62	5	57	....	26	7	19
Alexander	51	8	58	8	....	....	11 1/5	9 1/5	....	20 46	......	18 39	...	....	....	....	...	....	....	....
Alleghany	42	7	37	3	......	.....	10 35/37	8 2/3	...	20 31 5/7	14 66 2/3	19 00	.....	....	....	....	...	....	...	....
Anson	57	48	65	62	5,735 00	3,420 00	8	8.	...	20 06	18 40	17 60	13 56	43	....	43	....	35	2	33
Ashe	101	8	96	6	1,000 00	150 00	13	9.	....	20 00	18 00	16 00	16 00	74	23	51	....	3	...	3
Beaufort	74	42	48	34	7,138 00	2,976 00	10	9½	....	24 00	21 00	23 00	20 00	72	7	65	...	40	2	38
Bertie	64	55	57	53	5,183 00	5,165 00	12½	13½	....	24 46	22 25	25 82	22 56	61	....	61	....	55	....	55
Bladen	77	47	77	47	3,288 50	3,446 00	8	8	...	21 00	20 00	23 00	20 00	47	5	42	....	33	3	30
Brunswick	50	28	42	18	1,901 00	840 00	9	10		25 00	25 00	20 00	20 00	38	2	36	....	14	..	14
Buncombe	102	23	95	19	70,000 00	21,000 [illegible]	[illegible]7½	15½	36	30 02	30 02	25 00	25 00	89	13	67	7	31	17	12
Burke	68	16	52	10	3,223 00	752 00	[illegible]	12 8	...	20 95	20 20	21 45	21 45	43	17	26	....	7	5	2
Cabarrus	58	25	61	24	5,000 00	1,125 00	12⅔	11⅓	32	24 43	23 30	24 45	23 67	52	8	33	1	20	11	9
Caldwell	71	12	59	16	6,020 00	358 00	153	8 06	...	21 41	16 16	19 07	13 66	61	13	48	....	11	6	5
Camden	19	12	19	12	3,400 00	1,275.00	16	16	....	25 00	20 00	20 00	15 00	19	....	19	....	12	....	12
Carteret	25	10	27	7	4 500 00	1,040 00	10	11	....	25 40	19 95	19 00	20 00	34	.	34	....	11	....	11
Caswell	38	37	37	37	1,900 00	1,850 00	14	14	....	20 00	20 00	20 00	20 00	37	32	5	....	35	33	2
Catawba	78	23	74	21	....	....	13 7/25	9 23/25	..	25 96	21 96	22 70	....	74	13	61	....	19	14	5
Chatham	88	46	87	37	6,440 00	3,798 00	11½	11¾	....	21 47	19 68	23 22	21 10	73	20	53	....	42	14	28

Cherokee	48	3	46	3	3,950 00	125 00	14	12	40	23 00	18 00	21 00	15 00	47	27	20	...	3	
Chowan	20	13	19	13	2,665 00	2,001 00	16	16	...	30 00	25 00	27 50	25 00	20	...	20	...	13	...
Clay	17	2	18	2	6,000 00	100 00	12	6	...	18 00	16 00	15 00		17	10	7	...	2	
Cleveland	83	24	82	23	13,076 00	1,583 00	13$\frac{66}{83}$	14⅙	...	27 50	27 50	26 08	26 08	65	2	63	...	16	
Columbus	88	44	70	37	6,717 00	3 321 00	11$\frac{1}{10}$	12$\frac{8}{37}$	...	24 90	22 42	24 07	20 06	79	7	72	...	4	2
Craven	8	8	36	35	2,515 00	6,935 00	12	12	30	24 00	24 00	28 20	24 00	36	4	32	...	35	
Cumberland	85	59	78	59	6 612 00	4,483 00	8½	6¼	...	20 00	20 00	22 50	22 50	83	2	74	...	54	
Currituck	32	13	28	11	2,390 00	1,055 00	12.50	11.37	...	26 00	26 16	23 66	22 94	30	..	30	...	13	...
Dare	19	3	18	3	1,500 00	335 00	11	12	...	26 00	25 00	25 00	20 00	19	2	19	...	3	...
Davidson	100	31	98	30	6,942 00	1.175 00	13½	8⅖	...	22 50	20 00	20 50	18 00	70	18	51	...	21	1
Davie	45	17	45	17	2,594 00	1,190	10$\frac{1}{15}$	13$\frac{5}{17}$	...	27 07	20 19	21 76	21 25	38	21	15	...	13	1
Duplin	78	46	75	42	...	...	10⅔	8$\frac{1}{12}$	...	21 52	20 49	26 00	21 61	49	16	33	...	29	
Durham	40	27	40	26	...	...	17	15	36	30 00	27 50	30 00	25 00	40	...	40	...	27	...
Edgecombe	...	...	...	...	6.870 00	5,600 00				...	...	...	...	41	...	41	...	41	
Forsyth	70	22	70	23	66,350 00	13,135 00	16.84	15.25	...	27 18	25 77	24 71	22 85	72	6	65	1	19	
Franklin	55	46	59	57	...	...	13	11.20	...	26 00	24 20	26 00	21 75	...	...	...	...	...	...
Gaston	73	30	71	29	6 688 00	3,259 00	12.48	11.74	...	25 06	23 52	28 15	23 00	64	8	56	...	30	
Gates	33	22	31	22	3,195 00	2,393 75	12.29	17	...	21 87½	21 81¼	24 43¾	23 93¾	33	...	33	...	22	...
Graham	20	2	16	...	2,146 00	D0 00	13.33	...	...	25 67	20 25	...	...	20	10	10	...	...	...
Granville	41	41	40	41	5,900 00	4,500 00	16	17	...	25 00	25 00	25 00	22 50	38	...	38	...	37	
Greene	31	23	39	38	1,807 00	1,247 00	4.48	3.96	...	27 22	24 67	23 70	20 50	...	...	27	...	...	...
Guilford	98	39	96	39	25,850 00	7,300 00	14 88	15.35	40	31 00	24 68	25 92	23 10	84	20	55	4	38	2
Halifax	25	25	76	10	4,699 00	5,148 50	...	...	...	25 00	25 00	22 50	20 00	34	3	30	1	32	
Harnett	64	28	43	23	4,890 00	2,113 00	9$\frac{28}{43}$	8$\frac{8}{23}$	...	21 30	20 62	23 70	21 87	44	10	34	...	26	
Haywood	...	...	...	...	...	...	...	...	..	...	...	...	...	...	...	...	...	...	...
Henderson	52	11	...	...	...	...	13	12		25 00	20 00	25 00	20 00	...	...	...	...	...	...
Hertford	30	28	31	30	3,145 00	4,005 00	13	16	...	23 03	23 11	24 02	24 07	32	...	32	...	28	...
Hyde	29	14	27	22	3,515 00	1,255 00	12	12	...	24 00	24 00	24 00	24 00	28	...	28	...	17	...
Iredell	108	99	94	46	...	...	14	12	..	25 00	22 00	21 00	18 00	100	44	56	2	42	2
Jackson	43	3	37	2	5,860 00	540 30	13	14	...	26 40	20 07	23 30	...	27	3	22	...	3	
Johnston	109	40	101	36	11,768 00	3 034 00	15.80	11.66	...	32 20	24 80	27 80	23 75	90	...	90	...	35	...
Jones	26	21	26	21	2,075 00	1,165 00	5.50	6 50	...	20 00	20 00	25 00	25 00	33	4	29	...	18	
Lenoir	48	30	46	30	3,477 00	2,440 00	9.50	9.33	...	21 65	23 00	23 18	20 72	40	...	40	...	24	...

TABLE No. IV.—CONTINUED.

COUNTIES.	NUMBER OF SCHOOL DISTRICTS		NUMBER OF SCHOOLS TAUGHT.		VALUE OF PUBLIC SCHOOL PROPERTY.		AVERAGE L[illegible]TH OF TERM IN WEEKS.			AVERAGE SALARY OF TEACHERS PER MONTH.				NUMBER OF SCHOOL HOUSES					
														WHITE.				COLORE	
	White.	Colored.	White.	Colored.	White.	Colored.	White.	Colored.	City.	White Male.	White Female.	Colored Male.	Colored Female.	Numb'r.	Log.	Frame.	Brick.	Numb'r.	Log.
Lincoln	57	16	56	16	$ 11,100 00	$ 1,800 00	12	11	....	$ 25 16	$ 22 80	$ 24 40	$ 25 00	54	11	40	3	15	6
Macon	59	5	56	5	7,135 00	235 00	12	15	..	21 00	18 80	20 64	22 00	53	14	39	....	4	2
Madison	76	5	....	....	3,500 00	150 00	12	7	...	27 50	20 00	20 00	25 00	43	15	27	1	2	1
Martin	47	29	47	29	....	....	....	11	....	.....	.....	.....	.....	47	....	....	....	29	...
McDowell	56	13	52	12	3,876 00	994 00	11	11	...	24 25	20 25	22 25	17 80	30	10	20	....	8	1
Mg	72	61	176	129	8,000 00	3,700 00	11	7	36	30 06	27 52	24 54	22 16	72	19	52	1	44	22
Mitchell	62	4	56	2	6,000 00	500 00	11	13	...	22 00	21 00	....	16 00	44	14	30	....	3	1
Montgomery	52	20	52	20	4,042 00	948 00	10	9	....	21 75	20 50	20 80	18 00	51	8	43	....	16	1
Mre	91	42	82	36	4 886 00	3,183 00	11	10	....	23 75	20 50	23 75	21 50	69	6	63	....	42	7
Nash	67	45	45	38	4,925 00	3,200 00	11½	14	...	25 00	24 30	26 00	24 75	67	4	63	....	45	4
Nw Hanover	11	10	15	15	37,250 00	12,850 00	16	16	32	35 00	37 45	34 75	35 70	16	....	16	....	17	....
Northampton	48	48	45	46	4,340 00	5,261 00	14½	14½	....	27 57	23 24	26 03	24 85	37	3	34	....	40	1
Onslow	49	20	39	18	3,481 00	1,316 00	12	14	....	23 50	20 00	23 00	22 00	49	3	46	....	20	2
Orange	49	48	46	38	2,180 00	1,250 00	13	9½	..	24 50	23 00	22 50	20 00	36	16	21	....	24	17
Pamlico	24	12	25	11	2,043 00	716 00	6⅔	6	..	26 55	20 88	26 10	21 60	11	2	9	....	8	1
Pasquotank	22	18	22	18	12,050 00	4,550 00	18	17	36	30 00	25 00	27 00	25 00	22	....	21	1	20	....
Pender	52	39	38	32	4,080 00	3,110 00	11	11	....	22 71	19 82	24 00	22 25	49	4	45	...	36	7
Perquimans	29	19	30	19	4 300 00	2,475 00	14	14	....	26 50	23 30	27 25	25 80	32	....	32	...	19	....
Person	....	....	....	....	....	....	....	....	..	.....	.....	.....	.....	....	....	....	....	....	..
Pitt	98	56	....	....	4,600 00	2,800 00	14	14	....	25 10	20 00	27 50	20 50	98	....	98	....	56	2

Polk	32	13	30	13	1,870 00	255 00	12	11		25 75	22 40	21 50	19 25	34	7	27		12	7	
Randolph	113	27	100	25	13,540 00	2,540 00	16	15¼		26 00	24 25	24 00	22 00	95	20	75		23	10	
Richmond	63	60	63	54			14	18		25 00	25 00	20 00	20 00	40	14	26		34	10	
Robeson	95	66	86	50	5,500 25	5,354 00	9½	10		24 00		27 00		78	3	75		55	2	
Croatans		21		20		1,539 00		1-8 9/10					22 00	21	1	20				
Rockingham	67	47	71	47	9,856 00	3,953 00	15½	14		26 70	26 70	25 24	25 24	55	25	30		35	16	
Rowan	81	81	78	44	18,425 00	5,210 00	15¼	14½	36	27 50	24 75	22 83	19 12	71	26	43	2	32	18	
Rutherford	81	33	80	26	22,290 00	1,450 00	12	3½		29 37	29 37	25 50	25 50	20	54			17	12	
Sampson	91	56	85	53	7,001 00	3,534 25	11⅓	9⅓	36	23 45	21 40	24 03	21 28	77	22	55		51	17	
Stanly	70	10	68	10	3,792 00	580 00	8	8		30 00	30 00	28 00	28 00	55	4	51		8	2	
Stokes	82	24	75	18	5,277 00	810 00	10	9		22 66	20 60	22 00	21 07	80	64	16		19	17	
Surry	82	21	75	18	6,398 00	1,115 00	16	11		23 92	21 62	20 23	18 00	59	31	28	stone	15	8	
Swain	32	2	31	1	2,057 00	75 00	14	11		23 00	22 00		20 00	29	17	11	1	1		
Transylvania	33	3	32	3	3,350 00	300 00	10	13		24 00	20 00	20 00	16 00	33	6	27		3		
Tyrrell																				
Union	88	35	101	47	6,710 00	3,285 00	10	9		23 50	22 25	26 50	21 67	81	16	65		32	7	
Vance	32	32	32	32	3,300 00	2,975 00	16	18			27 00	27 50	25 00	28	4	24		32	10	
Wake	87	67	85	67	8,600 00	6,000 00	16	16		32 50	27 50	27 00	25 00	78		78		69		
Warren	33	29	37	34	3,955 00	1,994 00	16	16		21 70	21 70	19 94	19 94	36	2	31	3	30	2	
Washington	30	20	28	19	3,523 00	1,818 00	17½	16½		25 53	24 00	27 05	26 62	29		29		19		
Watauga	67	6	67	4	800 00	100 00	12	7		21 25	18 50	20 00		67	18	49		4	4	
Wayne	68	42	63	40	16,400 00	8,715 00	14	18	40	25 26	24 30	25 05	22 00	67		67	1	42		
Wilkes	103	21	98	18	5,910 00	685 00	12	10		20 00	17 00	19 00	17 00	72	33	39		11	9	
Wilson	47	31	41	31	12,635 00	4,780 00	13	15		28 75	26 00	29 46	26 85							
Yadkin	61	19	58	9	3,500 00	200 00	13	10		21 78	19 08	23 81	18 00	53	30	23		5		
Yancey	42	6	26	2			11	6		21 42	17 80	10 40								
Total	5,247	2,540	4,998	2,360	$ 644 309 75	$ 234,324 00	11.73	10.86	360	$23 21	$20 81	$21 54	$18 25	4,369	899	3,438	32	2,037	489	1,

TABLE No. V.

Number of Teachers Examined and Approved During the School Year Ending June 30, 1897, Showing Race, Sex and Grade.

Counties.	White. 1st Grade. Male.	Female.	Total.	2d Grade. Male.	Female.	Total.	3d Grade. Male.	Female.	Total.	Colored. 1st Grade. Male.	Female.	Total.	2d Grade. Male.	Female.	Total.	3d Grade. Male.	Female.	Total.	Total White. Male.	Female.	Total.	Total Colored. Male.	Female.	Total.
[illegible]	29	30	59	8	9	17	1	1	2	3	4	4	9	9	18	3	4	7	38	40	78	15	14	29
Alexander	24	6	30	13	1	14	....	....	...	1	1	2	4	1	5	...	....	....	....	....	....	5	2	7
Alleghany	23	2	.	14	1	3	3	....	3	....	....	....	3	...	....	1	...	4	37	3	40	4	..	47
Anson	15	27	42	6	6	12	....	....	...	12	3	15	10	3	13	6	8	14	40	12	54	36	14	65
Ashe	47	....	47	37	1	38	....	1	1	....	....	....	2	....	2	2	....	4	47	39	86	2	2	90
Beaufort	25	35	60	7	5	12	....	....	....	7	10	17	5	8	13	2	3	5	32	40	72	30	21	51
Bertie	3	31	34	6	12	18	..	2	2	14	11	25	16	21	37	2	8	70	9	44	53	32	40	72
Bladen	20	36	56	5	8	13	....	...	....	25	4	29	14	24	38	1	15	16	25	44	69	40	43	83
Brunswick	12	6	18	15	5	20	....	..	....	6	1	7	6	...	6	2	....	2	27	11	38	14	1	15
[illegible]	40	25	65	7	6	13	....	....	....	10	6	16	3	2	5	....	....	....	47	31	78	13	8	21
Burke	9	9	18	24	6	30	....	....	2	2	1	3	6	3	9	..	..	...	33	15	48	8	4	12
Cabarrus	20	15	35	20	3	23	1	1	2	8	7	15	3	11	14	..	1	1	41	19	60	11	19	30
Caldwell	27	19	46	8	4	12	....	....	....	2	1	3	7	2	9	1	....	1	35	23	58	10	3	13
[illegible]	6	3	9	1	....	1	....	....	....	3	2	5	4	2	6	...	3	3	7	3	10	7	7	14
Carteret	8	5	13	7	8	15	....	....	....	....	....	....	....	5	5	2	1	3	15	13	28	2	6	8
Caswell	1	15	16	2	5	7	...	1	....	4	4	8	7	9	16	...	....	...	3	21	24	11	13	24
Catawba	52	16	68	5	....	5	....	1	1	8	...	8	10	...	10	1	1	2	57	17	74	19	1	20
Chatham	30	20	50	21	19	40	1	1	2	12	2	14	16	11	27	3	3	6	52	40	92	31	16	47
[illegible]	11	6	17	18	3	21	....	....	....	..	...	...	.	..	...	..	1	1	29	9	38	....	1	1
Chowan	3	10	13	....	7	7	..	....	....	4	10	14	2	3	5	..	2	2	3	13	16	6	15	21
Clay	12	..	12	4	...	4	3	..	3	....	...	....	....	..	....	....	....	....	19	....	19	....	....	....

Cleveland	46	20	66	16	7	23	...	...	...	12	7	19	5	2	7	...	...	...	62	29	89	17	9	26
[redacted] mbus	26	25	51	8	5	13	...	1	1	18	9	27	8	11	19	4	...	4	34	35	69	30	20	50
Craven	6	35	41	4	11	15	...	...	...	12	19	31	5	29	34	...	...	...	10	46	56	17	48	65
[redacted]nd	26	30	56	6	10	6	2	4	6	20	25	45	7	2	9	3	2	5	34	44	78	30	29	59
[redacted]k	4	22	26	3	2	5	...	...	...	4	5	9	3	5	8	...	...	...	7	24	31	7	10	17
Dare	...	...	...	...	...	...	...	...	...	...	...	...	...	...	...	...	...	...	...	...	...	...	...	...
Davidson	65	23	88	6	...	6	...	...	...	18	3	21	9	6	15	...	...	...	71	23	94	27	9	36
Davie	37	10	47	6	7	13	1	1	2	1	1	2	15	2	17	...	...	...	43	18	61	16	3	19
Duplin	13	54	67	5	11	16	...	...	...	10	3	13	8	16	24	3	10	13	18	65	83	21	29	50
Durham	25	11	36	2	17	19	...	...	...	29	17	46	...	...	...	...	...	...	27	28	55	29	17	46
Edgecombe	2	19	21	1	16	17	...	7	7	10	4	14	11	12	23	6	11	17	3	42	45	27	27	54
Forsyth	47	16	63	14	2	16	...	...	...	17	2	19	6	3	9	...	1	1	61	18	79	23	6	29
[redacted]in	11	40	51	2	6	8	...	...	...	17	27	44	7	6	13	...	...	...	13	46	59	24	33	57
Gaston	28	29	57	10	8	18	...	...	...	6	2	8	9	6	15	2	1	3	38	37	75	17	9	26
Gates	4	12	16	4	6	10	...	1	1	2	5	7	5	6	11	...	2	2	8	19	27	7	13	20
[redacted]m	8	1	9	4	3	7	12	4	16	...	...	...	...	...	...	...	...	...	24	8	32	...	...	...
Granville	3	35	38	...	...	...	...	...	...	16	25	40	5	5	10	...	...	...	3	35	38	21	30	51
Greene	6	26	32	1	2	3	...	...	...	12	4	16	...	10	10	2	...	39	36	28	34	18	21	39
Guilford	27	21	48	18	36	54	...	2	2	7	5	12	14	8	22	2	2	4	45	59	23	20	16	39
Halifax	3	47	50	...	6	6	...	...	...	20	32	52	18	30	48	...	...	...	3	53	56	38	62	100
Harnett	4	5	9	4	1	5	...	...	...	1	...	1	2	4	6	...	...	...	8	6	14	3	4	7
[redacted]d	...	...	...	...	...	...	...	...	...	...	...	...	...	...	...	...	...	...	...	...	...	...	...	...
Henderson	...	...	...	...	...	...	...	...	...	...	...	...	...	...	...	...	...	...	...	...	...	...	...	...
Hertford	2	25	27	1	7	8	...	...	...	11	5	16	13	9	22	1	1	2	3	32	35	25	15	40
Hyde	14	8	22	3	1	4	...	...	...	1	7	8	5	11	16	...	1	1	17	9	26	6	19	25
Iredell	24	18	42	29	22	51	...	...	...	8	...	8	34	...	34	...	13	13	53	40	93	...	...	55
Jackson	9	7	16	4	4	8	...	...	...	...	...	...	2	...	...	...	...	...	13	11	24	2	...	2
Johnston	46	28	74	17	8	25	1	1	2	8	3	11	12	9	21	1	9	10	63	37	100	21	21	42
Jones	8	13	21	3	3	6	...	...	...	7	2	9	6	7	13	1	...	1	11	16	27	14	9	23
Lenoir	5	35	40	2	3	5	...	...	...	12	8	20	8	24	32	...	5	5	7	38	45	20	37	57
Lincoln	1	...	...	...	...	...	...	...	...	...	...	...	...	...	...	...	...	...	...	...	...	...	...	...
Macon	10	12	22	14	18	32	1	1	2	...	...	...	4	1	5	1	...	1	25	31	56	5	1	6
Madison	19	10	29	6	3	9	...	...	...	...	...	...	...	...	1	...	...	...	25	13	38	...	...	...

TABLE No. V.—Continued.

Counties.	White. 1st Grade. Male.	White. 1st Grade. Female.	White. 1st Grade. Total.	White. 2d Grade. Male.	White. 2d Grade. Female.	White. 2d Grade. Total.	White. 3d Grade. Male.	White. 3d Grade. Female.	White. 3d Grade. Total.	Colored. 1st Grade. Male.	Colored. 1st Grade. Female.	Colored. 1st Grade. Total.	Colored. 2d Grade. Male.	Colored. 2d Grade. Female.	Colored. 2d Grade. Total.	Colored. 3d Grade. Male.	Colored. 3d Grade. Female.	Colored. 3d Grade. Total.	Total White. Male.	Total White. Female.	Total White. Total.	Total Colored. Male.	Total Colored. Female.	Total Colored. Total.
Martin	13	5	24	6	20	26	...	...	...	12	1	13	9	7	16	1	4	5	19	25	44	22	14	34
McDowell	12	12	24	17	5	22	...	1	1	2	...	2	3	...	3	...	1	1	29	18	47	5	1	6
Mecklenburg	63	37	100	8	4	12	...	...	...	29	7	36	18	19	37	1	5	6	71	41	112	48	31	79
Mitchell	37	9	46	10	7	17	1	...	1	...	1	1	...	1	1	...	...	1	48	17	65	...	2	2
Montgomery	18	9	27	10	7	17	...	1	1	7	1	8	3	3	6	...	1	1	28	17	45	10	5	15
Moore	28	12	30	21	11	32	2	3	5	10	3	13	8	9	17	2	7	9	51	26	77	20	19	39
Nash	...	...	...	...	...	...	...	...	...	...	...	...	...	...	...	...	...	...	...	...	...	...	...	...
New Hanover	1	42	43	...	...	...	...	...	...	3	25	28	2	2	4	...	...	...	1	42	43	5	27	32
Northampton	12	25	37	4	5	9	...	1	1	8	5	13	19	14	33	...	1	1	16	31	47	27	20	47
Onslow	3	9	12	10	6	16	1	...	1	4	1	5	5	3	8	4	3	7	14	15	29	13	7	20
Orange	18	9	27	5	8	13	...	2	2	5	1	6	5	11	16	4	7	11	23	19	42	14	18	32
Pamlico	...	...	...	...	...	...	...	...	...	...	...	...	1	...	...	...	...	...	...	...	...	...	...	...
Pasquotank	4	11	15	4	4	8	...	...	...	4	1	5	9	7	16	...	1	1	8	15	23	13	9	22
Pender	2	17	19	3	7	10	1	...	1	12	3	15	8	7	15	4	3	7	6	24	30	24	13	37
Perquimans	4	10	14	3	9	12	...	1	...	1	4	4	8	4	5	9	...	..	7	19	26	8	9	17
Person	...	...	...	...	...	...	...	...	...	...	...	...	...	...	...	...	...	...	...	...	...	...	...	...
Pitt	9	25	34	4	20	24	...	2	2	12	4	16	7	15	22	...	3	3	13	47	60	19	22	41
Polk	9	4	13	8	14	22	3	1	4	2	1	3	3	4	7	1	3	4	20	19	39	6	8	14
Randolph	59	25	84	14	10	24	...	...	...	5	...	5	11	9	20	...	1	1	73	35	108	16	10	26
Richmond	13	11	24	11	6	17	...	...	...	11	9	20	14	17	31	...	...	...	24	17	41	25	26	51

Robeson	27	9	36	14	17	31	5	5	10	11	5	16	11	8	19	3	3	6	46	31	77	25	16	41
Croatans	4	1	4	6		6	1	1	1												11			
Rockingham	14	70	84	1	1	2				19	8	27	16	12	28	1	2	3	15	71	86	36	23	59
Rowan	43	10	53	14	13	27				6	3	9	21	9	30		2	2	57	23	80	27	14	41
Rutherford	33	20	53	16	17	33				3	2	5	13	12	25				49	37	86	16	14	39
Sampson	31	39	70	9	10	19		2	2	16	11	27	10	22	32	1	3	4	40	51	91	27	36	63
Stanly	44	18	62	1		11				5	4	9	2	3	5				45	18	63	7	7	14
Stokes	34		34	32		2	2		2	1		1	15		15	1		1	33	35	68	10	7	17
Surry	20	14	34	24	7	31	7		7	4		4	8	3	11	4	4	8	51	21	72	16	7	23
Swain	6	5	11	7	8	35	2	3	5		1	1							15	16	31		1	1
Transylvania	10	17	27	7	4	11	2	4	6	1	1	1	1		1		1	1	19	25	44	2	1	3
Tyrrell																								
Union	56	28	84	12	4	16				21	13	34	11	5	16	3	5	8	68	32	100	35	23	58
Vance		27	27							11	20	31	1	3	4		1	1		27	27	12	24	36
Wake																								
Warren	3	34	37							3	2	5							3	34	37	14	15	29
Washington	11	7	18	1	3	4				6	3	9	2	14	16		3	3	12	10	22	8	20	28
Watauga	24	5	29	14	2	16		1	1	1		1	1	1	2	3		3	38	8	46	5	1	6
Wayne	32	31	63	4	8	12				6	5	11	10	12	22		7	7	26	39	65	16	24	40
Wilkes	62	12	74	17	2	19	2		2	7	3	10	6	1	7	2		2	81	14	95	15	4	19
Wilson	19	22	41	1	1	2				23	17	40	5	28	33	2		2	20	23	43	30	45	75
Yadkin	34	4	38	21	4	25				4	1	5	4	2	6				55	8	63	6	1	7
Yancey	16	2	18	8		8										2		2	24	2	26	2		2
Total	1769	1599	3368	762	578	1340	54	57	111	675	239	914	617	606	1223	100	178	278	2481	2277	4758	1368	1249	2617

TABLE No. VI.—WHITE—1897.

Showing Number of Pupils of Different Ages from Six to Twenty-one Studying Different Branches.

s.	Six Years.	Seven Years.	Eight Years.	Nine Years.	Ten Years.	Eleven Years.	Twelve Years.	Thirteen Years.	Fourteen Years.	Fifteen Years.	Sixteen Years	Seventeen Years	Eighteen Years.	Nineteen Years.	Twenty Years.	Number Studying Arithmetic.	Number Studying Geography.	Number Studying Eng. Grammar.	Number Studying N. C. Histoy.	Number Studying U. S. Histoy.	Number Studying Physiology and Hygiene.
...	308	224	309	211	360	249	265	228	184	204	151	130	105	71	66	2,025	1,064	698	277	333	247
..	238	216	218	213	189	188	192	187	168	138	134	96	80	45	33	891	361	310	51	100	65
...	181	156	155	118	156	117	147	123	125	1	86	70	54	26	22	644	295	226	62	81	67
...	129	169	171	154	198	154	168	144	142	123	99	78	62	48	37	1,187	658	416	202	254	92
...	386	375	389	325	423	359	363	439	434	302	245	199	161	89	75	1, 66	616	497	86	146	149
..	182	261	201	237	219	163	177	131	169	120	112	110	60	52	45	2, 00	950	530	150	275	170
...	124	141	148	143	160	127	154	145	166	1	102	63	49	31	19	1,221	695	441	233	248	242
...	120	165	138	155	168	139	160	155	154	145	121	107	105	48	54	1,327	626	444	177	139	276
..	95	109	112	110	109	121	112	124	101	98	67	62	55	38	35	629	315	234	72	68	54
..	....	.....	....	.....	.....	.....	.....	.....	.....	....	....	.....	.....	.....	.....	2,594	1,310	835	213	381	664
...	...	...	...	...	...	...	...	...	...	...	...	...	...	...	...	...	...	...	...	...	...
...	188	214	212	234	207	212	299	199	215	170	157	94	90	51	26	1,429	745	373	247	217	128
...	219	191	198	210	255	211	213	166	187	169	132	12	68	45	25	1,040	670	323	67	195	122
..	63	59	66	55	72	70	68	63	50	45	30	36	25	16	8	425	222	135	90	89	55
..	110	98	92	101	87	95	100	96	106	82	81	68	72	53	35	96	324	267	125	110	150
...	90	88	95	100	125	130	140	13	107	57	63	58	61	75	23	954	754	659	82	208	95
...	340	354	412	348	434	321	363	337	281	214	160	124	66	47	13	1,954	1,105	615	317	282	153
..	268	248	277	256	324	239	299	261	275	33	204	163	132	90	68	2,182	996	618	411	182	182
...	187	207	204	193	182	177	185	175	169	159	125	97	82	39	40	778	384	299	50	125	105
...	51	56	63	47	59	64	48	57	43	41	29	28	17	27	9	504	229	115	83	70	52

Clay	....	....	....	....	....	....	....	....	....	....	....	....	....	....	....	....	....	....	....
Cl ead	463	416	396	486	476	417	448	356	365	291	261	146	170	111	101	2,270	1,056	817	300
Ibus	255	310	310	250	310	250	290	315	199	270	170	170	185	110	90	1,530	795	495	110
Craven	97	89	118	93	99	88	73	147	110	64	61	50	35	9	9	773	228	277	1
Cumberland	145	210	237	209	230	195	194	202	188	176	130	123	96	72	46	1,219	1,000	875	950
Currituck	....	....	....	....	....	....	....	....	....	....	....	....	....	....	....	....	....	....	....
Dare	65	70	89	90	88	86	93	100	98	100	90	64	45	7	6	443	237	219	91
Davidson	397	367	356	384	396	353	380	367	356	276	241	190	138	80	73	2,350	1,125	575	395
Davie	160	176	175	176	210	166	175	178	152	183	144	76	62	47	46	1,050	478	342	129
Duplin	240	200	272	210	250	231	151	236	212	199	180	116	105	56	65	2,074	944	575	352
Durham	80	189	170	188	262	147	165	166	147	110	73	73	36	18	18	921	460	368	368
Edgecombe	....	....	....	....	....	....	....	....	....	....	....	....	....	....	....	....	....	....	....
Forsyth	375	365	367	323	418	302	328	271	274	238	196	124	131	69	56	1,992	, 1	592	231
Franklin	135	187	176	189	217	208	209	204	163	158	1	64	55	35	30	1,555	736	503	182
Gaston	306	281	305	262	229	276	245	234	227	174	138	99	86	43	23	1,781	905	536	280
Gates	84	87	122	109	115	106	118	86	102	67	72	57	29	37	17	827	442	273	152
Graham	74	68	76	81	87	85	91	68	86	65	55	54	23	19	22	347	150	110	31
Granville	75	91	106	151	90	135	184	120	166	167	135	61	15	12	11	1,200	1 060	1,110	409
Gne	100	96	120	120	104	88	99	88	94	67	43	46	20	16	9	784	403	273	133
Cuilford	312	326	346	321	372	319	300	294	300	179	221	161	145	86	75	2,504	1,296	748	314
Halifax	149	192	222	220	264	249	275	206	204	178	159	178	79	48	20	1,740	952	603	280
Harnett	111	148	126	138	134	137	139	145	127	117	122	70	60	48	42	835	429	296	94
Haywood	....	....	....	....	....	....	....	....	....	....	....	....	....	....	....	....	....	....	....
Henderson	....	....	....	....	....	....	....	....	....	....	....	....	....	....	....	....	....	....	....
Hertford	81	98	112	114	1	126	111	97	83	63	60	46	30	14	15	828	477	242	149
Hyde	58	100	87	88	110	76	77	78	95	60	58	33	23	21	6	67	309	187	78
Iredell	298	324	329	394	325	300	360	340	315	320	330	300	287	230	106	2,100	1,000	694	320
Jackson	177	160	190	189	202	198	187	164	172	132	117	88	69	48	35	941	466	273	51
Johnston	375	420	448	422	497	370	452	380	369	298	265	214	163	122	69	2,929	1,036	862	334
Jones	94	88	115	109	108	99	123	97	97	98	73	48	55	26	28	728	417	234	136
Lenoir	135	150	171	118	184	121	150	148	138	102	82	69	47	36	20	1,243	662	331	171
Lincoln	263	245	285	233	262	220	234	210	212	178	162	111	68	37	34	1,423	658	433	291
Macon	207	218	238	218	239	203	230	208	199	187	167	129	90	74	60	1,134	582	259	59

TABLE No. VI.—WHITE—CONTINUED.

s.	Six Years.	Seven Years.	Eight Years.	Nine Years.	Ten Years.	Eleven Yeos.	Twelve Years.	Thirteen Years.	Fourteen Years.	Fifteen Yeos.	Sixteen Years.	Seventeen Years.	Eighteen Years.	Nineteen Years.	Twenty Years.	Number Studying Arithmetic.	Numb r Studying Geography.	Number Studying Eng. Grammar.	Number Studying N. C. Histoy.	Number Studying U. S. History.	Number Studying Physiology and Hygiene.
...	216	171	188	155	169	154	164	144	158	116	107	109	7 0	49	39	782	314	239	62	84	44
....																					
..	101	178	143	195	255	218	204	198	168	171	153	114	84	48	31	1,153	710	458	82	102	94
rg	514	577	543	592	618	505	583	510	518	411	310	267	197	122	80	3,945	2,424	1,636	735	1,190	493
...	308	297	303	267	321	281	275	318	322	227	159	148	105	77	37	90	497	291	46	114	105
ry .	261	215	198	190	275	193	185	179	182	201	163	83	95	45	35	850	460	315	180	95	180
....	288	209	220	230	243	280	280	260	215	156	153	110	96	68	48	1,498	592	493	187	146	299
....	138	189	230	198	194	181	104	147	93	95	76	47	49	51	46	1,110	530	436	153	143	58
ver.	85	120	183	211	226	216	198	167	135	96	50	25	9	...	...	1,721	1,721	1,721	1,721	1,721	1,721
ton.	118	1	148	149	165	146	171	150	117	116	115	76	50	33	29	1,169	715	483	292	295	213
..	138	121	150	137	145	133	160	159	2 7	125	114	93	76	46	57	1,133	756	418	272	84	352
....	123	160	165	164	171	156	174	130	138	133	119	89	71	51	46	1,206	687	414	363	278	151
...	109	107	136	110	85	100	105	112	110	98	76	72	50	36	19	829	411	237	142	57	57
k..	78	138	1	124	116	134	106	104	89	43	33	35	21	13	8	929	510	404	201	132	59
...	81	86	90	87	96	80	1	97	87	85	66	72	46	28	16	875	382	244	106	140	109
s .	110	109	107	108	109	82	113	89	78	55	57	44	34	24	11	803	443	240	135	129	78
...																					
...																					
....	130	110	102	110	132	104	115	88	93	88	72	61	45	34	13	675	315	232	14	48	179
....	510	400	523	416	435	415	465	426	405	283	425	275	260	365	100	3,987	2,134	1,351	784	719	903
...																					
...	234	288	323	293	313	280	308	286	289	246	191	215	119	89	53	2,139	1,211	791	259	338	204

ham	288	267	234	298	349	260	322	242	288	224	192	130	101	70	40	2, 99	1,186	655	250	490	169
....	219	220	258	413	433	430	456	435	407	340	263	225	166	86	59	2,953	1,613	833	567	514	331
rd..	421	332	418	330	400	340	372	280	315	260	232	160	130	110	80	2,015	854	725	176	220	190
....	215	279	286	278	326	266	294	300	243	241	201	172	138	82	47	2,336	1,048	842	392	489	390
....	178	255	292	261	297	263	271	250	243	217	181	144	109	74	67	1,332	638	423	148	199	143
....	268	240	262	268	312	267	304	265	245	229	167	142	119	53	38	1,473	863	519	191	227	184
....	391	352	351	311	365	297	321	279	293	253	225	154	119	76	65	1,848	908	680	245	357	164
....	....	....	....	....	....	....	....	....	....	....	....	....	....	....	....	....	....	....	....	....	....
ania.	160	157	148	151	148	143	140	137	136	135	134	133	130	90	70	700	400	600	50	100	175
....	....	....	....	....	....	....	....	....	....	....	....	....	....	....	....	....	....	....	....	....	....
....	423	418	480	398	512	380	487	388	329	260	224	169	103	89	....	2,234	1,130	831	264	247	171
....	68	77	95	93	89	98	80	79	63	56	43	41	34	17	6	801	476	368	116	156	298
....	421	560	560	559	591	563	576	503	480	390	260	275	147	148	71	2,849	1,784	1,413	820	496	1,002
....	53	71	79	90	73	89	86	78	70	51	54	20	22	12	6	697	440	208	80	202	144
ton	113	103	114	97	106	114	91	110	102	81	68	42	37	25	14	808	410	284	110	135	98
....	310	280	302	260	290	255	260	225	220	205	185	140	99	58	55	1,213	520	315	80	110	105
....	199	248	266	238	262	208	268	222	222	169	142	135	89	41	30	2,314	1,048	666	250	485	478
....	462	357	370	356	354	320	357	358	349	300	263	217	160	130	108	1,760	786	624	162	183	207
....	157	151	148	155	178	149	185	166	150	116	96	64	67	34	23	1,169	518	326	110	256	226
....	243	253	266	234	257	204	295	210	240	202	164	128	99	73	70	1 383	617	500	172	59	96
....	132	122	123	101	141	134	145	145	104	112	60	62	42	30	17	360	185	173	17	30	61
l....	16,858	17,333	18,489	17,582	19,575	17,115	18,460	16,764	16,139	13,524	11,605	8,943	7,079	4,899	3,299	117,732	61,809	42,515	18,330	21,377	18,259

TABLE No. VI.—COLORED—1897.

Showing Number of Pupils of Different Ages from Six to Twenty-one Studying Different Branches.

COUNTIES.	Six Years.	Seven Years.	Eight Years.	Nine Years.	Ten Years.	Eleven Years.	Twelve Years.	Thirteen Years.	Fourteen Years.	Fifteen Years.	Sixteen Years.	Seventeen Years.	Eighteen Years.	Nineteen Years.	Twenty Years.	Number Studying Arithmetic.	Number Studying Geography.	Number Studying Eng. Grammar.	Number Studying N. C. History.	Number Studying U. S. History.	Number Studying Physiology and Hygiene.
Alamance	1	110	1	96	122	83	117	121	115	118	67	62	47	40	26	710	373	104	43	109	222
Alexander	6	15	20	13	27	19	21	24	17	21	17	10	14	7	4	100	59	46	3	2	26
Alleghany	3	2	6	5	4	3	8	4	2	8	7	4	4	3	1	35	8	6	....	....	....
Anson	149	142	148	154	191	165	169	200	178	125	137	101	83	54	28	1,243	563	416	78	136	209
Ashe	10	13	10	4	7	9	11	7	14	10	9	13	11	4	5	43	26	9	1	1	1
Beaufort	113	108	140	136	119	140	175	150	197	128	117	101	63	30	18	1,200	550	300	115	215	500
Bertie	173	183	214	214	269	212	303	253	243	183	162	40	96	49	19	1,326	645	447	225	178	459
Bladen	90	134	126	134	164	152	192	180	157	167	130	110	102	58	45	996	466	418	86	107	346
Brunswick	33	16	53	49	70	40	68	70	68	53	55	43	20	22	16	308	126	68	6	18	87
Buncombe	...	...	...	...	...	...	...	...	...	...	...	...	...	...	...	349	166	109	20	105	167
Burke	...	...	...	...	...	...	...	...	...	...	...	...	...	...	...	...	...	...	...	...	...
Cabarrus	51	71	80	78	78	63	106	89	80	73	68	52	36	18	12	590	262	173	53	117	151
Caldwell	28	23	41	34	43	32	27	23	34	26	29	20	13	5	4	148	87	44	18	31	46
Camden	30	37	29	32	42	44	52	30	38	22	27	25	20	15	6	125	128	90	40	33	29
Carteret	28	31	22	36	30	34	37	29	18	9	11	7	9	8	3	109	68	60	27	41	16
Caswell	97	100	158	173	195	194	176	153	107	28	25	29	18	4	1	798	349	255	45	85	37
Catawba	60	63	50	62	59	41	58	58	54	41	42	39	27	15	8	303	156	98	26	39	150
Chatham	74	128	100	102	131	125	151	144	1	107	103	83	68	40	29	805	472	314	184	84	251
Cherokee	9	6	15	11	7	11	5	10	7	7	4	3	1	2	2	23	19	18	5	17	11
Chowan	73	76	80	104	96	80	95	82	74	57	50	33	26	8	6	834	540	375	207	253	536
Clay	....	....	....	....	...	...	....	....	...	....	....	....	....	....	....	....	....	....	....	....	.....

Cleveland	104	87	92	81	107	72	88	101	105	68	74	62	50	43	56	421	204	128	48	53
Columbus	133	105	84	105	70	84	98	112	91	84	91	42	28	20	14	329	116	116	70	63
Craven	173	190	198	232	237	244	266	308	221	152	157	136	99	55	43	1,571	1,043	928	209	786
Cumberland	332	221	289	260	265	234	267	268	205	193	147	120	100	74	50	1,562	672	428	256	647
Currituck	...	...	...	...	...	...	...	...	...	...	...	...	...	...	...	...	...	...	...	...
Dare	10	12	14	15	12	16	13	12	12	10	10	6	5	4	3	62	48	20	16	8
Davidson	55	61	50	59	67	60	52	66	54	51	42	28	22	13	10	394	188	104	38	51
Davie	53	52	57	56	53	47	61	50	62	46	43	41	20	21	12	336	201	112	45	50
Duplin	135	150	120	105	156	121	148	146	160	129	120	109	88	56	38	104	82	197	104	82
Durham	57	124	109	121	170	97	109	109	97	79	49	49	24	12	12	610	243	170	49	97
Edgecombe	...	...	...	...	...	...	...	...	...	...	...	...	...	...	...	...	...	...	...	...
Forsyth	144	113	109	116	112	87	118	82	88	70	77	58	52	32	25	600	431	343	56	72
Franklin	192	200	229	213	258	224	333	241	236	215	186	151	106	68	35	1,711	999	801	235	221
Gaston	67	99	115	96	121	93	121	95	98	78	56	57	52	16	13	665	309	131	53	71
Gates	47	76	93	97	121	84	106	101	104	109	84	75	50	40	13	623	345	199	55	68
Graham	...	...	...	...	...	...	...	...	...	...	...	...	...	...	...	...	...	...	...	...
[illegible]ile	122	134	224	156	133	200	268	242	178	246	201	89	22	20	15	1,500	1,308	907	500	347
[illegible]e	64	84	106	98	99	115	112	104	92	91	66	46	33	23	6	606	243	121	58	70
[illegible]d	122	149	126	141	170	138	159	131	127	128	106	89	61	35	25	936	329	429	114	178
Halifax	312	446	430	572	603	526	485	290	284	382	326	280	195	86	59	3,048	2,494	1,820	383	410
[illegible]ett	57	63	52	86	67	68	100	83	77	56	61	71	54	45	31	506	282	154	81	45
Haywood	...	...	...	...	...	...	...	...	...	...	...	...	...	...	...	...	...	...	...	...
Henderson	...	...	...	...	...	...	...	...	...	...	...	...	...	...	...	...	...	...	...	...
Hertford	95	141	150	160	158	186	189	182	159	157	140	91	81	42	35	774	529	380	106	205
Hyde	45	75	65	62	95	85	75	85	100	86	78	61	38	24	21	543	253	142	69	84
Iredell	110	107	88	75	60	55	48	42	115	106	105	104	107	110	112	675	340	200	105	92
Jackson	16	10	3	12	13	9	7	9	7	5	5	2	5	2	1	34	16	17	3	...
Johnston	113	121	1	129	148	124	145	173	142	153	125	93	71	59	24	889	291	266	165	165
Jones	54	73	77	75	102	71	86	93	98	104	60	64	34	29	17	1,037	550	300	125	152
Lenoir	148	161	180	157	158	126	151	165	144	139	117	66	60	31	23	707	434	196	130	95
Lincoln	56	61	74	52	76	66	64	65	61	54	30	24	18	10	...	309	115	140	17	23
Macon	13	10	18	15	14	18	22	16	8	13	11	4	2	4	1	56	43	27	6	14
Madison	...	...	...	...	...	...	...	...	...	...	...	1	...	1	1	...	...	...	...	...

TABLE No. VI.—COLORED—CONTINUED.

COUNTIES.	Six Years.	Seven Years.	Eight Years.	Nine Years.	Ten Years.	Eleven Years.	Twelve Years.	Thirteen Years.	Fourteen Years.	Fifteen Years.	Sixteen Years.	Seventeen Years.	Eighteen Years.	Nineteen Years.	Twenty Years.	Number Studying Arithmetic.	Number Studying Geography.	Number Studying Eng. Grammar.	Number Studying N. C. History.	Number Studying U. S. History.	Number Studying Physiology and Hygiene.
Martin	....	....	....	....	....	....	....	....	....	....	....	....	....	....	....	....	....	....	....	....	....
McDowell	30	41	46	63	62	60	68	43	40	5	1	2	....	1	....	138	147	63	18	15	16
[redacted]rg	496	495	509	522	546	429	534	523	425	398	334	236	177	72	42	2,457	1,240	795	295	530	310
[redacted]ll	5	7	8	4	13	4	9	8	6	7	6	3	3	3	4	48	11	12	6	....	7
Montgomery	65	70	70	55	60	65	75	60	60	50	55	35	40	25	30	340	235	175	65	45	105
Mre	102	89	94	134	125	106	100	124	109	96	81	70	59	26	18	772	431	287	154	88	432
Nash	106	103	152	89	168	164	179	130	172	158	123	89	67	58	31	847	516	373	102	107	332
New Hanover	112	159	249	276	282	262	241	218	183	131	72	27	14	6	...	2,232	2,232	2,232	2,232	2,232	2,232
Northampton	138	187	198	147	206	199	242	254	245	186	184	134	93	53	34	1,061	575	342	253	85	352
Onslow	54	73	69	63	83	72	93	90	93	80	82	63	32	36	20	580	330	189	111	85	155
Orange	78	95	100	89	126	99	89	84	67	46	54	40	48	25	9	558	343	195	46	56	160
Pamlico	30	24	35	26	30	27	46	56	19	52	54	30	20	26	11	224	112	85	40	54	170
Pasquotank	72	82	87	70	100	82	94	81	90	68	75	43	29	26	15	482	190	137	66	30	101
Pender	93	120	101	93	120	87	109	113	97	98	85	81	55	31	20	616	295	158	31	52	119
Perquimans	81	86	88	90	102	99	115	100	94	101	75	71	49	28	33	771	553	233	129	63	215
Person	....	....	....	....	....	....	....	....	....	....	....	....	....	....	....	....	....	....	....	....	....
Pitt	....	....	....	....	....	....	....	....	....	....	....	....	....	....	....	....	....	....	....	....	....
Polk	28	26	49	34	34	26	34	29	27	24	19	9	16	4	2	141	55	40	12	....	40
Randolph	94	76	95	97	79	63	52	80	75	70	21	12	18	17	10	801	314	231	84	61	191
Richmond	....	....	....	....	....	....	....	....	....	....	....	....	....	....	....	....	....	....	....	....	....
Robeson	176	194	212	220	224	205	233	203	189	176	134	117	98	47	29	1,202	516	216	138	106	73
Croatans	46	67	66	89	66	35	61	59	51	41	30	33	23	26	208	104	44	17	28	14	....

Rockingham..	115	168	167	194	177	167	207	189	224	163	143	96	76	42	22	1,147	704	419	145	159	158
Rowan....	113	117	101	139	121	100	121	119	127	100	83	96	54	29	39	740	374	237	68	119	104
Rutherford..	94	92	100	74	78	90	92	90	62	54	46	40	22	10	..	450	300	160	95	50	237
Sampson	101	132	141	141	186	159	187	186	150	176	168	150	88	55	49	1,353	566	412	155	189	537
Stanly	19	37	33	36	41	28	28	36	46	23	38	19	18	18	5	159	122	97	53	45	39
Stokes.	37	58	51	52	74	54	62	53	65	53	52	47	24	....		261	151	100	13	21	20
Surry	27	30	38	26	32	20	43	39	34	26	32	28	25	22	8	176	88	69	21	22	9
Swain	....	....	....	....	....	....	....	....	....	....	....	....	....	....	....	....	....	....	....	....	....
Transylvania	25	22	19	16	14	12	13	10	9	8	7	7	6	4	3	40	40	125	10	10	10
Tyrrell	....	....	....	....	....	....	....	....	....	....	....	....	....	....	....	....	....	....	....	....	....
Union	173	184	161	161	218	137	214	193	198	169	123	101	73	46	24	984	540	369	133	136	226
Vance	116	138	171	156	172	133	164	137	159	109	98	71	33	18	8	1,103	596	391	89	149	809
Wake	492	587	580	632	677	564	629	578	499	420	416	326	232	168	124	2 206	892	960	460	229	520
Warren	127	195	195	215	229	213	294	266	226	201	184	115	93	50	18	1,279	635	140	203	132	320
Washington	84	111	95	93	92	122	107	93	107	63	50	30	24	9	6	432	223	146	51	82	216
Watauga	4	3	3	2	2	3	11	3	3	2	1	1	3	1	2	20	6	7	....	4	....
Wayne..	155	170	192	184	169	175	162	198	141	145	104	80	76	33	20	1,198	467	309	159	156	291
Wilkes	61	44	40	40	44	37	46	35	27	26	15	21	10	7	..	213	119	74	47	42	52
Wilson	117	114	143	115	119	123	126	108	115	116	99	53	42	27	21	631	273	193	56	109	256
Yadkin	17	11	19	20	23	23	36	19	22	29	28	15	11	13	14	170	109	77	22	27	44
Yancey	3	1	3	4	2	1	2	5	1	2	1	1	2	2	1	8	4	5	1	2	2
Total	7,507	8,564	9,080	9,054	9,625	9,109	10,229	9,5[illegible]4	8,745	7,708	6,770	5,213	3,851	2,392	1,618	56,875	33,269	22,229	9,541	11,002	18,187

TABLE No. VII.—1897.

Showing Amount Apportioned to White and Colored, Assessed Value of Property of White and Colored, Insolvent Polls, Poll Tax Levied, and Amount Applied to Schools.

COUNTIES.	Amount Appo-tioned to Whites.	Amount Appo-tioned to Col o ed.	Assessed Value of Property of Whites.	Assessed Value of Property of Colored.	No. White Polls.	No. Colored Pol s.	No. of Insolvent White Polls.	No. of Insolvent Colored Polls.	Total Poll Tax Levied.	Amount Poll Tax Pa d for Schools.	Amount Actually Paid by Whites on Property and Polls	Amount Actually Paid by Col o ed on Property and Polls.
[illegible]e	$ 10,036 00	$ 3,422 00	$ 4,971,750 00	$ 80,630 00	2,667	743	80	90	$ 2 25	$ 1 50	$ 12,879 64	$ 1,074 63
Alexander	3,541 00	4 00	...	...	*1,515	.	...	..	1 93	1 56	*4,224 04	...
Alleghany	2,165 25	194 91	607,952 00	6,753 00	983	44	94	13		1 24	2,427 81	58 66
Anson	2,852 25	2,968 58	1,724,821 00	74,545 00	1,557	1,169	433	888	...	1 50	4,710 67	656 18
Ashe	*5,281 24	...	1,268,885 00	3, 00 00	2,349	53	*50	.	...	.	5,296 62	...
Beaufort	5,452 72	2,631 05	2.423,112 00	147,799 00	1,991	1,187	477	435	.	1 19	6,226 44	266 03
Bertie	5,742 50	5,520 40	2,539,933 00	252,580 00	1,470	1,445	63	165	2 10	1 50	6,680 85	2,354 83
Bladen	4,137 39	1,342 04	1,182,719 00	106,410 00	1,339	767	...	.	2 35	1 50	4,137 39	1,342 04
[illegible]k	2,727 14	10,327 10	9,826 20	937 50	1,071	563	50	170	2 00	1 50	3,551 06	758 25
Buncombe	19,476 90	4,212 70	9,055,598 00	148,594 00	5,201	1,296	670	1.345	2 00	1 50	23,082 76	1,235 00
[illegible]	5,481 75	979 60	1,354,266 00	33,110 00	1,644	203	...	...	3 00	1 50	2.466 00	304 50
Cabarrus	7,533 73	2,572 57	3,108,939 00	56,285 00	2,043	504	.	.	...	...	...	...
Caldwell	4,524 22	728 50	16,322 02	141 10	1,746	154	130	70	2 00	1 50	5,478 96	151 39
Camden	1,904 00	912 00	528,856 00	37,160 00	492	330	15	31	2 00	1 50	2,037 64	541 40
[illegible]	2,425 00	466 10	785,615 00	31,865 00	1,439	200	407	104	1 95	1 29	2,545 57	118 54
Caswell	2 830 90	2,830 90	1,333.369 00	50,019 00	1,011	892	100	300	.	1 50	...	...
Catawba	6,663 40	1,277 70	2,643,652 00	27,212 00	2,432	266	22	40	1 50	.	8,406 57	447 98
Chatham	6,265 60	3,763 10	2,671,309 00	109,497 00	2,366	859	..	.	2 15	1 50	...	...
Cherokee	4,038 40	147 25	1,339,247 00	2,132 00	1,198	27	172	17	3 75	1 50	3,255 70	33 60
Chowan	3,102 00	2,520 79	1,215,176 00	109,847 00	712	610	25	100	2 00	1 56	3,255 31	1,112 72

Clay	1,354 40	44 00	489,000 00	921 00	556	15			1 66	1 50		
Cleveland	8,903 10	2,277 10	3,015,421 00	72,523 00	2,860	485				1 56	*10,225 26	
[illegible]us	5 486 40	3,011 70	1,662,440 00	19,806 00	1,939	552	51	152		1 50	5,774 11	790 07
Craven	4,577 98	4,720 95	2,357,269 00	132,454 00	1,461	1,451					4,096 43	3,881 76
Cumberland	6,711 77	4,953 86			2,344	1,315				1 50		
Currituck	2,301 00	829 00	568,892 00	27,025 00	831	322	15	60	2 00	1 50	2,078 00	437 76
Dare	1,464 82	1,777 74	340,335 00	11,673 00	635	61	48	7	2 25	1 56	1,565 10	112 57
Davidson	8,996 64	1,876 92	3,252,502 00	43,445 00	2,852	285	175	125		1 56	10,132 50	505 70
Davie	3,445 00	1,298 00	1,564,558 00	33,509 00	1,404	278	211	122	2 00	1 50	4,366 63	279 61
Duplin	4,220 35	2,442 04	2,050,846 00	75,777 00	2,024	678	281	205	2 00	1 50	7,240 15	1,153 40
Durham	12,676 65	7,573 80	7,369,348 00	122,650 00	2,150	1,085	158	316	2 00		16,252 82	1,373 77
Edgecombe	6,271 41	4,516 03	3,566,672 00	97,937 00	1,601	1,871			2 00	1 50	8,053 37	4,532 41
Forsyth	11,153 00	4,746 00	7,026,543 00	146,150 00	3,574	1,371	350	702	2 00	1 50	19,211 08	2,319 57
Franklin	4,765 00	4,170 00	2,452,934 00	171,730 00	2,041	1,551	251	636	1 50	1 50	8,086 60	1,537 89
Gaston	6,184 87	2,445 88	3,183,769 00	54,241 00	2,364	705	482	189	2 00	1 50	11,046 00	
Gates	2,204 80	2,361 60	978,045 00	82,526 00	888	528	25	50	2 00	1 50	3,512 31	835 55
Graham	1,890 40	52 80	*605 779 00		554	5	50			1 29	1,912 40	635 00
Granville	5,128 85	5,122 43	*3,814,280 00		1,648	1,486	747		1 95	1 46		
Greene	3,055 00	2,255 00	1,323,497 00	64,596 00	995	723	46	72	2 27	1 56	3,934 46	1,244 15
Guilford	12,137 00	5,734 00	5,939,121 00	157,423 00	3,400	820	510	440	1 64		16,940 00	931 00
Halifax	3 679 78	4,997 45	3 316,793 00	315,182 00	1,698	2,414			2 00			
Harnett	2,219 50	1,110 50	1,393,914 00	49,058 00	1,573	519	271	195		1 50	4,984 98	543 97
Haywood												
Henderson	5,381 26	975 47	2 072,973 00	23,427 00	1,661	142			3 06			
Hertford	3,809 07	3,939 03	1,679,644 00	214 159 00	989	1,063	45	166	2 00	1 56	4,894 93	1,784 79
Hyde	2,519 93	1,142 07	937,226 00	37,375 00	867	507	61	123	2 69	1 50	2,896 01	643 27
Iredell	7,968 95	2,906 40	3,452,024 09	69 875 00	2,895	780						
Jackson	3,603 15	205 20	1,162,118 00	12,560 00	1,266	49	124	22	2 00	1 50	3,990 81	96 11
Johnston	12,504 00	3,175 00	3,149 549 00	83,744 00	3,427	901			1 56			
Jones	1,807 08	1,602 16	1,043,204 00	48,690 00	697	453	38	76	2 30	1 50	2,866 26	653 14
Lenoir	3 294 68	2,375 27	1,818,547 00	99,142 00	1,607	863			2 45	1 56	3,522 70	2,422 55
Lincoln	4,854 00	1,368 00	1,853,399 00	37,121 00	1,586	266			2 00		6,059 92	465 82

*White and Colored.

D.

Counties.	Amount Apportioned to Whites.	Amount Apportioned to Colored.	Assessed Value of Property of Whites.	Assessed Value of Property of Colored.	No. White Polls.	No. Colored Polls.	No. of Insolvent White Polls	No. of Insolvent Colored Polls.	Total Poll Tax Levied.	Amount Poll Tax Paid for Schools.	Amount Actually Paid by Whites on Property and Polls.	Amount Actually Paid by Colored on Property and Polls.
Macon	$ 4,123 00	$ 300 00	$ 1,073,152 00	$ 7,961 00	1,464	78	42	10	$	$ ..	$	$ ......
Madison	6,242 40	154 40	1,655,514 00	2,330 00	2,693	67	802	28	....	1 50	*10,086 04	....
Martin	5,304 90	3,144 30	1,883,239 00	120,090 00	1,245	888	48	140	....	....	1,867 50	1,332 00
McDowell	3,761 00	180 00	889,984 00	5,459 00	1,293	156	*95	.....	2 45	1 50	......	1, 00 00
Mecklenburg	20,122 00	9,780 00	9,230,766 00	268,010 00	3,783	2,052	*1,000	....	2 00	1 50	24,089 88	3,560 42
Mitchell	3,400 20	127 20	795,150 00	5,783 00	1,571	32	....	....	.	..	4,311 97	1,642 10
Montgomery	3,148 62	1,185 34	1,238,293 00	17,285 00	1,453	348	....	....	....	1 50	3,695 69	1,247 57
Moore	5,395 00	2,979 00	3,145,434 00	72,586 00	2,336	951	..	.	2 15	....	10,723 00	1,092 00
Nash	7,457 76	5,747 04	3,029,556 00	142,739 00	2,329	1,259	200	175	.	...	.....	......
New Hanover	....	.	6,403,029 00	453,810 00	1,546	1,425	518	1,077	2 10	1 50	11,525 45	816 86
Northampton	4,755 56	5,279 26	2,846,252 00	212,963 00	1,499	1,616	40	260	..	1 50	7,235 40	2,526 15
Onslow	3,706 00	1,402 00	1,612,303 00	51,411 00	1,387	438	25	139	1 50	1 50	4,123 00	541 03
Orange	.	.	...	.	1,393	612	.....	...	2 00	...	.	......
Pamlico	1,710 56	892 44	597,295 00	45,109 00	829	325	..	..	2 00	1 56	2,411 76	587 40
Pasquotank	3,315 00	2,715 00	1,972,769 00	157,635 00	1,027	853	4	7	2 00	1 56	4,766 62	1,493 34
Pender	2,365 54	2,335 11	1,550,211 00	93,212 00	938	782	98	301	2 00	1 56	4,129 85	923 34
Perquimans	2,830 00	2,270 00	1,281,332 00	106,714 00	848	546	30	48	1 50	1 50	3,856 67	1,000 46
Person	.	....	...	.	.	.	.	....	.	...	.....	.....
Pitt	8,671 26	6,431 69	3,289,952 00	96,937 00	2,463	1,962	*1,000	....	.....	1 56	8,764 28	3,235 20
Polk	2,028 05	564 45	173,328 00	2,806 00	712	98	25	15	....	..	.....	......
Randolph	9,820 00	1,790 00	3,616,941 00	45,218 00	3,521	383	400	....	..	....	12,380 19	655 89
Richmond	4,472 32	4,908 85	2,556,159 00	60,154 00	1,765	1,405	785	.....	.....	1 54	2,150 12	1,139 25

Robeson	6,766 60	8,190 30	550,025 00	6,893 00	2,716	2,288	*370		2 29	1 50	10,078 46	3,943 04
Rockingham	8,911 00	5,556 60	3,655,375 00	110,920 00	2,636	1,120	*999		1 50	1 56		
Rowan	10,626 00	3,697 50	4,996,211 00	118,976 00	2,927	578	247	119	1 95	1 23	13,271 61	802 52
Rutherford	6,590 75	1,773 25	2,238,672 00	48,856 00	2,615	469						
Sampson	5,746 20	3,463 00	1,838,572 00	73,792 00	2,616	844	150	250	2 15	1 50	6,963 42	978 82
Stanly	2,617 80	360 00	1,424,591 00	28,880 00	1,652	186	209	40	3 00	1 50	4,856 02	250 18
Stokes	6,765 62		1,733,969 00	26,089 00	2,333	368			2 00	1 50	6,594 77	515 39
Surry	7,732 50	1,166 65	2,573,316 00	36,081 00	3,[illegible]4	336				1 50	9,192 96	568 95
Swain	2,741 20	70 40	1,124,047 00	1,640 00	860	15			1 50	1 50	2,626 26	55 00
Transylvania	2,387 12	262 88	884,780 00	5,137 00	836	52				1 50	2,746 58	87 25
Tyrrell												
Union	6,501 75	2,887 40	3,091,923 00	69,088 00	2,611	738	222	202	2 69	1 56		
Vance	3,646 00	4,111 00	2,752,574 00	137,049 00	1,047	1,190				1 25	6,263 38	1,487 50
Wake	11,003 05	9,150 20	9,339,546 00	460,802 00	4,375	2,664	436	983		1 50	20,468 32	4,326 18
Warren	3,500 00	3,700 00	1,767,031 00	259,968 00	957	1,386			2 00	1 50	4,673 57	2,630 07
Washington	3,290 00	2,486 00	991,[illegible]08 00	65,467 00	870	676	19	40	2 00	1 50	3,272 02	1,257 16
Watauga	4,390 24	189 67	1,187,986 00	5,436 00	1,718	37	83	15	2 00	1 50	4,479 91	89 67
Wayne	8,770 00	7,089 00	5,226,696 00	242,194 00	2,716	1,441	221	450	1 50	1 50	13,440 83	1,888 24
Wilkes	6,069 00	643 30					*335					
Wilson	6,256 40	4,585 00	3,108,089 00	87,861 00	2,034	1,096			2 00	1 56	9,492 30	1,802 14
Yadkin	4,463 04	587 52	1,362,465 00	12,790 00	1,870	137	77	23	2 00		5,358 89	228 52
Yancey	3,041 18	87 78	512,512 00	800 00	1,439	31	121	4		1 50	3,081 02	47 94
Total	$ 485,203 75	$ 244,468 22	$211,301,836 00	$7,350,064 00	167,476	66,674	14,430	11,752	126 59	104 89	$ 507,273 60	$ 79,392 20

*White and Colored.

TABLE No. I.—1898.

School Fund Received by County Treasurer for the School Year Ending June 30, 1898.

COUNTIES.	State and County Poll Tax.	General Property Special Tax.	Special Property Tax. Local Acts.	Special Poll Tax. Local Acts	Fines, Forfeitures and Penalties.	Liquor Licenses.	Estray.	State Treasurer.	Other Sources.	Total Receipts.	Balance on Hand Last Report.
Alamance	$ 4,945 50	$ 8,531 14	$	$	$ 241 33	$	$	$ 728 37	$ 141 50	$ 14,587 84	$ 1,515 38
Alexander	2,254 13	1,707 14			55 00			334 98	81 00	4,432 25	197 02
Alleghany	1,407 00	1,187 57			97 75			253 71		2,946 03	1,587 75
Anson	2,342 70	3,622 86			145 06	190 00		711 72	671 51	11,208 68	3,524 83
Ashe	3,164 24	2,322 18			113 57	4 75		631 62	59 37	6,295 73	999 98
Beaufort	3,982 23	4,934 45			69 87	1,530 00		705 78	604 65	11,826 98	5,814 03
Bertie	4,314 04	4,798 49			209 59			709 11	866 57	10,897 80	4,559 54
Bladen	2,906 45	2,572 87	152 68	78 10	53 42		60	613 17	138 88	6,516 17	1,873 53
Brunswick	1,883 60	2,355 60			65 10	142 50		389 52	99 07	4,935 39	1,[illegible]87 20
Buncombe	6,100 21	17,104 89			323 40	1,425 00		1,310 04	1,364 29	29,045 62	7,360 96
Burke	2,311 83	2,904 86			285 19	190 00		559 53		0,323 41	1,124 33
Cabarrus	4,939 86	6,260 14			371 34			674 10	432 60	12,678 04	1,261 53
Caldwell	6,500 83				247 22			487 89		7,235 94	
Camden	1,086 63	1,385 12			49 02	90 00		166 86		2,845 62	229 64
Carteret	1,365 53	1,272 67			13 50	190 00		342 18	925 34	4,109 22	1,555 95
Caswell	1,963 42	2,110 31	57 00		119 00	997 50		441 18		6,091 16	2,569 28
Catawba	4,000 00	4,723 60			205 06			686 88		9,615 54	
Chatham	4,325 00	4,884 32			161 95			825 95	1,002 14	11,198 96	2,980 94
Cherokee	1,778 56	3,557 03	1,003 70	501 86	69 00			392 85	87 50	7,390 50	1,737 05
Chowan	1,973 70	2,789 50			103 13	1,420 86		273 75		6,706 60	
Clay		1,839 23			45 50			154 35	428 65	2,313 38	14 32
Cleveland	4,574 25	5,968 31			603 28	600 00		869 31	5,469 88	17,215 72	956 17

Columbus	3,468 48	4,579 77			68 60			683 37	230 72	9,030 84	4,896 50
Craven	5,256 90	5,489 88			120 36	3,200 00		640 35		14,826 49	1,441 41
Cumberland	1,875 00	8,231 50			33 73	2,400 00		833 94	272 00	13,646 17	3 16
Currituck								198 36			
Dare	669 00	318 42	84 86	21 00	83 32			134 46	19 50	1,330 50	585 14
Davidson	4,025 30	6,410 84	74 30	23 94	235 95			734 04	263 91	11,773 45	
Davie	2,077 65	2,741 05			114 70			421 83	66 00	5,426 23	114 93
Duplin	3,626 10	4,002 13			82 25	95 00	5 97	673 28	106 70	8,596 43	2,116 75
Durham	3,732 18	14,869 42			549 18	1,965 00		638 19	871 19	21,986 97	840 10
Edgecombe	13,317 35				471 81	3,144 50		775 53	3,426 40	21,195 59	3,977 35
Forsyth	4,873 28	9,131 54			496 71	1,000 00		979 29	1,321 18	17,802 00	4,549 85
Franklin	3,448 77	4,444 18			340 82	1,045 00		548 64	847 40	10,674 81	2,578 12
Gaston	5,092 50	6,262 19			573 00			904 48	324 92	13,157 09	2,049 74
Gates	2,016 91	2,243 82			40 55	356 25		357 48	85 00	5,000 01	2,458 70
Graham	645 00	1,179 17			34 00			132 57	12 00	2,002 74	
Granville	4,822 80	6,255 16			67 60	800 00		677 25	174 50	12,797 31	1,123 34
Greene	2,366 93	2,375 52			26 30	912 00		340 47	1,140 00	7,161 22	3,164 28
Guilford	6,992 42	11,042 83			554 46	1,100 00		978 30	77 50	20,743 50	510 38
Halifax	4,235 72	11,161 66			15 92	3,624 03		1,037 62	17 33	20,092 28	868 29
Harnett	2,566 43	2,589 25			49 75	475 00		513 73	126 50	6,320 65	1,469 56
Haywood								536 31			
Henderson	2 758 50	4,147 53			195 91	100 00		488 43		8,117 66	7,309 16
Hertford	2,594 58	3,680 64			78 17	522 50		477 63	101 50	7,455 02	
Hyde	1,952 44	1,715 35	317 68	144 30	16 55	285 00		303 75	447 00	5,268 28	3,322 68
Iredell	4,963 92	8,158 44			368 98	1,400 00		913 50	121 72	15,926 56	906 18
Jackson	2,014 20	2,217 27			113 30			378 90	981 84	5,705 51	8 90
Johnston	7,155 72	6,948 04			64 70	1,869 41		991 53	219 76	17,249 20	3,568 96
Jones	1,394 62	1,822 04			27 72	350 00		260 19	428 83	4,283 40	2,288 43
Lenoir	3,118 00	4,408 76			271 18	1,340 00		522 09	2,955 05	12,526 00	
Lincoln	2,537 73	3,507 66			179 10			479 70	70 00	6,774 39	608 99
Macon	2,199 54	1 956 30	93 34	37 15	30 69			380 70	88 35	4,786 07	113 95
Madison	4,536 64				143 70	332 50		434 31	170 80	5,617 95	1 14
Martin	2,896 31	3,851 83			36 11	1,852 50		518 67	111 75	9,267 17	9,052 40

TABLE No I.—Continued.

Counties.	State and County Poll Tax.	General Property Special Tax.	Special Property Tax. Local Acts.	Special Poll Tax. Local Acts.	Fines, Forfeitures and Penalties.	Liquor Licenses.	Estray.	State Treasurer.	Other Sources.	Total Receipts.	Balance on Hand Last Report.
McDowell	$	$	$	$	$	$	$	$ 389 70	$	$	$
Mecklenburg	10,083 16	18,855 72	237 74	54 00	165 67	3,211 01		1,204 56	1,971 60	35,783 45	5,601 63
Mitchell	1,914 11	1,739 93			118 57			520 47		4,293 08	
Montgomery	1,989 45	2,230 08	107 45		289 32			387 38	120 72	5,124 40	1,541 30
Moore	4,049 00	5,527 57			126 29			756 54	130 00	10,589 40	290 00
Nash	7,371 10	5,594 50			281 44	1,343 94		788 22	1,940 51	16,531 49	
New Hanover	3,152 90	13,177 90			23 01	12,360 00		684 81	12,805 23	42,203 85	6,404 34
Northampton	4,183 36		5,602 82		115 65	250 00		709 02	63 00	10,923 85	1,374 83
Onslow	2,436 75	2,766 86			46 00	389 50	4 67	367 65	268 50	6,279 93	2,154 98
Orange	2,000 00	3,285 59			120 95			433 35	57 00	5,896 89	
Pamlico	1,257 75	1,532 57			47 50			255 78		3,138 60	1,761 00
Pasquotank	2,500 96	5,001 92			71 90	969 00		391 87	76 25	9,011 90	566 87
Pender	2,427 52	2,952 70			1 05	100 00		444 60	96 00	6,021 87	2,499 89
Perquimans	2,034 08	2,750 03			52 28	403 75		320 04		5,816 16	138 30
Person	1,340 00	4,822 45			100 00			459 72		6,262 45	114 00
Pitt	5,950 50	5,[illegible]32 72			332 31	6,040 38		1,007 38	525 00	19,687 91	274 71
Polk	875 00	1,883 00	255 66		33 50	95 00		218 34		3,400 50	167 47
Randolph		12,188 14			399 95			909 45		13,497 54	
Richmond	3,892 50	5,221 64			201 08	700 00		875 75		10,890 97	4,615 36
Robeson	7,550 88	10,141 19			193 94			1,167 84	210 75	19,264 60	2,397 00
Rockingham	5,823 00	8,453 18			361 40	3,200 00		929 25	685 25	19,452 08	
Rowan	4,610 93	10,284 80			153 85	845 50		853 92	217 25	16,966 25	560 12
Rutherford	4,866 00	4,818 74			416 03			791 64	3,909 37	14,801 78	730 16

Sampson	4,418 93	3,383 82			120 85	950 00		876 60	481 57	10,231 77	1,353 84
Stanly	2,503 50	2,241 66			221 43			446 67	169 09	5,582 35	
Stokes	3,017 55	2,544 26			319 40	400 00		638 55		6,889 76	222 42
Surry	4,217 05	4,345 99			150 84	95 00		601 74	2,566 34	11,966 96	2,728 59
Swain	1,053 93	1,937 65						199 98		199 98	2,991 58
Transylvania	1,301 03	1,575 32			97 50			213 75		3,240 85	2,745 90
Tyrrell	1,063 05	873 09			8 30	10 00		150 84	54 00	2,159 28	1,558 55
Union	4,874 93	5,486 20			275 67	380 00		876 60	834 85	12,728 25	2,541 55
Vance	402 80	5,872 20			62 50	665 00		492 30	165 72	7,660 52	1,279 12
Wake	7,200 00	20,145 94	13,535 09		566 09	2,100 00		1,595 16	2,136 16	45,683 28	13,415 24
Warren	4,208 06	3,777 59			19 24	900 00		628 20	115 00	9,648 09	239 98
Washington	2,247 28	1,881 07			140 81	1,615 00		326 34	106 86	6,317 36	3,234 58
Watanga	2,460 98	2,029 63			223 26	47 50		419 22	285 74	5,466 33	450 34
Wayne	5,506 92	10,117 00			151 64	1,254 00		954 45	143 75	18,127 76	4,630 95
Wilkes	3,729 62	3,218 05			107 16	83 13		898 92		8,036 88	
Wilson	5,832 00	7,100 81			43 85	2,220 00		772 11	991 91	16,188 57	5,833 73
Yadkin	2,679 00	2,470 30			373 94			479 97	31 63	6,034 84	610 07
Yancey	1,659 37	922 70			86 89			247 40		3,200 26	134 97
Total	$ 318,933 58	$ 441,526 92	$ 21,522 32	$ 860 35	$ 15,653 50	$ 74,777 01	$11 24	$ 56,849 13	$ 57,170 35	$ 988,409 11	$ 176,341 19

*Due from Sheriff. Auctioneers, $70 80.

TABLE No. II—1898.

School Fund Disbursed by County Treasurer for School Year Ending June 30, 1898.

COUNTIES.	Paid Teachers of White Schools.	Paid Teachers of C°lor'd Schools.	Paid for School Houses and sites (white).	Paid for School Houses and sites (colored).	Paid County Superintendents	Paid for Institutes (white.)	Paid for Institutes (colored.)	Paid Treasurers' Commissions.	Paid Mileage and per diem Board of Education.	Paid Expenses of Board of Education.	Paid to City Schools.	Paid for other Purposes.	
Alamance	$ 8,768 43	$ 3,143 78	$ 1,192 64	$ 66 30	$ 327 00	$	$	$ 269 97	$ 47 20	$ 61 86	$	$ 633 07	$ 1
Alexander	3,614 31	404 10			106 00			84 98	44 75	8 70		71 00	
Alleghany	2,272 85	139 71	291 04	8 00	57 09			30 00	37 10	3 98		133 72	
Anson	3,051 30	2,233 09	342 81	425 50	355 70			120 87	120 90	8 00		357 35	
Ashe	4,939 60	209 30			345 00	47 00		125 47	57 95	11 77		19 70	
Beaufort	6,719 35	3,659 16	10 00	20 00	375 98			813 70	77 40	18 54		1,803 07	1
Bertie	6,328 90	5,114 59	339 10		237 00			252 69	75 60	21 68		771 13	1
Bladen	3,257 57	1,412 72	345 83	209 27	162 00			104 50	82 86	7 29		2,288 59	
Brunswick	2,461 83	1,490 25	167 25	108 50	126 00			152 48	68 80	9 91		650 24	
Buncombe	13,523 02	1,814 72	120 00	13 50	866 00	*100 00		525 68	199 20	411 33	5,994 00	3,272 27	2
Burke	3,786 02	847 45		6 00	52 50		29 00	105 64	65 70	22 30		473 22	
Cabarrus	5,658 02	1,951 16			135 65			242 28	17 00	93 41	3,710 85	552 99	1
Caldwell	4,836 05	508 29	1,229 30	89 00	315 46			141 19	57 00	24 75		26 85	
Camden	1,679 86	814 92			103 15			70 72	34 80				
Carteret	2,233 53	368 00			126 05			59 12	45 35	16 10		166 89	
Caswell	2,501 10	2,525 75	153 00	190 22	268 75					112 69			
Catawba	7,051 27				160 81			176 30	80 85		864 45	503 97	
Chatham	6,422 64	3,614 68	80 00		235 00			160 57		74 17		278 25	1
Cherokee	5,254 05	237 25	92 40					114 57	46 94	32 04	66 05		
Chowan	2,078 99	2,380 58	237 50	231 85	150 00			162 10	14 20	6 60		524 51	
Clay	1,545 04	72 16	346 75		12 00			45 54	30 00	15 04	254 80	1 00	
Cleveland	10 057 04	2,509 26	515 10	105 06	465 00	75 00	25 00	277 39	58 00	25 50		35 50	1

Columbus	4,839 85	2,572 89	210 00	30 00	316 59			66 10	42 50	39 50		621
Craven	6,752 25	6,682 50	257 58	378 03	374 00			295 08	119 30	35 85		154
Cumberland	6,509 41	4,803 59	40 00	42 50	210 56			253 44	40 70	18 00		977
Currituck												
Dare	1,252 98	160 60	116 34	5 35	115 77			42 68	50 00	6 35		
Davidson	8,001 33	1,403 42	598 74	173 82	212 50	4 00	2 50	219 87	43 80	29 60		
Davie	3,136 11	1,025 69	226 84		231 35			92 01	76 58	14 34		211
Duplin	4,742 42	2,041 66	1,275 05	115 00	313 00			172 36	82 30	7 83		87
Durham	8,927 63	6,165 75	1,690 27	173 00	328 86			37 08		42 30	3,750 00	1,406
Edgecombe	* 11,523 67				312 00	21 00	21 00	308 96		147 75	3,235 90	752
Forsyth	1,029 05				337 27			428 68	304 76		3,833 00	
Franklin	4,653 81	4,368 26			373 50			213 49	149 10			545
Gaston	7,311 14	2,811 31	779 26	111 03	84 00			224 36	46 40	7 00		223
Gates	2,210 78	1,623 00	100 00	90 00	81 00			91 65	63 70	13 81		1,019
Graham	1,590 03		121 83	25 00	8 00			38 77	52 45	7 66		159
Granville	6,776 10	4,809 76	160 00	463 50	365 00			253 76	79 00	15 07		20
Greene	3,821 66	2,475 71	286 17	413 85	41 85			145 45	77 75			185
Guilford	14,916 97	13,058 53	751 50	202 48	832 18			395 23				
Halifax	4,498 38	6,821 17	146 03	561 35	551 10			283 00	129 70	120 86	434 00	887
Harnett	4,038 16	1,428 30	216 38	206 65	298 00			220 20	54 00	20 48		
Haywood												
Henderson	4,991 53	999 62	181 00	22 09	141 45			141 31	46 90			
Hertford	3,023 00	3,238 33	333 24	148 17	220 49			111 32	67 80	42 38		108
Hyde	2,564 50	1,405 13			164 50			91 94	94 80	2 13		632
Iredell	7,775 62	2 506 85	1,180 37	188 54	343 35			271 58	65 50	41 44	1,435 00	42
Jackson	4,496 53	295 75	471 93		208 78			111 77		95 00		
Johnston	12,293 19	3,137 79	684 32	242 84	213 00			335 89	75 15	13 75		234
Jones	2,000 60	1,245 79	35 00		178 00			76 97	82 50	7 80		122
Lenoir	5 227 33	3,174 42	523 95	425 24	206 87			187 61	78 20			70
Lincoln	5,276 62	1,078 04			70 25	11 68	10 00	133 99	25 50			227
Macon	3,790 37	286 00	296 20		160 50			46 04	61 80			9
Madison	4,266 08	150 00	168 89					105 70		81 75		241
Martin	4,588 37	2,830 58	411 17	291 23	159 98			166 32	51 40	4 97		

*White and Colored. †Due Treasurer.

TABLE No. II—Continued.

Counties.	Paid Teachers of White Schools.	Paid Teachers of Color'd Schools.	Paid f o School Houses and sites (white).	Paid f o School Houses and sites (colored).	Paid County Superintendents	Paid f o Institutes (white.)	Paid f o Institutes (colored).	Paid Treasurers' Commissions.	Paid Mileage and per diem Board of Education.	Paid Expenses of Board of Education.	Paid to City Schools.	Paid for other Purposes.
McDowell..	$	$	$	$	$	$	$.	$	$. . . .	$. . . .	$.	$. . . . .
Mecklenburg.	15,665 26	6,423 69	53 25	24 05	610 50			699 82	107 85	. . . . .	9,479 36	2,912 38
Mitchell	3,815 29	171 11	19 44	. . . .	83 00	50 00	. . . .	78 00	64 24	12 00	. . . .	. . . . .
Montgomery .	2,629 50	1,018 74	. . . .	. . .	110 00	. . . . .		76 80	59 40	22 82	. . . . .	. . .
Moore	6,084 15	3,115 50	172 30	26 05	300 00		. . . . .	210 86	62 80	20 00	115 50	647 09
Nash..	8,054 55	4,478 15	1,770 64	765 31	382 56	. .	. . . . .	305 83	31 10	3 96	. . . .	167 93
New Hanover	11,350 00	8,125 00	14,097 43	40 00	1,800 00		. . . . .	796 10	. . . . .	659 05	. . . .	3,874 99
Northampton	5,377 73	4,690 44	458 00	28 74	615 00	4 50		235 31	64 55	175 53	. . . .	399 58
Onslow	3,277 75	1,022 27	348 97	158 85	313 75	. . .		96 15	88 65	17 55	. . . .	18 38
Orange	3,542 82	1,729 60	. .	5 45	221 89	. . . . .	. . .	118 72	85 40	. . . . .	. . . .	184 02
Pamlico .	1,710 46	733 28	181 63	11 13	114 77	. .	. . . . .	25 36	27 00	. . . . .	. . . .	. . .
Pasquotank	4,045 47	2,680 01	400 00	95 77	140 50	. . . . .		164 30	62 20	. . . . .	. . . .	836 11
Pender	2,077 72	1,516 98	633 25	498 91	304 31	. . . . .		94 53	82 60	12 25	. . . .	. . . .
Perquimans	2,246 14	1,717 00	477 82	866 14	109 10	. . .	. .	145 74	65 05	.	. .	. . . . . .
Person	3,022 70	2,063 81	77 20	310 90	. .	. . . . .		151 28	. . . .	225 75	. . . . .	121 70
Pitt	9,469 67	5,805 48	. . .	. . . .	258 97	. . . . .	. . . . .	351 98	77 13	. .	. . .	2,010 47
Polk	1,498 62	440 20	8 79	3 50	87 36	. . . .	. . . . .	45 31	48 00	6 50	. . . .	. . . .
Randolph .	10,667 77	1,520 37	. . . .	. . .	147 85	. . .		254 06	58 15	. . . . . .	. . . .	. . . .
Richmond .	4,374 62	4,765 27	701 05	347 16	113 96	. . . . .	. . . . .	209 83	79 16	110 56	. . . .	. . . . .
Robeson .	7,617 11	4,920 01	860 36	619 59	170 00	. . .		321 32	74 50	47 33	. . . .	75 00
Croatans	. . . . .	1,695 81	*88 00	. . . .	. . . .			. .	. . . .	. . . . . .	. . . .	. . .
Rockingham	7,477 26	3,938 09	807 93		. . . .	359 15	122 25	312 23	. . . . . .	507 32	2,252 60	3,522 63
Rowan.	10,271 20	3,400 50	416 45	226 64	264 00	. . . .	. . . . .	295 38	65 00	18 00	. . . .	107 00

8,561 66	1,953 87	1,219 53	180 50	425 00			256 09	117 20	91 01			12,804 86	2,727 08
6,836 73	3,883 90	100 83	98 75	228 00			227 01	108 40	10 00		84 20	11,577 82	8 79
4,410 90	430 06	169 45	2 34	84 00			103 36	66 00	8 40			5,274 51	307 84
5,334 16	1,089 10						197 78	99 67			6 50	6,727 21	384 97
11,521 62	1,054 20			138 20	19 80		251 51	110 50			1,468 74	14,564 57	130 98
195 99							3 99					199 98	‡2,991 58
1,920 60	242 08	9 60	1 00	84 34			55 11		22 00			2,811 04	3,175 71
1,196 83	427 69	122 90	35 50	75 25			40 11	40 50	2 25		250 65	2,191 68	1,526 15
9,180 44	3,270 83	387 07	67 80	314 43			261 32	83 00	29 45			13,594 34	1,675 46
3,811 23	3,880 99	194 48	82 00	245 69			179 95	68 20			714 97	9,177 51	237 87
20,879 79	14,737 33						889 73	382 13		1,650 00	8,076 46	46,645 44	12,483 08
2,812 18	3,402 03	349 27	1,286 55	281 96	5 60	25 00	179 32	62 05	8 41		553 89	8,966 26	921 81
3,383 69	2,248 64	270 29	123 27	321 58				40 00	13 93		737 65	7,281 83	2,270 11
4,662 10	143 00	103 75		156 77			102 14	21 30			20 00	5,209 06	707 61
7,018 08	3,991 36	550 50	629 21	227 50			315 58	113 20	59 40		118 25	16,455 08	6,303 63
6,361 57	768 50	124 05		123 50			153 17	111 85	16 00			7,658 64	378 24
7,732 04	5,403 51						284 74				1,101 37	14,521 86	7,500 44
4,890 90	645 16	113 33		110 00			118 86	92 05	2 86		88 64	6,062 10	582 81
3,003 87	135 96			84 00			64 00	44 10				3,332 03	3 20
$512,455 43	$228,033 97	$ 41,823 34	$ 12,117 28	$ 21,383 08	$697 73	$234 75	$ 18,071 05	$5 886 03	$3 903 61	$ 37,075 51	$ 49,501 18	$947,635 82	$210,274 20

or Croatans. †Due Treasurers ‡Due from Sheriff.

TABLE No. III.

Showing Number of Children Between Six and Twenty-one Years of Age, Number Enrolled, Average Attendance and Institute Sta in the Several Counties of the State During the School Year Ending June 30, 1898.

Counties.	Census of White Children.			Enrollment of White Children.			Average Attendance of White Children.	Census of Colored Children.			Enrollment of Colored Children.			Average Attendance of Colored Children.	Institutes.		No. Te… Atte…	
	Male.	Pemale.	Total.	Male.	Female.	Total.		Male.	Pemale.	Total.	Male.	Female.	Total.		White.	Colored.	W. Male.	W. Female.
Alamance	3,072	3,120	6,192	1,840	1,612	3,452	1,971	1,308	1,290	2,598	748	726	1,474	738	1	1	20	5
Alexander	2,159	2,155	4,314	1,440	1,442	2,882	1,386	191	193	384	180	183	363	237				
Alleghany	1,704	1,136	2,840	768	647	1,411	32	156	106	262	79	51	130	13				
Anson	2,016	1,817	3,833	1,043	952	1,995	1,410	2,104	2,012	4,106	1,195	1,287	2,482	1,708				
Ashe	3,628	3,203	6,831	1,457	2,051	3,508	2,650	156	146	306	91	83	174	15	1		52	
Beaufort	2,262	2,212	4,474	1,769	1,672	3,441	2,151	1,606	1,680	3,286	1,097	1,283	2,380	1,463				
Bertie	1,578	1,463	3,041	1,027	896	1,923	1,124	2,270	2,203	4,473	1,605	1,728	3,333	1,915				
Bladen	1,716	1,602	3,318	941	902	1,843	1,285	1,641	1,604	3,245	657	730	1,387	987				
Brunswick	1,336	1,226	2,562	904	835	1,739	2,307	978	1,011	1,989	505	54[illegible]	1,048	26				
Buncombe	6,277	6,012	12,789	3,000	3,442	6,442	4,500	1,307	1,321	2,628	500	450	950	525	1	1	31	4
Burke	.....		.....	1,025	964	1,989	.....	.....	.....	.....	252	258	510	347	1	1	10	1
Cabarrus	2,798	2,778	5,576	1,676	1,462	3,138	2,016	911	943	1,854	606	572	1,178	649				
Caldwell	2,430	2,407	4,821	1,606	1,389	2,995	1,584	399	380	779	226	228	454	204				
Camden	573	536	1,109	352	295	647	468	392	375	767	323	323	612	304				
Carteret	1,601	1,578	3,179	468	435	903	563	380	270	650	81	80	161	107				
Caswell	1,033	1,101	2,234	578	600	1,178	728	1,327	1,295	2,622	846	895	1,741	1,236				
Catawba	....		6,598	2,347	2,059	4,406	2,954	.....	.....	1,122	360	364	724	420	3		35	1
Chatham	2,866	2,646	5,412	1,880	1,627	3,507	2,314	1,592	1,554	3,146	958	1,075	2,033	1,283				
Cherokee	2,190	2,058	4,248	1,310	1,405	2,715	1,447	110	86	196	74	76	150	90				

Chowan	729	671	1,400	433	339	772	22	993	1,010	2,003	557	505	1,062	43	...	...	...	...
Clay	...	...	1,686	549	484	1,033	550	21	29	50	.....	.....	.....	.....	...	...	...	...
Cleveland	3,966	3,851	7,817	2,546	2,394	4,940	3,473	968	977	1,945	534	587	1,121	715	1	1	52	4
Columbus	2,588	2,511	5,099	1,883	1,730	3,613	2,384	1,228	1,404	2,632	1,127	927	2,054	1,231				
Craven	1,469	1,453	2,922	979	950	1,929	1,106	2,212	2,183	4,395	1,192	1,522	2,714	1,476				
Cumberland			6,394	1,296	1,302	2,598	23			5,047	1,286	1,477	2,763	27				
Currituck	803	744	1,547	522	447	969	604	388	387	775	268	275	543	289				
Dare	678	643	1,321	585	511	1, 06	840	87	72	159	75	60	135	120				
Davidson	3,628	3,468	7,096	2,446	2,157	4,571	3,045	677	653	1,330	385	359	744	462	1	1		
Davie	1,561	1,496	3,057	1,144	1,016	2,160	2,158	457	428	885	352	322	674	386				
Duplin	2,394	2,169	4,563	1,806	1,766	3,872	2,280	1,545	1,600	3,145	984	1,269	2,283	1,435				
Durham	2,565	2,498	5,063	936	804	1,740	1,066	1,540	1,595	3,135	790	801	1,591	816				
Edgecombe	1,626	1,622	3,248	793	945	1,738	658	2,831	2,770	5,601	1,407	1,761	3,168	870	2	2	2	3
Forsyth	3,860	3,626	7,486	2,130	1,800	3,930	2,292	1,700	1,695	3,395	590	571	1,161	658	1	1	50	1
Franklin	2,161	2,001	4,162	1,072	1,047	2,119	1,227	1,998	1,950	3,948	1,273	1,504	2,777	1,705				
Gaston	3,465	3,523	6,988	1,739	1,585	3,324	2,050	1,088	1,120	2,208	928	932	1,860	789				
Gates	1,041	923	1,964	768	709	1,477	825	922	916	1,838	624	689	1,313	792				
Graham	805	791	1,596	504	475	979	565	7	5	12								
Granville	1,984	1,890	3,874	963	947	1,910	1,126	2,162	2,066	4,228	1,182	1,364	2,546	1,319				
Greene	998	978	1,976	625	638	1,263	778	1,019	918	1,937	590	703	1,293	657				
Guilford	3,821	3,670	7,491	3,069	2,622	5,691	3,631	1,902	1,860	3,763	1,184	1,070	2,254	1,491	1	1	38	6
Halifax	1,777	1,799	3,576	759	843	1,600	982	3,508	3,596	7,104	1,623	2,177	3,800	2,233				
Harnett	2,040	1,866	3,906	1,541	1,325	2,866	1,824	956	956	1,912	501	617	1,118	701				
Haywood	2,870	3,100	5,871	2,593	2,748	5,341	3,974	105	118	218	97	89	186	157	3		37	3
Henderson	2,383	2,263	4,646	1,637	1,316	2,953	1,635	330	356	686	170	164	334	152				
Hertford	1,171	1,146	2,317	587	635	1,222	689	1,589	1,678	3,267	1,153	1,234	2,387	1,275	1	1	3	1
Hyde	1,013	844	1,857	657	545	1,202	808	739	739	1,478	591	609	1,200	828				
Iredell	3,750	3,522	7,272	2,334	2,193	4,527	2,882	1,279	1,274	2,553	812	842	1,654	934				
Jackson	1,985	1,956	3,941	1,450	1,304	2,754	1,505	110	106	216	84	84	168	107				
Johnston	4,162	3,900	8,062	2,898	2,470	5,368	2,931	1,473	1,468	2,941	844	951	1,795	1,015				
Jones	713	635	1,348	380	420	800	460	666	692	1,358	410	530	940	564				
Lenoir	1,792	1,657	3,449	893	827	1,720	1,024	1,283	1,155	2,438	862	850	1,712	1,062	1		8	3
Lincoln	2,247	2,135	4,382	1,475	1,320	2,795	1,862	591	572	1,163	376	413	789	470	1	1	19	1
Macon	2,101	1,990	4,091	1,549	1,330	2,879	1,648	121	149	270	73	76	149	78				

TABLE No. III—Continued.

Counties.	Census of White Children. Male.	Female.	Total.	Enrollment of White Children. Male.	Female.	Total.	Average Attendance of White Children.	Census of Colored Children. Male.	Female.	Total.	Enrollment of Colored Children. Male.	Female.	Total.	Average Attendance of Colored Children.	Institutes. White.	Colored.	No. T[…] Atte[…] W. Male.	W. Female.
Madison	3,924	3,804	7,728	2,354	2,104	4,458	2,416	77	78	155	25	39	64	41	5		33	3
Martin	1,514	1,280	2,794	1,446	1,252	2.698	1,354	1,408	1,305	2,713	1 372	1,234	2,606	1,107				
McDowell	1,800	1,730	3,530	1,178	1,053	2,231	1,150	361	419	780	229	217	443	221				
Mecklenburg	5,232	5,046	10,278	2,721	2,424	5,145	3,294	3,772	4,013	7,785	2,149	2,131	4,280	2,377				
Mitchell	2,843	2,993	5,836	1,900	2,100	4,000	1,000	100	80	180	60	40	100	33	1		25	1
Montgomery	1,983	1,843	3,826	1,120	840	1,960	33	525	505	1,030	384	434	818	31				
Moore	2,697	2,611	5,308	1,579	1,550	3,129	25	1,430	1,461	2,891	686	866	1,552	24				
Nash	2,570	2,526	5,100	1,352	1,344	2,696	1,518	1,957	1,827	3,784	999	1,174	2,173	1,026				
New Hanover	1,628	1,554	3,182	805	958	1,763	1,279	2,214	2,273	4,487	1,078	1,212	2,290	1,153				
Northampton	1,613	1,463	3,076	1,038	913	1,951	1,078	2,304	2,383	4,687	1,300	1,566	2,866	1,456	1		12	2
Onslow	1,523	1,303	2 826	1,355	1,197	2,552	1,437	715	820	1,525	424	450	874	469				
Orange	1,693	1,509	3,202	1,019	821	1,840	1,101	851	784	1,635	461	486	947	585				
Pamlico	897	894	1,791	716	676	1,392	954	534	529	1,063	180	285	465	26	1		3	
Pasquotank	1,453	1,452	2,505	702	601	1,303	950	1,250	1,000	2,250	560	500	1 060	690				
Pender	1,215	1,106	2,321	603	561	1,164	855	1,235	1,299	2,534	561	647	1,208	857				
Perquimans	928	826	1,754	608	594	1,202	760	950	863	1,818	712	627	1,339	870				
Person	1,799	1,585	3 384	714	579	1,293	26	1,346	1,337	2,683	479	635	1,114	22				
Pitt	2,737	2,420	5,157	1,599	1,608	3,207	21	2,551	2,543	5,094	1,277	1,479	2,753	26	1	1	9	5
Polk	1,034	907	1,941	685	612	1,297	693	292	264	556	189	172	361	185				
Randolph	4,358	4,112	8,470	2,818	2,475	5,593	3,576	760	720	1,480	542	566	1,118	742				
Richmond	2,335	2,297	4,632			3,920	22	2,641	2,892	5,533	.....	.....	4,589	48				

Robeson	3,239	3,080	6,319	2,435	2,329	4,764	3,045	1,787	2,577	4,364	5,239	1,787	1,961	3,748	1		32	22	
Croatans	823	741	1,564	601	554	1,155	677			.....		.....	.....	.....					
Rockingham	3,157	3,231	6,388	1,850	1,632	3,482	1 842	2,010	2,031	4.041	1,005	1,099	2,104	1,122					
Rowan	3,722	3,538	7,260	2.616	2.398	5,014	3,317	1,283	1,262	2,545	894	920	1,814	1.024					
Rutherford	3,500	3,342	6,842	2,212	1,979	4.191	2,686	905	923	1,828	508	575	1,083	679					
Sampson	3,041	2,945	5,986	1,964	1,794	3,758	2,523	1,858	1,968	3,826	1,052	1,332	2,384	1,492	1			23	
Stanly	2,374	2,251	4,625	1,772	1,434	3,206	46	352	300	652	189	184	373	37					
Stokes	2,975	2,662	5,637	1.853	1.588	3,441	2,386	534	485	1,019	351	350	701	1,256					
Surry	3,780	3,660	7,440	2 416	2,243	4,659	2.214	562	517	1,079	333	302	635	364	1				
Swain	1,380	1,460	2,840	1,055	877	1,932	941	50	32	82	12	8	20	12					
Transylvania	1,089	1,063	2,152	813	792	1,605	971	119	126	245	81	83	164	105					
Tyrrell	614	513	1,727	328	250	578	330	276	278	554	168	193	361	184					
Union	3,722	3,277	6.999	3,067	2,580	5,647	3,553	1,609	1,548	3,157	1,024	1,088	2,112	1,031					
Vance	1,020	1,049	2,069	563	521	1,084	19	1,717	1,627	3,344	1,017	1,118	2,135	32	1	1		15	
Wake	4,832	4,668	9,500	2,833	2,700	5,533	2,750	4,339	4,542	8,881	2,813	3,137	5,950	3,850					
Warren	1,009	976	1,985	529	510	1,039	590	2,514	2,488	5,002	1,396	1,644	3,040	1,696	1	1		23	
Washington	933	832	1,765	427	343	770	475	937	946	1,843	389	447	836	455					
Watauga	2,405	2,305	4,710	1,768	1,590	3,358	1.877	76	88	164	61	59	120	92					
Wayne	3,032	2,922	5,954	1,540	1,409	2,949	1,728	2.287	2,393	4,680	863	1,091	1,954	1,100					
Wilkes	4,594	4,460	9,054	2,750	2,565	5,320	3.001	465	525	985	270	309	579	396					
Wilson	2,404	2,123	4,527	1,230	1,285	2,515	1,507	1,749	1.778	3,527	932	1,092	2,024	984					
Yadkin	2,434	2,258	4,692	1,683	1,435	3,118	44	283	304	587	175	178	353	22					
Yancey	2,000	2,100	4,100	1,400	1,325	2,785	1,342	51	69	120	45	50	95	60	2		19	7	
Total	200,217	200,367	415,262	133,788	124,463	261,223	144,346	106,254	106,964	213,218	65,688	67,875	138,152	68,894	35	14	490	580	2

TABLE No. IV.

Reports Showing the Number of Public School Districts, Number of School Houses, Number of Schools Taught, Value of Public Schoo Average Length of Terms in Weeks, and Average Monthly Salary of Teachers in the Several Counties in the State during the School ing June 30, 1898.

COUNTIES.	NUMBER OF SCHOOL DISTRICTS		NUMBER OF SCHOOLS TAUGHT.		VALUE OF PUBLIC SCHOOL PROPERTY.		AVERAGE LENGTH OF TERM IN WEEKS.			AVERAGE SALARY OF TEACHERS PER MONTH.				NUMBER OF SCHOOL HOUSES.						
														WHITE.				COLORED.		
	White.	Colored.	White.	Colored.	White.	Colored.	White.	Colored.	City.	White Male.	White Female.	Colored Male.	Colored Female.	Numb'r.	Log.	Frame.	Brick.	Numb'r.	Log.	Frame.
Alamance	67	27	64	27	$ 16,340 00	$ 2,337 00	16.46	16.37	....	$26 25	$24 48	25 18	22 65	61	8	53	....	23	11	1
Alexander	50	8	49	8	4,025 00	285 00	14	14	....	20 00	18 00	16 00	16 00	50	15	35	....	8	4	
Alleghany	41	5	46	5	......	......	13	13	...	....	....	....	....	....	....	....	....	....	....	...
Anson	...	...	49	45	5.735 00	3,420 00	8	8	...	27 89	21 69	21 38	20 19	43	...	43	...	35	2	[illegible]
Ashe	100	8	97	7	7,114 0	100 00	9.25	11	....	18 93	18 33	17 14	.....	69	27	42	....	2	...	
Bart.	69	38	90	51	6,235 00	2,285 00	12	13	....	25 52	23 88	23 37	19 86	66	4	61	1	28	4	[illegible]
Bertie	64	55	64	55	5,583 00	5,400 00	16	14	....	24 25	24 00	24 50	24 00	63	....	63	....	54	....	[illegible]
Bladen	63	43	53	36	3,520 00	2,180 00	9	8	....	23 48	18 32	22 28	18 64	63	8	35	....	43	11	[illegible]
Brunswick	49	26	48	26	1,910 0	642 00	8	8	...	24 70	22 00	27 20	21 60	51	..	31	....	16	3	1
[illegible]	103	21	100	20	7,500 00	2,000 00	19	19	32	32 00	29 00	25 00	25 00	105	13	75	7	19	10	
Burke	64	16	49	11	....	....	10 33	10.50	...	25 00	25 00	23 00	23 00	43	17	26	..	7	5	
Cabarrus	57	24	57	20	12,130 00	2,840 00	16.10	13.58	36	27 50	27 04	23 40	21 80	54	6	47	1	16	5	1
Caldwell	75	13	73	12	4,640 00	700 00	12.20	13.09	....	20 51	19 51	18 12	18 33	...	....	75	..	...	....	1
Camden	20	12	18	12	2,000 00	1,160 00	16	12	....	21 66	23 57	20 54	19.42	19	....	19	....	12	....	1
Carteret	24	8	18	5	4,700 00	1,000 00	12.16	12	....	22 40	19 00	......	19 00	...	.	34	....	...	....	1
Caswell	39	36	37	36	1,500 00	1,200 00	11	13	..	24 75	25 25	24 25	23 15	36	23	13	...	36	11	2
Catawba	75	20	84	20	8,025 00	1,210 00	12.33	10.07	....	25 00	20 45	19 94	17 50	65	3	62	....	19	9	1
Chatham	86	45	85	44	6,060 00	2,565 00	13.05	14.08	....	23 62	20 43	22 00	20 28	70	16	54	....	35	9	2

Chowan	20	14	19	14	3,875 00	2,587 00	16.11	16		27 50	27 85	28 10	25 80	20	4			14		
Clay	17	1	17	1	3,550 00		13.18			21 02	20 00			16	2	14				
Cleveland	82	23	82	23	16 600 00	2,875 00	14.25	13.50	32	31 00	25 00	25 00	22 00	83		82	1	23		2
Columbus	86	45	84	44	8,580 00	2,415 00	11	9	20	23 00	24 17	24 80	21 60	83	5	78		44	4	4
Craven	35	35	29	30			14	14		28 00	28 00	26 00	26 00	35		34	1	35		3
Cumberland			70	57			12.75	11.33		23 80	23 75	20 90	22 06							
Currituck	32	13	31	13	2,525 00	1,050 00	13.31	10		22 67	22 08	25 02	24 50	29		11		13		1
Dare	16	3	16	3	1,650 00	350 00	11	12		30 00	25 00	25 00	20 00	21		21		3		
Davidson	92	24	95	23	7,020 00	1,390 00	66	58		24 75	22 75	20 00	20 43	80	28	52		25	16	
Davie	42	16	42	16	3,000 00	800 00	12	12.75		24 63	20 00	20 15	20 70							
Duplin	72	46	95	49	6,191 00	2,600 00	9.50	9		23 40	21 50	21 00	19 35	63	6	57		35	6	2
Durham	38	27	37	27	9,460 00	4,875 00	26	26	40	33 33	32 00	32 00	27 14	38	8	30		27	12	1
Edgecombe	40	42	42	41	6,600 00	6,440 00	21	19	34	32 00	28 53	28 75	23 00	40		40		42		4
Forsyth	73	22	73	22	66,895 00	13,850 00	16.49	16.10	36	28 00	23 12	24 64	22 50	73	3	70		22	7	1
Franklin	54	47	54	44	3,140 00	2,145 00	12.09	12.06		23 03	24 69	24 67	22 68	1	1			2		
Gaston			76	33	6,760 00	3,200 00	14	14.08		27 75	24 25	24 50	22 25	65	8	57		30	7	2
Gates	33	24	33	24	9,980 00	1,625 00	11	12		20 01	21 33	20 00	20 00	33		33		23		3
Graham	20		20		2,245 00	150 00	14			25 00	20 00			20	10	10		2		
Granville	57	43	51	43	5,300 00	4,465 00	19.22	17 00		27 29	26 41	24 86	24 01	44	8	36		36	12	2
Greene	32	24	32	23			15	15		29 44	24 87	23 7	21 40	32		32		24		2
Guilford	94	33	92	33	39,500 00	8,200 00	17.13	19.51	40	25 18	23 00	22 57	20 63	84	19	68	4	31	18	1
Halifax	47	68	47	68	6,002 00	7,845 00	12	14	16	26 00	26 64	22 66	22 85	32		32		53	12	4
Harnett	60	27	55	25	5,015 00	1,451 00	11.02	11.01		22 24	21 62	21 6	20 22	49	1	48		22	1	2
Haywood	58	3	54	3	8,475 00	500 00	14	14		25 50	23 00	22 50	25 00	48	15	31	2	2	1	
Henderson	57	11	51	9	10,460 00	925 00	13	16		30 87	23 93	22 26	21 75	48	2	46		9	2	
Hertford	33	32	33	32	3,542 00	4,560 00	16	16		20 00	20 00	22 50	22 50	33		33		32	3	2
Hyde	51	36	43	36	3,735 00	1,930 00	10	6.50		24 00	24 75	22 20	23 75	24		24		17		1
Iredell	92	37	91	34	18,188 00	4,405 00	14	13	32	26 33	24 37	21 19	20 28	92	25	66	1	34	17	1
Jackson	41	3	40	3	6,000 00	600 00	16	16.38		26 50	21 40	24 00		27	3	24		3	1	
Johnston	108	39	105	34	9,084 00	2,500 00	17	13.50		28 75	27 00	26 00	24 20	94		94		34		3
Jones	27	23	27	23	1,770 00	1,420 00	11.25	9		24 25	22 00	23 00	21 50	26	3	24		23	2	2
Lenoir	41	29	40	27	4,785 00	2,760 00	17.33	15.33		23 91	23 31	22 82	21 21	42		42		24		2

TABLE No. IV.—Continued.

Counties.	Number of School Districts		Number of Schools Taught.		Value of Public School Property.		Average Length of Term in Weeks.			Average Salary of Teachers per Month.				Number of School Houses.						
														White.				Colored.		
	White.	Colored.	White.	Colored.	White.	Colored.	White.	Colored.	City.	White Male.	White Female.	Colored Male.	Colored Female.	Numb'r.	Log.	Frame.	Brick.	Numb'r.	Log.	Frame
Lincoln	54	16	54	15	10,800 00	1,800 00	14	13	....	26 53	24 78	24 53	19 33	54	28	34	3	15	6	
Macon	57	4	54	4	7,135 00	350 00	13	17	....	22 10	20 00	16 33	18 00	60	14	46	...	4	2	
Madison	75	4	63	3	12,140 00	250 00	14	10	....	25 70	22 71	16 50	......	57	21	36	...	2	1	
Martin	49	30	49	30	6,000 00	2,300 00	14	14.50	....	27 00	27 00	26 00	26 00	49	1	49	...	30	...	
McDowell	56	13	54	11	3,200 00	375 00	9	10.50	....	24 13	20 45	22 29	18 24	25	7	18	...	5	1	
Mecklenburg	52	73	88	62	6,180 00	5,365 00	19	15	36	35 00	30 00	25 30	25 00	61	10	51	...	39	7	
Mitchell	92	4	52	4	11,600.00	200 00	10	8	....	22 50	20 00	18 00	15 00	55	9	46	...	...	...	
Montgomery	58	18	50	17	3,115 00	970 00	9.50	9	....	22 00	21 00	21 00	19 00	54	13	41	...	12	3	
Moore	..	....	81	40	4,395 00	2,633 00	12	12	....	24 50	21 50	24 00	21 00	71	..	71	...	40	...	
Nash	64	41	64	41	5,400 00	3,900 00	16.75	17	....	27 00	23 00	26 50	22 40	61	3	58	...	37	4	
New Hanover	15	16	15	16	37 250 00	12,850 00	24	24	32	.....	38 40	34 90	35 85	16	.	16	...	17	...	
Northampton	47	46	46	46	2,350 00	2,475 00	16	16	...	30 34	26 12	24 80	22 40	48	...	48	...	46	1	
Onslow	48	20	42	16	2,670 00	925 00	12	10	...	22 50	23 20	21 25	21 00	39	...	39	...	18		
Orange	48	25	44	22	5,290 00	3,140 00	14	12	...	24 20	23 70	22 96	21 07	44	22	22	...	34	20	
Pamlico	24	12	32	26	2,043 00	716 00	6.75	6.50	..	26 55	20 88	26 10	21 60	11	2	9	...	8	1	
Pasquotank	6	6	22	18	12,050 00	4,550 00	18	18	38	30 00	25 00	25 00	22 00	22	...	21	1	20	..	
Pender	44	37	33	25	3,035 00	2,460 00	9	9	...	22 77	22 16	21 92	21 60	43	5	38	..	38	13	
Perquimans	29	19	29	19	4,185 00	3,105 00	12.33	13	...	25 00	24 37	25 87	22 66	29	...	29	...	19	...	
Person	....	....	28	26	1,500 00	1,000 00	16	13	...	25 00	27 00	24 00	21 00	..	...	...	...	...	..	
Pitt	92	59	92	56	7,540 00	4,605 00	15	15	...	22 00	23 00	25 00	21 00	88	...	88	...	39	...	

Randolph ..	112	24	112	21	12,087 00	1,995 00	15	14	....	23 50	22 00	22 00	20 25	90	22	68	...	20	9	1
Richmond .	56	83	56	83	2,650 00	3,035 00	7	7	...	26 00	25 00	25 00	20 00	46	5	41	...	48	20	2
Robeson	95	63	117	70	5,155 00	3,455 00	8	12	...	28 49	22 63	26 59	25 36	71	3	68	...	44	1	4
Croatans .	22	....	27	...	1,385 00	....	8	..	...	25 00	.....	25 00	.....	...	...	...	...	...	...	.
Rockingham.	71	43	71	43	7,337 00	3,675 00	14	15	...	27 20	26 16	23 33	21 26	66	25	41	....	33	16	1
Rowan..	81	81	85	36	18,125 00	5,105 00	16	15	36	27 75	26 00	23 36	21 37	72	26	44	2	32	18	1
Rutherford..	72	27	68	23	7,135 00	833 00	15	14	...	28 83	24 87	21 77	19 32	61	10	51	..	25	9	1
Sampson	79	51	79	51	7,000 00	3,500 00	12	12	36	23 35	21 00	21 30	20 00	77	22	55	....	50	17	[illegible]
Stanly	70	10	69	10	3,792 00	580 00	8	8	...	28 00	28 00	23 00	23 00	55	4	51	....	8	2	
Stokes.	80	19	76	19	....	....	12.27	12.83	..	23 49	22 01	20 50	20 00	81	64	17	....	19	17	
Surry........	79	17	79	17	7,123 00	800 00	15	12	28	22 95	20 48	18 54	18 40	58	30	28	....	14	8	
Swain	35	1	34	1	3,220 00	40 00	12	13	...	22 92	23 10	.....	22 50	32	13	18	1	...	...	
Transylvania	32	3	32	3	2,855 00	275 00	12	10	...	25 66	22 43	27 25	20 00	32	5	27	....	3	...	
Tyrrell.....	24	8	24	8	1,940 00	685 00	8	7	...	23 00	22 50	22 50	22 50	26	..	26	...	8	....	
Union	86	32	86	32	6,655 00	1,950 00	15	15	15	24 00	24 00	22 00	21 00	8[illegible]	2	78	...	30	5	[illegible]
Vance	41	41	33	39	3,175 00	3,035 00	17.33	15	...	30 00	26 45	25 18	24 52	45	3	22	...	31	6	[illegible]
Wake........	92	75	92	74	7,640 00	19,402 00	17	17	34	29 57	27 17	28 45	24 90	64	2	62	...	49	4	[illegible]
Warren......	36	41	36	41	3,125 00	3,040 00	14	14	16	.....	21 25	24 43	20 50	32	1	31	...	39	...	[illegible]
Washington.	28	19	28	19	2,875 00	1,850 00	16	16	16	25 41	23 75	.....	23 98	28	...	28	...	18	...	1
Watauga.....	64	6	64	6	6,600 00	150 00	12	8	...	21 60	20 75	18 47	18 00	2	...	2	...	..	...	...
Wayne.....	68	42	67	38	17,025 00	9,730 00	15.28	18.49	40	27 83	25 60	24 33	22 37	68	...	67	1	42	..	[illegible]
Wilkes	108	18	107	17	5,235 00	500 00	11	9	...	22 50	20 00	19 00	18 00	83	24	49	...	18	12	
Wilson..	48	31	44	31	13,520 00	5,005 00	15	13	36	31 00	.....	26 75	.....	48	...	48	...	31	...	[illegible]
Yadkin	59	9	59	9	3,192 00	250 00	14	13	...	23 25	20 71	22 50	20 31	46	36	10	...	5	4	
Yancey	44	6	44	6	15,000 00	200 00	11	6	....	23 00	19 00	13 00	10 00	...	...	...	1	...	...	...
Total...	5,083	2,401	5,370	2,503	$ 683,363 00	$ 246,851 00	14.06	12.97	721	$24 66	$22 96	$21 64	$19 85	4,297	736	3,533	28	2,042	419	1,6[illegible]

TABLE No. V.

Number of Teachers Examined and Approved During the School Year Ending June 30, 1898, Showing Race, Sex and Grade.

COUNTIES.	WHITE.									COLORED.									TOTAL WHITE.			TOTAL COLORED.		
	1st Grade.			2d Grade.			3d Grade.			1st Grade.			2d Grade.			3d Grade.								
	Male.	Female.	Total.	Male.	Female.	Total.	Male.	Female.	Total.	Male.	Female.	Total.	Male.	Female.	Total.	Male.	Female.	Total.	Male.	Female.	Total.	Male.	Female.	Total.
Alamance	28	31	59	8	6	14				3	1	4	14	11	25				36	37	73	17	12	29
Alexander	35	4	39	9	2	11				1	1	2	5	2	7				44	6	50	6	3	9
Alleghany	5		5	25	2	27				1		1	2	1	3				30	2	32	3	1	4
Anson	15	19	34	4	5	9				5	2	7	17	6	23				19	24	43	22	8	30
Ashe	32	1	33	18	1	19							7		7				50	2	52	7		7
Beaufort	25	39	64	5	8	13				3	9	12	10	16	28				30	47	77	13	25	38
Bertie	8	30	38	4	18	22				10	11	21	8	19	27				12	48	60	18	30	48
Bladen	14	27	41	3	9	12				5	4	9	5	11	16				17	36	53	10	15	25
Brunswick	14	15	29	9	8	17				6		6	8	2	10				23	11	34	14	2	16
Buncombe	75	49	124	15	10	25				8	7	15	6	6	12				90	59	149	14	13	27
Burke	4	2	6	21	8	29				1		1	3	3	6				25	10	35	4	3	7
Cabarrus	28	33	61	5	2	7				4	10	14	6	8	14				33	35	68	10	18	28
Caldwell	34	19	53	10	4	14				4	1	5	4	2	6				44	23	67	8	3	11
Camden	9	7	16	3		3				6	1	7	4	6	10				12	7	19	10	7	17
Carteret	10	5	15	3	5	8							1	7	8				13	10	23	1	7	8
Caswell	3	14	17	3	5	8				7	3	10	4	9	13				6	19	25	11	10	21
Catawba	45	15	60	16	5	21				8	1	9	10	2	12				61	20	81	18	3	21
Chatham	26	19	45	18	19	37				10	1	11	16	10	26				44	38	82	26	11	37
Cherokee	21	1	22	15	7	22				1		1		2	2				36	8	44	1	3	4
Chowan	1	10	11	2	3	5				6	4	10	6	10	16				3	13	16	12	14	26
[illegible]	[illegible]	[illegible]	[illegible]	[illegible]	[illegible]	[illegible]				1		1							15	2	17	1		1

Cleveland	52	26	78	7	6	13				9	4	13	5	2	7				59	32	91	14	6	20
Columbus	20	21	41	10	2	12				14	4	18	1	3	4				30	23	53	15	7	22
Craven	3	37	40	2	4	6				5	12	17	14	15	29				5	41	46	19	27	46
Cumberland	30	31	61	3	4	7				15	30	45	7	7	14				33	35	68	22	37	59
Currituck	5	9	14	2	4	6				5	1	6	1	1	2				7	13	20	6	2	8
Dare	6	5	11	4	2	6					1	1	1	1	2				10	7	17	1	2	3
Davidson	31	13	44	35	15	50				2	2	4	9	7	16				66	28	94	11	9	20
Davie	18	4	22	6	4	10					1	1	10	3	13				24	8	32	10	4	14
Duplin	10	45	55	3	6	8				8	5	13	6	25	31				12	51	63	14	31	45
Durham	20	20	40	7	5	12				15	12	27	4	18	22				27	25	52	19	30	49
Edgecombe	4	17	21	2	11	13				9		9	13	13	26				6	28	34	22	13	35
Forsyth	28	6	34	10	12	22				12	1	3	12	5	17				38	18	56	14	6	20
Franklin	14	34	48	5	6	11				11	21	32	10	16	26				19	40	59	21	37	58
Gaston	20	11	31	29	18	47				3		3	18	10	28				49	29	78	21	10	31
Gates	3	19	22	2	2	4					4	4	8	9	17				5	21	26	8	13	21
Graham	8	1	9	4	7	11													12	8	20			
Granville	8	38	46		2	2				19	20	39	7	15	22				8	40	48	26	35	61
Greene	5	23	28							1	1	2	3	3	6				5	23	28	4	4	8
Guilford	20	16	36	14	21	35				6	3	9	9	5	14				34	37	71	15	8	23
Halifax	5	48	53		1	1				25	14	39	16	23	39				5	49	54	30	48	78
Harnett	21	8	29	10	5	15				6	3	9	6	3	9				31	13	44	12	6	18
Haywood	17	14	31	20	16	36					1	1	2		2				37	30	67	2	1	3
Henderson	11	14	25	1	1	2				1		1							12	15	27	2		2
Hertford	2	25	27		2	2				18	13	31	2	5	7				2	27	29	20	18	38
Hyde	6	13	19	7	3	10				6	6	12	4	1	5				13	16	29	10	7	17
Iredell	27	11	38	8	14	22				3		3	14	12	26				35	25	60	17	12	29
Jackson	15	14	29	1	8	9				1		1	4	1	5				16	22	38	5	1	6
Johnston	39	31	70	13	10	23				6	7	13	2	13	15				52	41	93	8	20	28
Jones	6	12	18	7	5	12				13	1	14	9	6	25				13	17	30	12	7	19
Lenoir	8	27	35	1	9	10				5	2	7	11	12	23				9	36	45	16	14	30
Lincoln	24	17	41	7	6	13				8		8	7	3	10				31	23	54	15	3	18
Macon	11	11	22	19	20	39							1	4	5				30	31	61	4	1	5
Madison	26	23	49	17	10	27							3		3				43	33	76	3		3

TABLE No. V.—Continued.

Counties.	White. 1st Grade. Male.	White. 1st Grade. Female.	White. 1st Grade. Total.	White. 2d Grade. Male.	White. 2d Grade. Female.	White. 2d Grade. Total.	White. 3d Grade. Male.	White. 3d Grade. Female.	White. 3d Grade. Total.	Colored. 1st Grade. Male.	Colored. 1st Grade. Female.	Colored. 1st Grade. Total.	Colored. 2d Grade. Male.	Colored. 2d Grade. Female.	Colored. 2d Grade. Total.	Colored. 3d Grade. Male.	Colored. 3d Grade. Female.	Colored. 3d Grade. Total.	Total White. Male.	Total White. Female.	Total White. Total.	Total Colored. Male.	Total Colored. Female.	Total Colored. Total.
Martin	11	6	17	14	25	39	....	....	....	9	3	12	10	17	27	....	....	....	25	31	56	19	20	39
McDowell	19	9	28	8	5	13	....	....	....	2	1	2	3		13	....	....	....	27	14	41	5	..	5
Marg.	25	15	40	1	..	1	....	....	....	16	3	19	10	12	22	....	....	....	26	15	41	26	15	41
Mitchell	24	11	35	13	4	17	....	....	....	....	....	....	2	2	4	....	....	....	37	15	52	2	2	4
Mgmery.	18	9	27	14	7	21	....	....	....	7	1	8	4	4	8	....	....	....	32	16	48	11	5	16
Moore	34	15	49	16	10	26	....	....	....	7	1	8	6	12	18	....	....	....	50	25	75	13	13	26
Nh	15	32	47	4	8	12	....	....	....	12	6	18	5	16	21	....	....	....	19	40	59	17	22	39
New Hanover	1	39	40	....	....	....	....	....	....	4	25	29	3	2	5	....	....	....	1	39	40	7	27	34
Northampton	12	13	25	6	5	11	....	....	....	4	3	7	13	5	18	....	....	....	18	18	36	17	8	25
Onslow	6	5	11	19	8	27	....	....	....	2		2	6	1	7	....	....	....	25	13	38	8	1	9
Orange	9	14	23	4	5	9	....	....	....	3	1	4	6	5	11	....	....	....	13	19	32	9	6	15
Pamlico	21	16	37	1	2	3	....	....	....	2	1	3	3	10	13	....	....	....	22	18	40	5	11	16
Pasquotank	16	13	29	4		4	....	....	....	8	8	16	3	..	3	....	....	....	20	13	33	11	8	19
Pr	4	18	22	4	6	10	....	....	....	8	2	10	7	11	18	....	....	....	8	24	32	15	13	28
ups	5	17	22	2	6	8	....	....	....	4	5	9	4	12	16	....	....	....	7	23	30	8	17	25
Person	4	15	19	2	6	8	....	....	....	2	1	3	9	13	22	....	....	....	6	21	27	11	14	25
Pitt	4	41	45	7	28	35	....	....	....	6	5	11	11	15	26	....	....	....	11	69	80	17	20	37
Polk	1	3	4	2	2	4	....	....	....	....	....	....		2	2	....	....	....	3	5	8	....	2	2
Rph	60	21	81	25	14	39	....	....	....	4	1	5	10	9	19	....	....	....	85	35	120	14	10	24
Richmond	6	13	19	5	18	23	....	....	....	10	2	12	6	10	16	....	....	....	11	31	42	16	12	28

Robeson	19	15	34	12	32	42				7	7	14	14	9	23				31	47	78	21	16	37
Croatans	4		4	4	1	5													8	1	9			
Rockingham	22	57	79	3	1	4				17	8	25	12	18	30				25	58	83	29	26	55
Rowan	38	20	58	18	10	28				5	4	9	15	11	26				56	30	86	20	15	35
Rutherford	17	17	34	18	19	37							10	15	25				35	36	71	10	15	25
Sampson	27	47	74	9	8	17				6	2	8	5	5	10				36	55	91	11	7	18
Stanly	41	15	56	6	2	8				5	3	8	1	1	2				47	17	64	6	4	10
Stokes	23	11	34	17	18	35				2	4	12	12	4	16				40	29	69	14	4	18
Surry	30	14	44	30	6	36				2	1	3	12	4	16				60	20	80	14	5	19
Swain	9	5	14	12	8	20					2	2							21	13	34		2	2
Transylvania	9	10	19	3	4	7				2		2		1	1				12	14	26	2	1	3
Tyrrell	8	1	9	3	2	5				2		2	1	3	4				11	3	14	3	3	6
Union	29	23	52	24	12	36				4	3	7	19	14	33				53	35	88	23	17	40
Vance	1	30	31		1	1				19	17	36	7	12	19				1	31	32	26	29	55
Wake	40	35	75	4	9	13				28	18	46	6	25	31				44	44	88	34	43	77
Warren		36	36							13	23	36	1	6	7					36	36	14	29	43
Washington	13	11	24	5	1	6				5	5	10	3	21	24				18	12	30	8	26	34
Watauga	22	10	32	14	2	16							4	1	5				36	12	48	4	1	5
Wayne	8	31	39	2	7	9				9	5	14	5	18	23				10	38	48	14	23	37
Wilkes	55	18	73	40	5	45				3		3	11	6	17				96	23	118	14	6	20
Wilson	18	18	36		5	5				10	7	17	1	5	6				18	23	41	11	12	23
Yadkin	12	3	15	4	3	7					1	1	2		2				15	6	22	2	1	3
Yancey	4	1	5	18	6	24													16	7	23			
Total	1604	1735	3339	852	688	1540				573	410	983	604	694	1298				2539	2415	2954	1156	1107	2263

TABLE No. VI.—WHITE—1898.

Showing Number of Pupils of Different Ages from Six to Twenty-one Studying Different Branches.

s.	Six Years.	Seven Years.	Eight Years.	Nine Years.	Ten Years.	Eleven Years.	Twelve Years.	Thirteen Years.	Fourteen Years.	Fifteen Years.	Sixteen Years	Seventeen Years.	Eighteen Years.	Nineteen Years.	Twenty Years.	Number Studying Arithmetic.	Number Studying Geography.	Number Studying Eng. Grammar.	Number Studying N. C. History.	Number Studying U. S. History.	Number Studying Physiology and Hygiene.
....	358	302	33	33	84	91	274	87	28	67	197	115	91	75	92	2 97	1, 28	60	259	423	39
....	329	275	90	25	180	70	325	75	30	60	90	5	200	5	10	2,770	1,894	,105	200	1, 00	00
....	124	104	121	142	114	136	112	04	95	91	64	58	28	22	.	92	48	94	51	70	79
....	143	186	44	162	00	70	185	177	36	148	06	70	68	48	33	1,307	74	99	259	69	28
....	425	368	97	356	88	97	373	33	42	67	70	192	149	98	73	1,66	77	619	97	195	196
....	313	280	56	295	82	90	286	37	257	191	193	118	105	61	50	82	1, 99	87	292	82	382
....	139	142	73	183	76	49	169	39	43	147	02	82	52	41	31	1,355	70	98	255	87	34
....	126	148	158	49	41	161	147	63	168	27	00	89	76	42	38	1.259	54	92	156	22	318
....	129	140	126	148	140	148	137	52	30	01	10	75	69	49	62	80	40	84	156	10	134
....																					
....																					
....	270	300	333	329	86	266	279	31	213	89	60	114	74	57	26	2, 25	1,211	92	373	34	320
....	272	260	249	236	6	46	214	85	226	72	70	106	84	102	40	51	78	79	60	06	93
....	40	51	65	63	63	58	64	55	53	51	25	25	24	4	4	32	25	21	63	77	39
....	84	60	67	94	86	106	75	80	54	40	32	15	8	10	12	8	183	146	89	77	65
....	80	91	103	121	113	93	115	07	85	75	70	52	40	20	13	9	6	65	126	30	90
....	259	371	466	360	69	42	313	330	304	76	183	116	88	71	33	,87	1, 21	68	333	66	205
....	272	270	335	290	9	97	285	65	288	238	226	148	139	78	68	2,360	1, 61	77	454	64	257
....	222	218	220	235	255	07	22	16	191	198	175	108	104	56	56	1,86	63	37	38	10	95
....	79	78	82	77	75	69	68	61	65	43	24	33	14	14	6	18	76	153	78	81	91

Clay	90	111	89	80	93	88	101	89	68	76	77	47	37	16	23	448	282	165	3
Cleveland	461	366	614	459	436	419	384	397	298	272	211	197	172	125	90	2,490	1,726	2,490	1,411
Columbus	313	277	335	293	282	271	333	283	289	231	219	181	139	114	102	1,745	909	581	219
Craven	96	91	116	92	98	89	76	151	116	68	62	54	39	11	13	792	246	299	116
Cumberland																1,770	909	656	245
Currituck	78	87	84	102	108	78	99	93	69	61	36	28	20	11	9	714	416	201	83
Dare	60	65	74	85	88	86	74	79	80	85	80	70	65	50	55	375	230	200	125
Davidson	389	384	396	384	384	394	390	358	341	328	256	210	148	97	59	2,573	1,327	836	394
Davie	179	168	190	175	186	170	191	181	162	142	149	79	64	49	24	894	542	543	191
Duplin	300	309	310	298	294	308	293	275	269	236	214	167	131	92	108	2,811	1,228	787	514
Durham	219	161	179	189	167	156	150	109	117	83	77	46	34	25	28	1,123	325	227	125
Edgecombe	193	165	181	187	165	166	125	134	107	124	79	53	37	16	4	1,337	694	496	180
Forsyth	369	383	376	391	338	350	324	385	297	234	197	147	105	71	63	1,872	1,056	631	211
Franklin	154	205	197	201	192	165	237	173	176	134	131	80	61	36	23	1,437	615	504	146
Gaston	372	324	354	321	308	253	297	236	243	195	160	116	78	40	27	1,872	1,034	580	345
Gates	89	113	117	143	160	133	137	133	108	92	83	61	46	21	17	1,029	588	364	165
Graham																			
Granville	176	194	221	201	222	194	228	226	204	183	173	109	110	59	46	1,431	802	592	275
Greene	115	131	122	116	123	94	125	106	94	94	53	44	35	15	16	904	402	264	108
Cuilford	396	335	423	444	386	353	345	326	323	267	223	183	137	96	85	2,760	1,466	926	988
Halifax	140	133	155	145	148	130	153	153	139	105	78	35	46	10	12	1,156	644	431	161
Harnett	267	259	236	217	245	245	256	222	196	200	172	132	101	53	64	1,597	703	489	193
Haywood	217	298	526	581	662	730	548	563	353	207	164	149	129	118	98	3,015	2,229	2,015	429
Henderson	265	245	261	254	253	223	257	251	245	183	154	105	96	70	49	1,582	828	559	74
Hertford	106	87	77	98	108	124	114	105	119	75	72	41	40	27	14	914	921	362	185
Hyde	90	129	124	123	117	86	79	98	56	65	43	23	12	12	8	807	434	309	114
Iredell	352	436	485	419	338	381	403	371	358	241	258	172	137	99	77	2,519	1,459	1,067	506
Jackson	257	208	243	219	233	210	262	192	215	174	158	102	88	52	44	1,366	641	394	168
Johnston	448	495	510	454	482	462	449	442	412	333	291	192	169	84	78	3,088	1,369	970	267
Jones	50	56	78	68	75	58	65	62	68	55	36	40	36	26	25	612	320	140	60
Lenoir	132	143	161	162	142	149	157	138	135	115	99	73	58	42	25	1,360	754	396	194
Lincoln	262	237	268	268	254	223	264	202	213	170	144	137	79	50	26	1,576	630	410	322
Macon	265	253	256	221	260	245	238	215	222	186	155	134	94	61	54	1,228	729	395	153

TABLE No. VI.—WHITE—Continued.

s.	Six Years.	Seven Years.	Eight Years.	Nine Years.	Ten Years.	Eleven Years.	Twelve Years.	Thirteen Years.	Fourteen Years.	Fifteen Years.	Sixteen Years.	Seventeen Years.	Eighteen Years.	Nineteen Years.	Twenty Years.	Number Studying Arithmetic.	Number Studying Geography.	Number Studying Eng. Grammar.	Number Studying N. C. History.	Number Studying U. S. History.	Number Studying Physiology and Hygiene.
....	467	58	44	63	378	384	384	53	245	268	34	194	138	173	106	1, 9	63	4	48	208	158
....	201	29	40	263	194	187	219	71	195	160	71	133	127	131	87	2, 38	1, 62	1, 4	6	500	785
..	195	166	06	56	177	173	201	74	188	202	31	102	68	49	32	1, 02	41	8	43	105	89
urg	454	40	496	81	499	47	531	89	363	319	68	217	141	73	47	3, 6	1, 9	1, 80	5	93	389
...	170	20	30	30	360	90	420	30	380	270	20	230	200	190	80	1, 00	55	20	....	00	50
y	181	75	61	42	147	96	42	65	133	118	20	91	69	88	42	82	67	04	9	29	28
....	227	47	72	244	284	73	266	89	258	207	89	154	123	69	57	1, 82	88	78	9	91	225
....	228	02	71	21	260	44	254	29	189	169	30	93	73	47	40	1, 60	86	96	38	00	182
ver.	85	24	87	25	230	20	02	71	139	100	52	27	11	4	...	1, 63	1.763	1,763	1. 63	1, 63	1,763
ton.	126	33	64	57	180	67	82	87	60	119	21	95	75	50	35	1,382	994	488	98	51	212
...	192	63	80	46	184	154	170	52	90	138	24	86	96	48	39	1, 9	9	74	31	91	1,265
....	112	146	83	62	189	56	77	49	130	122	05	81	50	40	36	1, 83	49	40	95	49	180
....	108	07	36	10	85	00	05	12	110	98	76	72	50	36	19	89	41	37	42	57	57
k..	94	54	22	46	136	53	26	34	94	47	33	32	19	13	...	97	60	40	25	46	67
....	78	01	99	84	102	07	00	05	94	73	65	58	56	28	15	83	09	96	42	43	145
s.	104	09	12	11	116	86	92	16	86	76	60	41	31	24	13	91	92	79	13	45	114
....	85	90	50	20	109	19	22	107	98	77	52	64	39	34	25	89	48	77	42	18	74
....	316	74	83	31	295	78	64	244	237	198	78	117	102	44	61	1, 82	93	53	69	40	167
....	506	87	536	423	468	400	65	403	396	256	98	242	200	312	95	3, 65	2, 87	1,231	93	1, 35	573
...	328	38	322	348	383	294	40	384	355	457	278	206	169	102	83	2, 72	1, 63	1,158	321	505	349

ttans	68	85	105	90	13	100	16	102	88	75	60	57	40	20	18	33	85	65	25	42	29
ham	34	235	318	323	298	305	99	317	255	96	177	15	92	62	23	2, 82	1, 21	82	84	54	232
.....	59	443	487	436	47	406	41	385	388	53	271	200	46	89	42	, 84	1, 98	1, 91	44	50	376
rd..	20	238	210	406	55	294	91	490	560	36	224	210	98	14	42	2, 92	1, 02	1, 03	58	94	416
.....	71	312	340	282	365	297	36	290	295	83	221	183	41	97	75	, 44	1, 79	91	50	496	464
.....	94	224	327	277	265	248	61	234	254	00	46	133	06	87	71	1, 63	77	93	86	25	171
.....	32	308	310	272	323	289	92	286	240	22	194	151	07	65	47	1, 33	90	51	35	75	300
.....	62	377	399	337	370	275	32	349	330	31	233	157	34	84	87	1, 95	91	64	20	30	188
.....	00	130	163	140	135	130	47	120	134	18	76	74	61	31	21	90	94	27	57	14	202
ania .	21	90	134	98	115	123	90	94	89	86	71	63	49	20	23	31	92	29	42	92	83
.....	59	67	64	65	56	69	56	64	55	69	44	26	26	10	11	44	68	02	96	66	24
.....	47	448	485	445	451	421	47	440	426	56	304	230	01	128	82	2,657	1, 98	1,480	87	43	229
.....	80	85	112	101	105	96	118	94	87	57	58	25	30	11	1	96	83	70	93	80	320
.....	36	319	383	340	398	326	77	320	302	73	244	179	64	74	61	2, 76	1, 43	1, 13	65	89	468
....	86	85	101	87	92	107	05	98	86	85	42	35	15	8	4	844	81	50	75	89	221
ton	71	66	58	77	66	56	82	58	61	88	41	37	19	18	8	462	48	56	73	92	62
.....	59	267	280	293	93	299	79	250	254	84	170	148	24	63	77	1,229	76	49	21	55	106
.....	86	236	259	289	294	223	86	254	235	20	241	125	86	68	23	1,969	1, 01	66	04	98	499
.....	438	436	485	427	464	434	43	396	409	78	310	233	97	133	164	2,262	90	66	26	93	313
.....	62	179	155	172	209	188	79	176	158	29	111	89	53	40	31	1,139	66	56	69	32	263
.....	37	246	261	226	247	197	83	234	193	22	167	128	17	76	48	1,427	69	95	81	10	84
.....	45	325	200	260	06	210	80	204	190	180	145	170	80	75	35	811	31	34	48	178	361
l ..	20,130	19,901	22,311	20,884	21,283	21,080	20,916	19,482	17,841	15,295	13,006	9,674	7,739	5,249	3,401	139,263	76,725	53,595	23,296	25,795	24,828

TABLE No. VI.—COLORED—1898.

Showing Number of Pupils of Different Ages from Six to Twenty-one Studying Different Branches.

Counties.	Six Years.	Seven Years.	Eight Years.	Nine Years.	Ten Years.	Eleven Years.	Twelve Years.	Thirteen Years.	Fourteen Years.	Fifteen Years.	Sixteen Years.	Seventeen Years.	Eighteen Years.	Nineteen Years.	Twenty Years.	Number Studying Arithmetic.	Number Studying Geography.	Number Studying Eng. Grammar.	Number Studying N. C. History.	Number Studying U. S. History.
Al[illegible]me	132	109	106	126	119	109	122	143	131	93	93	82	47	30	20	86	47	79	72	113
Al[illegible]der	5	7	8	30	40	20	35	175	53	25	30	40	5	....	....	20	104	60	25	25
[illegible]y	14	6	5	8	8	12	11	7	10	11	16	9	7	9	8	56	26	14	1	4
[illegible]n	147	179	181	184	220	194	259	220	221	92	181	133	95	48	25	1,313	69	59	90	177
[illegible]	13	12	17	13	9	10	14	15	14	17	13	12	2	5	7	65	32	27	9	5
Beaufort	154	195	211	193	217	160	211	187	189	164	140	120	88	47	25	1,515	62	58	60	410
Bertie	212	205	85	189	89	246	284	274	77	81	194	169	117	69	27	1, 34	98	50	260	215
B[illegible]n	60	91	99	107	98	97	137	126	116	125	96	69	62	39	45	63	211	183	22	31
Brunswick	67	85	123	80	80	69	69	72	86	75	72	49	40	30	34	810	40	284	149	148
[illegible]e	....	....	....	....	....	....	....	....	....	....	....	....	....	....	....	....	....	....	....	....
[illegible]e	....	....	....	....	....	....	....	....	....	....	....	....	....	....	....	....	....	....	....	....
[illegible]s	109	100	108	116	121	91	99	97	100	75	62	53	35	14	15	47	36	213	25	140
[illegible]l	39	45	40	37	34	21	32	30	32	48	22	21	28	12	13	35	115	69	18	36
[illegible]n	56	50	45	56	54	46	58	57	62	35	34	26	18	7	4	27	1	91	30	11
[illegible]t	22	13	13	16	18	7	14	6	17	5	9	6	5	2	4	63	45	14	1	1
[illegible]ll	30	130	157	141	168	150	186	151	157	119	97	70	47	20	18	856	59	181	47	126
[illegible]a	45	42	48	40	46	42	50	54	42	44	36	30	27	19	7	221	162	112	29	48
[illegible]m	117	146	164	145	76	155	195	210	149	35	156	112	88	45	28	1, 07	610	404	203	74
[illegible]e	18	15	16	11	5	14	13	11	10	7	6	13	3	6	2	66	47	26	....	15
[illegible]wan	85	87	111	113	111	99	96	95	113	83	57	50	31	18	5	867	474	362	232	314
[illegible]y	....	....	....	....	....	....	....	....	....	....	....	....	....	....	....	....	....	....	....	....

Clevel[illegible]d	78	166	165	66	67	62	91	70	80	59	49	27	37	21	23	48	462	40	340	420
[illegible]	150	159	170	134	154	146	151	163	137	128	137	100	95	69	42	28	68	40	242	234
Craven	175	195	201	235	48	250	275	315	231	156	163	132	104	17	14	65	1,102	86	208	823
[illegible]d	...	...	...	...	...	...	...	...	...	...	...	...	...	...	...	40	66	58	160	88
[illegible]k	43	34	48	52	54	49	42	44	38	37	27	26	17	11	3	288	152	22	32	33
Dare	12	10	11	14	9	15	12	8	5	9	10	6	5	5	4	30	20	15	17	15
Davidson	46	73	59	53	73	61	71	75	55	51	50	35	32	9	10	35	215	114	48	47
[illegible]e	48	51	51	55	49	63	62	62	49	46	35	59	32	14	12	314	175	97	19	38
Duplin	139	181	170	154	202	184	208	175	180	185	153	114	96	68	58	1, 97	537	33	131	125
[illegible]	167	168	144	148	145	122	141	123	102	91	74	58	57	30	23	83	278	191	90	67
Edgecombe	250	300	281	311	34	283	309	315	241	180	161	99	65	29	10	1, 72	752	90	144	259
Forsyth	77	66	77	81	89	89	79	94	87	86	86	62	40	28	19	88	334	211	79	48
Franklin	177	185	232	193	45	221	254	242	211	193	161	124	115	67	41	1, 62	977	69	224	253
[illegible]n	176	155	149	175	168	132	193	187	150	115	107	68	53	19	13	86	432	45	73	135
Gates	66	85	92	105	110	93	108	100	113	93	95	78	46	27	20	68	327	07	70	45
[illegible]m	...	...	...	...	...	...	...	...	...	...	...	...	...	...	...		...	...	...	...
[illegible]le	73	162	174	169	03	168	178	224	184	135	105	74	61	27	12	1,376	857	91	240	373
Greene	99	91	111	111	131	93	113	117	139	86	83	65	31	17	13	68	294	171	60	61
Guilford	118	140	133	133	165	141	154	134	125	98	87	86	65	48	13	54	422	84	88	151
Halifax	256	252	314	303	416	327	384	340	327	266	223	164	136	79	33	2, 96	1,106	35	289	213
[illegible]	76	76	78	98	89	98	97	85	80	83	68	65	65	38	22	615	289	182	99	61
[illegible]d	14	16	21	29	18	16	14	13	11	9	7	8	6	3	1	67	49	32	14	11
[illegible]n	35	34	24	30	22	31	22	34	31	22	15	16	11	10	5	197	67	108	1	19
[illegible]ord	28	68	118	112	75	209	138	105	119	75	73	41	40	27	14	914	921	62	185	202
Hyde	49	75	72	88	93	83	56	61	75	94	71	50	37	20	5	40	218	129	80	73
[illegible]ll	153	200	104	141	127	125	112	153	105	152	75	69	61	47	30	92	434	88	199	258
[illegible]n	18	17	16	12	14	12	12	15	15	14	7	4	5	7		107	84	56	8	44
[illegible]n	114	120	129	110	154	127	129	134	158	140	114	103	74	46	22	1,015	553	87	146	181
Jones	42	62	60	75	66	67	70	66	58	62	40	63	46	32	20	30	270	104	43	86
[illegible]ir	116	136	138	162	56	122	163	138	129	112	96	104	64	22	13	53	423	217	189	104
[illegible]n	55	76	62	61	65	47	59	65	56	39	57	46	25	15	5	97	168	108	15	49
[illegible]n	5	15	11	10	15	11	11	19	11	9	11	13	8	2	6	61	45	34	16	22
[illegible]n	4	4	5	5	3	9	4	6	6	6	1	4	3	...	4	26	14	...	...	4

TABLE No. VI.—COLORED—CONTINUED.

COUNTIES.	Six Years.	Seven Years.	Eight Years.	Nine Years.	Ten Years.	Eleven Years.	Twelve Years.	Thirteen Years.	Fourteen Years.	Fifteen Years.	Sixteen Years.	Seventeen Years.	Eighteen Years.	Nineteen Years.	Twenty Years.	Number Studying Arithmetic.	Number Studying Geography.	Number Studying Eng. Grammar.	Number Studying N. C. History.	Number Studying U. S. History.
[illegible]n	253	237	228	241	222	218	222	211	208	160	132	121	63	59	41	1,600	913	75	[illegible]	207
[illegible]ll	37	32	38	29	40	37	36	34	42	38	23	16	23	7	7	193	75	64	6	5
[illegible]g	370	347	401	361	414	388	407	370	347	286	263	175	112	74	25	2,259	[illegible]	[illegible]	72	372
Mitchell	5	5	10	10	8	8	10	4	7	10	8	5	5	1	1	20	10	....	....	.
[illegible]ery	54	48	58	68	64	63	70	50	72	88	50	64	32	24	13	441	[illegible]	87	87	53
Moore	108	121	136	135	124	131	156	127	128	122	93	76	42	31	22	923	417	43	26	86
Nash	167	177	[illegible]	197	221	160	185	191	178	133	106	99	62	34	15	1,374	[illegible]	41	40	130
New Hanover	116	165	85	282	288	268	247	224	189	134	75	27	14	6	....	2,290	2,[illegible]90	[illegible]	[illegible]90	2,290
[illegible]n	164	178	24	205	234	231	270	252	245	224	234	170	116	83	46	1,458	7[illegible]16	46	38	86
[illegible]	41	55	49	59	48	68	63	67	73	66	52	48	44	24	23	356	44	22	67	41
[illegible]e	85	68	1[illegible]6	63	92	63	79	60	71	75	66	48	29	23	19	522	271	22	70	55
[illegible]o	30	24	35	36	30	27	46	56	19	52	54	30	20	26	11	224	112	85	40	54
[illegible]k	92	94	87	76	85	100	97	82	94	67	78	40	27	26	15	484	90	41	67	30
[illegible]r	81	90	111	117	114	103	90	103	76	82	75	52	49	45	20	591	35	45	54	55
[illegible]s	108	106	[illegible]7	124	103	105	116	119	108	82	86	63	62	23	21	861	43	91	34	78
Person	52	95	97	111	95	95	131	101	95	65	90	30	26	18	13	337	20	46	58	48
Pitt	190	246	33	238	274	213	244	248	235	220	128	110	95	52	24	1,091	58	92	14	130
Polk	....	....	....	....	....	....	....	....	....	....	....	....	....	....	....	....	....	....	....	....
Randolph	97	[illegible]9	114	106	102	95	87	77	70	76	60	45	41	25	19	628	317	23	35	61
Richmond	....	....	....	....	....	....	....	....	....	....	....	....	....	....	....	....	....	....	....	....
[illegible]n	251	302	308	326	362	277	317	297	247	248	180	156	134	75	41	1,661	60	285	97	151
[illegible]n	126	183	[illegible]7	188	197	196	186	188	164	162	114	86	75	21	22	1,026	68	371	148	174

Rowan	55	160	178	142	63	51	163	50	117	126	91	83	55	30	21	848	467	304	82	157
Rutherford	57	68	59	96	37	84	95	116	38	80	50	60	28	4	11	413	208	111	24	41
Sampson	168	151	170	189	74	96	213	99	91	184	170	45	69	79	48	1,50[illegible]	578	436	156	312
Stanly	22	27	38	30	41	27	27	35	20	33	15	26	22	12	7	179	120	83	54	41
Stokes	48	65	62	39	62	48	69	46	74	74	47	34	22	21	10	290	198	127	29	34
Surry	37	50	38	59	48	42	43	65	51	34	46	28	29	20	17	352	176	9[illegible]	38	23
Swain	3	2	2	1	1	3	1	4	....	1	....	..	..	....	..	20	2	...	....	....
Transylvania	12	6	1	6	15	15	17	11	6	10	12	12	5	....	2	89	28	16	3	6
Tyrrell	27	42	32	43	28	29	25	31	21	18	20	7	5	6	5	141	68	46	21	28
Union	53	70	167	168	40	139	153	167	75	141	116	21	51	26	20	870	445	243	100	103
Vance	49	92	65	271	63	91	145	216	92	157	127	68	72	37	5	1,330	584	413	76	70
Wake	31	31	412	351	411	63	420	96	92	243	314	28	158	88	61	2,340	1,172	819	506	223
Warren	65	83	32	221	37	38	277	34	68	243	202	44	99	43	20	1,928	1,040	739	194	274
Washington	62	80	66	71	80	69	87	78	71	55	43	32	22	7	6	330	175	138	66	70
Watauga	11	19	7	9	15	11	10	8	9	6	11	3	7	2	5	39	17	8	1	5
Wayne	81	59	68	149	20	53	188	176	55	132	109	93	60	27	17	1,226	460	270	164	180
Wilkes	40	31	52	51	35	35	42	46	47	43	34	20	18	14	19	250	138	105	96	52
Wilson	44	130	186	143	49	35	166	130	54	103	97	66	54	37	27	641	319	213	76	94
Yadkin	26	27	18	30	27	17	28	25	30	29	23	18	20	10	27	186	112	78	33	30
Yancey	10	14	13	11	12	10	8	7	5	4	2		...	....	....	17	14	10	2	4
Total	8,495	[illegible],988	10,153	10,082	11,047	9,960	10,833	10,708	[illegible]	8,471	7,247	5,720	4,078	2,429	1,544	67,251	34,237	24,210	11,017	12,233

TABLE No. VII.—1898.

Showing Amount Apportioned to White and Colored, Assessed Value of Property of White and Colored, Insolvent Polls, Poll Tax Levied, and Amount Applied to Schools.

COUNTIES.	Amount Apportioned to Whites.	Amount Apportioned to Colored.	Assessed Value of Property of Whites.	Assessed Value of Property of Colored.	No. White Polls.	No. Colored Polls.	No. of Insolvent White Polls.	No. of Insolvent Colored Polls.	Total Poll Tax Levied.	Amount Poll Tax Paid for Schools.	Amount Actually Paid by Whites on Property and Polls.	Amount Actually Paid by Colored on Property and Polls.
[illegible]	$ 10,440 58	$ 3, 63 88	$ 4,464,702 00	$ 79, 9 00	2,749	780	100	150	$ 2 25	$ 1 50	$ 12, 81 82	$ 1,088 99
[illegible]	3,895 10	422 40	....	....	1,408	97	....	....	....	....	....	....
[illegible]	2,483 12	94 91	52, 94 00	6,770 00	1,041	47	....	....	....	....	1,351 50	67 68
Anson	3,066 40	3, 81 80	1,748, 96 00	79,315 00	1,608	1,286	*1,250	....	....	....	....	....
Ashe	5,716 25	36 70	1,350, 66 90	7, 74 00	2,524	58	140	10	2 00	1 9	5 66 44	88 74
Beaufort	6,041 98	4, 47 63	2, 66, 78 00	47, 24 00	2,195	1,352	107	279	2 40	....	7,384 88	1,549 15
Bertie	5,500 00	5, 95 00	2,744, 81 00	260 97 00	1,470	1,549	31	121	2 10	1 50	6, 72 69	2,599 37
Bladen	3,270 74	2, 71 36	1,477, 07 00	117, 58 00	1,400	781	47	93	1 50	30	4, 48 52	1,230 80
Brunswick	3,211 82	1, 82 81	1,002, 81 00	93, 58 00	1,080	567	37	73	2 45	1 29	3,149 51	806 16
[illegible]	....	....	9 91 01 00	150,487 00	5,508	1,364	600	1,372	....	75	26, 79 76	2,175 17
[illegible]	....	....	1,400, 85 00	30,873 00	1,750	177	....	....	2 70	1 29	4, 64 83	283 83
[illegible]	9,200 40	3,059 10	3 94, 32 00	63,285 00	2,208	631	....	....	2 45	1 56	....	....
[illegible]	4,917 42	91 58	1,602,033 00	13 91 00	1,837	185	53	27	2 00	1 50	....	....
[illegible]	1,917 00	86 00	527,621 00	37,890 00	489	325	9	24	2 00	1 50	2, 92	579 08
Carteret	3,154 00	76 00	39 92 00	35,182 00	1,466	213	318	71	....	1 50	2,745 19	230 10
[illegible]	2,767 92	2, 67 92	1,249 65 00	69 95 00	982	852	100	300	2 46	1 50	1,473 00	1,278 00
[illegible]	8,723 56	....	2,779,740 00	26,279 00	2,510	268	*61	....	1 92	1 50	*8,836 75	....
[illegible]	6,614 40	3, 75 20	2,674,747 00	107,853 00	2,409	941	....	....	2 29	1 50	....	....
[illegible]	4,248 00	96 00	1,331,303 00	1,947 0	1,106	24	162	16	2 90	....	3, 90 89	23 98
[illegible]	2,195 75	2, 87 01	1,270,977 00	128,462 00	756	774	25	100	2 00	1 29	3, 62 99	1,229 68

Clay	1,584 84	47 00	84668 00	856 00	532	14	....	....	....	....	......	......
[illegible]ld	9 426 00	2,343 60	*3,113.936 00	....	*3,461	...	*408	..	2 60	1 54	*10,542 56	.....
[illegible]us	5,608 90	2 895 20	1.520,373 00	121,940 00	1,976	69	39	119	.	1 50	4,839 85	2,512 89
[illegible]en	5,720 35	8.571 24	2,638,320 00	363 321 00	1.760	2,020	*1 399		3 20	1 29	......	......
[illegible]and	7.375 12	5,712 62	...	....	.....							
Currituck	2 706 [illegible]	1,052 98	598,359 00	27.562 00	924	337	20	63	2 00	1 50	2,463 05	554 01
Dare	1,604 40	190 80	352,309 25	10,902 85	655	60	....	...	....	...	1,479 15	97 02
Davidson	10,364 00	....	3,193,128 00	40,314 00	2,916	310	325	75	.....	1 50	11,156 74	537 57
Davie	....	...	1,527,305 00	31,892 00	1,380	264	65	58	2 00	....	.....	.....
Duplin	4 563 00	3,119 00	6 191 00	2,600 00	2,111	741	225	75	2 50	....	6,184 73	1,271 93
Durham	8 869 38	5,123 75	7,468,6[illegible]2 00	146,751 00	2.378	1,190	..		1 50	1 50	.....	...
Edgecombe	1,800 00	....	2,989,779 00	119,489 00	1,669	2,015	50	150	2 57	1 50	6,874 53	3,022 50
Forsyth	11,556 72	4 486 28	6,898 991 00	141,549 00	3,711	1,561	328	656	2 30	....	16,782 25	1,422 23
Franklin	4,741 43	4,635 94	2,452,207 00	171,825 00	2,049	1,602	162	558	2 42	..	6,495 06	1,540 11
Gaston	*12,644 49	....	3,391,051 00	58,742 00	2 499	734	210	...	2 00	1 50	11,371 69	....
Gates	2 749 60	2.573 20	1,248,120 00	84,198 00	868	519	18	50	2 00	1 50	3,511 62	834 06
Graham	1,765 50	13 20	602.408 00	....	573	4	66	...	....	...	.....	....
Granville	6,338 00	5.221 96	3,174,760 00	125.425 00	1,773	1.524	76	191	2 00	1 50	8 416 29	2,385 44
Greene	3,578 22	2,370 54	1,327,465 00	71, 66 00	1,011	760	2	....	2 54	1 19	......	....
Guilford	12.458 00	6,228 00	5 998,846 00	166 906 00	3 754	907	524	416	1 64	....	17,661 00	1,025 00
Halifax	*15,434 00	.....	3 422 587 00	311 695 00	1,804	2,568	....	....	2 15	..	....	......
Harnett	3,906 00	1,912 00	1,459 605 00	54,570 00	1,641	526	172	214	2 40	1 50	4,712 74	549 01
Haywood	5.870 00	218 00	1,705 840 00	9.371 00	1,994	37	*444	...	2 75	1 50	*4 975 90	..
Henderson	6,201 33	897 66	2,042,680 00	24,126 00	1,672	167	190	110	...	...	6 101 33	807 66
Hertford	3.400 25	3 462 02	1,927.001 00	222.179 00	962	1,073	27	138	2 00	1 50	4,737 83	1,867 67
Hyde	2 774 47	1,460 22	958,670 00	25,048 00	915	534	...	.....	2 45	...	2,975 72	837 67
Iredell	10,850 80	3.606 21	3.533,345 00	70,392 00	3.116	810	434	310	2 55	1 56	......	.....
Jackson	4, 00 00	231 47	1,141,838 00	[illegible],441 00	1.391	64	46	5	2 90	1 50	4 141 81	118 39
Johnston	*17.274 71	... .	3,165,538 00	112.977 00	3.550	971	*56	....	2 00	1 56	12.041 10	1,505 13
Jones	1,607 07	1,619 25	964,243 00	59.259 00	442	478	23	63	2 75	1 29	2,566 70	642 02
Lenoir	6,601 54	3.700 71	1,888,472 00	100,793 00	1,6[illegible]4	948	112	142	2 45	1 50	3,379 25	161 43
Lincoln	5,135 96	1,240 79	1,851,995 00	40 292 00	1.650	292	95	66	2 00	1 50	6,145 37	510 52

*White and Colored.

TABLE No. VII—Continued.

Counties.	Amount Apportioned to Whites.	Amount Apportioned to Colored.	Assessed Value of Property of Whites.	Assessed Value of Property of Colored.	No. White Polls.	No. Colored Polls.	No. of Insolvent White Polls	No. of Insolvent Colored Polls.	Total Poll Tax Levied	Amount Poll Tax Paid for Schools.	Amount Actually Paid by Whites on Property and Polls.	Amount Actually Paid by Colored on Property and Polls.
Macon........	$ 4,475 21	$ 270 71	$ 1,094,751 00	$ 7,147 00	1,496	78	30	3	$....	$ 1 65	$........	$ ....
Madison.......	6,336 94	127 10	1,570, 00 00	3,860 00	2,690	68	775	25	2 76	1 50	7,442 62	171 48
Martin	5,097 07	3,659 06	1,827,535 00	130, 00 00	1,302	914	11	150	1 10	1 50	5,242 56	1,605 00
Mll.....	2,118 00	468 00	913,498 00	7, 00 00	1,360	194	*243	......	2 45	1 50	.	....
Mecklenburg ..	14,031 29	8,489 35	8,975,382 00	297,985 00	4 286	2,665	747	..	2 00	1 50	*10,395 00	....
Mitchell..	3,501 60	108 00	855,049 00	6,851 00	1 610	31	75	10	.. .	1 50	3,953 00	58 53
Montgomery ..	3,809 70	988 56	1,287,344 00	17,042 00	1,480	404	46	43	2 30	.....	4,339 60	551 83
Moore.........	5,838 80	3,180 10	2,380,046 00	76,056 00	2,266	883	54	27	1 50	.....	8,451 57	1,125 00
Nash	7,639 50	5,676 00	3,033,391 00	139,641 00	2 413	1,366		....	.	....	8,572 87	2,013 51
New Hanover......		.. .	6,591,032 00	448,042 00	1,815	1,847	388	948	2 25	.....	11,9.0 03	793 12
Northampton	5,375 88	3,962 63	2, 60,473 00	212 091 00	1,536	1,657	20	64	2 54	1 36	7,399 90	2,386 28
Onslow	3 547 43	1,269 92	1,604,660 00	48,11 000	1,408	417	25	75	1 50	1 50	4,643 96	559 64
Orange	4,291 93	1,989 71	2,215 072 00	84,930 00	1,438	690	...	....	2 00	1 50	3,500 00	500 00
Pamlico..	1,928 80	1,045 80	597,295 00	45, 09 00	825	210	...	....	2 00	1 56	2,411 76	587 40
Pasquotank	3,999 80	3,340 10	2,073,551 00	158 330 00	1,028	838	..	...	2 00	1 56	4,682 91	1,847 43
Pender.	2,899 62	2,355 57	1,058,057 00	107,539 00	982	812	34	136	2 00	1 56	4,336 34	1,385 01
Perquimans....	2,726 31	2,087 30	1,300,872 00	113 546 00	856	604	21	45	2 20	1 50	4,018 14	1,11 038
Person	3 891 60	3,085 45	1,820,462 00	54,463 00	1,379	834	*363	....	2 00	..	6,673 09	1,359 40
Pitt...........	10,685 00	6,989 00	317,637 00	118,978 00	2,507	1,769	57	300	2 00	1 50	9,397 48	2,203 50
Polk..........	2,352 98	665 43	923,356 00	13,976 00	735	110	.....	..	..	.....	*2,849 74	...
Randolph	1987 00	1,850 00	3,694,172 00	42,920 00	3,610	453	8	10	2 25	1 50	12,754 85	756 75
Richmond......	[illegible]	5,210 60	2,643,658 00	71,980 00	1,783	1,375	200	400	1 54	1 50	7,000 00	3,500 00

Robeson	*13,260 80	...	3,326,718 00	280,973 00	2,887	2,377	250	350	2 00	1 50	9,943 37	3,549 25
Rockingham	8,943 20	5,657 40	3,888,883 00	1,021,000 00	,702	1,180	*625	.....	...	1 50	....	....
Rowan	10,890 00	3,817 50	5,223,038 10	128,344 [illegible]	3,161	792	204	92	1 77	...	14,577 48	1,178 07
Rutherford	6,842 00	1,828 00	2,231,210 00	43,254 00	3,237	507	248	125	2 65	1 50	8,780 84	903 90
Sampson	5,986 00	3,826 00	1,898,370 00	80,475 00	2,667	884	150	250	2 15	1 50	7,532 56	1,470 85
Stanly	4,871 46	300 00	1,445,556 00	26,230 00	1,629	182	148	46	3 00	1 50	4,665 27	250 21
Stokes	5,918 85	1,069 95	1,974,6 5 00	21,682 00	2,395	335	273	100	2 00	1 50	5,334 16	1,089 10
Surry	8,407 20	1,219 27	2,508,738 00	32,772 00	3,124	302	...	.....	1 50	1 50	9,192 96	568 95
Swain	3,169 15	73 33	1,072,546 86	3,929 00	805	[illegible]	54	6	3 00	...	....	....
Transylvania	2,334 16	254 60	890,253 00	5,250 00	850	63	55	20	2 70	...	2,877 46	103 75
Tyrrell	1,846 90	....	492,205 00	18,746 00	585	190	*29	.....	1 50	...	1,657 56	375 80
Union	*11,873 12	....	3,080,935 00	72,845 00	2,787	880	246	.....	.....	1 50	6,652 45	1,451 12
Vance	3,002 95	4,845 90	2,174,848 00	148,257 00	1,085	1,255	.....	.....	.....	...	....	....
Wake	16,666 25	15,533 00	9,360,797 00	511,946 00	4,549	2,D7	800	970	2 00	1 50	3,106 65	13,535 09
Warren	2,282 75	5,752 30	1,788,213 00	247,434 00	951	1,491	*90	.....	1 72	1 72	4,800 87	2,433 83
Washington	...	.....	1,0.9,575 00	73,390 00	925	754	14	88	2 00	1 50	3,257 45	1,281 76
Watauga	4,646 39	151 26	1,192,215 00	6,345 00	1,797	38	108	10	2 00	1 50	4,646 36	151 26
Wayne	9,081 00	7,020 00	4,555,616 00	250,594 00	2,845	1,503	140	265	.	1 50	13,415 87	2,304 00
[illegible]s.	6,790 50	738 75	*1,881,906 17	.....	2,788	190	268	44	1 50	...	....	....
Wilson	8, 48 60	6,348 60	3,257,772 00	114,135 00	2,772	1,166	...	...	2 00	...	11,053 36	1,879 45
Yadkin	5,255 04	657 44	1,372,530 00	12,501 00	1,940	156	185	15	1 50	1 50	3[illegible]75 55	283 93
Yancey	2,370 51	87 00	511,862 00	7,507 00	...	...	80	4	...	...	....	....
Total	$ 537,125 87	$ 224,672 63	$219,106,232 18	$9,476,283 85	178,793	71,363	14,718	10,716	$....	$..	$ 499,232 52	$ 90,696 57

*White and Colored.

LIST OF TEACHERS.

A request was made, and blanks sent out, to secure a list of the names of the teachers in the respective counties. The following names were taken from the lists of the Supervisors who complied with the request:

ALAMANCE COUNTY, N. C.

Union Ridge Academy, Union Ridge, Rev. T. W. Strowd.
Methodist Academy, Burlington, Prof. G. O. Green.
Union High School, Burlington, Prof. E. E. Britton.
Graham High School, Graham, Prof. W. P. White.
Swepsonville School, Swepsonville, Prof. E. Lee Fox.

Miss Mary Bason, Miss Connie Heuley, Burlington; Miss Berta Moring, Miss Irene Johnson, Miss Julia Long, Prof. W. P. Lawrence, Prof. J. O. Atkinson, Dr. J. U. Newman, Prof. S. A. Holleman, Prof. W. C. Wicker, Elon College.

ALEXANDER COUNTY, N. C.

Taylorsville Classical Institute, Taylorsville, Rev. J. A. White.
Hiddenite High School, Hiddenite, A. F. Sharpe.

Miss Nola Sharpe, Hiddenite; Miss Grace A. Sloan, O. F. Pool, W. L. Beach, Taylorsville; Mrs. Mamie Sharpe, Hiddenite.

ALLEGHANY COUNTY, N. C.

Sparta Institute, Sparta, S. W. Brown.
Whitehead Academy, Whitehead, E. L. Wagoner.

ANSON COUNTY, N. C.

Anson Institute, Wadesboro, Prof. D. A. McGregor.
Polkton Academy, Polkton, Prof. Humbert.
Ansonville High School, Ansonville, Prof. R. B. Clarke.

Morven Academy, Morven—Miss Virginia Lilly, Wadesboro; Mr. W. L. Clarke, Mr. L. M. Clarke, Miss Mary Dunlap, Cedar Hill; Prof. J. A. McRae, White Store; Prof. J. C. Hines, Morven.

ASHE COUNTY, N. C.

Creston Academy, Creston; C. H. Lowe.
Sutherland Seminary, Sutherland, W. H. Jones.
Nathan's Creek Academy, Nathan's Creek, R. E. Plummer.
Jefferson Academy, Jefferson, —— Parks.
Laurel Academy, Graybeal, E. C. Graybeal.
Lansing Academy, Lansing, W. H. Graybeal; J. H. Cole, Sutherland.

BEAUFORT COUNTY, N. C.

Aurora Academy, Aurora, Mrs. A. G. Lane.
Aurora High School, Aurora, Miss Sallie Bonner.
Trinity Classical School, Chocowinity, Rev. N. C. Hughes.
Alexander Academy, Edward, L. H. Ross.
Beckwith School, Washington, Mrs. S. T. Beckwith.
Quinn School, Washington, Miss Annie Quinn.
Bath High School, Bath, C. N. A. Yonce.

BERTIE COUNTY, N. C.

Bertie Academy, Windsor, R. L. Kerney.
Windsor Academy, Windsor, E. S. Askew.
Rosefield School, Windsor, Mrs. W. F. Gillam.
Coleraine Academy, Coleraine, Mrs. E. F. Etheridge.
Aulander Male and Female Academy, Aulander, Spright Dowell.
Roxobel Academy, Roxobel, Miss Mattie Luiesman.
Mdway School, Lewiston, Miss Rosa O. Speight.
Woodville Academy, Lewiston, Miss E. H. Clarke.
Miss Minnie Gray, Miss Helen Gillam, Windsor; Miss Della Poole, Miss Cheek, Aulander.

BRUNSWICK COUNTY, N. C.

Southport Collegiate Institute, Southport, Palmer Dalrymple.
Shallotte Academy, Shallotte, George Leonard.

BUNCOMBE COUNTY, N. C.

Normal and Collegiate Institute, Asheville, Rev. Thomas Lawrence.
Home Industrial School, Asheville, Miss Florence Stephenson.
Weaverville College, Weaverville, T. M. Yost.
Camp Academy, Leicester, A. L. Reynolds.
Farm School, Swannanoa, Rev. Samuel Jeffreys.
Collegiate Institute, Fair View, D. L. Ellis.
Skyland Institute, Asheville, T. J. Dickey.
Ravenscroft Church School, Asheville, Rev. McNeely Dubose.
Antioch Seminary, Democrat, G. K. Grant.
Morgan Hill Academy, Morgan Hill, J. J. Ammons.
Sand Hill High School, Acton, S. F. Venable.
Bingham School, Asheville, Robert Bingham.
Cove School, Weaverville, Miss Evangeline Garbold.
Young Men's Institute, (colored) Asheville, A. D. Baker.
Hominy Institute, Candler, O. F. Thompson.
Mt. Dale Academy, Barnardsville, Walter Hurst.
E. P. Stradley, C. B. Way, Asheville; Mrs. N. B. McDowell, Weaverville. D. L. Ellis, Mrs. D. L. Ellis, J. W. King, Asheville; Miss Mary Merrill, Fair View; A. H. Felmet, Acton.

Colored Teachers.—Miss Lillian Murray, Acton; Miss Lucy Johnson, Candler; R. D. Berthea, James W. Young, H. L. Watkins, West Asheville; J. S. Chambers, Asheville; A. B. Logan, Barnardsville; Miss Mary Coison, Fair View; Miss Annie McKesson, Asheville; Miss Olive Patton, Biltmore; Miss Lelia Rankin, Asheville; Miss Sallie Kilpatrick, Barnardsville; P. M. Flack, Alexander; J. H. Johnson, Mocksville.

CABARRUS COUNTY, N. C.

N. C. College, Mount Pleasant, Rev. M. G. G. Scherer, President.

Mount Amoena Female Seminary, Mount Pleasant, Rev. H. N. Miller.

Georgeville Academy, Georgeville, Prof. E. A. Griffin.

Poplar Tent Academy, Concord, W. W. Morris.

Miss Mattie Query, Harrisburg; Miss C. S. Scott, Miss Willie Weimer, Pioneer Mills; Miss S. S. Milles, Harrisburg; Edgar Bowers, George F. McAllister, Rev. J. H. C. Fisher, H. T. J. Ludwig, Miss Julia Hintz, Miss A. G. Seiber, Miss Bessie Simmers, Miss Leah Fisher, Miss Virgie Shoupe, Mount Pleasant.

CALDWELL COUNTY, N. C.

Lenoir Boys' School, Lenoir, Rhodes Massey.

Faucett Academy, Lenoir, E. M. Faucett.

Kirkwood Academy, Lenoir, Miss Emma Rankin.

Lenoir Academy, Lenoir, Mrs. Shell.

King's Creek Academy, King's Creek, I. H. McNeil.

Globe Academy, Globe, W. M. Francum.

Patterson Academy, Patterson, G. P. Jones.

Granite Falls Academy, Granite Falls, A. P. Sherrill.

W. L. Beach, Emanuel; J. J. Beach, King's Creek; E. B. Phillips, Lenoir.

CAMDEN COUNTY, N. C.

Old Trap, Old Trap, M. B. Burgess.

Oak Ridge, Riddle, L. V. Owen.

Belcross Academy, Belcross, Miss Kate Harris.

Shiloh Academy, Shiloh, C. B. Garrett.

CASWELL COUNTY, N. C.

Miss Mary Brown, Locust Hill, Miss Mary Brown.

Miss Carrie Herndon, Locust Hill, Miss Carrie Herndon.

Prof. N. Seiman, Youngsville, N. Seiman.

Miss Mary Jones, Youngsville, N. Seiman.

Miss Addie Lea, Blanch, Miss Addie Lea.

Mr. L. K. Miller, Leasburg, L. K. Miller.

Miss Fannie Wilson, Gatewood, Miss Fannie Wilson.

CHATHAM COUNTY, N. C.

Mt. Vernon Springs Academy, Mt. Vernon Springs, Rev. O. T. Edwards.

Thompson School, Siler City, J. A. W. Thompson.

Pittsboro Scientific Academy, Pittsboro, A. B. Stalvey.

Moncure Academy, Moncure, Allred.

Ore Hill Academy, Ore Hill, T. M. Watson.

Miss Fannie Thompson, Pittsboro; Miss Kate Hanks, Pittsboro; H. H. Siler, St. Lawrence.

CHEROKEE COUNTY, N. C.

Bellvue, S. W. Part, of Cherokee county, J. W. Lawing.

J. V. Parker, Marble; M. C Clark, Hanging Dog.

CHOWAN COUNTY, N. C.

Edenton Academy, Edenton, J. C. Kittnell.

Edenton Industrial Institute, Edenton, R. H. Riddick.

Mr. J. C Finch, Miss Ava Moore, Sophia C. Martin, Lucy Kittnell, Lucy L. Kipps, Edenton.

CLEVELAND COUNTY, N. C.

King's Mountain High School, King's Mountain. Dr. L. A. Bickle.

Grover High School, Grover, Mr. W. L. Howell.

Earl High School, Earl, A. E. Elliott.

Boiling Springs High School, Boiling Springs, D S. Lovelace.

Mooresboro High School, Mooresboro, D. F. Putman.

Cleveland Mills High School, Cleveland Mills, W. Banks Dowe.

Fallston High School, Fallston, S C. Thompson.

Waco High School, Waco, W. O. Goode.

Belwood High School, Belwood, Prof. Craven.

COLUMBUS COUNTY, N. C.

Prof. J. W. Jacobs, Rehoboth, Rosindale.

Rev. C. H. Mabrey, Vineland.

Miss Bessie Hoyle, Whitesville.

Prof. N. D. Johnson, Fair Bluff, Principal.

Miss Laura Snowden, Cerro Gordo.

Miss Georgania McFadgen, Lake Waccamaw, Principal.

Miss M. C. Applewhite, Cronly, Principal.

Miss Sarah M. Payne, Houb, Principal.

CRAVEN COUNTY, N. C.

Miss Mollie Heath, Mrs. Annie Ferebee, Mrs. Sarah Jenkins, Miss Mary Brown, Miss Mary Hendren, Miss Leah Jones, Miss Fannie Smallwood, Mr. T. R. Faust, Newbern.

CURRITUCK COUNTY, N. C.

Shawboro High School, Shawboro, Miss Kate Albertson.

Miss Mollie Goodson, Jarvisburg; Miss Emma Hines, Kittie Hawk; Miss Annie Upton, Coinjock; Miss Julia Poyner, Currituck.

DARE COUNTY, N. C.

Manteo, Manteo, N. C., Jas. D. Harris.

Wanchese Academy, Wanchese, Chas. R. Taylor.

Nova Midgett, Manteo; C. M. Midgett, (colored), Elizabeth City.

DAVIDSON COUNTY, N. C.

Thomasville High School, Thomasville, Prof. H. W. Reinhart.

Reeds Cross Roads, Michael, Rev. J. M. Bennett.

Yadkin College High School; Yadkin College, Prof. George W. Holmes.

High School, Denton, Prof. J. A. Stone.

Pilgrim Academy, Lexington, Rev. H. A. M. Holshouser.

Bethany High School, Miss Sue Siceloff, Bethany.

Holly Grove Academy, Ilex.

Hedrick's Grove, McKee, Rev. S. W. Beck.

Arcadia, Enterprise, R. H. Beisocker.

Arnold Academy, Arnold.

Miss Corinna Thomas, Thomasville; Mrs. O. A. Hege, Lexington.

DUPLIN COUNTY, N. C.

Sprunt Institute, Kenansville, Miss McFarland.

Warsaw High School, Warsaw, Rev. C. J. Wells.

Faison High School, Faison, Miss O. J. Ireland.

Magnolia High School, Magnolia, Thomas Sloan.

Oakland Academy, Wallace, Rev. R. W. Grizzard.

Miss Nellie Johnson, Warsaw; Miss Hattie Cox, Magnolia; Miss Winnie Faison, Faison; Rachel Winson, Miss Tipping, Miss Bumgarden, Miana Loften, Kenansville.

DURHAM COUNTY, N. C.

Patrick Henry Institute, 8½ miles S. W. Durham, Rev. R. T. Way.

Miss Cora Bolton's School, Miss Cora Bolton.

FORSYTH COUNTY, N. C.

Kernersville Academy, Kernersville; Rural Hall Academy, Rural Hall; Salem Female Academy, Salem; The Boys' School, Salem; A. J. Butner, Bethania.

FRANKLIN COUNTY, N. C.

Louisburg Academy, Louisburg, Mr. W. W. Boddie.

Franklinton High School, Franklinton, Darious Eatman.

Misses Yarborough's School, Youngsville, Misses F. and M. Yarborough.

Youngsville High School, Youngsville, Rev. Saudus Clapp.

Cedar Rock Academy, Cedar Rock, Spencer Chaplin.

Louisburg Female College, Louisburg, W. S. Davis.

Mapleville High School, Mapleville, Charles N. Beebe.

State Normal School, Franklinton, Rev. J. A. Savage.

Young Ladies' Training School, Franklinton, Miss Augusta Curtis.

Christian College, Franklinton, Prof. Reynolds.

Good Shepherd School, Louisburg, Mrs. Sallie B. Perry.

Mr. Sidney Mrs. James Long, W. Wilson, Rev. James Fuller, Miss Minnie Dunston, Rev. C. E. Tucker, Mr. Louis W. Neal, Miss Mary Baptist, Mr. H. E. Long, Franklinton; Miss B. R. Williamson, Louisburg.

GASTON COUNTY, N. C.

Gaston Female College, Dallas, S. A. Wolff.

St. Mary's College, Belmont, Right Rev. Leo Haid.

Belmont Academy, Belmont, F. T. Hall.

Cherryville Academy, Cherryville, Rev. J. J. George.

Gaston Institute, Gastonia, J. P. Reed.

Oakland Institute, Gastonia, B. Atkins.

Jones Institute, All Healing, Rev. C. A. Hamptou.

Lincoln Academy, King's Mountain, Miss Lillian S. Cathcurt.

GRANVILLE COUNTY, N. C.

Horner Military School, Oxford, J. C. Horner.

Female Seminary, Oxford, F. B. Hobgood.

Hilliard School, Oxford.

Masonic Orphan Asylum, Oxford, James W. Lawrence.

Tar River Academy, Oxford, T. J. Clements.

Creedmore Academy, Creedmore, L. T. Buchanan.

Miss B. C. Jordan, Oxford; Mrs. A. A. Hicks, Oxford.

Colored.—Mary Potter Memorial School, Rev. G. C. Shaw.

GUILFORD COUNTY, N. C.

G. F. College, Greensboro, Prof. Dred Peacock.

Oak Ridge Institute, Oak Ridge, J. A. and M. H. Holt.

Whitsett Institute, Whitsett, W. T. Whitsett.

Alamance Academy, Hinton, J. C. Wilson.

McLeansville Academy, McLeansville, Charles Cobb.

Bennett College, Greensboro, Dr. J. D. Chavis.

HALIFAX COUNTY, N. C.

Roanoke Institute, Weldon, Prof. J. A. Jones.

Vine Hill Male Academy, Scotland Neck, D. M. Prince.

Vine Hill Female Academy, Scotland Neck, Miss Lena Smith.

Littleton Supplemental School, Littleton.

Colored.—Scotland Neck Male Academy, Scotland Neck, G. T. Hill; Episcopal Missionary School, Littleton, V. N. Bond; Baptist Institute, Weldon, A. P. Robinson; Littleton Supplemental School, Littleton.

HARNETT COUNTY, N. C.

Buie's Creek Academy, Poe's, Rev. J. A. Campbell.

Dunn High School, Dunn, A. B. Hill.

Legal Academy, Legal, Rev. S. W. Oldham.

Bunnlevel Academy, Riverdale Academy, Bunnlevel; Lillington Academy, Lillington; P. D. Woodall, Poes; Lonnie Smith, Bradley's Store; Miss Lizzie Lanier, May; Miss Nannie Clements, Miss Emma Kivett, Lillington.

HAYWOOD COUNTY, N. C.

Clyde Academy, Clyde, J. G. McLaughlin.

Waynesville Academy, Waynesville, E. E. Mayee.

Canton Academy, Canton, R. L. Hoke.

Rock Spring School, Peru, Miss Clora Haynes

Bethel Academy, Sonoma. W. H. Phillips.

HYDE COUNTY, N. C.

Swan Quarter, Swan Quarter, Yinkie Swindell.

Fairfield, Fairfield.

Juniper Bay, Juniper Bay, E. O. Langston.

Miss Bettie Perry, Lake Comfort.

P. Mede Phelps, Lake Comfort.

C. Davis, Sladesville.

JACKSON COUNTY, N. C.

Cullowhee High School, Painter, Prof. Robert L. Madison.

Sylva Training School, Sylva, Mrs. Anna M. Chisholm.

W. D. Wike, Painter.

Z. V. Watson, Painter.

JONES COUNTY, N. C.

Trenton High School, Trenton, W. H. Rhodes.

Ida J. Hargett, Florence Wooten, Mattie Noble, John B. Koonce, Emma Thornton, Trenton; Ora L. Koonce, Comfort; Mamie Kinsey, Tuckahoe; G. G. Noble, Trenton; A. H. White, Polloksville.

LENOIR COUNTY, N. C.

Lewis School, Kinston. Dr. R. H. Lewis.

La Grange High School. La Grange, Newbold Bros.

High School, La Grange, Miss Lula Whitfield.

Mrs. Y. T. Ormond, G. B. Webb, Miss Minnie Edwards, Kinston; Mr. L. T. Rightsell, Falling Creek; Miss Fannie Payne, Miss Josephine Payne, Miss Dora Miller, Mrs. H. Archbell, Kinston.

LINCOLN COUNTY, N. C.

Piedmont Seminary, Lincolnton, J. C. Linney.
Ridge Academy, Henry, L. M. Wilson.
Denver Academy, Denver, W. M. Brooks.
J. C. Wessinger, Henry.

MACON COUNTY, N. C.

Franklin High Scool, Franklin, Prof. T. J. Johnson.
Flats High School, Flats, Mr. F. T. Gettis.
Highland High School, Highland. Mrs. L. W. Cralle.
St. Agnes High School, Franklin, Mrs. H. Dyer.
Colored.—B. T. Lacy, Maggie Holden, W. B. Harper, Franklin; J. H. Morrow, West Mills.

MADISON COUNTY, N. C.

Mars Hill College, Mars Hill, Prof. R L. Moore and Rev. S. W. Hall.
East Creek, Reek, Horace Sons.
Heat Springs, Heat Springs, J. E. Phillips.

MARTIN COUNTY, N. C.

Hamilton High School, Hamilton, G. W. Mewborn.
Everett Academy, Everett's, C. B. Grantham.
Robersonville Academy, Robersonville, Stephen Outerbridge.
Williamston Academy, Williamston, Mrs. Walter Hassell.
Jamesville High School, Jamesville, R. J. Peel.
W. E. Stubbs, L. L. Johnson, Jamesville; Mrs. Chloe Lanier, Williamston; M. T. Lawrence, Hamilton.
Colored.—Jamesville Academy, Jamesville, J. P. Butler; Williamston Academy, Williamston, W. L. Andrews; H. S. Mayo, Williamston.

MECKLENBURG COUNTY, N. C.

Huntersville High School, Huntersville, R. J. Cochran.
Bain Academy, Mint Hill. H. K. Reid.
Davidson Academy, Davidson, Spence.
Mount Zion Academy, Davidson, J. L. Bost.
Newell Academy, Newell, P. E. Wright.
Hopewell Academy, Hopewell, L. K. Glascow.
Paw Creek Academy, Sandifer, Harrison.
Dixie Academy, Dixie, C. C. Ore.
Shopton Academy, Shopton. L. O. McCutshen.
Ebenezer Academy, Griffith, R. B. Hunter.

Sharon Academy, Cottonwood, Thompson.
Mecklenburg Academy. Harrison, Morrison Brown.
Sardis Academy, Sardis, J C. Reid.
Matthews Academy, Matthews, J. N. Tolar.
Darita Academy, Darita, G. F. Johnson.

MITCHELL COUNTY, N. C.

Bowmar Academy, Bakersville, J. J. Britt.
Aaron Seminary, Montezuma, S. Ridemour.
Ledger School, Ledger, C. H. Wing.
Sprucepine School, Sprucepine, Miss J. English.
Toe River Academy, Plumtree, Chas. E. Greene.

MONTGOMERY COUNTY, N. C.

Mount Gilead Academy, Mount Gilead, R. H. Skeen.
Pekin Academy, Pekin, Kirk.
Troy Academy, Troy, D. W. Cochran.
Troy Peabody Academy, Troy, Rev. O Faduma.
Miss Ina Smitherman, Troy; Miss Mittie Lilly, Allenton Ferry; Miss Ada Saunders, Troy.

MOORE COUNTY, N. C.

Union Home School, Victor, J. E. Kelly.
Carthage Academic Institute, Carthage, R. T. Hurley.
Oak Grove Academy, Bensalem, T. M. Langley
Sanford High School, Sanford, J. A. W. Thompson.
Jonesboro High School, Jonesboro, Arthur Arrington.
Miss Adie StClair, Victor; Miss May Stewart, Carthage; Miss Mary H. Arnold, Pocket; Miss Annie Clegg, Carthage.
Colored.—H. D. Wood, Carthage.

NASH COUNTY, N. C.

Rocky Mount Collegiate Institute, Rocky Mount, W. H. Holmes Davis.
Carolina Institute, Nashville, N. L. Eure.
Spring Hope Academy, Spring Hope, F. L. Cornwell.
Mount Pleasant Academy, Glover, S. E. Eure.
Dortches Academy, Dortches, J. A. Bordgers.
Cedar Rock Academy, Ceder Rock, Spencer Chapell.
Whitaker Academy, Whitakers, Rev. Andrew Moore
Stanhope Academy, Finch, R. H. Wright.
Avents Academy, Avents, W. O. Dunn.
Philadelphia Academy, Dukes, Miss Florence Arrington.
Colored.—Nashville High School, Nashville, J. P. Humphrey; Miss Annie Lewis, Rocky Mount; Miss Laura Boddie, Nashville.

NORTHAMPTON COUNTY, N. C.

Garysburg Academy, Garysburg, Winston Parish.
Seaboard and Roanoke Institute, Seaboard, C. W. Harris.
Lasker High School, Lasker, Oscar McNewby.
Rich Square High School, Rich Square, S. B. Webb.
Severn High School, Severn, J. W. Fleetwood.
Pendleton Academy, Pendleton, J. R. Beale.
Woodland Academy, Woodland, N. W. Britton.
Jackson Female Academy, Jackson, Miss L. H. Whitfield.
Colored.—Garysburg High School, Garysburg, Rev. R. I. Walden.

ONSLOW COUNTY, N. C.

Richlands High School, Richlands, G. V. Tilley.
Richlands High School, Richlands, John Koonce.

ORANGE COUNTY, N. C.

Caldwell Institute, Caldwell Institute, Prof. Candler.
Damascus High School, Lindsay, Prof. Herbert Sholtz.
Rock Springs High School, Rock Springs, Rev. J. F. McDuffie.
Cedar Grove Academy, Ceder Grove, Prof. B. T. Hodge,
Miss Heartt's School, Hillsboro, Miss Alice Heartt.
The Wm. Bingham School, Mebane, Prof. Gray.
Hillsboro Male Academy, Hillsboro, Prof. Alsbrook.
Chapel Hill High School, Chapel Hill, Prof. Canada.
Miss Annie Woods, Rev. J. H. McCracken, Caldwell Institute; Miss Sarah Kollock. Hillsboro; Mr. Jesse Oldham, Mebane; Miss Lula Hendon, Chapel Hill.
Colored.—Mission School, Rock Spring; Mission School, Mebane, Rev. Hoskins; Mission School, Hillsboro, Rev. Hoskins; Mission School, Chapel Hill, Mr. Sosbin P. Berry.

PAMLICO COUNTY, N. C.

Pamlico Male and Female Institute, Bayboro, W. W. Cole.
Vandemere High School, Vandemere, C. H. Paul.
Grantsboro High School, Grantsboro, Irvin W. Rogers.
Miss Lucy Dees, Miss Anna Landis, Vandemere; Miss Amanda Baxter, Miss Jesse Herman, Stonewall; Miss Bessie Tucker, Oriental; J. E. English, Marribule.

PENDER COUNTY, N. C.

Burgaw High School, Burgaw, Rev. W. Farnell.
Colored.—Burgaw Academy, Burgaw, Rev. Summer.

PERQUIMANS COUNTY, N. C.

Hertford Academy, Hertford, W. G. Gaither.
Pleasant Valley Academy, Jacock, Miss Sallie M. Grant.

Belvidere Academy, Belvidere, Miss Lucy J. White.
Private School, Winfall, Miss Lucy Twine.
Private School, Winfall, Mrs. J. B. Whidbee.
Miss Helen Gaither, Miss Annie F. Stokes, Hertford; Miss Adelaide E. White, Belvidere.

PERSON COUNTY, N. C.

Bethel Hill Institute, Bethel Hill, Prof. Beam.
Roxboro Institute, Roxboro, Prof. Mason.
Roxboro Primary, Roxboro, Miss Sallie Street.
Brooksdale Academy, Roxboro, D. S. Parker.
Olive Hill Academy, Olive Hill, Miss Eugenia Bradsher.

PITT COUNTY, N. C.

Greenville High School, Greenville, Prof. W. H. Ragsdale.
Farmville Male and Female Academy, Farmville, Prof. W. E. Newborn.
Carolina Christian College, Ayden, Prof. A. F. Moon.
Bethel Academy, Bethel.
Winterville Academy, Winterville, Miss Mamie Cox.
Miss Maria E. Hill, Ayden; Mr. C. Dawson, Littlefield.
Cooper Gap, Cooper Gap Township, A. L. McMurray.
Mrs. Alice Missildine, Lyon.

RANDOLPH COUNTY, N. C.

Trinity High School, Trinity, R. M. Vestal.
Farmer Academy, Farmer, L. M. H. Reynolds.
Why Not Academy, Why Not, J. P. Boroughs.
Mount Olivet Academy, Erect, T. C. Hoyle.
Shiloah Academy, Moffitt, J. R. Miller.
Ramseur High School, Ramseur, D. M. Weatherly.
Ashboro High School, Ashboro, E. P. Mendenhall.
Liberty Normal School, Liberty, T. C. Amick.

RICHMOND COUNTY, N. C.

Laurinburgh High School, Laurinburgh, W. G. Quackenbush.
Gibson Academy, Gibson Station, F. D. Wycho.
Ellerbe Spring Academy, Ellerbe, J. C. Story.
Rockingham Academy, Rockingham, Gray R. King.
Pee Dee Factory School, Rockingham, Mrs. M. Thomas.
Midway Factory School, Rockingham, Miss Patt McRea.
Spring Hill Academy, Fontcol, A. A. McMillan.
Hoffman Academy, Hoffman, Miss Page.
Hamlet Academy, Hamlet, Miss Nellie Powers.

ROBESON COUNTY, N. C.

Red Springs Seminary, Red Springs, C. G. Vardell.
Robeson Institute, Lumberton, John Duckett.
St. Paul's High School, St. Paul, D. R. McRae.
Ashpole Institute, Ashpole, G. E. Linberry.
Lumber Bridge High School, Lumber Bridge, J. A. McArthur.
Maxton High School, Maxton, R. P. Johnson.
Parkton Institute, Parkton, J. G. Murphy.
Red Springs High School, Red Springs, D. R. McIver.
Bloomingdale, Sterling, W. R. Surles.
Miss Mattie Stansel, Miss Eliza Stansel, Allenton.
Colored.—Whitin Normal, Lumberton, D. P. Allen.

ROCKINGHAM COUNTY, N. C.

Reidsville Female Seminary, Reidsville, Miss Annie Hughes.
Mrs. W. M. Mebane, Madison; Mrs. B. W. Ray, Leaksville; Mrs. W. C. Wooten, Reidsville.

ROWAN COUNTY, N. C.

Church High School, Salisbury, Burton Craige.
Salisbury High School, Salisbury, Miss Josephine Coit.
Mrs. A. M. Coit, Miss Laura Coit, Salisbury.
Colored.—Livingston College, Salisbury, Rev. W. H. Gales; Normal School, Salisbury, Rev. J. O. Crosby.

RUTHERFORD COUNTY, N. C.

Rutherford Military Institute, Rutherfordton, Capt. W. T. R. Bell.
Sunshine Institute, Sunshine, Prof. D. M. Stallings.
Bostic Academy, Bostic, Prof. B. H. Budges.
Forest City Academy, Forest City, Prof. J. W. Smith.

SAMPSON COUNTY, N. C.

Oakhurst Academy, Chance, Street Brewer.
Oak Grove Academy, Timothy, J. F. Jackson.
Union Hill Academy, Giles Mills, J M. Page.
South River Baptist Institute, Autryville, C. M. McIntosh.
Glencoe High School, Herring, J. D. Ezzell.
Salem High School, Ora, Howard Barrett.
Kerr High School, Kerr, Isham Royall.
Beaver Dam High School, Newton Grove, M. Blockman.
Harrell's Store School, Harrell's Store, N. B. Cobb.
Well's Chapel, Harrell's Store, R. H. Gilbert.
Ida Bullard, Hayne; Sarah J. Owen, Roseboro; Lillie McIntosh, Autryville; Mrs. Cox, Newton Grove; Mrs. J. C. Wright, Coharie; W. H. Hobbs, E. M. Hobbs, Mittie Beaman, Clinton; G. I. Smith, Roseboro; Mettie Mints, Chance.

STANLY COUNTY, N. C.

Palmerville Academy, Palmerville, E. F. Eddins.
Norwood Academy, Norwood, A. P. Harris.
New London Academy, New London, John Spence.
Albemarle Academy, Albemarle, J. F. Bivens.
Miss Ella Coggin, Palmerville; Miss Mabel Turner, Norwood.

STOKES COUNTY, N. C.

Dalton Institute, Dalton, Prof. W. A. Flynt.
Sandy Ridge Institute, Sandy Ridge, Prof. Fleming.
Walnut Cove Institute, Walnut Cove, Prof. Small.
Germanton High School, Germanton, Prof. Harris.
Mountain View Institute, Mizpah, M. T. Chilton.

SURRY COUNTY, N. C.

Siloam High School, Siloam, Allen & Cundiff.

SWAIN COUNTY, N. C.

Whittier High School, Whittier, Rev. M. E. Merriam.
Bryson City School, Bryson City, L. Lee Marr.
J. Wilrich Gibbs, Whittier.

TRANSYLVANIA COUNTY, N. C.

Epworth, Brevard, Fitch Taylor.

TYRRELL COUNTY, N. C.

Columbia Academy, Columbia, J. J. Calhoon.

UNION COUNTY, N. C.

Monroe High School, Monroe, W. C. McAlister.
Union Institute, Unionville, O. C. Hamilton.
Wardlaw Academy, Wardlaw, C. R. Clegg.
Wingate Academy, Wingate, M. B. Dry.
Morgan Academy, Old Store, Newel.
Alton Academy, Alton, Mrs. Eva Belk.
Waxhaw Academy, Waxhaw, Rev. Hoone.
Marshville Academy, Monroe, Plummer Stewart.
E. C. Croxton, Marshville; L. D. Andrews, Monroe; Mrs. Rosa Chandler, Marshville.

VANCE COUNTY, N. C.

Prof. John A. Gilmer, Mrs. J. A. Gilmer, Miss Emma Hood, Prof. James Horner, Mrs. J. Horner, Mrs. Mariah Harris, Dr. M. Crachen, Mrs. W. Rowland, Mrs. W. Annson, Mrs. Norwood, Mrs. Ellen Daniel, Mrs. C. Hunter.

Colored.—Prof. Hawkins, Kittrell.

WAKE COUNTY, N. C.

Cary High School, Cary, E. L. Middleton.
Wakefield High School, Wakefield, Rev. A. A. Pippin.
Mt. Moriah M. & F. Academy, Auburn, J. P. Cannaday.
Eagle Rock Academy, Eagle Rock, S. T. Liles.
Bethlehem School, Marks Creek Township, J. E. Debnam
Wendell High School, Wendell, A. R. Flowers.
Greeen Level Academy, Ewing, J. M. Holding.
Wake Forest Academy, Wake Forest, W. C. Parker.
Colored.—Apex M. & F. Academy, Apex, W. H. Morris; Wakefield High School, Wakefield, G. W. Howell.

WARREN COUNTY, N. C.

Miss Lucy Hawkins' Private School, Warrenton, Miss Lucy Hawkins.
Mrs. Pendleton's Private School, Warrenton, Mrs. V. L. Pendleton.
Miss Brown's Private School, Warrenton, Miss Mattie Brown.
Warrenton High School, Warrenton, Profs. Graham and Hazg.
Littleton Female College, Littleton, Rev. J. M. Rhodes.
Wise High School, Wise, Miss Maggie M. Hodgins.
Warren Plains High School, Warren Plains, Miss Edna Allen.
Miss Annie Hawkins, Miss Lizzie Hawkins, Warrenton.
Colored.—Shiloh Institute, Warrenton, Rev. T. O. Fuller: J. P. Williams, Warrenton; Miss Sarah C. Johnson, Warrenton; Miss Carrie C. Thornton, Warrenton.

WASHINGTON COUNTY, N. C.

Plymouth High School, Plymouth, E. S. Edwards.
Plymouth Normal College, Plymouth, J. W. McDonald.
Plymouth Private College, Plymouth, Miss Marshie Latham.
Creswell Academy, Creswell, Mrs. Carrie Howell.
Roper High School, Roper. Miss Lelia Savage.
Miss Lee Robinson, Miss Gertie Woodard, Roper; Mrs. C. J. Dance (colored), R. R. Cartwright, J. C. Cardon, W. J. Hines, Plymouth.

WATAUGA COUNTY, N. C

Skyland Institute, Blowing Rock, Miss Annie Jackson.
Valle Crucis, Nallicincis, J. L. Nicholson, Miss Annie Dobbins.

WAYNE COUNTY, N. C.

Mount Olive High School, Mount Olive, M. W. Ball.
Fremont Seminary, Fremont, Mrs. W. H. Speight.

WILKES COUNTY, N. C.

Wilkesboro Academy, Wilkesboro, Prof. R. H. McNeil.
North Wilkesboro Seminary, North Wilkesboro, Rev. John W. Wilson.

Boomer High School, Boomer, Prof. W. S. Surratt.

Traphill Institute, Traphill, Prof. M. B. Joins.

Fair View College, Traphill, Prof. Johnson.

Moravian Falls Academy; Moravian Falls, Prof. Stepens.

Pleasant Grove Academy, Clingman, J. E. Hamton.

New Hope Academy, Purlier, James W. Blankenbekler.

Ronda High School, Ronda; Miss Mamie McEleve, Miss Gertrude Johnson, North Wilkesboro; Miss Juda Perlier, Moravian Fal s; Miss Mattie Sale, Brien Creek.

A. and I. Institute, North Wilkesboro, S. G. Walker.

WILSON COUNTY, N. C.

Elm City Academy, Elm City, James W. Hays.

Kinsey Female Seminary, Wilson, Joseph Kinsey.

Miss Wahala Griffin, Elm City; Miss Ida Warren, Conetoe; Miss Levici Edwards, Lawrence.

YADKIN COUNTY, N. C.

Yadkinville Normal, Yadkinville, Z. H. Dixon.

Union High School, East Bend, M. L. Matthews.

Y ikin Valley Institute, Boonville, R. B. Horn.

Jonesville, Academy, Jonesville, J. E. Johnson.

YANCEY COUNTY, N C.

Mountain City College, Bald Creek, E. W. Elliot.

Burnsville Academy, Burnsville, C. R. Hubbard.

Petterson Academy, Day Book, W. N. Peterson.

Blue Rock, Flinty, Josephine English.

Miss Maggie Ray, Bertie Aurther, Burnsville; Claud Davis, Bald Creek; C. C. Peterson, A. H. McCoun, Day Book.

NORTH CAROLINA TEACHERS' ASSEMBLY.

The North Carolina Teachers' Assembly was organized in 1884, and has held large and enthusiastic meetings each year since. Teachers from every grade and kind of our schools, from every department of our educational life; together with leaders in church and State have year after year gathered for consultation upon educational problems and conditions.

Experts have been secured to discuss the best and latest methods, and the full and free discussion always allowed has helped to solve many vexed problems.

The Assembly has been for fifteen years a potent factor in the educational life of North Carolina. Much of the best educational legislation, many changes in our educational systems, and some of our leading advances in the field of education originated in the work of the Teachers' Assembly.

The annual meetings are held the second Tuesday in June, and usually continue from one to two weeks. The Assembly is supported by yearly membership fees; the fee for males is $2, for females $1. Life certificates of membership are sold for $25.

The leading teachers of North Carolina have always been identified with the work of the Assembly, and it has received hearty support and encouragement from all classes of intelligent and progressive citizens.

The annual meetings of the Assembly are held at various points in the State, selected from time to time by the Executive Committee.

As an index of the Assembly's work we append a list of officers for 1898 and the programme of the last meeting.

ORGANIZATION FOR 1898.

PRESIDENT.

ALEXANDER GRAHAM, Superintendent City Schools, Charlotte.

SECRETARY AND TREASURER.

W. T. WHITSETT, Superintendent Whittsett Institute, Whitsett.

FIRST VICE-PRESIDENT.

W. H. RAGSDALE, Male Academy, Greenville.

VICE-PRESIDENTS.

J. O. ATKINSON, Elon College.
E. S. SHEPPE, City Schools, Reidsville.
E. P. MANGUM, City Schools, Wilson.
J. H. CLEWELL, Salem Female Academy.
W. H. PEGRAM, Trinity College, Durham.
B. F. SLEDD, Wake Forest College.
MISS MARGARET HILLIARD, Female Seminary, Oxford.

EXECUTIVE COMMITTE.

President, *ex-officio*, ALEXANDER GRAHAM.
Vice-President, *ex-officio*, W. H. RAGSDALE.
Secretary, *ex-officio*, W. T. WHITSETT.
C. H. MEBANE, Superintendent Public Instruction, Raleigh.
R. L. FLOWERS, Trinity College, Durham.
N. Y. GULLEY, Wake Forest College, Wake Forest.
G. A. GRIMSLEY, Superintendent City Schools, Greensboro.
D. MATT THOMPSON, Superintendent City Schools, Statesville.
A. Q. HOLLADAY, A. and M. College, Raleigh.

PROGRAMME NORTH CAROLINA TEACHERS' ASSEMBLY, ASHEVILLE, N. C., JUNE 14-18, 1898—FIFTEENTH ANNUAL SESSION.

TUESDAY, JUNE 14th.

8 P. M.

PRAYER, by Dr. J. S. Felix, Asheville.
ADDRESS OF WELCOME, by Hon. John W. Starnes, Asheville.
RESPONSE, by the President of the Assembly.

THE EDUCATIONAL INTERESTS OF NORTH CAROLINA—

(1) ACADAMIES AND HIGH SCHOOLS:

Supt. Robt. Bingham, Bingham School, Asheville, 10 m.
Prin. A. B. Justice, Winton Academy, Winton, 5 m.
Prin. J. C. Horner, Horner School, Oxford, 5 m.

(2) PUBLIC SCHOOLS OF THE STATE:

State Senator George E. Butler, Clinton, 10 m.
President L. L. Hobbs, Guilford College, 5 m.

(3) COLLEGES:

Prof. J. B. Carlyle, Wake Forest College, 10 m.
Prof. W. F. Massey, A. and M. College, Raleigh, 5 m.
Prof. C. L. Raper, Greensboro Female College, 5 m.
Prof. J. O. Atkinson, Elon College, 5 m.

(4) THE PEOPLE AND THE SCHOOLS:

Hon. Daniel L. Russell, Governor of North Carolina.
Col. Julian S. Carr, Durham, 5 m.
Col. John S. Cunningham, President N. C. State Fair, 5 m.
Prof. John Graham, President N. C. Farmers' Alliance, 5 m.

WEDNESDAY, JUNE 15th.

9:30 A. M.

THE TOWNSHIP SYSTEM IN NORTH CAROLINA—

Hon. Charles H. Mebane, State Supt. of Public Instruction.
Supt. M. C. S. Noble, Wilmington Graded Schools.
Prof. D. L. Ellis, County Supervisor for Buncombe County.

General Discussion.

10:45 A. M.

LOCAL TAXATION FOR SCHOOLS—

President C. D, McIver, State Normal and Indnstrial College.
Editor Josephus Daniels, News and Observer.

General Discussion.

12:00 M.

TEXTILE SCHOOLS—

D. A. Tompkins, of the D. A. Tompkins Co., Charlotte.

General Discussion.

AFTERNOON—RECREATION.

8:30 P. M.

ANNUAL ADDRESS by the President of the Assembly.

Prof. Alexander Graham, Supt. Charlotte City Schools.

THE X RAYS (with many experiments with a complete set of apparatus.)

Dr. H. L. Smith, Davidson College.

THURSDAY, JUNE 16th.

9:30 A. M.

OUR SECONDARY SCHOOLS—

Prin. J. Allan Holt, Oak Ridge Institute.
Prin. Hugh Morson, Raleigh Male Academy.
Prin. Holland Thompson, Concord High School.

General Discussion.

10:45 A. M.

ENGLISH IN OUR SCHOOLS—

Prof. Edwin Mims, Trinity College.
Prof. J. A. Bivins, Charlotte Graded Schools.
Prin. R. L. Madison, Cullowhee High School.

General Discussion.

12:00 M.

LITERATURE AS A CULTURE STUDY—

Prof. J. H. Clewell, Salem Female Academy.

General Discussion.

12:45 P. M.

A NATIONAL UNIVERSITY—

Mrs. J. R. Chamberlain, Raleigh.

4:00 P. M.

MUSIC RECITAL—

Prof. Albin Oswald Bauer, (Royal Conservatory, Leipzig, Germany,) Asheville College for Young Women.

8:30 P. M.

MODERN GREECE—

Dr. Eben Alexander, University of North Carolina.

9:30 P. M.

RECEPTION to members of Assembly, by Buncombe County Teachers.

FRIDAY, JUNE 17th.

9:30 A. M.

NORMAL TRAINING FOR TEACHERS—

Prof. P. P. Claxton, State Normal and Industrial College.

General Discussion.

THE POWER OF THE TEACHER'S PERSONALITY—

Editor J. W. Bailey, Biblical Recorder.

BUSINESS MEETING, Election of Officers of the Assembly, Choosing Place of Next Meeting, etc.

11:00 A. M.

EXHIBITION by pupils of N. C. School for Deaf and Dumb.

AFTERNOON—RECREATION.

2:30 P. M. to 6:00 P. M.

VISIT TO BILTMORE ESTATE. (Party will assemble at Public Square at 2:30 P. M.)

8:30 P. M.

THE TEACHER HIMSELF—

Dr. J. H. Kirkland, Chancellor Vanderbilt University.

Adjournment.

SATURDAY, JUNE 18.

RECREATION.

8:00 A. M. to 1 P. M.

VISIT TO BILTMORE ESTATE. (Party will assemble at Public Square at 8:00 A. M.)

2:00 P. M. to 7:00 P. M.

EXCURSION TO HOT SPRINGS, (Party will assemble at Southern Railway Station at 1:30 P. M. Railroad fare, round trip, $1.00.)

THE ASSOCIATION OF ACADEMIES OF NORTH CAROLINA.

This organization, embracing the principals and teachers of the private schools of North Carolina, was formed in the spring of 1897, and held the first meeting at Morehead City June 18–19, 1897.

Its first officers were: Hugh Morson, Raleigh Male Academy, Raleigh, President; J. M. Oldham, William Bingham School, Mebane, Vice-President; W. T. Whitsett, Whitsett Institute, Whitsett, Secretary and Treasurer.

The Association holds its annual meetings during the Christmas holidays. The annual meeting in Raleigh December 28–29, 1897, was attended by representatives from all the leading private schools of the State, and many prominent educators. Great interest was manifested, and the excellent papers, live discussions, and spirit of progress manifest in all its work, attracted the attention of the State to the work of the Association.

Some reforms as to courses of study, entrance at college, and other important matters, promise much good for the future of our schools.

A business meeting of the Association was held at Asheville June 16, 1898, but, as above stated, the regular work of the Association is done in the annual meeting in December.

The present officers of the Association are: J. Allen Holt, Oak Ridge Institute, President; Holland Thompson, Concord High School, Concord, Vice-President; W. T. Whitsett, Whitsett Institute, Whitsett, Secretary and Treasurer.

The membership roll of the Association embraces the following schools:

Raleigh Male Academy, Raleigh; Horner School, Oxford; Whitsett Institute, Whitsett; Bingham School,

Asheville; Oak Ridge Institute, Oak Ridge; Concord Hich School, Concord; Dr. Lewis' School, Kinston; Tarboro Male Academy, Tarboro; Winton Academy, Winton; Mars Hill College, Mars Hill; Turlington Institute, Smithfield; Cape Fear Academy, Wilmington; Graham Institute, Graham; Jefferson Academy, McLeansville; Cullowhee High School, Painter; Fairview Collegiate Institute, Fairview; Advance High School, Advance; St. Paul's School, Wilmington; University School, Augusta; Fayetteville Military Academy, Fayetteville; Penelope Academy, Penelope; Vine Hill Academy, Scotland Neck; Wilkesboro Academy, Wilkesboro; Lumber Bridge School, Lumber Bridge; La Grange School, La Grange; Mt. Olive School, Mt. Olive; Rich Square School, Rich Square; Dunn High School, Dunn; Hayesville School, Hayesville; Huntersville High School, Huntersville; Robeson Institute, Lumberton; Chapel Hill School, Chapel Hill; Trinity High School, Chocowinity; Cary High School, Cary; Wake Forest Academy, Wake Forest; Charlotte Military Institute, Charlotte; Selma Collegiate Institute, Selma; Jonesboro High School, Jonesboro; Tuckasiegee High School, Webster; Greenville Academy, Greenville; Buie's Creek Academy, Poe's; Rutherford Military Institute, Rutherfordton; NewberneAcademy, Newberne; Burlington High School, Burlington; Warrenton Academy, Warrenton; Bloomingdale School, Sterling; Bostic High School; Bostic; Union Home School, Victor; Hendersonville Institute, Hendersonville; Lexington Seminary, Lexington; Bain Academy, Mint Hill; Parochial School, Sylva; Elm City Academy, Elm City; Gaston Institute, Gastonia.

COUNTY INSTITUTES.

I publish the reports of the work done in the County Institutes by Profs. P. P. Claxton, J. Y. Joyner and Frank H. Curtis. Some work along this line was done by President Charles D. McIver and Supt. J. I. Faust. Also in some counties the Supervisors and local teachers did good Institute work of which I have no definite record.

These Institutes do a great deal of good among our teachers. Life, inspiration and enthusiasm are enkindled in the minds and hearts of the teachers thus being brought together under the guidance and supervision of wide-awake educators.

The desire for reading and study, for doing better and more systematic work on the part of the teachers, are among the good results to be seen where these Institutes are held.

COUNTY INSTITUTE WORK.

Greensboro, N. C., November 10, 1898.

Hon. C. H. Mebane,

Superintendent of Public Instruction:

Dear Sir—I have the honor to submit herewith a brief report of the County Institutes conducted in the summers of 1897 and 1898 as a part of my duties as a member of the faculty of the Normal and Industrial College. I conducted three of these Institutes in the summer of 1897, and seven in 1898. The following table gives the number of white teachers in attendance at the several Institutes. Only bona fide teachers were enrolled:

1897.	Males.	Females.	Total.
July 26-30—Alamance county.....	20	54	74
Aug. 2-6—Surry county..........	65	32	97
Aug. 16-20—Lincoln county......	16	35	51

1898.	Males.	Females.	Total.
June 6-10—Edgecombe county....	3	28	31
July 18-22—Randolph county.....	54	65	119
Aug. 1-6—Jackson county........	23	17	40
Aug. 8-12—Transylvania county...	5	7	12
Aug. 15-19—McDowell county....	14	13	27
Aug. 22-26—Rutherford county...	38	43	75
Sept. 12-19—Swain county.......	18	13	31

Total number of white teachers present at all Institutes 557

In Alamance and Lincoln I did some work in the Institutes for colored teachers, in session at the same time with those for the white teachers. There were 31 colored teachers enrolled in Alamance, and 18 in Lincoln. In Edgecombe a session was held for white teachers each morning from 9 to 12:30, and a session for colored teachers from 2 to 5 each afternoon. Forty-six colored teachers were enrolled. In Randolph the Institute for white teachers was held for only four days, and an Institute for colored teachers was held on Friday and Saturday, with an attendance of 23.. I worked in this only one day. Supervisor N. C. English conducted it on Saturday. In Surry and Transylvania the colored teachers attended the Institutes for white teachers, sitting apart in a place assigned them, as has been the custom in some of the western counties where there are very few colored teachers. There were fourteen colored teachers present in Surry, and two in Transylvania. A similar plan was followd in Rutherford the first three days of the session, thirty colored teachers being present. The Institute in this county was continued through two weeks, and was conducted the second week by Supervisor C. C. Gettys and some of the teachers of the county. During the second week separate sessions were held for the white and for colored teachers.

In most of the counties a very large per cent. of the

teachers of the county were present. The small attendance in Transylvanit was due largely to the fact that there were heavy rains every day of the week.

Superintendent E. P. Moses, of the Public Schools of Raleigh, was with me in McDowell, and rendered valuable assistance. I wish to express my thanks also to the County Supervisors of the several counties for their valuable assistance in calling the teachers together and making all necessary preparations for the meetings, and to teachers and citizens for their uniform courtesy and kindness.

Except in two instances, the Institutes began at 10 o'clock on Monday morning and closed at 4 o'clock on Friday afternoon. Two sessions, making, together, five and a half hours, were held daily. At each Institute two or three evening lectures were given on educational questions of general interest, and a public address was made on Friday. In this address the needs of better public schools in North Carolina and the means of securing them were discussed. The number of citizens present to hear these addresses varied from fifty to four or five hundred, the average being about two hundred and fifty. Frequently a large number of township committeemen were present, and at a few places a special meeting was held to discuss the duties of the committees and the best methods of organizing the schools of a township under the new law. Everywhere the importance of local taxation was emphasized, and the people urged to vote such a tax at the next opportunity. In July and August, 1897, by special appointment, I addressed the voters of a half dozen or more townships on this subject. In only two of these townships was the tax voted, but I have reason to believe that the labor was not wholly in vain in other townships, and that in most of them the tax will be voted at the next opportunity, as it will in forty per cent. of the townships in the State.

The regular sessions of the Institutes were devoted to a

study of the essential elements of the subjects taught in the public schools of the State, and to brief discussions of the fundamental principles of teaching, the best methods of procedure in the several subjects, and the means of securing prompt and regular attendance upon the schools.

In conclusion, I wish to recommend that the General Assembly be asked to make some provision for more systematic Institute work. An Institute of two weeks' length should be held in every county of the State every year. Two skilled teachers should be employed to conduct each Institute. A few sets of the best books on teaching should be furnished the Institute conductors, to be taken from place to place and put in the hands of the teachers and read by them at odd hours during the session of the Institute. Many of the teachers have never seen a book on teaching. It is not to be expected that the Institutes can ever do much to improve the scholarship of the teachers. This can be done only through the establishment of good public high schools, normal schools in which a large part of the time shall be given to the mastery of the subjects taught in the elementary schools, and a system of more rigid examinations, all of which must be provided before our public-school system can begin to accomplish the full purpose for which it exists.

Respectfully submitted,

P. P. CLAXTON.

Greensboro, N. C., October 21, 1898.

Hon. C. H. Mebane, Raleigh, N. C.:

Dear Sir—I have the honor to submit the following report of the Institute work done by me as a member of the faculty of the State Normal and Industrial College during the summers of 1898:

COUNTY.	DATE.	ENROLLMENT.			AV. AGE.		YEARS EXPERIENCE.		
		Males.	*Fem.*	*Total.*	*M.*	*F.*	*M.*	*F.*	*Aver.*
Robeson	June 20–24	33	22	55	28	22	6	2	..
Pitt	June 27, July 1	10	48	58	23		..	..	3
Onslow	July 18–22	21	17	38	..		$4\frac{3}{7}$	$4\frac{2}{17}$	..
Harnett	July 25–29	..	..	60	25		..	..	$5\frac{1}{3}$
Rowan	August 15–19	58	27	85	27		..	..	6
Cabarrus	Augdst 22–26	31	39	70	..		..	..	..
Total enrollment of white teachers				366					

I found the Supervisors of these counties teachers of successful experience, that were earnestly laboring for the advancement of the educational interests of their counties. In most of the counties the members of the Boards of Education manifested a commendable interest in the work of the Institute and contributed greatly to its success by their influence and their presence. The teachers were regular in their attendance, cordial in their co-operation, earnest and, in many instances, enthusiastic in their work. It is my fixed conviction that the majority of the four hundred teachers with whom I talked and worked in these Institutes are duty-loving and duty-doing men and women. Many of them have struggled into the presence of the truth, and, in spite of meagre opportunities, hampering environments and almost inconceivable discouragements, are successfully leading hundreds of our children into its blessed presence.

The general spirit of progress and improvement observable in most of the teachers of these six counties is admirable and encouraging.

To one who, for the past fifteen years, has been engaged in this educational work, and who, during each year, has mingled much and talked much, publicly and privately, with all classes of our people in the interest of public education, there is noticeable a very marked and hopeful change in their attitude toward the public schools. This change has come about so gradually that many whose work has not kept them in touch with the educational sentiment of the State are not conscious of the extent of it.

In each county, on the last day of the Institute, addresses on public education were delivered. In most of the counties the audiences were large. Still but a very small part of the taxpayers and patrons of the public schools were reached or will ever be reached by a few speeches delivered at one point in a large county.

Respectfully,

J. Y. JOYNER.

Hon. C. H. Mebane,

Superintendent of Public Instruction:

Sir—I have the honor to submit herewith a report of the work done by me as Institute Conductor.

The first County Institute which I conducted was held at Charlotte, Mecklenburg county, July 18-23. This Institute was held in the magnificent new courthous, and I had the honor of conducting the first Institute ever held in that building. At this Institute I was most ably assisted by Prof. J. G. Baird, Chairman of the County Board of Education, and Prof. Charles L. Coon, of the Charlotte Graded Schools. Prof. J. A. Bivens, of the Charlotte Graded Schools, gave a most interesting talk on what he called a typical lesson in nature study. This was greatly enjoyed.

County Supervisor R. B. Hunter did all in his power to make the Institute both pleasant and profitable to the teachers, and he succeeded admirably.

The total enrollment of teachers during the week was ninety-one, with a daily average attendance of sixty. The attendance of visitors during the week was most encouraging, the large court-room being filled at each session.

I am convinced that much and lasting good was accomplished, and that the teachers were greatly benefited. Such deep interest was manifested that, by a rising vote, it was unanimously decided to continue the Institute until Saturday afternoon instead of closing Friday afternoon, as at first intended.

The Institute was especially fortunate in having such distinguished speakers as Hon. C. H. Mebane, Dr. Henry Louis Smith, Dr. Charles D. McIver, Dr. E. W. Sikes Rev. Dr. Baron and others.

My second Institute was held at Lincolnton, Lincoln county, July 25-30. This was the third Institute which I have held in Lincoln county, and I was prepared for great things. In this I was disappointed. Lincoln county is to be congratulated upon the earnest devotion of her teachers to their profession.

The Institute was held in the courthouse, and the attendance of teachers and citizens alike was most encouraging. Every white teacher in the county, except one, was present, and that teacher was ill. Superintendent J. E. Hoover, himself a teacher of long and successful experience, did everything possible for the success of the Institute. He was present the entire week and frequently took part.

Lincoln county has long enjoyed the reputation of being one of the foremost counties, educationally, in the State, and she worthily sustains that well-earned reputation. As at Charlotte, an extra day was voted by the teachers, and the Institute did not close until Saturday afternoon, having had the largest attendance of teachers probably ever had by any Institute held in that county. Fine addresses were delivered by Hon. C. H. Mebane, Dr. E. W. Sikes, Prof. W. E. Mikel, of the University of Pennsylvania, and others.

From Lincoln county I went to Stanly county, where my next Institute was held, August 1-6. Owing to the distance, I was unable to reach Albamarle, the county seat, until Monday afternoon. Upon my arrival I found a large number of teachers assembled in the courthouse. Between seventy-five and one hundred teachers were enrolled, and the very deepest interest was manifsted during the entire week. Supt. J. A. Spence, Principal of Albemarle High School, is a young man, who takes a very deep interest in education, and is doing a good work for the schools of Stanly county. Prof. J. A. Bivins, of the Charlotte Graded Schools, assisted me during the week, and did most excellent work. He is progressive, enthusiastic and deeply in earnest.

The attendance during the entire week was remarkably good, and it has seldom been my privilege to address a more attentive and responsive body of teachers than the teachers of Stanly county.

My next Institute was held in Rockingham county, where one week was given to white teachers—August 8-13—and one week to colored teachers, August 15-20.

The attendance of teachers, both white and colored, was remarkably large, and a very deep interest was manifested. I have nowhere seen more progressive and enthusiastic teachers than in this county. It is no wonder that the schools of this county rank high, for County Supervisor E. P. Elington is doing all in his power for the upbuilding and improvement of the schools under his charge.

During my Institute work in Rockingham county I had no assistance, but the appreciative interest and attention of the teachers rendered the work both light and pleasant.

My Institute work closed at Wentworth on August 20, on account of having to take charge of the Mt. Airy Graded Schools. In leaving for Mt. Airy I was compelled to decline conducting four additional Institutes.

Including my work done at the Summer School at Wake Forest, I addressed about five hundred teachers and a large number of citizens. Everywhere I found a growing sentiment strongly favoring the public-school system.

There is a marked improvement in the scholarship and professional preparation of teachers, and this is a hopeful indication of better teaching, but it must be borne in mind that the teaching force of the counties is continually changing, almost a complete change being effected every four or five years. This is obvious to all Institute conductors.

The Institutes have met with a most cordial reception from school officers and citizens wherever they have been held.

All of the Supervisors of the counties in which I held Institutes were untiring in their efforts to make the meetings profitable and pleasant.

In all of the Institutes I tried to make the work of a thoroughly practical nature, such as could be utilized in the school-room. Instruction was given in all branches taught in the public school, and much emphasis was placed upon the "theory and practice of teaching." I always endeavored to show the teacher not only what to teach, but how to teach.

I cannot close my report without speaking of the great good the County Institute is to the teacher who avails himself of the opportunity offered by it. I find that the counties most progressive educationally are those that believe in Institutes and have them. The counties that do not believe in Institutes and do not have them are the counties that are non-progressive and backward.

Our public-school system is far from perfect. There are many defects and many things that can and ought to be improved, but on the whole there is much that bids us thank God and take courage. There are brighter days ahead for the public schools of North Carolina.

Respectfully submitted,

FRANK H. CURTIS.

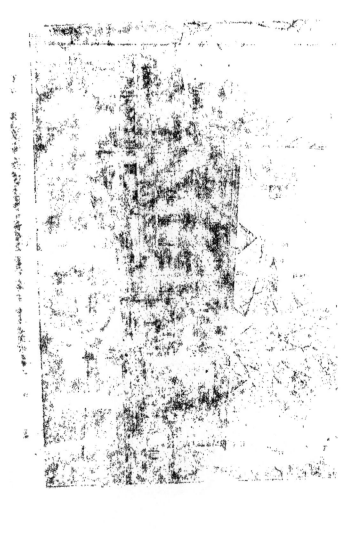

AGRICULTURAL AND MECHANICAL COLLEGE (COLORED), GREENSBORO, N. C.

CITY PUBLIC SCHOOLS.

I report in the following few pages a historical sketch and a brief outline of the work being done in some of our leading city schools:

GREENSBORO PUBLIC SCHOOLS.

Perhaps no other community in the South has a better population than Greensboro. Certainly there are few in which there is a better sentiment for education. This is due to the noble ancestry of her people and their devotion to the cause of religion and education. The foundation was laid just before the Revolution. To this section of the State came a sturdy people—the Scotch-Irish, Highlanders, Quakers and Moravians. They were lovers of truth and liberty. Among them came as missionaries ministers who were graduates of the New England colleges. They began the important work of religious and intellectual training that was to do so much for future generations.

To Guilford county, in the immediate vicinity of Greensboro, came the Scotch-Irish, of whom Caruthers says: "They have ever been the staunchest friends of liberty and of everything else that can elevate the character or promote the welfare of society. Combining the intelligence, orthodoxy and piety of the Scotch with the ardor and love of liberty peculiar to the Irish, they were the most efficient supporters of the American cause during the struggle for American independence, and they have done more for the support of learning, morality and religion than any other class of people.

The man who shaped their destiny and who builded better than he knew was Dr. David Caldwell. He came to Guilford as a missionary in 1765. He was the most noted of all the ministers who came to this State. In the next year he was ordained pastor of Alamance and Buffalo churches. During the same year he founded the first classical school in North Carolina. This school was in the vicinity of Greensboro, and it soon became so noted that it attracted students from all the States south of the Potomac.

Dr. Caldwell labored continuously in this community about sixty years. His school was the University of the South for nearly thirty years. His influence for good has never been equalled in the history of the State. He was a graduate of Princeton, a man of ripe scholarship and strong character, zealous and fearless. He imparted his zeal for education and religion to those around him. His zeal has been transmitted from time to time in the establishment of better educatioal advantages. This section has long been noted for its splendid private schools and colleges. Here was established the first system of public schools in the State supported by a special tax.

GREENSBORO FIRST.

In May, 1874, the people of Greensboro voted a special tax for the support of its public schools. There was a large vote cast, and only eight against the tax. The following was the tax voted:

1. On real and personal property, 25 cents on $100.
2. Poll, $2.
3. Purchase tax—general, 10 cents on $100.
4. Purchase tax—liquor, 20 cents on $100.
5. Drays, express wagons, carriages, etc., $5.
6. Itinerant merchants and peddlers, $25.
7. Billiard tables and bowling alleys, $50.
8. Liquor, $50; beer, $25.
9. Circus, $20 each day.
10. All other shows for reward, $5.
11. Hotels, restaurants and liveries, $25.

BUILDINGS.

The schools first begun in the public schoolhouse provided by the county. The building for the white children was remodeled and enlarged so that it contained five rooms and a chapel.

In 1886, when the town began to make more decided improvements, Judge Schenck, a member of the Board of Aldermen and Chairman of the School Committee, went to work to get a more creditable school building. The result was the handsome and commodious brick building on Lindsay street. In 1887 this was completed and equipped with the most modern school furniture. At this time there were two brick buildings—one for the white children and one for the colored.

During the session of 1890 and 1891 the schools had a wonderful growth. The large building on Lindsay street could no longer accommodate the white children. An elegant building for the primary department was erected on the same grounds.

In May, 1891, the corporate limits of the city were extended, and in September of the same year schools for both races were opened in South Greensboro. There were now four schools—two for white children and two for colored.

The growth of the schools continued from year to year, so that on the South side two tenement houses had to be rented to accommodate all applicants for admission. The necessity for more and better accommodations in this section was so urgent that in May, 1893, bonds were issued for the erection of the Ashboro Street building, one of the handsomest and best equipped public school buildings in the State.

It is a significant fact that Greefnsboro has not only provided splendid buildings for her own schools, but she has put forty-one thousand dollars in buildings for the Normal and Industrial College for white girls and the Agricultural and Mechanical College for the colored race.

GROWTH OF THE SCHOOLS.

The schools opened in 1875 with over one hundred pupils, and had an enrollment of 147 during the year. Fourteen years afterwards, in 1889, there were 285 enrolled. In 1890 and 1891 there were over six hundred. The number has increased yearly and kept up with the rapid growth of the city. The third school for the white children has been established. There were enrolled last year 1,096 white children and 452 colored. This year the enrollment during the first month is nearly as large as it was during the whole of last year.

Probably no other town in the State or in the South has a larger percentage of its school population enrolled in the public schools. The last report shows an enrollment of 74 per cent. of the white children and 62 per cent. of the colored. This means that at least 95 per cent. of the white children between the ages of six and sixteen are in school.

HIGH SCHOOL.

The most notable and gratifying growth in the history of the schools has been in the High School. In 1888 there were only thirty-seven enrolled in this department. In 1894 there were one hundred and fifty-seven. This year there are one hundren and seventy-one, and nearly half of them are boys.

The graduates of this department, without exception, have taken a high stand at Guilford College, Davidson and the University.

COURSE OF STUDY.

The session continues nine months during the year. The course of instruction covers a period of nine years. Those who complete it satisfactorily are prepared to enter the freshman class at college.

GOVERNMENT.

The schools are under the control of a Board of Education and the supervision of a superintendent. There are six members of the Board of Education. Two are elected every year by the Board of Aldermen for a term of three years. There is a faculty of progressive, experienced teachers, graduates of our best colleges, the State Normal and the University.

The present members of the Board of Education are: W. E. Stone, President; C. H. Ireland, Secretary; George S. Sergeant, W. E. Bevill, C. E. Holton and J. R. Mendenhall. G. A. Grimsley has been Superintendent since 1890.

LIBRARY.

In the Lindsay Street School there is a growing library of about five thousand volumes. It has a regular income and is one of the United States depositories for the publications of Congress. The books circulate among the children and are used largely in connection with their class work.

THE CHARLOTTE PUBLIC SCHOOLS.

The Charlotte public schools were established under an act passed through the Legislature in the spring of 1875. Captain Waring, Senator from Mecklenburg, introduced the bill allowing the people to vote a tax not to exceed 25 cents on property and 75 cents on the poll.

Ten cents on realty and 30 cents on the poll was the amount voted at the polls, which amount proved sufficient until several years ago the people voted again and increased the tax to 20 cents on the one hundred dollars, and 60 cents on the poll. The Charlotte Military Institute, together with twenty-eight acres of ground surrounding it, was purchased, and September, 1882, the public schools of Charlotte were opened for children between the ages of six and twenty-one.

Prof. T. J. Mitchell, of Ohio, with ten assistants in the white and eight in the colored school, which was situated on Fifth street, near Caldwell, was elected Superintendent. The schools flourished under his administration. He established during 1885 a training school for teachers, with Mrs. Eva D. Kellogg as teacher. When Mrs. Kellogg resigned, Prof. J. T. Corlew was chosen to conduct the training class, and also the Boys' High School. Professor Mitchell was elected, in 1886, President of Alabama Normal College, and Professor Corlew was elected Superintendent, and Mr. M. S. Salterman, of Ohio, was chosen teacher of the High School and training class. In the early spring of 1888 Mr. Corlew resigned, and Mr. Alexander Graham, of Fayetteville, N. C., was chosen to succeed him.

The following tables show the growth, total enrollment and daily attendance during the eleven years of Mr. Graham's administration. Total enrollment, white and colered, for eleven years:

1887-1888	1,288
1888-1889	1,368
1889-1890	1,500
1890-1891	1,579
1891-1892	1,523
1892-1893	1,758
1893-1894	2,017
1894-1895	2,098
1895-1896	2,142
1896-1897	2,234
1897-1898	2,254

Daily attendance, white and colored, for eleven years:

	Whites.	Col.
1887-1888	432	277
1888-1889	453	284
1889-1890	562	312
1890-1891	569	319
1891-1892	657	358
1892-1893	759	510
1893-1894	882	607
1894-1895	840	565
1895-1896	866	410
1896-1897	958	486
1897-1898	1029	443

The year 1898-1899 promises to eclipse all previous years. We have to-day a daily attendance of 1,300 pupils in the white school out of a total enrollment for September of 1,359. The colored school has a daily roll of 604 out of a total of 739. There are forty teachers in all—tweney-nine white and eleven colored. There are only seventy-five more white girls than boys in each school. Two new school buildings are to be erected—one for white and one for colored pupils.

The schools are popular with all of our people. Our school was represented in the graduating classes of the State University, Trinity College, Wake Forest and in the undergraduate classes of Davidson College in the past year. The State Normal at Greensboro and all the leading female colleges in North Carolina, South Carolina and Georgia had representatives from this school. The honors conferred speak in no uncertain tones of the quality of the work done in the Charlotte city schools.

Hoping this brief sketch will answer your purpose, congratulating you on the hopeful outlook of all our educational facilities in the State, commending your zeal and intelligent and painstaking interest in the cause of public schools and all institutions, State and denominational as well as the excellent private schools, and promising you always my continued support in your excellent administration, I beg to subscribe myself

Your friend,
ALEXANDER GRAHAM,
Supt. Charlotte City Public Schools.

October 14, 1894.

THE WILMINGTON PUBLIC SCHOOLS.

The city of Wilmington is divided into two public-school districts. There are three committeemen for each district, who, by special law, are permitted to unite and elect a Superintendent for all of the schools in the city.

The schools were organized upon their present basis sixteen years ago, when a Superintendent was employed to have the general management of the schools of both races. The Legislative act under which they are organized requires that the Superintendent shall be a practical teacher, and the committees interpret "practical teacher" to mean a teacher who not only has class-room experience, but such professional training as is derived only from frequent attendance upon summer schools, teachers' gatherings and educational meetings.

In the selection of teachers every effort is made to employ those who have hed professional training for the school-room. At present every teacher in the public schools of Wilmington has either attended a summer school or normal college, or has received special collegiate instruction fitting her for the work of teaching. The Superintendent conducts weekly teachers' meetings for the discussion of educational problems and for the study of the best methods of teaching.

CONSERVATIVE MANAGEMENT.

The management of the schools has been remarkably conservative. James H. Chadbourn, chairman of the committee in District No. 2, has served the schools for more than twenty-five years with ever-increasing zeal, enthusiasm and efficiency.

James F. Post, Jr., chairman of the committee in District No. 1 for the past five years, gives to the schools in his district the same business-like care and attention which were given to them by his prelecessor, the late Donald MacRae, one of Wilmington's most prominent citizens and as school committeeman during the twenty years preceding his death.

COURSE OF STUDY.

The course of study provides not only primary instruction, but thorough preparation for college entrance, and is the result of long and careful thought and investigation.

EQUIPMENT

There are separate buildings for the primary, grammar and high-school departments. The primary buildings were built especially for work in the lower grades, and have every appliance necessary for successful teaching.

The grammar-school buildings are models for comfort, arrangement and equipment. On the second story of each building there is a handsome assembly hall, brilliantly lighted, seated with five hundred opera seats and furnished with a piano, rostrum and drop-curtain for public occasions.

The recitation rooms are large, well-lighted, thoroughly ventilated and comfortably heated by an approved system of hot-water heating. The blackboards and maps are of the best quality, and single desks of the latest pattern are found in every room.

The high-school building is the only one in the State devoted exclusively to public high-school work. It is a handsome two-story structure, planned by an expert in school architecture. The school committee enjoys the free use of this most excellent building, through the kindness of the trustees, under the will of the late Mrs. Mary Hemenway, a Boston woman, whose generous work for the educational advancement of Wilmington has made her name a household word in every home in the city.

THE ENROLLMENT.

The enrollment has grown steadily for years, and represents every family in the city. During the year ending May 28, 1898, more than 3,000 pupils were enrolled.

The school committeemen, pupils and teachers are loyal to the schools and proud of them. The professional spirit of the teachers is ambitious, and the educational desires of the city are constantly growing stronger. With such conditions existing the growth of the school system of Wilmington is an encouraging fact.

RALEIGH PUBLIC SCHOOLS.

Hon. C. H. Mebane:

Dear Sir—I beg to acknowledge the receipt of your favor, requesting me to give you a short history of the graded schools of Raleigh.

In the fall of 1876 a public graded school was opened in Raleigh in the old Governor's Mansion, at the foot of Fayetteville street. The school was patriotically styled "The Centennial School," and the name remaineth unto this day. Capt. John E. Dugger, of Warrenton, N. C., was elected principal. The expenses of the school in excess of the public-school revenue were met by voluntary subscriptions of citizens.

In 1877, by authority of an act of the General Assembly and a popular vote, a special tax of one mill was levied upon the township for the support of this school and for the colored schools.

The Centennial School began its second year's work with 300 pupils and eight teachers, including the Superintendent.

The present Centennial School building was erected in 1885.

In 1887 the Murphy School for white children was opened in the northeastern part of the city.

In 1889 the special tax levy for schools was increased to two mills.

The school committee has recently rented a building on Halifax street to relieve the crowded condition of the Murphy School.

A lot in the western part of the city has been purchased, and we hope to be able to erect thereon a school building for white children in the near future.

There are four good buildings now in use for the colored children, erected or remodelled in 1884, 1885, 1887, 1897.

In the white schools there have been enrolled this session 1,194 pupils, taught by twenty-four teachers, including principals.

In the colored schools the enrollment is 1,229, with twenty teachers, including principals.

Meetings of teachers, by schools or by sections, are held on the afternoon of each school day in the month, except two.

A school is what the teachers make it. I believe that the teachers of the Raleigh schools are constantly and unselfishly striving to be worthy of their high calling, and to make their work worthy the confidence of the public.

Very respectfully,

EDWARD P. MOSES,

Superintendent.

WILSON PUBLIC SCHOOLS.

The Graded Schools of Wilson, N. C., were established in 1881. They were first supported by private subscription, although tuition was free, with certain restrictions.

Prof. J. L. Tomlinson was the first Superintendent. He organized the schools and began work in October, 1881. There were eight grades, with seven teachers. During the first year the enrollment was 274. At this time there was no connection between the schools for the whites and the schools for the negroes, although the negroes had a public school. Superintendent Tomlinson, with his corps of excellent teachers, made his influence felt throughout the State, and when the history of education in North Carolina is written, his name will occupy a deservedly high place.

In 1883 the question of support by taxation was agitated. The Legislature authorized the people to vote upon the question of taxation. The result was a victory for progress and civilization. From this time until the decision of the Supreme Court in regard to the "Dortch Bill," the schools were wisely managed and very successful.

Superintendent Tomlinson resigned in 1883, and Mr. John F. Bruton, now a prominent lawyer of Wilson and a Colonel in the State Guard, was elected superintendent. Colonel Bruton had been principal of the schools, and to him was due, in a large measure, their excellent discipline.

Prof. E. C. Branson, now Professor of Pedagogy, State Normal School, Athens, Ga., succeeded Colonel Bruton, and for two years managed the schools with great wisdom and ability. Superintendent Branson resigned to accept the superintendency of the Athens (Ga.) schools, and was succeeded by Prof. Collier Cobb, now Professor of Geology, University of North Carolina. Up to this time the growth of the schools had been steady and sure.

In 1886, upon the decision of the Supreme Court that the graded-school law was unconstitutional, the trustees were forced to return to the old system of support by subscription. Prof. P. P. Claxton, of the State Normal College, was the superintendent during the year 1886-1887, but his wise management and enthusiastic devotion to the interests of the schools could not turn the tide, and in 1887 the schools were closed. The handsome building and beautiful grounds passed into the hands of one of our wealthy and progressive citizens, and now, after remodeling and much improvement, is occupied by him as a residence.

From 1887 to 1891 there was no public school in Wilson, except that supported by the general school fund. In 1891 several citizens, seeing the necessity confronting them, began the agitation for the re-opening of a graded school. The question was again submitted to the people, and again was the school victorious. A new building was completed by October, 1891, and Superintendent J. I. Foust, now of the Goldsboro schools, was elected superintendent. The school was organized with six grades, a teacher for each grade. At the beginning of the second school year two new grades were added and the number of teachers increased to nine.

The school for the negroes was under the control of the same Board of Trustees as the school for the whites. The number of grades was seven, with five teachers.

Superintendent Foust served the schools for three years with much wisdom and prudence. Upon his resignation, Mr. G. W. Connor, a citizen of Wilson, but at that time principal of the Goldsboro schools, was elected superintendent. Under his administration the schools grew rapidly in usefulness and in the hearts of the people. The total enrollment in the two schools reached about 700.

In December, 1896, Mr. Connor resigned and entered the mercantile business as partner in the firm of J. C. Hadly & Co. He was succeeded by the present encumbent, Superintendent E. P, Mangum, whose efficiency is attested by the steady krowth of the schools during the past two years. The enrollment for the year of 1897-1898 in the two schools was 827, and the present enrollment is 121 in excess of that for the same period last year. The schools now have fifteen teachers besides the superintendent—ten white and five colored. The rate of taxation is 30 cents on the $100.

The teachers in the Wilson schools are second to none in the State. Their energy and their devotion to their work, laboring in perfect harmony with their superintendent, have rendered possible the present efficiency of the schools. Wilson is justly proud of her graded schools.

E. P. MANGUM,
Superintendent.

ASHEVILLE PUBLIC SCHOOLS.

The city of Asheville was made a special school district in 1887. A tax of sixteen and two-thirds cents on each hundred dollars of listed property, and fifty cents on each poll, was levied, and the city's public school property was turned over to a school committee of six members. This property consisted of a small wooden house belonging to the old colered district, a vacant lot and a small sum of money belonging to the white district. The old military academy on Montford avenue was purchased and repaired. The school opened in January, 1888, with more than 600 white applicants and 300 colored. The building on Orange street was completed by the fall of 1888, at a cost of about $11,000. Ten white teachers and one colored were added to the corps, and 1,200 children were admitted to the schools. A tax of thirty cents on property and ninety cents on polls was levied to raise $12,000, which was badly needed. This was continued the following year, but the rate was afterwards made twenty cents on property and sixty cents on polls, the maximum allowed by the amendment pased by the Legislature of 1889. The Legislature of

1891 pased a bill authorizing the city council to issue bonds of the city to the amount of $25,000. This act was ratified by an almost unanimous vote of the people. Three handsome brick buildings were erected in the summer of 1892—Montford, Bailey and Valley street buildings.

Another issue of $25,000 in bonds was made, and to-day the city has four handsome brick buildings in which to accommodate her children. The school tax received from the city is about $11,000, and from the county about $6,000. The schools are free from debt, are well equipped with modern conveniences, are thoroughly progressive and are patronized by every class of society, including visitors who spend their winters in the city.

There are thirty-one teachers, twenty-three white and eight colored, and one superintendent, who devotes his entire time to the schools.

It has always been the policy of the school committee to choose teachers according to fitness, regardless of geographical locality or sectarian views; and this wise policy has led to the selection of a fine corps of teachers, who keep in touch with every educational move.

The school committee is chosen by the Board of Aldermen. Two members are selected every two years, and serve for six years, without compensation.

The course of study in the Asheville schools extends through a period of ten years, and graduates are well prepared for college and university. Each building has a library for the pupils, to which additions are regularly made, and the teachers also have a growing library in each building for their own use. The enrollment for the session of 1898-'99 will reach 2,000.

J. D. EGGLESTON,
Superintendent.

DURHAM PUBLIC SCHOOLS.

Like many other institutions, the Durham Graded School had its ups and downs, its trials and difficulties, its friends and enemies. Owing to early education, the white people, for many years after the late civil war, could not cheerfully accept the new regime, could not realize that the colored population should have equal educational facilities with the whites; therefore they were opposed to a specific tax for educational purposes; also the old idea still existed that a man should not pay tax to help educate his neighbors' children.

The Durham Graded School had to battle against these ideas in the beginning, and fierce opposition and war was made against it by a number of the leading men of Durham, and as the first bill of incorporation did not provide equal facilities for the colored, that element also was opposed to it, but by energetic work on the part of a few the public was so thoroughly aroused that the citizens of Durham voted to sustain the school by a direct tax, and later the town voted to issue bonds to raise money for the purpose of erecting a suitable school building.

Some of the bitter opponents of the school, hoping to defeat it, refused to pay the tax levied for support, and this brought the matter up before the courts on constitutional grounds, and the Supreme Court of the State decided that, as the charter did not make equal provision for the colored, the bill was unconstitutional and void.

Nothing daunted, the friends of the school went to work and drew another charter, avoiding the former mistake, and provided equal facilities for both races, which was ratified by the citizens of Durham in 1887, after a bitter contest. Some of the opponents were not even satisfied until they tested the constitutionality of this last act. It might be said to the honor of the opponents that when the school became a fixed and final fact they withdrew further objec-

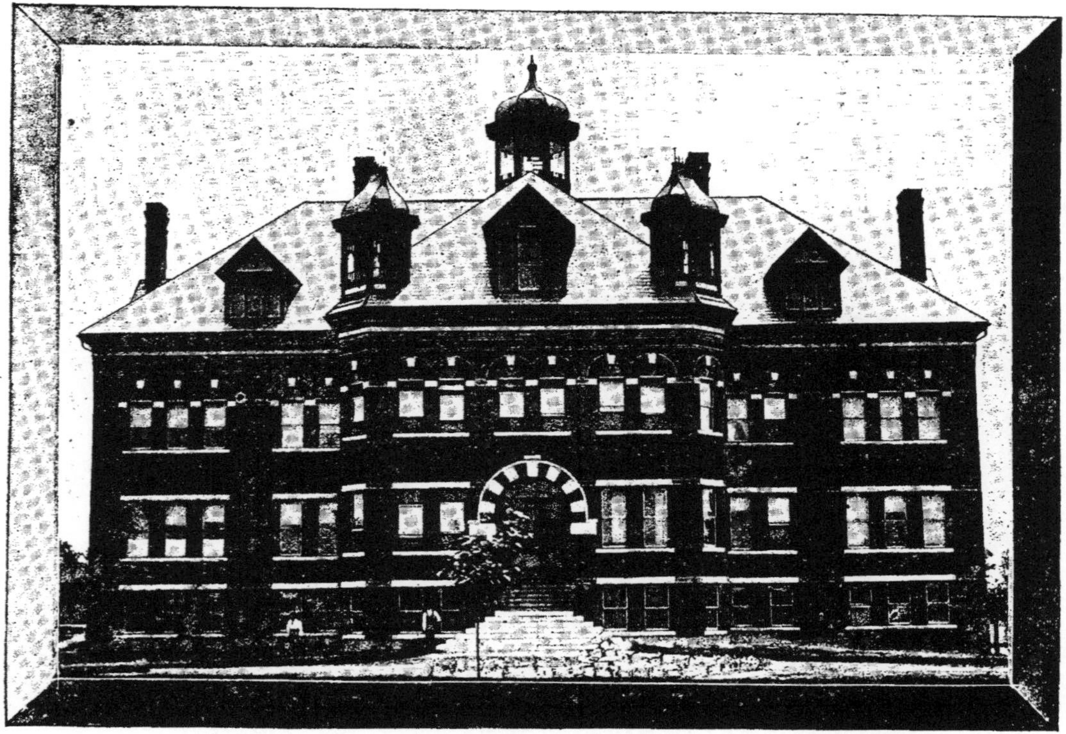

AGRICULTURAL AND MECHANICAL COLLEGE (COLORED) GREENSBORO, N. C.

tion, and instead of remaining enemies were among its warmest friends and supporters. Today it would be difficult to find an enemy to the school.

The first school was organized in 1882 by electing Prof. E. W. Kennedy superintendent, with a faculty of four or five teachers. The school was first opened in an old tobacco warehouse on Main street, with as few conveniences as possible and no comforts. In the face of all difficulties the school continued to grow in popularity and numbers.

After the Supreme Court had declared the first bill unconstitutional, the school was run one year by private subscriptions before another charter could be obtained from the Legislature. So earnest were the friends of the school, they determined that there should be no suspension of it, lest it might be the means of defeating the school altogether.

The colored school, under the new charter, was opened in a brick building, erected for a tobacco factory, and possessing many more conveniences and comforts than the building for the whites. In the year of 1890 the city issued $25,000 in bonds for the construction of a suitable building for the whites. This building was erected in 1891, with all the modern conveniences of heating, ventilation and sanitary measures. It is one of the best public-school buildings in the State.

The new building for whites was occupied in 1893, and in 1894 Prof. C. W. Toms succeeded Professor Kennedy as superintendent. During Professor Toms' administration as superintendent manual training was introduced into the school. Like all new departures, this branch had its friends and its enemies among the school committee, but by perseverance of certain friends the Board, in the year of 1894, voted to introduce manual training into the school, and elected Miss Beemis, from Pratt Institute, Brooklyn, N. Y., teacher of manual training.

So successful has this branch been that it has made

friends of all who at first opposed it, and has done much for the discipline of the school and for the training of the eye and hand as well as the mental faculties. The great want of the South to-day is trained mechanics and skilled artisans; and as manual training is a stepstone to this, it should be introduced in all the public schools of the South as rapidly as possible. It is the universal verdict of all the teachers in the Durham Graded School that manual training has been useful not only in discipline, but in stimulating the students in other studies.

A new graded-school building was erected for the colored in 1896, with all the conveniences and comforts necessary, at a cost of about $8,000. The principal, W. G. Pearson, is a colored man, and has proven himself to be a competent man for the place. Much to the regret of all Durhamites, Prof. Toms, tendered his resignation as superintendent , being elected to the faculty of the University, in 1897. His administration as superintendent of the school was eminently successful.

Prof. W. W. Flowers, a graduate of Trinity College, was elected to succeed Prof. Toms.

The schools enrolled in 1897, 870 whites, 390, colored.

These 1,260 pupils were instructed at a cost of one dollar a pupil per month. That the schools have been able to give instruction of a high order at such low rates is due to the fact that they have had committees who believe that a school, like any other enterprise, should be run on strictly business principles. They believe that the "best is good enough for children," and that the best is in the long run the cheapest. The most successful and the most influential men of Durham have given their time and thought to conducting the educational interests of the town. The present committee is composed of Messrs. Leo. D. Heartt, Chairman, S. F. Tomlinson, Secretary, J. S. Carr, B. N. Duke, W. H. Rogers, and M. H. Jones.

THE REIDSVILLE PUBLIC SCHOOLS.

These schools were incorporated by act of the Legislature in 1887, and were put into operation the same year. At first there was considerable opposition to the system from some of the largest property owners, but this has almost entirely disappeared. The enrollment has increased from 444 in 1887 to 805 in 1898. The schools have gradually won their way to the confidence and patronage of every class of citizens until they stand as fixed institutions of the community, firmly grounded in the affections of the people.

There are three buildings, two for the white and one for the colored race. The work is organized on the basis of ten grades, seven in the primary and grammar schools and three in the High Schools. Each grade below the High School is subdivided into two sections, with an interval of half a year between them; and promotions are made semi-annually, or oftener if the interests of the pupils require it. No pupil is held back or kept "marking time" on account of the slowness of others.

The High School, which is the crowning interest of the system, prepares its graduates for college or for practical life. The addition of a thorough course in book-keeping and business practice greatly enhances the value of the instruction in this department. Many students from a distance seek the advantages offered by the Reidsville schools every year.

Among the special features which have contributed more than any other agency to the efficiency of the training given in these schools are the Debating Work and the School Exposition. These were introduced by the present superintendent four years ago.

Debating is a part of the regular work in all grades above the fifth. The debates are held every other week. The children elect their own officers and manage the affairs of the debating societies in their respective grades, but all the pupils are required to participate in every debate. The subjects selected are usually drawn from American and English history, and from live current topics. This work reinforces all the other work of the school. It trains in the habit of independent investigation; it develops the power of thinking clearly upon any subject; and it is pre-eminently a training in the power of forcible, connected expression. The children become intensely interested in the debating work, and this interest passes easily into the domain of all their school duties.

The school exposition is held annually at the close of the session. It consists of specimens of the regular work of the pupils in all branches of study which are taken up about twice a month and bound into booklets. It does not show the occasional work of a few of the brightest pupils, but the regular work of all the pupils. No selections are made. The pupils are impressed with the fact that they must be careful to improve in neatness as well as in correctness every week. Instead of seeking to outstrip their fellows in an ignoble competition for prizes, rewards and distinctions, they catch the spirit of the true rivalship which makes them anxious to improve upon themselves—to beat their own best records. The exposition not only affords a strong incentive to pupils to do their best work at all times, but it opens the eyes of parents and other friends of education as to the work of the schools in the community. When a pupil is promoted his work goes with him, and, is made the basis of comparison during the next session. His new teacher sees what he did the previous year and how he did it. This knowledge is of great value to the teacher.

The schools are maintained at the small costs of about seventy-eight cents a pupil per month for tuition and every other expense. Fifteen teachers are employed, with E. S. Sheppe as superintendent and W. C. Allen, principal of the High School. The school library consists of several hundred volumes.

EDWIN S. SHEPPE,
Superintendent.

MT. AIRY UBLIC SCHOOLS.

To the Hon. Chas. H. Mebane, Superintendent of Public Instruction.

Sir:—I have the honor to submit herewith, in accordance with your request, a concise historical sketch of the Mount Airy Graded Schools.

I am informed that prior to the fall of 1896 no attempt had ever been made to consolidate the public school money, and to have only one public school in the town instead of the three or four public schools, which had previously existed and which had received the patronage of the public school fund, each school receiving its pro rata of said fund.

Prior to 1896 the amount received from the public school money did not exceed five hundred or six hundred dollars ($500 or $600) per annum for white education, and the length of the public school term was not more than four (4) months every second year.

In the fall of 1896 the public school fund was consolidated, and the several public schools heretofore existing in the town were united into one central public school. At that time no attempt whatever at gradation was made, and the school was simply conducted as an ungraded public school. In the spring of 1897 some classification was made and this formed the nucleus of the present graded system of schools.

Until the fall session of 1898 the school committee employed a principal to conduct the school, paying him a certain monthly amount, he furnishing and paying his assistant teachers. In the fall of 1898 the school was placed upon a more thoroughly graded basis. A superintendent was elected, and the teachers were employed and paid stated salaries by the school committee.

Up to this date (Nov. 21) the attendance this session has been very greatly in excess of the attendance of any previous entire session, and present indications are that the present enrollment will be greatly increased during this session.

The consolidation of the school funds in 1896 made the vote on local taxation a possibility when that proposition was placed before the voters of Mount Airy. This is one of the very few towns in the State that voted favorably upon local taxation, thereby making the graded school here a possibility.

At present the available funds for graded school purposes are as follows:

Public School funds from the State	$ 1,100
Anticipated donation from town	500
Duplication by the State	500
Special tax of 10c. on $100 of town property	600
Duplication by the State	600
Total	$ 3,300

The above is practicably the available funds for the current school years.

The total enrollment to date is:

White students	408
Colored students	125
Total	533

There are six white teachers and two colored teachers. The superintendent has his office in the building for white students, hears some advanced classes and has charge of both schools.

The course of study is advanced, thorough and well-graded.

The graded school system in Mt. Airy is firmly established, as evidenced by the wonderful increase in attendance during the present session, and by a great educational awakening among all of the citizens.

In no other way is it possible for all classes to provide as cheap, thorough and satisfactory educational advantages for their children as by the graded school system, and the people of Mt. Airy are fully imbued with this idea.

FRANK H. CURTISS.
Superintendent Graded Schools.

HIGH POINT PUBLIC SCHOOLS.

Just one year ago, September 20, 1897, the High Point graded school had its beginning.

It had been looked for, long and anxiously. Many strenuous efforts and much expended energy were necessary to bring it to pass. Like all reformations, it had its champions and its foes. But "heroes' hearts are not cast in common molds." The greater the pressure brought to bear against the graded school idea the greater did its supporters labor and sacrifice.

A great victory crowned their efforts. High Point, Guilford county, and the State were made happy to know that right had triumphed and a thousand more children had given to them golden opportunities for acquiring an education. Never was a struggle more honorable or noble.

With all due deference to High Point's twenty factories, the busy life they necessitate, and the markets of the world they fill, they will never yield greater dividends, or bring happier results than the school. They give employment, pay wages, train the muscle and lend art and skill. The school gives employment, diciplines the mind, awakens the intellect, quickens lofty purposes, builds character and determines destiny. The one is physical sustenance and growth, all of which is necessary; the other is moral development, christian growth, and leads to the eternal.

All honor, then, to those who, actuated thus, fought for years so nobly and so well. Their efforts may go down unappreciated by a few, but splendid specimens of young manhood and young womanhood will each year bring new lustre and added glory to their lives, and when dead, wreathe it upon their tombs—the work of their hands is immortal.

Already it has almost transformed the life of the children of the town. Frequently do we hear it remarked, "I can see a difference in the children since last year." It is now stimulating a healthy educational conscience among the citizens.

At the opening last year there were 386 bright, happy boys and girls present. They were grouped and given to christian teachers to guide and control.

The course that had been carefully outlined, together with the life, love and energy of our faculty dispelled every doubt and gave us a sea with scarcely a ripple or a wave.

Our numbers increased to 416. Energy and diligence deepened and broadened until "a prophecy of a glorious future" was aroused in the hearts of the people.

But, we let others give our history.

Says the North Carolina Journal of Education: "Probably no schools in North Carolina have ever begun more auspiciously than the public schools of High Point. The town itself is a progressive one, engaged largely in the manufacture of furniture and other wood-work. The people are thrifty and possessed of much public spirit.

After the school election last summer the committee was fortunate enough to secure, on very reasonable terms, the handsome building represented herewith, which they proceeded to remodlel and furnish, until it is now one of the finest and most perfectly equipped public buildings in the State.

Superintendent Crowell has gone to work energetically, and the people are supporting him with enthusiasm. The school for white children was organized with nine grades, and nearly 80 per cent. of the school population have been enrolled. An excellent beginning has been made on a school library. The Journal wishes the High Point schools great success. They will doubtless be worth more to the town than all its manufacturing plants, of which it is so justly proud."

Says the High Point Enterprise: "The Enterprise has watched the progress of our graded school very closely from the beginning and it gives us pleasure to say that now that the first year's work has been finished, the success of the school is far beyond our expectation. As a rule there is always trouble in starting off a big school and the first year's work is always accompanied by little misunderstandings, etc., due largely to the training of children in old fashioned schools.

"But not so in High Point. Our school has had smooth sailing almost all the way. The training of the children has been thorough, while the discipline was all that we could ask. If you had picked the country over you could not have found a man more suitable for the place than Mr. Crowell, and as for his corps of assistants they have been equally as successful in their work."

Says the Epworth League:

"While in High Point we visited the graded school of which Rev. G. H. Crowell is superintendent. They have one of the finest school buildings in the State. It is admirably arranged and the whole is heated with a furnace. There are now in attendance about 400 pupils. After going through all the departments, meeting the teachers and observing their work, we unhesitatingly pronounce it one of the best conducted graded schools we have seen. Bro. Crowell is beyond all question one of the best teachers in the State."

Says Bishop Rondthaler, "I can judge of the prosperity of your school by the interest of your people."

We might present you pages of such history, but we must refrain.

In conclusion I wish to state that the success of the past year characterized the opening of this year, for we graded about 130 new students, making the enrollment for the two years some over 600 pupils.

And not only has progress been made here, but the experience of the past year and all the information that could be derived from journals, books on method, summer school and the National Educational Association, have been inculcated into our course of work for the present year, and things are moving along now as if destined by fate to eclipse anything in the State.

Our course consists of nine grades distinctly marked and correllated. The year is divided into three terms. We have the best books. Our discipline is unexcelled. It is maintained by positiveness and kindness, and appeals to the child's honor. The teachers love and smile upon the students. The students reciprocate it. Our teachers are enthused with their work. We work together like brothers and sisters. We study the best pedogogical works—McMurray's Method in Recitation, McMurray on different subjects. We have model classes in teachers' meetings, and discuss government, discipline, nature work, etc., etc. If asked the key of our success, I believe it is "Common sense in an uncommon degree" exercised, together with an abiding faith in God and vital union with the same.

The wonder is that so much can come out of Nazareth. "Come and see," says the High Point Enterprise. "At the beginning of the second month of this term of our graded school everything is working so harmoniously that there is not even a shadow of a suggestion for an improvement. Our school has made the most remarkable record of any within our knowledge."

THE GOLDSBORO PUBLIC SCHOOLS.

The public schools of Goldsboro are a township organization, created by an act of the General Assembly of 1881; and ratified by a vote of the citizens a few months later. All of the leading citizens worked unceasingly for the establishment of the schools, especial credit being due the late Julius A. Bonitz, who at that time published the semi-weekly Messenger at Goldsboro.

The first session began in September, 1881. The schools were very fortunate in having as their first superintendent Mr. Edward P. Moses, who came from the Knoxville schools. By his efficient work and his enthusiam won the whole community. He, at this place, began the work that has made his name honored among the profession throughout the State and gave an impulse to education that is still felt. He was ably assisted in his work by Mr. E. W. Kennedy, afterwards Superintendent of the Durham schools; by Mr. P. P. Claxton, now Professor of Pedagogy at the Normal and Industrial College, and by Mr. E. A. Alderman, President of the State University.

After serving the schools with much wisdom for four years Mr. Moses was elected Superintendent of the Raleigh schools. He was succeeded by Mr. Alderman.

The law under which the schools were established provided that the taxes collected from whites should go to the white school and taxes from the negroes to the negro schools.

This law was declared unconstitutional by the Supreme Court of North Carolina during Mr. Alderman's superintendency. For a year the Goldsboro schools ceased to exist as a public institution, as no special school tax could be collected. Nevertheless the organization was preserved intact. A small tuition fee was charged those able to pay, and children whose parents were unable to pay were admitted free. The school was kept open to every child in the township by voluntary subscription—nearly every one in the community, able to do so, subscribing liberally for this purpose.

When the General Assembly met in 1887 a bill was enacted in harmony with the Constitution providing for the collection of taxes for the support of public schools in Goldsboro township, without discrimination on account of color. Before becoming effective, however, the question of imposing a special tax had to be submitted to a vote of the citizens of the township.

The election was carried imposing a tax of one dollar on each poll and thirty-three and one-third cents on every hundred dollars' worth of property for the purpose of maintaining schools in the township. The Board of Trustees have, however, never asked for the full amount, there being twenty cents on each poll and thirty cents on every hundred dollars' worth of property collected.

After serving three years as Principal and four years as Superintendent, Mr. Alderman resigned and was succeeded by Mr. James Y. Joyner.

After four year's faithful service Mr. Joyner was elected, in 1893, professor of English Literature at the Normal and Industrial College.

Mr. Logan D. Howell was elected to succeed Mr. Joyner. Mr. Howell superintended the schools for two years, at the expiration of which time he was elected to the superintendancy of the Raleigh schools. He was succeeded by Mr. J. O. Faust, the present superintendent.

LIBRARY.

In connection with the school there is a good library of about 2,000 well selected volumes. A librarian is employed whose sole duty is to care for the library.

The books are selected with reference to their adaptability to children and hence the library is used to strengthen and give interest to the work throughout the whole school.

THE BOARD OF TRUSTEES.

The school is governed by a Board of Trustees consisting of nine members. These are elected by the County Board of Education for a term of six years. The Board has always been composed of excellent men, who have willingly given much thought and time for the best interest of the school. This has contributed much to the high character of the school. The present Board is composed of the following gentlemen: Hon. Chas. A. Aycock, chairman; W. G. Britt, Treasurer; E. B. Borden, W. T. Yelverton, N. W. Musgrave, George Lungston, Dr. M. E. Robinson, Henry Weil and John W. Bryan.

The school has always been noted for its thoroughness from the primary grades through the high school. The course of study, among other subjects, embraces, Arithmetic, Algebra, Geometry, Latin (reading of Caesar, Cicero and Virgil) English and American Literature, Greek History, Roman History, American History, English History, History of North Carolina, Mythology, Civil Government, Physics, Botany and Mineralogy.

Its graduates always stand among the first at the University and in Colleges of the State.

One year has recently been added to the course of study, thus making ten full years for graduation.

J. I. FOUST,
Superintendent.

THE PLACE OF THE ACADEMY IN OUR EDUCATIONAL SYSTEM.

BY W. T. WHITSETT, PH. D , PRESIDENT WHITSETT INSTITUTE.

The academies and high schools of North Carolina have played a significant part in the educational development of our State. Nearly thirty years before our University welcomed her first student, and at a time when our white population did not exceed twenty thousand, Dr. David Caldwell's preparatory school was attracting students from every State south of the Potomac. This Princeton graduate from his log cabin in Guilford county furnished to the State lawyers, judges, physicians, ministers, such men as Judge Murphy, Judge McCoy, Dr. Samuel E. McCorkle, and others of no less renown, five of his students becoming Governors of different States.

In 1749 the first act establishing a free school by the government of North Carolina was passed, and only a dozen years later Tate's Academy in Orange county, and Crowfield Academy two miles from the present site of Davidson College were training many of the leading spirits of the Revolution. In these schools were trained such leaders and thinkers as Dr. McKee, the scholarly divine; Dr. James Hall, the military parson; Ephraim Brevard, author of the Mecklenburg Declaration of Independence, and others whose lives showed the power of culture in making kingly men. A reference to the records will show that at the close of the eighteenth century North Carolina had more than twenty-five incorporated academies for the training of her people.

During the past one hundred years our academies have been doing work that compares favorably with the advancement made along other educational lines in the State.

Of the more than one hundred secondary schools now reporting from North Carolina, no one will claim that they all rank with the few conspicuous New England fitting schools, still we may justly claim that these schools have done their part of the work comparatively as well as the public schools and colleges of North Carolina have done their work which properly lies within their sphere. During the century we have not been without preparatory schools, whose work has been well done; and it is true that more students from distant states have been attracted to our borders by the reputation of our preparatory schools than by our colleges. It would be easy to criticise the work done in many of these secondary schools, but it would not be difficult to criticise the collegiate instruction of the same period. A State whose public school system is even now in process of re-adjustment, and whose advocates of higher education sometimes fail to agreed upon very important particulars, does not seem to be in a logical position to criticise unduly her secondary schools; because these academies, as a matter of self-preservation, must adjust themselves to the public school on the one hand and to the college on the other. Their survival alone is an answer as to how well they have discharged their duty to education.

The Utopian dream of our educators of the day, when a student may pass from the free public schools to his college classes, well prepared for regular entrance, will hardly be realized in this generation. We have those among us who will always prefer the private secondary school with its healthful personal supervision and oversight, and its power of developing individuality. For these, and other reasons, our academies may be regarded as having a permanent place in our educational system.

The graded school is pre-eminently the school for the larger town. This, though, does not solve the problem of the people of our smaller towns and the country. They must have academies and high schools. Let us come then to consider the special work of the academy in our educational system. If other conditions were ideal, and the correlation and adjustment of other parts of our educational structure were perfect, we might be expected to speak of an ideal academy. Our limited time may be better spent in considering the duties of the academy today—under present conditions—to the educational work of the State.

The constant discussion of the educational problem in North Carolina gives us hope for the future. The subject is ever new. So long as untrained minds are requiring instruction and development the problem will not grow old. The key-note of all our difficulty was struck by the president of Johns Hopkins University when he recently said: "Underlying all our deficiencies there is the want of organization and correlation. It is not likely that American education will be satisfactory to the most thoughtful people until it is far more systematic than it is at present—until the rations of all grades from the kindergarten to the professional schools are adjusted to one another by such a definite consensus as will be binding like the common law. We lose now a great deal of time at every transfer station. Every higher grade blames the lower for not affording better preparation. For example, not long ago when the teachers of a celebrated university set forth the pitiable English of the undergraduates, and threw the blame on the fitting schools, the fitting schools passed the complaint on to the lower schools, and they in turn to parents, so that it really seemed as if Dr. Holmes' witticism was true—'To become a good scholar be sure and have good grandparents."

Let it be understood, then, that as we speak o fthe special work of the academy in our educational system, we speak of its work under present actual conditions. No reasonable mind can expect perfection on the part of our academies

LINDSEY STREET PUBLIC SCHOOL, GREENSBORO, N. C.

and high schools, while some among us are so dissatisfied with our public schools as to pronounce them a "delusion and a snare;" while of our institutions bearing the name of college and university, a recent writer of great authority in the new German Cyclopaedia of Education says that of over five hundred of this name in the United States only nine are entitled to rank with those of Europe.

The academy is really deserving of less criticism than any other portion of our educational work. It is forced to adapt itself to the preparation afforded by the public schools on the one hand, and to the demand of the colleges on the other. In some respects, to be mentioned later on, it is a law unto itself; but in many respects it is governed by outside educational conditions.

The students in our academies are largely drawn from our public schools. Let us consider then first the special relation of the academy to our public school system. When we remember that a majority of our public school teachers have had no training other than that afforded by the academy, we must admit the vital relation of the academy to the public schools. One hundred inquiries were recently mailed to teachers in every county in this State asking where preparation was obtained for the work of teaching; seventy six replies were received, and of these six had received college training, while fifty-eight had been students in academies and high schools. This would seem to indicate that our secondary schools are in a position to exert a very decided influence upon the public school work of the State. There are those among us who believe that owing to this condition all our secondary schools of the better class should offer some special preparation to those who intend to become public school teachers. So long as so many of our public school teachers receive no other training, save that given in the high school, it would be well to have some special help for this class in our secondary schools. With the present requirements for three school teachers, our academies can easily prepare students for first grade certificates by giving, in addition to the regular literary course offered in the academy, some training in normal methods, and by this means convert the student into the teacher. If you will pardon the personal reference—five years ago this course was first given in the school with which I am connected. It was popular from the beginning. It had only one purpose—to give to the struggling boy or girl such help as would secure a first grade certificate to teach in our public schools. Three or four books upon the history of education, and elementary psychology with special reference to the teacher's work, are carefully studied. Latin and algebra for five months are required in addition to the studies required for the public schools. This course has helped numbers to get started in the work of teaching, and no student completing the course has yet failed to obtain a first grade certificate. Twenty or thirty have taken this course with us year after year, and our experience shows that in this special work of furnishing teachers for public schools the academy is an important factor. The literary attainment of the student wishing this special elementary normal training is such as to forbid his entrance at a first class college, hence he turns to the high school.

Another important phase of this question is the high school as an institution preparatory for business and life. Ridicule as we may the idea of a business course preparing for actual duties in five to ten months, the fact remains that many of our schools will continue to offer such courses, and hundreds will continue in the future as in the past to enroll as students in the work. This State of ours, which a generation ago was one of the six richest in the American Union, is now, excepting Idaho alone, the poorest, hence many of our children can have only a few months at most in our academies. Such being true, our academies have a special and very important work in seeing that every means possible as to discipline, cost, and opportunities afford the greatest possible good in the least possible time to that class unable to spend more than a limited time in school. Practical courses in the fundamental branches, special training in business methods and customs, condensed statements of the laws of commerce—in all these lines the attempt is being made to give much in a short time with a view to saving both time and money. In our towns hundreds of young men are filling positions in the world of industrial activity whose only preparation has been that above indicated. If so many are to have no further equipment for the duties of life than our academies furnish, the responsibility upon the academy becomes all the greater. The large numbers attending our secondary schools compared with the number who are in college is sufficient evidence that the academy of today is the only alma mater for a majority of our business men. In this hasty review of actual conditions we cannot fail to see that as a preparation for business and for life we must not ignore the secondary schools of North Carolina. How necessary, then, that in its moral and social atmosphere; in its proper attitude to industrial development; in the actual knowledge imparted; and above all in the making of men into types of true citizenship, we see to it that our secondary schools do their full duty, and realize the magnitude of their special work in our educational system.

Now we must briefly consider the duty of the high school as to the preparation of students for our colleges. The number of students that pass from high school to college is small, when compared with the numbers who become teachers in the public schools, who go into actual business, and who quit school with the training acquired in the high school. We shall attempt to give no reason for this. It may be because of poverty, or for lack of that encourage-men to obtain higher education, which can only be afforded when our higher institutions have ample endowments; it may be in some cases on account of inadequate preparation on the part of the academy, or because the academy failed to give to the student an educational enthusiasm; but whatever the reason in special cases, the number passing from high school to college is small. We say nothing of the fact that pupils are received into some of our colleges before they are prepared, and the preparatory school then blamed; but overlooking this, and overlooking the large numbers who are allowed to enter upon conditions, and to enter to take optional courses, our colleges are not getting their just proportion of students from our academies. The academy has its special work in our educational system, certainly the college has its special work also, and the more harmonious the relations existing between them, and the more exact the subdivisions of the work each shall do, the greater the number of students our academies will furnish to the colleges. Every reputable academy has a certain definite course of study. Students who are allowed to enter colleges without a certificate showing the completion of the course should not have their failure charged against the academy. Those who have this certificate, and who then fail, are certainly witnesses against the preparatory school. Let us be just and entirely reasonable in our conduct along this important line. Our colleges need the help of the teachers in our academies. Often it is that the teacher of the preparatory school exerts the influence that sends a student to a higher institution, and in some instances exerts the influence that keeps the student from going. Let us remember that the student is in the high school at an age when he is very susceptible to influence, and entirely open to conviction. Let the college be careless as to the entrance of students, taking them from the high school before they are really prepared for collegiate work, and we need not be surprised if the preparatory school retaliate by holding boys who should be in college, and even by persuading some to finish their school days by a course of business training in the preparatory school. Justice and harmony would be better for the academy, better for the college, and inconceivably better for the student. The "academy attachment" of the college in order to swell its numbers will surely lead to the "graduation attachment" of the otherwise excellent high school in order to retain its students. Our public schools, academies and colleges can certainly afford to be frank with each other. No one can be deceived in this matter except the student. Let a college refuse to accept the students from an academy until they have completed the preparatory course, and have a certificate showing this, and it is to that very college that the academy will do all in its power to direct students when they are really prepared. The day when the successful boy was spoken of as a graduate of "Blank College" and the unsuccessful one as being from "Blank Academy" thus giving no praise and all blame to the preparatory school, has about passed.

Justice is here the part of wisdom. Let praise and let censure fall where they are due. Our leading academies are responding to every reasonabl demand that is being made unon them. They are broadening the preparation afforded in literature; in the beginnings of science; and in a more exact study of languages. The recent awakening of our colleges to the importance of our mother tongue; to the need of more and better facilities for scientific and industrial research; and to the fact that an educated man of today has greater demands made both on his body and mind than was true a generation ago—these awakenings show us that even some of our colleges have not attained to educational perfection.

Nothing but a spirit of just regard, an da desire to secure harmonious relations and connected development, should be allowed to enter into these questions. Kindly criticism may be met by providing remedies for existing evils; bitterness will lead only to a worse condition. In the preparation of a student for college the academy has its special work, give it every opportunity to do it, and then demand that it be well done. In a recent pamphlet issued by one of the higher institutions in North Carolina these words were used: "The best place for preparation is a good preparatory school.' This idea enforced by every institution in North Carolina bearing the name of college would do much to improve the standard of education, and would tend to diminish the friction that sometimes exists between our preparatory and higher schools. The college should be a stimulant to the high school, the high school to the public school. The utmost sympathy and good will should exist. The high school is the college for many from the great middle class of our society. Hon. John Eaton, while United States Commissioner of Education, often declared that our academies and high schools should be made mandatory in our educational system. He contended that it was the duty of a state not alone to support its elementary schools but its high schools as well. In Massachusetts we find dozens of towns today voluntarily supporting academies and high schools which by law they are not obliged to do. When public taxation supports our elementary schools, and our institutions for higher education, it may well be contended that it is only reasonable and logical to support in like manner our secondary schools as a connecting link. But we have no time in this hurried discussion for argument on this question. Suffice to say, that as North Carolina gives nothing in the way of public money to the support of her secondary schools, certainly an intelligent citizenship may give kindly sympathy and co-operation to those who, as a matter of private enterprise and patriotic duty, are devoting their lives to the training of youth in our academies and high schools.

Time forbids a further discussion of other important phases of this question. It is to be hoped that a more perfect adjustment and harmony may soon characterize the work of the public school, the academy and the college. It is not a time for fault-finding among the different parts of our educational system. The cloud of over thirty three per cent. of illiterate voters in the South calls for every educational agency possible for our enlightenment. The loss from unskilled and ignorant labor here in the South would educate fifty times over every one of our children. No people in the Old or the New World ever accomplished so much in so short a time against such formidable opposition. But we are only beginning. Let us never forget that in connection with general education for all of our people of every rank and condition, go "industrial success, productive industry, renumerative wages, national independence, and well-being."

Ignorance is always slavery. All honor then to our academies and secondary schools of whatever name, that, without endowment from private benefactors, or aid from the State, have done what they could for our educational development. We owe much to them, for the school-house and the church house are ever among the chief agencies in the making of men.

HISTORICAL SKETCH

OF THE

OFFICE OF SUPERINTENDENT OF PUBLIC INSTRUCTION.

BY C. H. MEBANE, SUPERINTENDENT OF PUBLIC INSTRUCTION.

The General Assembly of North Carolina passed, in 1852, an act. Section 1 is thus:

"That there shall be appointed a Superintendent of Common Schools for the State; the said officer to be chosen by the Legislature, and to hold his office two years from the time of his election: Provided, that this act shall not be so construed as to prevent the Superintendent for the time being from continuing in office until a successor is duly appointed."

Sec. 6. Duty of Superintendent of Common Schools.

"That it shall be the duty of the first Superintendent of Common Schools for the State, appointed under the provisions of this act, to collect accurate and full information of the condition and operation of the system of free or common schools in each county in the State." * * *

After a collection of statistics as to conditions, etc., we find this:

"Which report shall be transmitted by the Governor to the Legislature of the State."

"Sec. 7. That it shall be the duty of the Superintendent of Common Schools for the State to superintend the operations of the system of common schools, and to see that the laws in relation thereto are enforced; to call on the chairman of the different Boards of County Superintendents who fail to make returns to him according to the provisions of this act," etc.

"Sec. 12. That the Superintendent of Common Schools for the State shall be allowed for his services the sum of one thousand five hundred dollars per annum, to be paid out of the moneys o fthe Library Fund by the Treasurer of the State."

Section 13 is very interesting on the subject of politics, although this act was passed in 1852:

"Be it further enacted, That if the Superintendent of Common Schools for the State shall wilfully and habitually neglect his duties as specified in this act, or shall use his official position for the purpose of propagating sectarian or political party doctrines, he shall be liable to be removed by the President and Directors of the Literary Board," etc.

It will be well to bear in mind that there was created by the General Assembly of 1825 a Literary Board. This board had charge and management of the public fund for common schools. The common-school system went into operation in the year 1840. This Literary Board was the executive head of the common schools until the election of Rev. C. H. Wiley, in 1852.

THE SUPERINTENDENTS.

The reports of Dr. Wiley are not even to be found in the office of the Superintendent of Public Instruction now. The only reports of his to be found as public property, so far as I know, are those in the State Library. For this reason I shall publish, at length, some of his official records in order that the public of today may know something of the heroic efforts put forth by this great pioneer in the public educational work of North Carolina.

Forty-six years ago this great man was traveling, speaking and toiling for the education of all the white children of North Carolina.

I would not for one moment, if I could, detract from or

underestimate any of the honors ever bestowed by our people upon our gallant heroes in battle or upon distinguished sons in the various avocations of life in making up our historic record as a State of which every true North Carolinian is proud; but when I read of the toil, of the great opposition and obstacles overcome by Dr. Wiley for the cause of public education, I, for one, want to place him among the great sons of North Carolina.

I hope, at no distant day, we may have within our State some splendid public school or institution of learning erected to the memory of the man who labored so faithfully for thirteen years for popular education.

Even amidst the dark and gloomy years of the terrible war betwen the North and the South he was found at his post of duty. Most assuredly no ordinary man could or would do what he did through the troublesome years from 1861 to 1865.

Hon. John C. Scarborough, ex-Superintendent of Public Instruction, informs me that Dr. Wiley was in his office, in the west room, top floor, of the State capitol when Sherman and his men entered Raleigh at the south end of Fayetteville street, at what was then the Governor's Mansion, now the Centennial Graded School building. He saw from the south window of his office the march up Fayetteville street in April, 1865.

From this time until the adoption of the Constitution of 1868, when "Canby" controlled North and South Carolina at will as a military district, there was no school system, and of course no public schools.

The Constitution of 1868 provided for the office of "State Superintendent of Public Instruction." This name we have kept until the present time.

Rev. S. S. Ashley, from Cape Cod, known among our people as a "carpet-bagger," a term aplied to those men who came to North Carolina from the North to rule over us in those days, came into office in 1868 or 1869. It has been said that he was a very good man in his purposes, but was a fanatic on the subject of negro equality and mixed schools. He was elected at the same time W. W. Holden was elected Governor. Mr. Ashley appointed one "Bishop" Hood, a negro Methodist preacher, as Assistant State Superintendent.

Mr. Scarborough says: "Ashley's salary was, I think, $2,500. The Assistant, I think, received $1,500. Ashley had clerks and expenses in plenty."

The people elected a Democratic Legislature in 1870. Holden was impeached and turned out of office by this Legislature, and the expenses in the office of Ashley were cut down. The office of Assistant Superintendent was abolished; also the clerks. Traveling expenses were taken away and the salary reduced to $1,500 per annum.

During the year 1870 Mr. Ashley resigned, and Alexander McIver was appointed to fill the vacancy.

The Republicans, in 1872, nominated and elected an aged man, James Reed, who was a man of most excellent life and character. Mr. Reed died before the day for his inauguration. Todd R. Caldwell, the Governor, thought he had the right to appoint a successor to Elder Reed. He appointed Hon. Kemp P. Battle to the position. Mr. McIver refused to turn over the office to Mr. Battle, on the ground that Mr. Reed, having died before he could be legally inducted into office, he claimed that there was no vacancy, as no successor to himself had been qualified, even if he had been elected.

A case was agreed upon to test the claim of McIver. It was tried before the Supreme Court, and McIver was declared by the court to be entitled to the office.

McIver was in the office until Janury, 1875, when Stephen D. Pool, who was elected over Thomas R. Purnell, the Republican candidate in 1874, took the office. Mr. Pool served until July 1, 1876, having applied a considerable sum of the Peabody Fund given to North Carolina that year to his own private use in payment for a house and lot in Raleigh. His party forced him to resign, and Brogden, who became Governor on the death of Todd R. Caldwell, appointed John Pool, a cousin of Stephen D. Pool, to fill out the six months of the unexpired term of Stephen D. Pool.

Hon. John C. Scarborough was elected in August, 1876, and took charge of the office January 1, 1877, and served until January, 1885.

Maj. S. M. Finger was elected in 1884, took charge of the office in January, 1885, and served until January 1, 1893.

Hon. John C. Scarborough was elected again in 1892, took charge January 1, 1893, and served until January 1, 1897.

C. H. Mebane, the present incumbent, was elected in November, 1896, and took charge of the office in January, 1897.

I am indebted to ex-Superintendent Scarborough for most of the historic information contained in the last few pages in regard to the office of Superintendent of Public Instruction.

Rev. C. H. Wiley, the first Superintendent of Common Schools (as the schools were then called) said in his first report in regard to the territory:

"The territory of the State is very large, and, except in ten or twelve counties there are no facilities for rapid traveling from one section to another.

"I have to go generally in a private conveyance, and in this way two-thirds of my time is lost by being spent upon the road.

"The presence of the Superintendent, in one sense, ought to be felt imediately in every section. In short, the Superintendent, like the chief executive head of all systems, ought to be present, enquiring, advisin, suggesting and enforcing at many places at once; and to infuse himself into all the parts with a rapidity of motion and power or ubiquity of which his body is incapable.."

COMMON SCHOOLS, ACADEMIES AND COLLEGES.

I most heartily endorse Mr. Wiley's words in the following:

"Let it be universally understood that colleges, academies and common schools are all bound up in one common interest, and that the common schools are to the academies and colleges what the back county is to commercial cities. From them must come the supplies, and therefore the more intimate the connection the better for all concerned. I suggest that every new academy make itself a normal school, and that it agree to educate every term a number of poor boys or girls on their promise to teach common schools till they are able to pay the cost."

UNIVERSITY AND COMMON SCHOOLS.

Dr. Wiley said: "The University and the common schools were founded on the same principle, to-wit, that by founding an institution at the public charge it would greatly diminish the cost of instruction to each individual; but the authorities did not recognize and acknowledge this intimate relationship, and the common schools became a sort of castaway, and their designation passed into disgrace among certain classes. And yet, common, as denoting general, and applied to the interests of the masses, cannot be more plebeian than universal, which embraces the whole.

"But, as with reference to our schools, the two words are identical in meaning, and they imply that the institutions which bear the names are the interests and should exercise the care of all the people.

"It will be a gloomy day for North Carolina when these two institutions become antagonistic; and if we are not given over to blindness we will see to it that both are properly sustained; that their intimate connection is recognized, their exertions directed to the same end.

"Our University is worthy of our pride and fostering care; our common schools constitute a twin interest and should be recognized as one of the most dignified and the most important concern of the State."

DENOMINATIONAL COLLEGES.

Dr. Wiley said: "Of course I am not to be understood as casting reflection on other colleges and seminaries of learning, whether founded by individual enterprise or by the liberal zeal of religious denominations. Though the State has no official connection with these, I have uniformly exhibited my great interest in their success, and my sense of the vast good they have done and are doing; but my purpose is to show that, after all their noble exertions, there is still a wide field to be occupied by the State, and which the State only can occupy fully. I take occasion also to say that in the schools founded by religious denominations in North Carolina bigotry has not been tolerated, and a wise and just forbearance is generally manifested in regard to doctrinal tenets and disputes. But we have no security that such disputes will not arise some day and injure the cause of education, if we have no other schools."

MORALITY AND DISCIPLINE.

The same writer said: "To make a nation truly great and happy, its heart and mind should both be educated, and the undue cultivation of one of these to the neglect of the other will lead to inevitable injury. Among a population wholly ignorant, wicked and designing, men avail themselves of the pious and reverential tendencies of the human heart to enslave and oppress the multitude in the name of religion, while people educated with the soul idea that the chief end of man is to make money and acquire power, and to use them for the indulgence of his passions, will, in the end, first become slaves to their appetites and then to a more self-denying race. Extreme care therefore, should be taken to improve the heart and subdue its passions as the mind is enlightened; and a grave responsibility rests on every teacher, as well as parent, to enforce on children the injunction to remember their Creator in the days of their youth. Religion and education must go together; and while contemplating the possibility of a future generation of North Carolinians wholly enlightened and universally able to take care of themselves, in a worldly point of view, I cannot but feel a deep solicitude that it should not be an infidel generation, devoted to Mammon and ready to abuse itself to all the strange gods which the wicked inventions of men may create.

"To enforce, however, wholesome morality is not more important than to guard against all sectarian influences in our public schools, and those who have their direction should have constantly at heart these two cardinal objects.

"As far as my influence would extend, I have exerted it, and shall continue to exert it in favor of the employment of teachers whose morals are wholly above reproach; and while the word of God, the common creed of all Christian nominations, has not been recommended as a text-book for the schools, every child should have access to it and be allowed to read it and judge and choose for itself. This is in accordance with our fundamental political doctrine, and it is in accordance with the idea that man is a responsible free agent, each individual accountable for his own life and opinions to the one Divine Master of all.

"It is my desire that all children shall be taught to read, and taught by those whose lives illustrate the beauties of a heart disciplined to good; and that, when enabled to read, they be allowed to read for themselves the relation of heaven's will to man."

FREE SCHOOLS.

"It seems to be thought, in some places, that a free school is one where entire freedom of action is to be guaranteed to the pupil; and, entertaining these erroneous notions, parents not infrequently prevent the improvement of their children by refusing to permit them to be corrected or submit to discipline necessary to chasten and restrain the wayward disposition and the puissent passions of youth.

"Even kings and emperors have those who are to inherit their power carefully instructed in youth, causing them to undergo the most thorough training to develop all those qualities which make the self-reliant hero, and reduce to subjection those passions and tendencies which, if allowed to grow with our growth, render the man a mere child in the great conflicts of life. And if all the people would follow this example there would not be one king to own and rule a nation. Each individual citizen would be a sovereign, considerate to equals, but acknowledging no superior.

"I wish to see our common schools turning out a generation of men and women with childish appetites subdued and indolent propensities overcome, and with all the sovereign attributes of free citizens and of the mothers of free men, in a state of healthv development. It should be a maxim, known and received of all, that free children do not make free men. * * * They must be trained, but trained as delicate beings, full of keen susceptibilities, of generous emotions and of loving natures; and while the noxious weeds are carefully eradicated, not one harmless blossom should be touched, whether the blossom be the promise of future fruit or the mere embellishment of a kindly soil.

ASHEBORO STREET PUBLIC SCHOOL, GREENSBORO, N. C.

ATTACHMENT TO HOME.

"While an arrogant and self-sufficient egotism is as disgusting and sinful in nations as in individuals, a proper self-respect and love of home are essential to the welfare of each. They are virtues in themselves, and the parents of a whole family of other virtues. Till that millennial era, when we will regard the world as our country and all men our kindred, they lie at the foundation of most improvements. They are the promoters of benevolent enterprises and of self-denials, lead to those sublime sacrifices which constitute true patriotism and promote those institutions which make home comfortable and secure. Efforts to promote the love of home in the plastic nature of childhood are peculiarly becoming in North Carolina, a State where the want of this attachment and its ruinous effects are eloquently recorded in deserted farms, in wide wastes of guttered sedge-fields, in neglected resources, in the absence of improvements, and in the hardships, sacrifices and sorrows of constant emigration.

"Our State has long been regarded by its own citizens as a mere nursery to grow up in; and, from my earliest youth, I have witnessed the sad effects of this in the families of my acquaintance, many of such being scattered from the homes of their nativity over the wide southwest, some without bettering their fortunes, some to become ever afterwards unsettled, and not a few to find graves by the wild roadside. Such is the experience of all, or nearly all. As a private sitizen, I have long resolved in my mind plans for the removal of this infatuation; and, as I have intimated in another place, I undertook a series of North Carolina Readers to be used in our schools, partly with the object in view named above."

TIME—PATIENCE.

"Time is necessary to the growth and development of great enterprises. Even the Deity, infinite in power and resources, took six days to create and fashion the world, thereby teaching us an important lesson.

"The common schools of the German States, of Scotland and of Massachusetts, in their present condition, are the result of the patient labor of many years, and in some of the places named have been maturing for centuries; and if we could attain to the same successful state of things in ten or twenty years, we would be a most remarkable people—too far advanced in knowledge to need a system of common schools at all.

"It is, therefore, very absurd to compare ourselves with these States in their present condition, and thus to draw conclusions unfavorable to our ability to mature a good system of public schools. We are doing vastly better than the pioneer States did in the infancy of their progress; and this undoubted fact, and the glorious eminence which those pioneer States in the cause of general education, have finally reached, should fill us with hope, nerve us with energy and induce us to be patient in continued efforts. Standing at the head of our system of comon schools and surveying all its parts, I can see it advancing and gathering strength; and I can see where, in the last year, obstructions have been overcome, jarring machinery adjusted and weak points fortified. But I can see, also, a vast deal that is yet to be done—work for a long life of activity, steady and patient effort. The field for the engineer-in-chief, so to speak, had to be cleared and a way marked out for my successor; and this consideration, and the fact that it was necessary to make almost unnatural efforts to revive hopes, devolved upon me an amount of care, responsibility and exertion of which few persons are aware. I trust I have entertained a full sense of these responsibilities, and it has been an object of prayerful solicitude with me to mark out such a path as will lead, in the end, to results that will make the office a blessing to humanity. Of course I have not confined myself to the mere routine of official prescribed duties. No law can fully prescribe all the duties which ought to devolve on the head of such a system. They must often be suggested by his own heart and regulated by his own mind; and there are a thousand springs to touch, a thousand things to do, which can only be known to the public, like the imperceptible growth of a tree or plant in their final results. We may slough and hoe and weed our corn; but after all this, its life and growth depend on an infinite variety of little operations which nature performs without parade or ostentation, and with the use of means which we would regard as contemptible.

"Our people should be in continual expectation, always looking and working for better things; but they must have patience and a disposition to co-operate with those having charge of the system of common schools. They must not expect miracles, but they ought to strengthen the hands of the chief executive and to wait the developments of time. The machinery is vast, complicated, weak in many points and operating in a difficult field; but let us give it a fair trial, with proper managers, properly supported, with time and means to clear the way, smooth the joints, overhaul and examine and fit in and strengthen all the parts, and we will succeed."

STATISTICS.

"The census of 1840 was the first which undertook to ascertain the condition and progress of education among the people of the United States. According to the returns of that enumeration, taken before our common schools went into operation, the condition of things in North Carolina, with respect to schools and general intelligence, was as follows, towit:

Number of colleges and universities	2
Number of academies and grammar schools	141
Number of primary and common (county) schools	632
Whole number of schools, academies and colleges	775

"There are at school as follows:

	Scholars.
At college	158
At academies	4,398
At all other schools	14,937
Total of children at school	19,483

"The number of whites over twenty years old who could not read and write was 56,609, and, according to the census of 1850, our white population had increased but little. We now have in the State—

Males colleges	5
Female, so-called	6
St. Mary's and Salem Schools	2
Total	13

"Of academies I have not yet accurate data; but there are not less than 200—perhaps 300.

"The number of students at male colleges now is, perhaps, between 500 and 600; number at female colleges (including Salem School and St. Mary's), not less than 1,000. There are also several male colleges on the way, and two or three—at least three—female colleges.

"The number of students at academies, select and private classical schools, cannot be less than 7,000.

"By the census of 1850 (of which I have seen the general outlines) the whole number of white children at school in North Carolina during that year was 100,591.

"The common schools had been in operation about nine years, and the increase of white population in that time only about 12 per cent. The increase in the number of children at school was as follows: In 1840, 19,483; in 1850, 100,591—or five hundred per cent. gain in nine years!

"Whole number of common schools in 1840, 632. In 1853, by my returns, there were 2,131 schools taught in seventy counties, and perhaps full 2,500 in all. Increase in common schools in thirteen years, 400 per cent. The increase in colleges has been about 250 per cent., and in academies at least 100 per cent.

"By returns made to me, as the tables in this report will show, the number of children now attending common schools in seventy counties is 83,873, and the number in the counties not heard from, and the number not reported, may be safely estimated at 12,000 more, making at least 95,000 who attended common schools in 1853, against 14,937 in 1840, being an increase of over 600 per cent. in the number attending primary and common schools. That this action of the common schools has not been an unhealthy one, injuring the quality of education and breaking down better schools, we have the bold and indisputable fact (and facts are stubborn arguments) that colleges and academies have made an average increase of 150 to 200 per cent. (an unexampled one), and that the course of studies has, every year, been made more thorough and practical.

"There were 632 primary and common or country schools in 1840, and I am thoroughly convinced that if all our 2,500 common schools are not as good as those 632 subscription schools were (and certainly they are not, by a good deal), yet that there are more than 1,000 common schools now in operation which, in all respects, are equal to the 632 schools heretofore in existence. I am convinced that for every two good subscription schools broken down by the common schools we have at least three equally good common schools and one academy somewhere else, or two good schools for one, besides three or four other schools not so good for every one thus interfered with.

"The whole income of the public-school fund of the United States in 1850, aside from that raised by taxation, donations, etc., was only two million five hundred and odd thousand dollars, and this income of the public fund of North Carolina (aside from swamp lands and county taxes) equal to more than one-twentieth of the whole.

"The whole amount expended in the United States was nine millions and something over five hundred thousand dollars, and in North Carolina about $175,000 on common schools.

"The whole number of public schools was about 81,000; and therefore the average amount expended in the United States was about $117 to the school; the average amount in North Carolina about $70 to the school taught, and at least $56 for every district in the State, or every four miles square of territory.

"The average time during which all the schools are taught in the year, for the whole State, is about four months; and the whole number of white children between the ages of five and twenty-one years cannot be short of 195,000; and of these we may consider that at least 55,000 are between the ages of five and eight, and eighteen and twenty-one; and we may calculate that of those at this age the number who have not yet commenced going to school, and who have finished their education, is at least 30,000.

CONCLUSION IN 1854.

"Great are our inducements to labor. Perhaps fully one-sixth of the free grown-up people of North Carolina cannot read the word of God. Two hundred thousand children are growing up among us—two hundred thousand immortal souls whose minds will be living records for all eternity to read the manner in which the happy people of this heaven-favored land made use of their boasted privileges, records from which the Almighty Father of Spirits will pronounce judgment on those to whom their training was committed. Our eyes are running over all the earth, looking for happy revolutions in favor of light and progress, and here we have growing up an army of two thousand souls who, if properly trained and armed, would be enough to preserve for the whole world the oracles of liberty and of the religion of Jesus Christ. That liberty and that religion are the hopes of man in time and eternity; and here, on this broad area of fifty thousand square miles, we can find and perpetuate by the blessings of heaven at least one unconquerable commonwealth, where men can be happy in time with bright hopes of a blessed immortality.

"The 'good time coming' will arrive when each one improves his own part of God's domain. Here is one field of labor in the cause of progress.

"In the spring of the past year I was in Currituck, in sight of the spot where the Anglo-Saxon first landed and took possession of this continent, claiming it from the Indians because he came to improve the earth, which the original owners had failed to do.

"In early autumn I made an address at Cherokee, and there, among my audience an attentive listener, was a fine-looking Indian, one of the small remnant of those original lords of the soil whom we have driven before us to the verge of the continent. I could not but feel that he was a witness for or against us before the courts of high heaven, and I ardently hoped that some of his race might be left to see that we had vindicated our right to the country by founding and sustaining those institutions which will insure general and individual happiness, and progress, peace, security and virtue. We have these considerations to impel us to further action, and further inducements are furnished by the experience of the past and the hopes of the future exhibited in the reliable statistics I have made.

"Our position was not high; but, looking to the statistics of this report, what may we not expect by the time we have had the experience in such things of Connecticut or Massachusetts?

"Our position is not high, but in no county on earth can greater industrial, commercial and educational progress be made in the next ten years than it is in our power easily to accomplish for North Carolina. To look back, then, or turn back, would cover us with eternal shame, while to go forward will be just as easy—more profitable every way, to everybody, individually and collectively, and a thousand times more honorable.

"In conclusion, I must ask pardon for the length of this report, which could not well have been curtailed, considering that it is the first of the kind in our history and relates to matters deeply interesting to all the friends of human happiness. I avail myself of the occasion to offer to your Excellency and to the members of the Literary Board my thanks for the prompt and liberal manner in which you have generally sustained and aided me in my views, plans and regulations.

C. H. WILEY,
"Supt. of Common Schools
for the State.

Raleigh, N. C., Jan. 24, 1854."

The first report made was to his Excellency David S. Reid, Governor of the State of North Carolina. The second annual report was made by Mr. Wiley to his Excellency Warren Winslow, Governor of North Carolina, on December 13th, 1854. In this report we find three things discussed asking necessary legislation for the success of the common-school system:

First. "A stricter and more uniform and patient attention to the execution of the law."

Second. "The wise oversight and constant exertion by some systematic means for the improvement of teachers."

Third. "A third vital point presented by our present organization, and needing constant care and attention, is the discipline in the schools."

It is interesting to know what individual was considered by Mr. Wiley as the father of common schools in North Carolina. He calls "Bartlett Yancey the immediate father of the common schools of North Carolina."

SKETCH OF THE HISTORY OF EDUCATION IN NORTH CAROLINA.

BY C. H. WILEY, SUPERINTENDENT OF COMMON SCHOOLS.

GENERAL VIEW.

1855.

The connection between history and progress is obvious. History, it has been well said, is philosophy teaching by example; and all that does not come to us by revelation from Heaven, is taught by the lessons of experience. Without letters, however, we could know only the experience of one generation, and we could know even that but imperfectly, as there would be no medium by which its scattered facts could be collected and displayed in all their mutual bearings and dependence, and their general tendency and philosophy ascertained.

Hence, since the invention of letters, at least and especially since the art of printing has been made easy, it has been the custom of all governments among civilized people, and in fact of all permanent associations and societies, to keep a record of their proceedings, while many of the more enlightened, and in fact all who aim at good ends, make periodical publications of their proceedings, to expose them to general criticism, diffuse information and invite suggestions, receiving and examining in return the journals of other governments and other societies.

This power of collecting, condensing, and preserving all the scattered facts connected with its operations, is the life principle of every institution; this, and this only can insure permanent progress and improvement to any merely human invention. If it is organized without any provision of this sort, it is a body without a soul; it may have life and exist, but its existence will be an unreasoning and unremembering one, and its progress accidental and uncertain, and not marked by any gradual and continuous improvement.

If such an organism is necessary to the growth and expansion of all institutions, how much more so to one whose very object is the cultivation of letters and the diffusion of information among all the people. The government of North Carolina, with a wise and beneficent purpose, undertook to establish schools for the education of all the children of the State, and acting upon the best lights of experience then before it, and following the successful examples of other States and governments, adopted what is called the Common School system.

Information in regard to the experience of other countries was acknowledged and felt to be necessary while maturing this plan; but unfortunately our statesmen left out the very principle which had furnished them with light from other quarters. Without designing it, our system was adopted with no sufficient means to record its own experience and now, after nearly fourteen years of experiment in the dark, it is found necessary to institute a searching review of past operations, that we may be able to take a reckoning and see where we are, and whither we are tending.

First, then, what is our position with reference to general education? This position of course will be a relative one—relative as compared with our own past station, and the situation and condition of other free and enlightened States.

The State of North Carolina is peculiar in every respect. The attempt to colonize the country directly from Europe failed, in a great measure at least; and as our coast seemed to be without good harbors and bays, and without navigable rivers flowing from the interior, while the regions first presented to the eyes of those coming from the east, appeared difficult to subdue, from the immense marshes and swamps (now some of the best farming lands in the world) direct emigration hither from the old World received an early check.

The prevailing bigotry and intolerance, a little modified by travel, found their way from the old haunts of monopoly, to the distant settlements of the new world; and men to escape from these, altogether, deserted the little farms but recently won by hard toil from the savage, on this Western continent, and plunged into the unbroken forests and interminable swamps of what is now North Carolina. Universities, Colleges, and ecclesical establishments were, in their minds, identified with the intolerance and monopoly which governed such institutions in Europe; and while these people were piously inclined, and seekers after truth, they were not zealous in the building of churches and the founding of Literary Societies.

The subsequent history of the colony and province of North Carolina, down to the time of the revolution, was not favorable to the cause of general education, except simply as the mental and moral faculties of the people were disciplined by converse with nature in her rude solitudes, and by the habits of independent thought and self-reliance and by the expansion of ideas caused by the situation of the scattered colonist in a far off wilderness. Schools were necessarily few and feebly supported.

Small colonies of emigrants from different nations and States, with diverse habits and prejudices, began to dot the country with thrifty settlements; but no one of these settlements maintained a ruling influence and gave directions and character to the others, while there was a want of cohesion among the colonies—and no uniformity in their general aim. The principle of individual independence, and of opposition to central influence and absorption was developed to a great extent for that era; and these characteristics of our early settlements furnish the key to all our after history, clearly indicating the origin of a good principle carried here to injurious extremes.

When centralizing power and authority did come, they were not of a character to give the people a distaste for the unquestionable evils growing out of their former somewhat patriarchal state; the power came from those who imposed it with a view solely to the interests of the governing few, and was thus too selfish even to promote its own ends. The proprietaries of Carolina, reaping only trouble and disaster, from their unwise attempts to reduce the people to a race of homogenious servants, transferred their authority and interests to the Crown of Great Britain; and the new sovereign, not superior to the narrow policy of that day, was not much more happy in its experiments. There was a sort of general government, and a few necessary regulations concerning the general safety, and the administration of justice between man and man were enforced; but the central power was mostly felt, not in efforts to mould the masses into a united population in pursuit of the public good, but in the executions and oppressions of its officers and its multiplied inventions for extortion.

The officers of the law were felt to be not the ministers of God for good, to execute wrath upon him that doeth evil, but a set of self seekers, wholly disregardful of popular feeling, rights and interests—in fact were a swarm-devouring locusts that came warping on the eastern wind, creating everywhere alarm and distrust, and enhancing the long cherished hatred of the source from whence they sprang, the central or general governing power.

Thus, down to the period of the revolution, the people of North Carolina were united in nothing but in dislike of the reigning powers; were bound together by no general sympathies except a common love of liberty. There lives were absorbed in struggles for existence and for independence, and the efforts to obtain the latter were localized and without any general system. Of course, the cause of general education languished—of course, the people in their corporate, organic capacity made no successful effort to foster the care of letters. There was no university—there was no college—there was no successful high school—diffusing a general light and influence, no systematic attempts to promote common schools. Individuals, small communities, and religious bodies made some exertions, and a few fountains were open, and sent their refreshing waters over occasional green spots in this wide and parched territory; but as a general thing the people received their education in the schools of adversity, and were prepared to act as they did act, the part of heroic men, by the teachings of the pecular and special providential circumstances which surrounded them.

They were prepared to heed the voice that called for union in defence of right and liberty; but independence secured, our population again manifested its well founded jealousy of central power. Our State was the last but one to espouse the federal government, and the same causes which induced this wise caution in coming into the union, prevented an active and sympathetic co-operation of all parts of the State in any general plan of the public or State progress. In this a just principal was carried to excess: it was not the design of providence that men should be independent of each other. The interests of all mankind sustain a mutual dependence on each other; and in every single State is organized society, and such states and societies are undoubtedly essential; the welfare and happiness of each individual are promoted by contributions to the general good. The very right and liberties of each are secured, and secured alone, by surrendering a part of his time and means to the body politic; and where that body politic is controlled by the impartial voice of all its constituent members, as it is here, we are happily exempted from the dangerous liability to err in surrendering too much of the individual to the public.

Our backwardness in contributing to the general welfare, has undoubtedly been felt to a greater or less extent in some of the hardships under which our people have labored—and to say the truth, we have not prospered in a manner worthy of the glorious privileges which we have enjoyed for three quarters of a century.

We have been much divided—we have neglected our resources, and instead of making a thorough examination of the advantages and capabilities of that part of God's creation on which we have been planted, with fostering skies above us, with a healthful climate and enticing scenery around us, we have been straining our eyes to far distant lands, and teaching our children that North Carolina was not their home, but a nursery from which they were to be transplanted to other regions. Such is a short, but I believe, accurate glimpse of the history of our State, with reference to its progress in general improvements.

PARTICULAR EFFORTS TO PROMOTE THE CAUSE OF GENERAL EDUCATION.

Of these there have been few that resulted in any practical good.

Those who took a prominent part in the struggle of independence were aware of the intimate connection between education and freedom, and of the importance of the former to the preservation of the latter. Providence bestowed upon us at the Revolution, privileges never before granted to any people, in the same ample extent; privileges which are accompanied by a corresponding responsibilities, and to be properly enjoyed and secured require a national and individual character superior to that of former generations.

God himself, in the workings of his wonderful providence, educated the race achieved Revolution, for that great struggle and for its mighty result; he had selected his agents and carried them far from all the haunts of corruption and of fashionable vice, cutting them off from all the trammels of human invention and opinions, and planting them in a wilderness to be nurtured by nature, an by her light to study to reverlation of Heaven, and the conclusions of philosophy. They were trained in school admirably suited to form and foster the virtures necessary in republicanism but with the Revolution this State of trial and preparation was to cease, and men were to be left to try what many had long sought, the experiment of self-government.

Our fathers seem to understand that they received this boon with an implied promise to work up the standard which it presupposes; and in the Constitution of our State, ratified at Halifax, December 18th, 1776, is the following clause, Section 41.

(That a school or schools shall be established by the Legislature for the convenient instruction of youth, with such salaries to the masters, paid by the public, as may enable them to instruct at low prices; and all useful learning shall be duly encouraged and promoted in one or more universities.) The first clause is the parent of our present common school system; but how long was this offspring held back in the womb.

This constitutional enactment, binding the consciences of all our legislators since, seems to have been before its time: there is in it a wisdom and reach of thought, which even at the present day, we are hardly realizing in North Carolina. In the first place we should observe the character of the schools which the Legislature is enjoined to establish, schools (with such salaries to the masters, paid by the public, as may enable them to instruct at low prices),

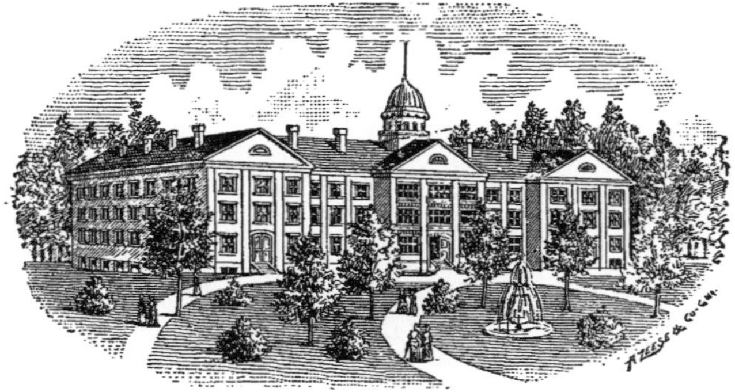

GREENSBORO FEMALE COLLEGE, GREENSBORO, N. C.

the obvious meaning of which is, that a public fund is to be raised of such an amount that individuals would have to subscribe but little to each particular school. These schools were, therefore, not to be charity schools, as each parent was expected to pay something; but the burden of educating all the children was to be equalized, as a public necessity, by making much of it a public charge, to be paid as other public taxes, or paid according to the means of each.

Those who fought through the seven years' war of the Revolution, many of them sacrificing all of their estates in the cause, subsisting on bread and herring, and seeing their dearest ones wasted away by disease and privation, were likely to know the nature and extent of these privileges for which they were struggling; and in their first fundamental organic laws, ratified in the very midst of the conflict, at the very hour that they were going forth to meet the storm that darkened all the horizon, solemnly enjoying that posterity for whose benefit they were going out to be sacrificed, to educate the children of the State, at the public expense. How then can we declaim against taxes judiciously laid for this purpose, as contrary to our privileges gained in the War of Independence, a war which our fathers assumed in the very act of enjoining these duties on those who were to reap a fruit of severe labors! How far, indeed, must we have descended from the standard of '76 when we repudiate as a grievous burden, a duty consecrated as one of the glorious privileges of the free, by our heroic progenitors, by being placed by them upon the immortal scroll on which they recorded the inestimable rights their decendants should enjoy, dictated by souls that were looking camly in the face of all the horrors of a protracted civil war incurred for their rights!

We should notice in the next place the near relationship implied by the makers of our Constitution, between a system of common schools, made cheap to the people, and a university for the encouragement and promotion (of all useful learning.) A university and common schools, were, or seemed to be, regarded as parts of one system, identified in origin, aim and interests, beneficial to each other, and essential to the prosperity and dignity of the State. And in the last place we may observe, in commenting on this clause, that the order observed in innumerating educational institutions to be founded by the State, is different from that which we have adopted in practice, but it is never the less corect and philosophical, and shows that the founders of our government imbrace a wide scope in many of their views, and examine the relations of cause and effect with more care than their decendants have generally done.

Common schools—schools for the instruction of the masses, were to precede universities; and it would seem to be reasonable that these higher seminaries should be the natural off-shoot of a general system of primary schools, the crowning cope of the educational structure, and not its foundation, as they are not sufficiently broad and pervading in their influence as to support a massive superstructure.

It is somewhat, if not altogether doubtful, whether a university would ever educate a nation or defuse a popular desire for information and notwithstanding to general admirable management at Chapel Hill, for the first fifty years years of the noble institution there, we observe little of its reflected light in the progress and improvement of people in the State, on the contrary the gulf between the few and many was widened; and our favored young men, after receiving a high culture at college, would only feel the more enclined to desert a community where they find their education would not be appreciated. Had the University been based on a good system of primary schools, the result would have been very different; its prosperity, founded on a vastly greater number of tributary streams, would have been greater, its relation to the popular interests better understood, and its usefulness at home greatly enhansed.

This University, founded at Chapel Hill, by virtue of an act passed in 1789, was the result of the first practical effort of the Legislature to carry out the provisions of the Constitution.

Its beginnings were small, and the endowments by the State very inconsiderable; but it had by nature a vigorous constitution, and in spite of its many difficulties, it continued to grow and prosper, until it has reached a very eminent and honorable position.

This prosperity is owing in part to the efficient management of its trustees and faculty, it having been especially favored in its presidents—and in part to the necessities and characteristics of our people.

We were sadly deficient in good schools; but as a general thing we have felt our ignorance and have been willing to be enlightened.

One college, however, was not more than sufficient for the wealth and aristocracy of the State; and notwithstanding the republican manners prevailing at Chapel Hill, and the efforts to make the college accessible to all, its influence was but little felt for many years, among the middle and lower classes.

The Legislature, by the granting of lotteries, helped to give a small foundation to a few academies; and this, and the mere granting of charters and corporate privileges, was the only substantial aid furnished to the cause of general instruction. There were men, however, who felt the necessity of the times and the duties of statesmen; and among these was the late Judge Murphey, who, in the language of the recent contributor to the University Magazine, was a philosopher and statesman, whose views were greatly in advance of the generation to which he belonged. As chairman of the Committtee of Education, in the Senate of the State, in the year 1819, he made an elaborate report indicating that he fully understood and appreciated the requirements of that clause of the Constitution, which I have before quoted. The report covered the whole ground of public instruction, and embraced in its recommendation, primary schools, academies, a university and an asylum for the deaf and dumb; but, although it made a sensation at the time, it soon passed from the public memory.

In the meantime there was a gradually increasing interest in education of the higher kind; and to meet the wants of the times an occasional new academy would spring up in a position where it was likely to be well patronized by the more wealthy class.

From the first the facilities for improvement furnished to the masses were very indifferent; and down to a period within the memory of the middle aged; and even of the younger portion of our citizens, our voluntary subscription system of old field-schools was, to say the least, utterly inadequate to the necessities of the times, giving no promise of ever effecting, within any reasonable period, the object of those who framed the clause of the Constitution before alluded to.

The school houses were few and far between—located in the more thickly settled neighborhoods, and bad as are our common school houses, not at all equal to them, as a general thing, in comfort and convenience of arrangement, while there was not a house of any kind expressly dedicated to the purposes of teaching, for every ten miles square of territory in the State.

The teachers, as a class, were indifferent scholars; and I say this with high respect for a race, among whom there were some useful and devoted public servants and benefactors; but, much as we complain now, salaries then were a good deal lower than what they now are; and even had they been equal or larger, the advantage in this respect would still belong to the modern cash incomes, promptly paid, over the uncertain earnings which were often delayed, and part of which were very frequently paid in barter. There were a great multitude of little collections to make, and men of active business habits were not eager to engage in a calling whose small profits were as hard to collect as they were to make. The lazy, the lame, the eccentric, the crippled, were but too often the old-field teachers; and while many of them could not write their own "articles" (as agreement between teachers and parents were called) a collection of those written by the masters would form a literary curiosity as unique in style, spelling, and chirography as any contribution of the kind could now be made by any class of teachers.

*It was not at all uncommon to find these houses without a ground or loft floor, with chimneys built of sticks and dirt. Fuel was supplied by brush for which the children were sent out, every few hous to gather, and about the fire there was a perpetual scramble for the inside position, while the young men and women, and older children, ciphered out doors in the sun, forming very social but not stiudious little parties on the sunny side of all the surrounding trees.

The studies pursued were spelling, reading, writing and arithmetic; and if those who applied themselves to them in the old schools succeeded better as men and women, than those who now study in our common schools, it is another illustration of the advantages of early hardships, while the praise is due mainly to the energy, industry and perseverance of the pupil, and not to the schools.

Grammar and geography were almost wholly unknown in the best of these schools, and many of our middle-aged people who now read the newspapers teaming with news from the four corners of the earth, all knit together with railroads and telegraphs, feel and complain of their ignorance of the latter study, and would give much to be able to trace upon the map the connections and bearings of countries, formerly seldom heard of, and now mixed up with their nearest political and religious interests, and affecting the prices even of their produce and labor.

The method of teaching was extremely primitive; to look on the book and make a decent, droning noise of any kind, not out of the common key, would insure him immunity from all potent rod—while this habit of noise, pleasant as it is as a reminiscence, because it was the music of our early years, was anything else than an advantage to those who really wished to bend their minds to study. Hence all these, and all who claim to be such, were allowed to pursue their studies out of doors! and among the white heads with which the sunny landscapes would blossom, perhaps one in every ten would be following out some useful train of thought, or diving into the mysteries of Dillworth and Pike. He would "work out the sum" for all the others, and as blackboards were unknown, the scholar had but to run in, hold up his slate to the teacher, get an approving nod, and return to his amusements. There were no lectures, few explanations, no oral instruction; to get through the book, was the great end, and to whip well, the paramount means. Few and indifferent as these schools were they were not generally kept for a longer term than the great majority of common schools now are, and the attendance was equally uncertain and irregular. The schools were generally limited to a quarter of three months, during the coldest part of the winter; and as families with two children would subscribe half a scholar the house would often be jammed with sixty students, and as often hold fifteen or twenty.

Half a scholar!—Why can't we remember when five children would biennially get the benefit of the teaching due half a scholar for three months—that is, when one and half months schooling every year, or every two years would be divided among three to five children, making six to ten days or more apiece! The good old times, which, divested of all romance, of all the tender fancies which naturally cluster around a recollection of our childhood, were times which tried the souls of those who wished to gain a good education, and which throw their still lingering shadows upon the present age.

In the year 1825 the State made a step forward, by committing itself in its corporate capacity to the principles of public schools for the instruction of all the people; thus, for the first time, since the adoption of the Constitution in 1776, recognizing the obligations which it imposes, and adopting the initiatory measures for their practical fulfillment.

*The writer wishes it distinctly understood that he fully appreciates the good teachers under the old-field system, and that he honors and respects their memory. He was personally acquainted with and instructed by a few of this kind; and in different parts of the State were a number of such, but altogether they did not amount to perhaps one-fourth or fifth the present number of our schools. For the memory of some of these, he cherishes a grateful recollection and some of them, good teachers, are yet with us. But how few they are compared with our wants.

The act, which it is unnecessary to quote, made a provision for the raising and vesting of a permanent fund, the proceeds of which, when sufficiently large, were to be applied to the support of a system of common schools. And this act is the immediate father of our present system.

Let us now for a moment glance at the present condition of things and compare it with our situation twenty years ago.

The very imperfect picture which I drew of our educational history does not do us injustice: it is imperfect mainly as it fails to exhibit in their startling force, all the dark coloring which would be displayed by minute statement of all the facts and figures on which the general conclusion are founded.

It was stated there was not a school house for every ten miles square of territory in the State—and perhaps it would be entirely just to assert, that there was not one for every fifteen miles square. There were two male colleges—Wake Forest was incorporated in 1833; and there was the Salem Female School, occupying the position of a college.

There was not a single high school, a very useful kind of seminary intermediate between academies and colleges, and there were a few good classical academies, the whole number of male and female institutions of this kind, not amounting together, to more than half the number of counties, if indeed, to one-third.

Nearly every institution of this sort was founded with exclusive reference to the rich: and in how many of them could be found a native teacher, male or female.

Even those of our own young men, who resorted to teaching as a means of raising funds to continue their educations, went out of the State, believing that wealth and a desire for improvement, were not sufficiently concentrated here to afford immediate and profitable temporary employment of this kind, to those who only wish to teach for a few sessions.

No one can ever dream of going out into the highways, and inviting the people to come into the feasts of learning: and when the poor come unbidden, they took the lowest seats and worked hard for what they got. Unfortunately, as a natural result of this state of things, the common people (as the masses were termed), and their old-field schools, were not unfrequently the themes for a display of professional wit and sarcasm; thus inculcating in the minds of the young scholar as a fundamental idea, a want of confidence in the people and a belief in their hostility to liberal accomplishments—and as a set off, the old-field teacher and the old-field graduate were not indisposed to measures of retaliation, boasting on the stump, in the Forum, and even in the sacred desk that they had never rubbed their back against the white-washed walls of academies

All the industrial interest felt the blasting effects of this unwholesome condition of things. The educated and the uneducated grew up with a carefully inculcated dislike for home—the latter looking to other States as opening wider fields for exertion in the race of improvement, the former taught to believe that talents and acquirement could not be appreciated in North Carolina. It is no exaggeration to say that the State was a great encampment, while the inhabitants looked on themselves as tented only for a season; and every year the highways were crowded with hundreds of emigrants, whose sacrifices and losses in selling out and moving would have paid for twenty years of their share of public taxes, sufficient to have given to their homes all the fancied advantages of those regions, whither they went to be taxed and suffer with disease.

The resourses of the State were wholly neglected; and even till a very recent period, masses of gold worth hundreds of dollars, lay unnoticed, and when seen unrecognized as of any value, upon the soil of our guttered hills.

A purchaser of lands could easily find a seller in every owner indeed almost every house and plantation exhibited in their decaying aspect the most unmistakable words: "For Sale," this melancholy sentence was plowed in deep black characters upon the whole State, and even the flag that waved over the capitol, indicating the sessions of the Assembly, was regarded by our neighbors of Virginia and South Carolina as an autioneer's sign.

What is our present position? I will begin my answer to this question with an extract from my first annual report as Superintendent of Common Schools, a report based on information not as extensive or as favorable as that now in my possession.

I believe that I do not over-estimate our progress; and I am equally confident in the opinion that the average quality of the education which can now be obtained in our common schools is fully as good as that now obtained in the subscription schools. I believe it is better; but it would occupy too much time and space to go into the argument to prove it, and therefore, I will not now state it as a settled fact.

I admit that a considerable number of those who now attend school go but a few days in the year, and learn but little; but it must be borne in mind as a very important consideration, that many of these are the children of those who never went a day to school themselves. Into a mind wholly ignorant, it is hard for the light to penetrate and a man who does not know the alphabet is not sufficiently enlightened to feel his ignorance, or to appreciate a higher state of improvements. He is not upon the ladder of knowledge at all, and can, therefore, see no one above him; but as soon as he makes his start, he can begin to understand his relative position. Hence the children of ignorant parents who get a little smarttering of knowledge at our common schools will feel their wants when they take their positions life—and their children, if the same facilities remain, will be much better educated. This is a conclusion that cannot be gainsaid; and as a large majority of the children of that large part of our population who can not head at all, are learning a little at our common schools, we may boldly assert that in the second generation that dark belt that covers the sixth of our moral surface will nearly wholly disappear, leaving only a dim outline to indicate its former existence.

To sum up, for nearly every four miles square of territory in the State, there is a school house, and of our fifty thousand square miles, not one hundredth part of it is out of reach of the schools.

There are, perhaps three thousand school houses—and from Currituck to Cherokee they are accessible to more than ninety-nine hundredths of all our population, reaching to the shores of every lake and river, to the heart of every swamp, and to the top of every mountain.

The temple is erected, and its lights are burning, feeble and dim, I admit, in many places, but the lights of an inextinguishable fire are burning in every dark valley, in every deep cove, in every marsh, and bog and fend. Low these three thousand lamps to one siuated, as many of our people are, within view of only one of these tapers, shedding, perhaps, a dim and flickering light, the prospect may not appear very bright or encouraging; but to behold them as it has been my business and pleasure to behold these three thousand lights, grouped in one grand chandalier, and from the ocean to the smoky mountains, penetrating every square foot of fifty thousand square miles of land of shadows with the cheering beams of knowledge, is well calculated to fill the coldest breast with emotions of enthusiasm, and to arrest the hand of the most daring invader of this constellation of hope!

And here I feel impelled to make a small disgression, in order to call attention to a very important consideration growing out of this matter, and which has made a forcible impression on my mind. Whoever travels over North Carolina will meet with great apparent diversity of character, manners and interests; and if he be much attached to the ways and feelings of his own community, will hardly ever feel himself at home from the time he crosses the boundaries of his county.

I remember that while travelling in the mountains on the business of my office, I was accompanied by a Methodist clergyman from the middle of the State; and as I saw a Methodist pulpit open for him everywhere, even in the

Indian settlements, I was more than ever impressed with the energy and all-pervading influences of that church.

For myself I found also one common point of attraction between me and the citizens of different sections, and but one common interest, and only one, which we all studied and felt. The east regards all the up-country mountainous; in the mountains all the east is characterized as "low lands." Different sections and different counties know little of the wants and manners and characters of other sections and counties, while no pains were taken to gain information of this sort; and as our Legislatures too often show, we are, or have been, a divided people.

We seem to have nothing in common but our name and our honorable revolutionary history; and for this reason have not been animated by those common sympathies and hopes which so materially help to make a great people. But from Roanoke Island to the last earthly home of the Cherokees—at the fisheries, in the turpentine forest, among the copper mines, and on the highest mountains there are common schools, governed by common laws, based on common principles, experiencing a common history, advancing with a common step towards a common end, and such a state of things cannot fail, in time, to produce great results by the homogenious spirit and the kindred sympathies which it will inevitably impart to our corporation, now so diversified in these respects.

But to proceed with the synopsis of our educational history. We have now about three thousand common school houses, pervading by their influences every mile of territory in the State; we have annually more than one hundred thousand children attending these schools, and nearly two hundred thousand in every period of two or three years, in contrast with eight hundred or one thousand school houses formerly in existence, and the forty or fifty thousand pupils which they numbered.

Instead of the old prejudice among the collegians and

academicans against the schools of the people, the colleges and academies are vying with each other in efforts to enlist the popular sympathies; and for the former dislikes among the colleges and academies, every community almost is trying to have a college or high school, or academy of its own, while all of these already established become more prosperous every year. There is a universal spirit of education, and, considering our former position, without a parallel in the history of any country, all demonstrating the excellent material of which our population is composed, and their high susceptibilities when once started on the right course, and properly encouraged.

And this spirit is again reflected in the industrial progress of the people, in their growing confidence in themselves and attachment to home, and the general disposition to make permanent investments in, and to try the resources of their own country.

I have had very considerable opportunities of observing closely, the general condition of things in North Carolina, and those who are familiar only with the more obvious phenomena, exhibited only on the surface, have no idea of the leaven that is working beneath. A great moral revolution is silently going on; a universal change is coming over the spirit o fthe people. One small circumstance will illustrate this; and though it may seem trivial in itself, it is a most significant sign. There is a greater demand for building material than was ever known before in North Carolina, and the demand is everywhere felt, and among all classes of society. It is by no means all demanded for new and fine houses, but much of it is for the finishing of old dwellings carelessly erected in a former age, when people builded only for a temporary shelter. In some counties almost every second man is looking out for plank, and many tenements awkwardly erected ten, twenty, or more years ago, are now being refitted and arranged for the comfort of families who feel that they and their children are permanently located.

Such is a very brief statement of the progress and condition of our educational and industrial interests, but though brief, it already occupies so much space that it would be out of the question to advance the arguments, statistics and investigations on which these general conclusions and assertions are based.

They are believed to be accurate and reliable, and they bring us to a point of view from which we can ascertain our real position and see which way to steer our course.

Comparing ourselves with ourselves, we have done much; and most of this has been accomplished within that short period of time during which we have endeavored to carry into practical effect the sacred injunction of the Constitution. For the time that Bartlett Yancey and his compeers recognized the obligation in that fundamental law, we have accomplished more for the cause of education than in all our previous history; but we stil stand far below the proud heights to which it was intended we should attain, and which have been nearly reached by other States and countries. This is a distinction which is exceedingly important for us to remember; we should look behind us and before us both.

We have made a long stride forward—let us remember this—but we still have a very imperfect system of common schools, yet in its infancy, full of the complaints incident to its age, exposed to many dangers and needing a watchful and tender parent's wise, constant and fostering care.

OUR COMMON SCHOOLS—THEIR HISTORY AND CONDITION.

The difficulties under which our common school system had to labor were of two kinds, to-wit: Those which grew naturally out of the condition of things, and the State of public opinion, and those which were incident to the particular kind of organization which we adopted. If we will attend carefully to these, we will know what remedies are needed; and this is one of the greatest usages of history, teaching us how to avoid the errors of the past.

The obstacles naturally in the way of any system of district schools were many and formidable; but they were not of a character to deter us from the attempt which we are making, because many of them are obstacles to other improvements, and must be overcome before we can become a great State. First among these was a very diversified character of our people, and the local prejudice hedging in almost every county from the cordial co-operation with its sister counties in any great work designed for the common good.

The common schools were a common interest, requiring joint efforts and united wishes. The whole machinery was of a character demanding as necessary to its successful operation, a community animated with one heart and zealous of the common welfare.

A perfectly homogenious population will never be found and is not desirable; but it is possible and consistent with the practicable endorsement of the most liberal republicanism to have a whole people distinguished by certain leading elements of character, and in their aggregate capacity, and since a public duty, breathing kindred sentiments, and making united efforts.

As before intimated, a good principal had been carried here to injurious extremes; and it was our misfortune to have a State so much like a confederation of independent communities, as to be unable to work harmoniously together, in the traces of a system complicated in its parts, but uniform in its action, and requiring the joint exertions of all.

This was a great difficulty—and it is one which must be overcome by time and patience.

The jarring elements of a disunited community of different races are not to be moulded into harmonious nationalities in a day; and to work out such results, nothing is more effectual than a good system of common schools, wisely, patiently and efficiently managed. And thus, this greatest of obstacles to the greatness of the State and the success of the school, is one which the schools only can effectually overcome.

Secondly.—The common schools were an entire novelty to our people—a people tenacious of old habits, and justly suspicious of the innovation. By experience we knew nothing of such things; and the system was not to grow up among us by slow degrees, from small beginnings, and gradually to work its way into the popular heart. Such had been its history and progress in Scotland, in Prussia, in Massachusetts. In these States its orgigin is hid in the remote past, and its high perfections are the results of centuries of trial.

From these we borrowed it in its mature form, and planted it on our soil; and without waiting for it to strike its roots into the earth, we expect it instantly to flourish and overshadow us as it has done for the people in its native clime.

The expectation was utterly unreasonable—and then, because a miraclous event did not occur, we are disposed, with as little reason, to become impatient, and to lose our faith.

We had no experience in common schools, we had no one able and authorized and required to teach us; and instead of comparing ourselves with ourselves, and judging the condition of the present by the past, we looked at the results of centuries in other countries, and made this a standard of our growth. To have reached this standard in ten or fifteen years would have been contrary to the laws

SCOTIA SEMINARY, CONCORD, N. C.

of nature, and a positive miracle; and because we did not reach it, and had no way of determining our real situation by contrasting with the past, we imagine that we have failed, we become faint in heart, and we utter complaints and criminations, and look back longingly to the Egypt behind us.

This system of common schools, to be successful in the high sense, implied moral revolution; it imposed new duties on the entire mass of our population, it was based on new ideas that had to become thoroughly rooted in every mind, and it opposed and sought to reverse old prejudices and old habits.

Nothing but the Spirit of God can so change and remould individual or national character, in a day, a year, or a decade of years; human agencies in such matters, work by slow degrees, applying themselves most effectually to the new generation, meeting them on the threshold of state of action, and assigning them their part, while he has no lessons to unlearn. To expect to remodel merely by the passage of the law, and not by the working of that law on successive generations, the whole habits and minds of the nation, is to expect an impossibility; and when we seriously look for and insist on such results, we are making ourselves equal with the children for whom we are seeking to provide means of instruction.

Thirdly.—We felt and acknowledged that we were ignorant. One-sixth part of our population could not read, and of those classed among the readers, how manw could write a plain note of hand, or read so as to be understood? I would willingly draw a veil over these things but our best and dearest interests demand that we and our children should know them and hold them in perpetual rememberance. The ignorance of the State was a misfortune, not the fault or disgrace of the people; but it was ignorance, nevertheless, and in its nature presented a strong resisting medium to the whole machinery of the common schools, to their principle of action, to their workings and their end. It presented obstacles in every step; it met with barricades at every turn, it enveloped it in a continual cloud of dust and smoke. Could an illiterate community anywhere manage, with perfect success, a perfect system of education? The idea involves an absurdity; and in such a sphere and system itself must necessarily be imperfect, compared with those where all have been educated, and its movements must be slower and awkward. It has to clear its tracks; it is here a kind of car that has to make the road on which it is to run. Hence it in the popular mind will act and react on each other, and when the way is made smooth in the latter the former will assume a more perfect form, and run its destined course with a more even and speedy motion.

Fourthly.—Many of us entertain erronious notions as to the objects of our system of common schools; and unfortunately the name helps the deception. Some of those who entertain these notions were its staunchest friends; they were men of education, of liberal views, and of humane feeling. It was supposed that common schools were intended for what is styled the common people—a sort of charity school for the poor. Now charity is a leading virtue; but real charity is that of the mind, that which humbles the person in whose breast it springs, and elevates and honors those for whom it is entertained. But that charity which bestows good on the poor, with an implied understanding that they must take them in humility, and enjoy them out of the sight of the giver, is not always appreciated; and certainly to a free people, the idea that because they were poor, their very children must be fenced off to themselves, in schools intended only for them, was by no means a pleasant one, and while I make all due allowances for those who fell into this notion—while I admit their intentions to have been good, and their dispositions liberal, and attribute their errors wholly to the times, and to the want of more information in such things, and not at all to their hearts and impulses—as citizens of North Carolina, I am proud of the fact that her poorest people disdain to receive an education under such terms, with such an understanding.

This opinion, indicated in our practice, was injurious in two ways; it prevented many from sending to school, and it kept part of the more intelligent portion from taking an active part in the management of the school. They would give their money, but money was the least of our wants, as it could be easily raised, while its wise and beneficial application, and the assumption of some labor and pains by all classes, to secure this end, were the great things needed. The design of a common school system is not to educate the poor with the means bestowed in charity; it is to bring education within the reach of all by making it a public burden, according to the means of each. Thus each one pays a public tax, according to his ability, to secure a government and the administration of the laws; and the individual who contributes the tax on one poll is politically the equal of him who pays for one hundred.

This is the only way to secure an efficient government, and the certain administration of justice. It is also the surest and vastly the cheapest way of bringing education within the reach of all.

Fifth.—We expected the common school system to work itself; we suppose it to be in the nature of a labor-saving machine, taking off our hands both the cost and trouble of instructing the rising generation. We, therefore, grumbled at every task, and assumed with a protest the duties of every office assigned to us—forgetting that in every county a vigilant scrutiny and active oversight, by the people, and a free expression of public opinion are necessary to the purity and usefulness of all institutions. But it was natural for us to make the mistake we did, as the common school system was, in its nature, a public work, and each individual considered himself free from responsibility, and not specially called on for private exertions. All these difficulties, each one in itself a serious obstacle, had to be met and overcome, and were the natural results of our conditions; and in addition to these, the thinness of the population in many sections, the broad distinction in societies in others, caused embarrassments of no light order.

Lastly.—We opened several thousand schools and we had only some one thousand teachers to take charge of them. It is not uncommon to hear the remark, that our common school system is inferior to the old subscription plan, because the teachers are inferior to the old-field masters—a conclusion not at al warranted by the premises, while these premises are by no means granted. Admittitng the assumption that common school teachers are inferior as a class, we justly infer from this a strong and fatal reflection on the old system, for it demonstrates the former state of ignorance and the great paucity of schools. Most of the old teachers are stil employed, and if the average quality has deteriorated, it shows that these old teachers are in a decided minority, and that thus there were formerly not half enough schools for the country.

We still have many of the old class—and with them, and with the addition which thirteen years has supplied, there is still not more than half a supply of competent teachers—and this affords abundant testimony of the melancholy condition of education formerly among the masses. We had not teachers for our three thousand schools, and teachers were, therefore made of indifferent material; but this was an evil which only the schools could remedy, and which they will undoubtedly remedy in the course of time. The old-field teachers, to the meritorious men and women, among whom I wish to do full justice, did not readily fall into the spirit of the new system; like all people honestly devoted to any useful calling, they had their opinions and prejudices, and their pride and their long followed habits, rendering the best of them often the least disposed to lay aside their cherished laurels and their authoritative positions, to begin a new race with for influence and position with young competitors, on a new field, and before new judges.

Nor do they readily recognize the merit of those young pretenders who now suddenly emerge from obscurity, the medium of common schools—and who, by the facilities now afforded, are prepared to teach, after not more than half of the time, cost and labor, spent in preparations that were formerly deemed requisite. Nevertheless the supply is increasing and the quality is improving; and the best manufactory in the world is the common school system itsent. And if we had begun with an expensive Normal School for the education of teachers, these highly educated teachers would have done as our educated young men have generaly done, they would have exiled themselves to other States. The general ignorance and apathy here, instead of being an incentive to take part among us and labor here, would have only formed inducements to carry them off to more open fields.

But the common schools made first a demand for teachers—and in the second place, they will gradually so enlighten the general mind as to enable it to demand and appreciate good teachers. A way is open thus to increase the numbers, and improve the character of teaching; and with no other means and measures than those now in vogue. If these are efficiently and judiciously followed up for ten years, I boldly and confidently venture the opinion, that the supply and qualifications of teachers in North Carolina will be made more satisfactory than any results that could be obtained by any totally different means within our reach. Young men and young women will emerge, and are emerging, from the humblest walks in life, and avail themselves of the means of gradual and certain elevation which the common schools afford—and taught first in these schools, trained in them, and owing all their progress to them, they will better understand their character, and they will be more devoted to their success and perpetuity. But the measures to which I allude, must be fully and vigorously carried out in their letter and their spirit—and time must be allowed for their natural development, our whole machinery being of character, considering our former history and condition, our prejudices and settled habits, to apply itself more usefully to new generations moulded by its genius.

The best common school teachers should naturally spring from the schools themselves if they contain the principle of life within them; and the ability and tendency to produce teachers will be one good test by which to judge the character of the system. It has already sent out efficient laborers, and the tendency to produce such by the natural operations of the schools, and the means of producing them, should be the subject of constant watchfulness. They have been so to me.

And this brings me to the second-class of obstacles with which our system of common schools has to contend, to-wit: the imperfections of the system itself.

I come to this subject with a good deal of embarrassment; for it is one in regard to which there has been a great variety of opinions; and it is one also which has not been always regarded from the right point of view, as few persons have been in the habit of properly estimating or regarding that all the natural difficulties in the way of any good system of education, holding the particular plan itself responsible for all the results.

I also feel some delicacy, from the position which I occupy, in expressing my opinion; but I know that every consideration of personal diffidence should be forgotten while I am called on by the Legislature of the State to express my views.

Impressed with the sense of duty, I shall endeavor to overcome all sensibility, and to state my honest convictions freely, and however much I may dislike to have to utter them, while in office, I. take the occasion to say distinctly, that they are firmly entertained. I have a high respect for some of opposite or different opinions; but I am strongly convinced of the justness of part of my own conclusion, and feel bound, under the law, to give them unequivocal utterance.

Our system was good, so far as it went, but it liked one essential element of success. It was a mere system, a machine of human invention; and like all other human systems, it needed, of course, a motive power, and a guiding genius.

No one will deny this. When we undertake to build a railroad, or start a mnufacturing company—indeed when we would sink a shaft in search of mineral, or lay off a garden, or start a farm, we first look about for engineers, mineralogists, florists, overseers, whose profession it is to understand the particular kind of business we are about to engage in.

On every farm—and every mine and factory—on every railroad and canal and in every bank, there is an executive, controlling head, appointed to superintend the whole business; to watch all operations; to gather up all its scattered facts, and deduce from them general principles, and to keep the owners and those interested constantly apprised of the progress and condition of things.

On large farms, even, and at the fisheries, it is customary to keep a record of every occurence, for guidance in the future; and, as intimated at the beginning of this report, all governments, and all societies, and all institutions, among civilized people, are endowed with the power of perpetuating their experience, and this is the only way of advancing in knowledge.

The power of remembering fact and collecting and collating them, and thus reducing the general scope and bearing, is the power of indefinite expansion and improvement. This distinguishes mind from instinct, while the power of transmitting the memory and conclusions of one generation of another distinguishes the civilized mind from the savage.

Without the ability or recording our experience, we could not improve beyond given point; the experience and knowledge of one generation would be the experience and knowledge of all generations. The first man would arrive at the ultimathule—the farthest point of possible progress—and every succeeding race would begin and end at the same place. Besides, it is just important in all institutions covering a wide field of operations, to be able to collect facts as to record them; they cannot be recorded till they are collected. Each individual sees only the facts in his vicinity—each subordinate officer observes the obstacles and dangers of his own beat only.

One see a morass, one sees a river, one a mountain, and one a sterile plain; and each one, if the observation of all could not be collected, would decide that the danger to all is apparent danger in his path, and prescribe a remedy and issue a general order which might prove destructive to all the others. Hence there would be a thousand contradictory assertions as to the difficulties in the way. The army against a mountain, and the officer in command here captain with a swamp before him would drive the whole would lead it into the desert. So on the field of battle (and every human invention has to battle its way through a resisting medium), so, on the field of battle without a general officer to survey the whole embattled line of his forces and his enemies, there would be unutterable confusion and a pitiable waste of energy.

Thus a head is necessary to the existence and progress of every kind of business, if it were only to collect facts and record them; in that case it would act only as a memory of th institution, and as such only, be indispensible.

But in any extended system of operations, it has uses nearly equally important; it must see the existing regulations carried out, hold all subordinates to a strict accountability, itself accountable to the stockholders at large, explain doubtful points, decide disputes, diffuse information, and infuse energy into all the parts.

All the facts are admitted: We admit them in our daily practice, in everything.

How was it with our common schools?

While we suppose that in the management for these we were acting on our own views altogether, and refusing to have a distinct head, we were at the very time still controlled by the opinions of one eminent mind which had thoughts for us all, and had necessarily, from the time and circumstances under which it reasoned, arrived at some impracticable conclusions.

The late patriotic Judge Murphey was the first, as before stated, who seemed to understand and feel the full obligations in regard to the general education imposed on us by our Constitution, and by our inestimable privileges, earned at a dear cost by those who formed that constitution; and in the report prepared by him and submitted to the Assembly in the year 1819, a general plan of the common school system was distinctly shadowed forth.

Of course it was to have a guiding, remembering, and

recording head, and to make this head the more useful and efficientan d to give to it the greater dignity, and to insure to it a thorough knowledge of all our sectional interests, it was to consist of several eminent citizens, and to be a distinct corporation and power in the State, with an imposing name, and considerable authority.

There were to be six directors, to be styled "the Board of Public Institution," three were to reside east of Raleigh and three west; and the governor was to be ex-officio the president of the board. They were authorized to employ a secretary and were to be empowered, subject to limitation by law, to locate the academies directed to be established as part of the common school system, to determine the number and title of the professors, to examine and appoint the professors, and regulate their compensation, and that of teachers; to appoint, in the first instance, the trustees of several academies; to prescribe the course of study in the academies and high schools; to provide some just and practicable mode of advancing from the primary school to the academies, and from the academies to the universities, as many of the meritorious children educated at the expense of the State, as could thus be educated by the public funds, after first carrying out the whole system of schools as recommended. They were to have power to enact and alter rules and by-laws, and to recommend to the General Assembly, from time to time, laws in relation to education, &c.

They were also annually (sessions of Assembly were then annually) to submit to the General Assembly at or near the commencement of the session, a view of the State of public education within the State, embracing the history of the progress or declension of the University in the year next preceding, and illustrating its natural condition and future prospects, and also setting forth the condition of the fund committed to their trust for public instruction. They had other powers and duties—as it will be seen, were to manage the funds as well as to act at the head of the school system.

In the year 1825, as before related, the State took the first step towards establishing common schools, by making provision for the raising of a fund for that purpose; and in the year 1836, Judge Murphey's plan, so far as relates merely to the creation of a Literary Board, was carried out. It was enacted that there should be a "Board of Literature in this State," to be called "The President and Directors of the Literary Fund of North Carolina;" so called, because there was then only a fund, and no public schools. This board became mere trustees of the fund—they have been useful as such, and as such only have tried to be useful, it being impossible, in the nature of things, that they could, without immense cost to the State, efficiently discharge the duties of head of the public schools, as originally intended by Judge Murphey.

Nevertheless, when we established our system of public schools this Literary Board was made the nominal head—and thus, as I stated, we were still under the influence of the erronious conclusion of one active intellect which thought for us twenty years before.

This board, however, was but a nominal head, divested of all the powers necessary to make it useful as such; and so we launched our experiment, so new to our people, so complicated, so liable to difficulty, and cut ourselves off from all direct communication with it.

Considering the obstacles in the way and the interests at stake, does it not seem remarkable, when we look back, that we did not try to devise means for keeping the public fully apprised of the progress of things! If we could divest ourselves of the prejudices which habit has fostered, we would be really astonished, after taking a retrospective view, to find there had been no worse confusion, and no greater despondency.

The Assembly which first convened after the adoption

of the system, fraught with such momentous interest, must naturally have felt a lively concern to know what had been done—what difficulties had been met, what ones overcome, what good had been accomplished, what danger still threatened, what hopes might be cherished, what expectations encouraged.

Instead, however, of a careful and circumstantial statement of the progress and condition of things, the official overseer, the Literary Board, honestly reports its inability to discharge the duties which ought to devolve on the head of the system—and they honestly recommend a change, in the law, in this respect. The change was not effected, and to each succeeding Assembly the recommendation of the Literary Board is repeated, and the report of facts connected with common schools more and more general and unsatisfactory. There finally seems a complete divorce between the State and its schoools, and apparently disowned by the State, they are hardly claimed by the public or repudiated by the friends of the old system and by many of the more wealthy and intelligent, and seem to belong to nobobdy, to be cared for by nobody, and to be, in the affairs of the State, like poor relations quartered on the bounty of great men, seated at their banquets, but kept from a freezing distance from the lord of the feast, neglected by the waiters, and rudely elbowed by the other guests.

All at the table take their cue from the proprietor at the head, and as he gives an equivocal recognition to the new comer, his favorities give a polite stare and turn their backs, and the genius of common schools, like many other poor geniuses, is desolate in the hall of feasting.

At the end of the first year we did not know even how many schools had been established, nor yet at the end of the second or third or fourth (nor do we yet know) we did not know what was taught, nor who was taught, how many attended school, how many did not, nor how long the schools were taught; we did not know what counties obeyed the law and what ones did not; we did not know what disbursing officers were faithful, or what ones speculated on the public moneys; we never heard what counties succeeded best, what difficulties were encountered in the division of the school fund, among the districts, how districts were laid off, how teachers discharged their duties, what demand there was for teachers, or whether the supply was increasing, or whether the people were learning to make a good use of the system. A few good and true men sent up their annual reports from their counties, and all their facts in figures, their suggestions and recommendations sleep securely in the dust and rubbish of some huge old boxes and shelves that adorn the sides of the executive offices.

Thus, till two years ago we had no experience, for we had no recording memory; as far as general conclusions were concerned, based on general facts, we were where we started, and we might have continued for many years without improving by experience, or learning lessons from our history. The knowledge of each was derived from his own observation only, and hence so many contradictory complaints, so many jarring opinions, so many doubts, such injurious changes from injudicious legislatures, such discrepancies and imperfections in the details of the law, such contrariety of construction and practice in different counties, such neglect in accounting officers, such a general laxity in the entire machinery.

There are many other imperfections in the law, but its great radical effect was the want of organism by which the system could observe and note its own deficiencies, ascertain its own progress and record its own experience. A general superintendent of common schools can not by any powers the law may give him at once make good schools where there are bad ones, transform poor teachers into efficient ones, turn bleak log tenements into comfortable houses, or send to school all the children who refuse to go; he cannot create good committees, or active superintendents, nor an intelligent, public-spirited population. He can not say to the crippled "rise up and walk;" he can not work miracles.

But a single, intelligent, faithful executive head, aided by the patriotic legislatures, could, in the first place, give dignity and importance to the common school system, exciting the respect, and enlisting the aid of all classes of citizens, showing by his very existence, to all the pensioners of the commonwealth, that "common schools" was an honored guest, and to be treated accordingly, by high and low. He could have kept the whole machinery in active operation; he could have seen and collected and reported back, for the information of all, all the various facts in its experience; he could have kept us constantly aware of the progress made; he could have caused a strict accountability to be enforced on all subordinate officers, thus avoiding a fruitful source of doubts, disaffection and confusion in many localities; he could have infused confidence by being known to be a source of information, a hearer and reporter of complaints, and a judge of disputes, and he could have continually diffused information, making common schools here and elsewhere his study. By means of such an organization the vitality of the whole system would have been increased, its errors more readily perceived, and its capabilities better understood. Therefore, under such a system, there would have been more maturely devised and consistent legislation, more uniformity of action, and more zeal and interest manifested on the part of our leading citizens.

This last consideration is one not to be overlooked; and I feel confident that the mere creation of the office of Superintendent of common schools, two years ago, added at least ten per cent. to the hope of the assistant by the confidence which it infused into a large and respectable class who had lost all interest in the schools for the want of better management.

This fact, and the fact that intelligent teachers and prominent and public-spirited citizens can have their views brought together, heard and respected, and can thus be induced to labor with new zeal, would of themselves justify the office; and I feel fully warranted in these conclusions by what I know from actual observation and from my correspondence and intercourse with the friends of education in various sections of the State. Much more could be added on this subject, but it seems hardly necessary to occupy farther time on a question which, in every State where there has been the least experience in these things, has been decided the same way.

I would, however, respectfully submit one more view, arising from our peculiar situation; and it is one which, it does seem to me, ought to be decisive. This view grows out of two admitted propositions, to wit: First, that our system has languished for the want of public confidence and interests, while to enlist these would be to give it new life and vigor; and secondly, that the creation of the office of superindendent awakens new hopes all over the State. Now it follows that to abolish it (this new office) will be to extinguish those hopes and cause the whole system inevitably to collapse, in public estimation, into a more despondent condition than ever. The hope of better things, ardently cherished, will of itself cause that better time to come; for it will supply the energies and the means to bring it on. When hope is gone, enterprise fail. Let this office be abolished and despair will fill the horizon, now lighted with the signs of promise; it would be a step at least apparently backwards, and bring confusion along our whole line in the very crisis of our engagement with the opposing forces of general education.

In view of these things—in view of the momentous issues at stake, considerations of momentary popularity, of evanescent political expediency, dwindle into utter significance; while the vast results looming in the future call on us to forget, in this, all our factitious distinctions, and side by side march up to our great destiny, knowing only that we are men, patriots, republicans, christians, joint inheritors of inestimable privileges, and trustees of the most precious temporal hopes of the world!

For more specific recommendations and suggestions as to modifications of our common school laws, I refer to part third of this report.

A BRIEF ACCOUNT OF THE MANNER IN WHICH THE SUPERINTENDENT OF THE COMMON SCHOOLS HAS DISCHARGED THE DUTIES OF HIS OFFICE.

According to my humble sense of the duties of the office which I have had the honor to fill for nearly two years, they are not limited to the mere requirements of law, nor can they be fully defined wtihin the limits of any statute.

The position is one of vast responsibility; it is that of official head of assistants which purposes to unfold the intellects and direct the thoughts of two hundred thousand immortal souls just entering on the stage of an endless existence. It is intimately connected with the progress of the State, and with the peace and welfare of all its citizens; and it thus opens up a field where philanthropy and intellect of the purest and highest order can find ample scope for all their powers. And there are a thousand little springs, invisible to the casual observer, to be delicately touched, a thousand nameless duties to be performed, a thousand crosses and difficulties which, like those incident to the condition apparent, are unknown to the world at large.

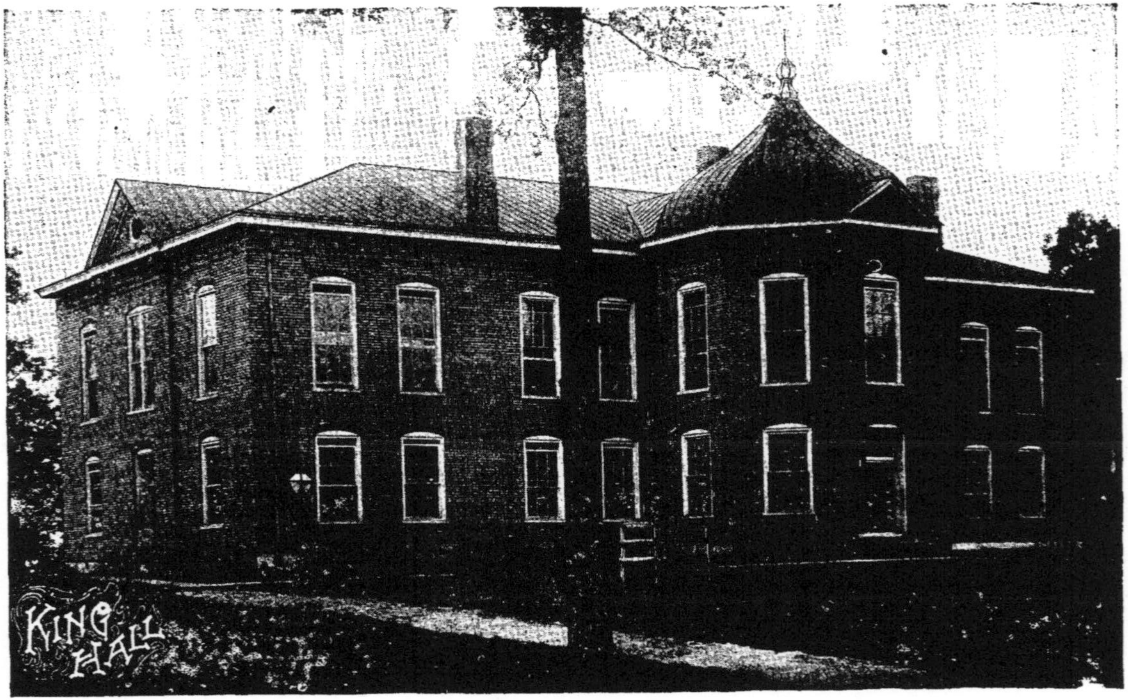

GUILFORD COLLEGE, GUILFORD COLLEGE, N. C.

There should be that highest rank of ability, the power to seize on detached facts to refer them to their leading cause, and thus arrive at general laws, of cause and effect; and there should be the ability, equally a part of real greatness, to observe and appreciate the minutest incidents, the little seeds that grow, bud by bud, and leaf by leaf, into giant trees.

Conscious of my own inability—conscious of my own responsibilities, and aware that expectation was on the stretch, that from our previous history, the path of the new officer was beset with many difficulties, doubts, and temptations, I trust I will be pardoned for saying that I entered on my duties with a trembling solicitude and constant prayer to God that he would support and guide me, and make me an humble means of doing good.

I hope it will also not be considered out of place for me to say that I made at the start, two unalterable resolutions with myself, for these will give the key in part to all my subsequent course, and furnish an answer to questions respecting reasons for particular action. The first was to do what I deemed right, regardless of all personal consequences, and of all expectations. To carry this resolution out in its letter and its spirit, required some patience and self-denial; for it is easy for a superintendent, and especially for the first officer of the kind, to keep himself prominently before the public and to appear to be doing much while the public were also looking for "strong measures" and new movements of some sort or other; but considering the imperfect state of our knowledge in regard to our common school—considering the history of the past, and the condition of the present, the best interest of the public demanded caution and patient investigation in the superintendent, before taking any decided steps; and while his friends were looking for some brilliant attempt or achievement, it was a painful duty to have to disappoint them while making a careful reconnoissance of the whole field, closely observing cause and effect. I am tracing things to their remote sources. It was felt that to be really useful, a superintendent must at first adopt this Fabian policy, and forego the pleasure of an open display of his prowess on a rashly chosen occasion, and that he must keep his eyes steadily fixed on the great end, that of making the office a real blessing, and never forget it, or negyect it, to gratify any particular expectation, to win applause, or to avoid censure. I hope I have strictly adhered to this resolution, and now, at the end of my term, it affords me more consolation than any reward which earthly power could bestow.

The second resolution was to do nothing violently, but to introduce every change and every form with as little confusion as possible; in other words, to plant still deeper in the popular mind every good principal which had taken root, and to graft new principles on those already acclimated and used to the soil, instead of digging up and planting over.

In short the object was to help nature, and so to imitate and carry on now reforms as to have them interwoven with the habits and manners of the people, and thus to fit and cleave to the popular heart and mind. Upon the subject of the last means of educating the masses there are two extreme opinions: one closs contend that the whole subject should be left to itself, while another would open schools and force everybody to go. In this, as in all other things, there is a golden mean: we should act as we do with our farms—we do not leave to the weeds and grass, simply because a hot-house system is not to be commended. We cultivate continually and carefully; but we do it knowing it is God that giveth the increase, following the methods which He, through nature, points out, and waiting for the early and latter rain. Entering on the dicharge of my duties with these views, I have divided my time among, and given my attention to, six different objects, all, of course, having in view the same great end.

These objects were, to gain information for my own guidance, to let teachers, officers and childıen know and feel that the State, in its organized capacity, was really, as well as theoretically, interested in the schools, and looking in at every school-house, to diffuse information on common school subjects in general, and in regard to our own system, its objects, histories and necessities in particular, to have the laws in force carried out, to make the system a means of supplying its own great want in the manufacture and constant improvement of teachers, and to initiate useful reforms in the methods of executing the spirit of the law, in the discipline of the school houses, and by the books calculated to produce permanent impressions.

To obtain the first desideratum it was necessary to adopt a variety of means. To visit all the counties in North Carolina and see all the officers of the schools, and others interested, would monopolize the entire time of the superintendent for a period longer than that of two years. It had been my fortune, before my election to office, to travel over a considerable portion o fthe State with a view of learning its history, Geography and social conditions; and soon after the ajournment of the last Assembly, I set out to visit various sections with a view of increasing my knowledge, and of delivering lectures to those interested in schools. The notices of my intended visits were necessarily short—and as the season was sometimes an inclement one, sometimes a busy one, and there was no excitement to draw out the people, the audiences were small, though generally very attentive. This, I knew, was a slow way of reaching all the people—and the impressions produced by a speech are generally of an evanescent character. But I had to travel, and while doing so, I very generally made an address at the county seats of the counties visited. Various invitations were given to me to make addresses at colleges and academies—but I felt constrained to decline most of these, as they would have taken too much of my time from the more immediate business of my office.

During the first year of my term I was in thirty-six counties, mostly in the extreme of the States bordering on other States; this year I have not been able to travel much. The time spent in these travels, though considerable, has not been unprofitable; and I have the satisfaction of believing that I am now tolerably well acquainted with the geographical position and the social condition and habits of every section, if not every county in North Carolina. One very important piece of information gained by these visits to different counties is this: Under our loose method of managing a system of common schools heretofore, some very important parts of the law have been, in many places, almost entirely neglected. One of the most essential provisions of the school laws requires a board of county superintendents to keep a true and just account of all moneys received and expended by them—when and of whom received, and for what and to whom paid—and the balance, if any, remaining on hand; to lay the same before the comcommitttee of finance of their respective counties, and if no committee of finance, then before the clerk of the county court, together with the vouchers in support of the charges therein made, on or before the second Monday in October of each year, which account it shall be the duty of the said committee of finance to examine, or the clerk of the court, as the case may be, carefully to examine, and if found correct, to certify the same. A copy of this account, with various additional items of information, was to be filed with the clerk of the Board and recorded, one sent to the Literary Board, (now to the Superintendent) and one posted at the court house door. One of these provisions, that in regard to disbursements of moneys, is of vital importance: if it is neglected or never enforced, we all know what abuses might be practiced. But besides vast sums of money which might be lost, still greater evils would accrue: persons, dissatisfied with the schools could go to the records, and finding there no satisfactory accounts of the application of the school moneys, could easily poison the general mind in that community, having strong apparent evidence to corroborate their assertions that the whole system was an evil.

What is the general condition of these records? This is a question I dislike to have to answer fully, for fear it may cause all blame to fall on those officers who are only entitled to share with us all. The blame justly belongs to the peculiar organization of the system; the simple solution of the ugly-looking state of things in the fact that there was really no apparent use in making a report which, if not made was not called for, and when made was heard of no more, the accounting and non-accounting officers standing in the same category. Well, if we were now to seek for a legal account of all the moneys disbursed, to be found in the annual statement of the board or its chairman, and certified by the finance committee and recorded, the search would be vain for a very considerable part of it—a part amounting in the aggragate to a vast sum. The condition of the record is very bad, to say the least: but there has been a many honest chairman, who has served the public faithfully, who could not now show the regular annual endorsements of the finance committee according to law. We have no right, however, to pass these and sue others against whom there is the same prima facie evidence; and we have no moral right to sue all, and put them now to the trouble of proving what they did with the public monies, since we did not, at the proper time, enforce a compliance with the requirements of the law. Except, therefore, in cases where there is evidence of fraud, aside from the mere want of the record by law required, it seems best to me, after seeing what I have, to let the past go, every one taking a share of the blame, and to take good care of the future. We are taught to pray to be delivered daily from temptation, and if we send out large sums, and require no accounts of their application, imposing also heavy duties on the disbursers of these sums, with small compensation, we are exposing them to a double temptation.

Upon this subject I would call attention to the suggestions and recommendation in the third part of this report. The matter is one of leading importance, and if it were not, if it were a little thing, it should be remembered when every little member is diseased, the whole body is in danger. But this touches the most vital part of the system; and among a people less honest and trustworthy than ours, a course of conduct like that which we have followed would have given rise to an immense system of fraud, and cause the loss, by this time, of half million dollars.

As a setoff to this unfavorable appearance found in the record, I was glad to see that certain physical obstacles to the success of district schools were not so serious as apprehended. I have feared that the marshes and swamps in the eats, and the mountains, would prove barriers in those regions, not to be overcome; and that in consequence many of the children would necessarily always be out of reach of the school-houses. I therefore made careful investigation in regard to this matter, and so favorable is the information given on the spot, by experienced school officers, that our people in the more favored middle districts of the State would hardly credit it. I was uniformly informed that but very few families were necessarily cut off from the schools, and, without intending to draw distinctions the least invidious, I would, for general encouragement, make a passing allusion to difficulties encountered and overcome in the mountains.

I have seen boys going three miles to school, and have talked with them, and I found that they considered two miles and two miles and a half a very moderate walk even in mid-winter, when snow and ice and sleet are common. Some few of the school-houses I saw were small, made of unhewn logs, and open on all sides—and into these, in weather which only mountaineeers can endure, would be crowded forty to seventy children of all ages, and in all kinds of clothing.

Many of these schools, in the mountain counties, last only two to two and one half months; and yet, let any one examine the children as they come, and see how many he will find tolerably keen set for an education. I mention this to show that what are called facilities of education are good or bad, according to circumstances; and that notwithstanding the complaints, the children of the mountains would consider the means, in my native county for instance, as very ample. Some material parts of the law I found, by observation, by my correspondence, and by questions referred to me, were carried out in different ways in different sections. For instances, in the division of the school fund among the districts, there has been a great diversity and practice, while the provisions of the law are hardly ever literally carried out. In some counties the districts are laid off large, and there are several school-houses in each;—a method objectionable, in my judgment, for various reasons. In the many disputes liable to occur, and always occurring in regard to the location of school-houses, there is one decisive method of arriving at a just conclusion (except where there are natural barriers, such as swamps, rivers, mountains, &c.), and this is to place it in the center. But in large districts, with several schools in each, this principle cannot be applied; and on the other hand, as long as there are contentions about the proper place for a school-house, the system cannot be said to have made a permanent beginning. In these matters I have been often called on for advice, and I would have felt bound, without this call, to give my opinion, the result of and observation extended over the State, and of a comparison of views with men of experience, in different parts. For information as to action in the matter, and for a further account of the difficulties encountered in this part of our system, I refer to the 6th head of this part of my report.

My plan of gaining information in short, was as follows: To see, by actual observation, the field of operations, and know the physical and moral difficulties in the way, as well as to get a general idea of the method of proceeding, and its actual results in different sections, making it a point to inspect every peculiar locality, and see the State of things in every variety of climate, interest and population; to correspond with experienced persons in various sections; to send out circulars with questions to the chairman of each county. And finally, that I might be ever in view with the workings of our system, and see it continually in practice, I have thought it important to keep my office in the country, near some central point, where there are good mail facilities, &c., and this was of farther consequence to me, as it kept me beyond the reach of the claims of society, and thus enabled me to devote my pursuits that, to me, most precious part of time, the evenings and mornings, in towns, generally given up to social intercourse. I am in a country school district, forming, in its location and inhabitants, about a fair sample. I am surrounded by such and have made it a rule not to interfere specially in them, but to watch continually the course of things, and the operation of general principles. It may be well to add that I have a large circle of intimate acquaintances, and a number of relatives of both sexes, engaged in teaching in most every kind of school—and in these I have an opportunity of feeling and realizing, as a friend, the influence of measures in regard to teachers.

In short I have, I believe, had opportunities of viewing things from every point of view—and of feeling the operations of the system in all their practicable bearings. My views are, therefore, not inconsiderately given; and my conclusions in regard to common schools have been so formed, that while I am generally rather inclined to be diffident, perhaps too much so, in these I feel entirely confident.

My next object was to let all persons interested immediately, feel that the State was in earnest in its professions of regard for common schools.

A new compilation of the acts in force was prepared—and with it was a plain synopsis of the laws, forms, an address, with suggestions to the teachers, pupils, officers, and friends of our system, an index, &c., of which a large edition was printed, and copies sent, according to law, to the chairman of the Boards of Superintendents, to be distributed to all officers of the system, clerks of the court, &c. &c.

Circulars, explaining the new order of things, requesting information and assistance, and urging new efforts, were also issued to all the chairmen; and to let teachers and pupils feel that the State was actually looking into each school-house, a short address, with advice to teachers and pupils and the assurance of the interest of the State in each and signed by the State's representatives, were sent to the chairman to be posted against the wall of every school-house. This being the first call of the kind made by the State, would, perhaps, be hardly understood at first, in some places; for, I regret to say, that there were teachers and pupils who, from the former course of things, had very undefined ideas respecting their connections, as teachers and pupils, with the State. It was thought that the address would put both on inquiry, and that it would help the teacher to enforce good discipline by appealing to the authority of the government, while the pupils, hourly seeing the government's definition of the master's duties before their eyes, would know how to appreciate his good and bad conduct, honoring the former and reproving the latter.

Obvious motives would prevent these addresses from being stuck up in many places; and as this is the shortest method of conveying information to all interested in regard to common schools, and as plain and correct definitions of the reciprocal duties of pupils and teachers to each other, and of the duties of all to the common parent of all, kept constantly before the eyes of the school, cannot fail to do good, while it also tends to foster the idea that the State is watching every school, a recommendation on this subject will be found in the proper place.

The connection between the State and its schools is not altogether like that between the government and every other interest under its control. Instead of being more distant and formal it should be essentially parental, manifested by an appearance of constant solicitude, the commonwealth, through its representative, not merely discharging the duty of enforcing the law, &c., of having every regulation strictly comlied with, but indicating that its eyes are fixed perpetually on the schools with a parent's yearning affection, while it is ever ready to exhort, to reprove, to counsel and to command.

I have endeavored to diffuse information by a pretty extensive correspondence, by lectures, by communications to the Governor, intended for publication, by handbills, circulars to examining committees to county superintendents, by books, &c., &c. The information conveyed by speeches only is not of a lasting character, and I became fully impressed with the belief that this department of labor alone (the diffusion of knowledge,) might employ much of the thoughts and exertions of the superintendent.

The history, objects, character and necessities of common schools should be graven on the hearts and minds of the people—should and must become as familiar to them as the contens of their almanacs. On this subject no exertions had been made. The common schools were not even mentioned in our statistical or familiar literature.

Our publications were all so silent in regard to them that other States did not know we had a system, and while we were advancing with more rapid strides than any Southern State, we did not have credit for any efforts at all. This want of knowledge abroad, however, did not hurt us here, except, as it often induced our reading people—people who read a good deal and do not look about them much at home—to believe that we were really in the rear of everybody. But the want of information at home has been reflected in the confusion and despondency of things, and it has been my study and aim to have common schools kept before the eyes of all classes, in all the common vehicles of information in papers and circulars, school books, public meetings, conventions, college exercises, &c., &c. This field is a very wide one, and to carry out fully the views which I entertain will require time and exertion. Already there are public signs indicating the springs that have been touched. Both political parties in their conventions adopted common schools on their platforms, this mere adoption doing much good by infusing confidence. College students speak on common schools, college professor become interested in preparing books for them, newspapers have opportunities of publishing statistics and signs of progress, and our whole literature, our calendarial and familiar literature at least, will in time, if the plan initiated is pursued in all its ramifications, become redolent of common schools.

As part of the rather extended operations began or attempted in this line, I have made arrangements to publish a common school catechism, to be used as a text book in all the schools; the work to be small, containing short lessons, in questions and answers, as to the origin, history, and progress of common schools generally; their history, character, and objects here; the duties of parents, teachers, and children in regard to them; the name and style of the State, names of its Governors, &c., name and style of the United States, names of Presidents, &c., and the fact that this is a free republican government of the people, and the only one on earth, and the duty and privilege of all its citizens of improving these privileges and securing them by habits of piety, morality, public and private honor and fidelity, &c. Pupils daily or weekly catechised as to the duties of their teachers, will form a tribunal to judge their teachers, and teachers thus catechising their pupils will surely feel restrained from those careless habits which they are calling on their students to learn to condemn. Children will see also if their parents are performing the duties to their schools, which parents, according to this catechism, ought to perform; and they will point out the passages neglected, and thus bring those things home more directly and influentially to the breasts of all concerned.

According to a rule established with myself, I intended to have no pecuniary interest in this little work, direct or indirect. I have already corresponded with a respectable publishing house, and contracted to give them the copyright, and requiring them to furnish the work as cheap as possible. My many engagements have prevented me from finishing it. I need not say it will contain no party or secretarian matter. When party spirit of any kind gets into the management of our schools, it is time to shut them up. It is a consolation to me to reflect that I have never inquired as to the party politics of the school officers, &c., with whom I have had to deal, except the information came unsought; and that in religion I have desired every child to be left free to choose its own form of worship, or be guided by parents and pastors, wishing only and especially that the minds of all be imbued with reverence for the God that made us and who will judge us, and be put on inquiry for themselves, or under the guidance of their parents and pastors, as to the means of reconciliation to him.

The peculiarly mercenary and utilitarian character of many of our people has caused infidelity to take deep hold in some of the American school systems; and in the thousands of "new improved" school books issuing from the press, in the social circle, in school, in all they see and hear, children are taught that "the chief end of man is to make money," and t orise to dignity as congressmen or presidents. There are many nice things about humanity and kindness, &c., but humanity and kindness and all the virtues have their origin at least in nature, and as national characteristics in piety and condition to God. The result of this real, practicable infidelity among the educated at the North is a debasement of the mind to the most absurd chimeras. A race highly educated, taugh that the chief good is money, find out the soul has other wants and immortal interests, and not unfrequently give themselves up to such miserable delusions as spiritual sappings, socialism, &c., &c.

Would that it could be our destiny to occupy the golden mean between schools of superstition and atheism and to raise up a well educated people with the idea, on the one side, that all are the creatures of the infinitely wise being who has made a revelation of His will known, and on the other, that each one must answer to Him for himself and must, therefore, examine, choose and decide for himself. The creed of all christions is the same—that there is one God and one Redeemer revealed in the flesh who has secured a way of escape from the general doom pronounced on Adam; where more is attempted to be taught in the public schools there should be an inflexible opposition, for whatever the motive, the end is an establishment of some particular form of worship at the expense of other forms, and consequent injury. The other teaching must be at the domestic fireside, and in the sanctuary.

Laws not enforced or enacted without a provision for their uniform enforcement are a real nuisance; and as far as it has been in my power, I have endeavored to have the school laws executed, having reference to their spirit, where there are inconsistencies, and remembering also the peculiar condition of things, reports from chairman not having been heretofore strictly required, and old habits could not be immediately performed, and at the end of the last school year several counties failed to comply with the law. After waiting a reasonable time, I sent a respectful notice of delinquency to the chairman not heard from, and by early spring I was enabled to finish my annual report to the Governor, and to give an account of operation in most of the counties. Defalcations were alleged against several chairmens—but in one instance only I deemed the evidence laid before me of such importance as to justify and investigation under my direction. Doubtless a great deal of money has been misappropriated, but who can distinguish the innocent from the guilty? The past is gone. But I was called on in one county, in a matter that I deemed authiritative, to point out a method of investigation, &c. I did so: the result I have not heard. Doubtless there had been great carelessness, and in several instances this carelessness, even for the last year, has been worthy of censure at least. Considering everything, however, the want of means of information, the loose way of doing things heretofore, &c., I have thought that the public interests did not demand an official account of the rumors I have heard, nor a circumstance of account of irregularities and negligence growing necessarily out of the former condition of things.

The recommendation which I make in another place in regard to the reports of chairman, it seems to me, is essential, and with this means of detecting financial errors in chairman, and the habit of requiring reports there will be no necessity of making new examples of severity.

The duties imposed on the chairman are troublesome, and while a dishonest man could easily have appropriated money to his own use, and the careless one could make his place an easy one, a faithful chairman could find employment for a good deal of time and trouble and care, more than commensurate with his pay.

The duties of this office should be simplified, the penalties on the committeemen, &c., reduced, the school year re-arranged, and the whole law rendered more consistent and plain, and then all its parts should be strictly enforced.

Instead of enforcing the requirements as to the method of dividing the school fund in each county—requirements not practicable in many places—I have made recommendations to the various boards of county superintendents, with a view of arresting disputes on this subject, and of securing the accomplishment of the greatest possible good by the means on hand.

A copy of my recommendations on this subject will be found in the Appendix to this report.

Nothing is of more service in the transaction of public business, by the people, than a good supply of useful blanks. They are suggestive—they make the labor easy, and insure uniform and fuller returns—and they often include principles.

A good deal of attention has, therefore, been given to this subject—new forms for committees and chairmen introduced, &c., &c. Eome little confusion necessarily followed; but it is believed that the new arrangements are a decided improvement. They were approved by the Literary Board; and if the full supply, and some others needed, were kept in the proper hands, good results would follow.

All these little things help to increase the general deficiency; and if every little screw that is loose were properly adjusted it would wonderfully change the whole aspect of things. Special care has been directed to the improvements of the law in regard to the examination of teachers but this subject more properly FALLS UNDER ANOTHER HEAD.

District committees are an important part of the school machinery; and as some diversity of opinion have long existed as to the best method of getting good committees, I have taken some pains to collect information on this point. The superintendent has no direct authority over these, but it is his business to see how all parts of the machinery work; and this is one of the most delicate and difficult, as well as useful. Committees will improve as common schools diffuse information, and new generations come on. The general diffusion of a spirit of education and strict attention to other parts of the law will also help. But in the meantime, some modification of the law is called for; and after a good deal of consultation and observation, I honestly recommend the plan to be found under the proper head.

I have had some correspondence with committees, and made efforts in various ways to stimulate them to a strict attention to the schools; and to insure the performance of one duty, have sent out forms on which they are to make their returns of each school, with drafts for the teacher's salary. When filled out it will exhibit in full, the school operation.

A great want of our system, as before stated, is a supply of good teachers—and an all important question arises, "How are they to be got."

To create a corps of good teachers it is necessary to have not merely well educated men and women, in the common sense, they must be devoted to teaching, and they must understand the nature and wants of common schools. Experience shows that the graduates of colleges, from whatever sphere in life they start, are not apt to follow teaching—most of those who follow any profession study law or medicine.

GUILFORD COLLEGE, GUILFORD COLLEGE, N. C.

To secure a supply of teachers trained to the calling, a Normal school is often spoken of. Would this plan fill our present wants? Supposing the school to contain four classes, with eighty-two in each class, (the number of counties in North Carolina), so that one for each county might graduate each year, there would be three hundred and twenty-eight students. It would require at least ten professors or teachers to instruct these; and the salary of these, allowing $1,000 only to each, would be the interest on something over $166,000, (one hundred and sixty-six thousand dollars.) Allowing the board, books, and clothes of students to average $150 only to each, the yearly cost of 328 students would be $49,200 (forty-nine thousand and two hundred dollars) or the interest on something over $800,000.

Thus, then, to educate one teacher for each county annually, would take an investment of $960,000 (nine hundred and sixty thousand dollars) besides the cost of buildings: and if the State paid only half the cost it would take $500,000. By this means we could get one teacher for every thirty-five or forty districts in one year, and in twenty or twenty-five years would have teachers for half the schools. A larger number of Normal schools would not diminish the cost; and it would not do to furnish only tuition, as that is trifle compared with the cost of board and clothing.

Partiality, from family, political, or personal influences, would be felt in the selection of pupils for the Normal school or schools, and considering the small number of teachers which our means could supply, I cannot see that such schools would meet our present necessities, while their immense cost would, by taking this sum from the common schools, greatly cripple their energies.

Common schools, in their organization, may furnish a system for training teachers, and with our present law a little modified and rigidly enforced, more will be done to relieve our present necessities than can be effected in any other way.

The substance of our regulation on this subject is as follows: The act of 1852 requires that no one shall teach a common school and receive the public monies therefor unless he has a certificate as to moral character and literary qualifications from the committee of examination of the county where the school is taught, which certificate must also not be more than one year old. The examining committee is to have at its head a chairman of the board of county superintendents, the object being to give the chairman an opportunity of having a committee that will act, appointed, and of advising and deliberating with it.

Now, by the approbation of the Literary Board, I have prepared the form of certificate to be used in all cases, according to which form the rank of the teacher is designated by figures, figure one denoting the highest proficiency and figure five the lowest.

This method of grading the teacher is recommended by many obvious considerations; it excites emulation, it encourages merit, it puts committees on their gaurd, it enables the examining committee to see who are improving, and when one takes out the lowest number, and cannot reach higher next year, he can be refused a certificate without exciting complaint.

To the examining committees I have issued annual circulars, the last of which is appended; and I have also prepared new forms of returns for chairman, on which the names and rank of each teacher's license in the year are to be recorded.

As a further stimulus to teachers, I have recommended to the chairman to inscribe the names and rank of the teachers on the copy of their report, to be posted at the court house door, to be seen by all.

Now, with some farther exemptions from other public duties and burdens, in favor of members of examining committees, so as to insure a committee that will act, with a provision recommended in another place, as to the formation of teachers' libraries in each county, and with a strict enforcement of the law by an efficient head, we have in each county a school for teachers, admirably adapted to our wants.

Having to rely somewhat on themselves in efforts at improvement, and operated on by public opinion, they will be more likely to succeed in life than those immured in colleges, at the public expense, and shut out from the eyes of the world; and when they gain information it will be practicable, lasting, and connected with experience in the common school.

In many counties now they are rigidly examined every year; and fro one xamination to another, many of these teachers are thinking of the next trial, and preparing for it. It is in fact a fine school to insure their own success in life, as well as to insure good teachers in time, and the result of my careful observation and inquiry and exertions on this subject is a firm conviction that it would be very unwise not to continue on in the course now carefully matured.

To all the chairmen in the State, this, among other questions, was this year propopunded: "What is your observation of the effect of examining committees?

Fifty-five answers were given—one said bad—one said no change yet—four were yet in doubt, but hopeful, and forty-nine were of the impression that the effect was decidedly good under present regulations.

In short, I will candidly confess my firm belief that the efforts of the superintendent and others, to make the system furnish a supply of teachers without additional cost, are likely to result in good, and if consistently preserved in, must effect a decided alteration for the better.

An enumeration of all my efforts under the sixth branch of my lavors, to wit, the initiation of useful reforms, would lead to a repetion of some things already mentioned. I have desired to have teachers to understand and constantly to feel that there was a pressure on them from behind—to have a full supply of useful, simple and suggestive forms—to secure some satisfactory and equitable method of dividing the school fund in each county, so as to make it do the most good, keeping in view that the principle of equality in facilities for instruction, and not equality in money, was the end to be aimed at.

I have made effort, involving sacrifices of all labor, time and interest, to secure uniformity in the use of text books, and have tried also to secure a series of books that would, in time, create a revolution in the mind of our State.

I have, with this view, refused to recommend any geography for the use of our school, till allowed to correct the text in regard to North Carolina; and having selected a work which seemed best suited to our school, I asked and obtained permission to add an Appendix giving a condensed, but full account of our State. I also helped to prepare a new map of the State for this work, with all our railroads, plankroads, intended routes, &c., &c., and this special Appendix, and this large map of North Carolina (large for the work, or concessions to our State was never made in any work to any State before.

It was made the duty of the Superintendent of common schools to appoint agents and attorneys in the different counties to look after claims of this kind, escheats, power of attorney, instructions, &c,, &c., to be sent out, intending to adopt an efficient system of operations.

In the meantime a suit to contest the right to this property was made up between the trustees of the University and the Literary Board for decision in the Supreme court of the United States; and the president of the latter then suggested that if suits to cover escheats were brought by the Literary Board, and any fail, the University, if it succeeded in gaining this property, might not allow the cost expended by the loosing party. I, therefore, proposed to the executive committee of the trustees of the University to permit me to collect escheats for the Literary fund, till the decision of the suit alluded to, with the understanding that if the University gained the suit it was to allow all the cost incurred in the efforts to collect and receive only the balance, &c., &c.

This proposition was finally referred for consideration to the committees of trustees, to be held this winter in Raleigh; and thus no satisfactory conclusion has yet been arrived at.

Something ought to be done immediately. I have been informed of several instances where property, now the subject of escheat, would in a short time belong to private individuals by claims matured by possession under color of title.

But for the conflicting claims to this species of property, I could have collected a handsome sum during the last two years; and considering the intrinsic importance of the subjec, as well as the unnatural attitude of the University and of the common schools towards each other, it is proper and right that the Legislature should interfere in such a way as to reconcile these twin interests, and place both on a substantial foundation. It has been a great object with me to have the University and the common schools identified, in the popular mind, as parts of one system; and when, from want of means or other causes they assume a hostile attitude towards each other, the cause of education will be much embarrassed. The trustees and faculty of the former seem disposed to take similar views; and it is to be hoped that the guardians of the latter, interest will see that justice is done to both. It was my purpose to have said more upon this subject of text books, as a means of awakening an interest in North Carolina, and in the schools, and to have given a detail account of my labors on this subject. This report, however, has already grown to an inconvenient length; and I must fere, for a general statement of my course in this respect, to the circulars in the Appendix.

In conclusion, I feel it my duty to state my candid conviction as to the usefulness of the Superintendent of common schools for the last two years; and I trust I shall do so without any undue regard for my individual view, or any egotistical sense of my personal exertions. I speak of the office and the officer, not knowing myself in this connection.

The creation of the office gave a decided impetus to the schools because it increased confidence and encouraged the belief that the common schools system was hereafter to be carefully managed and watched over by the State. Except to one in my position, surveying the whole field, and seeing the great want of confidence and its immense importance of this apparently simple consideration: from accounts sent to me from various sections, and from my own observation, I believe that this one step added a considerable per cent to the hopes of the system. Then the fact that there is an officer clothed with a superintending trust, ever watching the whole field, intent on trying to remedy every defect, pushing every advantage, keeping a lookout for dangr, holding all agents to a strict accountability, and pressing continually on the backs of teachers, still keeps up the public confidence, enlists as aids to the superintendent the leading minds of the country, the clergy, who pervade all parts, the professional men, the colleges and the gentlemen of leisure and literary taste.

All these, and the students of colleges, become assistants to the Superintendet, having now a rallying point, a bond of union, and a common center, where their minds can meet and be directed to tangible and common ends.

This, in addition to what has already been said of the office, while it may be added, that to abolish it will in all probability tend to increase confusion, to discourage a large class of citizens, and to create a general depression and belief that the system is uncertain, not understood, changeable, and of doubtful utility.

On the other hand it is not to be denied that the officer may be inefficient and even injurious by his policy; that he may make but little exertion to do good, or may employ his time and great opportunities in doing mischief by seeking his own ends and the advantage of his friends, or by inculcating pernicious doctrines. We have, however, to trust fallible men in many responsible situations; and the best we can do is to throw around them such restraints as the nature of things will permit, and to use every exertion to keep the people, with whom is the heart and conservatism of the country, well informed, and in a situation to form correct opinions of all public matters. All who are opposed to this are enemies of freedom; men can have but one motive for keeping their fellow-beings in ignorance, while they themselves want light. That motive is to gain and to keep undue advantages for themselves at the expense of the multitude: it is the motive which made Nimrod a hunter of men, and which will govern his descendants until that good time when, by God's blessing, men will be able to discern the fowler's snare, and the meek shall inherit the earth.

Till then every office and every officer is a necessary evil; the mere cost of the office as a general thing is a small matter, in this country, while we have to direct the influence of evil passions in the incumbent, and in the management of the office.

This one may be prostituted and be made a curse: but the cost of it is a matter of no moment whatever, considering the immense interests at stake and the sum expended on them. To abolish it for the cost would be truly a farthing-wise and pound-foolish policy; and if other offices in the system are kept up (offices as liable to be abused), it is well to keep up this as a necessary part of the machinery.

This head can have much influence in directing the studies of the schools, in introducing modes of instruction, in regulating rules of teaching, and in practically modifying the system, in making it produce natural off-shoots of higher schools: all of which I have attempted, with, I hope, some success, and with a view simply of adding to the utility of the system. But at the same time all efforts of this kind might, with greater efficiency, be turned to evil; the office, in all its bearings, might be perverted, and become a fountain of mischief, sending forth corrupt waters through the young hearts and minds of the State.

Human nature is erring and selfish, and human passions leave their slime on everything; but may we not reasonably hope for good officers, and watchful legislatures, and intelligent people, if the system is kept up, and good men in all departments exert their influence for good, in all branches of the government, and invoke God's blessing on them? We ought to hope for the best and continually strive to do well, leaving it to the disposer of all events to order every well-meant effort to happy results.

CONCLUSION.

The history and condition of general education in North Carolina are such, that the incumbent of this office, with a proper sense of his responsibilities, cannot confine himself, in his annual report, to a bare statement of facts and figures.

The financial question has not been the one of greatest interest or trial in the management of our system of common schools; and the chief obstacles being of a character which general intelligence only can finally remove, there cannot be too much discussion or interchange of opinion.

One object of the office of general superintendent in

every common school system is to promote an active circulation of ideas among its friends and agents, and to meet and answer the objections of its opponents, and reports, therefore, from such officers, very generally and properly contain more or less of history and discussion.

One occupying the standpoint afforded by this office, and surveying the field now before me, is peculiarly tempted to indulge in such things; and for myself, I own to a conflict between my disposition to be brief in every written communication, and a desire to keep before the public a fair and full view of considerations, as well as of facts, important for all to know.

Indeed, in every enterprise, we can best encounter the future, after a calm survey of the past; and nowhere and in no undertaking is a knowledge of the past so essntial as it is to the people of North Carolina in estimating the condition, advantages and prospects of their present system of common schools.

But I have dwelt on these things in former reports, and information from this office is now reaching the public through so many avenues that iti s hardly necessary to go over ground occupied in former communications.

Our difficulties, as before stated, were not pecuniary; and to meet emergnecies of a moral character, we have had to call out moral resources and agencies.

The system of means has been complicated and the operations varied, but all tending to a common end; and now the elements of our strength are rapidly converging into a more compact array, and the combinations and the points of attack are better understood by all concerned.

Our ranks, to continue the figure, are closing up; and though I have never despaired I am now more certain of the success of our system of common schools than ever before.

There are dark as well as bright sides to the picture

which it presents; but the whole view is highly satisfactory, and more encouraging than at any former period.

As intimated in the first part of this report, people are also beginning to make more sober and practical calculations; and every revulsion which sweeps away the inflations of airy speculations must result to the benefit of the common schools.

Far, far be it from me to rejoice at those reverses which cause any class to feel the pressure of pecuniary necessities; I only mean to say that such pressures, aggravated often by over-sanguine adventures in doubtful enterprises, though involving in distress the economical as well as the more rash, are sure to cause favorable views of a system of education which is so cheap, and which needs only patience and personal attention on the part of all the people to render it efficient.

The past year has been indeed one of trial to all classes, the most industrious and the most honest suffering as severely as any other portion of the community; but while we deplore these misfortunes, it is a consolation to reflect that one good and noble enterprise, and one in which every citizen is vitally interested, stands unharmed, and reflects an unclouded promise.

No community can be long prostrated with such sources of mental life unimpared; and the State whose entire population is so supplied with means of intellectual and moral development has a vitality, an elasticity, and immortal vigor which no pecuniary reverses can ever destroy.

National wealth and national power are the outward expression of popular intelligence and virtue; and while the latter remain the former will be as certain to follow as the verdure which the sunshine and rains of spring call forth upon a bountiful soil.

In the common schools, in a free government, and in a pure and free gospel, our State has an inheritance far more valuable than the entire coinage of all the mints of the world; and while these resources remain we need have no fears for the happy condition of our posterity here to the remotest periods of time.

Our system of common schools, though so rich in intrinsic worth, makes but little external show; it employs but few kinds of officers and at moderate expense, while nowhere in the world are schools equally good, so plainly housed.

All the trappings of the system, so to speak, are extremely republican; and the whole institution is patriarchal in its character, and not likely to impress strangers except by its results.

These are now attracting general attention abroad, and three of the most distinguished States of the South, and long considered our superiors in many things, are not ashamed to look to us for light and information on this important subject.

Virginia, South Carolina and Georgia are disposed to copy our example; many leading citizens in each of these noble commonwealths openly acknowledge our superiority in educational facilities, and point to our course as worthy of imitation.

Doubtless when these States take the field for common school they will act with their usual boldness, and improve on our model, but we have greatly the start in time and experience, and if true to ourselves we may expect certainly to maintain our foremost position.

Perhaps no State in the South has so respectable an educational system as North Carolina, and surely, surely this is saying much for a State which was once behind all her sisters.

The colleges and classical schools of the State are much frequentel by youths from the Southwest and South; and teachers, in plain country neighborhoods, teaching in rude but comfortable buildings, of a kind to be found nowhere else, used for such purposes, number pupils from States as far South as Louisiana, Florida and Texas.

It is the character of our population and the intrinsic excellence of the course of instruction that brings this distant patronage; and it is a fact not generally thought of that our State derives a large pecuniary profit from its educational character. It is safe to estimate that our schools bring into the State, or cause to be expended here from abroad, not less than $200,000 annually; and in a few years the sum will be at least half a million—more than the entire expense of the common school system.

The moral atmosphere here is peculiarly adapted to the training of youth and good classical teachers have been very successful and well rewarded. The business of teaching has been and will be profitable here: and even in common schools the wages will compare well with the profits of labor of other kinds in any place.

Considering the expense of living here, the certainty of the pay, and the little delay and trouble in obtaining it, I am inclined to believe that the prices of teaching common schools in North Carolina are better than any State in the Union; and I speak after some consideration, and with a knowledge of the vexations, formalities and impediments in the way of collecting bills even for public schools in some other and more distinguished States.

The wages of no class of persons so numerous, are more promptly paid in any business in any part of this country, or in the world; and nowhere else are teachers or employees enabled to authenticate and collect their claims in a manner so simple and inexpensive.

Our character as a people, our pursuits, material resources and geographical position, peculiarly fit us for the successful management of schools; and if we will only be true to ourselves, North Carolina will share very largely in the education of the children of the South.

For this proud and advantageous position she will be

mainly indebted to the sober and virtuous habits of her population; and she will hold a position just as long as, and no longer than, her people are distinguished by these characteristics.

But all true virtue and morality are the offspring of true religion; and this brings us to the great and certain conclusion that religion is the only sure foundation of national prosperity.

This position is destined to become a fixed elementary principle of political economy; and while the light upon the subject will become brighter and the evidence more and more conclusive and overwhelming, it seems impossible even now, and without recurring to the plain teachings of the Bible, to look at the past and present condition of the world, and doubt it.

The object of all education, therefore, should be, not to learn us to dispense with the agency of God, in our affairs, but to lead us more directly to Him—to open up the mind to the Truths of His revealed Word, and to prepare the heart for submission to His control.

Education is only a blessing as a means of leading to these results, and the improper prejudices raised against it are due to the fact that promoters of (vain babblings, and oppositions of science, false so called), have, in certain places, confounded the means with the end.

All the inventions and the institutions of man are powerless in themselves to eradicate a single passion of the natural human heart; and any educational system, based on any other idea, will inevitably become a nursery of pernicious principles.

Religion can only bind men into a national brotherhood of honest, forbearing and mutually supporting citizens—and without a real change of the heart, naturally selfish and depraved in all men, by the operation of God's spirit and through faith in Jesus Christ, education is but a change of manners and not of character. The whole world lieth in wickedness, and Christ is its only hope; and if we build our educational system on this Rock it will stand, when all others not so established, are swept away.

We are to build on it by always recognizing this principle in all our efforts at improvement, by allowing free course to God's appointed means, by encouraging a free Gospel, and by acknowledging, in acts and words, that however diligent we labor, it is all in vain, without the guidance and the blessing of Him, of whom and to whom are all things.

Permit me, in concluding this report, to offer a slight expression of my grateful sense of your Excellency's personal kindness to me, of the uniform courtesy which has marked our official intercourse, and of your firm, consistent and enlightened support of the cause of popular education.

I have ever found in your Excellency and in the Literary Board a patriotic desire to promote the true interests of the people, by giving a liberal support to all means designed to increase the efficiency of the common schools.

With much respect,

Your obedient servant,

C. H. WILEY,

Superintendent of Common Schools for the State.

Raleigh, N. C., Jan. 18, 1858.

CONDITION AND PROGRESS OF THE COMMON SCHOOL SYSTEM DURING THE YEAR 1859.

The remarks under the above head in my report for the year 1858 will answer, with slight variation, for the year 1859.

A system like that of our common schools does not undergo sudden changes in the ordinary course of its operations; and although it makes steady progress, and this onward movement is, each year, more rapid, yet the common observer could not mark the change between periods only one year apart. For instance, there is generally an increasing attendance at school each year, and each year the increase is greater. From 1857 to 1858 the increase was about 3.145; from 1858 to 1859 about 4,335, a material advance, but only to be ascertained by careful statistics.

The system makes progress not only in accomplishing good, but in the increase and development of its own energies, and the more consistent and efficient working of its machinery; but, as suggested in former reports, pretences of great and sudden changes for the better should, in the very nature of things, be suspected.

The revolution which the common school system proposes to make in the character of the whole white population of the State is one of those vast moral results which cannot be briefly accomplished except by miracles; and if the end can be attained in the course of two or three generations, the time and means will be nobly employed.

The march of such a system as faintly depicted in the foregoing statistics, with all its vast material and moral resources, and the great sweep of its pathway conterminous in physical space, with the limits of the State, and in moral influence commensurate with all its infinite extent of honest interests, hopes and fears, must be slow, but it is a spectacle of the true moral sublime; a progress whose every measured step is a victory of christian civilization, and a permanent acquisition to the beneficient resources of society.

The following sketch is taken from the History of Education in North Carolina, by Charles Lee Smith, in 1888:

THE PUBLIC SCHOOLS.—ORIGIN OF THE SYSTEM.

North Carolina was one of the first States to make constitutional provision for both the common and the higher education of her citizens. The heroes of 1776 recognized that liberty and enlightment were complements of each other, and that the surest safeguard to democratic government is education. So in the initial constitution of the State it was declared: "That a school or schools shall be established by the legislature for the convenient instruction of youth, with such salaries to the masters, paid by the public, as may enable them to instruct at low prices; and all useful learning shall be duly encouraged in one or more universities."

The above, then, is the foundation of the public school system; but such was the financial condition of the State in the early years of its history that a half century elapsed before the fair promise of the Constitution was realized, even in a measure, in so far as it related to common schools. The University, which was chartered in 1789, and began the work of instruction in 1795, was doubtless instrumental in educating public sentiment to the importance of a State system of schools.

Not until 1816 did the public authorities take any action on this question. In that year Gov. Miller, in his message to the General Assembly, called attention to the need of public schools, and recommended that some action be taken looking to their establishment. The legislature appointed a committee, with the Hon. Archibald D. Murphey as chairman, to report upon the subject of "affording means of education to every one, however indigent." Judge

MEMORIAL HALL—GUILFORD COLLEGE, GUILFORD COLLEGE, N. C.

Murphey has been called the father of our public school system, and well does he deserve this title.

On December 19th, 1816, Judge Murphey, in behalf of the committtee, submitted a report urging the establishment of "a judicious system of public education." This report, which he drafted, is worthy of close study. The first part is devoted to a learned dissertation upon the benefits of education and the needs of the State University. Following this are suggestions for a school system. "This general system," says the report, "must include a graduation of schools regularly supporting each other, from the one in which the first rudiments of education are taught, to that in which the highest branches of the sciences are cultivated. It is to the first schools in this gradation that your committee beg leave to draw the attention of the legislature at this time, because in them will be taught the learning indispensible to all—reading, writing, and arithmetic. These schools must be scattered over every section of the State, for in them education must be commenced, and in them it will terminate as to more than one-half of the community. They will be the most difficult of organization and the most expensive to the State; but they will be the most useful, inasmuch as all the citizens will be taught in them, and many of the children are destined never to pass to any other."

No action was taken at this session of the legislature, and Judge Murphey was made chairman of a committee to investigate the subject more fully and report at the next session. He was much interested in this subject, and before submitting his report in 1817 he not only made a careful study of education in the New England States, but also visited Europe to examine the continetal school system. The result of his study and observations are embodied in the report of the committee, a voluminous but well written and eminently suggestive document.

A comparison with the reports as published in the records of the General Assembly for 1816 and 1817 shows that their main provisions are excellently summarized in the following extract from the admirable historical sketch of the North Carolina State School System in the report of the Commissioner of Education U. S. for 1876:

"The report (of 1816) went on to suggest that from the youth educated in these schools at State expense teachers should be selected for schools in which they might be qualified to teach, and that discreet persons should be appointed in each county to superintend and manage the concerns of the sectional schools which should be established, to designate the children who should be educated in whole or in part at the public expense, and to apply the funds which should be consecrated to the purposes of these schools. It closed with a recommendation that the two houses should appoint three persons to digest a system of public instruction founded upon the general principles which had been stated, and to submit the same to the next General Assembly.

"The house concurring with the senate on this motion, a committee was appointed, with the same gentleman as chairman, which made an elaborate report at the session of 1817. This new report recommended the formation of a fund for public instruction, and the constitution of a board to manage the fund and carry into execution the plan of public instruction contemplated. This plan was one which was meant to make the progress of education natural and easy, beginning with primary schools in which the first rudiments of learning were to be taught, and proceeding to academies, in which youth were to be instructed in languages, ancient and modern history, mathematics, and other branches of science, preparatory to entering the University, in which instruction should be given in all the higher branches of the sciences and the principles of the useful arts. An institution for the deaf and dumb was also included in the plan.

"For the elementary instruction to be given it was proposed to divide each county in the State into two or more townships, and to have one or more primary schools established in each township, which should provide a lot of ground of not less than four acres, and erect thereon a sufficient house, and vest it in the board of public instruction. For secondary training this board waws to divide the State into ten academic districts and have an academy erected in each district, the State to meet one-third of the expenses of the erection and the site, and furnish one-third of the sum required for salaries of teachers, on condition of their instructing a certain number of poor children free of charge. As to the superior instruction which was meant to crown the whole, the legislature was urged to provide the needed funds for sustaining and carrying forward the then struggling University. For gnitting the whole together came the board of public instruction to be constituted, which was to consist of the Governor of the State as president, and six directors, to be appointed by the general assembly. This board was to have power to locate the several academies to be established; to determine the number and titles of the professorships therein; to examine, appoint, and regulate the compensation of the professors and the teachers; to appoint, in the first instance, the trustees; to prescribe the course of instruction and discipline according to the general rules which should be first fixed by law; and to provide some just mode of advancing from the primary schools to the academies, and from the academies to the University, as many of the most meritorious children educated at the public expense as the proceeds of the funds for public instruction should suffice to maintain and educate."

Thew riter just quoted adds that "No better, more compact, or more connected scheme for the formation of a

State system of instruction could well have been devised at that quite early day. The main fault in it was that it undertook too much, viz.: to maintain as well as educate the children of the poor—an undertaking quite beyond the means of a State yet sparsely settled, and with the burdens of a recent war still weighing on the people. It was the expense which this portion of the plan involved that seems to have killed the project, for though the bill met with favor from the legislature, was ordered to be printed, and put into a form for passage, the consideration of the large sums it would annually require to carry out its liberal provisions induced a pause, and that pause was fatal to it. Instead of eliminating from it the one specially impracticable feature and trying to work out the practicable ones, its advocates desired and urged its passage as a whole, and so friends fell from it and it failed."

HISTORY OF PUBLIC SCHOOLS.

BY DR. STEPHEN B. WEEKS.

1. REORGANIZATION AND GROWTH, 1852–1861.

2. THE CIVIL WAR AND THE END OF THE OLD REGIME.

The following pages, containing much valuable historical information as to our public schools, are copied from "Beginnings of the Common-school System in the South," by Dr. Weeks, of the Bureau of Education, Washington, D. C.

It is my earnest desire that my report may give to the people of to-day, as well as those in the years to come, a general knowledge, at least, of the subject of public schools from their origin to the present time, trusting that the trials, toils and cares, as well as the obstacles overcome in the past, may be a means of inspiration and life to the friends of public education at present and in the future.

Dr. Weeks has been a close student of North Carolina history, and is well prepared to write of us and for us. I take pleasure in handing down to our people the valuable information contained in the following pages by Dr. Weeks:

REORGANIZATION AND GROWTH, 1852 1861.

The common-school system had begun in 1838 with considerable means, and the small impression that it created on the thinking people of the State and on the public generally proves that it was not considered a part of the governmental machinery, but as a local interest, with which local authorities could deal largely at their discretion.

The law of 1825 had provided that the distribution of the literary fund should be on the basis of the free white population, but the act of 1840 changed the basis from white to Federal population. Governor Manly, in his message to the legislature of 1850-'51, claimed that the rule adopted in 1840 carried "on its face a violation of the spirit and object of the injunction of the constitution; is a breach of the public faith given by the legislature of 1825; is at variance with the rule in other Southern States; divides the fund, not according to the public necessity, but the wealth of the people, and is in itself unequal and unjust. The advocates o fthe existing system defended their side with equal vigor, and thus were sown the seeds of dissention and jealousy with which Dr. Wiley had to deal during the whole of his administration.

"The system, as then organized, was not only deficient in its organization, but in accountability, uniformity, and its general management. For a period of ten years about $90,000 have been placed annually in the hands of the various school committees of the State, a sum larger than the whole amount of the State's revenue paid into the public treasury during that period. This large sum, forming an aggregate of nearly a million of dollars, has within this brief period been spent, and yet no adequate provision has been made, much less enforcd, for even informing the people or their representatives of what has become of it or how it has been spent."

*Manly's message to the legislature of 1850-51 (p. 19). The growth of the literary fund is shown by the following figures:

1850-51:	
Receipts	$129,255.24
Disbursements	94,596.41
1851-52:	
Receipts	137,380.41
Disbursements	161,472.33
1852-53:	
Receipts	192,250.75
Disbursements	139,865.16
1853-54:	
Receipts	196,090.25
Disbursements	169,983.32

Governor Manly substantiates his charges by saying further that he had published in 1849 an edition (6,000 copies) of the laws of the assembly relating to the public schools (the first of the kind), and had distributed the same, together with an appendix of precedents and appropriate forms of returns. These laws required that the chairman of the board of county superintendents of each county should, within fifteen days of the 1st of November, report in writing to the literary board his school accounts, credited by the proper county authorities, together with the number in the schools for the previous year, and the length of time the schools had been kept open. But this duty was performed by only seven superintendents throughout the whole State within the specified time. Several came in later, so that at the time of the report to the legislature forty-one had been received. This was a little more than one-half. It was found that there was still in the hands of the chairmen an aggregate of school funds amounting to $90,000. Estimating a like amount in the hands of those who had made no returns, it might be said that $180,000 lay unemployed and not used for school purposes, besides an indefinite amount in the hands of former chairmen and not used for school purposes.

Governor Manly continues his message in the following strain:

"Those [chairmen] who choose to do so submit them [their accounts] to the committees of finance or county court clerks, while those who fail to do so escape forfeiture or censure. It may be safely stated that thousands of dollars remain from year to year in the hands of superintendents, and if a rigid settlement were enforced the public would be astonished at the aggregate sum thus withheld from its legitimate destination. The whole fund annually distributed, although large, is yet inadequate to the public exigency.

"According to the provisions of the existing law, the

several county courts may, in their discretion, levy a tax as other taxes are levied for county purposes, not less than one-half of the amount annually received from the literary fund . . . Some of the counties, with commendable spirit, levy a fair tax; others levy a very small one,, while very many of the counties levy no tax at all. Hence it results that in those counties dependent solely on the literary fund, the sum they receive, when subdivided among a large number of districts, is so small for each that many of the districts have no schools at all and derive no benefit from the provision. . . . . Our people do not take hold of the subject with that energy and spirit essential to success. A general listlessness prevails. Those that can afford it send their children elsewhere to school, while the poorer classes keep theirs at home to work. Throughout the State you see everywhere on the highways schoolhouses deserted, the doors broken from their hinges, and the grass growing in the yard. Why is this? Besides those already alluded to, one prominent cause, doubtless, is the difficulty of procuring proper teachers, qualified by education and good morals, to direct the young. . . . In some of the counties, I am happy to be able to say, their schools are well managed, and are accomplishing with marked effect the beneficent results aimed at by the law, and it is to be hoped that such is the case in others. But there is no official information on the subject, and what I design to say is that the very want of this information demonstrates the absolute necessity of some radical amendment. This necessity suggests the expediency of creating a new office in the government to take general charge of the whole business, in accordance with the practice in other States and with the earnest and repeated recommendation of my predecessors. . . . Having been a member of the literary board from its organization, and having bestowed some attention upon the subject, I feel, in conclusion, fully warranted in recommending as the most effectual means of attaining the ends referred to, the appointment of a general superintendent of common schools for the State.*

Under such pressure as this from the governor, the literary board, and other officials, progress was made toward reform. When it is remembered that the annual income of the literary fund was more than the income of the State, and that this amount was spent and subjected to no general supervision, the importance of such supervision may be easily seen.

The legislature of 1848-'49 had considered bills for the appointment of a general superintendent, but while rejecting them, had authorized county superintendents at a salary of $250 each. In the legislature of 1850-'51, Dr. Wiley, who was then a member of the house of commons from Guilford County, introduced a bill for the appointment of a State superintendent. The bill had able and enlightened friends in both houses; it received favorable consideration and a large vote, but failed to pass.

Dr. Wiley was also a member of the assembly of 1852-'53' and through his influence a bill for a superintendent was introduced by Mr. Cherry, of Bertie. Another bill to divide the funds among the counties in the ratio of their white population, and one to provide for the education of teachers at Normal, Davidson and Wake Forest colleges, were also introduced, but these failed to pass.

The "Act to provide for the appointment of a superintendent of common schools, and for other purposes," stands as chapter 18 in the Public Acts of 1852. It is the corner-stone on which was built up the best system of common schools in the South before the war, and, in brief, is as follows:

It provides for a superintendent of common schools for the State, to be chosen by the legislature and to hold office

*This message emphasizes and summarizes the report which Governor Manly had made to the same legislature as chairman of the literary board.

for two years. County chairmen were to make their reports to the superintendent on or before the third Monday in November, and to include, among other items the number of certificates granted to teachers, male and female. In each county there was to be "a committee of examination," consisting of not more than five members, "whose duty it shall be to examine into the qualification, both mental and moral, of all such persons as may apply for employment as teachers in any of the common schools." Certificates issued to teachers were good for one year, and only in the county where issued, and in the absence of such certificate payment might be refused. The State superintendent was to collect information concerning the condition and operation of the common schools in the counties, and to report the same to the governor for the benefit of the legislature. He was to superintend the operation of the schools, see that the laws were enforced, and look after escheated property. The State treasurer was to furnish him an annual statement of the sums disbursed to the counties, and he was to issue annually to the examining committees "a circular letter of instructions and suggestions as to the qualifications of teachers." He was to prepare and furnish blanks for the use of county officers and to compile and arrange the laws on the subject, together with such other instructions as were necessary. He was to make an annual report to the governor, reviewing the work of the schools and including statistics, of which "the governor shall cause 150 copies to be printed in cheap pamphlet form, 50 copies for his own use, and 100 copies for the use of the said general superintendent," who was "as often as possible" to deliver public lectures on the subject of education. His salary was $1,500.

The funds of the literary board, principal, in 1852, were invested as follows:

1.	5,322 shares stock in Bank of Cape Fear	$ 532,200.00
2.	5,027 shares stock in the Bank of the State	502,700.00
3.	Bonds of Raleigh and Gaston Railroad Company, indorsed by the State, due January 1, 1860	140,000.00
4.	Bonds on Wilmington and Raleigh Railroad Company, secured by mortgages and deed of trust on the property of the company in 1837 and 1840	85,000.00
5.	Bonds endorsed by the State	50,000.00
6.	Bonds endorsed by the State	2,250.00
7.	Bond of State issued for stock in Fayettevslle and Western Plank Road	2,000.00
8.	Bond executeu according to act of assemply	39,808.55
9.	Bond executen according to act of assembly	552.00
10.	Bond of Wake Forest College	6,169 52
11.	Bond of Floral College	2,000.00
12.	Bond of Greensboro Female College	7,000.00
13.	Bond of Chowan Female Institute	3,000.00
1s.	The whole of the swamp lands of the State, reclaimed and unreclaimed, not granted and held by individuals prior to the year 1826, estimated at 1,500,000 acres, heretofore valued at	150,000.00
15.	State bonds issued in 1852, purchased by the board	10,500.00
16.	Three bonds on on J. W. Keeling and others for swamp lands, $755 each	10,000.00
17.	Four bonds on Thomas Sparrow and others for swamp lands	125.60
18.	Four bonds on Allen Grist and others for swamp lands	296.00
19.	One bond on Nathaniel Credle and others for swamp lands	125.00
20.	One bond on W. D. Cooke, showing a small balanca.	
21.	One bond of N. S. King, believed to be of no value	268.00
22.	One bond of William D. Cooke and others	1,000.00
23.	Amount of cash in bank of Cape Fear to credit of boarn (principal money)	1,000.00
		$1,538,995.46

After securing a new and improved act for the schools, and providing for a superintendent of common schools, came the still more difficult task of finding the proper man to fill the office. Dr. Wiley was then a member of the legislature from Guilford County. He was a Whig in politics and a lawyer by profession, while the legislature was Democratic. But the activity displayed by him in advancing the interests of the schools pointed him out as the man for the place. He was elected, without the slightest solicitation on his part, and by a large majority, in December, 1852, and entered upon his duties January 1, 1853.

In the estimation of all others, as well as himself, the superintendent was "all things to the schools, and had to be, for a time, a guide to them, to public sentiment and to the legislature, with no guide or support for himself in the community or in the neighboring States." Dr. Wiley was already well and favorably known to the people of the State.

Calvin Henderson Wiley was born near Greensboro, Guilford County, N. C., February 3, 1819, and was the son of David L. and Anne Woodburn Wiley. His father's family was of Scotch-Irish stock. William Wiley, his great-grandfather, removed from Pennsylvania in 1754, and bought lands from Lord Granville in the Alamance section of Guilford. His grandfather, David Wiley, was a Regulator in 1771, and later a soldier in the Revolution. While still a boy he showed a taste for books and reading, and was sent to Caldwell Institute in Greensboro and was there prepared for the University of North Carolina. He was graduated from that institution in 1840, and already numbered among his friends some of the political leaders of the State. He studied law, was admitted to the bar in 1841, and located in Oxford. In addition to his practice of law he edited the Oxford Mercury, 1841-'43. Not content with these two activities, he entered the field of romance and published, in 1847, his first novel, called "Alamance, or the Great and Final Experiment," which was redolent of the soil of his native section. A second novel, "Roanoke, or Where is Utopia?" appeared in Sartain's Magazine in 1849. In 1851 he was invited and urged to go to Charlotte to edit a Whig paper, but declined. During that year, however, he associated himself with W. D. Cooke in editing the Southern Weekly Post, in Raleigh. The first number appeared December 6, 1851, and was "edited chiefly" by Wiley. Cooke was the publisher. It was devoted to the general upbuilding of North Carolina. The announcement of this paper, evidently the work of Wiley, strikes the keynote of the policy which his paper, and he in all his subsequent work, was to pursue:

"It is a fact worthy of being universally known that North Carolina is considered by bookmakers the best mart in the world for uncurrent and trashy productions, and the very refuse of literary quackery is sent out here and circulated among our people. For most of the works of this sort Northern publishers have agencies all over North Carolina, and thus while there are none to circulate our own book, and the people are kept in ignorance of their own history and of the character and resources of their State, they are drugged with foreign narcotics and heavily taxed for the benefit of fabrics that will not sell and can not be sold where they are manufactured."

It was with the hope of doing away with or improving on this state of affairs that Dr. Wiley entered politics in 1850 as a Whig member of the House of Commons from Guilford County, and began efforts for that series of educational reforms which have put him among the leading educational statesmen of the South. He assumed his duties as superintendent of common schools January 1, 1853. During the whole period of his incumbency much of the superintendent's time was taken up with the routine and clerical duties of the office, for he was allowed no clerk. His correspondence with local school officers was heavy and much of it trivial. He prepared digests of the school laws, gave directions and made suggestions to teachers and to committees, made many speeches in all parts of the State, and published many articles in the papers. He was forced, moreover, to meet many attacks on himself and on the system, as a whole, from its enemies, open and concealed. It was said that he wasted his time or used it for his private interests, while he complained that the newspapers failed to devote a proper attention to educational affairs, since few were apparently interested, and that there were none to stir up a community on education against the coming of the superintendent, while there were plenty to arouse enthusiasm when a politician was to speak. But in the midst of criticism and abuse Dr. Wiley steadily refused to follow the policy which would keep his own name most prominently before the public. He chose rather to do the humbler work, which was no less necessary, but which brought him little personal credit. He was willing to work for the future. His first official duty was to prepare a new digest of the State laws relating to the schools then in force. These laws went no further back than the act of 1844-'45. To the collection of acts was added a statement of the forms in which the principal of the literary fund was invested; specimens of the forms to be used by the county chairmen in their reports to the State superintendent, and by the school committees to the county chairmen, regulations, a circular to the chairmen, and an address by the general superintendent "to the officers of the common schools and to the friends of education in North Carolina," were included in his first official publication.

In the spring of 1853 Dr. Wiley began the active prosecution of his duties. He made a tour in his buggy from the middle part of the State to Currituck Court House, in the extreme east, and delivered addresses, according to previous arrangements, at each county seat. In the summer and fall het raveled in the same way to Murphy, in Cherokee County, in the extreme southwest. It is evident that trips of this kind would require a large amount of time, but they were made during the whole period of his incumbency, and during the earlier part were necessarily by private conveyance. But as the means of travel became better, public mthods were used more, and less time was spent on the road. But these early tours by private conveyance, while they were paid for by the superintendent out of his own pocket, and cost for the first year nearly half of his salary, were of great service. The disabilities and conveniences of different localities were observd; visits were made to districts distinguished by special or good features and to some schools laboring under peculiar disadvantages. The history and progress of the schools in the counties visited was inquired into, the friends of the system, teachers and school officers were interviewed and the system discussed. Further, the superintendent made use of the public press at every opportunity. There were many misconceptions of the work. These had to be corrected and its true mission and spirit made known. Uniformity had to be fostered, and a healthy public spirit created. The friends of the schools had to be discovered, supplied with arguments and every effort made to keep the movement clear from sectional, partisan and sectarian prejudices. Special efforts were made to show to academies, high schools and colleges their interest in the common schools and to enlist the sympathy and co-operation of ministers of all denominations.

"At that day all of these points, some of which now seem elementary, had to be fixed, and some of them after a hard struggle, and the whole system had to be purged of the fatal taint of charity once adhering to it, and especially and after a protracted effort, lifted from the position of a beneficence to a class to that of a fundamental interest of all the State."

These earnest efforts met with great success. The higher schools were brought to see their interest and duties in the superintendent's labors, and denominationalism was kept out of the work. It was the same in the matter of politics. Dr. Wiley, a Whig, was elected by a Democratic legislature. He retained and voted on his political convictions, but from the day he went into office had no stronger friends than W. W. Holden, of The Standard, and W. J. Yates, of The Charlotte Democrat, who were the leaders of the Democratic press.* In the same way all the governors, from 1853 until the close of the war, were Democrats, as were most of the other State officers, but they were the friends of Dr. Wiley, and held up his hands to the fullest extent. It is safe to say that he won his position through merit, and retained it largely through a self-respecting neglect of his political interests, for on one occasion the Democrats in the legislature moved his re-election early in the session to anticipate the rise of party feeling and to lessen the chances for a Democratic opponent.

The first annual report of Dr. Wiley was made to Governor David S. Reid, and is dated January 24, 1854. It is mainly a review of the situation, pointing out the weaknesses and difficulties of the schools and the character of the work needed for the future, while the survey of what had already been done occupies a subordinate place. It may be well to summarize the situation as it then appeared.

He gives the extent and character of his travels from one end of the State to the other, for the most part by private conveyance, for only in ten or twelve counties could access be had to the county seat in any other way. In his future travels he was to be governed, to some extent, by the character of the reports received, his object being to visit the counties that sent in the least satisfactory reports, to find out the difficulties in their way, to give them advice and information.

"Every citizen of the State ought to be spoken to. . . . I hope in due time to reach every man. . . . There is also now a source, however imperfect, of information and a tribunal to decide or give opinions, and almost daily applications to me demonstrate to me the injuries and discouragements heretofore resulting from doubts never solved, difficulties never settled, and inquiries never answered."

*But neither of these papers, so far as I know, nor the Raleigh Register, the Whig organ, interested themselves to any great extent in the agitation which brought about the appointment of a superintendent. This honor was left to the Raleigh Star.

GUILFORD COLLEGE, GUILFORD COLLEGE, N. C.

To promote the efficiency and uniformity of the system, he prepared a form of certificate to be given to the teacher by the committee of examination. "The grads are from No. 1, the highest, to No. 5, the lowest, on the studies of spelling, reading, writing, arithmetic, geography and grammar." Under the law the chairman of the county superintendents was authorized to refuse payment to a teacher who held no certificate. These certificates were good only in the county where issued, and were to be renewed annually. From these it was hoped that the happiest results would follow.

"A crying evil in the State was the multiplicity and frequent change of text-books, by which expenses are accumulated on parents and guardians, the progress of the school retarded, and teachers greatly embarrassed by having large schools with nearly every child in a class by itself. I have often been called on to interfere in this matter, and have felt it my duty to use such exertions as the law would authorize. The object of my efforts was, first, to drive from our schools bad books; second, to prevent frequent and injurious changes—injurious alike to parents and to pupils: and third, to secure the use of a uniform series, whereby expense would be avoided and teachers would be enabled to arrange their pupils in classes."*

His efforts were directed largely to securing the best books for the schools.

"Not willing to recommend for the use of the schools of the State books which do it injustice, I notified publishers that I would not approve of any geography unless I was allowed to alter and correct the text so far as relates to North Carolina. The publishers of different works consented, and, having selected Mitchell's Intermediate Geography as best suited under all the circumstances for our

*As early as 1853 there was a proposition from Pasquotank county to furnish books to the pupils at government expedse. The proposition was renewed from time to time from other quarters.

common schools, I prepared an appendix, which, in a new edition o fthe work, with a full and new map of North Cara-lina, is now coming out. . . . The new edition will be worthy of the patronage of all our schools and will contain, besides the new map, several engravings illustrating the description of our State. . . . The time is coming when very material changes will be effected in the routes of commerce. All things considered, the finest agricultural country in the world is the valley of the Mississippi and its tributaries. . . . Between the nearer Atlantic and this vast granary of the West and Southwest stands the interposing barrier of the Alleghany Mountains, long thought to be an impassable wall, and a limit to the iron track of commerce. But modern science has overcome greater difficulties to secure that modern desideratum, the shortest passage, and the gallant States of Virginia and Georgia are already storming these heights with every prospect of success. South Carolina will follow in the assault, and none of these have so great inducements to undertake the enterprise as the people of North Carolina. Nearly midway of the Atlantic coast, in a temperate and healthy climate, is the unchangeable, safe and capacious harbor of Beaufort; and from hence through our fertile upland slopes and the gorges of our own beautiful mountains, lies the shortest route to the great Southwest. To foreshadow the grand commercial destiny we might attain on the youthful mind of the State and prepare it to grasp and realize the magnificent consummation, I took much pains to have all the proposed railroads over the mountains and their bearings and connections made familiar to the publishers of the geography in question. . . . The State already occupies in the work the largest space of any other, with its railroad routes noticed, and Beaufort handsomely described."

In the matter of school Readers Dr. Wiley did not make a recommendation, for reasons as follows:

"It is well known that a few years ago I undertook to make a series of North Carolina Readers, and published the most important number, for advanced schools, containing a familiar history and description of the State, with compositions in prose and verse by distinguished North Carolinians. Its object was obvious; and to all acquainted with our peculiar position, our desponding and erroneous estimate of our resources, and the history of that singular and remarkable exodus or emigration which for years has retarded our progress in every species of improvement, the uses of such a work, well compiled, were fully apparent."

For these and other reasons, Dr. Wiley had it at heart to make a good series of home readers. His own book had been recommended by all the colleges and many academies before his appointment as superintendent, but he knew its defects, and also dtermined to make no profit out of any school book used during his term of office. He thereupon began negotiations to induce some publisher to take the reader at the original cost, on condition that he would employ Professor Hubbard, of the University, "or some other person, of equal taste and ability, to alter my work and complete the series."

Dr. Wiley proposed also, under an arrangement which he termed "medical school," to give the few individuals in a community who were accustomed to spend money for education in private schools at a distance a large control in the public schools of their district, thus securing a better school for the home district, arousing interest in the home school, and saving money.

The prospects and necessity of normal schools were also considered. Teachers were already being educated in the Normal College in Randolph county in return for a loan made by the State. "Let it be universally understood," he adds, "that colleges, academies, and common schools are all bound up in one common interest and that the common schools are to the academies and colleges what the back country is to commercial cities."

The subject of escheats was discussed. These had been transferred to the University after the State had exhausted its resources in trying to enforce payment. Later they were retransferred to the literary fund, and a suit was brought in the Supreme court of the United States to test the legality of the act. Agents were appointed to hunt up this species of property and prosecute the claims of the literary fund. * He combats vigorously the strange and foolish idea that a free school was a place—

"where entire freedom of action is to be guaranteed to the pupil; and, entertaining these erroneous notions, parents not unfrequently prevent the improvement of their children by refusing to permit them to be corrected or submit to discipline necessary to chasten and restrain the wayward disposition and the prurient passions of youth.

"Efforts to promote the love of home in the plastic nature of childhood are peculiarly becoming in North Carolina, a State where the want of this attachment and its ruinous effects are eloquently recorded in deserted farms, in wide wastes of guttered sedge fields, in neglected resources in the absence of improvements, and in the hardships, sacrifices, and sorrows of constant emigration. Our State has long been regarded by its own citizens as a mere nursery to grow up in, and, from my earliest youth, I have witnessed the sad effects of this in the families of my acquaintance, many of such being scattered from the homes of their nativity over the wide Southwest."

He adds statistics of the progress of the schools since 1840. In 1850 the schools had been in operation about nine years, and the increase of the white population had been about 12 per cent. In 1840 there were 19,483 pupils in schools of all grades; in 1850 there were 100,591, or an

*In 1855 escheats had been restoren to the univerfity.—Manly to Wiley, February 16, 1898

increase of 500 per cent. In 1840 there were 632 schools; in 1850 there were 2,131 schools in 70 counties, and perhaps 2,500 in all; increase in thirteen years, 400 per cent. In 1840 the pupils in the common schools were 14,937; in 1853 there were 83,873 in 70 counties, which would indicate 95,000 for the whole State, or an increase of 600 per cent. During the same period the colleges and academies increased in attendance by 150 to 200 per cent. The value of the apparatus was three times as much, the number of grammars and geographies sold five times as many, and the number of good scholars three times as many. It was not claimed that all the common schools were as good as the subscription schools broken down, but it was claimed for every one thus broken down there were two just as good in its place, besides three or four other schools not so good. The average time during which the schools were kept open was, for the whole State, about four months. From the progress made in these ten years Dr. Wiley estimated that the nexet generation would have 50 per cent les of ignorance than the one then on the stage of action.

"I feel bound to say that money is not our greatest want, and that the places where the highest salaries are paid are not generally those which have succeeded best. We want more efficient management, a constant embodiment and expression of public opinion, a watchful supervision, a liberal course of legislation, good officers, and patience and energy in all having an official position in the system."

Again, he says in his special report on the same subject:

"I admit that a considerable number of those who attend school go but a few days in the year and learn but little; but it must be borne in mind as a very important consideration that many of these are the children of those who never went a day to school themselves. Into a mind wholly ignorant it is hard for the light to penetrate, and a man who does not know the alphabet is not sufficiently enlightened to feel his ignorance or to appreciate a higher state of improvement. He is not upon the ladder of knowledge at all, and can, therefore, see no one above him, but as soon as he makes a start he can begin to understand his relative position. Hence the children of ignorant parents, who get a little smattering of knowledge at our common schools, will feel their wants when they take their positions in life, and their children, if the same facilities remain, will be much better educated. This is a conclusion that cannot be gainsaid, and as a large majority of the children of that large part of our population who cannot read at all are learning a little at our common schools, we may boldly assert that in the second generation that dark belt that covers the sixth of our moral surface will nearly wholly disappear, leaving only a dim outline to indicate its former existence."

With the founding of the common schools came two great problems to their managers:

"First. How were eight hundred to a thousand old-field school-teachers to be utilized in a system of one genius, one law, and one end, when to each his own school had long been the educational world, of which he was the center and sovereign? These teachers were our only capital, of the kind with which to begin, and we all know that it is easier to prepare a new generation of employees in any business than to break in old ones long accustomed to their own diverse ways."

But the managers of the common schools could not wait, and they had no means of training, besides it would have been unjust an dimpolitic to set aside the old-field veterans as a class, while their opposition to the new system would have insured its failure. "And yet to work them into a homogeneous and progressive system under a general law, to subject them to annual examinations and licensure, and to grade their attainments, was a task requiring the greatest patience, tact, and powers of organization."

The next question was how to find the 1,500 or 2,000 more teachers that were needed at once, for the position was considered humble and the salary was small. The situation was delicate and the superintendent was aware of its character. The conclusion was reached that the common schools must both multiply and improve the teachers whom they needed. There was no other practicable method.

The first step was the establishing of examining boards in all the counties. This was no easy task, for there was no salary and no influence attached, and its objects seemed to aim at individual freedom and made it unpopular, but after awhile these examining boards were paid and their value increased. The certificates issued allowed the party to teach for one year and in one county only. It was found that perpetual permission to teach caused retrogression on the part of the party holding such a certificate, and confining the license to one county was necessary to give such counties as desired it an opportunity to raise the standard of their own schools. Few young people dependent on their own resources cared to go into the schools, but the superintendent used all available means to bring to the attention of such people a realization of the avenue of advancement open to them through the schools. To carry out these plans it was necessary to begin with low grades. His rule was to authorize the issue of certificates to persons who could teach only spelling, reading, writing, and arithmetic, and who received low grades on those subjects, but none were to be relicensed with such a grade, and all with grades below the first were expected to improve with each new examination. Under such an arrangement it was possible to make the requirements for No. 1 exacting. Of the successes of this system Dr. Wiley says:

"Progress could be more easily marked when there were so many grades; even the least advancement could be graded, and advancement became the order of the day. Some of the very best teachers and most useful members of society grew from the lowest grades; young persons, shut in by poverty and thirsting for knowledge, would follow my advice and teach on low certificates, studying as they taught, and as they acquired means would attend higher schools, and then go on step by step to the most respectable positions in life."

There were at this time few women in the schools. In some counties there were none. He urged repeatedly that they be encouraged to teach. In his second annual letter to county superintendents he says:

"Encourage as much as possible the very poor, and especially poor females, to become teachers......

"There is, however, a class, a numerous class, who are hired out to field labor, and many of these, if properly awakened, could become excellent teachers, and make more than twice as much as by their present occupations..

"But a helpless female, who can not push her fortune in the world, and yet is born dependent on the labor of her own hands, when started on such a career, fairly electrifies surrounding ignorance and prejudice and is a standing miracle performed by means of our common schools. Imagine a girl—you can see them in your own neighborhood—a girl with natural sensibilities and capabilities—for heart and mind are inherited bv all ranks and classes—but from her very infancy pushed into rude contact with the world, it being necessary for her own existence or that of her parents that she be hired out to wages. What is the hope before her? In the factories she may make $4 to $6 per month, and may preserve her character, though inhaling a noisome atmosphere. In the fields she may earn $3 per month...... Or such a one may, for board and coarse clothes, go into domestic service......

"There is another road open to such a one, leading from want and social inferiority to independence, to respect, and to usefulness and happiness, and it lies through our common schools......

"And females, for certain classes, make the best teachers. They are more patient, more easily win the affections of the young, and are more likely to mold to virtuous and refined sentiments the plastic nature of childhood."

The schools needed all the help and encouragement that could be drawn from the enthusiasm of their superintendent, for his correspondence shows that the complaints were neither few in number nor insignificant in character. Many districts were careless. In some cases the money was not appropriated and no schools were held for several years. Many of the teachers were incompetent. The committees had to take as teachers persons who had never studied English grammar or geography. It was necessary to employ those who could only spell and read and who had only a moderate knowledge of arithmetic, for these were the only kind to be had, while in some districts no children were far enough advanced to study grammar. Many school committees refused to serve. Some, if not actually dishonest, were careless, ad there had been no machinery by which they could be brought to a strict account. In some counties, prior to 1853, there had been no chairman for two years and in some sections the common schools were patronized only by those who were too poor to do better, and from one county it was reported that some districts had had no schools in four or five years. There was sometimes trouble with the county chairmen, who either failed or refused to report, and in a few cases it was found necessary to fine them for their neglect. In some cases, so imperfectly was the common school idea recognized, people moved into the school house and had to be dispossessed by process of law. In some places there was trouble over the age limit. Persons over 21 years of age would attend the schools and thus crowd out the younger pupils. Trouble also arose from the passing of pupils from one school district to another. One case was reported where the teacher was required to receive pupils coming from another district, but to charge them tuition, which the committee undertook to appropriate for their own benefit! Some counties would now and then refuse to levy any tax at all for the schools, and the amount due from the literary fund was too small to be of any practical value. The schools were usually held in the fall, since this was the season when pupils could be most easily spared from the work of the farm; they were then crowded with the larger boys and girls, who monopolized the teacher and cut out the smaller pupils. It was proposed to obviate this difficulty by holding two sessions instead, one in the fall and one in the spring, for young pupils especially. The latter were to be taught by women, who were cheaper than men. The question of the teaching of free negroes in the common schools also came up, and there was at least one case where a committeeman insisted that they attend. There was also more or less discussion as to whether "silent" schools were superior to "noisy" schools, or vice versa. New committees on coming into office would sometimes expel the teacher employed by the former committee and put in a new one, or they would notify him to quit and refuse to pay his salary.

These were some of the many questions that came to the superintendent for adjudication and settlement. There was also talk of repealing the law. This had, of course, a depressing effect on the superintendent and shows itself in his report. Dr. Wiley discusses in his second report the leading features of the schools as follows:

A stricter and more uniform and patient attention to the execution of the law. Annual reports from the counties should be insisted on, together with a certificate as to the correctness of the accounts from the committee of finance, authenticated by the clerk of the county court. This requirement would compel more accurate accounts to be kept, for while the greater part of the money had passed through honest hands; "doubtless a sum sufficent to pay a superintendent for twenty years has been carelessly handled, to say the least." When the county chairmen found that strict accounts were not required of them, they in turn relaxed their requirements, and after twelve years there was "a universal complaint that committees will not make the proper returns."

The second subject demanding careful attention, wise oversight, and constant exertion by some systematic means, was the improvement of teachers. There had been great complaint in regard to them; some were incompetent, some were unfaithful, and he emphasizes the fact that it is not always the want of money which makes indifferent teachers. The salaries paid were not large, but poor teachers were paid as much as good ones, and still better ones might be employed for the same money.

"On the contrary, large salaries under the old regulations would often enhance the nuisance; it would be an inducement to imposters and adventurers to swarm among us in pursuit of the sums thrown out to attract the attention and excite the enterprise of such characters. Have it understood that $50 to $75 per month were to be paid to those who would fill in so many days in a school house, and that no evidence of moral character, and no certificate as to mental qualifications from those capable of judging, and no reports of the manner in which they had discharged their duties were to be required, and you will have not the merely indifferent teachers and respectable and moral persons now so much complained of, but every ignorant neighborhood, from the seaboard to the mountains, infested and overrun by plausible, worthless, and dangerous characters, setting on foot all sorts of intrigues, imposing on the credulity of the simple-minded, and even conspiring with local speculators to obtain and divide with them the tempting spoils."

Normal schools were needed, but they were rather the result than the cause of an advanced state of education. Teachers were to be examined yearly. This was found to be a hard rule to enforce, but the examining committee were steadily supported by the superintendent, and as refractory teachers saw that the officers supported each other, they were glad to give in and pass the examinations. Further, the schools were beginning to command the sympathy and respect of other branches of education:

"Professors in colleges, male and female, reposing a confidence for which I am grateful, have tried to strengthen my hands, and I have felt proud of the fact that since my term of office began common schools have enlisted interest and received respect in every male college and nearly every female one in the State, and from the conventions of both political parties."

Another means of improvement recommended to teachers was the formation of teachers' library associations.

"Every trade and profession should be learning by experience; but how many teachers in North Carolina have read one single book giving an account of the experience and improvements in their profession in other places?...... The legislature should pass a general act of incorporation, giving corporate existence and privileges, on certain conditions, to the chairman of the board of county superintendents, and the teachers of each county and committees of examination; and an appropriation of $1 or more for each school district.... should be made for a foundation. Let the chairman be librarian, with a certain remuneration, and let each teacher pay 50 cents, more or less, annually, for the privilege of membership. The superintendent can furnish or recommend a list of books, in conjunction with the chairman; and each teacher who joins should have the fact stated on his certificate.... These associations will increase in consequence; they will form meeting places for teachers to assemble and discuss the affairs of education, and furnish proper places for lectures by superintendents and others; besides, when the minds of teachers are thus brought in contact, the superior intellects will diffuse themselves and be reflected in the action of all the teachers in the association."

In an Appendix to this report Dr. Wiley emphasizes still more the necessity of organizing, throughout the State, teachers' library associations.

"With such an organization the following effects may be confidently anticipated: The first appropriation, small as it is, would buy a sufficient number of copies of Page's work on teaching, Northend's, or any other, for all the teachers in the county. Some four or five works on such subjects might be selected and enough of each purchased to have one book, at the least, for every member. And if only one-third of the common-school teachers of North Carolina could be induced to read the most indifferent work on teaching, what a vast change would soon be perceptible!.... Scatter judiciously over the State good copies of any good work on teaching and it will create a revolution. Hitherto we have never seen or heard of any other plan than the old provincial one, with no blackboard, no oral instruction, no lectures, no inducement to study but the whip, no evidence of proficiency but the sum stated on the slate, without a word as to how it was arrived at, no admitted indications of industry but a loud babel of sounds, etc. Teachers have no fixed plans for their own improvement—none for the scholars. The only labor is to fill out the time; the only object to get the public money."

Other objects to be secured by the teachers' library associations were the insuring an active person as the head of the examining committee and insuring a committee. Further than this, a communion of feeling and ideas would be effected among the teachers:

"They will have something to distinguish them as a class—a common bond of union, a place to meet and exchange thoughts.... Teachers will feel themselves enhanced in public estimation, and they will have a body, a society, to defend, to promote, to improve; and by all efforts to elevate their society and make it respected they will be individually benefited."

These library associations would also furnish vital mediums through which to effect the interest and progress of common schools and enlist the aid of public-spirited and philanthropic citizens. The views of the superintendent on these and similar lines are reinforced by extracts from the reports of State superintendents and others.

Another vital point demanding constant care and attention was the discipline in the schools. "How often do I hear the complaint that teachers consider that they have to fill out merely a certain number of days, and make it their greatest object to kill time instead of improving it." It was charged that bad habits were not forgotten and no good ones acquired; parents were put to expense and children put back by a constant change of books, while no efforts were made to classify the children, "and a school of fifty scholars will have forty classes, each class thus having but a very few minutes to recite in and the teacher no time for lectures, explanations, or oral instructions. Seven hours are enough for school hours in the twenty-four; and ten recitations, fifteen at the furthest, are as many as can be well made and heard in seven hours, except recitations by those learning their letters. Oral instruction is coming more and more in vogue." Dr. Wiley then recounts his efforts to bring about a proper classification of the children:

"I determined, if possible, to make arrangements to have the children classified, and to get into use one uniform system of good books, to insure this end of classifying the pupils, to save cost, to have good sources of instruction in the schools, and to have the young mind of the State in its plastic condition learning about North Carolina and learning to love the State and to take an interest in its institutions. This of itself would make a great revolution in time. How could we feel an abiding interest in the common schools, or in any other institution of the State, when under the old way of doing things we were educated to love and respect every other country and the affairs of every other country more than our own?"

Of his own duties he says:

"The head of the common school system ought to study; like the leader of an army, he ought to have the whole field before him and to initiate every general movement with great care. He ought to study other systems as well as our own; he needs a previous preparation just as much as a lawyer, engineer, or physician.... Knowing that States never do things as well or carefully as individuals or private companies, I have endeavored to prepare myself in the midst of the duties of the office. I have read and written on the road, and procured and studied all the lights I could, and, as I could catch time, endeavored to look over our whole system and examine it in its details and in its general bearings."

Of the need and importance of teachers' institutes he says:

"When traveling, to acquaint myself with the character of the State, I often undertook to deliver lectures, and I was of opinion that many who heard me began to feel a new interest in the cause. But many of our so-called intelligent people would not attend, looking on the whole common school machinery as not intended for them; and they, whom they called the common people, had no excitement to draw them out, no example of interest set by others, while teachers, afraid, no doubt, of exposing themselves in some way, rarely ever attended. Hence, speech making in North Carolina was not calculated much to advance the cause."

Then, mindful of the criticisms which came pouring in on him and of the political sword suspended always above his head, he modestly says of his own work:

"I was conscious that more was expected of me than could be accomplished by mortal man, in the time, with even more means at his disposal—that I was, in fact, expected to do in two short years, with none to help and all to criticise, what legislators and officers and people, by cheerful co-operation and patient effort, with full confidence in each other and every disposition to strengthen the hands of each other, ought to be proud to be able to accomplish in ten or twenty years, and what it had taken such efforts longer time to effect in other places. I felt, too —not a pleasant reflection to a sensitive mind—that while I was spending freely in books, in postage, in travels, and neglecting more profitable sources of revenue, and not saving much of my salary, some were thinking I was growing rich on the public money and robbing the schools, which had lost many thousands for the want of a more efficient organization and which contributed to my salary about 50 cents each, or in the ratio of three-quarters of 1 cent to the child, while I was trying to save twenty times that amount to each on the single small item of books alone.... I will be excused for saying, in conclusion, that the subject is the most important one which can possibly come before our legislature, and that in common schools the people are infinitely more interested than in all the other literary institutions of the country."

The year 1855 opened with a revisal and reenactment of the school law. There had been much opposition to the new system developed. There had been rumors that the law of 1852 was to be repealed and a return to the old decentralized, do-nothing system inaugurated—a "system of nominal supervision and actual indifference." But these fears were groundless. The return to the old system was not inaugurated, and Dr. Wiley was reelected to the place of superintendent without opposition and by political opponents.

ADMINISTRATION BUILDING—SHAW UNIVERSITY, RALEIGH, N. C.

There is a vein of hope and encouragement in the third annual report for the year ending December 31, 1855.

Before noticing the report it may be well to consider the new law: The act ratified February 10, 1855, defined the sources of revenue of the literary fund, directed the management of the swamp lands, and regulated the common schools. Under the act the distribution was to be on the basis of Federal population as it had been under the earlier law, the appointment of a general superintendent was renewed, and each county was to have not more than ten nor less than five local superintendents or committeemen. The chairman of these superintendents was to give bond, and his compensation was 2 1-2 per cent.; the counties were to levy a tax not less in amount than one-half of the estimated amount to be received from the literary fund. In addition to these, three school committeemen were to be chosen annually by popular vote. These two boards were to have control of the schools and to make reports to the State superintendent. The efforts of the superintendent were directed largely to introducing new ideas, to improving the quality of the teachers, and to securing punctuality and faithfulness in the disbursement of money.

Only in two cases did the failure to report on the use of money indicate its misapplication, and one of these was taken into the courts more as a matter of warning to others than with the idea of prosecution. A more general knowledge of the school law and of its objects and a stricter attention to its requirements was needed. Dr. Wiley desired to secure good examining committees by providing for the payment of their expenses, but in this he failed. He wished also to organize the teachers into associations. One of the matters that attracted the attention of the superintendent continually and enlisted his best efforts was the desire to spread throughout the State a more general knowledge of its history and resources and correct false impressions. The common-school class "imbibed their first ideas from books, in which North Carolina, whenever it was necessary to mention the State, was represented in such a way as to make impressions anything else but pleasant to young imaginations." On the misrepresentations and manifest injustice to the State Dr. Wiley rings the changes time and time again. It was against such ideas as these that he had prepared his reader and the North Carolina edition of Mitchell's Geography, and so persistent and enthusiastic was he that before the war began his reader had been adopted in most of the schools of the State, and there was more knowledge of the State and a better appreciation of its resources than at any previous time. He was also busily engaged during this year in superintending the making of the first and second numbers of his readers.

"In a short time our whole school literature will be changed; a new spirit will breathe from the pages where our children get their first and most lasting impressions, and it is impossible not to foresee from this a great and thorough revolution in public sentiment and feeling, producing a more homogeneous and public-spirited population, inspiring respect for the common schools as a great hope of a growing and prosperous Commonwealth and reflected in all our industrial, social and educational characteristics."

He repeats his suggestions in favor of teachers' library associations which he had previously made, and emphasizes their importance in fostering the growth of knowledge of methods of teaching and of the history of the schools of the State. That this knowledge was necessary is evident from the fact that while the American Almanac, published in Boston, had some mention of common schools in North Carolina, there was none in either of the two leading almanacs published in the State.

But while there were defects and weaknesses, the report for the year, as a whole, was satisfactory. The reports from the counties, while not complete, were more complete than they had been in any previous year. There were then about 9,000 pupils in academies and about 1,000 in colleges. The male colleges numbered 5, the female 9, the academies about 300, and the common schools about 3,500. The whole number of counties was 85; the whole number of districts in 75 counties reporting was 2,995; the whole number of schools taught in 71 counties, 1,905; whole number of children in 70 counties, 189,562; whole number attending schools in 73 counties, 112,632, and those in counties not reporting would have probably swelled the number to 130,000. The number of teachers licensed in 57 counties was 1,369; the average length of the school term was about four months; the salaries ranged from $10 to $13 in Watauga County, and $11 to $15 in Madison, to from $25 to $40 in Carteret and New Hanover. According to the observations of the superintendent, "In all essential points the common-school system of North Carolina has undergone an entire and quiet revolution in the last three years." Reports had improved, salaries had improved, and "our social condition more than that of apparently better favored regions has helped to foster this system of schools, and our masses, nearly all of them being of the middle class, are becoming molded into a homogeneous population, intelligent, eminently republican, sober, calculating, moral and conservative."

The report of the superintendent for 1856, coming within less than a year after that for 1855, is more like a special report. In this report the chief matters discussed are the publication of the school journal and the organization of a State Teachers' Association. These subjects are treated at length later. In his annual letter to the county superintendents, whose duty it was to examine teachers, he notes the progress that had been made in the teachers in the last five years. Then there were perhaps two hundred teachers who held certificates of character and qualifications from examining committees, and these were for an indefinite period. In 1856 there were 2,000 such teachers, all under the spur of annual examinations—

"and of these a considerable proportion are continually improving, while some of the old incorrigible nuisances are each year cut off and their connection with our educational system severed forever. These are great facts; they show that while we are getting rid of bad material we are supplying its place with that which is better, while of those who still continue to teach an important number are improving. . . . It is right to be predisposed in favor of those who have stood high heretofore; but ever remember that while the teacher may depreciate in morals and in intelligence, and thus lose his relative position, he may also lose it by the increasing knowledge of the community. A high standard of qualification five years ago is not a high standard now; and, therefore, let me urge on you the importance of granting no certificates without actual examinations. These examinations are not a thorough test, but they are a spur to candidates, and cause many of them to be constantly endeavoring to improve, and that is the great point."

Dr. Wiley urges repeatedly that mental qualifications should never be substituted for "unimpeachable integrity and moral character."

The fifth annual report was for the year 1857-'58, but was made to the Assembly of 1858-'59. It notes satisfactory progress throughout the whole of the State, but there were still many things that needed attention and improvement. The superintendent notes that at that time the number of schools taught in any one year was not in itself an indication of increasing or failing energies in the system, for many districts preferred to have a long term once in two years than a short term each year. A considerable number of schoolhouses had been closed for temporary reasons—some for repairs, others to be rebuilt or removed to a more convenient location. "Notwithstanding the hardness of the times, there is quite a spirit of improvement of this kind, and in some places the schools have been stopped that the districts may be laid off on a better plan." The estimated value of school houses and lots was $350,000. The sum expended in the 76 counties reporting was $226,238.49; the sum expended in the whole State was probably $253,000. The sum left over in the hands of chairmen in 76 counties was $157,519.60, or perhaps $175,000 for the whole State. The number of certificates to teach granted and reported was 2,256, which included 214 women teachers or more. There were perhaps not fifty who taught without license, while a few years before not one in forty had been licensed. At least three-fourths of all the teachers taught grammar and geography, while fifteen years before this time these subjects were not taught in one-fifth of the schools. The average length of the school was four months; the average attendance was 40 pupils, and the average salary about $24 per month, varying in different locations and at different seasons from $15 to $40. The average amount expended on each pupil was $1.66 2-3, while the average cost to each parent for all the expenditures of the common schools was about 66 2-3 cents per annum. The entire cost of administering the school fund, including expenses of every sort other than teachers' salaries, was less than $13,000. This meant that about 95 per cent. of the entire fund was paid to teachers.

For the year ending with September, 1857, the whole number of districts reported was 3,190, of which 2,516 were taught. The number of male children in these counties between 5 and 21 was reported as 91,938, the females 81,134; the boys attending school were 55,477; the girls 42,167.

The chairman of the board of county superintendents was now becoming of more importance and value than he had been in the past. He was now something more than an honest man and a good financier.

"These officers and the committees of examination manifest a much more enlightened sense of the spirit of their obligations, and very generally the regulations for the improvement of teachers and for enhancing the usefulness of chairman, are better understood and better appreciated. The capacity of the system for great and continued improvement is settled beyond dispute, the good already done is known and more properly estimated. Insufficient local officers are now much less likely to escape an awakened public attention, and a healthy and vigorous public opinion is bringing to light the defalcations and abuses of those who once freely speculated on the public funds. . . . There are now, comparatively speaking, no frontiers, no colonies, no obscure territories in which such persons can take refuge and be a law unto themselves."

These sentences indicate practices which had grown up in many quarters. Chairmen were required to give bond for the money passing through their hands, but in many counties they were allowed to hold over from year to year without renewing their bonds, which not only produced vexatious lawsuits, but in some cases actual loss to the schools. The legislature finally declared that the bond of a chairman was good against him and his sureties as long as he continued in office under the bond and until he settled his accounts with his successor, or gave a new bond. They were also required to renew the bond annually.

Dr. Wiley reviews the prospect of the future with hope and encouragement:

"A united people, a healthy and vigorous public sentiment, a vast educational combination, animated with one impulse and guided by fixed, uniform and general principles, and all operating to one end, the improvement of our common schools. . . . Every unimproving and unimprovable teacher in the State will be cut off after one year's trial; and none will be licensed for one year without proving a good moral character and showing respectable mental attainments. The entire corps of teachers will be organized into disciplined bodies, the members losing their isolation and feeling themselves to be parts of a great system, learning ideas from each other, zealous of the reputation of their order, and feeling that they are acting in the light of a public opinion from whose scrutiny they can not escape."

A plan for a series of district normal schools was proposed, which were to be inexpensive and were intended primarily for female teachers.

Th success of the common-school system of North Carolina had been so marked that it was attracting general attention abroad:

"Three of the most distinguished States of the South, and long considered our superiors in many things, are not ashamed to look to us for light and information on this important subject. Virginia, South Carolina and Georgia are disposed to copy our example; many leading citizens in each of these noble Commonwealths, openly acknowledge our superiority in educational facilities and point to our course as worthy of imitation. . . . Perhaps no State in the South has so respectable an educational system as North Carolina; and surely this is saying much for a State which was once behind all her sisters."

It was estimated that the schools brought into the State not less than $250,000 annually. This was due largely to the prominent position which the University of North Carolina then occupied among Southern colleges. During the year 1858-'59, out of 456 students in the institution 39 were from Tennessee; Louisiana had 28; Mississippi, 26; Alabama, 21; South Carolina, 15; Texas, 15; Georgia, 14; Virginia, 8; Kentucky, 4; Florida, 4; Arkansas, 2; Iowa, 1; New York, 1.

A matter which gave the school authorities much trouble was the distribution of the school fund. It produced hardship in the large districts if the same amount was given to each, and in the small ones if the division was made on the basis of numbers. The solution arrived at was that the districts should be so arranged that there should be only one school in each, and where it was necessary to have a very small district this was considered as having an average number of children. Wherever this plan was adopted it gave satisfaction and put an end to disputes. Another matter that gave considerable dissatisfaction, but which continued to be the plan of administration, was the distribution of the school fund on the basis of Federal rather than white population.

The report for 1858 indicates that the progress of the schools as a whole was favorable. It opens, however, with the characteristic and necessary complaint that some of the counties were slow in making their returns, and that therefore the reports were necessarily imperfect. There was in this, as in earlier reports, a manifest and laborious effort to figure ignorance out of existence. Still, the progress of the schools was very favorable.' The sums reported as in the hands of chairmen of 71 counties (out of 85) during the year was $371,320.07; the disbursements were $221,132.50, leaving a balance on hand of $152,173.87, a part of which was to be paid out soon for schools still in session. The number of districts reported was 3,237; number of schools taught, 2,602; boys reported, 82,642; in school, 57,700; girls reported, 74,582; in school, 44,587;* average length of school term, 3.7 months; average salary, $23.62; teachers licensed, 1,994, of whom 205 were women. The hopeful manifestations of progress were an evidently increasing sense of responsibility on the part of subordinate officers; more energetic and enlightened action on the part of boards of county superintendents; the general, gradual, but certain, elevation of the standard of teachers' qualifi-

*Corrected returns show that the whole number of boys and girls taught in 1858 was 115,855.

cations; obvious influence for good among all classes and in various places, caused by unceasing efforts to disseminate useful information and statistics; the successful formation of associations intended to combine the exertions of the friends of all classes of general education; the general disapparance of prejudice and the difficulties arising from prejudice and ignorance, and an increasing animation and hopefulness on the part of friends in every part of the State.

Chairmen of boards of county superintendents took more pains, as a general rule, and acted more on system, and there was less opportunity for malfeasance in office, and temptation to careless handling of money was cut off; maps of the counties and of the districts were prepared, and more visits were made to the schools.

A new school register was printed and sent out in course of the year. "Its advantages as a history of our schools are obvious, while it will be a material aid to the teacher in preserving order and in stimulating the industry of the pupils, who will not fail to remember that their actions and progress are being recorded."

The idea of school libraries was emphasized and a proposition made to erect teachers' halls in each county. The want of convenient and comfortable places of meeting had been a drawback on the usefulness of the examining committees.

"These halls would in time be filled with libraries for the use of teachers and common school officers, and they would furnish tempting inducements for the formation of teachers' associations. They would furnish points of contact and intercommunication for the teachers of each county, thus tending to destroy that isolation and indifference to the opinion of others so much in the way of their improvement and so repressive of a proper public spirit and interest in their calling; and here also the friends of the cause could and would have opportunities of meeting the teachers and officers, and would, from time to time, have courses of lectures delivered for their especial benefit. These halls and their purposes would be standing appeals to the patriotic, the benevolent, and public-spirited—and natives of the county, prospering in business in distant States and countries, Members of Congress, and public bodies would make donations of books, documents, maps, reports, periodicals, and minerals. They would be external signs of the progress of a moral cause, improving the senses and exciting the patriotic pride and generous emulation—considerations not to be neglected by the friends of common schools. The State would also doubtless contribute public documents, and these halls would in time become, next to the churches and court houses, the most useful and indispensable public buildings of the several counties."

As to the schools in general, Dr. Wiley is very modest:

"The common schools of the State make little show in the world. The houses are generally plain, the teachers modest and unpretending, and a vast majority of the officers are the hard-working and simple-minded yeomanry of the country. Even the chief executive head of the system has no office in the capitol, and there is not connected with any of the operations of the schools any of those pompous externals which command the respect and admiration of the vulgar-minded. But like every great cause, this one is striking its roots into the hearts and minds of the masses of the common people, and the philosopher can easily see that here is the nursery of power and dominion."

The reports for 1859 and 1860 were both made to the assembly of 1860-61, although printed and published separately. They begin with the usual complaint at the vice of tardiness which had characterized the local school officers from the beginning; but notwithstanding such defects, the progress of the schools was satisfactory. Returns had been made by 81 of the counties, but many of them were defective in one respect or another. The labor of educating the local officials up to the knowledge of the importance of full, accurate, and early returns was great. In the leading facts the reports for 1859 and 1860 differed only in degree, not in kind, from those for other years. Several of the counties were redistricted by actual surveys and in some cases the schools had been closed temporarily. The disposition to build new and better houses was on the increase. The salaries reached the maximum of the ante-bellum period in 1859, being $28 on an average, but fell in 1860 to $26. The receipts of school money was $379,842.64 1-4 in 1859 and the disbursements $235,410.57 1-2, against $408,566.32 received and $255,641.12 disbursed in 1860. As has been stated already, the sums reported as remaining in hand were liable to be paid out in part for schools in operation at the time of the report but not yet finished. A new phase of the report appears in 1859 for the first time with the reports from the various counties of the amount of school taxes collected during the year. This was done in accord with an act passed in 1858-59. Imperfect reports for the year ending September, 1859, show that in 59 counties $73,160 had been collected. The largest amount collected in any one county was $3,905.04 in Guilford; Mecklenburg came next with $3,449.98. In 1860 the amount in 65 counties was $75,929.88, making an average of $1,168.02 to the county. This average would have made for the State taxes amounting to $100,449.72. The districts as reported in 1859 were 3,373; in 1860, 3,488; schools taught, 1859, 2,758; in 1860, 2,854; boys reported 93,494; in school, 61,496; girls reported in 1859, 86,878; in 1859, 93,494; in school, 61,496; boys reported in 1860 in school, 47,442; girls reported in 1860, 88,037; in school, 45,558; teachers licensed, 1859, 1,843; women, 156; teachers licensed in 1860, 2,164; women, 315. There was in these, as in former reports, a strenuous effort to figure ignorance out of the State, with the same lack of success. It was always impossible to get Dr. Wiley's actual figures up to his estimates.*

Nearly all of the teachers were compelled to undergo annual examinations, and these were becoming more rigid from year to year. The number of women teachers was increasing, and there was not as much disparity between their wages and those of men as in other States.

"Nor should there be, for females make much the best teachers of primary schools, and it is sincerely to be hoped that the pecuniary inducements to engage them in the most honorable calling of teaching, as well as the great need of their services and the good to be accomplished by them, will soon enlist a much larger number in this cause. At present the proportion of female teachers is not greater than one in twelve of the whole number, and it ought to be at least one-half."

There is less emphasis in these later reports on the series of North Carolina readers and on the North Carolina edition of Mitchell's Geography, the probable reason being that these had been introduced already and had secured a firm foothold. But the subject of a uniformity of text-books is discussed with considerable fullness in the report for 1859. Dr. Wiley confessed that "the nuisance arising from the diversity and bad character of text-books is yet far from being removed," but still he argued against putting absolute power over this matter into the hands of the school authorities or in those of the superintendent. This subject makes him forget his true position and leads him off into a discussion of the great political topic of the day and its relations to the education of the ruling race, which is renewed in even more vigorous language in the report for 1860.

In his eighth letter of suggestions and instructions the

*According to the census of 1860 the total school tax of North Carolina for the year ending June 1, 1860, was $94,731 and the total school attendance, 116,567.

superintendent discusses the growing need of a graded system, and in 1859 the educational association appointed a committee to investigate the matter. The disadvantage of the system in use lay in the fact that it was horizontal, furnishing but one grade of education for all, and thus meeting only the demand for an elementary education.

"This first and chief necessity being overcome, we now want schools that will enable all classes to obtain such a practical or business education as they may desire.... If we had remained without common schools, we never would have needed a general system of graded schools, all kinds of education remaining at a very low point. But by furnishing the elements of knowledge to all, a great many naturally want more light; and therefore, if we would have graded schools to suit all, we must build on the common school system, and never for a moment think of abolishing it. To abolish it is to take away all foundation for graded schools, or for any general system. It has now laid a broad and durable basis for graded schools; and let us build all our hopes of improvement on this.... The first and chief point, then, to which I would direct your attention in this letter is this, to wit: To keep before you the fact that graded schools are becoming more and more necessary to supply the primary educational wants of the community. .... Until the popular mind is better prepared for such things it would be unprofitable and very troublesome to undertake, generally, to establish graded schools; and still there are increasing wants which point to such a sysytem as a coming necessity."

He urges, therefore, that at least one thoroughly qualified teacher should be secured for each school, and that no certificate should be granted to "any other class, unless it be to females who will teach summer schools composed of the smaller children."

Of the general success of the system in 1860 he says:

"The educational system of North Carolina is now artracting the favorable attention of the States south, west, and north of us.... All modern statistical publications give us a rank far in advance of the position which we occupied in such works a few years ago; and without referring to numerous other facts equally significant, our moral influence may be illustrated by the fact that the superintendent of common schools was pressingly invited to visit, free of expense, the legislature of the most powerful State south of us [Georgia], to aid in preparing a system of public instruction similar to ours. He receives constant inquiries from abroad in regard to our plan; and beyond all doubt our schools, including those of all grades, are now the greatest temporal interest of the State.... North Carolina has the start of all her Southern sisters in educational matters.... If, then, she is true to herself, and justly comprehends the plain logic of the facts of her situation, she will now.... prudently and courageously advance in the direction which leads alike to safety, to peace, and to prosperity .... Such action is not merely important as likely to lead to future greatness; it is also a defensive and imperative necessity of the present. If the Union remains, no one will deny the importance, to our peace as well as honor, of having a strong and prosperous State, able to command the respect of her confederates; if the Union is dissolved, then North Carolina is our only country for the present, and our present security and future hopes will depend on her power to stand alone or honorably to compete with rivals in a new confederacy."

In 1860-61 the Assembly passed an act modifying the method of choosing district committeemen, by which, while the election was put into the hands of the county superintendents, the people were given the power by means of petition to dictate the parties to be elected. Provisions were renewed by which copies of the North Carolina Educational Journal were to be sent to all school officers and paid for out of the school fund. The State Teachers' Association was chartered and given a small appropriation, and a plan for a teachers' or normal school was unanimously recommended by this association in November, 1860. The main features of this proposed plan were "that it springs as a natural, upward growth from the common school system, and is not a foreign idea ingrafted on it; it will not be a burden to the State or literary fund; it allows the people of the several counties to act on their own discretion when ready to act: it does not require all the counties to act together, but permits such as are ready for it to adopt the plan, others to follow when they choose."

This scheme had two defects. It was permissive, and it expected good schools at an insignificant outlay of money. It was bitterly attacked in the newspapers, and it was claimed that at each session of the legislature this or some similar scheme was gotten up to "throw dust into the eyes of the members' and get the superintendent re-elected. It was said that $10,000 had been wasted on one normal school already. The proposed scheme came to naught. This was not an unusual attack, for the success the system had attained under great difficulties had not saved it; but as an offset we may quote the reports from Granville county that the healthfulness of the system was being manifest in the building of new school houses of brick and stone, and from Chowan county, where the system was making itself felt in more intelligent jurors.

The Civil War and the End of the Old Regime.

Having traced the history of the common schools in North Carolina from the earliest times down to the beginning of the civil war, we must now trace their struggle for bare existence through that momentous epoch. In the meantime it may be desirable to review their condition in 1860-61, in order to see the powers at their command to meet the strain that was now to be put upon them. This cannot be done better than in the language of Dr. Wiley himself:

"The first superintendent went into office in January, 1852 [1853], and nine years afterwards, to wit, in January, 1861, the system of common schools was an established interest, respected and cherished by all parties and classes. It had fought its way against strong antagonisms, it had cleared its path of formidable obstructions, and now its character and capabilities were understood and appreciated and it had arrived at that point whence more rapid advancement and higher development were reasonable expectations. The machinery committed to subordinate officials was worked smoothly and efficiently by men trained to their duties. The number of local officers was over 10,000, and the great majority of these had become familiar with the management of the system, understood its laws, and were in sympathy with each other and with their head; public opinion had been enlightened by all possible means, and the whole educational force of the State had been welded together. The cause of education in all departments had made rapid progress, and North Carolina was acknowledged to be the banner State of the South, not only for her common schools, but in academic and collegiate progress....

"Our progress excited attention and interest in every part of the Union. The superintendent was applied to from various Southern States for copies of our common-school laws, and for suggestions and plans, and was invited to visit the legislature of Georgia, with offers of expenses, and, being unable to go, was asked for an essay, which the chairman of one of the committees on education in that body incorporated into an elaborate report to it. The means for the regular and systematic improvement of teachers had been carefully matured, and were working their accomplishment; the body of teachers, as a whole, had been completely revolutionized, and the superintend-

ESTEY HALL—SHAW UNIVERSITY, RALEIGH, N. C.

ent's persistent efforts had infused into it a large element, constantly increasing, of refining and elevating female influence.

"The State Educational Association, and the appliances for its usefulness, and especially its journal, had been firmly established at the cost of much exertion, and of considerable pecuniary outlay....

"The continued efforts of the superintendent were also ripening into systematic efforts to save and make available that vast, long-neglected, and somewhat mythical resource of the literary board called the swamp lands; and through this means a beginning was made to ascertain the location, titles, and qualities of these, and to protect them from squatters and timber getters. In the meantime all legislation on the subject of education of every kind and on the literary fund had become systematic. Through the influence of the superintendent the policy of making loans of the funds to individuals and to private institutions was discontinued, and for important reasons, the speaker of the two houses of the legislature, without solicitation from the superintendent, had adopted the habit of consulting him about the committees on education, * and these committees sat jointly, inviting the superintendent to attend as a consulting or corresponding member, and every bill relative to education in any of its branches, and to the school fund or school taxes, was submitted to him.

"The State Educational Association was ramifying into county societies, the superintendent was organizing, without public aid, teachers' institutes, and under his influence county superintendents were visiting their districts, in some instances making re-surveys of their counties, and were making out maps for their use and that of the superintendent. . . .

"Heretofore the system, in machinery, was horizontal,

*Dr. Wiley virtually dictated these committees.

though often it cropped upward by voluntary effort to higher developments. The superintendent had pointed out its availabilities in this respect, and he had legislative provision made to enable parties wishing higher grades to secure them in a way just to all. One or several individuals, for instance, contributing means equal to or greater than the fund coming to the district, were authorized to make bargains with the school committee whereby these parties could select the teacher from among those regularly licensed, and manage the school, always in a way not to prejudice the rights of any of the children. This was in accordance with the genius of common schools—people whose children were to receive only an English education were not taxed to promote special studies useful only to a class, and thos desiring to pursue such studies could do so economically and under the moral restraints of home, through the working of the common schools. Arrangements of this kind were becoming common, there were a number of admirable schools of the kind in the State, and cases could be mentioned of ladies thus highly educated and of men afterwards distinguished who were thus prepared for college.

"But a different machinery was needed in the cities and larger towns paying heavy sums of school taxes, and the beginning of the late war found the superintendent just preparing to launch a carefully matured system of graded schools." . . .

To this review may be added the following statistics for 1840 and 1860, taken from Governor Ellis's message to the General Assembly of 1860-'61.

	1840.	1860.
Number of male colleges	3	6
Number of female colleges	1	13
Number of academies and select schools	141	350
Number of primary schools	632	4,000
Total	777	4,369
Number of students in colleges	158	900
Number of students, female colleges	125	1,500
Number of students in academies and select schools	4,398	15,000
Number of students in primary schools	14,000	160,000
Total	18,681	177,400

The movement of North Carolina toward the cause of secession was slow and deliberate. The State legislature of 1860-'61 had refused at first to consider the question; then provision was made for calling a convention. This was defeated by popular vote in February, 1861. Then all the surrounding States seceded, and President Lincoln made his call on her for troops. It was not until then that the secession sentiment became predominant. The State seceded May 20, 1861. There was then danger that the people, having been slow and deliberate in making up their minds to enter the Confederacy, would now, with that fixed purpose before them, sacrifice all other interests of the war. It became obvious to a calm observer that there was danger of uprooting State institutions, and with them those ideas of local self-government and independence which are necessary for freedom.

These new perils to the school system, just now coming to maturity, "filled the superintendent with unspeakable concern, and the anxiety lest the result of years of toil and prayer should be suddenly blasted in the very dawn of triumph will never be known on earth outside of his own mind and heart. But his duty was to stand by his trust, to continue at his post, and there to serve his Divine Master and his generation."

It was evident that efforts would be made to exploit the school fund for war purposes, and against this effort Dr. Wiley tried to fortify himself. On May 4, 1861, he addressed a circular to the county superintendents, in which he recited the necessity the State was under to borrow money for war needs; that some persons, without due reflection, might propose to take the proceeds of the common school fund. This action would create a panic and produce the impression that the people of the State were not patriotic enough to pay a moderate tax for war purposes. He was anxious to aid the State and at the same time to save the school fund. To do this he proposed that the unexpended balances of the school fund which remained over in the various counties from year to year should be invested in State bonds taken at par. This investment would amount to something like the interest on a loan of a million of dollars.

"This would enhance our sense of our own resources, and would be a most useful and most gratifying achievement.... Of course the market value of State bonds is now below par, but if we secure our independence and the State does not repudiate, these bonds will soon be valuable, and can be converted into cash when needed. If we are subjected or the State repudiates her bonds we will be so hopelessly ruined that it will make little difference how our county funds are invested. By such an investment the counties will get interest on money not now needed, and they may save themselves from a much worse resort."

It does not appear that this suggestion was ever put into operation. In fact, it is not probable that it would have saved, under any circumstances, the fund from the attacks that were made on it.

The first legislature to assemble after the beginning of

the war had to make provisions necessary for carrying it on. It was then that Dr. Wiley feared an attack on the literary fund. Before the meeting of the Legislature he "asked and received permission to attend the meeting of the Governor's Council, at which were matured the first executive recommendations for the impending crisis. The Governor was in feeble health, wasting with consumption and the weight of public cares, and the meeting was at his residence. The superintendent was kindly received and patiently listened to on that memorable occasion, and then and there was fixed a policy which will ever be honorable to the State. It was suggested that the school fund of over $2,000,000 would seem large to some, and a ready means for the prosecution of the war and to save taxation, and that under these plausible pretexts the slumbering opposition to the schools would unite short-sighted friends, and by a temperary suspension aim to destroy them forever. And it was argued that though the fund was indeed a large one, in one sense, it was but an inconsiderable item in the expenses about to be incurred, and that if we were able to engage in hostilities at all we were able to do so without it; that if it was desired to popularize the war it would be most injudicious to begin it by the suspension of a system which was the poor man's life, and which would be so essential to the orphans of the soldiers called to surrender their lives for the common good; and that now when it was aimed to vindicate Southern civilization before the world it would surely be an unwise step to begin by the voluntary destruction of an efficient system of popular instruction; that no people could or would be free who were unable or unwilling to educate their children. True independence would be based on moral character and on popular intelligence and industrial development, and thus in the momentous struggle about to begin it would impart confidence to the public mind to see the State enter the contest with the apparent assurance that her interior interests were not endangered by her course; that war under any circuhstances was destructive for the time, and that the pending contest might be long and exhausting; and that it was the part of wisdom and patriotism so to act that the end should find the fewest possible desolations to be reoaired, and no permanent weakening of the elements of social elevation. These considerations prevailed, and the executive power of the State, represented by the Governor and his Council, entered into an informal but solemn agreement with the Superintendent of common schools to oppose, with him, all attempts to seize the fund for war purposes, or to suspend the schools, and the compact was faithfully observed by Governor Ellis and his three (two) successors during the war, and by their constitutional advisers."

The North Carolina Educational Association also added its pleadings for the integrity of the school fund, and in a memorial to the State convention in November, 1861, asked that, "by an amendment to the constitution the proceeds of the common school fund be sacredly and permanently secured to their original purpose." The memorial recites that while—

"The proceeds of the school fund would be barely sufficient to equip and keep in the field for military operations about 100 men, as now applied they give life to some 4,000 schools and are furnishing an elementary education to over 150,000 children. This much they now directly accomplish, and their certain tendency is to widen and deepen among the masses the spirit of education, and thus to sustain that vast superstructure of classical schools, seminaries, and colleges which constitutes the present glory of North Carolina and the great hope of the future of the State."

It was well that Dr. Wiley and the educational association had thus prepared themselves against the day of attack, for it came soon after the Legislature met.* The measure was introduced into the Senate and was backed by parties of the highest standing. The Superintendent in the meantime had sent circulars to the school boards of the counties, apprising them of and warning them against the effort. These local school officers were usually men of position and influence in their respective communities, and their answers were generally in favor of the school fund. Governor John M. Morehead was then a member of the State Senate, and led the defense of the fund. The attempt was defeated, but it reappeared again and again in new forms and in both branches. It was protracted and strong, and closed only with the adjournment. With the end of this legislature the fight was practically won. Succeeding Governors followed in the steps of Governor Ellis, and succeedeing legislatures respected the action of the earlier body.*

The distribution of funds to the schools during the war period was about as follows: In May, 1861, the local school authorities were assured that there would be no permanent falling off in the school fund, but during this year only one-half of the dividend due was paid out, and this was not made payable until April 1, 1862. This delay was due to the great and inevitable pressure brought to bear upon the

†The first extra session of the assembly met May 1, 1861, and adjourned May 13 until June 25. In the meantime an ordinance of the State convention changed the date of reassembling. The second extra session begon August 15, 1861. and adjourned September 23. 1861. On September the 9th Mr. Chandler introduced a bill "to provent the collection of tax for common-schools purposes during the war." (Senate J., 36, 104.) This act became a law on September 21. (Laws of 1861, 2d extra, ch. 31.) It repealed that section of the code which required the county courts to levy and collect a tax for school purposes, but provided that the act was not to apply "to those counties where the justices, a majority being present, shall elect to lay such rax."

*From the account prepared by Dr. Wiley and printed in the North Carolina Educational Journal, 1881-1883. The Journals of the legislature of 1861 fail to mention this fight.

treasury at the outbreak of the war and under which the literary fund, like the school fund of 1754, was temporarily diverted. This pressure was finally relieved. In October, 1862, $100,000 was distributed. This was the largest semi-annual dividend ever paid, but it was intended to cover a dividend and a half formerly withheld.

This irregularity brought down wrath upon the head of the system. Jonathan Worth, of Randolph County, one of the earliest and most steadfast friends of the schools, and afterwards Governor, writes to Dr. Wiley under date of June 6, 1862:

"It seems to be the pleasure of the literary board to assume legislative power over the literary fund and to disregard the will of the Legislature and of the convention. Neither the board nor the treasurer, even with your assent, has any right to withhold or direct the fund as they have been doing. They had no right to declare a dividend last fall and postpone its payment till this spring. It was a legislative usurpation, and I think a reprehensible usurpation, after the repeated refusals of the General Assembly to allow any encroachment on this fund. I believe fhe convention also refused to interefere with it. If the board had previously made illegitimate dividends, so that there was no money in the treasurer's hands, then they made dividends they ought not to have made and they were culpably negligent of the treasurer's accounts. The uncertainty which their illegal action occasions is about as pernicious to the school system as would be a diversion of the income of the fund to the ordinary or war expenses of the State by an act of the General Assembly."

From this time on, so far as I have been able to learn, this fund was paid regularly. But the counties were not always as faithful to their educational trust as was the State. As has been said, a law of 1861 released them from the requirement to levy taxes to support the schools. Some counties, as Edgecombe in 1862, and Mecklenburg, voted to use the school money for war purposes. Others, as Granville, refused to levy taxes for the support of schools, and said that they must stop until the war was over. Others seem to have let them fall into abeyance and die. They did not think their death even a mater of sufficient importance to be reported to the Superintendent. But such cases were the exception, not the rule.

the rule.

In his ninth annual report, for 1861-'62 (Doc, 9. sess. 1862-'63), Dr. Wiley discusses the situation as it then appeared.

The legislature of 1860-'61 (chap. 19) changed the school year to make it more convenient and uniform. The county chairmen, under the new law, were required to report on or before the third Monday in April, at the end of the school term instead of the middle. The labor of adjustment to the new requirements and to pressure of war made these reports more irregular than usual, but official reports were received from 65 counties. The receipts reported on 60 counties, including balances, was $220,312.99; disbursements, $117,924.50; on hand, $104,336.46. The number of children reported in 46 counties was, boys, 57,157; girls, 54,890; sex not stated, 6,755; total, 118,802. The number of districts in 58 counties was 2,621; the children attending school in 59 counties, 52,018, or 29,122 boys, 22,838 girls, and 58 sex not given; number of licenses granted and reported, 1,233—962 to men, 271 to to women; schools reported, 1,556; average length of schools, 2.8 months.

The Superintendent felt authorized to say that more children were taught in the counties officially heard from than were actually reported, that this discrepancy was due to the nature of the schools, and that as many as 60,000 children had been in school in the State.

"Let it be borne in mind, in connection with these facts, that our common school system had to encounter during the past year not only the difficulties naturally incident to revolution and war, but trials which, in times of peace, would greatly impair the energies of any enterprise. The novelty and the all-absorbing interest of the tremendous struggle in which our country is engaged necessarily distracted the minds of all classes of the community, and until we became used to revolution in our political relations and to a state of war a great many would naturally feel indisposed to devote much attention to the usual avocations of life. There were also some who supposed that our contest for independence would be of brief duration, and that all the agencies of society could be suspended during the struggle, without injury, and others, still more short-sighted, seemed to think that a war for political, commercial, social, and intellectual independence could be waged with better results by arresting or destroying all those springs of life on which natural wealth and greatness are founded."

Another difficulty was that of procuring text-books. This became so pronounced that the writing and publication of text-books grew into an important business interest in the Confederate States.

"The cheerful radiance of letters has not been for a moment extinguished even during the deepest gloom and the most terrible throes of this great crisis; and in the midst of shock with which the whole continent trembles, our public schools gave birth to an enterprise worth more to the independence and character of the South than all the money ever expended on them."

The method of procedure in the matter of schoolbooks was a question of some delicacy. Some thought that the publication of books ought to be encouraged by a bounty from the State; others that there should be a tribunal to decide on the manuscript to be published; and nearly all that there should be a protctive tariff in favor of local or State talent. The State Educational Association finally determind that 'the whole educational influence of North Carolina could be pledged to sustain, when worthy, home publications in preference to any other, whatever might be the difference in price or mechanical execution."

The Superintendent was embrassed as to the proper action to be pursued by himself on the publication of a work.

"But after careful consideration I adopted the plan of not recommending any home series of works for exclusive use, but of indorsing all that I deemed worthy of public confidence and patronage.. . . . My indorsement of a book as Superintendent of common schools simply brings it to the notice of all our school authorities and warrants them in introducing it without fear into the common schools, while the recommendation, not being special and exclusive, is not in the way of rival claimants of public favor."

The report for 1863 resumes the review:

"The present generation does not need to be told that it was hard to keep up a general educational system in any part of the Confederate States of America during the year 1863. . . . . and it is, therefore, a subject of devout gratitude to me to be able to announce that our common schools still live and are still full of glorious promise. Through all this dark night of storm their cheerful radiance has been seen on every hill and in every valley of our dear old State; and while the whole continent reels with the shock of terrible and ruthless war, covering the face of nature with ruin and desolation, there are here scattered through the wilderness hundreds of humming hives, where thousands of youthful minds are busily learning those peaceful arts which, under the blessing of God, are to preserve our civilization and to aid in perpetuating the liberty and independence for which this generation is manfully contending. This prospect more than repays all the toils, anxieties, and vigils of those to whose keeping is committed the great moral trust; and if the labors, denials, and responsibilities of those who nurse our educational system are unnoticed in this stirring and martial age, they have in their own hearts a consolation infintely more valuable than any reward the world can confer."

Reports had been received during 1863 from about 60 counties, but these were inexact and ununiform. The whole number of districts as reported in 47 counties was 2,149; the number of schools taught in 50 counties was 1,076; teachers licensed in 44 counties, 872, of whom 348 were women; children attending school in 50 counties, boys, 18,977; girls, 16,518; total, 35,495; average length of school year, three months; average salary per month, $25; the receipts of money in 54 counties was $240,685.38; the disbursements, $81,588.56, not including money then on hand for schools not finished. There had been an increasing difficulty in securing a supply of teachers; as the war went on the difficulty became greater, for school-teachers were not exempt from conscription in North Carolina (as they were in Georgia), but "the increasing number of female teachers not only gives promise of an ultimate supply of laborers for all our schools, but it is a sure augury of their greater efficiency."

The depreciation of the currency had made it impossible to employ teachers in some districts with the funds due them; some waited until the funds accumulated; in others the schools were taught, but the drafts held back with the hope of obtaining funds of a higher market value. In some it was found impossible to get active committees, for the reason that "nearly every man of that useful class, who is willing to assume, without remuneration, responsibilities in behalf of popular education and improvement, is gone to the army."

It was estimated that during this year the schools were attended by 50,000 children. Says Dr. Wiley:

"The future historian of this stirring age will not fail to find evidences of the moral energy which this fact implies;

for he will see that these schools had to be chiefly supplied with books written and printed in the State after the commencement of the revolution and in face of incredible difficulties, that they were all regularly visited by a State Journal of Education at a time when periodical literature was at a low ebb, and that educational associations still held their meetings, and still discussed plans for popular improvement."

Dr. Wiley then proceeds to point out the weakness of the school system as it stood and to suggest a remedy. The great defect of the system was that it was a horizontal one, "furnishing one kind of education for children of all ages and of every degree of advancement." As the school system elevated the standard of popular intelligence, there was an increasing necessity for higher ones. In this report (1863) and in a circular letter addressed to the authorities and people of North Carolina this year it was proposed to organize a series of graded or high schools in connection with the common schools of the State," the first and immediate purpose being to furnish facilities for a thorough business education to young men disabled in the army and to the children of indigent soldiers, while a second and important object will be to promote the general interests of the people of the State." The plan was now proposed that "in addition to the annual distribution from the literary fund for common school purposes, an additional amount should be appropriated to such counties as should raise a like or greater sum by taxes—the amount to be employed in supporting graded or higher schools for the education of disabled soldiers and the indigent children of those who have entered the army for teachers and for other useful and honarble occupations." To advance this purpose agents were appointed in each county to agitate for and advance the interests of these schools. As a reward these agents were to have exemption from service in the home guards, and they were to strive to secure donations for a county fund, to secure buildings in a convenient and healthy locality, and to enlist the sympathy and interest of the county authorites and of the public.

The subject of graded schools had been discussed by the North Carolina Educational Association in 1859, and a commmittee had been appointed on the matter. A bill for the creation of graded schools was introduced in the legislature of 1863, by William S. Harris, of Cabarrus. It had been approved by the literary board and was warmly pressed by the Governor. It passed the House, but not before being crippled by an amendment to the effect that 20 per cent of the fund be given to all the counties, and that the local authorites be left to decide the question of graded schools for themselves, this amendment being due to the false idea that 20 per cent of the whole school fund was to be set aside and given to such counties ar organized graded schools. The bill in its amended form passed the House and was sent to the Senate. It was reported back favorably from the committee, but was tabled for lack of time. This was the end of the efforts in the session of 1863.

An act to grade the common schools was passed December 23, 1864. It provided that the president and directors of the literary fund should not "for any purpose whatever, except the want of income, diminish the usual semi-annual appropriations to what are now known as the common schools of the State, and these appropriatons, with the county taxes, levied under existing laws for school purposes, shall be applied as heretofore. But when the income of the literary fund shall exceed those appropriations, the president and directors of the fund shall apply such portion of the surplus as they deem proper to the use of graded schools, dividing the amount among all the counties in the same ratio with other distributions." It also provided that when any indivdual made a subscription to a school amounting to more than that derived from the public, he was to be allowed to appoint the teacher and fix the salary and the length of the school term. When the funds allowed a school to be kept more than six months, the surplus was to be put into school buildings, books, and apparatus. When funds would justify, the school was to be divided into the primary and high school departments, and it was the duty of the Superintendent to recommend a course of study for the higher department.

The inherent defects in this law were enough to cause its failure, had there been no other.

The passage in the message of Governor Vance to this Assembly, which deals with education, deserves being put on record, not only for the sentiments expressed, but because of the fact that it is one of the last official expressions of North Carolina on the subject of education while a member of the Southern Confederacy.

Governor Vance said (November 21, 1864):

"The subject of our common schools is one which I beg you will not forget amid the great concerns of the war. The efforts making by the friends of education, with our zealous and indefatigable Superintendent at their head, to prevent the public from losing sight of this great interest, is worthy of our admiration. I earnestly recommend to your consideration the whole subject, and especially the system of graded schools advocated by the Superintendent, for which memorials will be presented by the literary board and the Educational Association of North Carolina. I also suggest that regular teachers be exempted from State miltary duty whilst employed in teaching. Though fully aware of the importance of their vocation, I have not felt at liberty to excuse them under existing laws.* The com-

*The extra session, June 30 to July 7, 1863, exempted "All persons engaged in editing or publishing classical or common-school books and all persons actually engaged in printing or binding such books." (House Journal, p. 44.) By chapter 18 of the laws of this session one editor for each newspaper, the necessary compositors, mail carriers, professors in colleges, and teachers in acadmies were exempted from service in the home guards.

mon schools should surely be kept going at every cost; and if sufficient inducements can be offered to disabled soldiers and educated women to take hold of them, the necessary males should be exempted. . . . It is with pride that I observe the publicaton in our State of various new school books, creditable alike to the authors, and to the public which has demanded them. Our great system of common schools is, after all, our only true and solid foundation for public education and demands your constant and fostering care."

The continued fall of Confederate currency was another cause of trouble. The funding bill which took effect April 1, 1864, put county chairmen in uncertainty whether the school funds in their hands should be thus scaled. They had only a choice between funding in Confederate bonds or further depreciation.* They asked Dr. Wiley for advice. He was himself brought into sore trouble over the depreciation. His salary was not enough "to board a horse," and so he concluded in 1864 to live without it. "Throughout the war I have devoted myself to the schools, and have tried to live on a salary averaging $200 in par funds for four years." When the Board came in the spring of 1865 to pay his $2,000 salary for 1864, they offered it in State coupons and Confederate currency, which at the then rate of depreciation made his salary for 1864 amount to $700 in the curency of 1864.

But notwithstanding all of the storms and stress of the war period, the light of the common schools—now changed to public schools so as to include the primary and graded schools—shone on. And Dr. Wiley stated in a speech before the State Educational Association in 1874, that he was receiving reports from school officers in different parts of the State at the time he heard of the surren-

*On May 28, 1864, county chairmen who had invested in Confederate bonds were authorized by act to sell these bonds and distribute the proceeds among the districts.

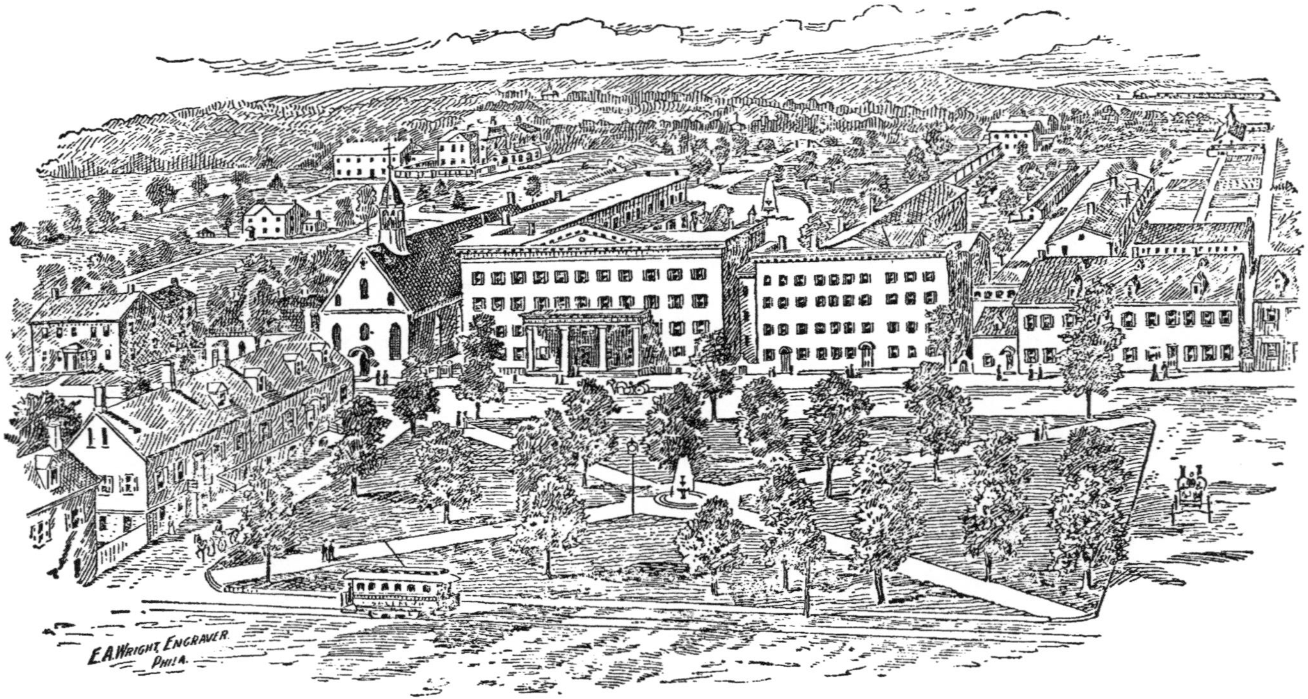

SALEM FEMALE ACADEMY, SALEM, N. C.

der of Gen. Joseph E. Johnston, April 26, 1865* The schools were closed at the end of the war only because of the loss of funds. The disposition has been manifested from time to time to change the form of these investments. It was the general policy to encourage Confederate securites, but it was a difficult matter to change the investment, especially one of a fiduciary character, and as the principal of the literary fund was in what was then the best possible securities—bank and railroad stock—it seemed that there could be no reason for a change.

Early in the war Dr. Wiley had recommended to the Literary Board that they agree to make no change in the investment. The policy was adopted and was followed to the end of the war. One of the results was that while the fund was not invested in Confederate securities, and was thus saved from destruction direct, it was retained as a part of the capital stock of the banks of the State and of Cape Fear, which was invested in these securities, and perished in the wreck of the old banking system after the close of the war. But there still remained to the banks, according to Dr. Wiley, a considerable amount of assets. Further, some of the county chairmen had invested the county school funds in Confederate bonds, which were lost. Besides this, the war made the collection of interest, notes, etc., more difficult. In 1863 the Literary Board complained to the Legislature of the carelessness with which the proofs of indebtedness, certificates of stock, etc., had been kept, and an act to define further the duties of the treasurer of the Literary Fund was passed December 14, 1863, to cover the necessities of the case. Dr. Wiley says also that the financial system of the schools had been conducted on such a simple and admirable basis that little loss or confusion was brought about by the collapse and surrender of the Southern armies and that $10,000 in good

*Report 1874-75, p. 37.

currency would have paid all outstanding debts to teachers, officers and printers. But the sum was wanting, and a part of these debts fell on him in his personal capacity.

Dr. Wiley remained in office after the close of hostilities and until the Constitutional Convention declared by ordinance on October 19, 1865, that all offices of the State in existence on April 26, 1865, should be vacated.* His last report as Superintendent accompanies the message of Governor Worth to the Assembly of 1865-66, is dated January 18, 1866, and forms pages 23-36 of Document 47, session of 1865-66. This report contains no statistics and no definite information on the condition of the schools in the last days of the war, but has some suggestions of value. He reviews the fortunes of the school fund in the war period; the need of money, of men, and of text-books:

"To the lasting honor of North Carolina her public schools survived the terrible shock of cruel war, and the State of the South which furnished most material and the greatest number and the bravest troops to the war did more than all the others for the cause of popular education. The common schools lived and discharged their useful mission through all the gloom and trials of the conflict, and when the last gun was fired, and veteran armies once hostile were meeting and embracing in peace upon our soil, the doors were still open and they numbered their pupils by the scores of thousands. . . . The feeling universal among the people is that the schools must not go down."

Dr. Wiley emphasized the necessity of making some arrangement by which the State would be relieved from the poverty then threatening. Many families had lost their support, many men were crippled for life, and many children were left orphans. The way of escape from pending dangers was thought to be through the school and the training of teachers.

*Ordinances, pp. 25-26.

He suggested the use of the remaining principal of the literary fund for the needs of the hour. He proposed to make distribution to schools and not to counties, so that it would all be used at once and none be allowed to lie idle. He said the board then owned in good stock about $880,-000.. By his scheme $200,000 could be expended per year for four years and there would still be left to the State from $150,000 to $500,000.

In connection with the use of the principal of the literary fund he suggests two plans: (1) "To issue certificates of indebtedness, in sums convenient for general circulation, bearing 1 per cent interest, receivable for all State dues, and to be redeemed in four, five, or six years." (2) "To convert the stocks of the fund into national securities and establish a national bank under the management of the literary board." But neither of these plans was adopted. The disposition of the remaining funds will be considered later.

At another time he addressed a letter to the legislature developing another plan by which he hoped to save the schools from the impending ruin. He says:

"Permit me to impress upon all a consideration which is sometimes overlooked in the discussion of the subject in hand; and that is, that the public schools are by constitutional provision, by law, and by established ideas, a part, and an essential part, of our State machinery, and, indeed, of our civilization. They are, for instance, as much a fixed institution of the State as the University, the lunatic asylum, or the institution for the deaf and dumb and the blind; and for every one to be benefited by either of these latter there are five hundred interested in the former. . . . These schools, be it remembered, do not propose now to be a burden to the State. They ask only permission to use their own capital to the best advantage, a capital which the State has no more moral right to seize than it has to appropriate the property of the University. The assets of the school fund are small compared with what they have been; but they are still of immense importance to a people who appreciate the blessings of education, and who have clear perception of the deplorable consequences that will follow the suspension of the public schools. . . . Let us look this straight in the face if we would appreciate the importance of our resources. To suspend the public schools is to destroy them; and to break them up at such a time is to risk utter demoralization, to add the most melancholy wreck of all the ruins with which we are surrounded. . . . Let it be added, that the abandonment of the cause of education will be regarded in this enlightened age as a certain indication of hopeless bankruptcy or of inferior and retrograding civilization; and either of these conclusions will be fatal to our credit and blast a thousand hopes built on expectations of capital of enterprise from abroad. I believe that there is not one of your body but would regret to see extinguished forever those thousands of lights which have shed a cheerful radiance over every hill and valley of our good old State, from the ocean to the Smoky Mountains. . . . Permit me to say with emphasis that; in my judgment, there is no such necessity, and that the people generally, poor as they know the State to be, do not believe this. To-day the common school system is the most solvent institution of the State. It is both able to pay its own way and aid the State. Why do I say so? It owes no debts, and it has assets that will soon and certainly be worth at least a million of dollars." . . .

Dr. Wiley then proceeds to develop a plan by which the literary board was to be authorized by the State to issue $400,000 in "certificates of indebtedness.' He says:

"If payable in two years, our teachers will be glad to get them, and if not receivable for taxes, they would pass. They would in no sense be bills of credit, for bidden by the Constitution of the United States. They would be the notes of a corporation, like bank notes, but not taxable as such, and based on a fixed capital. If made receivable for taxes, they would be the best relief which the State could afford for the people. They would be put into circulation in every school district, and by this universal diffusion be of infinite service in relieving the monetary pressure. Two hundred thousand dollars thus diffused would be equal in its relief to half a million or a million loaned by banks; and the State must do something to furnish a circulating medium. Here is a plan, simple, practicable, constitutional, and operating impartially as the dews of Heaven, and while it furnishes means everywhere to pay taxes, it keeps in life the most important institution of the State, and enables the people to educate their children."

The plan was warmly indorsed by the Governor, but nothing came of it.

So deep was Dr. Wiley's interest in the subject that he adds by way of postscript:

"I feel bound to warn the friends of the schools against the insidious policy of suspension. Had this policy prevailed when it was urged the first year of the war, the fund would be now all gone; if it prevails now, the fund will never accumulate, but be fritted away on other institutions. I hear there is a plan on foot to turn the poorer classes over to county systems, to be supported by county taxes. This is to degrade a noble State system into a pauper establishment that has heretofore miserably failed in a sister State, and which has been denounced by the best men in it. It would render poor white men worse off in educational facilities than the freemen; and while the world is trying to elevate these latter in the social scale, we would be taking steps to degrade our working classes." *

But the appeal was without effect. The schools went down in the general ruin that followed the beginning of reconstruction.

It now only remains for me to trace briefly the subse-

*Dr. Wiley had been one of the first to advocate the education of the negro.

quent fortune of the remainder of the literary fund and to give the leading facts in the private life of Dr. Wiley.

On July 4, 1868, the State was again reorganized by turning out all of the old officers and putting in others who had been elected under the Constitution of 1868. Under the new regime Rev. S. S. Ashley was made Superintendent of Public Instruction. His first report was made to the General Assembly for the session of 1868-'69, is dated November 10, 1868, and addressed to Provisional Governor Holden. The system was again reconstructed under the law of April 12, 1869, and Ashley continued in office until 1872. His report of November 10, 1868, contained a summary of the character and value of the literary fund which had escaped the wreck of war. The old literary fund was now known as the Educational Fund and owned stock as follows:

Cape Fear Navigation Company, 650 shares, at $50	$ 32,500
Bank of North Carolina, 5,027 shares, $100	502,700
Bank of Cape Fear, 5,444 shares, at $100	544,400
Wilmington and Manchester Railroad, 2,000 shares, at $100	200,000
Wilmington and Weldon Railroad, 4,000, at $100	400,000
Total	$1,679,600

The bank stock, amounting to $1,047,100, was supposed to be nearly or quite worthless, and a thorough examination of the affairs of the banks was recommended. The affairs of the Wilmington and Machester Railroad were undergoing an investigation. The corporation was bankrupt and "the prospect that this stock will be a source of income to the educational fund is not promising." The stock of the Wilmington and Weldon road "will probably become again profitable to the holders." The stock of the Cape

Fear Navigation Company, of which the State owned 650 shares, was at that time "of no pecuniary benefit to the school fund. For twenty-nine years, ending with September, 1863, the annual dividends punctually paid to the State amounted to $1,300." The swamp lands were at that time of no percuniary benefit. The amount derived from the tax on auctioneers and from the entry of vacant lands was about $1,500; the tax from retailers from October, 1867, to October, 1868, was $6,762.50. The fund also owned 6 per cent coupon bonds, dated prior to May 20, 1861, and amounting January 1, 1866, to $20,600. It had been increased by three 6 per cent certificates of indebtedness given by the State as follows:

Certificate dated June 1, 1867	$320,070.50
Certificate dated October 24, 1867	30,273.50
Certificate dated January 16, 1868	32,701.00
Total	$383,045.00

The total income of the school fund from all sources was $32,982.70. This represents all, and more than all, that had been saved from the great fund which had been accumulated and devoted to the common schools.

During the next year (1869) all the railroad stock belonging to the fund was sold to W. T. Walters, of Baltimore. He paid for the 4,000 shares of Wilmington and Weldon Railroad $148,000, and for the 2,000 shares of the Wilmington and Manchester road $10,000. This money was invested in new State bonds, and the Superintendent says:

"The sale of these stocks will realize to the board a permanent paying capital of not less than $450,000. The original investment was $600,000. The loss, therefore, will not exceed $150,000. It is certainly cause for congratulation and encouragement that so large a sum has been rescued from a condition of utter unavailability and made to contribute yearly to the support of public schools."

May 1, 1869, the stock of the Cape Fear Navigation Company was also sold for $3,250, or at the rate of 10 cents on the dollar.

There were, besides these funds, stocks amounting to $1,097,100, which were considered as worthless (Bank of North Carolina, $502,700: Bank of Cape Fear, $544,400, and Roanoke Navigation Company, $50,000). When the Bank of North Carolina went into bankruptcy, an effort was made to protect the interests of the educational fund, and—

"By the advice of able legal counsel proceedings were instituted against the assignee in bankruptcy of the Bank of North Carolina to establish the right of the Board of Education to prove their stock in said bank as a debt against its assets in bankruptcy. The matter was argued before Chief Justice Chase at the late June term of the Circuit Court of the United States for this district, and the decision of the Chief Justice was against the board. An appeal was taken to the Supreme Court of the United States, but in view of the uncertainty of gaining the case and of the great expense attending its prosecution, the appeal was withdrawn. The bank stock aforesaid owned by the board may therefore be considered worthless."

"The Roanoke Navigation stock should be valuable; accordingly the board hopes to turn it to account," but it was then not available. After deducting these amounts it was found that the "net public school fund" was "not less than $968,242.43" on November 1, 1869.

In the report of Superintendent Ashley for 1870-'71 the only source of revenue of the public schools mentioned are the State tax on polls, county tax on polls, special tax of one-twelfth of 1 per cent, and a tax on retailers of spirituous liquors. It was reported that the stock in the Bank of Cape Fear was worthless and could not be relied on for "future percuniary availability." Efforts had been made to sell the Roanoke Navigation stock, but to no purpose.

There was due to the board from the State as accrued and unpaid interest on coupon and certificates of indebtedness $60,291.75, besides $27,000 interest for one year on $450,000 in special-tax bonds purchased by the board from the proceeds of the sale of railroad stock. The total interest then due from the State was $87,291.75. I have been able to find no evidence that this sum was ever paid, unless it is included in the "special appropriation," made during the year 1870-'71, of $92,976.04.

The fortunes of the old literary fund may be summarized as follows: In 1860 this fund amounted to more than $2,000,000. The failure of the banks in whose stock a part of the principal was invested reduced this fund to less than $1,000,000 in 1869. This consisted in depreciated railroad stock, which was sold at from 10 to 37 cents on the dollar. The money thus realized was invested in North Carolina special-tax bonds, bought at a discount. These were repudiated by the State.

From that time (1870) practically all the support of the public schools has been derived from the annual State, county and municipal taxes.*

---

*It seems that there was a slight effort made after this to accumulate an educational fund. The report for 1872-73 gives, under the head of "Permanent Fund," $23,307.26½, which had been derived from entries on vacant lands, fines, and a balance on hand from the previous year. Of this sum, $16,218.75 was invested in United states bonds. The receipts of the "income fund" included "interest on United States bonds" and "dividends Roanoke Navigation Company." These are the only items in this report which indicate that they might have come from the old literary fund.

For the year 1873-74 the navigation dividends and interest on United States bonds amounted to $1,748.25. There was also an investment of $19,404.29 in United States bonds. These interest items amounted in 1874-75 to $2,461.50. There was then a further investment of $13,682.50 in United States bonds.

These bonds seem to have been carried from year to year as a part of the assets of the educational fund until 1881, when they were sold under the direction of the legislature. They then amounted to $91,500 and were sold for $106,224 25. The fund also owned $99,200 in State bonds, which were offered for sale in 1882, but not sold.

Perhaps the last official act of Dr. Wiley in the position which he had honored so much was writing a pamphlet on the swamp lands of the State, which was published in 1867. It now only remains for me to notice his work as a private citizen in other capacities.

Dr. Wiley felt himself called to preach at an early period in his educational career. He studied theology and was licensed by Orange Presbytery in 1855. He was ordained sine titulo in 1866 and never held a settled pastorate. He was one of the executive committee to found the North Carolina Presbyterian and a contributor to its columns. His work for the schools had brought him a knowledge of the undeveloped lands and other resources of the State, and, when the development boom came after the war, was solicited to beome a partner in many schemes looking to exploiting these resources. In 1867 he was elected corresponding secretary of the North Carolina Land Company, at a salary of $1,000 a year, and began work January 15, 1868. The company proposed to invest in and develop the swamp lands of the State, and Dr. Wiley's business was to collect information for pamphlets which were to be circulated abroad. He also sought to make better known the resources of the State by calling a convention of the leading literary men of the State in Raleigh in July, 1869.

On June 1, 1869, he became the general agent for the American Bible Society for middle and eastern Tennessee, and took up his residence in Jonesboro, Tenn. In March, 1874, on the resignation of Rev. P. A. Strobel, he was transferred to a similar position in North Carolina, and removed to Winston, N. C. In 1876 South Carolina was added to his field. He remained in this work until his death.

Dr. Wiley would have been made the candidate of the Conservatives for superintendent of public instruction in 1872 had he not been kept out by political disability. Dr. Nereus Mendenhall became the candidate, but the party went down in defeat. In 1876 he was again proposed as a candidate on the Conservative ticket, and would, no doubt, have been elected but for his own sense of duty. He regretted that the public schools had been brought into political debate, but "in view of the situation and of what is expected of candidates nominated on party platforms, the arena where honorable and good men not of my vocation may lawfully strive is closed to me by my sense of the obligations of my sacred calling."* During his later years he devoted himself as far as possible to advancing local educational interests, helped to establish the graded school in Winston, N. C., and was the chairman of its school board from its organization until his death.

He served the State as superintendent of common schools for thirteen years. He was a Whig in politics, and was twice elected by the Whigs and five times by the Democrats. He was a trustee of the University of North Carolina from 1875 until his death, and, although he never held a regular charge, preached frequently to Presbyterian and other congregations. He received the degree of D. D. from the University of North Carolian in 1881, to whose interest he had been always devoted. He married Miss Mittie Towles in Raleigh, N. C., February 25, 1862. To this union seven children were born, of whim five still survive. Dr. Wiley died in Winston, N. C., January 11, 1887. According to a personal friend, who knew him intimately, he "was very agreeable in social life. He was simple, gentle, unpretending, gracious, genial. He had a genuine fund of quiet humor, not anecdotical, but spontaneous and innocent. He was a guileless man—true, sincere, lovable."

*Dated at Winston, June, 7. 1876.

SKETCHES

OF SOME OF

THE OLD OR EXTINCT SCHOOLS

IN THE

COUNTIES OF NORTH CAROLINA.

BY

KEMP P. BATTLE, LL. D.,

PROFESSOR OF HISTORY UNIVERSITY OF NORTH CAROLINA.

1898.

PREPARED AT THE REQUEST OF

HON. C. H. MEBANE, SUPERINTENDENT OF PUBLIC INTTRUCTION.

INTRODUCTORY AND EXPLANATORY.

The following paper, voluminous as it is, contains notices of necessarily only a portion of the "old schools" of North Carolina, for moral reasons.

1st. It is almost certain that even in Colonial times, certainly afterwards, there were schools not mentioned in history. Among Christian communities instruction of the children was an ordinary and necessary duty. It is believed that many pastors, missionaries, lay-readers, gave or provided such instruction, and the records of the same, if any were kept, have been lost. We often find accidentally official records of church organizations not older than seventy or eighty years in private hands, sometimes at the beginning or end of old books of accounts. And in many communities intelligent old gentlemen or ladies, whose memories were valuable treasturies of important facts, have been allowed to die, without notes having been taken of those memories by an intelligent survivor. Frequently have we been met in searches after important transactions by the answer, "Grandfather or grandmother had a box of such papers, but they were burnt, or rats nibbled them into shavings and made nests in them." Rats making nests of priceless, irreplaceable ancestral papers and historical documents!

2nd. Information about institutions, which have come down to us, has been obtained only fragmentarily. There are large vacant gaps. And my sources of information in many counties, though tolerably complete as to some schools, are meagre, and totally deficient as to others.

3rd. Although I made application by letters, enclosing stamps for reply, in some counties, I failed to find the intelligent citizen who would take the trouble to send the information asked for. Hence some counties, viz., Rockingham, Lenoir—several others—have not justice done to their educational history.

In truth, accurate and full sketches of the schools of no county can be made without a visit of some length being made to that county, and investigation into all sources of information possible.

I render cordial thanks to all who have given me assistance. I know by experience how worrying it is to be called on to neglect ordinary avocations to engage in novel and perplexing enquiries.

It will be noticed by my readers, if there be any, that I have occasionally given minutely the charges for board and tuition, courses of instruction and other items of information. This will give a rough idea of the others, which were not greatly different, as all the teachers had the same general views. It would be tedious beyond endurance to repeat these items as to all.

I have also recorded incidents of a humorous nature. My object was to give some idea of the relations between teacher and pupil—the manners of the old school-room.

If it be complained that more details are given about some schools and teachers than others, the answer is simply, that I happened to have more accessible information about them, or having described one for some reason I thought it unnecessary to describe the others. I have had no conscious preference in the matter. If it is thought that I have mentioned that teachers were University men more often than I did in regard to other institutions, I answer that I gave similar credit to other institutions whenever it came to my knowledge, and, secondly, for many years the University was the only source for male teachers of collegiate training. Wake Forest, as Wake Forest Institute, opened in 1834, Davidson Colege in 1837, and Trinity, or Union Institute, in 1838.

It is humiliating to our State pride that for many years after the Revolution trustees of institutions sought patrons by advertising that their teachers were "Graduates of a Northern College," or simply "from the North." Notice under "Bertie" how trustees sometimes ordered lady teachers through commisison merchants.

From a literary point of view, it would be better to give the older counties first and then, in order, those subsequently formed from time to time, out of their area, and this was at first my intention. But for convenience of reference the plan of taking the counties in alphabetical order is greatly preferable. I adopt that plan wherever advisable, giving cross references.

It is to be hoped that this incomplete paper, with all its defects, will keep alive the names of many worthy men and women, who did great good in their day, and further, will stimulate some active young teacher in each county to make thorough investigations and write a full history of its educational institutions.

At the risk of offending students of history I give in advance lists of authorities in the lump rather than in detail at the bottom of each page.

K. P. B.

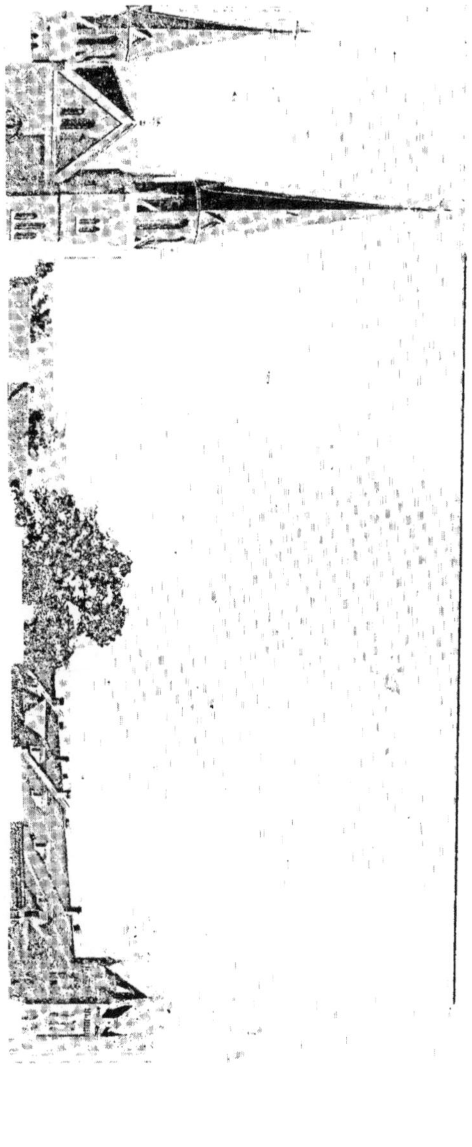

SCHOOLS IN TENNESSEE WHEN PART OF NORTH CAROLINA.

Two institutions, in the present limits of Tennessee. should be mentioned as having been incorporated, when a part of North Carolina, viz.:

MARTIN ACADEMY, named in honor of Governor Nathaniel Martin, incorporated 1783. In 1795 the name was changed to Washington College. Samuel Doak was for a long time its efficient President, the first classical teacher west of the Alleghanies. The institution is still doing good work.

DAVIDSON ACADEMY, incorporated in 1785. Rev. Thomas B. Craighead was President. Among the trustees were Hugh Williamson and Col. Wm. Polk. The State donated to it 240 acres of land, reserved to the State, most remote from the Salt Springs, near Nashville. The location was sold for $12,000. In 1806 the school was rechartered as Cumberland College, and in 1826 as the University of Nashville.. While named College of Cumberland the eschated and unclaimed lands given as bounties to North Carolina Continental soldiers, and which North Carolina donated to the University of North Carolina, were claimed by the General Assembly of Tennessee as belonging to that State, but by compromise allowed the University of North Carolina to have one-third, and gave one-third to the College of Cumberland and one-third to the College of East Tennessee. The University of North Carolina realized about $200,000, from her share, which constituted its endowment before the civil war, but the College of Cumberland appears not to have prospered with her share, for in 1875 the University of Nashville was merged into the Peabody Normal School.

SPORADIC EDUCATIONAL MOVEMENTS.

In 1754 George Vaughan, a London merchant, offered to give £1,000 annually for the education of Indians in the Province of North Carolina. The bequest was to take effect after the death of his nephew, John Sampson. The General Assembly made the counter proposal that if he would change the donation so as to be for general education, they would add £6,000 to it. On his acceptance the money was voted but was used for the French-Indian war, and so Vaughan's benevolent scheme came to an end.

An educational movement in 1820, which proved abortive, was the Western College of North Carolina. This was intended to be a State University for Western Carolina, was to be located "southwest of the Yadkin river," but the projectors soon found the undertaking to be too costly and it was abandoned.

It is worthy of note that as early as 1827, "certain persons associated themselves together for the instruction of the Dealf and Dumb, and formed an Institution" for that purpose. In that year the General Assembly granted a charter to this institution and all future associates, but strange to say the names of none of the members is given, nor is the name of any county mentioned. Nothing further appears in the laws about the movement.

ATTEMPTS TO OBTAIN PUBLIC SCHOOLS FOILED.

The Constitution of 1776, section 41, ordains, "That a school or schools shall be established by the Legislature for the convenient instruction of youth, with such salaries, paid by the public, as may enable them to instruct at low prices."

When we read the elaborate charters of Liberty Hall Academy, Martin Academy, Morgan Academy, Davidson Academy, Rowan Academy, Granville Hall, Science Hall, near Hillsboro, Grove Academy, Pittsboro Academy, and others, passed during the Revolution and soon afterwards, it seems to be clear that the projectors hoped to make these schools obtain help "from the public," i. e., the General Assembly. This was thwarted by a proviso at the end of the charters.

LIST OF AUTHORITIES.

Martin's, Wheeler's, Wilson's Histories.

Colonial Records.

Acts of Assembly, from 1777 to 1871.

Foote's Sketches.

Caruthers' Caldwell.

Rumple's Rowan.

Centenary of Davidson.

Battle's History of Raleigh.

Church History of North Carolina, especially Bishop Cheshire's Note.

K. P. Battle's History of the University of North Carolina in the Centennial Catalogue.

Life of Jacob Mordecai, by Gratz Mordecai.

W. S. Harris' Sketch of Poplar Tent Congregation.

W. A. Graham's Memoir of Chief Justice Ruffin.

Miss Fries' History of Forsyth County.

Smith's History of Education in North Carolina.

Bernheim's German Settlements and the Lutheran Church.

Branson's Directory, 1878.

Memoir of Dr. Witherspoon, by Chief Justice Nash.

Especially Dr. S. B. Weeks' "Beginnings of the Common-school System in the South," and

Raper's Church and Private Schools in North Carolina.

Dr. Weeks also furnished me prospectuses of various schools from the collection of Rev. Calvin H. Wiley, D. D., and a list made by Dr. Wiley of the schools in 1856.

I found considerable material by searching the files of

The North Carolina Gazette for 1877-'78;

The North Carolina Chronicle, 1790-'91;

The Raleigh Register, 1800-1860.

For information by letter I am indebted to the following:

Alamance—Mr. S. A. White, Maj. J. W. Wilson, Rev. Dr. W. S. Long.

Alleghany—Hon. R. A. Daugton, Mr. S. W. Brown.

Anson—Hon. R. T. Bennett.

Beaufort—Stephen C. Bragaw, Mrs. R. H. Lewis, Mrs. L. C. Phillips.

Bertie—Hon. F. D. Winston, Mr. E. B. Outlaw, Mr. E. S. Etheridge.

Brunswick—John N. Bennett, Esq., Hon. A. M. Waddell.

Buncombe—Supt. John W. Starnes, Mr. L. P. McLoud, F. A. Sondley, Esq.

Burke—Maj. J. W. Wilson, S. B. Erwin, Esq.

Cabarrus—Col. P. B. Means, Mr. H. M. Thompson.

Caldwell—Dr. J. M. Spainhour.

Caswell—Hon. Giles Mebane.

Catawba—Hon. M. L. McCorkle.

Chowan—Col. R. B. Creecy.

Chatham—J. J. Jackson, Esq.

Cherokee—Capt. T. J. Cooper, Jr.

Cleveland—Hon. S. A. Anthony.

Craven—Mrs. S. A. Taylor, Mrs. Roberts, Mr. B. B. Lane, Jr.

Cumberland—Hon. R. P. Buxton, Prof. A. Graham.

Currituck—C. M. Ferebee, Esq., Hon. T. J. Jarvis.

Davidson—Hon. F. C. Robbins.

Davie—G. M. Bingham, Esq., Col. A. S. Buford.

Duplin—Mr. Stephen Graham.

Edgecombe—W. H. Johnston, Esq., Hon. Fred. Phillips.

Franklin—Mr. W. W. Boddie, W. S. Battle, Esq.

Granville—Rev. J. M. Horner, Mr. J. W. Hays.

Greene—W. H. Austin, Esq.

Halifax—T. L. Whitaker, Hon. J. B. Batchelor, R. H. Smith, Esq., Dr. Willis Alston.

Harnett—Prof. A. Graham.

Henderson—Dr. R. H. Lewis, of Kinston.

Hertford—Pulaski Cowper, Esq.

Hyde—J. T. Mann, Esq.

Iredell—Prof. D. Matt. Thompson.

Johnston—Mr. Ira T. Turlington, Mr. J. D. Parker.

Jones—F. W. Foscue, Esq.

Lenoir—Dr. R. H. Lewis.

Lincoln—A. Nixon, Esq., Hon. M. L. McCorckle.

Macon—Hon. Kope Elias.

Madison—Mr. M. A. Chandley, Hon. John A. Hendricks.

Martin—Mr. J. M. Siterson.

Mecklenburg—Prof. A. Graham.

Mitchell—J. E. Jimerson.

Moore—Donald L. St. Clair.

Nash—W. L. Thorp, Esq., W. S. Battle, Esq., Thomas H. Battle, Esq.

New Hanover—James G. Burr, Esq., Rev. Robert Strange, D. D.

Northampton—Rev. Charles Fetter.

Onslow—J. E. Koonce.

Orange—Hon. Giles Mebane, S. A. White, Esq., Col. Cadwallader Jones, Maj. R. Bingham, Charles W. Johnston, Esq.

Pasquotank—Prof. S. L. Sheep.
Perquimans—Prof. W. G. Gaither, Mr. Josiah Nicholson.
Person—J. S. Merritt, Esq.
Randolph—Hon. M. S. Robins.
Richmond—M. M. McIver, Esq.
Robeson—D. P. McEachern, Esq.
Rowan—Rev. Dr. J. Rumple.
Sampson—Rev. J. L. Stewart, L. C. Hubbard, Esq.
Surry—Porter Graves, Ssq.
Tyrrell—Mark Majette, Esq.
Vance—Rev. Charles Fetter.
Wake—C. B. Root, Esq.
Warren—Mrs. Ellen Mordecai.
Watauga—Messrs. D. B. Dougherty and B. B. Dougherty.
Washington—S. B. Spruill, Esq.
Wayne—Mr. E. D. Broadhurst.
Wilson—Mr. George W. Connor.
Yadkin—Hon. Richmond Pearson.
Yancey—Mr. D. M. Ray.

ALAMANCE.

Formed from Orange in 1849.

Incorporated Schools.—Graham Institute, chartered 1851; Jefferson Academy, chartered 1861; Graham High School, chartered 1879; Graham Normal College, chartered 1881.

For earliest teachers and schools, see under "Orange."

In 1813 John H. Pickard opened a classical school near the residences of Rev. William Paisley and Mr. James Mebane. For his further services, see "Caswell."

About 1830 Jonathan Worth, afterwards a prominent lawyer and Treasurer and Governor of the State, taught at what was known as Providence Church, near the point where Graham station is located. He was succeeded by Burcheet, a scholarly and progresive man, by whose urgency a good library was purchased. Then came Dr. Wiliam F. Bason (1838 to 1840), a thorough teacher, afterwards, as a dentist, accumulating a handsome fortune. Rev. John R. Holt began teaching about 1840 at this place, and had a good school until the Normal College at Graham was opened. He had already been in charge of a school in the southern part of the county.

In 1850-'51-'52 Rev. William Nelson, of Robeson County, and his wife, born ——— Lacy, of Virginia, conducted a flourishing female school in Graham. They were assisted by Miss Paisley, of Guilford.

The Graham Institute was inaugurated in 1851 by Rev. W. H. Doherty, A. M., who was trained at the Royal Belfast Institution in Ireland. He had been senior professor in Antioch College in Ohio. His institute was under the control of the Christian (Methodist) denomination, but the instruction was general. It was merged into the Graham Normal College, Rev. D. A. Long, D. D., and Rev. W. S. Long, D. D., being joint principals for two years. Then the latter became sole principal until its close in 1888, when he asumed the presidency of the newly-incorporated Elon College.

It was in this county, at a place called Melville, doubtless in honor of the stern Scotch educator and preacher, Andrew Melville, that Rev. Dr. Alexander Wilson had his excellent school from 1852 until his death in 18.. This excellent man merits especial notice.

Alexander Wilson was born in County Down, Ireland, at Ballylesson. His father, of the same name, was wealthy, but lost his property by standing security for friends. Young Alexander received an excellent early education, with a view to becoming a physician. Obtaining a diploma from the governor and directors of Apothecaries' Hall, Dublin, entitling him to practice, he emigrated to America about 1818 in search of a location. Concluding to teach temporarily, he became assistant to Rev. Dr. William McPheeters in his famous school at Raleigh. Here his standing was so high that he was warmly recommended to be principal of the school at Williamsboro, as will be mentioned under the head of "Granville." In 1831 he was ordained a minister of the Presbyterian church, and, resigning his post as teacher, became pastor of Grassy Creek Church in Granville. In about two years he was called by his Presbytery to take charge of the Caldwell Institute at Greensboro, inaugurated under brilliant auspices. In recognition of his learning and success as principal, the University, in 1839, conferred on him the degree of Doctor of Divinity.

In 1845, owing to much sickness, supposed to be caused by a millpond, the school was removed to Hillsboro. In 1852 he removed to Alamance County, at a place called Burnt Shop, which name he changed to Melville. Here, until his death, he had a select private classical school of great reputation, far and wide, for its high moral and literary works. His charity was almost boundless. His executor found among his papers notes given by students to the amount of about $20,000, of which no one knew but himself. At the University and the colleges no students exhibited preparation superior to those prepared by him.

ALEXANDER.

Formed from Iredell, Caldwell and Wilkes in 1846.

In 1856 there was a Baptist college at Taylorsville. At this place also was the York Collegiate Institute, founded by Rev. Brantley York, of the Methodist Episcopal Church, South. He was a teacher of wide reputation, and the author of a school-book of merit—York's Grammar.

ALLEGHANY.

Formed in 1859 from Ashe.

There are schools of merit in this county, but I have been unable to obtain any facts in regard to those prior to existing institutions.

ANSON.

Formed from Bladen in 1749.

Stokes Seminary, chartered 1791; Sneedsboro Academy, chartered 1800; Wadesboro Academy, chartered 1802; Spring Grove Academy, chartered 1821; Culpepper Academy, chartered 1822; Meltonsville Academy, chartered 1822; Wadesboro Academy, amended 1829; Morven Academy, chartered 1833; Oak Grove Academy, chartered 1842; Carolina Female College, chartered 1849; Anson Institute, chartered 1854.

The Wadesboro Academy had the privilege of raising $1,000 by lottery.

Not one of these schools now exist by virtue of its charter, nor have any official records of them been found. Hon. R. T. Bennett has collected what unwritten memories there are. From them it appears that the earliest teachers of boys at Wadesboro, remembered, was a Mr. Robert L. Edmonds, succeeded by Parson Wright. Afterwards were Rev. Burke and Philip Wiley, Episcopal clergymen, and then "Sandy" Smith and Wiley Smith. Generally, it is true that Wadesboro has enjoyed classical school advantages for the past seventy-five years.

After Wiley Smith (above named) came ——— Clancy, William Richardson, ——— O'Hanlon, and during and directly after the civil war, ——— Lindsey. About 1854 came Booker Winfree, affectionately called "Old Booker," a man of merit, with singular ways. It was his custom to call in the pupils with "Oh, yes! Oh, yes!

come into school," to have "grace" at noon and benediction at the closing. All the larger boys, in fair weather, studied under trees, in the shade of the building or in the genial sunshine, as seemed pleasant to them. The girls and the little boys remained under the master's eye.

Gouldsfork Academy, five miles from Wadesboro, attained distinction in the two decades before the civil war. It was presided over by ——— Douglas, of South Carolina, and then successively by Fred. A. Shepherd, now of Nashville, Tenn., Hon. R. P. Buxton and P. H. B. Threadgill.

At Lilesville, in recent years, taught Rev. Mr. Jordan, Capt. J. T. Bradley, Rev. J. B. Lindsey and Rev. N. B. Cobb, D. D. Forty years ago —— Sutton had a school for boys eight miles south of Wadesboro.

About 1820 Miss Norton had a flourishing school for girls at Wadesboro.

I find a most ambitious advertisement in 1821, three-fourths of a column, by Mrs. Robert L. Edmonds, of her taking charge of Wadesboro Female Seminary. She was assisted by Miss Haskins, of New York. Her husband, who had the degree of Master of Arts, delivered lectures, but had no part of the management. The blank form of what was called a "judgment book," to be sent to patrons, conveying information as to numerous points of scholarship and conduct, was printed. Board and tuition were furnished at $130 per annum.

Anson Institute, incorporated in 1854, had as its principal Alexander McIver, since professor of mathematics at Davidson College and the State University, and State Superintendent of Public Instruction. His successors were Silas C. Lindsley and Rev. James E. Morrison. The latter was a graduate of the University in 1825. After giving up the Institute he removed to the Mineral Spring, near New Morven, one mile west of Old Morven, and had a well-conducted private school until his death, a few years ago.

"A few years after the stars fell," which phenomenon was in 1833, Mrs. Bogle assumed the reins of power, Then there was a mixed school, presided over by a Frenchman, —— Ange.

Other well-patronized private schools for girls were subsequently ably conducted by Mrs. Anne C. Hall, and then by Miss Mary Ann Shepherd.

Carolina Female College, at Ansonville, ten miles north of Wadesboro, was opened for students in 1851 in a building costing twenty thousand dollars. Its first president, Rev. Alexander B. Smith, of Anson County, served about two years. Rev. Tracy R. Walsh, for about ten years, was his successor. The school had a high reputation and had a large patronage, but was wrecked by dissensions among the trustees arising, it is said, from hot party feeling. Its doors were closed in 1862 for two years, when efforts were made to revive it by Rev. J. R. Griffith and James E. Blankenship, successively, with considerable measure of success. It was finally closed in 1868, but was afterwards used as a high school. In 1861 the property was offered to the South Carolina Methodist Episcopal Conference on condition that a $10,000 debt on it should be paid. This was never done.

ASHE.

Formed in 1799 from Wilkes.

I have not been able to procure information about the old schools of Ashe.

BEAUFORT.

Formed in 1705 as a precinct of Bath, called Archdale until about 1812. Made a county in 1738.

In this county was the first town in the State—Bath—

established in 1704. The first public library was here. There is no direct evidence of any schools, but probably those who officiated as lay readers also taught the children of the parish, as Brickell, who wrote in 1830, states.

Incorporated Schools.—Washington Academy, chartered 1808; Durham Creek Academy, chartered 1822; Lincoln Academy, chartered 1829; Bath Academy, chartered 1830; Washington Academy, again chartered 1834; Bellevue Academy, chartered 1861.

Of these the Bath Academy had exemptions from militia service.

I cannot ascertain details about any of them. In the period 1830-'50 there was a flourishing school for females at Washington, under the management of a very accomplished and able lady—Miss Mary McCotta. On her marriage with Rev. Thomas Owen, the twain removed to Tarboro and established a school there. Among the other teachers of Washington were William Bogart and ——— Wiley.

Washington Academy was in operation in 1856, and in or near Washington, at that date, were a select female school, Sans Souci Female School, two primary schools and a parochial school.

The property of the Washington Academy is now rented to the public schools.

BERTIE.

Formed in 1722; precinct of Bath until 1738.

The incorporated schools in this county were: Windsor Academy, chartered 1806; Indian Woods Academy, chartered 1807; Bertie Union Academy, chartered 1823; Coleraine Academy, chartered 1825; Oak Grove Academy, chartered 1832; Windsor Female Academy, chartered 1850; Windsor Male Academy, chartered 1850; Coleraine Female Academy, chartered 1850.

By the kindness of Hon. Frank D. Winston, and of his mother, a native of the county, sister of the gallant Col. F. W. Bird, I am able to give some particulars of some of these schools.

Indian Ridge had as its teacher Mr. McGuire. Among its pupils was Jonathan S. Tayloe, long clerk of the county court, and one of the purest and best informed men in his county. Another was Rev. Joseph Pender, afterwards of Tennessee. On re-visiting the ruins of his old school, Mr. Pender exclaimed:

"The house is gone, the chimney stands,
And the schoolboys wander in foreign lands."

This couplet applies to scores of abandoned academies in our State. I am indebted for this reminiscence to Capt. E. R. Outlaw, who lives near the site of the Indian Ridge Academy.

BERTIE UNION ACADEMY.—This was located at a place called Hotel, afterwards Woodville; hence the school was afterwards called Woodville Academy. It was justly celebrated for its excellence. Among its patrons were many Bertie people, who emigrated to the southwest. The attendance reached about 150, many children boarding at the Hotel, which was on the great Edenton and Halifax road. Two teachers were employed—a man, at $500, and a woman, at $300—both having free board and washing. Among the teachers were Rev. A. M. Craig, —— Thompson, —— Hicks, of Granville; Dr. Hatch, John H. Garmon, Jr., James L. Allfriend and John T. Trerevant, of Virginia. Among the lady teachers were Miss Eliza Bond, of Bertie County; Miss Viola Knapp, of Vermont; Miss Susan D. Bugbee, of Rhode Island; Miss Caroline Clemens, of Massachusetts. It was customary to order a lady teacher through commission merchants, there being then no "Teachers' Agencies."

Adramatic incident was connected with one of the teachers. He had begun his term of service as William Williams, an excellent man in behavior and scholarship. One day the community was shocked by his being arrested for stealing a horse and buggy. He was carried off, and, on his trial, proved that he had engaged a man to return the horse and buggy, and the hireling was the thief. He was honorably acquitted and resumed his real name of Allfriend. On being called out ot the school once by an unknown man, a bright little pupil, on his return, asked: "What is your name now, Mr. Allfriend?"

Mr. Trerevant was accustomed to have elaborate examinations, ending with a drama. Shakespeare's "Julius Caesar" was once selected. At the first rehearsal, Joseph Pugh, a grown young man, who impersonated Caesar, did not repose on his bier with the still dignity proper to a corpse, whereupon the irate schoolmaster fell upon him with a hickory switch. This was resisted, and a rough-and-tumble fight ensued, "which lasted half a mile down the road." The bystanders must have thought that Trerevant was acting Brutus or Cassius.

The Oak Grove Academy was two miles from Windsor. Abram Poindexter was the earliest teacher, afterwards, an eminent Baptist preacher, half-brother of another eminent Baptist preacher, William Hill Jordan. Mrs. Winston remembers that her two brothers were regular pupils, and if either was sick she, a tot of four years, was seated in his place—a practice not uncommon in our State. Owing to the excellence of this school, the Windsor Academy was not successful. The closing exercises were attended by visitors from all the Albemarle section.

Other teachers were Eason Jones, a lawyer of Virginia; John H. Garmon, Jr., of Massachusetts, an eminent man in English grammar; and —— Metcalf, afterwards a physician in Florida.

In 1840 Patrick Henry Winston, Jr., so called to disguish him from a learned old bachelor lawyer of the same name, then of Wadesboro, afterwards of Raleigh, took charge of the school. His salary was $400 a year ,and also board and washing. He saved money enough to enable him to graduate at Columbian University in Washington City, and at Judge Battle's law school at Chapel Hill, and, after marrying, in 1846, was employed again at a salary of $400 yearly, with the privilege of practicing in the county and superior courts of Bertie, Martin and Washington. In 1847 he secured as his successor James Banks, an able teacher, afterwards a prominent lawyer of the Cape Fear section and of Florida.

Another teacher was Rev. Andrew M. Craig, a Baptist minister of much force, and with great gifts as a teacher—free in the use of the rod, but always just. James B. Jordan, a graduate of Brown University, and of the law school of our University, was also one of the teachers—a lawyer of brilliant promise, who died in service in 1862. After the war, came Thomas Turner Allen, a lawyer, of whom great things were expected, but he died in early manhood.

The academy, after a distinguished career of usefulness, has now over its door "T. ———, coffin-maker and wheelwright. Sweet cider, 10 cts."

Coleraine Academy had the following teachers, beginning in 1854: J. J. Freeman, John M. Puttich, Malachi Horton, Edward Jordan and Albert L. Adkins. It flourished moderately until 1861.

BLADEN.

Formed in 1734 from New Hanover; precinct of Bath until 1738.

Incorporated Schools.—Bladen Academy, chartered 1797; Elizabethtown Academy, chartered 1810; Cape Fear Academy, chartered 1854.

In 1808 the Bladen Acader··· was authorized to rent out the fishery opposite the town Commons for three years and use the proceeds, but this—one of the earliest public gifts to educaton—was repealed in the following year.

No information could be obtained in regard to the schools of Bladen.

In 1856 there was an academy at Prospect Halll, and Cape Fear High School at Cape Fear.

BRUNSWICK.

Formed from New Hanover and Bladen in 1764.

The only incorporated school of the old days in Brunswick was Smithville Academy, chartered 1798. It had numerous trustees, and was authorized to raise $7,000 by lottery. The ambitious project is said to have been a failure.

Hon. A. M. Waddell writes me that his mother, daughter of Alfred Moore, Jr., and granddaughter of Judge Alfred Moore, attended a school of which Mrs. Clitherall (born Burgwin) was the principal. This was in the twenties, at Smithville.

At Shalotte, about 1812, Thomas Hudson began to teach, succeeded by Mr. Acrefoot in 1820; about 1832 by Jonathan Wilkinson; in 1837 by Edward J. Bernard, both highly regarded, especially the latter; in 1848, John K. Burns; in 1850, Daniel K. Bennett; in 1851, Robert H. Beatty had schools at the same place. In 1879 Eureka Shoolhouse was built at Shalotte, and was used for about thirteen years, the puipls running from 40 to 73. George Leonard was principal most of that period. In 1892 the citizens built an academy ,of which Mr. Leonard is the head.

At Smithville (now Southport) Hartford Jones was the teacher about 1838-'39, and was acceptable; soon afterwards John K. Burns, gifted in imparting instruction,

MISSIONARY TRAINING SCHOOL—SHAW UNIVERSITY, RALEIGH, N. C.

but with the fatal defect of occasional devotion to alcohol. About 1850, Rev. James H. Brent, as Principal, with Mr. Murphy and Miss Sallie Brent, Assistants, began an academic school at Smithville (Southport) with about 120 pupils, and was successful for a few years. An academy was built for them in 1853. The same year Rev. W. M. Moore succeeded Mr. Murphy. Then Mr. Brent resigned and afterwards the academy sometimes prospered and at other times languished. In 1854 J. G. Sewall was Principal, in 1858-'59 Dr. J. A. Wainwright had 78 pupils. About 1880 Dr. Murphy had a successful school. It is now on floo tide, under command of Palmer Dalryimple.

In 1858-'59 and again in 1872, John N. Bennnett had successful schools at Town Creek.

BUNCOMBE.

Formed in 1791 from Burke and Rutherford.

Incorporated Academies.—Union Hill Academy, chartered 1805; Asheville Academy, chartered 1818; Sulphur Spring Academy, chartered 1834; Asheville Female Academy chartered 1840; Newton Academy, chartered 1849; Holston Conference Female College, chartered 1854; Bascom College, at Leicester, chartered 1859; Newton Academy, chartered amended 1879.

The Union Hill Academv was established on eight acres, given by Wm. Forster. In 1809 a lottery was authorized to raise $5.000 to complete the buildings and establish an academy for females in Asheville. In 1849 the institution was merged into Newton Academy. It was situate on the road between Biltmore and Asheville. The land was donated, as stated, by Wm. Forster, in 1803 to trustees, "for a place of residence for a preacher of the gospel, teacher of a Latin and English school, or either, as may be thought proper." The trustees elected the school and they were incorporated as mentioned. In 1809 Forster gave this corporation three and a half acres more. Rev. George Newton, a Presbyterian preacher, a man of ability, learning, piety and winning manners, was at the head of this school from 1797 to 1814, at the same time preaching here and at other places in the county. Governor David L. Swain and many other men of mark were taught by him, assisted by Rev. Mr. Parker. They bore strong testimony to the thoroughness of his teaching. In 1814 he removed to Shelbyville, in Tennessee, and became president of Dickson Academy. He died about 1841. In 1803 the Rev. Francis Asbury, the eminent Methodist divine, says of him: "I spent a night under the roof of my very dear brother in Christ, George Newton, a Presbyterian minister; an Isrealite indeed." While he was Moderator of the Presbytery, held at Unity Church in 1800, a petition to the justices of the county was adopted asking them to enforce more strictly the laws against intemperance, profane swearing, Sabbath breaking and other crimes. The county court favored the petition.

The earliest school in Buncombe was by ROBERT HENDERSON, on the Swannanoa, 1790 to 1800. He afterwards became eminent as a surveyor and lawyer.

Another school for boys, of local fame, was about seven miles north of Asheville, on Ream's Creek. It was taught successively by Robert Wood, J. H. Calfee, J. K. McCarthy, J. M. Campbell, H. A. Yost, J. A. Reagan and aided in equipping the late Senator Zebulon B. Vance and other prominent men. The building was burned in 1871, and near it grew up Weaverville College.

Col. Stephen Lee's classical and mathematical school was established two miles east of Asheville, in Chunn's Cora, in 1844. It continued almost without interruption, except during a short service of Colonel Lee in the Confederate army. Its patronage extended from Virginia to Texas, being especially strong in South Carolina, of which State he was a native.

SAND HILL ACADEMY was very prominent from about 1845 to 1870. It was situate seven miles west of Asheville, on Hominy Creek. Students, male and female, attended it from other counties and from South Carolina, Georgia and Tennessee. Here were trained men of the greatest influence in Western North Carolina. The teachers were Jacob Hood, Wm. H. Graves, T. C. Collins, J. J. Osborne and W. S. Barnes.

MALE ACADEMY FOR THE TOWN OF ACHEVILLE.—This academy was located on land donated in 1858 by N. W. Woodfin and James W. Potter. The teachers were from time to time Messrs. D. A. Dupree, Tuck, Nye, Holmes, J. W. Starnes and Mrs. Hutsell.

In 1878 Prof. S. F. Venable obtained a lease of the premises, and for twelve years was principal with signal ability and success, training hundreds of young men for college and the various avocations of life. In 1888 he sold his lease to the school committee of Asheville, and in 1890, on account of health impaired by reason of a wound received in a battle near Atlanta, removed to the country and continues his work on a smaller scale.

Among the earlier schools were Asheville Female Seminary, of which John Dickson, M. D., and Rev. Dr. Erastus Rowley were principals. It did good work until it was merged into the Asheville Female College, under charge of the Holston Conference. It was under the control of the Methodists, but the instruction was general. It did good work. Among the graduates was Mrs. A. T. Summey, who procured a reunion of her graduating class in 1892. Five out of the six of the class, from 60 to 62 years of age, were present and they telegraphed greetings to Dr. Rowley, in Kentucky, 85 years old.

A very remarkable teacher in Buncombe is Mrs. Mary Ann Hutsell, born in Wells. She has taught in all parts of the county, noted for thoroughness and rigid discipline enforced by a six-foot birch. Her age may be inferred from the fact that she taught, and doubtless whipped, the father of Superintendent John W. Starnes, who died in 1897 at the age of eighty.

THE RAVENSCROFT SCHOOL was established in 1855 on 13 1-2 acres now in the heart of Asheville, bought by contributions from various persons for a Protestant Episcopal Church school. It was conducted as a classical institution as its chief object for some years, Rev. Dr. Jarvis Buxton being principal. At the close of the civil war it was reorganized solely as a Theological School. In 1886 it was decided to revive the Diocesan School for boys and to devote the Ravenscroft building to this purpose. Mr. Schoenberger, a Northern man, gave $11,000 for the erection of a building for a training school for the ministry.

The Principals of Ravenscroft have been Rev. Jarvis Buxton, D. D.; Rev. Lucias Holmes, Rev. George Wilmer, Rev. F. J. Murdoch, D. D., and Rev. D. H. Buel, D. D.

I am indebted for the information about Buncombe to Supt. John W. Starnes, Mr. L. P. McCloud and the excellent address of Mr. F. A. Sondley on the "Asheville Centennial," and Rev. Dr. Jarvis Buxton.

BURKE.

Formed in 1777 from Rowan.

The incorporated schools of Burke are.—Morgan Academy, chartered 1783; Morganton Academy, chartered 1823; Morganton Academy, chartered 1844; Rutherford Academy, chartered 1859; Rutherford Seminary, chartered 1863; Table Rock Seminary, chartered 1867.

Morgan Academy was chartered in the same act with Martin Academy, in Washington County, Tennessee.

It was provided that neither should be held to be one of the schools commanded by the Constitution, which ordains that the salaries of the masters should be paid by the public. In the act of 1823 it was recited that "there has been for many years an academy existing at Morganton, with a flourishing male and female school attached to it," and that "it has been heretofore managed only as a private school, although considerable funds have been given it, both by private donations and acts of the legislature, without incorporating said academy." From this it appears that succession under the act of 1783 was not kept up.

By a supplemental act in 1823 the trustees were authorized to lay out streets, lanes and alleys, and lay off lots in the academy's land, and the same shall be a part of the town of Morganton.

By the act of 1844 a new corporation was created and new trustees appointed, the property of the old academy to vest in them.

These changes indicate a rather varied fortune of the school.

The following information about the schooools and teachers of Burke is derived from Mr. S. Bulow Erwin, a former citizen.

One of the earlier teachers was D. W. Conway, who had a school in a log cabin not far from Col. W. W. Erwin's Belvidere plantation. He wrote and published Conway's Arithmetic, between 1815 and 1825. He is mentioned again, under "Coldwell." In 1830 Rev. Mr. Eddy taught in Morganton. He was succeeeded by Rev. John Silliman, pastor of the Presbyterian Church. One peculiarity of his teaching was the passing over of English grammar and entering directly on the Latin by those intending to take a classical course. In 1835-'36 a Burke County man was the teacher, Thomas Washington Scott, remarkably successful in the English branches, and a writer of verses.

He probably was head of the first free school in Morganton, about 1845-'46. The next teacher was Noble A. Penland, of Buncombe, and then, in 1837, an accomplished English and classical scholar, Wm. Ramsay, of Pennsylvania, had a flourishing academy. Then came G. Zelotes Adams, of Georgia, an eccentric writer of poetry, by some thought to have merit. After him came Rev. John M. Wilson, pastor of the Presbyterian Church for several years.

Near Quaker Meadows a Mr. Hill had a good classical school, at which Col. W. W. Avery and others were prepared for college. This was before and after 1830.

Stoney Hill Academy was under the management of a very able teacher and disciplinarian, 1834-'36, Mr. Robert Rhodes, of Sampson. Once he laid the lash on the back of a future Governor, Tod R. Caldwell, who fled to his home, seeking for parental sympathy. Soon was discerned through the cracks of the log school house the boy returning in miserable haste, with his father, John Caldwell, closely following, hickory in hand. He urged upon the teacher to repeat the punishment for every transgression of the laws.

Of the female teachers in Morganton, about 1830 and afterwards, were Misses Maria and Harriet Allen, of Pennsylvania; also Miss McIlwaine, sister of the Bishop of Ohio, also from Pennsylvania, Miss Cowan and Miss Correns. Of the above Miss Harriet Allen married a Mr. Schenck, of Lincolnton; Miss McIlwaine, a Dr. Butt, of Lincolnton, and Miss Correns, a Mr. Moore, of Lincoln County.

CABARRUS.

Formed in 1792 fro Mecklenburk.

The incorporated institutions are—Poplar Tent Academy, chartered 1810; Rocky River Academy, chartered 1812; Rocky River Academy, chartered 1833; North

Carolina College, chartered 1859 Biddle University, chartered 1877, Zion Wesley, chartered 1879.

The Popular Tent School was flourishing long before its incorporation. It was situate near the Meeting-House, seven miles west of Concord. The pastor of the congregation, Rev. Robert Archibald, a graduate of Princeton University, began teaching in 1778, and was very successful. One of his pupils was Charles Wilson Harris, a graduate of Princeton with highest honor, who was the first Professor of Mathematics at the University of North Carolina. As he induced Joseph Caldwell to take charge of the State University, Poplar Tent materially affected for good its early career. In 1784-'85 Samuel Harris, afterwards a Tutor in Princeton University, very promising, but dying early, took temporary charge of the school. Then Mr. Archibald resumed teaching until in 1794, when he was deposed for hersy, having become a Universalist. He then became intemperate and was murdered by a desperado in Georgia. Foote says that his people mourned over him as over a fallen star. In truth, the people of Poplar Tent were fortunate in their teachers. Charles Caldwell, M. D., afterwards a distinguished savant of Philadelphia and then of Kentucky, at one time taught here. Thomas Allison, noted for his mathematical abilities, and an excellent man, was, as "Master Allison," in control for many years. But the most eminent, not excelled by any in all the land, North or South, was Rev. Dr. John Robinson, eminent as a preacher as well, who, with the exception of three years' service in Fayetteville, 1806-'09, had charge of the classical school from 1801 to 1806 and from 1809 until his death in 1843. The University of North Carolina honored him with the degrees of A. M. and then of D. D. He was a man of extraordinary virtues and talents. In addition to the usual branches in classical schools he gave instruction in theology, and many of the best ministers in North and South Carolina owed their training to him. Among the laymen were Governors Owen and Nathaniel Alexander, of North Carolina, and Governors Israel Pickens and John Murphy, of Alabama; Representatives D. M. Forney, H. W. Conner and D. M. Barringer, and very many others in high position and in the humbler but quite as useful walks of life.

After Dr. Robinson Daniel Coleman, afterwards Assistant Postmaster-General and State Solicitor-General, was a teacher. And then Jefferson Conly, and Rev. Addi E. Thom, Wm. H. Stanley, killed in the battle of Newbern in the civil war, and Wm. G. Weddington, who died in service in the Army of Northern Virginia. Wm. H. Owen, Tutor of Languages in the State University, and the Professor and acting President of Wake Forest College, and Stephen Frontis, and following him, B. W. Mebane, and then Jos. M. Morrison, brought up the tale of instructors to a recent date.

ROCKY RIVER ACADEMY was under the charge of Rev. John Makemie Wilson, the pastor of the church of that name and of Philadelphia. He taught for about thirty years, from 1801, with such power that it is said twenty-five of his pupils became ministers of the gospel. Among them were Rev. Robert Hall Morrison, D. D., and Rev. J. E. Morrison, D. D.

The next teachers successively were —— Graves and R. J. McDowell, and after an interval Geo. M. Gibbs, Archibald Neely, H. H. Kimmons and E. C. Alexander successively. Major S. C. Lindsley, of Greensboro, taught about five years with, perhaps, the largest attendance in the history of the academy. He was followed by Knykendale and J. T. Horry, while James Campbell was principal just before and during part of the war.

After the war the teachers were ——— Carr, a Davidson College student; then Rev. P. M. Custer, who had a large patronage; then —— Osborne, followed by —— Davie, with indifferent success.

In the 50's there was a good male and female school at Concord, and in the same locality was a successful school called Rocky Ridge.

At Mount Pleasant was the West Carolina Male Academy, of considerable reputation.

CALDWELL.

Formed in 1841 from Burke and Wilkes.

Incorporated Schools.—Davenport Female College, chartered 1859; Globe Academy, chartered 1873.

The first school in the county was taught under a large beech tree, about five miles from Lenoir, on the road to Patterson, a fine spring gushing from its roots. The teacher's name is unknown, but he must have been a man of parts, as his patronage was among the best men of the neighborhood for miles around. Among his students were Col. Wm. Davenport, Col. Thomas Lenoir, Captain Edmund Jones, Sr., Alexander Perkins and other members of that family from Johns River. After some years a log hut was built under the old tree and the school continued until the Master's death, about the beginning of this century.

The next school, about one hundred years ago, was at Litttlejohn's Church, seven miles from Lenoir, on the Morganton road. The first teacher is unknown, but he was a man of reputation and success. At a later date G. W. F. Gates (German, Gaeter), a man of learning and skilled in imparting instruction, was teacher. He had an unfortunate habit of disappearing for months at a time, especially on visits to Peter Stewart Ney, probably indulging together in the flowing bowl, as both were afflicted with craving for strong drink. About 1830 Major E. P. Miller built a school-house near Mary's Grove, two miles from Lenoir, and after teaching there for ten years in his spasmodic way, Gates disappeared and was never heard of afterwards.

From 1800 to 1820 a good school for many years was established near Baird's Iron Furnace, on Gunpowder Creek, and another, two miles from Lenoir, on the Indian Grave Gap road. This was later under Col. Wm. Greenway, for several years a successful teacher, especially in mathematics. He was a surveyor and his work may be seen in many of the deeds for land in his day. After him came Levi Saxton, Gen. C. W. Clarke and Rev. Nathan Clarke, all of whom practiced corporal punishment to a painful extent.

Col. Wm. Greenway also taught at a school on Zack's Fork, about three miles from Lenoir, followed by Wm. Prestwood and others. There was another school seven miles east from Lenoir, under different teachers, known as the Blair school-house.

A very successful school was established by D. W. Conway, near Lovelady Ford, on the Catawba. As stated under "Burke" he published an arthmetic, which was used by many schools for fifty miles around. Only one copy is known to exist. Another school-house in the three first decades of the century was near Fairfield Cemetery, at the spring, the teachers being Col. Wm. Greenway, Wm. Prestwood and others.

About 1800 Andrew H. Tuttle came to the county as a peddler from Connecticut. Some years afterwards he became principal of a well-patronized school, six miles south of Lenoir.

In 1842 Rev. Thomas S. W. Mott established a school at Belvoir, three miles southwest of Lenoir, which attracted pupils from all sections of the State. Among them was Junius Wheeler, of Hertford County, afterwards Professor at the West Point Military Academy.

In 1842-'43 Cape Taylor and Rev. Dr. Jarvis Buxton

taught succcessively at Montrose Academy in Lenoir. Both were good teachers. Then in 1844 Miss Emma J. Taylor began and continued the school for twelve years, ably assisted by her sisters. It was of such excellence that its patronage extended to several States. In 1857 the name was changed to Kirkwood School, but its reputation was not diminished under the management of Mrs. Jesse Rankin and daughters. Miss Emily L. Rankin is now in charge, but limits the number of her pupils.

In 1852 Col. Wm. Davenport, Hon. James C. Harper, Gen. S. F. Patterson and Col. Edmund W. Jones established the Yadkin Valley High School, near Patterson, and on the recommendation of Wm. J. Bingham, of the Bingham School, employed Capt. E. W. Faucette to take charge of it. He proved to be possessed of such excellent qualifications as an instructor as to attract pupils in large numbers from distant regions. His success led to his election as president of Concord Female College in 1858, and after two years as president of Statesville Female College. Remaining here one year he returned to Lenoir and took charge of the Finley High School and conducted it to signal success. After some years he removed to Tennessee, but has returned and still has a good school.

In 1855-'56 the citizens of Lenoir, with a population of about 300, erected Davenport Female College at a cost of $20,000, and donated it to the South Carolina Conference of the Methodist Episcopal Church, South. Rev. Henry M. Mood was elected president, with an accomplished corps of assistants and the school was soon filled with pupils from this State, South Carolina and Georgia. It was very flourishing until the civil war. Mr. Mood gave place to Rev. Richard N. Price in 1861, and he the next year to Rev. A. G. Stacey, who was in charge when Federal troops, in 1865, robbed the institution of books, apparatus, bed clothing, in fact, of all moveable property.

A small day school was kept up by Rev. George F. Round until the change in the Conference boundary in 1870, when Rev. Samuel Sander was elected president, and for four years had a flourishing school. Rev. W. M. Robey was then made president and in February 14th, 1877, the main building was burned. In 1883 $4,000 was subscribed to aid in re-building, when the school was again opened with W. W. H. Sanborn, and in 1888 J. D. Minnich, as president.

Since the war High Schools have been erected in various part of the county, and have been well patronized; such as Globe, Amherst, Gamewell, Hibriten, Hoover, King's Creek, Hudson, Patterson, Granite Falls and Lenoir Academies.

CAMDEN.

Formed in 1777 from Pasquotank.

Incorporated Schools.—Camden Academy, chartered 1819; Shiloh Academy, chartered 1831.

CARTERET.

Formed 1722; precinct of Bath until 1738.

Incorporated Schools.—Portsmouth Academy, chartered 1807; Carteret Academy, chartered 1810; Milton Male Academy, chartered 1823; Beaufort Male and Female Academy, chartered 1842.

Of these, Portsmouth Academy was allowed to raise $800 by a lottery.

In 1856 Mr. W. J. Langdon was principal of a female school at Beaufort. It was afterwards removed to High Point.

Shortly before the Civil War the Atlantic Female School was opened, at Morehead City, manned by a large faculty, of which Rev. Levi Branson, A. M., was principal. Mrs. Branson was teacher of French; N. B. Webster, A. M., lecturer on the natural sciences; Rev. C. P. Jones, instructor in Belles-Lettres; Miss Nannie S. Davis, teacher of music and painting; Miss Susan E. Suggs, assistant in the Literary Department; Miss Emily Branson, assistant in music. The prospectus says: "This institution is intended to supply a vacancy in position and female training, not hitherto filled. * * * It is now time to set a new standard. The next generation of men must have wives of a mental and bodily activity far surpassing anything that has hitherto been required. Our daughters must have a bold and heroic refinement, that will serve at home, or on the battlefield, if necessary. We intend to have scientific lecturing enough to start the mind into noble and energetic thought; text-book exercise sufficient to secure accuracy, and gymnastic training to insure the best bodily health and vigor."

It is to be regretted that this laudable enterprise was cut short by war.

The Atlantic Military Institute was located in Beaufort about 1860.

James H. Swindell and George W. Arrington were teachers of reputation at Beaufort.

CASWELL.

Formed 1777 from Orange.

Incorporated Schools.—Caswell Academy, chartered 1802; Hico Academy, chartered 1804; Milton Female Academy, chartered 1818; Milton Female Institute, chartered 1844; Dan River Institute, chartered 1846; Milton Male Institute, chartered 1849; Yanceyville Seminary, chartered 1864.

CASWELL ACADEMY was located in Yanceyville. Rev. Hugh Shaw and Bartlett Yancey were the teachers for the first two years. It then languished until 1808, when it was made prosperous by John W. Caldwell, son of Rev. Dr. David Caldwell. Yancey was afterwards a speaker of the senate for ten terms, and member of the Federal House of Representatives. He drew the act for the creation of the Literary Fund in 1825. James Kerr assisted Mr. Caldwell in 1811. In 1818 John H. Hinton, who had been tutor in the University, was principal. Dabney Rainey also taught here, highly respected.

HICO ACADEMY was near the "Red House," in the southeast part of the county. Rev. Hugh Shaw was the first teacher. In 1813 Abel Graham was in charge, assisted by —— Holbrook. In 1820 Mahlon Kenyon, a "graduate of Northern College," advertised to teach the classics, preparator to entering the State University.

Bartlett Yancey especially praised Robert H. Childers for his skill in teaching reading, arithmetic and penmanship.

In 1840 a Miss Spencer was principal of Calm Retreat Academy, in this county, and Lorenzo Lea was in charge of the Leasburg Academy, on the road from Henderson to Danville.

In 1856 there were Dan River Institute, at Yanceyville, A. C. Lindsay being principal; Female Institute at Yanceyville; Male School at Milton, T. R. McIver, principal; Female School at Milton, W. Presson, M. D., principal.

Fort many years Miss Margaret Smith, a Northern lady, called by the citizens "Queen Bess," had an excellent school in Milton. The academy was in a beautiful grove, and was in the hands of trustees, now all dead. The building is no longer used as a school.

Rev. John H. Pickard, a Presbyterian clergyman, established a female school, with Miss Forbis and other assistants, about twelve miles east of Reidsville. It had large influence for good.

In the neighborhood of Locust Hill there was a good female, school taught by Miss Balantyne, a Northern lady.

Rev. Solomon Lea, about the middle of the century, had a very fine school in Leasburg. He was a graduate of the State University, and at one time was principal of the Greensboro Methodist Female College, a local preacher and a most useful and pious citizen.

CATAWBA.

Formed in 1842 from Lincoln.

The incorporated schools are: Catawba College, chartered 1852; Newton Female Academy, chartered 1870; Concordia College, chartered 1881; Mount St. Joseph's, chartered 1883.

Up to 1842 tradition has it that only "old-field schools" were had in the county. The first classical school was taught on Mountain Creek by ex-Judge Matthew L. McCorckle, and then by —— Ramsey, of Rowan.

In 1845 was an academy at Wilfong's Mills, taught by Rev. Jerry Ingold.

In 1848 David Berrier opened a classical school in Newton. He was succeeded by Thomas Boyd, of Pennsylvania, who was afterwards a Congressman from Illinois.

CATAWBA COLLEGE, at Newton, belongs to the German Reformed Church. Rev. Mr. Albert, of Pennsylvania, was the first president; then for four years Mr. Hildreth H. Smith, afterwards professor of modern languages in the State University. He was succeeded by Rev. Mr. Smythe, of Maine. During the incumbency of these teachers the institution was only a high school, but Rev. A. S. Vaughan, of Pennsylvania, raised an endowment of $25,000 and restored the college curriculum. In 1865 Rev. J. C. Clapp, D. D., reorganized the school, and called it Catawba High School. The next year Maj. Sidney M. Finger, afterwards State Superintendent of Public Instruction, joined Dr. Clapp and was teacher of mathematics and Latin until 1874, when he retired and Dr. Clapp was sole principal until 1885, when the name of

Catawba College was restored under him as president. He is a graduate of Amherst College, and is at the head of his profession.

CHATHAM.

Formed in 1770 from Orange.

Incorporated Schools.—Pittsboro Academy, chartered 1786; Blakely Academy, chartered 1817; Haywood Academy, chartered 1818; Tick Creek Academy, chartered 1831; Haywood Academy, again chartered 1832; New Hope Academy, chartered 1855; Wilson Academy, chartered 1864; Tyson's Creek Academy, chartered 1881.

It is pleasant to note that the school of "Tick Creek" bore that offensive name only two years, in 1833 being changed to Caldwell Academy.

The Pittsboro Academy was allowed to raise $700 by a lottery. The most eminent teacher was Rev. William Bingham, father of William J. Bingham and grandfather of Col. William and Maj. Robert Bingham, who was professor of ancient languages in the University of North Carolina, 1801-'05. The school, seeming to have been closed. was re-opened April 1, 1805. The advertisement states that board could be had for $50 or $60 for the two terms. The tuition was $13 for five months if the classics were studied; otherwise $8. Professor Bingham was an honor graduate of the University of Glasgow, a Scotch-Irishman of Ulster; emigrated about 1788 on account of political troubles, landing in Delaware, and thence removing to Wilmington, N. C. He here preached and established a classical school. I find him among the first subscribers to erecting the buildings of the University. As the wealthier inhabitants of the lower Cape Fear either settled permanently or spent their summers on the hills of Chatham, he transferred his school, about 1795, to Pittsboro, and remained until his transfer to the Uni-

MEDICAL DORMITORY—SHAW UNIVERSITY, RALEIGH, N. C.

versity. After his second settlement in Pittsboro he was very successful for several years, but, concluding that Orange was a superior location, removed to Hillsboro. (See "Orange.")

Mr. Bingham was a man of great ability and skill as a teacher, in which respects he was perhaps excelled by his son, William James Bingham. He married Annie Jean, daughter of Colonel Slingsby, of the English army, who was in command in Wilmington during the Revolutionary war, highly regarded by the Americans for his humanity and justice. His family remained in Wilmington after peace was declared. William J. Bingham was born in Chapel Hill during the professorship of his father, in the house built for the president, now (1898) occupied by Professor Gore. He continued at Pittsboro until 1808.

The name of Pittsboro Academy was changed to Blakely, in honor of Capt. Johnston Blakely, who distinguished himself in the War of 1812 and was lost with his vessel, the Wasp. The General Assembly adopted his daughter, Udna M., and paid her a pension of $600 annually for many years.

Under Bingham the school was prosperous. Among its pupils were James F. Taylor, State solicitor; Charles Manll, Governor; Basil Manly, D. D., President of the University of Alabama, and Matthias E. Manly, judge of the Supreme Court of North Carolina.

There were many teachers after Bingham, often young men preparing for the profession. Of those who made teaching a business were Capt. Peter Lemeasurier, and, in the forties, J. M. Lovejoy, and Morgan Closs, a brother of Rev. Dr. William Closs, of the Methodist Church, of blessed memory. Since the civil war was Capt. C. B. Denson, afterwards of Raleigh.

There was also at Pittsboro in the forties a school for young ladies, of wide reputation, called Kelvin, at first under the widow of Solicitor General Edward Jones, and, in 1835, under Miss Charlotte Jones, his daughter. After her marriage to William Hill Hardin,, it was under their joint management.

In 1844 the Pittsboro Female Seminary had as its principal Rev. William Thornton, assisted by Miss Maria J. Holmes.

About 1860, for some years Rev. R. B. Sutton, D. D., an Episcopal minister, was master of a very good school in Locust Hill Academy in Pittsboro.

HAYWOOD ACADEMY was incorporated when there were strong hopes of making a large city in the forks of the Deep and the Haw. When the capitol was burnt, in 1831, efforts were made to make this the seat of government, as, in 1792, land and money were donated to locate here the State University. In 1835 the principal of the academy was Zachariah Wilson.

In 1856 there was here a female school also.

PLEASANT HILL ACADEMY was of considerable importance, under the able management of Rev. Baxter Clegg in 1839. It was six miles south of Pittsboro. He taught not only classics, but Algebra, Geometry, Surveying, etc., at prices, $30, $24 and $20 per annum. Board was $6 per month.

In 1856 there was a school at Mt. Vernon.

CHEROKEE.

Formed in 1839 from Macon.

Incorporated Schools.—Shoal Creek Male Academy, chartered 1859.

The education of the children of the county was mostly from the school fund, and after that was exhausted the teachers continued the schools by getting subscription from the neighbors.

CLAY.

Formed in 1861 from Cherokee.

Incorporated Schools.—Hayes' High School, chartered 1883.

CHOWAN.

Formed in 1672. A precinct of Albemarle until 1738; then a county.

The incorporated schools were—Edenton Academy, chartered 1770; Smith Academy, chartered 1782; Edenton Academy, amended 1800; Sandy Ridge Academy, chartered 1833; Edenton Academy, amended 1844.

The first teacher in Chowan County was Charles Griffin, lay reader of St. Paul's Parish, of whom some particulars are given under the head of Pasquotank.

The next was Mr. —— Marshburn, in 1712, at a place called Sarum, near the Virginia line and near two Indian towns, in one of which was the chief of the Chowan Indians. The Missionary, Rainsford, praises the proficiency of the children in reading and writing, and in the principles of the Christian religion. There is good ground for believing that the missionaries and lay-readers in early Colonial times, as a rule, added teaching of the elementary branches at least to their regular functions.

About 1763 a classical school was ably taught at Bandou, on the Chowan, about fifteen miles above Edenton, by Rev. David Earl, of the Church of England, and his daughter, Miss Ann (Nancy) Earl. Mr. Eearl was Rector of St. Paul's Parish, Edenton, and was of wide influence for good in the Albemarle section. The eminent physician of Raleigh, the late Charles Earl Johnson, was one of his lineal descendants.

The 1770 charter of the Edenton Academy recites that two lots had been bought by voluntary subscription and a conventient school-house erected thereon. The master must be a member of the Church of England, recommended by the trustees and licensed by the Governor. The trustees were very prominent men, Joseph Blount, Joseph Hewes, the signer of the Declaration of Independence; Robert Hardy, Thomas Jones, the eminent lawyer, probably the draughtsman of our Constitution of 1776; George Blair, Richard Bromrigg, and Samuel Johnston, afterwards Judge and Governor.

The religious views of the teachers in practice were not investigated. Rev. Charles Pettigrew, afterwards Episcopal Bishop-elect, took charge in June, 1773, under license signed by Governor Josiah Martin, when he was a Presbyterian. And Rev. Jonathan Otis Freeman, D. D., a Presbyterian minister, was once principal, as was Mr. John Avery, a Congregationalist, in 1814.

Mr. Freeman, for his teaching, received $600, and $400 for "delivering lectures to the students on the Sabbath." In 1811 he gave place to Rev. Frederick W. Hatch, of Maryland. In 1812 Mr. Avery began his charge and continued until 1824, becoming an Episcopalian in 1817. He was Rector of St. Paul's Church until 1835.

By the kindness of the excellent Nestor of the Press in North Carolina, Col. R. B. Creecy, I am able to give some details of the principal and of the school in 1819-'24.

Rev. John Avery was a native of Connecticut, a graduate of Yales, a classmate of George E. Badger. He was learned, absent-minded, a sharp disciplinarian, a good man, but indifferent preacher. His punishments were for light offences a high, pointed "Fool's cap," and keeping in after school; for grave offences, the whip. Fighting boys were made to play "wrap-jacket," or "hot-jacket" before all the school, i. e., each, armed with a switch, forced to scourge the other This gladiatorial display was greatly enjoyed by all but the participants. Every two pupils had a joint desk and were called "desk-mates;" Dr. Cheshire, of Tarboro, being Col. Creecy's desk-mate. Play hours were spent in fighting, the big boys "sicking" the little ones on, playing baseball, "fives," hop-scotch, mumble-the-peg, running foot-races, and fighting chickens. Col. Creecy, when about nine years old, bought a cock when on his way to school. Being surprised by the coming of the teacher, he hid his purchase in his desk. By and by, fearing that his pet would be smothered, he raised the lid an inch and peeped in. The rooster, reminded of the peep of day, gave a lusty crow and brought the avenging scourge on the back of his owner, as he

"Hung his head in fear and shame,
And to the awful presence came."

There were about 200 boys and girls, the school being the pride of the town. The girls were taught together in the upper room by Mr. Follett, of Connecticut, a genial, good man, who afterwards was promoted downwards to the boys in the lower room. In 1824 the female department was under George W. Barney, and then under Rev. Thomas Meredith, the founder of the Biblical Recorder. The boys were presided over by Rev. Joseph H. Saunders, late a tutor in the University of North Carolina, father of Secretary of State William L. Saunders, the father afterwards sacrificing his life in caring for yellow-fever patients in Pensacola. Another principal was Robert R. Heath, of New Hampshire, afterwards a distinguished judge.

The examinations and closing exercises, of Commencements," lasted three days, and were attended by the best people of Chowan and other counties. The trustees sat together and occasionally asked questions. The last exercise was the bestowal of prizes for scholarship and deportment, by the hands of some eminent man, followed by an address. Colonel Creecy's prize, the highest, in 1826, was delivered to him by James Iredell, the younger, then member of the House of Commons from Edenton, the next year chosen Governor, and the next Senator of the United States.

This academy was opened in 1856. And in Edenton there was likewise then a small female school.

Smith Academy was the gift of Robert Smith· a lawyer and merchant of Edenton. It was chartered in 1782. Judge James Iredell, Governor Samuel Johnston and Dr. Hugh Williamson were among the trustees. The General Assembly gave to it six acres of the Common's land.

CLEVELAND.

Formed in 1841 from Rutherford and Lincoln.

Incorporated Schools.—Male and Female Academy, near Shelby, chartered 1849.

By the charter of this school the Commissioner of Public Buildings was directed to subscribe $600 for every $200 paid by citizens for erecting the buildings.

In 1856 J. M. Newsom was principal.

COLUMBUS.

Formed in 1808 from Bladen and Brunswick.

In 1850 Columbus Academy, at Whiteville, was in operation.

CRAVEN.

Formed in 1712. Precinct of Bath until 1838.

Incorpated Schools.—Newbern Academy, chartered 1764; Adam's Creek Academy, chartered 1798; Newbern Female Charitable Seminary, chartered 1812; Griffin's Free School, chartered 1833; St. Phillip's Episcopal Singing Society, chartered 1867; Mt. Vernon Academy, chartered 1871.

The Newbern Academy was begun by Thomas Tomlinson as a private enterprise. In about two years it was taken up by the citizens and the charter of 1764 was obtained. The trustees was Rev. James Reed, Rector of the Parish; John Williams, Joseph Leech, Thomas Clifford

Howe, Thomas Hasler, Richard Cogdell, and Richard Fenner. The principal, who had previously taught in Fayetteville, was the second professional teacher in the State, so far as we know, Charles Griffin being the first. He was a most worthy man in all respects. Rev. Mr. Reed was the most active in getting up funds for the erection of the school building, which was of wood, forty-five feet by thirty. Mr. Tomlinson was paid from his thirty pupils about $300 per annum, and the Society for the Propagation of the Gospel added $50 the first year and $75 thereafter. In 1766 a tax on distilled spirits imported into Neuse river, of one penny a gallon, for seven years, was imposed for the purpose of employing an assistant teacher and paying the debts incurred by the trustees. Under this James McCartney, afterwards a minister in Granville, was engaged. In return for this appropriation ten poor scholars were to be admitted free of tuition, which was $16 per annum. By the same act the subscribers to the school were to choose the trustees, who were a self-perpetuating body, under the name of the "Incorparoted Society for Promoting and Establishing the Public School in New Berne." The purpose of the promoters was that "the rising generation may be brought up in the principles of the Christian religion, and fitted for the several offices and purposes of life." In 1772 the trustees became offended with Mr. Tomlinson for some reason—probably for disciplining some pupils—and requested him to resign, which he did, and removed to Rhode Island. He was one of the ablest teachers in colonial times.

The act of 1766 required that the master should be a member of the Church of England, chosen by the trustees and licensed by the Governor. From the prominence of Rev. Mr. Reed in caring for the school, and the devotion to it of part of the church grounds, it was probably considered to be a church school. At any rate, there is no contemporary complaint of this requisition. It may be of interest that the General Assembly of 1768, 1769, 1770 and 1771 met in this building.

After the departure of Tomlinson, we have only incidental notices of the teachers of the Newbern Academy. In 1778 Joseph Blyth advertises that he will teach in it Latin, English, Arithmetic, Geometry, Trigonometry and "several others of the most useful branches of mathematics, according to the best and most improved methods," and George Harrison at the same time offers to teach at another place English and French. It is thought that Solomon Halling, M. D., was master about 1792, until he entered on the work of the ministry. Thomas Pitt Irving, A. M., was principal in 1795 and until 1813. During his term of service the old academy building was burned, as was "Tryon's Palace," which the General Assembly allowed to be used for school purposes, and then authority was given to raise $700 by lottery. Mr. Loving was the rector of the Episcopal Church, as was also Rev. George Strebech, assisted by Rev. John Phillips and Rev. John Curtis Clay, all of whom were teachers in the school.

The old Newbern Academy did a great work. In Tomlinson's old building were taught such men as Gaston, Stanley, Spaight, and later came Badger, Hawks and the like. Newbern was one of the chief centres of culture in the State, and that culture was promoted by this institution.

After John Curtis Clay's incumbency, came in succession Rev. Edward B. Freeman, D. D., Frederick Freeman, Robert G. Moore, William B. Wadsworth and Edward Hughes, coming up to about 1840, and then "Messrs. Mayhew, Gordon and Bryant guided the institution to the beginning of the Civil War."

In 1866 the election of trustees was given by act of Assembly to the voters of the town, the term of office being one year, and groups so arranged that one-third go out of office annually.

In 1861 W. H. Doherty, A. M., late president of Graham College, as principal, assisted, among others, by Henry C. Thompson, a first-honor graduate of our University, and Col. J. V. Jordan, as teacher of military drill, opened in the academy a school for both sexes. It is noticeable that co-education is called in the prospectus "united education," and that corporal punishments were not to be employed. A department for the education of teachers was promised.

The Griffin Free School was founded by Moses Griffin, who died in 1816, leaving about $75,000 by will, to be devoted to the establishment of a free school. Junius Moore and his wife, of Wilmington, were the first superintendents. Then came Rev. William V. Hawks; then Miss A. S. Ellis, and fourthly, Miss Mary Oliver. The investments were all lost by the Civil War, except about $4,000 worth of land, including the school property, which has been sold and converted into interest-bearing securities. The interest of this is used for part payment of the salary of Mrs. Hannah Harrison, born Gibble, who is principal of an excellent parish school, which kept its doors open since 1853, even during the troublous times of the war.

In 1856 there was a female school in Newbern, of which W. H. Mayhew was principal.

CUMBERLAND.

Formed in 1754 from Bladen.

The incorporated schools are: Fayetteville Seminary, chartered 1799; Fayetteville Academy chartered 1809; Female Orphan Asylum Society, chartered 1813; Fayetteville School Association, chartered 1814; Fayetteville School of Industry, chartered 1830; Flea Hill Academy, chartered 1831; Ravenscroft Academy, chartered 1831; Donaldson Academy and Labor School, chartered 1832; Silver Run Academy, chartered 1832; Cumberland Academy, chartered 1852; Fayetteville Female High School, chartered 1855; United Baptist Association, chartered 1855; Fayetteville Military Academy, chartered 1864.

In regard to the above I note that the Fayetteville Academy was in place of the Seminary chartered in 1799.

The euphonious names of Flea Hill and Tick Creek were attached to literary institutions at the same session of the General Assembly. Rather in contradiction to the habits of the animals thus honored, the Flea kept its place and the Tick was chased away.

The first teacher in Fayetteville, known, was in 1791, the Rev. David Ker, an emigrant from North Ireland. He was also in charge of the Presbyterian congregation, receiving for the school $400, and the same as preacher. In 1795, as the first "Preaching Professor" in the University of North Carolina, his chair being that of "the Humanites," he received the first students of that institution. Here he became latitudinarian in his religious views, lost his place, studied law and was appointed by Jefferson, through the influence of Senator Stone, marshal, and then judge of the Mississippi territory. He died in 1810.

The second teacher was Rev. John Robinson, D. D., entering on his duties in 1801 at a salary of $1,000. He found them too much for his strength, and after a year was succeeded by Rev. Andrew Flinn, D. D., later a master of the University Grammar School. In 1805 he resigned, and afterwards was pastor of a church in Charleston. His successor was Rev. Dr. John Robinson, a second time, remaining three years and going back to Poplar Tent. In 1808 Rev. William Leftwich Turner was in charge, resigning in 1813.

All these teachers were zealous and efficient, especially Drs. Flinn and Robinson.

It is probable that the succeeding Presbyterian preachers, viz., Jesse H. Turner, William D. Snodgrass, R. H. Morrison, James E. Hamner, Josiah Kilpatrick, Henry A.

Roland, James W. Douglas, were likewise teachers of the academy, but Foote does not so state.

The Fayetteville Academy building was on a lot adjoining that of the Episcopal Church. Both were burned in the "great fire of 1831," and the Academy lot was sold to private parties. Miss Mabel Bingham was one of the teachers, and after the burning had a prosperous school for small girls for many years. After 1831 the schools were mainly denominational. The Episcopalians started the Ravenscroft School on Ramsay street, with Charles Stuart as principal. It was for several years very successful, attracting pupils from abroad, especially from Wilmington. Stuart was a vigorous wielder of the switch and chewer of tobacco. On his removal to his former residence, Virginia, the school passed away.

The Donaldson Academy was started in 1832 under control of the Presbyterians, on Hay Mount. The rivalry between the two schools was great, the favorite mode of showing it by the pupils being ducking one another in the swimming hole in Cross creek. This academy was endowed largely by the Donaldson family, one of whom, Robert Donaldson, settled at Hyde Park, on the Hudson, and bequeathed the bulk of his fortune to the University of North Carolina, which did not take effect because the will was not executed as required by the laws of New York. The Principal was an eminent teacher, Rev. Simeon Colton, D. D. Being accused before the Presbytery of heresy, on account of his opinion as to the permissibility of marrying sisters of deceased wives, the pupils attended the trial in a body and showed their interest by noisy clamor. After the trial, Dr. Colton removed to Harnett county. He was learned in many ways—so well versed in analytical chemistry as to be called as an expert in a celebrated poisoning case.

Among the successors in the superintendency of the Donaldson Academy were Rev. W. Johnson, of Robeson, and —— Ely, of Masachusetts.

The last Principal who taught and sent men to college from this academy before it was burnt was Alexander Graham, afterwards superintendent of the graded school of Fayetteville, and now of those of Charlotte. He had 505 pupils in a co-operative school, not supported by city taxes, the largest ever held in the academy—the largest of that kind in the State. It was remarkable, perhaps unique, in furnishing all school-books free of charge.

The Fayetteville Female Seminary was begun in 1854; Rev. W. E. Pell, of the Methodist Church, afterwards editor, with Maj. Seaton Gales, of the Raleigh Sentinel, being the first Principal. Mr. William K. Blake, a brilliant graduate of the University, succeeded him, and then came Mr. Thomas Hooper. The institution did not exist longer than the beginning of the Civil War.

CURRITUCK.

Precinct of Albemarle until 1738.

Incorporated Schools.—Currituck Seminary of Learning, chartered 1789; Pleasant Grove Academy, chartered 1835.

It is of interest that the Currituck Seminary, alone of all the charters, calls the Principal of the school "Provost."

The most important school of this county was Indian Town Academy, built by William Ferebee, Sr., in 1761, and burned during the "negro raid" of 1862. It was on land reserved by the Lords Proprietors in 1704 to the Yeopim (pronounced Yawpim) Indians, the country around being called Coretuck (Currituck) in imitation of the call of a wild goose. Their chief town was by the Indians called Culong, and by the whites Indian Town. In 1840, by permission of the General Assembly, the Indians sold their lands and, with their king, John Durant, left the State.

The lands were bought by a very intelligent class of people, such as Thomas McKnight, Col. Gideon Lamb,

Col. Solomon Perkins, John Humphries, Thomas Pool Williams, Maj. Taylor Jones, Gen. Peter Dange, Gen. Isaac Gregory, William Ferebee, Sr.· all of them military officers or members of the legislative bodies before and after the Revolution. The Indian Town Academy was on the plantation of William Ferebee, Sr., known as Culong, which descended to Thomas Cooper Ferebee, Sr., and from him to Thomas Cooper Ferebee, Sr., and was sold by the latter since Civil War.

The teachers worthy of mention were Ezekiel Gilman, of Massachusetts, a graduate of Harvard, who came to Currituck in 1840 and still resides there at the ripe age of 83. He taught for fifty consecutive years, in some instances having under his charge father, son and grandson. He is a man of learning and well preserved, mentally and physically.

Indian Town Academy was the early educator of many very useful men. One family, that of Wm. Ferebee, furnished si xmembers of the legislature, of whom two—Joseph and William—were officers in the Revolutionary army; one, Samuel, was a member of the Convention of 1789, and the last survivor; another, George, was a member of the convention of 1835, and still another, Dennis D., was a colonel in the Confederate army and a member of the convention of 1861.

DARE.

Formed in 1870 from Currituck, Tyrrell and Hyde.

For the school of this county see "Currituck."

DAVIDSON.

Formed in 1822 from Rowan.

Incorporated Schools.—Lexington Academy, chartered 1825; Clemmonsville Academy, chartered 1833; Glen Anna Female Seminary, chartered 1854; Yadkin Institute, chartered 1854; Shiloh Academy, chartered 1881.

All the above had a measure of success, but have been discontinued, with the exception of Yadkin Institute, which was changed to Yadkin College in 1865, and Shiloh Academy.

GLEN-ANNA FEMALE SEMINARY was designed as a feeder to Greensboro Female College, but "no sectarian influences were allowed." The first principal was Miss Branson and then Miss Ellen E. Morphis. —— Shelton was steward and his wife matron. Tuition, per session of five months, was $2, $10 and $12; Piano music, $20; French, $5; board, $6 per month.

Glen-Anna was bought by Rev. Dr. C. F. Deems, when president of Greensboro Female College, and owned for several years and supervised by him. He called it after the first name of his wife. Prior to his purchase it was a successful school, under the management of Mrs. Charles Moch, and was called Sylva Grove Female Seminary. The property passed into the hands of John W. Thomas, who erected a $12,000 building and secured for it an able corps of teachers. Miss P. L. Lathrop was principal in 1858. It had a large success until the Civil War. Mr. Thomas kept it up, though languishing throughout the war. In 1867 the name was changed to Thomasville Female College. On the death of Mr. Thomas in 1873, it was closed. In 1874 Mr. H. W. Reinhart purchased the property and for ten years had a large patronage. In 1884 Rev. J. N. Stallings became co-owner and co-principal. It began to lose its hold on the public for some reason, was transferred to High Point in 1889, and after about four years was closed.

YADKIN COLLEGE, at first Yadkin Institute, was opened in 1856, under the patronage of the Methodist Protestant Church. George W. Hege was the first President and it had good patronage until the Civil War. In 1867 H. T. Phillips, aided by F. T. Walser, reorganized the college. Rev. J. C. Deans joined Mr. Phillips in 1871. In 1873 President S. Simpson a man of enegry and talent, took charge and had fair success. He procured the erection of a large new building. On his resigning his place for a professorship in Western Maryland College, the institution, as a college, was closed for a time. Rev. A. R. Morgan, now a missionary in Japan, opened it as a high school, and it was so continued by George W. Holmes. Under the guidance of Mr. Holmes its functions as a college have been resumed.

DAVIE.

Formed in 1836 from Rowan.

The first classical school in this county (then part of Rowan) was taught by Peter Stewart Ney, the subject of an interesting volume by Rev. James A. Weston.

Its patronage extended over several counties. It was situated about one mile from Mocksville, near a church namey Joppa. Three years afterwards he taught at what was known as the Dan Foster school-house. He had about thirty pupils at each, many of whom were of full age, some being girls sixteen years old and over.

This remarkable man, who made a profound impression on all with whom he come in contact as a man of learning, and high character, arrived in the United States in 1819. His bearing, conversation, skill in horsemanship, fencing and military tactics and numerous wounds, together with his evidently being a Frenchman, showed that he had probably been a cavalry officer in Napolieon's army. He showed an acquaintance, which his friends thought to be familiar, with Latin, Greek and Hebrew, spoke good English and wrote indifferent poetry. He was a faithful and successful teacher, kind in temper and terrible only to the idle and wayward. He was honorable and of irreproachable conduct, except in the matter of temperance. He drank ardent spirits regularly, often to excess. When intoxicated, and occasionally when some thought him sober, he encouraged the belief that he was the celebrated Marshal Michael Ney, whose execution was alleged to have been a sham. He was by his pupils and patrons, who condoned his vice on account of his good qualities, regarded with affection and admiration. Many think that Mr. Weston has proved that he was truly the Marshal, others that the claim was the hallucination of alcohol. Certainly he was an interesting character.

Peter Stuart Ney taught in Brownsville, South Carolina, in Davite County, then Rowan, between 1820 and 1830, then in Mecklenburg County, in Virginia. Returning to North Carolina about 1830, he had schools in Lincoln, Iredell, Davie, Cabarrus, and Rowan, then in Darlington District, S. C., and in Lincoln and Rowan counties, in North Carolina, until his death, in 1846. His salary was $200 per ten months and his board. In addition to his knowledge of languages he was a skilled mathematician. The numbers of his pupils was about thirty. He was very liberal in giving free tuition, deducting the amount, if required by the trustees, out of his salary.

Other teachers in Davie, at Mocksville or very near the town, were—1830-'36: Wm. Buford, father of Col. A. S. Buford, once president of the Richmond & Danville R. R. Co., of high reputation. After him was A. G. Miller, and then —— Armfield, followed by Rev. John Tilllett, Robert E. Troy, Rev. Baxter Clegg (1840-'55). Then there were Rev. —— Campbell, Samuel Davis, Jacob Eaton (1862-'74), Miss Mattie Eaton (1875 to 1883), and afterwards successively, Rev. E. M. Dowum, —— Bander, Maxcy L. John and George E. Barnett (1893-'97). The attendance on these schools averaged about fifty.

Of the above Rev. Baxter Clegg had largest reputation, having pupils from Mecklenburg, Cabarrus, Rowan, Iredell, and other counties. He had great influence upon the young in stimulating desire for education, and upon the people at large, morally and socially. (See "Chatham.")

GEORGE H. CROWELL,
PRINCIPAL HIGH POINT PUBLIC SCHOOLS, HIGH POINT, N. C.

In 1856 there were male and female academies at Mocksville, a mixed school at Smith's Grove, and another at Clemmonsville.

From 1854 to 1860 J. H. Foote and Samuel O. Tatum, and from 1878 to 1881 J. F. Brower taught about sixty pupils at Union Academy, near Farmington.

In the Academy at Farmington S. W. Finch, O. B. Eaton and Lemuel Cash were successively principals, from 1884 to the incumbency of Miss Jessie Chaffin, now in charge.

The following have been teachers in the county, within the last twenty years:

C. F. Rominger, Ed. Alderman, J. T. Alderman, 1876-'84; Rev. J. N. Stallings, Jerusalem, 1896; Rev. A. K. Murchison, Advance Academy, 1888; B. K. Mason and C. M. Sheets, Advance Academy, 1892-'94.

All the forgoing teachers were well qualified, but with the exception of Peter S. Ney and Rev. Baxter Clegg, their patronage was local.

Chief Justice R. M. Pearson opened his celebrated law-school in Mocksville in 1842. The school was afterwards removed to the part of Surry, now Yadkin, and will receive further notice under "Yadkin."

COKESBURY SCHOOL, though of short duration, is of much interest because it was the first educational institution established by the Methodists in North Carolina. It was a classical school, situate in Davie County, near the Yadkin, and was begun about 1893. Rev James Parks was the first and only teacher. Its name was a combination of Coke and Arbury, the great pioneers of Methodism. Asbury visited it and preached in its building.

DUPLIN.

Formed in 1749 from New Hanover.

Incorporated Schools.—Grove Academy, chartered 1785; Union Meeting House Academy, chartered 1801;

Goshen Academy, chartered 1813; Free School in Duplin, chartered 1814; Williams, Academy, chartered 1825; Bethel Academy, chartered 1828; Union Academy, chartered 1829; Hannah Moore Academy, chartered 1834; Franklin Academy, chartered 1842; Washington Academy, chartered 1844; Dunn-Faison Academy, chartered 1844; Warsaw High School, chartered 1857; La Place School, chartered 1864; Lane Field Academy, chartered 1873.

GROVE ACADEMY is the oldest and most eminent of the schools of Duplin. As early as 1790 there was an advertisement, signed by Thos. Routledge, President, offering full instruction in Greek and Latin and the Sciences. It is known that the Rev. Samuel Stanford was its teacher in 1795, and long afterwards. Between 1830 and 1840 Andrew Manspeaker had charge. From 1845 to and after the Civil War, a graduate of the University of Edinburgh, an accomplished scholar, and excellent man, Rev. James Sprunt, D. D., was its head. Under his management patronage was drawn from adjoining counties. After him was Samuel W. Clements, a graduate of the University of North Carolina, for many years. After high reputation for many years, the site of this school, the intellectual nourisher of Vice-President Wm. R. King, Col. Thomas Kenan, member of Congress in the old days; Col. Thomas S. Kenan, Attorney-General and Clerk of the Supreme Court of our days, and many other useful citizens, with its beautiful grove, is now a corn-field.

THE HANNAH MOORE ACADEMY was a flourishing institution for females.

LANE FIELD ACADEMY was quite flourishing in its day.

FRIENDSHIP ACADEMY was very successful, under the management of Rev. Malcolm Connelly.

FRANKLIN SCIENTIFIC AND MILITARY INSTITUTE, situate three miles from Mount Olive, was begun in 1858, by Richard W. Millard, of Duplin, and

Claudius B. Denson, of Virginia, as joint Principals. Philosophical, Chemical and Astronomical apparatus, maps, charts, etc., were procured. Besides Latin and Greek, French and German were offered. The terms were $40, $30 and $20 per ten months, for the Senior, Junior and Preparatory departments. Board, $8 per month, including washing, fuel and lights. Exercises in military tactics and gymnastics were required. This important enterprise was of course ruined by the exigencies of the great war.

DURHAM.

Formed in 1881 from Orange and Wake.

It was within the limits of this county that Rev. John Chavis, a freeman of color, taught a classical school, about seventy years ago. He was a preacher in the Presbyterian Church and was highly regarded by the best men of his community, both as a teacher and as a man. Among his pupils were Willie P. Mangum and other best citizens of Orange.

For the schools of Durham. see "Orange."

EDGECOMBE.

Formed in 1732. A precinct of Bath until 1738.

Incorporated Schools.—Tarboro Academy, chartered 1793; Tarboro Academy, chartered again 1813; Hopewell Academy, chartered 1822; Friendship Academy, chartered 1823; Town Creek Academy, chartered 1823; Mount Prospect Academy, chartered 1824; Harmony Grove Academy, chartered 1824; Pleasant Grove Academy, chartered 1825; New Hope Academy, chartered 1826; Columbia Academy, chartered 1827; Hickory Grove Academy, chartered 1830; Conetoe Academy, chartered 1835; Hopewell Academy, chartered 1840; New Hope Academy, chartered 1842; Toisnot Academy, chartered 1846; Tarboro

Academy, chartere again 1846; Tarboro Academy, chartered again 1870; Edgecombe Female Seminary, chartered 1873.

The only schools of much note within Edgecombe County were in Tarboro.

The names of the early teachers have been allowed to pass away. From an old letter I learn that George S. Phillips, whose father, Rev. John Phillips, was prominent in reorganizing the Episcopal Church in North Carolina, was principal of the Academy in 1819, but not successful as a disciplinarian. Dr. Jeremiah Battle, in his sketch of Edgecombe in 1810, states that there was no school of such importance as to prevent parents from sending their sons out of the county.

THE TARBORO MALE ACADEMY has kept up with more or less efficiency and with occasional interruptions since its establishment. In 1821 I find Mr. Robert S. Hall, a graduate of our University, as principal. The tuition was $16 and $22 for ten months. Frequent changes were made in the teaching force. In 1844 Josiah H. Brooks took charge and it flourished for several years. Robert H. Winborne, a promient physician of Chowan County, a grauduate of our University in 1847, was one of the principals. Frank S. Wiliamson, likewise a graduate of the same institution, succeeded in 1859, and conducted it very efficiently until the building was destroyed by fire about 1885. He then established a private schoool.

The school for females has had also varied fortunes. Miss Anna Phillips, daughter of Rev. John Phillips, said by an intelligent contemporary to have possessed all the Christian graces, was its head about 1820. For years prior to 1845, Misses Anna and Ellen Ragsdale, by their excellent management, secured a wide patronage. During that year Rev. Thomas R. Owen, and his wife, the latter having been a teacher of great repute at Washington N. C., began their career of eminent usefulness. About 1864 they gave

way to Mrs. General W. D. Pender, daughter of Hon. Augustin Shepherd, and Miss —— Anthony, likewise able teachers. On the marriage of the latter to Wm. H. Johnson, Mrs. Pender became sole principal. She retired about 1880 and D. G. Gillespie, now in charge, succeeded. As a matter of course the Graded School has drawn largely from its patronage.

Mount Prospect Academy was built by Exum Lewis on his plantation, about 1820, and was a mixed school of importance. The teachers were, successively, James C. Carey, George Pendleton, both of Virginia; Philip Wiley, afterwards an Episcopal minister; Eugene Casey, from Ireland; then Alexander Bellamy, afterwards of Florida; then Frederick Phillips, grandfather of the ex-Judge of the same name.

FORSYTH.

Formed in 1848 from Stokes.

Incorporated Schools.—Kernersville High School, chartered 1863; Salem Female Academy, established 1802, chartered 1866.

The admirable Salem Female Academy does not come within the scope of my enquiry, as it is still in existence.

It is believed that the German and Moravian settlers of this region had their children taught from the beginning. We have evidence that there was a school for boys as early as 1794 on the public square at Salem. The classics were not taught, but German was. The limits of ages was from six to fourteen.

The Military School, founded by Col. A. C. Davis, near Winston, was organized with what was considered a fair promise of a successful career. It was removed from La Grange, in Lenoir County. It was found, however, after several years of usefulness, that the patronage did not justify its continuance and it was closed in.

FRANKLIN.

Formed in 1779 from Bertie.

Incorporated Schools.—Franklin Academy, chartered 1786; Franklin Academy, again chartered 1802; Louisburg Female Academy, chartered 1814; Midway Academy, chartered 1821; Midway Academy, again chartered 1842; Franklin Institute, at Cedar Rock, chartered 1846; Franklinton Female Academy, chartered 1846; Female Academy, in Franklinton, chartered 1851; Franklinton Male and Female Institute, chartered 1854.

In 1854 it was provided that the Louisburg Female Academy should convey its property to the Louisburg Female College Company.

In 1851 the charter of the Franklinton Female Academy was repealed.

The citizens of Louisburg, from the first, provided for the education of their children. In 1779, when the town was laid off, 12 1-2 acres were set aside for a school for males, and on the opposite side of the main street a like area for females. The trustees were selected by the town authorities, and seemed to have been faithful in attending to their duties.

We have not a complete list of the teachers in these academies.

There must have been a cessation of exercises prior to 1802, as the charter was re-enacted then. The opening at that date was with promise of great things. In 1804 I find an advertisement by the principal, Matthew Dickinson, asserting that instruction would be given in ethics and metaphysics, Latin, Greek, Hebrew, French, Italian and the higher branches of Metaphysics and Philosophy, viz., Algebra, Geometry, Trigonametry, Conic sections, altimetry, longimetry, Mensuration of superfices and solids, Surveying, Navigation, Natural Philosophy and Astronomy.

At the close of the session there were to be orations and

a comedy, in which the pupils were the actors. The address was to be by the eminent lawyer, Judge John Haywood. It was stated that Dickenson was of Yale College, and he seemed to have aspired to supersede the State University. This ambitious scheme must have met with failure, as, in 1809, we find James Bogle and in 1811 Davis H. Mayhew, assisted by Mr. Hillman, in charge of the male academy. In 1820 both the male and female academies were under the joint management of Miss Ann Benedict and Mr. Fitch Wheeler, both of Connecticut, the latter of Yale College. John La Taste was over the music. In 1830 Miss Mary Ramsey, assisted by Miss Mary Earl, was over the females. In 1831 John B. Bobbitt, who had gained eminence in Halifax and Nash, a graduate of our University in 1809, was over the males, while his wife was principal of the female department, and they so continued for about ten years.

The patronage under them was extensive. An old pupil gives me his reminiscences of the instruction of Mr. Bobbitt. As he approached the academy he heard a loud humming noise. When he entered he found the teacher sitting in a chair, leaning against the wall, with his feet in the rounds. He was reading a book. The boys were sitting on backless wooden benches, with their faces to the walls and backs towards the teacher. All were studying aloud. When a class was ready to recite, they stood in front of the teacher and he heard their lessons with his eyes shut. There was very little discipline—no punishment for missing the lessons.

I myself was, in 1839, a pupil of Mrs. Bobbitt. There were 40 or 50 pupils, of all ages, from 18 down to 7. There were a few boys of tender age, but most of the pupils were of the other sex. There was no instruction given, except repeating lessons previously assigned. The girls behaved with all decorum. For example, they once discussed whether they might decently turn somersets in sight of the boys in a pile of leaves. A daring pioneer of woman's rights advocated the pastime, provided the lower skirts should be confined by a cincture, but she could not get a second. When the trustees came for the examination at the close of the session, we were previously given the two or three words which we would be required to spell. I do not know whether this "pious fraud" was committed with the larger pupils. Mrs. Bobbitt kept good order, but did not often inflict whipping. Standing in a corner, with or without the dunce's cap, and "keeping in" after school were the punishments. In the advertisement of their coming, in 1831, it was stated that they had taught previously in this institution acceptably.

In 1842, the Bobbitts giving place on acount of old age, A. H. Ray was principal of the male academy, and he and his wife of the female branch, assisted by Miss E. M. Curtis in the music department. In 1855, by authority of the General Assembly, the trustees leased for $40 per annum the female academy grounds to the Louisburg Female College Company, which tore down the old building and erected a handsome new building, with adequate recitations and dormitories. The first President under the new arrangement was J. P. Nelson; then Columbus Andrews; then James Southgate, who was Principal during the war, until it was closed.

The Principal of the male academy after A. H. Ray was Matthew S. Davis, who graduated at our University in 1855. This was also closed by the war.

In 1822 Rev. Charles Appewhite Hill, of the Methodist Church, an able teacher, who had been in charge of a school in Warrenton, opened Midway Academy for boys, half way between Warrenton and Louisburg, and continued it until his death, in 1831. His charges were $100 a year for board and tuition. He was succeeded by John J. Wyche. Mr. Hill was a graduate of our University in

1816, and was State Senator from Franklin four terms. Mr. Wyche graduated at the same institution in 1825, and was tutor therein. He was afterwards a professor of Jefferson College, Mississippi.

In 1839 John Y. Hicks was principal of Herndon Academy, which was probably in this county. He was an uncommonly good teacher, likewise worked in Nash and Wake; at Raleigh in 1843, and then removed to Macon County, where he taught and became a member of the House of Commons. I remember his as dignified, kindly and resorting to the rod only in extreme cases.

There was also in 1856 a flourishing academy at Cedar Rock.

GASTON.

Formed in 1847 from Lincoln.

Incorporated Schools.—King's Mountain High School, chartered 1883.

In 1856 there were small schools at Woodlawn, at Dallas and Mountain Island.

I regret that I have been unable to obtain information concerning the extinct schools. I feel sure there were many.

GATES.

Formed in 1779 from Hertford.

Incorporated Schools.—Spring Hill Academy, chartered 1820; Sunbury Academy, chartered 1832; Gatesville Academy, chartered 1832.

In 1850 there was a Female Institute at Buckland, of which Samuel E. Smith was Principal.

GRAHAM.

Formed in 1872 from Cherokee.

GRANVILLE.

Formed in 1746 from Edgecombe.

Incorporated Schools.—Granville Hall, chartered 1779; Williamsboro Franklin Library Society (school included), chartered 1799; Montpelier Academy, chartered 1810; Oxford Academy, chartered 1811; Williamsboro Academy, chartered 1813; Ford Creek Academy, chartered 1835; Tar River Academy, chartered 1850; Oxford Baptist Female College, chartered 1851; Granville Institute, chartered 1854; Oak Hill Military Academy, chartered 1861; Tally Ho Female Academy, chartered 1861; Horner School, chartered 1883.

Of the above, Montpelier Academy is described as being on the land of W. M. Sneed; Oxford Academy on the land of T. B. Littlejohn, near the courthouse.

In addition to these, it appears from the statement of Rev. Dr. C. H. Wiley that there were in 1856 R. H. Graves' Select School at Brownsville; Male Academy at Island Creek, T. H. Brame, Principal; High School at Oak Hill; Male Academy at Knap of Reeds.

This county is distinguished for its efforts in the cause of education. In addition to its excellent schools, it made an effort to secure the location of the University within its limits. When a ballot was had, in 1792, for the centre of a circle of fifteen miles radius, within which it was to be placed, Goshen and Williamsboro were two of the places placed in nomination.

One of the earliest and best teachers in the State was a Scotch-Irish Presbyterian, a preacher of influence, so great that he was one of those selected by Governor Tryon to pacify the Regulators, a delegate to the Provincial Congress of 1775, who presided in the committee of the whole; also acting as its chaplain—Henry Pattillo. He spent at least twelve years teaching and preaching in Orange and Granville. One of his schools was in Williamsboro; another was called "Granville Hall," incorporated in 1779, when the country was convulsed with war. The Governor, Caswell; the Speakers of the two houses, Nash and Benbury; a signer of the Declaration, Penn, and Brigadier General Person, were with Pattillo and other leading men, the trustees. Great things were expected of the enterprise. It is recorded that liberal subscriptions were made to it, and the trustees were instructed by the charter to purchase 500 acres of land and erect buildings thereon for the school, but even the site is not now known. Pattillo published, besides a volume of sermons, a school-book, probably the first in the State, a geography by question and answer, a creditable producttion. It was printed in 1796 by Abraham Hodge ,and dedicated to General Davie.

I regret that I am unable to give all the teachers of the Oxford Academy. In 1815 the Principal was Rev. James W. Thompson, assisted by Thomas H. Willie and Miss Ann C. McIntyre. There was also a female department, and the two departments have continued ever since, giving to Oxford, even before the advent of the famous schools of Horner and Graves and of J. H. Horner alone, a wide reputation as an educational centre.

Col. R. B. Creecy pays the following tribute to the teachers of the Academy in Oxford about 1822: It was "considered the best school in North Carolina, the teacher, James D. Johnson, a fine scholar, a Presbyterian of the straightest sect." * * * "The school was an example of education, with some features now obsolete, that might be imitated in those days of reconstructed systems of education."

In 1835 Rev. Thomas S. W. Mott, an Episcopal minister, was the head, a man of decided ability. In 1839 the principals were D. F. Robertson and Rev. Thomas H. Willie. In 1843 it was John J. Wyche, who was described under the head of "Franklin County." He was succeeded by Edward Hubbell Hicks, who taught until 1852, when

James H. Horner, the eminent educator, became principal and held the place for two years.

In 1830 the "North Carolina Literary, Scientific and Military School" was opened at Oxford by Capt. D. H. Bingham. Pupils over fourteen years of age were to pay $175, and under that age $160 for tuition and board. Clothing and books were extras. He removed to Raleigh the next year.

As said above, the Female branch of the Academy was as a rule successful in its work. I have not succeeded in recovering many of the teachers. Among them were Benjamin Sumner, afterwards of Licolnton, a University man, and then Samuel L. Venable and Mrs. E. F. Venable, about 1860.

St. John's College, designed to be an institution of learning, under control of the Masonic order in this State, had a checkered history. It was projected in 1850, a beautiful site purchased, and a handsome building finished by 1857, the property, however ,subject to a mortgage of $7,000. As there was no endowment it was determined to open a school in the building. This was done with much ceremony, Rev. Dr. Francis L. Hawks, the historian and eloquent divine, delivering an address before a numerous company. The principal of the school was Ashbel G. Brown, late Adjunct Professor of Ancient Languages in the University, and his assistant was James Campbell. The next chief was Thomas C. Tuley, who held the post for three or four years, when it was converted into a Female College or school, and John H. Mills, Rev. J. H. Phillips and Rev. C. B. Riddick, successively, were the teachers. The property was then sold under mortgage and the Grand Lodge became the purchaser, and, under the advocacy of John H. Mills, its first superintendent, was changed into the Oxford Orphan Asylum.

The Oxford Female College was opened in 1851, under

AUDITORIUM AND DORMITORY (NEW)—INSTITUTION FOR THE DEAF AND DUMB AND THE BLIND.
WHITE DEPARTMENT.

Baptist auspices, Rev. Samuel Wait, President. Owing to financial difficulties, the property was sold to J. H. Mills in 1857, and afterwards passed into the control of its present owner and superintendent, F. P. Hobgood.

Williamsboro Academy was always under control of Trustees who endeavored to secure the best teachers. In 1805 the principal was John Vick, who agreed to teach all the usual branches, including the classics. In 1815 we find Andrew Rhea, Professor of Ancient Languages in the University, 1800-'14. The tuition was then $20 per ten months and board $60. In 1821 there was secured one destined to become very eminent as a teacher, Rev. Alexander Wilson, who will be more particularly mentioned under Guilford. Dr. Wm. McPheeters, of Raleigh, under whom he had been teaching, certified that he ranked among the first academic instructors of the State, and Chief Justice J. L. Taylor, Solicitor James F. Taylor, and others joined in the certificate. He advertised to give instruction in "the different branches established by the University of North Carolina": Tuition $25 and $16 for 10 months, and $70 for board. Among the trustees of this Academy were Bishop John S. Ravenscroft, Chief Justice Pleasant Henderson, State Treasurer Wm. Robards, United States Senator Nathaniel Macon.

Ralph Henry Graves, a distinguished teacher, graduate and Tutor of Mathematics in our University, 1837-'43, had for many years a school of wide patronage in this county. It was called Belmont Academy, and he was assisted by William H. Owen, likewise a gradate and Tutor of the University and Professor and Acting Professor of Wake Forest College. Prof. Graves was a successful teacher in classical schools in several counties for about forty years.

Among the schools of Granville should be included the Law School of Chief Justice Leonard Henderson, at Williamsboro. Chief Justice R. M. Pearson and Judge

Wm. H. Battle, of the Supreme Court of this State, bore testimony to its efficiency and wide usefulness, and in their own law-schools adopted his method of teaching, by "familiar questions and answers."

GREENE.

Formed in 1799 from Glasgow, which was from Johnston, with a slice of Craven.

Incorporated Schoools.—Greene Academy, chartered 1804; Snow Hill Academy, chartered 1812; Greene Academy, again chartered 1813; Hookerton Academy, chartered 1817; Hookerton Academy, again chartered 1834; Oak Grove Academy, chartered 1825.

The charter of the Hookerton Academy allowed every $5 subscriber to vote for trustees, and the like amount was a qualification for holding the office. In 1819 the General Assembly authorized the trustees to make $2,000 by holding a lottery. In 1827 the Hookerton Library Association was chartered.

GUILFORD.

Formed in 1770 from Rowan and Orange.

The Incorported Schools are.—David Caldwell Academy, chartered 1798; Thisbe Academy, chartered 1809; Greensboro Academy, chartered 1816; Greensboro Female Academy, chartered 1820; New Garden Boarding School, chartered 1833; Greensboro Academy and Manual Labor School, chartered 1833; Caldwell Institute, chartered 1836; Greensboro Female College, chartered 1838; Union Institute Academy, chartered 1840; Greensboro High School, chartered 1846; Woodburn Female Seminary, chartered 1855; Greensboro Female College, chartered 1870; Oak Ridge Institute, chartered 1881.

Of the above the Greensboro Female Academy of 1820 was under the same trustees as the Male Academy. The

Greensboro High School of 1846 replaced the Caldwell Institute.

The most noted school in the State was in this county, that of David Caldwell, a graduate of Princeton in 1761 and in 1810, was the first who received the degree of Doctor of Divinity from our University. It was organized about 1767, and, with the exception of the interruption caused by the British warrior, under Cornwallis, continued until two years before his death in 1824, at the age of 99 years. He was active in efforts to tranquillize the Regulators, and in the Revolutionary struggle was so ardent a Whig that his library and books were burned. He was a member of the Constitutional Congress of November, 1776, at Halifax, and of the Convention of 1788, in which he voted with the majority against immediate ratification of the Constitution of the United States. He was urged by the Trustees of the University to take charge in 1795 of the opening institution. He was an able and thorough instructor in the classics, mathematics, belle-letters and Theology, and many of the leaders of North Carolina, and other States in ecclesiastical, as well as lay occupations, obtained their higher education from him. His school was about three miles northwest of Greensboro. Besides his labors as a teacher he was pastor of Buffalo and Alamance churches (Presbyterian).

It must not be supposed that Dr. Caldwell had the only school in the county. Among others after the Revolutionary War—Rev. Mr. Benthahn had a German school in the southeast part of the county.

Rev. Wm. D. Paisley organized a school for boys in Greensboro about 1820. About 1828 Rev. Silas C. Lindsley was his successor and did good work until called off to an educational movement on a larger scale.

In 1833 the Presbytery of Orange resolved to found a classical school for males. It was located in Greensboro, and named Caldwell Institute. It is usually stated that the name was in honor of Rev. Dr. Joseph Caldwell, who at that time, by his career as President of the University then drawing to a close, and by his labors in behalf of Public Schools, was especially before the eyes of the public, but it seems certain that the committee on Organization had in mind also the long and successful work of Dr. David Caldwell near the site selected. Rev. Alexander Wilson as Principal, and Rev. Silas C. Lindsley as assistants, were placed in charge. Besides the subjects taught in the best classical schools, instruction was given in the Evidences of Christianity, the Bible and the Westminster Catechism. A short sketch of Dr. Wilson is given under Alamance.

Rev. John A. Gretter was added as a teacher after two years, and was succeeded in 1844 by Ralph H. Graves. In the next year, owing to much sickness, caused probably by a neighboring mill-pond, the school was removed to Hillsboro.

The Greensboro High School was chartered to take the place of the emigrating Caldwell Institute, with John M. Morehead, John M. Dicks, John A. Gilmer and other worthy Trustees. The first principal was Rev. Eli W. Caruthers, a native of Rowan, a graduate of Princeton, made in 1854 doctor of divinity by our University, successor of Dr. David Caldwell in the pastorate of Buffalo and Alamance churches, another of the life of David Caldwell and of two volumes, on the Revolutionary history of North Carolina. The associates of Dr. Caruthers were Rev. John A. Gretter, D.D., long the respected minister of the Presbyterian church in Greensboro, Rev. Silas C. Lindsley, also a Presbyterian preacher and Dr. Joseph A. McLean.

After service of two years Dr. Caruthers resigned and the school was under charge of Dr. Gretter as Principal and Rev. Mr. Grimsley and for years did work of the highest order.

In 1856 a male academy here was conducted by J. D. Campbell, as Principal.

MAIN BUILDING HIGH POINT PUBLIC SCHOOLS HIGH POINT, N. C.

Dr. Caruthers about 1847 opened a classical school at a place called Alamance, nine miles east of Greensboro, and conducted it for some years, in addition to his duties as pastor. Being of anti-war sentiments his Alamance congregation requested his resignation, which was given in 1861. He died a bachelor in 1865.

Rev. Wm. D. Paisley, the organizer of the Presbyterian church in Greensboro, also taught a girls' school shortly prior to 1830. After him came successively Miss Judith Mendenhall, Miss Ann D. Salmon, then Miss Umphries, then about 1836 Miss Mary Ann Hoge, and with her a lady who afterwards was the wife of Robert G. Lindsay. In 1840 John M. Morehead, who next year became Governor of North Carolina, erected on a large and centrally located site a four-story brick building and established Edgeworth Female Seminary. Miss Hoge was chosen Principal, and with an able Faculty, attracted a wide patronage. Among the teachers were Misses Emily Hubbard and Eliza Rose, Misses Nash and Kolloch, Rev. John A. Gretter and Profs. Breite and Brandt, the two latter in music. In 1844, on the death of Miss Hoge, Dr. and Mrs. D. P. Weir succeeded, and the next year Rev. Gilbert Morgan and wife, who introduced the collegiate plan, with four classes, and a preparatory department to train young girls to enter the lowest class. The expenses were, for 10 months, board and tuition $150, piano $40, guitar $30, drawing $20, printing $20, Latin, Greek and French each $20, wax-work $20, shell-work $10, silk and worsted work $10. In the first collegiate year were taught Arithmetic, English, Latin and Greek grammars, spelling and analysis, Dictionary, Geography, History of United States, Book of Commerce, Mythology, Jewish Antiquities, Watts on the Mead, French, Latin or Greek Language, "with one ornamental branch." and Lectures on Self-knowledge and Self-Culture.

In the 2nd year the course included Algebra, Geometry, Rhetoric, Botany, Natural Theology, Ancient and Mediaeval History, Geography of the Heavens and Blair's Lectures.

In the 3rd year were Natural Philosophy, the English Language, its Etymology, Lexicography and History, Astronomy, Physiology, Alexander's Evidences.

In the 4th year were Philosophy of the Mind, Astronomy, Kame's Elements, Critical Study of Milton and Shakespeare, Constitution of the United States, Principles of Interpretation, Moral Philosophy, Guizot on Civilization, Butler's Analogy, Lectures on Harmony of Truth, or Method and Plea of Self-education.

The school prospered greatly. Mr. Morgan in 1850 was succeeded by Prof. Richard Sterling, of Virginia, under whom there was still further increase until it was closed in 1862 by reason of the war. In 1868 Rev. J. M. M. Caldwell, grandson of Dr. David Caldwell, leased the property and the school regained much of its patronage. In 1871 he removed to Rome, Georgia, and Edgeworth Seminary became a thing of the past.

Prof. Sterling was the author of the Southern "Second Reader," and "Fourth Reader," and in conjunction with Prof. Campbell, "Our Own Third Reader," and "The Southern Primer."

The Female Normal School, at High Point, was projected by Rev. W. I. Langdon, Proprietor, in 1858. The circular shows a most intelligent plan. Very liberal terms are offered those desiring to be teachers, in the way of tuition and other expenses loaned. A brick building, 100 feet by 47 feet, four stories high, capable of accommodating 125 boarding pupils, in rooms heated by fire places, and thus well ventilated, were provided. It was ruined by the war.

Major Wm. Bingham Lynch, grandson of Wm. Bingham, the elder, founded an excellent school at High Point about 1880, after retiring from the Bingham School at Mebane. He conducted it ably, using military government and drill, for several years, when threatened ill-health made it prudent for him to remove to Florida in 1883, where he is still engaged in the work of education. (See "Orange.")

HALIFAX.

Formed in 1758 from Edgecombe.

Incorporated Schools.—Vine Hill Academy, chartered 1809; Springfield Academy, chartered 1810; Union Academy, chartered 1814; Enfield Academy, chartered 1819; Farmersville Academy, chartered 1820; Eglantine Academy, chartered 1847.

In 1810 Vine Hill Academy had permission from the General Assembly to raise $500 by a lottery.

By the kindness of Mr. T. S. Whitaker, of Enfield, I have the following facts about the old schools of Halifax:

WHITAERK'S CHAPEL, five and a half miles from Enfield, had as its teachers between 1820 and 1850: McLean, Cassudy, Strange, John Beavans, R. H. Whitaker, Jones, Wm. Richardson, Cassady, Rev. G. T. Whitaker, A. Coningland, M. T. Whitaker, Ex-Attorney General Batchelor was a pupil of this school in 1838, and bears testimony to its high standing. His teacher was Richardson.

FARMWELL ACADEMY, near Ringwood. About 1830, John B. Tate; Horne 1837, Jackson, Judge, David W. Kerr, Wm. C. Doub, ——— Bass and ——— Garrett.

ELBA ACADEMY, near Brinkleyville. From 1854 to 1860 Rev. J. H. Page was Principal.

SHELL CASTLE, near Enfield. 1855 to 1860, Miss Denning.

In 1856 Major Fred H. Jones had a school near Halifax.

ENFIELD ACADEMY has been in existence since 1859, and is still doing good work.

Vine Hill Academy, in Scotland Neck, has been engaged in it's beneficent work for 90 years. It was attended by men like B. F. Moore and Judge Wm. H. Battle. As it is still in operation it's history does not belong to this paper.

In 1839 there was La Valle's School near Halifax "under two Northern ladies."

A few years prior to the Civil War Miss Sue Williams was Principal of Roanoke Female Seminary, near Palmyra.

About eighty years ago there was a good school in the upper part of the county at Webb's Cross Roads. The teacher was Wm. E. Webb, who was Professor of Ancient Languages in the State University, 1799-1800.

A. W. McLean, noted as a severe disciplinarian, taught probably at the Farmwell Grove Academy about sixty years ago.

In Halifax town, Kelly Hines, Andrew and Edward Coningland, the latter afterwards a prominent lawyer, had good schools about 1840.

HARNETT. Formed in 1855 from Cumberland.

At Summerville in this county General Alexander D. McLean, had a successful school for 38 years.

To the same village after 1850 Rev. Dr. Simeon Colter, mentioned in "Cumberland," transferred his teaching after he left Donaldson Academy in Fayetteville.

HAYWOOD.

Formed in 1808 from Buncombe.

Incorporated Schools.—Green Hill Academy, chartered 1809; Green Hill Academy, again chartered 1833; Richland Institute, chartered 1861; Waynesville Baptist College, chartered 1867.

HENDERSON.

Formed in 1838 from Buncombe.

After efforts extending from 1858 to 1882, Judson Col-

INDUSTRIAL BUILDING AND HEATING PLANT (NEW)—INSTITUTION FOR THE DEAF AND DUMB AND THE BLIND.

lege ,originally chartered as Western North Carolina Bapsist College, was opened under the control of the Baptists. Rev. J. B. Boone, with a corps of able teachers, had control for six years. He was succeeded by Richard H. Lewis, M. D., of Kinston, an experienced and able teacher. In 1892 the college property was sold to foreclose an old mortgage, passed into private hands, and Dr. Lewis returned to Kinston.

Judson College was a co-educational institution. It was divided into a Primary, a Preparatory, and a College Department. A fair idea of the scope of instruction may be had by noting the third, or last, year of the Preparatory and the third, or last, year of the College Departments. In the former were Mathematics, Arithmetic, Elementary Algebra.

English—Grammar, Composition and Rhetoric, Studies in English Literature, History of the United States.

Latin—Grammar, Caesar.

Greek—First Lessons, Grammar.

The studies of the third, or Senior, year of the college course, were:

Logics, Political Economy, Moral Science, Psychology, English Literature, General History, Evidences of Christianity.

Optional—French, Grammar, Bookkeeping, Music, Art.

In the second year, Mathematics was carried through Analytical Geometry and Calculus; Greek into Demosthenese, and Sophocles; Latin into Virgil, Horace, Tacitus, Livy.

In 1890-'91 there were six teachers, including the Principal, and 114 students.

HERTFORD.

Formed in 1759 from Chowan, Bertie and Northampton. Incorporated Schools.—Murfreesborough Academy, chartered 1797; Hertford Academy, chartered 1809; Spring Field Academy, chartered 1826; Murfreesborough Academy, again chartered 1830; Buckhorn Academy, chartered 1847; Chowan Female Institute, chartered 1849; Wesleyan Female College, chartered 1852.

I have no information about the earliest schools of Hertford. Mr. Pulaski Cowper furnishes interesting items beginning with 1840.

Wm. Bogart taught school in the old Buckhorn Academy, in Manning's Neck, now Como, about that date. He was succceeded by John Kimberly, a Northern man, afterwards Professor of Agricultural Chemistry in our University, and then came Mr. ——— Warner. About 1848, after Warner's departure, Mr. Kimberly opened a school at Buckhorn. George W. Neal was his pupil and assistant, and after graduating at the University, was his succcessor. Probably Dr. Robert H. Winborne taught here a short while. After the Civil War Julian Picot, took charge of the school, and still holds it.

At Murfreesborough Mrs. Harriet Banks, a most estimable lady, was chief of a mixed school for many years, beginning before 1840. Before her death she had a large boarding and day school for girls only. After her death the Academy was opened by John Lamb Pritchard, afterwards a Baptist preacher, an excellent man, who died in early life. After him Rev. A. McDowell, a graduate of Wake Forest College, took charge of the old Bank's Academy, and it was soon merged into the Chowan Baptist Female Institute.

After the sale of the Banks Academy to the Chowan Baptist Female Institute, a new Academy for boys was built, its first teacher being Mr. ——— Seward, of Connecticut, about 1844-'45. His successor was Amos T. Ackerman, of New York, who removed to Georgia, and was Attorney-General of the United States under President Grant. He is remembered by his pupils as being strict to the extreme of brutality. He is said to have inflicted 315 stripes on a boy in one whipping. Then came Edward J. Carter, and after him W. W. Manning, brother of Thos. C. Manning, Chief Justice of Louisiana, and uncle of John Manning, Professor of Law in our University. He himself had been a Judge in Alabama. His successor was James A. Delk, a graduate of the University.

About 1854 Jesse J. Yeates, afterwards a prminent lawyer and member of Congress, had a good school at Harrellsville.

Judson Cobb was head of a large school for boys and girls, about three miles from Murfreesborough. Mr. Alfred Darden employed teachers for a large school at his residence the same distance from that place, among the teachers being a daughter of Rev. Thomas Meredith.

At the residence of Captain Colin W. Barnes, father of the late Judge David H. Barnes, near the Northampton line, Rev. B. S. Bronson, a graduate of Yale, was Principal of a school.

Swift and Lyon had charge of the old Jackson Academy about 1851, and were followed by a Mr. —— Studley.

HYDE.

Formed 1705. Called Wickham until 1712. Precinct of Bath until 1738.

Incorporated Schools.—Rush Academy, chartered, additional trustees, 1832.

There were no schools in Hyde of more than local reputation. James H. Swindell, just after the Civil War, had probably the most noted, with about one hundred pupils, from all sections of the county. Its true name was Chapel Hiss Academy, though it was commonly called Amity Academy, because near a Methodist Church of that name.

He was a very severe disciplinarian, thought by some to have been excessively severe.

The teachers before the Civil War were, as a rule, freely given to the use of the rod. In one there was a veritable Declaration of Independence and successful Revolution. The teacher, James Young, was extremely unpopular with the pupils. One morning he found the school-house closed and doors and windows barricaded by the larger scholars, while the little ones had been sent home. He was notified that he must quit teaching in the county. He pleaded and threatened in vain. The boys "held the fort" all day and next morning renewed the contest. He yielded, and turning to other work, was successful in life and at his death left a good estate.

The following were the chief old schools and teachers of Hyde, approximately:

AT LAKE LANDING.—1825 to 1840, Arnold Gray Timothy Windley, ——— Vaughan; 1840, Philip Brody; 1844, Joseph Young; 1844 to 1850, ——— McGlynn, R. J. Wynee, Rev. Wesley Reid, Rev. Wm. E. Pell, Rev. ——— Terry, Simeon Rich; 1850 to 1860, Selby Watson, Thomas Mayhew, Benjamin Watson, ——— Gurganus, John Harris, Charles Anderson, A. McC. Jones; 1865 to 1878, J. H. Swindell, A. H. Hamlin, ——— Price, Rev. N. E. Price.

FEMALE TEACHERS AT LAKE LANDING.—1850 to 1860, Miss E. M. Parker, Miss Day, Miss Norton, Miss Blalock, Miss Remington, Mrs. Desmond, Miss Patterson, Miss Thoyer.; 1865 to 1875, Miss Caroline Borrow, Miss Henrietta Borrow, Miss Laura Borrow, Miss Annie Gibbs, Miss Clara Hoyt, Miss Emmeline Spencer, Miss Annie Spencer.

NEAR SWAN QUARTER.—Clement Lassiter, Washington Carrawan. Lassiter was murdered by Carrawan, who was a Baptist preacher, moved by jealousy, which was generally thought to have been unfounded. After conviction Carrawan drew a pistol and shot one of the lawyers for the prosecution, E. J. Warren, afterwards Judge, who was saved by the thickness of his overcoat. The prisoner then drew another pistol and shot himself through the head.

IREDELL.

Incorporated Schools.—Clio's Academy, chartered 1814; Statesville Academy, chartered 1815; Ebenezer Academy, chartered 1821; Mocksville Academy, chartered 1826; Poplar Grove Academy, chartered 1834; Statesville Male Academy, chartered 1849; Snow Creek Male Academy, chartered 1849; New Institute, chartered 1854; Olin High School, chartered 1857; Olin Agricultural and Mechanical College, chartered 1867; Centre Point Institute, chartered 1879.

Of the above, Clio's Academy had been in operation as Clio's Nursery since about 1775. It was changed to Statesville Academy in 1815.

New Institute was changed to Olin High School, and that to Olin Agricultural and Mechanical College.

The first school within the limits of this county, of which we have certain information, was the celebrated Crowfield Academy, established at Belle Mont, the old manor of Col. Alexander Osborne, as early as 1760. This was about two and a half miles northeast of Davidson College. It was continued until 1780, when the British invasion caused it to be closed. Dr. David Ker, the first Presiding Professor of the State University, and Charles Caldwell, M. D., afterwards Medical Professor in Philadelphia and elsewhere, taught here. It is said that Dr. David Caldwell was a teacher here and also Mr. McEwene. Many able men owe their education to it, e. g., Rev. Dr. ——— McRee, Dr. Sam'l E. McCorkle, Rev. Dr. James Hall, Dr. Epraim Brevard.

CLIO'S NURSERY—SCIENCE HALL.—These institutions were under the charge of Rev. James Hall, D. D., a Presbyterian minister, graduate of Princeton, Captain of cavalry and chaplain in the Revolutionary War. The degree of D. D. was conferred on him by his alma mater and the University of North Carolina. He opened Clio's Nursery, certainly as early as 1778, probably three years earlier. It was located on Snow Creek, and was the intellectual parent of many eminent men, such as Dr. ——— Waddel, of South Carolina, Judges Laurie, Harris and Smith.

Dr. Hall likewise purchased some apparatus in physics and opened Science Hall for advanced instruction. He had likewise a course in Theology. He thus had one of the best "Log Colleges" of that age, of vast benefit to those unable to secure the advantages of University training at distant points. Among the laity, who called Science Hall their alma mater, were Governor Israel Pickens, of Alabama; Joseph Pearson, member of Congress from North Carolina; Judge Williams, of Tennessee. Among the clergy were Drs. John Brown, of Georgia; Andrew Flinn, of South Carolina; John Robinson, of Poplar Tent.

Dr. Hall also aided his community by establishing a circulating library, and organizing debating societies. He likewise published an English Grammar. He made a donation of sixty volumes to the University.

The last years of this good man were clouded by melancholy. He died in 1826, at the age of 82.

Clio's Academy was removed to Statesville in 1815. The Principal was a worthy successor to Dr. Hall, John N. Mushatt, of Connecticut, a graduate of Yale College. He was a pastor of the Associate Reformed Presbyterian Church, and as such organized the first church of that denomination in Iredell County. He came to North Carolina about 1810 and married a daughter of General Wm. Lee Davidson. Shortly before 1830 he taught the Academy in Lincolnton.

Mushatt's school had a wide patronage. Among his pupils were Governor Wm. A. Graham, and Chief Justice R. M. Pearson, who were prepared for the University by him, both graduating there with first honor. They bove testimony to the excellence of his methods. He was a strict but just disciplinarian, whipping grown young men who broke his laws.

About 1830 he removed to Lownder County, Ala., and about 1838, one of his sons attended Davidson College.

Acccording to Prof. D. Matt. Thompson the true history of Dr. Hall's school is as folows:

Clio Lyceum was nine miles north of Statesville, near Snow Creek Church. The principal teachers were —— Stevenson, Dr. Charles Caldwell and Dr. James Hall. The school-house—of logs—was burnt in 1810, after continuing from 1776.

Rev. Dr. James Hall's Grammar School, six miles northeast of Statesville, near Bethany, the successor to Clio Lyceum, opened about 1810 and continued until "the 50's." The teachers were Dr. James Hall, to 1816, then Robert Hall to 1823, then Wm. A. Hall for two years, followed by Hugh R. Hall, for about 25 years.

Peter Stuart Ney, mentioned under the head of Davie, taught at OAK HIL ACADEMY, in this county, from 1826 to 1838. He had the reputation of being an accomplished teacher and good disciplinarian. The most obstinate boy nearing manhood quailed before his angry eye. He died near Third Creek, Rowan County, in 1846. (See "Davie.")

Fourteen miles northeast of Statesville was the Olin High School, at Olin, under able teachers, Rev. B. Clegg, as Principal and A. Haywood Merritt, Assistant. Discipline was maintained by a system of demerit marks, the scale of which is as follows:

Absence from Recitation	5
Absence from Prayers	5
Absence from Church	5
Tardiness in any duty	1
Leaving seat	2
Leaving Recitation Room	2
Leaving Church	3
Failure to prepare Recitation	3
Disorder in Recitation Room	1 to 25
Disorder in Study Room	1 to 25
Disorder at Prayers	5
Disorder at Church	10
Profanity	25
Drinking ardent spirits	50
Other misdemeanors	1 to 100

Incurring 100 demerits in one session of five months led to dismission. A "little boy," however, incurring 20 demerits in one month, was forced to cancel them by taking a whipping.

Tuition was $40 for 41 weeks, in the classical department. In the English department, $20 to $30. Contingent fee, $1. Board, exclusive of lights, $8 per month.

STATESVILLE FEMALE COLLEGE, may properly come under the title of this paper, although it has been revived under an able leader, Rev. John B. Burwell. It was established by the Concord Presbytery in 1857. The first Principal, the able teacher in Lenoir, Caldwell County, Rev. J. M. M. Caldwell, and Rev. E. F. Rockwell, D. D., were subsequent Presidents. From 1877 to 1884, Mrs. Eliza N. Grant and Miss Margaret E. Mitchell, daughters of Rev. Dr. Elisha Mitchell, of the State University, were successful Principals. In 1885, on the death of Mrs. Grant, Miss Fannie Everitt was Principal until 1894. It was then closed until Mr. Burwell took charge in 1896.

JACKSON.

Formed in 1851 from Haywood and Macon.

JOHNSTON.

Formed in 1746 from Craven. Slices of Orange and Duplin added.

Incorporated Schools.—Smithfield Academy, chartered 1819; Sardis Academy, chartered 1821; Johnston Academy, chartered 1849.

The first school building of any size in Johnston was erected at Smithfield about 1820, but I have not discovered who taught in it until 1840, when W. H. Guy was Principal. After him came ——— Brooks, of New York. He was succceeeded by W. H. Watson, who was at one time a member of the General Assembly. Then ——— Brooks, from the North; then E. W. Adams, Abel Wellon, and E. S. Parker, late State Solicitor. In 1866 Rev. W. B. Jones, then J. L. Davis. In 1886 Prof. Ira T. Turlington's Academy superceded it.

THE JOHNSTON ACADEMY, a mixed school, is often called the Leachburg Academy from the place where it was situated. Dr. J. T. Leach was the prime mover in its organization, which was in 1849. The teachers up to the Civil War were Dr. ——— Wyche, then George M. White, a first honor graduate of the University, who became a lawyer in Bladen; then Wm. J. Whyte, likewise a University graduate; then William L. Crocker, a graduate of Wake Forest College; then John W. Stuart, of Randolph-Macon College; then John B. Williams; then Miss ———. Yancey, who married Mr. ——— Fasnach, of Raleigh. At the close of the war Boar W. Young took charge and has kept it since. The school has turned out many useful men—was in its greatest prosperity under John W. Stuart, about 1855-'58.

About 1850 Henry L. Winton and his wife, from the North, established a school at Roxboro, about a mile from the present village of Clayton, and continued it about three years.

About 1855 Rev. W. B. Jones, a native of the county, opened a school at Clayton. He was assisted at first by ——— Cheek, of Orange, and then by Hannibal Parker, of Wake. In 1856 Mr. Jones married an accomplished Northern lady, Miss Delia Wright, who taught music and other branches. The school was prosperous, having 100 pupils, with five or six counties represented.

In 1854 E. D. Barbee was head of Union Academy, in the southwest part of the county.

Daniel Finleyson was a teacher of private schools about 1830, and John S. Powell about 1856, and W. H. Gery and W. H. Watson had schools about 1840.

From about 1870 to 1885 there was a school near Bentonville, called ANTIOCH, with E. D. Snead, as master, which trained many persons who taught in the public schools.

In 1885-'87 Ira T. Turlington, now Principal of the flourishing Smithfield Academy, had a good school, known as PLEASANT HILL ACADEMY, in the southewestern part of the county.

From 1880 to 1885 Mr. ——— White was Principal of WENTWORTH ACADEMY in the southern part of the county, large enough to require one or more assistants.

From 1875 to 1890, about five miles from Wentworth, an important Academy named GLENWOOD. Mr. Craven, as Principal, with three or four assistants, conducted it very successfully. It had an average attendance of 75.

JONES.

Formed in 1779 from Craven.

Incorporated Schoools.—Trenton Academy, chartered 1807; Trenton Academy, again chartered 1818; Trenton Academy, new trustees, chartered 1830; Cypress Creek Academy.

The following have been teachers in Jones County, some with good repute.

Littlebery Hudson, of South Carolina, 1833; H. H. Willard, of Virginia, 1837; G. H. Throop, of Virginia, 1843; H. F. Curtis, of Connecticut, 1844; E. F. Sanderson, of North Carolina, 1848; W. S. Byrd, of North Carolina, 1850; Wesley Mortal, of England, 1840; E. W. Haywood, of North Carolina, 1845; ——— White, of Raleigh, 1849; T. J. Whitaker, of North Carolina, 1855; Joseph Kinsey, of North Carolina, 1865; Wm. Russell, of North Carolina, 1866; C. H. Koonce, of North Carolina, 1868; —— Miller, of North Carolina, 1870.

Of the above Joseph Kinsey had afterwards a flourishing school at La Grange, in Lenoir County, and now has one in Wilson.

Miss May Pasteur, in 1839, was the first music teacher in Jones.

LENOIR.

Formed in 1791 from Dobbs, which was from Johnston, with a slice of Craven.

Incorporated Schools.—Dobbs' Academy, chartered 1785; Spring Hill Seminary, chartered 1802; Fairfield School, chartered 1817; Combridge Academy, chartered 1826; Moseley Hall Academy, chartered 1828; Union Academy, chartered 1842; Kinston Academy, chartered 1851.

Of the above Spring Hill Academy had the privilege of exemption from taxation for 99 years, and it was declared that it should not be considered as one of the schools required by the Constitution.

The teachers in Kinston Academy from 1849 were Hon. George V. Strong, his brother, W. A. Strong, Rev. ———

Gordon, Mr. Frarier. After the war the school was under Rev. Joseph E. Foy, D. D.

Mr. Midyette had a separate school.

Kinston College was built in the 80's.

Dr. Richard H. Lewis, an able veteran teacher, has been Principal of an Academy in Kinston for eighteen years. (See "Henderson.")

At La Grange Joseph H. Kinsey had a flourishing school for many years.

Col. A. C. Davis was Principal at the same place of a largely attended military school, which he transferred to Winston.

LINCOLN.

Formed in 1779 from Tryon, which was from Mecklenburg.

Incorporated Schools.—Pleasant Retreat Academy, chartered 1813; Lincolnton Female Academy, chartered 1821.

In 1825 there was a flourishing school taught by John Mushatt, a notice of whom is under "Iredell." He had about one hundred pupils. In the case of Taylor vs. Shuford, 4th Hawks, he was appointed by the Court to locate the southern boundary line of Earl Granville, in Lincoln County, which had not been run further west than the Catawba River. He ascertained it by astronomical observations.

About 1835 George W. Morrow, of Orange County, a graduate of the University, had a very flourishing school at Lincolnton. He was assited by his wife, daughter of a teacher of Orange, Rev. Elijah Graves. He died after a year's service, and John Dickey took his place. At the same time there was a female school of about one hundred, presided over by the Misses Smith. In 1842 Peter S. Ney, described under "Davie," had a classical school at Catawba Springs, six miles from Beattie's Ford. It is related of him

PHARMACY BUILDING—SHAW UNIVERSITY, RALEIGH, N. C.

that he was one of the few teachers who successfully resisted the old custom of barring out the teacher at Christmas. He used a large stick of wood on the door as a battering ram, with such terrifying effect that the pupils surrendered at discretion. One of the larger boys raised a plank and hid under the floor. There he soon fell asleep and betrayed his presence by most audible snoring. Thereupon the master raised the plank, and using it as a paddle, came down on the most exposed part of the body of the urchin, lying face downward, with a blow as demorlaizing as that inflicted by Marshal Ney on the Russians at Borodino.

Mr. Alfred Nixon finds in the old records that there were schools in Lincoln at a very early date. For example, the original grant in 1767 to the 67 acres of the David's Church, Lutheran and Reformed, has among the descriptions "including a school house." That school, he says, has been maintained uninterruptedly to this day. The deed to the oldest church in Lincolnton was made in 1788 to the "Dutch Lutherans and Dutch Presbyterians" for "the intent and purpose of building thereon a meeting-house for public worship, school-houses, both Dutch and English, and a place for the burial of the dead."

Schools of a high grade were maintained at an early day in the east Lincoln, at Triangle and Unity Churches.

M'DOWELL.

Formed in 1842 from Burke, with slice of Rutherford.

MACON.

Formed in 1828 from Haywood.

Incorporated Schools.—Tuckasegee Baptist High School, near Holley Springs, chartered 1869; Smith's Bridge High School, chartered 1879.

Michael Francis, a man of ability, afterwards a lawyer, State Senator and State. Solicitor, was Principal of an Academy in Franklin in 1836.

Afterwards Daniel McCoy took charge of the same school.

In 1840 John Y. Hicks, who had gained a good repute as a teacher in Nash, Franklin and Wake (at Raleigh), assumed the charge of the Franklin Academy. He was a member of the House of Commons, 1846-'50.

About 1850 Mr. Dabney taught at Holly Springs.

Between 1853 and 1860 Leonidas F. Siler, who had graduated at the State University with high honor, was Principals of the school at Franklin.

MADISON.

Formed in 1857 from Buncombe and Yancey.

Incorporated Schools.—Transmontane College, chartered 1859; Mars Hill Academy, chartered 1859.

Mr. M. A. Chandley, Superior Court Clerk of Madison, who was once himself a pedagogue, kindly gives me a description of the schools of Madison in the old days, when it was part of Buncombe. Although in other counties I did not attempt to sketch the public schools, I cannot omit the opportunity of giving so life-like a picture of those in the transmontane country.

"The common schools generally began about the first day of August and continued one or two months. The teachers were paid from ten to thirty dollars per month, the latter considered a very high price. The exercises began about 7 o'clock in the morning and lasted until about sunset, with one hour's recess at noon for dinner and recreation. The children spelt and read aloud, the louder the better—all at once—and the noise could be heard for a long distance.

"About 11 o'clock a. m. the pupils were ordered to get

their 'heart-lessons,' generally about a page of Webster's Blue-back Spelling-book. All would begin to read and spell aloud. Then all were made to "toe a mark," and spell and turn each other down. When this exercise was finished they were called on to spell their numbers, beginning with 'one,' until the pupil at the foot was reached. Each must remember his or her number so that at the next 'heart-lesson' the class should begin arranged as at the close of the last preceding contest.

"The school-houses were cabins, generally old abandoned houses, and the benches were made of logs, split in the middle, with flat sides up. There were two legs at each end about two feet long, so that the feet of the small children would dangle above the floor. The only books used were Webster's Elementary Spelling-book and Fowler's Arithmetic. The teacher, who had studied to the double Rule of Three in the latter, was thought to be very well educated. Geography and Grammar were not thought of." I echo Mr. Chandley's conclusion: "Honor to these schools, however, for if it had not been for them, perhaps, the writer would never have been able to write his name!"

The teachers before the war were Neeley Tweed, John Chandley, Ira Proffit, John B. Hale, Aaron Treadway, John Anderson.

MARTIN.

Formed in 1774 from Halifax and Tyrrell.

Incorporated Schools.—Williamston Academy, chartered 1816; Bachelor's Academy, chartered 1826; Williams' Academy, chartered 1830; Williamston Academy, again chartered 1835; Hamilton Female Institute, chartered 1851.

I find that the trustees of Williamston Academy advertised for a teacher, offering $500 salary or the privilege of taking all the tuition money.

I regret that I have been unable to ascertain any facts about the early history of the schools of Martin.

In 1850 the Williamston Academy was taught by ——— Whitley and McLane. In 1854 by ——— Matthews and George W. Neal, a graduate of the State University.

In 1858 the Principals were Asa Mattthews and S. W. Matthews; in 1856, ——— Brett; in 1860, H. L. Chase. About 1868-'72 the Academy was under Prof. Silvester Hassell, likewise a graduate of the University.

A High School was taught at Jamesville in the 50's by B. H. Scoville.

In 1870 S. W. Outerbridge founded an Academy at Robersonville, and is still in charge.

MECKLENBURG.

Formed in 1762 from Anson.

Incorporated Schools.—Queen's Museum, chartered 1770; Queen's Museum, again chartered 1771. Both disallowed by the King. Liberty Hall Academy, chartered 1777; New Providence Academy, chartered 1811; Liberty Male and Female Academy, chartered 1821; Liberty Male and Female Academy, again chartered 1838; Mallard Creek Classical School, chartered 1834; Mecklenburg Female College, chartered 1867.

Foote, in his "Sketches of North Carolina," states that wherever the Scotch-Irish settled a pastor was secured, and a classical school followed. He instances "Sugar Creek, Poplar Tent, Centre Bethany, Buffalo, Thyatira Grove, Wilmington, and the churches occupied by Pattillo, in Orange and Granville." The history of Mecklenburg, settled largely by this virile people, supports this assertion.

THE SUGAR (once Sugaw, or Shugaw) CREEK SCHOOL was probably the oldest in this section, the first teacher being Joseph Alexander, assisted by Mr. ——— Benedict. The attempt to merge this into the QUEEN'S MUSEUM in 1770 and 1771, under a charter from the Colonial Assembly, failed because, according to the ideas of that day when Church and State were united, the King declined to approve the legislative act unless the master should be required to be a member of the Church of England, licensed by the Governor. In other words the master of an incorporated institution was regarded as a State officer. Sugar Creek Academy was continued on its original site. In 1805 it went under the charge of Rev. Samuel C. Caldwell, son of Dr. David Caldwell, who carried it on for years. His loveable temper caused him to be described as "like the sunshine and showers of April."

After North Carolina claimed the powers of a sovereign State, the General Assembly, in April, 1777, incorporated LIBERTY HALL ACADEMY in place of the Queen's Museum. Among the trustees were such historic names as Thomas Polk, Abraham Alexander, Waightstill Avery; Ephraim Brevard, Adelai Osborne, John McKnitt Alexander, David Caldwell, Sam'l E. McCorkle, James Hall. Dr. Isaac Alexander was named as President in the act. The President and trustees were required to take an oath to discharge their trusts properly. The teachers were called "Professors and Tutors," so that the organization was that of a college. Power was given to receive donations, erect buildings, provide a public library, to grant certificates certifying the literary merit of the students. The trustees had power to fill vacancies in their body, and to suspend or remove the President, Professor and Tutors for cause. Some watchful member evidently scented an attack on the State Treasury,, so that a proviso was added that the State should not be obliged to support the Academy, and that it should not be considered one of those mentioned in the State Constitution.

The salary of the President was, in January, 1778, fixed at £195, to be occasionally increased in proportion to the prices of provisions. Dr. Isaac V. Alexander was the first President, continuing for a year, then Robert Brownfield accepted the charge for a year. Alexander McWhorter,

D. D., of New Jersey, an able and vigorous man, who had visited the country as a Missionary in 1764, was induced to undertake the duties, but the British invasion broke up the institution in 1780. The course of instruction was not far behind that of Princeton. It was the first effort to found a college in North Carolina. Presbyterians, ambitious to secure higher education, were forced to repair to Princeton or to Mount Zion College, in Winnsborough, South Carolina.

After peace Thomas Henderson inaugurated a High School in Charlotte, which was largely patronized for many years.

It is stated in the preamble of the 1777 charter of Liberty Hall that "a very promising experiment had been made at a Seminary in the County of Mecklenburg, and a number of youths there taught have made great advancements in the knowledge of the learned languages, and in the rudiments of the arts and sciences, in the course of a finished education, which they have since completed at various colleges in different parts of America. The spirit of education was evidently abroad in Mecklenburg.

Rev. James Wallis, awarded the honorary degree of Master of Arts in 1810, by the State University, of which he was a trustee, had a school noted for its excellence at NEW PROVIDENCE, now called Providence, about twelve miles southeast of Charlotte. He appears to have taught until his death, in 1829, nearly forty years. In 1811 he procured a charter of the New Providence Academy, of which he was the first named trustee, and the Principal. His successor in the pastorate was Rev. Dr. Robert Hall Morrison, first President of Davidson College. He was succeeded by Rev. Samuel Williamson, D. D., second President of Davidson College, who had charge of the school as well as congregation. Rev. Cyrus Johnston, D. D., came after Dr. Williamson and taught the Providence Academy several years.

Rev. Wm. Richardson, the uncle and foster father of Wm. Richardson Davie, was the first pastor of New Providence. It was here that Rev. Jethro Rumple, D. D., had his first charge, though he was not Principal of the Academy. That position was held by Mr. ——— Kuhendall, a good teacher.

CHARLOTTE FEMALE INSTITUTE was organized in 1857, and conducted to great success by Rev. Robert Burwell, D. D. (University of North Carolina) and his wife, soon assisted by his son, John B., famous afterwards as Principal of Peace Institute, Raleigh. He was succeeded in 1872 by Rev. R. H. Chapman, who, in 1875, gave place to Rev. Taylor Martin. In 1878 Rev. W. R. Atkinson took the Presidency and held it for several years. On his removal to Columbia, S. C., to a similar position, the Institute was closed.

THE NORTH CAROLINA MILITARY INSTITUTE was inaugurated in 1858 by Gen. Daniel H. Hill, assisted by Col. C. C. Lee and Gen. James H. Lane. It was very successful and furnished many drill-masters and company officers to the Confederate army. The exercises were broken up by the war, and for a while a school for girls was held in the buildings by Rev. Mr. Stacy. Then Col. J. P. Thomas revived the male school, but it was closed in 1882 on his transfer to the Citadel Academy at Charleston, as Professor.

As at first organized, the session lasted, without intermission, throughout the year, the months of August and September being spent campaigning in the mountains of North Carolina. At the end of the second year cadets received a furlough of two months.

There were a Scientific and a Primary department. In the former the West Point Curriculum was closely followed, and the students were required to board in the buildings and to be under military discipline.

There was a Primary department, which aimed to prepare students for any college. Such of these students as boarded in the buildings were likewise under military discipline.

The Institute provided board, lodging, fuel, lights, washing, arms, equipments, medical attendance, uniforms and all clothing, except underclothes, for $300 per annum. No extra charges.

The buildings are now used by the Graded School, Alexander Graham, Superintendent.

MITCHELL.

Formed in 1861 from Yancey, with slices of Watauga, Caldwell, Burke and McDowell.

My informant writes that he has not been able to ascertain that there were any old schools of note in this county, but that in recent years there have been very good teachers, with successful results at Bowman Academy, in Bakersville.

MOORE.

Formed in 1784 from Cumberland.

Incorporated Schools.—Peasley's Academy, chartered 1799; Solemn Grove Academy, chartered 1804; Mt. Parnassus Academy, chartered 1809; Euphronean Academy, chartered 1811; Silvester Academy, chartered 1833; Carthage Male and Female Academy, chartered 1844; Jonesboro High School, chartered 1881.

The names of some of the early chartered academies suggest classical training. I regret that I have been unable to obtain the names of their teachers.

THE M'MILLAN ACADEMY, near Deep River, was conducted for many years by Rev. Murdoch McMillan, a Presbyterian, assisted by his wife. He was a pupil of Dr. David Caldwell, and, in addition to his work as teacher, preached twice a month at Buffalo. Both he and his wife were very estimable, and their academy, which was for both sexes, was successful until their removal to Alabama, in 1830.

THE JACKSON SPRINGS ACADEMY building was erected on the land of its Principal, Rev. Hugh McLaurin, a Presbyterian preacher, by the labors of himself and his neighbors. Here he conducted a classical school, attended by pupils from Moore, Robeson, Richmond and other counties. He is described by Prof. Alexander McIver as a stout, energetic, bold and fearless man—fortitur in re, if not suaviter in modo. In 1851 he removed to Alabama, and the Jacksin Springs Academy was no more.

THE CARTHAGE ACADEMY.—In 1842 Rev. A. C. McNeill and his wife were employed by the trustees of the Carthage Male and Female Academies, and these were combined into the Carthage Academy. A new building was erected for the school on land donated by the late Judge Samuel J. Person, a graduate of the State University. The teachers were noted for scholarship, thoroughness and good discipline, and patronage was gathered from many counties and several States. Some dissatisfaction being expressed in regard to the strict discipline of Mrs. McNeill, she and her husband emigrated to Alabama.

CANE CREEK HIGH SCHOOL was situated about three miles from Cameron. Its first Principal was Prof. W. McMillan, an alumnus of the State University, of Robeson County. It had extensive patronage. Among its pupils were Evander J. McIver, once Superintendent of Public Instruction in Alabama; Judge James D. McIver, of this State, and his brother, Judge Alexander McIver, of Texas; Rev. Dr. Daniel McGilvary, missionary in Siam; Dr. Hector Turner, of the Convention of 1861. It was closed by the hardships of the Civil War.

POCKET ACADEMY, about five miles from Jonesboro, under the management of Mr. Daniel McIntyre, of the Bingham School, aided by his wife, the daughter of Gen. A. D. McLean, was, just after the Civil War, a signal benefit to the youth of Moore. Mrs. McIntyre was a pupil of Rev. Dr. Moses D. Hoge, of Richmond, Virginia, and was cultivated in mind and manners.

THE KELLY SCHOOL was begun shortly before 1880 by John E. Kelly, an alumnus of Davidson College, and continued for four years. He had rare powers of inspiring enthusiasm and imparting instruction, and his school was very successful. He is now, and has been for years, Principal of Union Home School.

The old schools of Moore were taught, as a rule, by men of good scholarship and wise conduct. To those already mentioned should be added the names of Peter McNab, Angus R. Kelly, William Buie, the McCrimmons and the McIvers.

In 1856, besides the Academy at Carthage, there was a classical school at Carbonton and an English school at Mechanics' Hall, as appears by the report of Dr. Calvin H. Wiley.

MONTGOMERY.

Formed in 1779 from Anson.

Incorporated Schools.—Montgomery Seminary, chartered 1797; Lawrenceville Academy, chartered 1818; Davidson Academy, chartered 1824.

Montgomery Seminary is described in the charter as near the town of Henderson, which name has disappeared.

L. D. Andrews (see "Randolph") taught at Mt. Gilead for some time after the Civil War.

NASH.

Formed in 1777 from Edgecombe.

Incorporated Schools.—Hilliardston Academy, chartered 1818; Nashville Male and Female Academy, chartered 1826; Nashville Male and Female Academy, again chartered 1847; Rocky Mount Academy, chartered 1828;

Stony Hill Academy, chartered 1828; Stanhope Academy, chartered 1883.

In 1856 there were The Morning Star Institute, Nashville; Masonic Male School, of which M. Y. Chappell was Principal.

As early as 1810 there was, as appears by the "Description of Edgecombe County," by Dr. Jeremiah Battle, an Academy at Westrayville, in Nash, of dignity sufficient to attract pupils from Edgecombe. The teacher was John B. Bobbitt, who began here his long and honorable career. He left about 1815, and the reputation of this Academy was short-lived. It was five miles from Rocky Mount, on the road to Nashville, and its establishment was due to the energy and liberality of Samuel Westray, Esq., the elder.

Hilliardston Academy was likewise a successful school. It had male and female departments, with separate buildings. The first teacher of the male department was Thomas G. Stone, afterwards a farmer and State Senator of Franklin.

Of the Female Department, Misses Mary and Ann Ragsdale were the first teachers.

The buildings were on the land of James C. Hillard and the school was fostered by him, Wm. Burt and John and Peter Arrington.

Among its pupils were Archibald H. Arrington, a member of Congress of the Confederacy, Rev. Mark Bennett, and many other good men.

About 1826 Hecor and Ragsdale had a good school near the Goodson Falls, above Rocky Mount.

About 1833 John Y. Hicks (mentioned again under Franklin, Macon and Wake) was a very acceptable Principal of the Nashville Male Academy.

About 1835 Martin R. Garrett was the master of the Stoney Hill Academy. Afterwards Captain J. H. Tharp and then D. S. Richardson.

D. S. Richardson in the 40's had a large school at Castalia, thence removed to Wilson.

NEW HANOVER.

Formed in 1729. Precinct of Bath until 1738.

Incorporated Schools.—Innes Academy, chartered 1783; Public School, chartered 1800; Wilmington Academy, chartered 1803; New Hanover Academy, chartered 1833; Rockfish Academy, chartered 1834; Female Institute, near Black Creek, chartered 1846; Topsail, chartered 1851; Union (at Harold's Store), chartered 1854; Rocky Point, chartered 1867.

The "Public School," above mentioned, was not a school supported by the public. It was for all the people, as opposed to a limited private school.

A Presbyterian clergyman, Rev. James Tate, established a classical school in Wilmington in 1760. Here he taught acceptably for eighteen years, when, on account of his unbending Whig principles, he was forced to leave and carry on his pastoral works in the Hawfields. His name stands high in the annals of our State.

A teacher of the eighteenth century was R. Harley, who opened a classical school in Wilmington about 1776. His terms were, for reading and writing, 30 shillings ($3) per quarter; for the same, with Arithmetic, 35 shillings ($3.50); the same, with Latin, 5 shillings per quarter, $4). He also offered himself as a land conveyancer, so that he was probably a fairly educated English lawyer who had drifted to these shores.

It is supposed that Rev. Wm. Bingham began his classical school in Wilmington about 1788, and had great success until he removed to Chatham (vide "Chatham" and "Orange.")

JUNES ACADEMY was founded by Col. James Junes the first in our State to show a broad and generous spirit in behalf of public education. By birth a Scotchman, he served with distinction as Captain in the army, which made an unsuccessful attack on Carthagena. He was one ot the council of Governor Johnston. He commanded the North Carolina troops in the French and Indian war and on the death of Col. Fry, was the ranking officer of all the Colonial forces. Governor Dinwiddie called him "an officer of unblemished character, of great reputation for bravery and conduct." While at Winchester in 1754 he executed his will, of which the following is an extract: "I give and bequeath at the death of my loving wife, Jean Innes, my plantation, called Point Pleasant, and the opposite marsh lands over the river, two negro young women, one negro young man, and their increase, all the stock of cattle and hogs, half the stock of horses belonging to the plantation, with all my books and one hundred pounds sterling, or the equivalent thereto in the currency of the country, for the use of a free school for the benefit of the youth of North Carolina; and to see that this part of the will be duly executed at the time, I appoint the Colonel of the New Hanover Regiment, the parson of the Wilmington Church [St. James Episcopla], the vestry for the time being, or a majority of them, as they from time to time shall be chosen or appointed." He also bequeathed a bell to the Parish Church of Cannisbay, in Caithness, and £100 sterling to the poor of the Parish. The lands devised are about twelve miles above Wilmington, and, including the swamp-land, were about five thousand acres. They are a wilderness of forest and marsh, with not a building on the tract. The owner is Samuel Davis. There is no tradition even as to what became of the negroes. They were probably carried off by the British or escaped during their occupancy of Wilmington.

Col. Innnes died in 1759, and his will was then proved. Owing to the continuance of the life of his widow, and probably the troubles of the war, the execution of the bequest for the school was not considered until 1783. At that time there was, from all that we can learn, no rector or vestry of St. James' Church. An act of Assembly was procured vesting the property bequeathed in Trustees, viz: Hon. Samuel Ashe, Archibald Maclaine, Wm. Hill, Thomas McGuire, John Ingram, John Hay, Hon. Edward Starkey, John Lillington, and Robert Shaw. In 1788 nothing had been done and the Assembly increased the Trustees to thirty. I have been unable to ascertain the facts in regard to the school, then established, if one was started. It must have been on a small scale, as we find that an act was passed in 1803 for the relief of "Innes Academy," which recites that a quorum of the Trustees could not be procured, and others were named, with authority to sell the Point Pleasant lands and reinvest in other land.

At the same session of the Assembly the WILMINGTON ACADEMY was chartered, the Trustees being among the most influential in the lower Cape Fear country, viz: Joshua Granger Wright, Samuel Russell Jocelyr, Nathaniel Hill, James W. Walker and Benjamin Smith. As the price obtained for the Innes lands must have been very small, owing to the destruction of the buildings and long neglect, it was possibly subscribed to the Wilmington Academy, and hence its name was superseded by the latter. In the three acts of 1783, 1788 and 1803 the name is spelt Innis, which, at least, indicates the pronunciation of the name of this, one of the most worthy of North Carolina citizens.

The Wilmington Academy was liberally supported by the people of Wilmington. The Academy building was on the site of the City Hall and was not removed until 1856 or 1857. The first Principal was the Rev. Dr. Solomon Hailing, of the Episcopal Church, a man of learning, who had served as Senior Surgeon in the Department of the South, and after the war took holy orders. After faithful and successful service as teacher, he removed to Georgetown, in South Carolina, and died in 1810.

His successor was John Rogers, who afterwards had a prominent school at Hillsboro. (See Orange.)

Rev. Adam Empie, D. D., Rector of St. James Parish, was the next to assume charge of the Academy, but soon resigned it in order to open a private select school, of excellent repute. He was an exemplary man, of wide usefulness and influence, of learning and real worth. Marrying a daughter of Judge Johsua G. Wright, he left numerous descendants to inherit his virtues.

The next teacher was a marked contrast to his predecessors. He was a stern disciplinarian, and gave the impression to his pupils of deriving pleasure from the infliction of pain. Corporal punishment was inflicted on boys and girls alike for the slightest mistake in recitation or the least impropriety of behavior. Such is the testimony of one of his pupils now living, a man of recognized intelligence and accuracy.

The succeeding masters of the Academy, in the lively language of the excellent gentleman from whom this information is derived, were "the Rev. Mr. Lathrop, Mr. ——— Hartshorn with his slender legs and spectacles on nose, Wm. Lowry, a good natured, double-joined Irish man, who subsequently removed to Alabama, where he became a Judge; ——— Joy, whose name was a misnomer, for he was never known to laugh aloud, ——— Wilkes, who was an adept to squirting tobacco juice from his lips and could send it in a continuous stream almost any distance, and strike the bull's eye every time; Rev. John Burke, who delighted in the classics, and in calling the roll of the school, would never use the Christian name, but would substitute the Latin: thus, Jones, Primus, Jones, secundus, Jones, tertius, and other teachers who hal flourishing schools in the Academy building, but after awhile it was allowed to fall into decay, was not used for educational purposes and in consequence the corporation became extinct. But during its existence it exerted a strong influence for good."

In Wilmington, as in Newbern, Edenton and many other towns dancing was considered a part of polite education. General Davie expressed much gratification that polished French refugees from Hayti and emigrants from France could be procured. One of the best markers in Wilmington appears to have been —— Clay, who, among other beautiful figures, promised to instruct in the mysteries of Parsby's Rigadvon.

NORTHAMPTON.

Formed in 1741, from Bertie.

Incorporated Schools.—Northampton Female Seminary, chartered 1833; North Carolina Male and Female Academy, chartered 1836.

The last of the above charters was amendatory of the first. It contained a donation by the State of a lot in the town of Jackson.

In 1839 James H. Wood advertised that he had secured the services of a lady Principal from Mrs. Willard's school at Troy, N. Y., and she would open a school for females on his plantation. Board and tuition for five months $40.

Mr. Julian Picot taught for many years at Buckhorn in this county. He had a well earned reputation.

Rev. Charles Fetter was Principal of the Jackson Male Academy for four years, succeeding A. J. Britton. In 1878 he was elected Principal of the new Academy at Garysburg, which position he held until the Fall of 1885, with the exception of one year.

Rev. Vernon Janson taught at Seaboard in 1880.

LEONARD MEDICAL BUILDING—SHAW UNIVERSITY, RALEIGH, N. C.

ONSLOW.

Formed in 1734. Precinct of Bath until 1738.

Incorporated Schools.—New Town, of Swansboro Academy, chartered 1783; Richlands Academy, chartered 1783; Onslow Academy, chartered 1791; Onslow Academy, again chartered 1809; Swansboro Academy, again chartered 1810; Swansboro Academy, again chartered 1824; Richlands Academy, again chartered 1815; Male and Female Academy of Swansboro, chartered 1857; Richland Female Academy, chartered 1866.

Of the above the Richlands Academy, a classical school, was flourishing for the twelve years before the Civil War, and was patronized by five adjoining counties. The Principal was L. G. Woodward, a graduate of Dickinson College in Pennsylvania. Occasionally the members reached seventy, making an assistant necessary.

There were various subscription schools, some of a high order, inaugurated by a number of neighbors, employing a teacher, often from the North, for the purpose of instructing their children primarily. Other pupils were, however, admitted. Whipping was a common punishment for violation of rules or shirking of tasks, rather than expulsion. This punishment was only used for students of mature age.

ORANGE.

Formed in 1751, from Granville, Johnston and Bladen.

Incorporated Schools.—Science Hall, chartered 1779; Science Hall, amended 1784; Hillsboro Academy, chartered 1814; Prospect Hill Female Academy, chartered 1818; Bingham Academy, chartered 1819; Hillsboro Female Academy, chartered 1824; Bethmont Academy, chartered 1829; Junto Academy, chartered 1838; Fairfield Academy, chartered 1840; Caldwell Institute, chartered 1846; Cedar

Grove Academy, chartered 1851; Hillsboro Academy, chartered 1852; Hillsboro Military Academy, chartered 1861; Bingham School, chartered 1864; Little River Select Academy, chartered 1866; Hillsboro Military Academy, changed to North Carolina Military and Polytechnic Academy 1867.

The projectors of Science Hall evidently hoped for great things. Among the Trustees were Wm. Hooper, the signer of the Declaration of Independence; Governors Martin and Burke, Nathaniel Rochester, the founder of the city of Rochester in New York. The privileges of Liberty Hall Academy were given to it. In 1784 the old Episcopal church was allowed to be repaired and used as a Union church on Sundays, and for the school on week days. If an Episcopalian and one of another denomination applied, the former was to have the preference. The liberty granted to Liberty Hall Academy to issue certificates of proficiency was restricted so as not to include collegiate degrees. The Trustees failing to act, others, were appointed by the Act of 1784. The right to raise $1,000 by lottery was given. As "Rev. Mr. Frazier" was the last named, in a modest way, of the Trustees of 1779, I conjecture that he was the first teacher. I know no other.

The earliest settlers of Orange, including its daughters, Caswell, Person, Alamance and Durham, were plain but intelligent people, mainly Scotch-Irish. The first regularly organized churches were by the Quakers and Presbyterians; when Rev. McAden visited North Carolina in 1755 there were churches and almost certainly schools at Hawfields, Eno and Hyco. A Rev. Pattillo had a school at Hawfields before moving to Granville. In the sketch of that county he is farther noticed.

Richard Stanford, who was a member of Congress, and who married a daughter of another member of Congress, Gen. Alexander Mebane, a very examplary man, had a largely patronized classical school at the Burnt Shop, afterwards Melville. One of his pupils was Thomas Hart Benton, the eminent Senator from Missouri, and another was John Taylor, thirty years Clerk of the Superior Court of Orange, and ancestor of the late Prof. R. H. Graves.

Rev. John DeBow, a Presbyterian preacher, uncle of Archibald DeBow Murphey, the eminent lawyer and promoter of education, once Professor of Languages in the State University, and Rev. Wm. Hodge, who was a co-laborer with the great revivalist, McCready, 1800-1810, also taught in the Hawfields before entering the University.

The next teacher at Hawfields was Rev. Wm. Paisley, whose labors continued from about 1800 to 1820. He afterwards labored in Greensboro as was seen under "Guilford." He was a learned and useful man.

Rev. Elijah Graves was a noted teacher about 1830, near White Cross, a Presbyterian minister, father of Richard Stanford Graves, once Treasurer of Mississippi, and of Mrs. Wm. Thompson, long keeper of a boarding house in Chapel Hill, herself, when the wife of Morrow, teacher in Lincolnton, as assistant to her husband. (See Lincoln.)

One of the most worty of the old teachers, Benjamin Burnside, although not versed in the classics, whose work was in Orange and Guilford, should be recorded. He took charge in his old age of one of the first free schools, with many pupils, a few miles northeast of Mebane. Among these children were grandchildren of those he had trained in his youthful days.

Daniel Turrentine, described by one who knew him as "a great teacher," taught in the Hawfield section from 1800 to about 1830. Among his children were James C. Turrentine, for sixteen years Sheriff of Orange, at one time a teacher, John Turrentine, for many years a successful teacher, surveyor, and gifted as a conversationalist, from whom are descended the Turrentines in and near Burlington, Samuel, Joseph and William Turrentine, all teachers, good scholars, especially gifted in permanship. Rev. Samuel Bryant Turrentine, Presiding Elder of the Charlotte District, is the son of William.

Judge Jesse Turner, of Arkansas, who recently died, aged 90, honored and beloved, was one of the pupils of Daniel Turrentine.

Rev. Daniel Kerr, a minister of the Christian church, who had a scholarly reputation, carried on a good school, called Junto, formerly Mt. Pleasant Academy. Besides teaching well, he preached every Sunday and edited "The Christian Sun." He was a very bright Mason and was supported by his fraternity, after old age incapacitated him from labor.

BINGHAM SCHOOL.

Wm. Bingham, who has been noticed under "New Hanover" and "Chatham," after leaving Pittsboro, about 1808, taught for a short while at Hillsboro. The court towns were the scenes of frequent and vilest dissipation and for this reason the charter of the University forbids its location within five miles of any one of them. This suggests a reason why Wm. Bingham, and many others of our ablest teachers transferred their work to the country.

Mr. Bingham soon moved his to a place which he named Mount Repose, two miles east of the Cross Roads Church, five miles north of Mebane, about one mile from the point where David Kerr's Junto Academy was located, about two miles north of the site of Wm. Paisley's school, about ten miles northwest of Hillsboro. Here, in a moral community, on his own land he had a classical school for boys, famous for thoroughness and firm but kindly discipline.

Hon. Giles Mebane, now living at Milton, full of years and honors, gives me the following description of this famous schoolmarker. "In appearance he was about five, six inches tall, no surplus flesh, weighing 150 or 160 pounds; very quick and brisk in his movements; walked erect, like a well-drilled soldier; was bald—the boys nick-named him "Old Slick," walked three miles to church on Sunday, leading his boarders; was reasonably talkative and sometimes jocose but never undignified. He whipped with well trimmed hickories, of which he kept a supply equal to the demand. He whipped in discharge of a duty to his patrons, rather than to punish the boys. Whipping was imported from Ireland, but lost nothing of its usefulness in America as administered by the elder Bingham. The school-house was of logs with one chimney and one stove. In front of the door was a leaf arbor for study in good weather. On one occasion I was dancing furiously under the arbor. The old gentleman came to the door and said: "Aye! Aye! Giles!" The matter ended there. He had several log cabins built near his house and in them the boys lodged and studied such books as Caesar and Virgil, and imbided classical ideas. His reputation as an educator drew scholars from a distance. When I was at the school there was one from Virginia and one from New Orleans. The average number was 35 or 40. He had no assistant. His son, Wm. J., did not resemble him." I add that Mr. Mebane was a pupil of his son as well as of the father and was never punished which shows that their dreaded severity was only applied to the unruly.

Wm. Bingham ended his most valuable life work at Mt. Repose in 1825. His widow removed with her son, Robert Bingham, M. D., to his home near Paris, Tennessee, where she died in 1858. The shares of the heirs, except his own and that of his sister, Mary Slingsby, wife of Rev. Thomas Lynch, of the Orange Presbytery, were bought by Wm. J. Bingham, and conveyed to Mrs. Lynch, and the tract now belongs to her heirs.

Wm. James, the eldest son of Wm. Bingham, graduated at the State University with highest honors in 1825, and was studying law with Chief Justice Thomas Ruffin when his father died.

He felt obliged to take up his father's work, as well as the burden of being the chief support of his family. He began his eminent career as a teacher at once at Mt. Repose, but remained there only two years.

We have only detached glimpses into the history of Hillsboro Academy. There are long gaps. In 1805 Richard Henderson, of Kentucky, a nephew of Chief Justice Henderson, late a Tutor of the University, afterwards a lawyer of high standing in Kentucky, had charge; in 1815 one Graham and a Miss Farley. In 1818 Rev. John Witherspoon, D. D. LL. D., was the Principal. Being also Pastor of the Presbyterian church, he induced Mr. John Rogers, who had been teaching in Wilmington with high reputation, to join him.

In 1824 Mr. Rogers was sole Principal, his school attracting patronage from distant sections. Col. Cadwallader Jones, an excellent gentleman, State Solicitor, when a resident of Hillsboro, who furnishes me the information, was sent to this academy when his father resided in Halifax. Among the pupils were the late Judge Thomas S. Ashe, the late Bishop Cicero Hawks, of Missouri. Rogers was from Ireland, and a good scholar. He married a sister of Congressman Wm. Barry Grove, of Fayetteville.

In 1828 the Turstees offered the Principalship to Wm. J. Bingham, which he accepted on condition that he should have the uncontrolled management, and should be paid no salary other than the tuition money. He had great success. I find an advertisement of 1830. His tuition was $30 for ten months; board $10 per month. His remarkable ability was soon recognized and his reputation repidly grew. In 1844 he removed to a farm which he bought, called Oaks, in the western part of the county, and limited the number of his pupils to thirty. His instruction was thorough, his discipline was rigid but just. Boys whom no one else could manage were sent to him with almost invariable good results. For grave offences he used the lash, vigorously applied; for lesser offences he introduced digging up stumps. His course of studies led up as high as the Sophomore classes of Universities and Colleges. Certificates that men had finished with him were often accepted as sufficient qualifications for taking charge of classical schools. He advanced his tuition to a point higher than was ever before reached in this State—$150 for ten months.

In 1857 he associated with him his sons, Wm. and Robert, who had graduated at the University with first honors, and the limit of students was increased to sixty. As Robert was in active service throughout the Civil War, he gave up in 1863 the practical management of the school to his other son, Col. Wm. Bingham and died February 19th, 1866. The continuation of the history of the Bingham School does not come within the scope of this paper.

During the latter part of the period of his mastership of the Hillsboro Academy, Wm. J. Bingham had as his partner his brother, Rev. John A. Bingham. He had an Engineering Department, presided over by John Hough, while French was taught by Jean Odeud. The tuition in the classical department was in 1834 $42, and in the others $30 each, for ten weeks. Rev. John Bingham was a very able man, but his career was shortened by pulmonary consumption.

James H. Norwood was Principal of the Academy, but resigned it in 1845 and advertised for a select school.

In 1835 Wm. E. Anderson, brother of Professor Walker Anderson, of the State University, who was afterwards

Chief Justice of Florida Territory, had a select school near Hillsboro, called Lochiel.

From 1825 for many years there was, under the general superintency of Rev. Wm. M. Green, afterwards Professor in the State University an dthen Bishop of Mississippi, a well patronized school for females called Hillsboro Female Seminary. The principal teacher was Miss Maria L. Spear, whose mode of teaching was an anticipation of the best Graded School methods.

This Seminary was succeeded by the Mr. and Mrs. John Burwell Female Sshool, which had equal success until 1857, when they were carried to Charlotte by superior inducements offered.

Their school was succeeded by another excellent institution, the Select Boarding and Day School for Young Ladies, by Misses Nash and Miss Kolloch. The Misses Nash were daughters of Chief Justice Nash and Miss Kollock their cousin. They continued their beneficent ministration nearly to this day.

An important educational enterprise was the Hillsboro Military Academy, projected by Col. C. C. Tew in 1859. After opening well, it was closed by the Civil War, Col. Tew entering the army and being killed at Sharpsburg. About 1872 Messrs. Horner and Graves closed their school at Oxford and re-opened it in the handsome Tew building. The change did not meet with success. First Mr. Horner, after about two years, returne dto Oxford and after two years more Mr. Graves also left, and the doors were permanently closed for educational purposes. Col. Tew's charges were $315 for ten months board and tuition.

Wm. Bingham Lynch, a grandson of Wm. Bingham, had a well managed select school near Mebane, which was closed when he entered the Confederate service. After the war he went into partnership with Maj. Robert Bingham in the Bingham School at Mebane, then opened a school with military government at High Point and then on account of his health removed to Florida, where he is still a teacher. He graduated at the State University with highest honors in 1857. (See Guilford.)

Rev. John R. Holt taught in this county with success.

A school of high reputation for good work, whose patronage extended beyond the limits of this State, was that of Samuel W. Hughes, a graduate of Hampden-Sidney College. He was an assistant of Wm. J. Bingham for several years. In 1844 he opened a classical schol for boys at Cedar Grove and taught without intermission until his death in 1884. The average number of his pupils was about fifty. President George T. Winston was one of them. Rev. Dr. Charles Phillips, who entrusted his son Rev. Dr. A. L. Phillips to his care, said of him. "He taught his pupils to love the truth, to be patient in finding it, and to be strong through the finding of it." Among his children were Rev. A. K. Hughes and Sheriff John Hughes.

One of the best classical schools for boys in the State was that connected with the State University. It was organized in 1796 and continued until about 1820. At first it was considered a part of the University but after a few years there was almost a total separation. Among the teachers were Andrew Flinn, 1804, afterwards D. D.; Mathew Troy, 1805, a prominent lawyer of Salisbury; Rev. W. L. Turner, 1808; George Johnstone, 1809; Abner W. Clopton, afterwards the private clergyman of John Randolph of Roanoke; James Craig, of Orange.

In 1843 Hon. William H. Battle, then Judge of the Superior Court, afterwards Judge of the Supreme Court, inaugurated his law-school, modelled afte rthat of Chief Justice Henderson (see "Granville"), of whom he was a warm admirer. He was assisted by Hon. Samuel F. Phillips, afterwards Solicitor General of the United States. In 1845 the school, by their consent, was made a department of the State University. In it were trained many of the ablest lawyers and judges of the South.

PAMLICO.

Formed in 1871, from Beaufort and Craven.

PASQUOTANK.

Formed in 1672. Precinct of Albemarle until 1738.

Incorporated Schools.—Vixonton Academy, chartered 1804; Elizabeth City Academy, chartered 1807; Newland Academy, chartered 1809; Elizabeth City Academy, again chartered 1820.

Vixonton Academy was authorized to raise $2,000 by lottery.

Newland Academy was in the upper part of the county.

In 1867 the Trustees of Elizabeth City Academy were authorized to sell one of its lots.

Pasquotank can boast of having had the first teacher of ability and the first school which history has recorded. Charles Griffin came from the West Indies in 1705, and made a profound impression for good on the community where he labored. Rev. Wm. Gordon writes in 1709 that he was surprised at the "order, decency and seriousness with which the congregation performed public worship," that the people were more "industrious, careful and cleanly," than elsewhere, all owing to the young lay-reader and school teacher, Charles Griffin. He mentions as a signal proof of his ability that "even the Quakers themselves send their children to his schools, though he has prayers twice a day and obliges them to their responses and all the other decencies of behavior as well as others." In 1708 Rev. James Adams was his successor, while he removed to Chowan. Here, according to a subsequent letter of missionary Gordon, he "fell into notorious sin and joined the Quakers."

Dr. Hawks and other historians leave the brilliant young teacher with this beclouded reputation, but we learn from Bishop Meade's "Old Churches and Families of Virginia," that he afterwards was a clergyman of the Church of England—that he taught an Indian school at Christina in Virginia, and was then a Professor of William and Mary College.

As to the other schools and teachers of Pasquotank my information is meagre. By the kindness of Prof. L. L. Sheep, of Elizabeth City, I have the following:

In the thirties, a brother of the great war Secretary, Edwin M. Stanton, taught in the Elizabeth City Academy. He wa safterwards a member of Congress from Tennessee and Territorial Governor of Kansas, in the troublous days. About the same time a parochial (Episcopalian) school was carried on by Rev. Jarvis Buxton, afterwards rector at Fayetteville for many years.

In the forties George A. Sargent and Zara Hamilton were Principal of the Academy. They also had a school at Salem in the southern part of the county, about the same period, where James Howlet previously taught.

The most noted for learning and severe discipline of all the Pasquotank teachers were David and Robert Lindsay, of Scotland.

In the Baptist parsonage in the fifties, John B. Lyon, a native of the county, had a private school of much note.

From about 1844 until the capture of the town by the Federal troops, Rev. Edward M. Forbes, of the Episcopal Church, a graduate of the State University, had a school of considerable repute in the old Episcopal Church, patronized by all denominations.

Of the Vixonton Academy, Captain Wm. Mullen was master in the thirties, and afterwards S. B. Bagley.

PERQUIMANS.

Formed in 1672. A precinct of Albemarle until 1738.

Incorporated Schools.—Union Hall School, chartered 1806; Pleasant Grove Academy, chartered 1816; New Prospect Academy, chartered 1817; Concord Academy, chartered 1820; Woodville Academy, chartered 1830; Harvey's Neck Academy, chartered 1831; Pleasant Grove Academy, again chartered 1838; Perquimans Academy, chartered 1849; Perquimans Male and Female, chartered 1861; Perquimans Male and Female, again chartered 1867.

Union Hall School is described as near "Old Vicks," a corruption from "Old Neck.' It was in existence for some time prior to its incorporation.

New Prospect Academy was described as near Oak Grove, on Little River.

The Belvidere Academy, a classical school, has been doing excellent work since 1835. It is under the control of the Society of Friends, but not sectarian in its teachings or patronage. It has had the following teachers among others: Ed. S. Gifford, of Massachusetts, 1835-'7. Dr. John Winslow; 1838-'41. Dr. Caleb Winslow, 1843-'44. Joseph R. Parker, 1865-'67. Timothy Nicholson, 1848-'55. John W. Albertson, 1846. W. A. Symmes, 1870-'73. Messrs. E. W. Nicholson and M. J. White have been masters since 1882. Among the pupils were Judges Geo. W. Brooks and John W. Albertson, the latter being also a teacher, Thomas G. Skinner, M. C., and many of the best men of the Albemarle section.

The first Principal of Perquimans Academy in 1848 was John Kimberly, afterwards a Professor in the University. (See "Hertford.") Then came Rev. Benjamin S. Bronson, ———— Bennet, W. H. Weatherly, James M. Mullen, now a Judge in Virginia, and George B. Gordon. In 1870

Wm. G. Gaither took charge of the male department, when Mrs. A. E. Barrow was in charge of the Female department. Then the two were united and the principalship devolved on Mr. Gaither for twelve consecutive years. He had an assistant from time to time. Messrs. Winslow, May S. M. Gattis, Hammond, J. C. Kittrell. In 1897 Mr. Gaither again took charge of the school which is taught according to the most improved methods. The old building was burnt in 1835 and was rebuilt the same year.

In 1856 there was a Male Academy at Newby Bridge.

According to tradition Levi Munden and Rev. Hezekiah G. Leigh had schools at Durant's Neck.

PENDER.

Formed in 1875 from New Hanover.

Incorporated Schools.—Burgaw Male and Female School, chartered 1879. Some of the schools named under "New Hanover" were within the limits of this county. (See "New Hanover.")

PERSON.

Formed in 1791 from Caswell.

Incorporated Schools.—Arcadia Academy, chartered 1833.

Arcadia Academy was situated between Oxford and Milton. Its Principal was Benjamin Sumner, a first honor graduate of the State University, who afterwards settled in Lincolnton. A building was erected for the accommodation of boarders. The terms were $100 for ten months for board and tuition.

Bethel Academy was near Woodsdale, the Rev. T. J. Horner, being Principal.

About 1850 James Woody had a good male school at Roxboro, and Mrs. Mm. O. Bowler a female school of like character. The male school was in charge of James I. Baird in 1856, and then successively Rev. J. H. Brent and Hazell Norwood were successful Principals of institutions at the same place. Their successors were John Baity, Wm. Rowland, the last in 1856.

PITT.

Formed in 1760 from Beaufort.

Incorporated Schools.—Pitt Acdemy, in Greenville, late Martinboro, chartered 1786; Greenville Academy, chartered 1814; Greenville Female Academy, chartered 1830; Clemons Academy, chartered 1830; Contentnea Academy, chartered 1831; Jordan Plain Academy, chartered 1831; Midway Male and Female Academy, chartered 1849; Aurora Male and Female College, chartered 1869.

The Trustees of Pitt Academy under the charter of 1786 were Richard Caswell, Hugh Williamson, Wm. Blount, John Simpson, James Armstrong, James Gorham, John Hawkes, John Williams, Robert Williams, Arthur Forbes, Benjamin Moy, John Moy and Reading Blount. It is observable that the name given in place of Martinboro was not Greeneville, but Greenesville, which is the lawful spelling unless a subsequent Act of Assembly eliminated the s.

It was provided that this Academy should not be deemed to be one of those whose formation and support were commanded by the Constitution.

In 1856 there was a male and Female High School at Marlboro.

POLK.

Formed in 1855 from Rutherford and Henderson.

Incorporated School.—Columbus Normal School, chartered 1857.

In 1856 there was a High School at Columbus.

RANDOLPH.

Formed in 1779 from Guilford.

Incorporated Schools.—Unity Academy, chartered 1798; New Hope Academy, chartered 1824; Sandy Creek Academy, chartered 1828 Randolph Female Academy, chartered 1839; Ashboro Male Academy, chartered 1842; Franklinsville Academy, chartered 1851; Normal College, chartered 1852; Ashboro Male and Female Academies united, chartered 1854; Mt. Olivet Academy, chartered 1857; Trinity College, chartered 1859.

Normal College of 1852 took the place of Union Institute and was merged 1859 into Trinity College.

Unity Academy some time after its charter was granted had a period of prosperity, under the management of L. D. Andrews, who subsequently taught at Oak Grove Academy till 1861, and is now teaching at Monroe.

Sandy Creek Academy about 1850 was prosperous, with Sampson C. Fox as the master, but has long since been discontinued.

In the Ashboro Female Academy, an accomplished lady from the North, taught very acceptably. Miss Stickney, afterwards Mrs. David G. Worth. Josiah H. Brooks had charge of the Male Academy with success. After the union of the two Academies Rev. Dr. Simeon Colton and his wife were Principals, with exceedingly high reputations. (Vide Cumberland.)

Middleton Academy was built not far from that at Franklinsville and under the very able management of Samuel H. Wiley attracted good patronage. The able lawyer, State Senator and Speaker of the House, Marmaduke S. Robins, kept up the fame of the school 1857-'60. It was burned in 1865.

Mt. Olivet Academy had a good reputation under Dr. John Holt, but afterwards was abandoned.

Science Hill was a good school for some years under Josiah H. Brooks, above mentioned, and at the beginning of the Civil War under Marmaduke S. Robins.

RICHMOND.

Formed in 1779 from Anson.

Incorporated Schools.—Richmond Academy, chartered 1788; Cedar Grove Academy, chartered 1804; Laurel Hill Academy, chartered 1809; Hickory Grove Academy, chartered 1827; Richmond Academy, again chartered 1846; Richmond Academy, amended 1883.

No liquor to be sold in three miles of Laurinburg (so spelt) High School 1852.

Hickory Grove Academy is described as being on the land of John Carmichael. The name of Laurinburg is misspelled, as the town is named after the McLaurin family, who have lived there since the battle of Culloden. Rev. G. B. Scott was Principal in 1856.

Richmond Academy is now known as Rockingham Academy.

In 1856 there was an Academy at Montpelier and a school at Spring Hill.

ROBESON.

Formed in 1786 from Bladen.

Incorporated Schools.—Lumberton Academy, chartered 1793; Raft Swamps Academy, chartered 1793; Mt. Clio Academy, chartered 1806; Zion Parnassus Academy, chartered 1808; Philadelphus Academy, chartered 1812; Lumberton Academy, again, chartered 1819; Lumberton Academy, again chartered 1823; Oak Forest Academy, chartered 1826; White Oak Academy, chartered 1828; Cool Spring Academy, chartered 1831; Pine Grove Academy, chartered 1833; Lumberton Academy, again chartered

MAIN BUILDING NORTH CAROLINA SCHOOL FOR DEAF AND DUMB, MORGANTON, N. C.

1849; Antioch Academy, chartered 1849; Robeson Institute, chartered 1851; Chicora Collegiate Institute, chartered 1864; Edenborough Medical College, chartered 1867.

Lumberton Academy was authorized to raise $5,000 by a lottery. In 1797 the town commons was authorized to be sold for its benefit. The repeated Acts seem to show that its prosperity was fitful.

Zion Parnassus is described as being in Richland Swamp —the incongruity of two mountains being located in a swamp not being perceived.

Mt. Clio Academy was authorized to raise $800 by a lottery.

In 1852 it was enacted that no liquor should be sold within three miles of Robeson Institute.

The Edinborough Medical College was allowed to grant diplomas. The Principal was Dr. Hector McLean. It was situate in the northern part of the county and was discontinued at his death.

In 1856 Dr. Calvin H. Wiley reported as existing—

Floral Female College, at Gilopolis.

Robeson Institute, at St. Paul's.

Philadelphus Institute.

Union Institute, at Clay Valley.

Antioch Institute, Male and Female School ,in Lumberton.

Spring Hill Academy, at Brooklyn.

Floral College, for females, was established in 1841, and reached an average attendance of one hundred. It was located near Shoe Heel, now Maxton. Rev. John R. McIntosh was its first Principal, at the same time pastor of Centre Presbyterian church at the same locality. He was succeeded by Rev. Daniel Johnson, who continued until the Civil War. After the war Rev. Gilbert Morgan, Rev. Archibald Baker, and Messrs. J. C. Southerland, J. L. McLean, Rev. Dr. Luther McKinnon and Major J. R. Mc-

Lean, were Principals. It at one period had patronage from several counties of North and South Carolina, but it became involved in debt, was sold on mortgage and about fifteen years ago lost its influence.

Robeson Institute was a mixed school. Rev. John Calvin McNair, Rev. Malcolm McNair and Mrs. Effie McE. SinClair were the Principals. Rev. John Calvin McNair, after graduating at the State University, and teaching a while, entered the University of Edinburgh for advanced education in theology. He died there, having devised his property, then of considerable amount—land, slaves and securities, to his mother for life, and then to the State University, for establishing a lectureship on the Harmony of Religion and Science. The life estate did not fall in until most of the property was lost; litigation ensued about the land, and the proceeds of its sale, shortly to be had, will probably be so small as to require many years of accumulation to enable the University to carry the pious wishes into effect.

Tusculum (Male) Academy was established 1866 or 1867 in the western part of the county. Rev. Malcolm McNair, a graduate of the University, was its Principal. Mr. McNair had also a flourishing institution at St. Pauls.

ROCKINGHAM.

Formed in 1785 from Guilford.

Incorporated Schools.—Clio Montana Seminary, chartered 1801; Madison Academy, chartered 1819; Leaksville Female Academy, chartered 1819; Shady Grove Academy, chartered 1825; Leaksville Male Academy, chartered 1860.

The Leaksville Female Academy was authorized to raise $6,000 by a lottery.

I have endeavored in vain to get information about the old schools of this county.

ROWAN.

Formed in 1753 from Anson.

Incorporated Schools.—Salisbury Academy, chartered 1784; Salisbury Academy, chartered 1798; Salisbury Female Academy, chartered 1838; Salisbury Female Academy, amended 1851.

The first Salisbury Academy was the famous Liberty Hall Academy, of Charlotte, transferred to Salisbury. The Act, (Laws of 1884, First session—Chapter 29) shows that it was expected to be a high institution of learning for the whole Judicial District of Salisbury. Its title is "An Act for the Encouragement of Learning in the District of Salisbury." The preamble is interesting. It shows that the Trustees of the old institution petitioned for the change of location, alleging that "from various reasons the Liberty Hall Academy is in an entire state of decay, and that it would be more eligible to have an academy for the education of youth at or near Salisbury." There is a most ambitious list of Trustees, mostly new. Among them are Governor Nathaniel Martin and David Caldwell, of Guilford, Judge Samuel Spencer, of Anson, Col. Wm. Henry Harrington, of Richmond, Wm. Sharpe, M. C., and James Hall, of Iredell, Col. Joseph Winston, of Surry. Wm. Hill, of New Hanover, Joseph Dickson, M. C. and Gen. Charles McDowell, of Burke, besides leading wealthy and enlightened men of Mecklenburg, Cabarrus and Rowan. There are only seven of the original Trustees. Full corporate privileges are given, but it is odd, that while in the preamble it is ostentatiously declared that "the General Assembly are at all time disposed to give every proper encouragement for the promotion of learning, religion and virtue," the cautious proviso is added to the last section of the Act: "This seminary shall not be construed to be any one of those mentioned in and intended by the Constitution." All proper encouragement but not a dollar in cash!

There is no record of any realization of the dreams of the projectors of this great enterprise. On the contrary, fourteen years afterwards a new Salisbury Academy was chartered, with an entirely different Board of Trustees, with no allusion to the old. In 1815 a teacher was advertised, stating "the Main Building was nearly finished," and by 1818 I find the Salisbury Male and Female Academy in full operation. It must not be assumed that good schools had not existed in Salisbury before this. Among the teachers was Matthew Troy, a graduate of the University, who taught with reputation in the Preparatory School in 1805.

The famous Zion Parnassus School of Rev. Samuel Eusebias McCorckle, D. D., was situate 10 miles west of Salisbury, near Thyatira Church. He was a Scotch-Irish Presbyterian and gave instruction in the usual thorough manner of the clergyman of that race. Of the first graduates of the University of the State, seven in number, six were pupils of his. He gave likewise theological training, and also offered special instruction to those desiring to become teachers. How far this very early, if not the first "Normal School" in America, succeeded we have no means of knowing. He was very liberal in donating tuition and use of books to the needy. Such was his commanding reputation that his friends confidently expected his election as President of the University years before the choice of Caldwell in 1804.

General John Etcele's annoyance at Governor Davie's throwing his overpowering influence against it, was so great as to break up their old friendship for several years. Davie thought that executive ability was more needed for that office than deep learning and that McCorckle lacked it. The good doctor's friendship for the University was not impaired. He continued to be a warm supporter until his death. He was one of the charter Trustees, and delivered the sermon at the laying of the corner-stone in 1895, which was printed and which justifies the reputation he had among his contemporaries.

Dr. McCorckle was born in Pennsylvania in 1746, was brought to Rowan by his parents when ten years old, was prepared for Princeton by Dr. David Caldwell, graduated there in 1772, was ordained pastor over Thyatira congregation in 1777 and died in 1811. He was granted the doctorate by the State University.

The Lutherans as early as 1773 had a scholarly teacher in Rowan, Rev. Gottfried Anrendt.

In 1788 Rev. Carl August Gottleb Storch had a German School in Salisbury, and taught Hebrew as an elective study in the Academy.

I add that in the throes of the Civil War, in 1862, Edward Payson Hall published a card, couched in eloquent language, offering to teach anywhere within the limits of Rowan, but not outside.

RUTHERFORD.

Formed in 1779 from Tryon, which was from Mecklenburg, with a slice of Burke.

Incorporated Schools.—Rutherford Academy, chartered 1806; Rutherford Male and Female Academy, chartered 1838.

In 1856 C. H. Wiley reported a Female Institute at Rutherfordton, of which Rev. Erastus Rowley was Principal; a male school at the same place, of which Mr. Davis was chief.

After the Civil War there were Rutherfordton Female Academy, taught by Miss Lizzie Guthrie; Burnt Chimney Academy, by Mrs. W. H. Logan; Royster Academy, at Burnt Chimney, by Mr. and Mrs. Royster; and Rutherfordton School, by Miss Maggie Logan.

SAMPSON.

Formed in 1784 from Duplin, with a slice of New Hanover.

Incorporated Schools.—Clinton Academy, chartered 1821; Line Academy, chartered 1825; Holly Grove Academy, chartered 1827; Spring Vale Academy, chartered 1834; Clinton Female Institute, chartered 1851; Franklin Academy, chartered 1870.

There was a school of some note at a place called the Kornegay House, in the eastern part of the county, not far from the site of Duplin's old courthouse, about 1830, Dr. Fields being Principal.

It was superseded by Spring Vale Academy, not far from its site, which was a very flourishing institution, to the outbreak of the war, the pupils averaging about 80, sometimes reaching 100, from Sampson, Duplin, Wayne and Bladen. The teachers, sucessively, were Joseph S. Rhodes, George W. Johnson, Angus C. McNeill, Miss Bizzell, John G. Elliott, Solomon J. Faison.

Of these, John G. Elliott deserves special notice. He was at the University with James K. Polk, and walked fifty miles to the University in 1847 in order to greet him. He was a good classical scholar, eccentric in manner, devoted to his calling as a teacher and extremely charitable in giving tuition; high-principled, but agreeing with no one in religious views. He was a philanthropist-teacher. His personal appearance was peculiar. He was so thin and cadaverous that from his youth he was known as "Ghost Elliott," and, falling into the humor, he added "G.' (for ghost) to his Christian name. Rev. Dr. C. F. Deems describes him as he appeared in 1855: "Small, thin, washed out by multitudinous ablutions, built after the architectural design of an interrogation mark, with a disproportionately large head, the white hair on which was cropped to a length measured exactly by the thickness of the comb, he was a man whose appearance attracted attention everywhere. In some departments he was very learned, and his solid acquirements dominated his eccentricities and won for him the respect of a large class of citizens." I add that he was accustomed to ride intellectual hobbies. I remember him at the University Commencement of 1847, when President Polk and a brilliant collection of visitors were on the Hill, he would talk of nothing else than Greek adverbs and prepositions.

Clinton has had good schools since about 1825. There was an academy building for males on the lot where the Female Academy now stands. It was taught by a Mr. Litcom, and later by a Mr. Clark, and later still by Rev. Malcolm Conoly, of the Presbyterian Church. This building was burned and another for males was erected about 1858 in the western part of the town. Curtis Lee was the first teacher, but, his health failing, his place was taken by Thomas Williams, from Portsmouth. Then, in 1861, came Rev. George Gibbs and young Mr. Burkhead, a nephew of Rev. Dr. Burkhead, of the Methodist Conference. He volunteered for the war and was killed, and Mr. Gibbs continued, with an average attendance of about 75.

Teachers of the male schools in and near Clinton, besides the above, have been A. A. McKay (afterwards Judge), Mr. Boston, from Ireland; Mr. Williams, B. F. Grady (afterwards member of Congress), Murdock McCloud and James H. Murphy.

About 1850 the Clinton Female College was built. Luke C. Graves, of Massachusetts, but late of Warrenton, was the first Principal, and ultimately owned it. It was very prosperous, having a patronage of 150 to 175. After the Civil War, Luke Graves died and his son Thomas became owner. He, with his uncle, Nelson Graves, had a good school, respectable for numbers. Afterwards the property passed into other hands, but the school has been continued, sometimes for both boys and girls, with an average attendance of 100 to 125. The teachers have been Rev. J. L. Stewart, Hon. B. F. Grady, Rev. John N. Stallings, D. B. Nicholson, F. R. Cooper and others.

STANLY.

Formed in 1841 from Montgomery.

I do not find any incorporated schools for several decades after the formation of the county. Since 1870, H. W. Spink had a very good school at Albemarle, called Prospect Academy. At Mineral Springs, O. C. Hamilton was Principal of a school called Yadkin Academy.

In 1856 Mr. Wiley reported Centre Academy at Norwood, Long Creek Academy, Wolf Level Academy, Female Academy at Albemarle.

STOKES.

Formed in 1789 from Surry.

Incorporated Schools.—Germantown Academy, chartered 1809; Barshavia Academy, chartered 1832; Good Spring Grammar School, chartered 1832; Pleasant Hill Academy, chartered 1833; Germantown Academy, again chartered 1834; Bethania Literary Society and Academy, chartered 1844.

The first Germantown Academy had the privilege of raising $500 by lottery.

In 1856 Mr. Wiley reported Masonic Institute at Germantown, Female Institute at Germantown, Female Seminary at Danbury.

In 1878 W. A. Flynt was Principal of a very good classical school, called Dalton Institute, at Dalton.

SURRY.

Formed in 1770 from Rowan.

Incorporated Schools.—Jonesville Academy, chartered

1818; Franklin Academy, chartered 1833; Rockford Male and Female Seminary, chartered 1867.

First among the old schools of Surry was one taught by Professor Hickman, 1811-'20, about two miles from the site of Mt. Airy, patronized not only by Surry, but by adjoining counties of North Carolina and Virginia. Here were trained the scions of the families of Franklin, Martin, Moore and others. Judge John M. Cloud was one of the pupils.

Later, in 1836, Professor Blakely, a well-educated Virginian, had a successful school of 100 boys at "The Old Hollow Meeting House," about a mile west of Mt. Airy, for five years or more. He removed to Georgia and was succeeded by F. M. Gambrill, of Wilkes. Judge Jesse F. Graves was one of the pupils, and Jonathan X. Couter, who achieved much reputation in the Confederate Navy, received his appointment to Annapolis while a student here.

In the fifties Mr. West and his wife, who held a high place among the educators of their day, had a well-patronized mixed school at Rockford. After some years of service here they removed to Mt. Airy and had separate schools for boys, widely celebrated, attracting pupils from Virginia, South Carolina, Georgia and Alabama. They were succeeded by Mr. Reed and his wife, who also taught for some years with success.

THE ROCKFORD MALE AND FEMALE SEMINARY, after the cutting off of Yadkin, was held in the old courthouse and was flourishing.

After the Civil War Rufus H. Smith gained a wide reputation as a thorough and faithful teacher at Mt. Airy, until 1878. He was assisted by Gavin H. Lindsay.

The name of Miss Lizzie Gilmer, now living, should be held in honor for the great good she has accomplished by her forty years' labors in educating the girls of Surry.

In 1878 Mr. Guss Grayham had the male school at Mt.

Airy, Miss Lizzie Gilmer the female school at the same place, and Miss Lucy C. Journey, an accomplished teacher, the female school at Dobson.

SWAIN.

Formed in 1871 from Jackson and Macon.

In 1878 the following schools were reported:

Academy at Charleston, E. M. Scruggs.

Academy at Nantahalah, H. D. Welch.

Academy at Nantahalah, A. H. Welch.

Academy at Nantahalah, John McHan.

Academy at Nantahalah, J. H. McHan.

Academy at Nantahalah, Solomon McHan.

Academy at Nantahalah, J. S. Smiley.

Academy at Forks of Tennessee, D. Lester.

Academy at Ocona Lufty, George Bradley.

Academy at Charleston, Davis Whiteside.

TRANSYLVANIA.

Formed in 1861 from Henderson, with a slice of Jackson.

In 1878 the following schools were reported in this county:

Brevard Seminary, W. L. Norwood, Principal.

Davidson's River Academy, G. F. Robertson, Principal.

TYRRELL.

Formed in 1729. Precinct of Albemarle until 1738.

Chartered Schools.—Pike Academy, in Little Alligator, chartered 1819; Swain's Academy, chartered 1842.

Joseph Phelps had a school of local fame in this county in 1797.

Pike Academy was in existence prior to its charter.

Scuppernong and Albemarle Schools, in Scuppernong township.

As a rule, when a school was maintained in one the other was vacant.

In 1843 the teacher was J. B. McGowen, of New York. His successor in 1847 was Heber C. Murphy, of Maryland, educated at Hobart College. After about four years' service he became a minister in the Episcopal Church. The next master was Broughton W. Foster, of Vermont, son of a distinguished Congregational preacher, graduate of Dartmouth College, a young man of very high standing and literary attainments, an excellent teacher. He had a select school of 35. The next Principal was Edward C. Brabble, a former pupil of Foster, who graduated at Dartmouth and had experience in teaching in Massachusetts. He was a gallant Confederate soldier, won promotion to the colonelcy of the Thirty-third North Carolina Regiment, and died in service.

After the war Mr. Webb, of the State University, taught until about 1870.

Isaac Newton Tillett, of the same institution, had the school until about 1873, succeeded by —— Walthall for one year, and then it went down.

COLUMBIA HIGH SCHOOL.—In 1844 Miss Mary Mann, a lady of intelligence, began the school. Her successor was Samuel Terry, M. D., of New York, once in the United States Navy. In 1847 George W. Adamson, of New York, well educated, had charge, and then Lemuel Rice, a scholarly man, who was Principal until 1856. Then Mrs. Caroline Alexander and her daughter, Martha F., the latter a graduate of Salem Female Academy, subsequently the wife of Dennis Simmons, of Williamston. In 1859 Broughton W. Foster became Principal, until 1865. Then, successively, Rev. Marmaduke Rhodes, a Baptist preacher of this State; P. H. Wilkins, of Virginia; J. A. Cohoon, an alumnus of Trinity College; Ab. Alexander, M. D., in 1874; Harper Alexander, an alumnus of Randolph-Macon College; Edmund Alexander, of Randolph-

Macon; M. D. L. Newberry; Starke Hassell, a graduate of Wake Forest College; then W. S. Dunston, a graduate of the State University, conducted the school successfully until 1892. It is still in operation, J. J. Cohoon being Principal.

The average attendance was about 30, but larger under the management of Messrs. Dunston and Cohoon.

Rev. James E. Mann, afterwards Presiding Elder in the Methodist Episcopal Church, was in charge of a private school at Gum Neck about 1850. He was succeeded by Samuel Terry, above mentioned, for a number of years.

The school was suspended by the war. It was resumed in 1868, under the mastership of J. A. Cohoon, who kept it open for four years.

UNION.

Formed in 1842 from Anson, with a slice of Mecklenburg.

In 1878 Monroe High School had as its Principal J. D. Hodges.

Grove Spring Academy was also in operation at Griffinville, with H. Hale as Principal.

VANCE.

Formed in 1881 from Granville, with slices of Warren and Franklin.

Incorporated Schools.—Henderson Academy, chartered 1842; Kittrell Spring Academy, chartered 1856; Kittrell Spring Female College, chartered 1867.

The Mathematical and Classical School of Thomas J. Horner and son at Henderson had for years a just celebrity.

In 1843 Rev. R. M. Chapman had a school near Henderson.

The Henderson Male Academy opened with William H. Bass and R. Macon as teachers.

After the close of the war Mr. (now Rev.) Frederick Fetter, late tutor in the University, opened a classical school in Henderson, which had a good patronage. He was soon joined by his brother, Mr. (now Rev.) Charles Fetter, and then by his father, Prof. Manual Fetter. In 1872 the school was removed to Kittrell, the father going to the Military School at Charlotte. In 1874 Rev. Charles Fetter moved to Northampton.

In 1877 C. G. Davenport was master of a school for both sexes at the same place.

WAKE.

Formed in 1770 from Johnston, with slices of Cumberland and Orange.

Incorporated Schools.—Raleigh Academy, chartered 1801; Forest Hill Academy, chartered 1818; Raleigh Female Benevolent Society, chartered 1821; Wake Union Academy, chartered 1824; Wake Forest Pleasant Grove Academy, chartered 1826; Pomona, chartered 1826; Woodville Academy, chartered 1829; Spring Field Academy, 1830; Rolesville Academy, chartered 1832; Episcopal School of North Carolina, chartered 1833; Literary and Manual Labor Institution, chartered 1833; Wake Forest College, chartered 1838; Forestville Female Academy, chartered 1849; Morning Sun Academy, chartered 1854; Springfield Institute, chartered 1856; Colored Educational Association of North Carolina, chartered 1867.

The city of Raleigh was located as the seat of government in 1792. The most active man in working for the early inauguration of schools was Joseph Gales, editor of the Republican organ, The Raleigh Register. The first Trustees of the Raleigh Academy were John Ingles, William White, Nathaniel Jones, Henry Seawell, Simon Turner, William Boylan, John Marshall and Joseph Gales. Of these, White was State Treasurer; Jones, State Senator; Seawell, then Commoner, afterwards Judge; Boylan, editor of the Federalist paper, The Minerva. Jones subscribed $100 and was made President, and Gales Secretary. One month afterwards $800 was reported as subscribed, and soon, on Burke Square, by permission of the General Assembly, one building was erected for males and another for females. In an extraordinary fit of generosity the use of the State rock quarry was granted for five years by the General Assembly to the Academy, the preamble of the act apologizing by stating that they were "of no profit to the State."

The Academy was opened in January, 1804. Rev. Marin Detargney, of Princeton and the College of Maryland, was Principal; Chesley Daniel, a graduate and tutor of the State University, was his assistant. Miss Charlotte Brodie was teacher of needle-work. Greek, Latin, Spanish, French, Mathematics, Astronomy, Navigation and the English branches were offered at $5 per quarter; the English branches alone, at $3; for needel-work, free.

The school had eminent success. Public examinations were held, and the Trustees detailed to report upon them. The reports show the following classes: One in Philosophy and Astronomy; one in Horace; one in Virgil; one in Caesar; one in Selecti Veterii; one in Erasmus; one in Aesop's Fables; one in Corderii; and two in Latin Grammar. There was no Greek class.

In the English branches there was one class in Geography; a first, second, third and fourth class in English Grammar; one in English Reading; one in Writing; and a first and second in Spelling.

In the female department there were a first, second, third, fourth and fifth class in Spelling; a like number in Reading; four classes in English Grammar; one in parsing in Blair's Lectures; two in Geography; two in Writing;

three in Embroidery; one in Tambour Work; one in Cotton Floss Work; one in Alphabetical Samples.

The examinations occupied Thursday and Friday. On Saturday the students read compositions and pronounced speeches to "large and respectable audiences." Those who did best were publicly mentioned.

At the close, in 1809, the students presented a comedv called "Sighs or the Daughter," and the farce of "Trick Upon Trick," for the benefit of the Polemic Library, probably connected with the school. At night was a ball—dancing, of course—attended by the older pupils.

It will be noticed that much Latin was taught the boys and none to the girls. On the other hand, the damsels had industrial training and the boys none.

In 1810 the Trustees secured the services of Rev. Wm. McPheeters, of Virginia, who was to be not only Principal of the Academy, but "Pastor of the City." He was a man of learning and strongest character, an admirable teacher, kind to all, but inflexibly severe on offenders. Under him the patronage was large. He had able assistants. Among them was Alexander Wilson, afterwards a Rev. Dr. and James Grant, afterwards a Judge in Iowa and a benefactor of his Alma Mater, the State University.

Among the assistants in the Female department, over which Dr. McPheeters had general charge, was a music teacher of celebrity, Thomas Sambourne. After his death his wife continued at the same vocation, until 1813, when she set up for herself. In the same year came Miss Bosworth, advertised as a "perfect mistress of the polite and fashionable accomplishments of drawing, and every kind of needle-work." In 1815 was employed Rev. Josiah Crudup, Jr., a Baptist preacher, afterwards a member of Congress, a formidable opponent of Willie P. Mangum. In 1820 we find Miss Nye, Mr. Barlow, "from the North," and Miss Yancey.

The Raleigh Academy had a wide and justly earned celebrity. Such was its high standing that a Mr. Edmondson inauguarted a school preparatory to it. It trained many of the leaders, not only of North Carolina, but of Virginia and the State south of us.

Dr. McPheeters was elected a Trustee of the University in 1812 and was honored by it with the degree of D. D. in 1819. He preached in the State House until the completion of the Presbyterian church in 1817. He gave up the Academy in 1833. In 1837 he spent a year in Fayetteville in charge of a large female seminary and then was forced to resign from bad health. For the same reason he declined the Presidency of Davidson College, but was able to have a small school of fifteen boys at Raleigh. He died in 1842, after a life most useful and honorable.

During the early work of Dr. McPheeters the Sorcastrian system of teaching was introduced in Raleigh. John Evans offered to teach poor children by that system for $10 per annum. Later Mrs. Peat established an "Infant School," the forerunner of our Kindergarten.

In 1822 Chief Justice John Lewis Taylor opened a law-school at his residence. After his death it was discontinued.

In 1820 J. H. Hassam had a private school in opposition to the Academy, but it had only moderate success.

In the 30's P. Le Messurier conducted a classical school.

In 1831 James Grant opened a private school, also offering French at recess to young ladies.

In the same year Captain D. H. Bingham, transferred his "North Carolina Literary, Scientific and Military Academy" from Oxford to Raleigh. His school was in the dwelling of Chief Justice Taylor, lately deceased, afterwards the home of Judge R. M. Saunders, and now of Captain S. A. Ashe.

NEW BUILDING NORTH CAROLINA SCHOOL FOR THE DEAF AND DUMB, MORGANTON, N. C.

BAPTIST FEMALE UNIVERSITY, RALEIGH, N. C.

In 1835 Robert G. Allison was in charge of the male department of the Raleigh Academy.

The Episcopal School of North Carolina.—The sum of about $1,200 was pledged by members of the Episcopal church, payable mostly in five years, for the establishment of a school for boys at Raleigh. The tract of 159 1-2 acres, about one mile west of the capitol, on which is now St. Mary's School, was bought and buildings erected thereon by mortgaging the property. The school was opened in June, 1834, with a large patronage—83 boarders and 20 day scholars the first year. Rev. Dr. Joseph G. Cogswell, afterwards the eminent librarian of Astor Library, was Principal. He was a graduate of Harvard and a Professor of Mineralogy in that University. He then spent six years in Europe perfecting himself in the German, French and Italian languages and literature, obtaining the degree of Doctor of Philosophy at Gottingen. He likewise studied educational methods and on his return resigned his professorship at Harvard and for ten years was Principal of the Round Hill school in Massachusetts. After all this experience he lacked the tact to manage the large number of boys who flocked to the Episcopal school from all quarters, including Mississippi, Florida, Alabama, Louisiana, Georgia, South Carolina, Virginia, Tennessee (99 in all) during the first year. His assistants, Rev. Joseph H. Saunders and John DeBerniere Hooper could not supply his defects. The boys became so very unruly, and the disorder so flagrant that the subsequent masters were unable to rectify it. At one time there were 135 pupils, but after six years experience the public confidence was withdrawn and the school was closed. Eventually the mortgage was foreclosed and the whole property passed into the hands of Duncan Cameron, and was rented to Rev. Dr. A. Smedes, becoming the famous St. Mary's School for girls, which, as it still exists, does not come within the scope of this paper.

The Principals of the Episcopal school for boys after Dr. Cogswell were Rev. Dr. Adam Empie, W. J. DeBerniere Hooper, afterwards Professor of Latin, and also of Greek in the State University, and Rev. Dr. Moses A. Curtis, the eminent Botanist. The terms at first were $175 for boarders for ten months and $50 for day pupils—afterwards raised to $200 and subsequently reduced to $150 and $40 for classical studies—$32 for English.

In 1839 W. G. Catlin had the old Raleigh Academy.

The next year Rev. John G. Backhouse, in the mornings, and Rev. Edwin Geer in the afternoons, had a well taught school in one of the buildings of the Episcopal school. Then in the Raleigh Academy John Y. Hicks (see "Macon,) was its Principal for a year, succeeded by Silas Bigelow, of Virginia, a loveable old man and fair teacher. Robert Gray, a graduate of Belfast College in Ireland, a superior teacher, in 1844 started the Raleigh Institute, enlarged the next year into the North Carolina Literary, Scientific and Military Academy, with himself as Principal and Instructor in Mathematics; O. A. Buck, a native of New Hampshire, in charge of Military Tactics; S. N. Botsford, of Experimental Chemistry and Philosophy; M. Maily, of French. A cheap uniform was prescribed. There were to be six hours of study. Instead of play there were Gymnastics and Military Exercises. Politeness, neatness and punctuality were to be cultivated. The school was short-lived.

Jefferson Madison Lovejoy, "Old Jeff," a native of Vermont, and graduate of Middleburg College, came from Pittsboro to Raleigh in 1843 and established his excellent school, first at his home and then at the Academy on Burke Square. In 1846, in consequence of the military spirit engendered by the Mexican War, he adopted the military feature, with Captain W. F. Disbrow as instructor, also teaching mathematics. He soon, however, dropped the military department, conducting a flourishing, classical institute, called the Metropolitan School, until 1866, when he took charge of Vine Hill Academy in Halifax. He returned about 1873 and taught until his death, in 1877, but did not, probably, regain his old fame. While he had eccentricities of manner, he was in his prime an uncommonly good teacher, thorough, strict, but not cruel—a terror to bad boys. While Mr. Lovejoy was absent from Raleigh 1866-'72, first S. G. Ryan, then Thos. B. Bailey, were principals of the Raleigh Academy. Later teachers, prior to Morson's Academy, now existing, have been J. M. White, J. J. Fray, C. H. Scott, Rev. Joseph M. Atkinson, D. D. and C. B. Denson.

Among the Female Schools in Raleigh no longer existing was the Raleigh Female Seminary, started about 1860, with T. H. Brame, as President, and R. G. Heflin as Professor. Wm. C. Doub was afterwards Principal. The success was not such as to warrant its continuance. Rev. Bennet T. Blake was likewise in charge of that or a similar school.

Nor should be unrecorded a school for young children of remarkable excellence, conducted by a very gifted woman, Mrs. Eliza F. Taylor, widow of an eminent lawyer, James F. Taylor, State Solicitor. It was begun not far from 1835 and continued over 20 years with unimpaired popularity. It was at her house that Judge Gaston wrote "Carolina!" and it was her daughter who adopted the tune, and, assisted by Rev. Dr. Joseph Blount Cheshire, first sang it.

In the county between 1830 and 1840 there was a Pleasant Grove Academy, of which A. D. Crenshaw was Principal.

The Wake Forest Pleasant Grove Academy, incorporated in 1826, was quite an ambitious enterprise. It was situate on the Oxford road 12 miles North of Raleigh. The Principal was Daniel W. Kerr. (See Alamance.) In addition to the classics and the English branches, he offered needle-work, drawing and painting, music. Teaching by the Lancastrian system was to be by Edward S. Fouches. Board could be had in the neighboring families at $4 per month. In 1845 we find Miss Martha R. Richardson to be Principal.

In 1834 Anderson Page advertised a school for Females at Oak Mount, stating that there was a male school in a mile of the same.

In 1839, near Soapstone, Stimson H. Whitaker opened a school.

In 1847 Rev. Dr. Aldert Smedes, on a small tract of land, about seven miles west of Raleigh, opened a church classical school called Trinity, of which he was Rector. Daily prayer was offered in the school, with daily examinations in Holy Scripture; fasts and festivals were duly observed, and catechizing on Sundays.

Rev. Fordyce M. Hubbard, D. D., was the first Principal. On his election as Professor in the State University he was succeeded by Rev. Mr. Bobbitt. After three years the school was closed. Its highest number of pupils at one time was nineteen.

In the 40's the Misses Owen, sisters of Prof. W. H. Owen, had a Female Boarding School at Wake Forest College.

WARREN.

Formed in 1779 from Bute, with slice of Granville. Bute was from Granville.

Incorporated Schools.—Warrenton Academy, chartered 1786; Nutbush Mineral Springs Academy, chartered 1810; Schocco Female Academy, chartered 1820; Shady Grove Male and Female Academy, chartered 1822; Warren Academy, chartered 1826; Princeton Acodemy, chartered 1833; Ridgeway Academy, chartered 1842; Warrenton Female

College, chartered 1857; Central Institute for Young Ladies, chartered 1883.

The Nutbush Mineral Spring Academy is described as being on the land of John Simms.

The Warren Academy was on Joseph W. Hawkins' land and built by him.

The Princeton Academy was on Dennis O'Bryan's land.

Rev. Charles Pettigrew, D. D., who was elected Bishop of North Carolina in 1794, but not ordained, when a young man was master of a school at Bertie Court-house, beginning 1766, under the patronage of Senator Benjamin Hawkins, Gen. Jethro Sumner.

The charter of Warrenton Academy in 1786 is in very many respect like that of Liberty Hall Academy. There was the same attempt to attract patronage from abroad by having as Trustees prominent men from a distance. Rev. Henry Patillo (See Granville) headed the list. Then came Wm. R. Davie, Nicholas Long and Willie Jones, of Halifax, and General Thomas Person, of Granville. Of the Warren Trustees were Benjamin Hawkins, one of the first Senators of the United States, and Nathaniel Macon, besides others of the leading citizens. They were allowed to raise $2,000 by a lottery, the details of which are set forth in the Act. There were one prize of $1,000, one of $500, fourteen of $100, twenty of $50, fifty of $20, three hundred of $10, two hundred and fifty of $4. The 2,500 tickets were to be sold at $4 each, of which 1,864 were blanks and 636 were prizes. It thus appears that there was about one chance in three of drawing any prize, and one out of 2,500 of getting the $1,000. The managers, appointed by the Trustees, were to give bond with good security for the performance of duty.

It was provided also in the charter that the Academy Should not be regarded as one commanded in the Constitution.

The Warrenton Academy was for years a power in the land. One of the earliest teachers was a Mr. Halbert, who advertised to teach Virgil, Horace, Ovid, Xenophon, Homer and Euclid.

One of the greatest teachers in the last century in the State was Rev. Marcus George, who was for years Principal of this school. Chief Justice Thomas Ruffin, Weldon N. Edwards, President of the Convention of 1861, and Col. Cadwallader Jones, of Hillsboro, were pupils of his, and classmates. They bore testimony to his excellence as a man, as a scholar and as a teacher. "He whipped powerful," they used to say. Governor Davie had such admiration that he endeavored, by authority of the Trustees, to induce him to accept a professorship in the University.

Among his assistants was a man of peculiar gifts, Wm. Augustus Richards, a Tutor in the University afterwards. He was well educated in London, became a sailor, deserted at Norfolk and joined a strolling theatrical company. At Warrenton he left the stage and became a good teacher, especially in elocution.

A successor of Mr. George in 1816 was Rev. Charles Applewhite Hill, likewise a most worthy man. (See Franklin.) During his incumbency John Forrest, Jr., opened a classical school in opposition. In 1820 Mr. Hill resigned the Academy and was Principal of a private school offering instruction in classics and mathematics as far as trigonometry and surveying. The Principal of the Academy was then Rev. George W. Freeman, afterwards Bishop of Arkansas.

Among teachers of subsequent period should be mentioned R. A. Errell in the 40's and Captain John E. Dugger, the latter being the first Superintendent of the Graded School of Raleigh, one of the pioneers of such schools in the State.

In the county were Midway Academy, between Shocco and Jones' Spring, in the 40's, of which John H. Barlow as master, and Grove Hill Academy about 1840, conducted by John Y. Hicks. (See Wake.)

In 1849 Rev. Dr. Wm. Hooper and his son-in-law, Professor J. DeBerniere Hooper, opened a "Family School" for boys near Littleton, the charge being $200 for ten months, board and tuition, with $20 extra for modern languages. The success was not sufficient to warrant long continuance.

Female schools of Warren have been for a hundred years conspicuous for their excellence. In the latter part of the last century Wm. and S. Falkener, his wife, had a school for "young ladies and gentlemen of tender age," which was projected on lines in advance of that age. They say, "conscious how much depends upon a vigilant attention to the early bent of inclination, every preceptive duty shall be diligently exercised. Persuasion and excitement will be preferred to coercion, their literary pursuits so varied as to suit the genius, induce emulation and render [children] eager of improvement." It is to be regretted that we have not the details of this experiment. It was probably successful, as Mrs. Falkner continued it for some years after the death of her husband. The charge for tuition and board was $105, certainly as late as 1805.

The Mordecai School.—Warrenton Female Academy. One of the very best schools for females ever had in the State was opened by Jacob Moredcai, as Principal, on January 1st, 1809. It was called the Warrenton Female Seminary, and had the unlimited confidence of a wide circle of patrons. Mr. Mordecai was assisted by his eldest son, Moses, afterwards an eminent lawyer of Raleigh, and his daughters, Misses Rachel and Ellen, and a younger son, Solomon. A. C. Miller was music teacher, and Mr. La Taste. Achille Plunkett, once a wealthy West India planter, forced away by an insurrection of the negroes, was Miller's successor. The number of students was from 75 to 100.

In 1817 leading citizens of Wilmington, Granville, Halifax, Petersburg, Fayetteville, Hillsboro, as well as Warren, united in an unqualified endorsement of the school.

Jacob Mordecai was born in Philadelphia, April 11th, 1762. He was for many years a merchant, but being a good scholar and fond of literary pursuits, after some financial reverses, concluded to adopt the profession of a teacher in which he was so successful, notwithstanding his Jewish faith. After giving up his school he purchased a farm near Richmond, Va., but failed in this venture and spent the remnant of his useful life in that city, dying in August, 1838. He left very distinguished sons, Moses, lawyer in Raleigh; Samuel, merchant in Richmond; author of "Richmond in Bygone Days;" Solomon, physician in Mobile, Ala.; George Washington, lawyer, railroad and bank President; Alfred, Major in the U. S. Army, scientific investigator and author. Augustus, was a highly respected farmer of Virginia. His daughters, too, were highly gifted.

In 1818 Joseph Andrews and Thomas P. Jones succeeded Mr. Mordecai and conducted the Academy for some years. They advertised that they had five teachers, and were prepared to teach "music, drawing and dancing, plain needle and muslin work," with use of maps and globes, and extensive apparatus for Natural Philosophy and Chemistry, and an Orrery. Terms were $150 for ten months, board and tuition, with music, drawing and dancing extra. They attempted too much and in 1822 the property was sold under mortgage.

After this Mrs. Caroline Plunkett, widow of Achille Plunkett, who was a daughter of Jacob Mordecai, was Principal of the Academy, on the same lines as when her father was in charge. How long her work continued has not been ascertained, but she was teaching in 1830, probably later.

In 1841 a successful effort was made to revive the Warrenton Female Academy, the Trustees buying very eligible property for the purpose. Rev. N. Z. Graves, a Presbyterian preacher of Vermont, was the first Principal, with Julius Wilcox as assistant, Mrs. Sarah A. Nichols being teacher of music. They had a good patronage, but in 1846 Daniel Turner, son of Governor Turner, an ex-member of Congress, who, with his wife, a daughter of Francis S. Key, had been conducting a select boarding school at their residence in the county, obtained a lease of the Academy property and conducted a successful school until their removal to California in 1856. It passed then into the hands of Methodist Trustees who obtained a charter for the Warrenton Female College. Rev. Thomas S. Campbell was the first President and two years afterwards Edward E. Parham, there being under their management, with able assistants, an average of one hundred pupils until diminished by the Civil War. Mr. Parham kept the doors open for most of the war and until 1866. About 1870 Dr. Turner and Mr. Jones had a school here but in 1873 removed to Greensboro and the College ceased to exist, although Mrs. Mary Williams and Miss Lucy Hawkins have a private school of high reputation in the building.

The Warrenton Collegiate Institute was founded in 1846 by Rev. N. Z. Graves, and his brother-in-law, Julius Wilcox. Two years afterwards they associated with themselves Luke C. Graves. In 1853 the latter was succeeded by Edwin L. Barrett. In 1859 Mr. Graves retired and Mr. Wilcox was Principal until he died in 1865, when his widow, Mrs. M. J. J. Wilcox conducted the school until 1880. All the teachers were most worthy and capable.

Shocco Springs, in the days when travelling by the family coach was usual, was a fashionable summer resort and therefore attracted the attention of teachers. Here the Marquis de Cluzrey, an emigre French nobleman, about the beginning of the century, taught the true Parisian accent to those not engrossed with the frivolities of dancing and card-playing. Here the Shocco Female Seminary had a good patronage for some years. In the 20's the Principal was Dr. Thomas Cottrell. In 1830 Mrs. Mary J. Lucas had charge.

In 1821 there was a school for both sexes under Rev. Rufus Wiley and Rev. Philip Wiley. In 1839 Alban Hart had a classical school at the same place.

Nor should if be forgotten that A. D. Smith, of Warren county, in 1830 advertised a new system of penmanship, by which "bad writers write an elegant hand in two or three days." Would that we could bring him to life again!

WASHINGTON.

Formed in 1799 from Tyrrell.

Frazier's Academy was once a school of well-merited reputation in this county. It was established by a Sctoch-Irishman of that name soon after the Revolutionary War, who taught for so long a period as to acquire the admiring epithet of "old Mr. Frazier." After his death it was continued by different teachers until 1850. It was situate about 1 1-2 miles east of Mackey's Ferry, and about 10 miles from Plymouth.

WATAUGA.

Formed in 1849 from Ashe, with slices of Wilkes, Caldwell and Yancey.

A very important educational enterprise in this county was the institute at Valle Crucis, founded by Bishop L. S. Ives, of the Protestant Episcopal Church in 1844. It was intended to be a Theological School and a centre of missions. A classical school was opened as a preparation to the theological, while the latter was to train up a native ministry on the soil. The enterprise seemed full of promise for five or six years, when it was ruined by the secession of the Bishop into the Roman Church.

Boone Classical High School was very successful from 1866 to 1879, the teachers being: H. C. Dixon, 1866-'69, J. S. Hill, 1874-'76, J. F. Spainhour and J. S. Hill, 1879-'81. The patronage of the latter reached 100.

Cove Creek Academy was a classical school of like success from 1885 to 1891, with J. S. Martin, E. S. Blackburn, and W. M. Francum successively, as Princilpals.

New River Academy, at Horton, was under W. R. Spainhour in 1888-'89. The next year J. F. and W. R. Spainhour had charge; the next year Mr. Hendren, and then W. M. Francum.

Elk Knob Academy, at Norris, is a classical school started by R. H. Cline in 1886. Wm. Laws, Jacob Wike, M. H. Norris, and Rev. J. L. Deaton have been the teachers since.

Zionville Academy, with W. R. Spainhour as Principal, had a short year's life in 1889.

WAYNE.

Formed in 1779 from Dobbs, which was from Johnston, with a slice of Craven.

Incorporated Schools.—Waynesboro Academy, chartered 1810; Free School in Wayne County, chartered 1813; Waynesboro Academy, again chartered 1832; Everettesville Female Academy, chartered 1847; Macon Academy, chartered 1849; Wayne Female College, chartered 1857; Goldsboro Female College, chartered 1867.

The terms "Free School" probably meant undenominational.

In the first half of this century the Fremont School, in the northern part of the county, was a classical school of high rank.

There were similar academies at Falling Creek and at

Everittsville. At all three places the teachers did not remain long enough to leave a permanent memory.

WAYNE FEMALE COLLEGE, an institution of high rank and large patronage, was inaugurated under control of the Methodists in 1857, with Rev. James H. Brent as President. It first occupied the old wooden Borden Hotel, but soon the funds were increased by stock subscriptions and a large brick building on ample grounds was erected. Dr. S. Morgan Closs was President one year. Rev. S. Milton Frost, D. D., a graduate of the State University, was President from 1857 to 1862 when the building was taken for a Confederate hospital. In 1866 Dr. S. Morgan Closs attempted to revive the college. President E. W. Adams continued the attempt, procuring a change of the name to Goldsboro Female College, but the adverse influences resulting from the war caused its final closing in 1871. Private schools were successively carried on in the building for ten years afterwards by Rev. N. Z. Graves, Prof. Manuel Fetter, long in charge of the Greek chair at the State University, and R. P. Troy, when the property was leased for the Graded School.

WILKES.

Formed in 1777 from Surry, with a slice of Burke.

Incorporated Schools.—Philomathian Academy, chartered 1804; Wilkesboro Academy, chartered 1810; Wilkesboro Academy, again chartered 1819.

"At a very early period in this century there was a notable "Grammar School," with John Harrison as Principal. It was described as "ten miles below the courthouse." Latin and Greek were offered. The tuition was $10 for ten months, and board could be had at $25 per year.

The only teacher of the Wilkesboro Academy whose name I have been able to recover is that of Rev. Peter McMillan, whose tuition was fifty per cent. higher than

Mr. Harrison's, and the board from 75 to 100 per cent. higher.

WILSON.

Formed in 1855 from Edgecombe, with slices of Nash, Johnston and Wayne.

Wilson Collegiate Institute was a school of much promise. The buildings were erected and furniture purchased, and Rev. Dr. Charles F. Deems, afterwards of the Church of the Strangers, New York, was offered control, with the gift of a majority of the stock. He accepted, and chose Miss Mary Wade Speed as Principal of the Seminary for the girls, while Capt. James D. Radcliff was in charge of the boys. The school was dedicated as St. Austin's Institute, and the exercises opened in 1859. Dr. Deems resigned after four years. The operations were suspended by the Civil War.

Wilson had another large academy building and school under control of the Primitive Baptists. Mr. E. W. Adams conducted it for several years.

In 1859 D. S. Richardson, a Northern man, with a faculty of eight other instructors, including his wife, had charge of schools, both for males and females. These were the Wilson Female Seminary and Wilson Male Academy. The next year the latter was changed to the Wilson Classical and Scientific Gymnasium. The buildings and boarding-houses of the two schools were separate. The departments were, of the male school: first, the Preparatory; second, Classical; third, Literary and Scientific; the second, preparing boys for college, the third being a curriculum of four years, to prepare the students to be "practical men." The Seminary had likewise three departments: first, the Preparatory; second, the Regular Collegiate, and third, the Department of the Fine Arts.

The turmoil of the Civil War broke up this ambitious scheme. After its close Mr. Richardson reopened the school, followed by J. B. Williams and E. M. Nadal. The property then changed hands, and from 1872 to 1886 Sylvester Hassell, a first-honor graduate of the State University, conducted a mixed school of wide patronage. A Female Seminary, under control of Prof. J. DeB. Hooper, and his father-in-law, Rev. Dr. Wm. Hooper, was, on the transfer of the former to the chair of Greek and French in 1875, combined with Professor Hassell's school, under the name of Wilson College. There were five professors of known ability and of reputation, assisted by five lady instructors. In 1886 Silas E. Warren, Principal, changed the name to Wilson Collegiate Institute, and continued it until his death, in 1894.

The Faculty of Wilson College in 1875 was a strong one, as follows: Sylvester Hassell, A. M., President, Ethics; J. B. Brewer, A. M., Mathematics, Chemistry; J. H. Foy, Ancient and Modern Languages; D. G. Gillespie, Bookkeeping, Banking; E. M. Nadal, Mathematics; Miss Mollie A. Southall, Music; Mrs. J. B. Brewer, Instructor in Music; Miss Bettie A. Chandler and Mrs. S. V. Briggs, English Branches; Miss Bertha Tripp, Drawing, Painting.

The Graded School, which diverted patronage from Wilson College, is not now held in either of the old school buildings, but in one of its own.

In 1897 Mr. Joseph Kinsey, a veteran and able teacher, moved his school here.

YADKIN.

Formed in 1850 from Surry.

This fragment of old Surry is distinguished as containing the celebrated Law School of Chief Justice Richmond M. Pearson, who was on the Superior Court bench twelve years and then on the Supreme Court bench for thirty years, most of the time as Chief Justice. I find the first advertisement of his school in a newspaper of 1842, when he resided at Mocksville. In it he promises to use the method of teaching adopted by Chief Justice Henderson—familiar questioning on points of law. In 1847 he removed to his plantation in Surry, now Yadkin, named by him Richmond Hill, and there were collected students from all parts of this and other States. The total number who received instruction from him has been estimated as high as seven hundred, including some of the greatest legal lights in the South. After his death, in 1878, the survivors of his students erected a handsome monument to his memory in Oakwood Cemetery, Raleigh.

YANCEY.

Formed in 1833 from Burke and Buncombe.

Prof. Stephen Adams was the first noted teacher of Yancey. He began about 1845, and for ten or twelve years had a good graded academy at Burnsville. After his death Prof. J. E. Rheim, of this State, taught seven or eight years. Both were graduates of good schools.

There never was a chartered educational institution in the county.

ADDENDA.

Since forwarding the foregoing paper to the Superintendent of Public Instruction I have received other information of interest.

From that well-posted antiquarian, Rev. Dr. J. D. Hufham, I get the following:

"Two brothers, John and Joe Elliott, both Yale men, came out from New England in the closing years of the last century and became the pioneers of higher education in the region which borders the Neuse and extends south to the Cape Fear. Joe taught a large school at Spring Hill, Lenoir County. It was greatly prosperous as late as 1812-'13, and many of his boys, among them William D. Mosely, Governor of Florida, went to the University." * *

Dr. Hufham further states that John Elliott's school was even superior to his brother's, situated in Duplin County, three miles north of Faison, called Green Academy. Maj. H. W. Husted, afterwards a lawyer of repute, who graduated at Yale, taught here. The father of Dr. Hufham, Rev. George W. Hufham, went from this school to the University. The eminent teacher, John Ghost Elliott, mentioned under Sampson County, was a son of John Elliott, who married a Cogdale, a relative of George E. Badger.

Dr. Hufham adds: "Up to 1830 there were no Baptist schools in North Carolina. There were schools which were taught by Baptists. There early grew up a custom of establishing schools near the churches. * * * There was such a school in the New England settlement at Sandy Creek, also among the churches of the upper valley of the Yadkin and elsewhere. Henry Abbott, the most prominent Baptist preacher of his day, taught both before and after he entered the ministry. Others did the same."

DURHAM COUNTY.—Dr. S. B. Weeks gives me some interesting points about Rev. John Chavis, the Presbyterian negro preacher and teacher. He was born, free, in Granville County, about 1763, a full-blooded negro; received a classical education under Dr. Witherspoon at Princeton. He was admitted to the Orange Presbytery in 1805. He preached often to the whites at Shiloh, Nutbush and Island churches. His language was free from negroisms, and his preaching clear and interesting. He was a good Latin and Greek scholar, and taught in Granville, west Wake, Chatham, and perhaps east Orange counties. Among his pupils, besides Senator Mangum and Governor Manly, were sons of Chief Justice Henderson and other leading men. He often visited his former pupils, and was received by them with the highest respect. Dr. Weeks shows me some of his letters to Senator Mangum. They prove that the Senator treated him as a friend, and are well written. One of them, dated in 1837, was a vigorous protest against the Petition for Emancipation, sent to Congress by the Abolitionists, as injurious to the colored race. Owing to the Nat Turner Insurrection in 1831 the General Assembly prohibited preaching by negroes. He submitted and was provided for by his Presbytery. One of his sermons was published. He died in 1830.

LENOIR COUNTY.—By the kindness of the veteran teacher, Dr. R. H. Lewis, of Kinston, I give more particular information about the schools of Kinston.

Judge George V. Strong and his brother, William A. Strong, were over Kinston Academy prior to the Civil War.

Kinston College began operation in 1882 under Richard H. Lewis, M. D., as President. He presided over it until 1889, when it ceased to be a corporation and passed into private hands, who kept it until about four years ago.

Dr. Lewis was Principal of "Kinston Collegiate Institute" from 1877 until his transfer to Kinston College, in 1882.

Kinston Female Seminary was under the charge of the Misses Patrick.

Vide supra, the school of Mr. Joseph Elliott at Spring Hill.

M'DOWELL COUNTY.—Among the teachers of this county between 1850 and 1860 were B. W. Craig, J. W. Biddix and William F. Craig.

MARTIN COUNTY.—I am indebted to Mrs. Nannie E .Jones, a daughter of Mr. J. M. Lovejoy, for the following:

"Mr. James H. Horner, afterwards of Oxford, taught at Hamilton, 1848-'50. He was succeeded by Mr. Swain, of Washington County, and then J. W. De Ford, of Pennsylvania.

PITT COUNTY.—Jefferson Madison Lovejoy, mentioned as teaching in Chatham and Wake, came from Vermont, first to Greenville, and was Principal of a school there. Here he married Miss Virginia Steptoe.

WAKE COUNTY.—A recent most interesting address by Rev. Dr. Thomas E. Skinner recalls to my mind that Rev. Thomas E. Meredith, the eminent founder of the Biblical Recorder, was, in 1848 and for some years subsequently, the Principal of a female school in Raleigh.

WARREN COUNTY.—Among the head-masters of Warrenton Male Academy about 1825-'30 was Rev. James H. Otey, afterwards Bishop of Tennessee, and then Rev. George W. Freeman, afterwards Bishop of Arkansas.

EARLY LEGISLATION FOR PUBLIC SCHOOLS.

I include in the following few pages some of the acts pertaining to public education. These acts furnish very interesting reading to all who are interested in our educational history.

ENACTED BY A GENERAL ASSEMBLY, BEGUN AND HELD AT RALEIGH, ON THE TWENTY-FIRST DAY OF NOVEMBER, IN THE YEAR OF OUR LORD ONE THOUSAND EIGHT HUNDRED AND TWENTY-FIVE, AND IN THE FORTY-NINTH YEAR OF THE INDEPENDENCE OF THE SAID STATE.

1825.

AN ACT TO CREATE A FUND FOR THE ESTABLISHMENT OF COMMON SCHOOLS.

Be it enacted by the General Assembly of the State of North Carolina, and it is hereby enacted by the authority of the same:

That a fund for the support of common and convenient schools for the instruction of youth, in several counties of this State, be and the same is hereby appropriated, consisting of the dividends arising from the stock now held, and which may hereafter be acquired by the State in the Banks of Newbern and Cape Fear, and which has not heretofore been pledged and set apart for internal improvement; the dividend arising from stock which is owned by the State in the Cape Fear Navigation Company, Roanoke Navigation Company, and the Clubfoot and Harlow Creek Canal Company; the tax imposed by law on licenses to the retailers of spiritous liquors and auctioneers; the unexpended balance of the Agricultural fund, wihch, by the act of the Legislature, is directed to be paid into the Public Treasury; all moneys paid to the State for entries of vacant lands. (excepting the Cherokee lands;) the sum of twenty one thousand and ninety dollars, which was paid by this State to certain Cherokee Indians, for reservations to land secured to them by treaty, when the said sum shall be received from the United States by this State; and of all the vacant and unappropriated swamp lands in this State; together with such sums of money as the Legislature may hereafter find it convenient to appropriate from time to time.

Sec. II. Be it further enacted: That all sums of money which have accrued since the first day of November last, or which may hereafter accrue as aforesaid, shall be, and the same is hereby vested in the Governor of the State, the Chief Justice of the Supreme Court, the Speaker of the Senate, the Speaker of the House of Commons, and the Treasurer of the State, for the time being; and they and their successors in office are hereby constituted a body corporate and politic, under the name of the President and Directors of the Literary Fund, with power to sue, and be sued, plead and be impleaded, and to hold real and personal property, and to sell, dispose of, or improve the same, to effect the purpose of promoting learning and the instruction of youth. The Governor shall be President of the Board, and any three of the Directors shall constitute a quorum for the transaction of business relative to the said fund; and, in the absence of the Governor, they shall have authority to appoint a President for the time of such absence. They shall cause to be kept by the Treasurer of the State a regular account of all such sums of money as may belong to the said fund, the manner in which the same has been applied and vested, and they shall make an annual report thereof to the Legislature, with such recommendations for the improvement of the same, as to them shall seem expedient.

Sec. III. Be it further enacted, That the President and Directors of the fund hereby created are authoribed to vest any part or whole of the said fund, in the stock of any of the Banks of this State, or of the United States, or in the stock of the Government of the United States and at all times to change, alter and dispose of the same, and of any real and personal estate belonging to the said fund, in such manner, and upon such terms, as may, in their opinion, be best calculated to improve the value thereof.

Sec. 4. Be it further enacted, That the fund hereby created shall be applied to the instruction of such children as it may hereafter be deemed expedient by the Legislature to instruct in the common principles of reading, writing and arithmetic; and whenever, in the opinion of the Legislature, the said fund shall have sufficiently accumulated, the proceeds thereof shall be divided among the several counties, in proportion to the free white population of each, to be managed and applied in such way as the Legislature shall hereafter authorize and direct.

ACTS—1830 AND 1831.

AN ACT TO RAISE A FUND TO ESTALISH FREE SCHOOLS IN THE COUNTY OF JOHNSTON, AND FOR THE GOVERNMENT THEREOF.

Sec. 1. Be it enacted by the General Assembly of the State of North Carolina, and it is hereby enacted by the authority of the same:

That the County Court of Johnston county may, at the first court which shall be held after the first day of May next, and annually thereafter, at least ten justices of the peace being present, lay a tax, and cause it to be levied on all the property in said county which is liable to be taxed for State or county purposes, equal to not more than twenty-five per cent. per annum, on the whole amount of

State and county and parish taxes levied in said county, which shall be collected, held and used as a school fund for said county of Johnston, according to the rules and regulations hereinafter prescribed.

Sec. 2. Be it further enacted by the authority aforesaid, That it shall be the duty of the sheriff or other collecting officer of said county to collect and account for the said taxes, under the directions of the county court, according to the rules and regulations by law created for collecting other taxes in said county, and he may be required to give a bond to the chairman of said court, in the penal sum of two thousand dollars, conditioned for the faithful collecting and accounting for said taxes.

Sec. 3. Be it further enacted by the authority aforesaid, That it shall be the duty of the clerk of the county court to take and receive from the sheriff the taxes aforesaid, who shall keep an account thereof, and hold the said monies in his office subject to the direction and control of the persons who are hereinafter authorized to manage the said fund, and the clerk shall give a bond with security, in the sum of two thousand dollars conditioned for the faithful discharge of the duties imposed by this act, and the honest accounting for the funds aforesaid.

Sec. 4. Be it further enacted by the authority aforesaid, That the county court aforesaid shall cause an election to be held for one trustee in each Captain's district in said county, each district electing its own trustee, of which election public notice shall be given, and in the said election each free white man who is taxed under this law shall have one vote, and the said trustees shall constitute a board, and hold their appointments for two years from the time of their appointment, and the said board shall be styled: "The Trustees of the Central County School of Johnston County."

Sec. 5. Be it further enacted by the authority aforesaid, That the election of trustees shall be held at such time and places as the county court shall direct, within six months after the period when the tax is laid by this act shall fall due, and biennially thereafter, and the said trustees, after their appointment, shall be notified thereof by the Clerk of the County Court, and shall, within 20 days thereafter, assemble, at Smithfield, and appoint one of their body President, another Secretary, and give notice by advertisement of their proceedings, so that the citizens may know who the said President and trustees are.

Sec. 6. Be it further enacted by the authority aforesaid, That the trustees shall have power and authority to make rules and orders for their own government, and compel the obedience and attendance of the members of the board by fines, to be by them fixed, and which fines shall be recoverable by a warrant before any magistrate, in the name of the clerk of the county court and his successor in office, and when collected go to increase the school fund aforesaid.

Sec. 7. Be it further enacted by the authority aforesaid, That the said trustees shall, as soon as it can be done with the fund aforesaid, purchase a site and erect a school house or school houses in said county for the education of youths, with a farm attached, if thought advisable, and the same shall be the principal or central school of said county, but the selection of said site shall be approved by the county court before the same is purchased and approved, and the title of the said site and the land attached to it shall be made to the clerk of the county court, and his sucessor in office, in trust, for the use of trustees aforesaid, and the purposes declared in this act.

Sec. 8. Be it further enacted by authority aforesaid, That the trustees aforesaid shall have power to select from the several districts in said county, always having the same number from each district, poor and indigent male children, who shall be educated at said school in the English language only, and such indigent children shall be boarded together and clothed out of the said fund during the time of their attendance at said school, free from any charge, and the said trustees shall have power to require, under such rules as they may prescribe, of any person taught at said school, that he shall teach others either in his trade or his books in said school, or other free school, to be organized in said county, until he shall come to the age of 21 years; or they may require of him, if they think it best, after he has been educated as aforesaid, to aid in the cultivation of the farm aforesaid, for the time aforesaid, and no child whose father is living shall be admitted in said school, unless his father will in writing under seal agree to submit, and cause his son to submit, to such regulations, which agreement shall be made with the trustees aforesaid and entered into by a deed executed to the Clerk of the County Court aforesaid and his successor in office, in trust for the board aforesaid, and no orphan child shall be admitted in said school unless he shall have been bound as an apprentice to said trustees and their successors by the County Court, and the said trustees and their successors are hereby declared to be able and capable in law to have apprentices bound to them, provided always, that the said trustees shall furnish the said child during the term of service aforesaid his necessary clothes and board; and provided, further, that they may allow the parents, guardians or friends of said child to pay to the fund aforesaid a reasonable compensation for the education of said child aforesaid, and therfeby release from him the obligation aforesaid, which compensation shall be fixed by a majority of said trustees at a regular meeting of the board.

Sec. 9. Be it further enacted by the authority aforesaid, That the said trustees shall have power and authority, with the fund aforesaid, to employ a teacher of said school and some competent person to manage the farm attached to it, upon such terms that they may be able to agree on, and they shall report in writing every six months to the County Court the progress and condition of said school, and the conduct of the scholars by name, and render with said report an account of the funds of the disbursements thereof.

Sec. 10. Be it further enacted by the authority aforesaid. That the said trustees may have power and authority to admit in said school other students, not exceeding 10, until the fund shall be in a condition to warrant an entire exclusion of all but the free scholars, and the rates of tuition and board of said scholars shall be uniform, but in no case shall any scholar who pays tuition be admitted over the age of thirteen years.

Sec. 11. Be it further enacted by authority aforesaid, That when the fund by this act created will justify, and the interest of the school require it, the trustees aforesaid may employ one or more artificers as instructors of the youth belonging to said school, and prescribe rules for the government both of the boys and master.

Sec. 12. Be it further enacted by the authority aforesaid, That the trustees aforesaid may make such allowance as they may think reasonable to the Clerk of the County Court for acting as their treasurer, and the Clerk shall be entitled to no other compensation for his services, and he shall be entitled to no fees for apprentices bound to said trustees.

Sec. 13. Be it further enacted by the authorities aforesaid, That the President of said Central School shall have full power to call said board of trustees together when- of whom, exclusive of the President, shall constitute a quorum for the transaction of business in all things except in the expenditure of the funds, and in that case it shall require a majority of the whole number to constitute a quorum.

The following is interesting to the children of the present generation:

ACTS OF THE LEGISLATURE 1830-1831—CHAPTER SIX.

An act to prevent all persons from teaching slaves to read or write, the use of figures excepted.

Whereas, the teaching of slaves to read and write has a tendency to excite dissatisfaction in their minds, and to produce insurrection and rebellion, to the manifest injury of the citizen of this State:

Therefore, Be it enacted by the General Assembly of the State of North Carolina and it is hereby enacted by the authority of the same,

That any free person, who shall hereafter teach or attempt to teach any slave within this State to read and write, the use of figures excepted, or shall give or sell to such slave or slaves any books or pamphlets, shall be liable to indictment in any court of record in this State having jurisdiction thereof, and upon conviction, shall, at the discretion of the court, if a white man or woman, be fined not less than one hundred dollars, nor more than two hundred dollars, or imprisoned, and if a free person of color, shall be fined, imprisoned, or whipped, at the discretion of the court, not exceeding thirty-nine lashes, nor less than twenty lashes.

2. Be it further enacted, That if any slave shall hereafter teach, or attempt to teach, any other slave to read or write, the use of figures excepted, he or she may be carried before any justice of the peace, and on conviction thereof, shall be sentenced to receive thirty nine lashes on his or her bare back.

3. Be it further enacted, That the judges of the Superior Courts and the justices of the county courts shall give this act in charge to the grand jurors of their respective counties.

CHAPEL—SHAW UNIVERSITY, RALEIGH, N. C.

PART II.

State Colleges and Institutions, Denominational Colleges, High Schools and Academies

OF

NORTH CAROLINA.

INTRODUCTION.

The following letter was sent to the respective schools of the State:

DEAR SIR:—I am anxious that the next biennial report that is sent out from this office shall show, not only what North Carolina is doing in the public schools and State institutions, but also shall show what our denominational colleges and high schools are doing—the academies, private schools, and in fact, want all the educational interests of the State to be represented in this report.

In order to do this, a considerable extra expense will be incurred, and in order to meet this expense, I have decided to offer space in this report at exactly what it will cost the State to print it.

We want a short, concise history of the various schools, academies, and colleges, and an outline of what has been done and is being done. Do not mention what you expect to do. I hope you will do greater things in the future, but want this report to show what is being done now.

Would be glad to have a cut of your building and faculty to publish.

The State Printer estimates the cost to be about $1.50 per page.

This is a very reasonable expense to the schools, and will do them a great deal of good as well as the State.

This report will be sent to every State in the United States, as well as distributed throughout North Carolina.

I expect to have a brief general history of the work done by the denominational colleges, and especially what the academies did for us as a State in early years.

I hope you will give this matter your careful consideration.

Let me hear from you as soon as possible, also designate how much space you will want.

Very truly yours,

C. H. MEBANE,
Superintendent Public Instruction.

In the great struggles that have been made for the cause of education in North Carolina, the denominational colleges, high schools and academies, have done a great work, and it affords me pleasure to recognize these institutions in making up our educational history. In fact, had it not been for these voluntary institutions, we would have had no educational advantages during all the years previous to the establishing of the University of our State. Also had it not been for these institutions since the establishing of the University, many thousands of the best and most intelligent citizens of North Carolin, who have been a blessing to the State as well as the church, would have been compelled to go through life with all the burdens and disadvantages to which ignorant people are always subject.

The writer himself would as soon think of forgetting his own parents, as to think of not honoring such institutions, because had it not been for these he would have been among those who would have been compelled to grovel in darkness, along with thousands of others.

The writer rejoices over what the University and State institutions have done and are doing, that the work of the University and its influence are felt to-day as never before, within the borders of our State, as well as without the State. Long may this Historic Institution continue to grow in usefulness and power for the good of our State. The writer rejoices none the less over what these voluntary institutions have done and are doing, for our citizeship, doing this, too, without the aid of the strong arm of the State.

All these heroic men and institutions have asked of the State has been the privilege to work, and I am proud to say, they have done this work right well. I express to these men and their work the sincere gratitude of thousands of worthy young men and young women of this State.

I have endeavored to bring about a closer relation and a deeper sympathy among the State institutions and the private and denominational institutions.

The higher institutions of the State can never educate the masses of our people, neither can the private higher institutions. Both of these classes of institutions should feel a deeper interest in, not only each other's welfare, but especially should they feel a common interest in the public schools.

What a field for educational labor, what a gathering into the collegs of the State and the private institutions, when

BELL STREET PUBLIC SCHOOL, STATESVILLE.

that long looked-for glad day comes, that each child will receive practical public school education; then will our colleges be full to overflowing; then, indeed, will we have to tear down our college rooms and private school houses and build greater ones.

The Presidents of the respective institutions represented in these pages prepared these sketches at my request.

UNIVERSITY OF NORTH CAROLINA.

CHAPEL HILL, N. C. Oct. 10, 1898.

Hon. C. H. Mebane, Superintendent Public Instruction, Raleigh, N. C.

DEAR SIR:—I herewith submit a report of the equipment, enrollment, and condition of the University of North Carolina. In obedience to a mandate of the State Constitution, the University of North Carolina was established one hundred and ten years ago. At seven different epochs the people in Convention or by Charter have imposed upon the General Assembly the duty to support and maintain this University. It has the distinction of being the first University established by legislative action in the South, and the second in the American Union.

The present Constitution, Article 9, section 6, says: "The General Assembly shall provide for the election of Trustees of the University of North Carolina, in whom, when chosen, shall be vested all the privileges, rights, franchises and endowments thereof, in anywise granted to or conferred upon the Trustees of said University, and the General Assembly may make such provisions, laws and regulations, from time to time, as may be necessary and expedient for the *maintenance and management* of said University."

During these years the University has rendered noble public service to this State and to the entire South. It may be doubted whether the University of any other Southern State contains such a distinguished roll of alumni, including: One President of the United States, two Vice-Presidents, eight Cabinet Officers, six Ministers to Foreign Courts, twenty United States and Confederate State Senators, eighteen Governors of States, twenty-two Justices of the Supreme Court, sixteen Generals, four Bishops, twenty College President's, fifty-nine Professors in

Colleges and Universities, and many useful citizens in all walks of life.

It is not too much to say that sons of the University have been prominent in every movement for Public Schools, in scientific agriculture, for industrial development, medicine, higher education and justice, and that their influence has stimulated the growth of all other Colleges in the State. The University is not a separate isolated institution, but belongs to the State, in the sense that the Capitol does or the Supreme Court building. Relying upon the promise of the State to maintain and support the University, various citizens have from time to time given money and land, to be used on trust forever for the purposes of the University. The property of the University includes six hundred acres of land, fifteen buildings, a library of thirty thousand volumes and ten thousand pamphlets, valuable scientific apparatus and about one hundred thousand dollars of invested funds. The valuation of this property is about half a million dollars.

The University comprises the following departments:

The College for Undergraduates.

The University or Graduate School.

The Law School.

The Medical School.

The School of Pharmacy.

The Summer School for Teachers.

In the College Department there are three general courses of study, leading to the following degrees: Bachelor or Arts, Bachelor of Philosophy, and Bachelor of Science. These courses furnish a broad foundation for liberal culture and require ordinarily four years to complete them. The following subjects are taught in the College Department:

1. Greek Language and Literature	8	Courses
2. Latin Language and Literature	14	"
3. Classical Philology	3	"
4. German Language and Literature	3	"
5. French Language and Literature	3	"
6. English Language and Literature	14	"
7. Philosophy	5	
8. History and Historical Research	7	
9. Political and Social Science	4	
10. Political Economy	2	
11. Mathematics	4	
12. Drawing and Surveying	2	
13. Physics	2	
14. Chemistry	9	
15. Biology	6	
16. Geology	8	
17. Pedagogy	6	
18. Spanish Language	2	"
	105	Courses

The Graduate School offers special advanced instruction in a total of seventy-five courses. This instruction leads to the degrees of Master of Arts, Master of Philosophy, Master of Science, and Doctor of Philosophy. The Law School, the Medical School and the School of Pharmacy are conducted by experienced professors, and give the most advanced training leading to those professions.

1. LAW SCHOOL.—The Law School provides two courses of study, each extending over a period of one college year. Instruction is given by means of text-books, lectures, the study of leading cases, and moot courts. Special lectures are given by the resident instructors and by members of the bar on such subjects as have been greatly modified by our statutes or by the development of our civilization.

During the summer two classes in law are conducted by Professors Manning and Biggs. The text-books used are the same with those required in Course 1.

The summer session begins on the first day of July and ends on the Thursday before the last Monday in September.

The fee for admission into either class is thirty dollars for tuition, and three dollars for registration; for admission into both classes, sixty dollars for tuition and three dollars for registration.

2. MEDICAL SCHOOL.—The Medical School provides two courses of study, for which are claimed the advantages derived from good equipment and small classes. Each student has the opportunity of seeing the various demonstrations and experiments, and receives direct personal instruction.

Special emphasis is laid upon anatomical instruction, and an abundance of dissecting material is provided. The two years' course here is accepted as equivalent of two years work in the best Northern colleges.

3. SCHOOL OF PHARMACY.—The School of Pharmacy offers instruction covering a period of two college years. The laboratory equipment for this instruction is admirable, and a certificate of the school will enable the receipient to receive license with very little difficulty.

4. SUMMER SCHOOL.—The University also maintains a summer school for four weeks in June and July, for the benefit of teachers and others who are unable to attend its regular sessions. Instruction is given in all subjects pertaining to common schools, and to the theory and art of teaching, besides careful work in the ancient and modern languages. A faculty of twenty-five teachers give instruction in this school.

The faculty of the University consists of the President and nineteen full Professors, five Instructors, six assistants and five officers. These Professors and Instructors are men of Christian character, and were trained in the best Universities of this country and of Europe. They are rich in culture and devotion to their duty.

EDWIN ANDERSON ALDERMAN, D. C. L.,

President and Professor of Political and Social Science.

Ph. B., Univ. of N. C., 1882; D. C. L., Univ. of the South 1896; Supt. City Schools, 1885-89; State Institute Conductor, 1889-92; Professor of History State Normal College, 1892-93 Professor of Pedagogy, Univ. of N. C., 1893-96; President, 1896.

KEMP PLUMMER BATTLE, LL. D.,

Alumni Professor of History

A. B, Univ. of N. C., 1849; A. M., 1852; LL D, Davidson College; 1879; Tutor Univ. of N. C., 1850-54; State Treasurer 1866-68; University Trustee, 1862-68, 1874-98; President Univ. of N. C., 1876-91; Professor, 1891.

FRANCIS PRESTON VENABLE, PH. D.,

Smith Professor of General and Analytical Chemistry.

Universities of Virginia, 1874-79; Bouv 1880; Gottingen, 1881; Berlin, 1889; Ph. D., Gottingen 1881; University High School, New Orleans, La., 1877-78; Professor Univ. of N. C., 1880.

JOSEPH AUSTIN HOLMES, S. B.,

Cornell University, 1876-80; Prof. Natural History, Univ. of N. C., 1881; State Geologist 189—.

JOSHUA WALKER GORE, C. E.,

Professor of Physics.

Richmond College 1871-73; Univ. of Virginia, 1873-75; C. E., 1875; Fellow Johns Hopkins, 1876-78; Professor South Western Baptist Univ., 1878-81; Assistant Univ. of Virginia, 1881-82; Professor Univ. of N. C., 1882.

JOHN MANNING, LL, D.,

Professor of Law.

A. B., Univ. of N. C.,.1850; A. M., 1854; LL. D., 1883; member 41st Congress; Commission to codify Statute Law 1883; Professor Univ. of N. C., 1881.

THOMAS HUME, D. D. LL D.,

Professor of the English Language and Literature.

A. B., and A. M., Richmond College, Univ. of Virginia; D. D., Richmond College; LL. D., Wake Forest College; Professor Univ. of N. C., 1885.

WALTER DALLAM TOY, M. A.,

Professor of Modern Languages.

M. A., Univ. of Virginia, 1882; Univ. of Leipsic, 1882-83; Berlin, 1883-84; La Sorboune and College de France, 1885; Professor Univ. of N. C., 1885.

EBEN ALEXANDER. PH. D. LL. D.,

Professor of the Greek Language and Literature.

A. B, Yale 1873; Ph. D., Maryville 1886; LL. D., Univ. of N. C., 1893; Instructor Univ. of Tenn., 1873-77; Professor 1877-86; Professor Univ. of N. C., 1886; U. S Minister to Greece 1893-97.

WILLIAM COIN, C. E.,

Professor of Mathematics.

N. C. Military and Polytechnic Academy, 1866; Civil Engineer 1866-74 Professor Carolina Military Institute, 1874 80; Professor S. C. Military Academy, 1882 89; Professor Univ. of North Carolina, 1883.

RICHARD HENRY WHITEHEAD, A. B., M. D.,

Professor of Anatomy.

A. B., Wake Forest, 1886; M. D., Univ. of Virginia, 1887; Graduate Student, Univ. of Pennsylvania and of New York; Demonstrator of Anatomy, Univ of Virginia, 1881-89; Professor Univ. of N. C., 1890.

HENRY HORACE WILLIAMS, A. M., B D.,

Professor of Philosophy.

A. B., A. M., Univ. of N. C., 1883; B. D., Yale Univ., 1888; Graduate Student, Harvard Univ., 1888-90; Williams Fellow, 1889; Professor, Trinity College, 1884; Professor, Univ of N. C., 1890.

HENRY VAN PETERS WILSON, PH. D.,

Professor of Biology.

A. B., Johns Hopkins Univ., 1883; Ph. D., 1888; Bruce Fellow, 1858-89; Assistant U. S. Fish Commission, 1889 90; Professur Univ. of N. C., 1891.

KARL POMEROY HARRINGTON, A. M.,

Professor of Latin.

A. B., Wesleyan Univ., 1882; A. M., 1885; graduate Student, Wesleyan Univ., 1882; Univ. Berlin, 1887 89; Yale Univ., 1890-91; in Greece and Rome, 1889; Tutor Wesleyan Univ., 1889-91; Professor, Univ. of N. C. 1891.

COLLIER COBB, A. M.,

Professor of Geology.

A. B., Harvard University, 1889; A. M., 1894; Assistant, Harvard University, 1888-90; Instructor, M. I. T., 1890-92; Lecturer, Boston University, 1891-91; Assistant U. S. Geological Survey, 1886-92; Professor Univ. of N. C., 1892.

CHARLES BASKERVILLE, PH. D.,

Associate Professor of Chemistry.

B. S., Univ. of N. C., 1892; Ph. D., 1895; Gradute Student, Vanderbilt Univ. and Univ. of Berlin; Assistant in Chemistry, Univ. of N. C., 1891-93; Instructor 1893-94; Associate Professor, 1894.

CHARLES STAPLES MANGUM, A. B., M. D.,

Professor of Physiology and Materia Medica.

A. B., Univ. of N. C., 1891; M. D., Jefferson Medical College, 1894; Assistant Demonstrator of Anatomy, 1894-95; Professor, Univ. of N. C., 1896.

EDWARD VERNON HOWELL, A. B., PH. G.

Professor of Pharmacy.

A. B., Wake Forest College, 1892; Ph. G., Phil. College of Pharmacy, 1894; Professor Univ. of N. C., 1897.

HENRY FARRAR LINSCOTT, PH. D.,

Associate Professor of Classical Philology.

A. B., Boarding College, 1892; A. M., 1893; Fellow Univ. of Chicago, 1893-95; Ph. D., 1895; Instructor, Brown Univ., 1895-96; Instructor, Univ. of N. C., 1896-97; Associate Professor, 1897.

MARCUS CICERO STEPHENS NOBLE.

Professor of Pedagogy

Davidson College, 1875-76; Univ. of N. C., 1877-79; Commandant Bingham School, 1879-82; Superintendent of Schools, Wilmington, 1882-98; Professor Univ. of N. C., 1898.

JAMES CRAWFORD BIGGS, PH. B.,

Associate Professor of Law.

Ph. B., Univ. of N. C., 1893; University Law School 1893-94; Professor St. Albans 1893; Mayor of Oxford, N. C., 1897 and '98; Associate Prosessor Univ. of N. C., 1898.

SAMUEL MAY, A. B.,

Instructor in Modern Languages.

A. B., Harvard University 1896; Instructor University of North Carolina 1896.

WILLIAM CUNNINGHAM SMITH, PH. B.,

Instructor in English.

Ph. B., University of North Carolina 1896; Student Harvard University, 1897; Instructor University of N. C, 1896.

ARCHIBALD HENDERSON, A. B.,

Instructor in Mathematics.

A. B, University of North Carolina, 1895; Instructor, 1898.

JAMES WILLIAM CALDER.

Instructor in Physical Culture.

Student in Gymnasium of Y. M. C. A., Brooklyn and New York, and Davidson College, 1898; Junior Director Brooklyn Y. M. C. A. Gymnasium; Director Charlotte, N. C., and Davidson College.

The total fall registration, less duplicates, up to November 1st, 1898, in all departments, is six hundred and fifteen, sub-divided as follows: College, 349; Law, 71; Medicine, 41; Pharmacy, 19, and Summer School, 147. This is the largest enrollment in the history of the University at this time, exclusive of the Summer School. The Senior Class numbers fifty-seven members, an increase of fifty per cent. over last year. The number of counties represented in North Carolina is eighty-three, and the number of States of the Union, fourteen, including the District of Columbia. The counties sending the largest delegations are as follows: Orange, Forsyth, Mecklenburg, Guilford, Wake, New Hanover, Cabarrus, Richmond, Cumberland, Wayne, Halifax, Rowan, Johnston, Durham, Buncombe, Anson, Wilson and Iredell. In view of these facts, it may be said that, between the Virgina line and the Gulf of Mexico, this University ranks first in numbers and achievements, and it does this on less money than any Southern University.

The total registration for the last academic year, fall and spring, in all departments, including the Summer School, was six hundred and ninety. It will thus be seen that thirteen hundred and eleven young men have received instruction at the University in the last year and a half. No American University, with the same means at its disposal, can exhibit a prouder record of public service.

The constant aim of the University has been to reach the people and to serve them. During the past two years it has loaned nearly six thousand dollars from the Deems Fund, thereby aiding eighty men. The Deems Fund is the bequest of Charles F. Deems and Wm. H. Vanderbilt. During the past twenty years it has aided nearly one thousand young men by loans and scholarships. The University is now giving free tuition to nearly one hundred and fifty students under the operation of State laws and by private philanthrophy. Nine-tenths of these men could not otherwise be educated. Over one-half of the students are the sons of farmers and two-thirds of them are here as the result of some sacrifice. Nearly one-third are supporting themselves by money which they have earned or borrowed. Seventy-five or eighty students are boarding themselves by labor, waiting upon their fellow-students in Commons Hall and at private clubs; managing boarding clubs, setting type, working in laboratories, serving as stenographers and typewriters, selling books and clothing, giving private instruction to other students, teaching classes in the village, clerking in the stores and doing many other kinds of work. It is no exaggeration to say that the University, by its loan funds, scholarships and opportunities for labor makes it possible for any worthy boy, however poor, to obtain in North Carolina as good an education as rich boys obtain elsewhere.

The University has well appointed laboratories in Physics, Chemistry, Biology, Geology, Mineralogy, Pharmacy and Bacteriology. The equipment of apparatus and supplies for lecture and experimental work is excellent, and every facility is offered for thorough instruction in all scientific subjects.

SOCIETIES.

The Literary Societies offer facilities for practice in debate, oratory, declamation and essay writing. Each Society owns a large, well furnished hall, the walls of which are hung with oil portraits of illustrious members.

The Societies for special culture, the Elisha Mitchell Scientific Society, the Philological Society, and the Shakspere Club offer unusual facilities for original research and study.

The Young Men's Christian Association meets four times each week. It is active and useful.

The North Carolina Historical Society is located at the University. It has some valuable historical material. Its work is open to all students.

Through the beneficence of Mrs. Frederick Baker a Commons hall has been established where wholesome, well, prepared food is served in a handsome dinning-room. Good food may be had for eight dollars a month. The students wait upon the table and manage the affairs of the institution, and it has proven a great help for the physical as well as the financial well-being of the students. The income of certain bequests of the University affords seventy-eight scholarships. Free tuition is given in the college to sons of ministers and candidates for the ministry, to young men under bodily infirmity, to public school teachers and those who intend to teach.

NECESSARY EXPENSES.

The necessary expenses at the University are very moderate. It is believed that no other similar institution in the United States offers equal advantages at so small a cost.

The dues payable at the beginning of each of the two terms are as follows :

Tuition	$30.00
Annual fee	5.00
Medical and Infirmary fee	3.00
Gymnasium fee	1.25
Library fee	2.00
	$41.25

MORALITY AND RELIGION.

The University recognizes religion and morality as the basis of character. Daily morning prayers are held in Gerard Hall. All students are required to be present, unless excused by special request of parents.

Regular services are held in the Baptist, Methodist, Episcopalian and Presbyterian churches twice a week and oftener. Bible classes for young men are taught in each church by members of the Faculty.

The Young Men's Christian Association meets every week-day night except Friday and Saturday.

Elective courses are offered in the study of the English Bible and in New Testament Greek. There is, also, a special class, meeting each Sunday morning, for the study of the Bible.

There are five eminent preachers elected by the Trustees as preachers to the University each year. These are chosen from the different denominations of Christian people.

The following have been chosen for the last two years: Rev. Robert Strange, D. D., Rev. L. B. Turnbull, D. D., Rev. C W. Byrd, D. D., Rev. J. W. Carter, D. D., Rev. P. H. Hoge, D. D., Rev. H. A. Swope, D. D., Rev. H. E. Rondthaler, Rev. S. B. Turrentine, D. D.

COST TO THE STATE.

The University receives from the State this year a $25,-000 appropriation. The appropriation, if collected *per*

SHAW HALL—SHAW UNIVERSITY, RALEIGH, N. C.

capita, would amount to about 1 3-5 cents per annum to each inhabitant; but the tax is paid entirely by property, and *the mass of the people in the State really contribute little or nothing to its support.* A man who pays only a *poll-tax* contributes *nothing.* A man *listed* at $100 pays less than one cent annually to the regular appropriation; at $500 less than 5 cents; at $1,000 less than 10 cents, at $5,000 less than 50 cents. The average tax-payer is listed at less than $500, and therefore pays less than 5 cents. About nine-tenths of the tax-payers pay *less than 10 cents a year* for an appropriation of $25,000 for the support of the University.

The tax for the University does not come from the public school fund. It is a tax on property alone, and its advantages accrue to the sons of the poor. It is a tax of the property holders for the benefit of themselves, their neighbors and the State It is an application of Chrstianity to government.

THE UNIVERSITY AND THE PUBLIC SCHOOLS.

The University is the logical head of the entire system of public educational institutions. This is the American idea, and every State in the Union has a University at the head of its school system.

The University, through Caldwell, Murphy and Wiley, established the public schools in the past and the two departments of education are inseparably linked together. The University has always been foremost in fostering and developing the schools. For the last fifteen years, more than half of each graduating class have gone into the public school service. The Normal Schools began at the Univerity, and the Teachers' Institutes were carried on by University men.

The University maintains a department for the training of teachers and a Summer School for those who are already teaching, and who are unable to attend its regular sessions.

During the past year 263 students, who are teachers or intend to teach, attended these schools.

The University thus saves the State the expense of a separate Normal School for male teachers, which in other States costs more than our entire University.

The motto here is "Lux Libertas." Here the truth is sought—whether in nature, in literature, in law, or in society. Here is where sanity reigns and judgment is sober, and toleration prevails, and humility seems a virtue. Here we would see things straight and clear, with vision undimmed by passion or prejudice or zealotry. Here men may meet on the level of equal opportunity, and may rise by the might of merit to the quiet power of Christian manhood. A university is a mighty piece of social machinery, but it can never be an organ or a propagandist. It does not stand for the rich as against the poor, nor for the poor as against the rich, but for rich and poor alike, that each may know the best of the other. It does not stand to bend to any breeze of popular delusion, but rather to withstand, and to lead the people in quiet ways to the larger view. It does not exist to lie snugly and cozily in the arms of power, but rather to remind power of its high duty; to approve when that power is nobly used, to condemn when tyrannously put forth, whether by States or individuals.

A university is a discoverer of truth, a conservator of ideas, a sower of seed, a missionary of democracies, a storehouse of high traditions. It has no passion, save of the truth and the betterment of men; no warfare, save against ignorance; no enemies, save those of the dark. Born of the people, nourished by the commonwealth, it stands as the servant, but not as the slave, of the public good, fortunate if it can reach out strong hands of help to all classes and conditions of men, high or low, rich or poor, quickening them into the better life. Institutions, like men in all self-governing communities, cannot assume the grand air. They must have unfaltering faith in the final rectitude of public impulse, and sublime patience with the blundering masses, alone on their toilsome march to economic, civil and religious liberty. De Tocqueville, sixty years ago, declared that democracy was the most difficult form of government. Social regenerative forces must, therefore, be patient with Demos, as Demos has been patient with the king. Daɪk, indeed, would be the hour in the life of an American State when it should be withrut some high institution of learning, begotten of public sagacity, nourished by civic patriotism, and creating in the hearts of its sons that gratitude to the State for its manifestation of heart and conscience, which constitutes the real strength of States, by implanting in the hearts of those who have been made strong by the collective will, the desire to serve, in their turn, the thronging future.

This is not the University of any class, but of all classes. The youth who gather here to learn the ways of manhood shall breathe the breath of freedom and learn to look squarely in the bright face of truth. To those who enter upon life endowed at the outset with brains or wealth, or influence, we offer the equipment of sane judgment, of trained minds, and sympathetic hearts of noble use of their mighty powers; and there shall blow through our halls forever, please God, the wholesome breezes of sympathy and helpfulness for the dim, toiling thousands, who work in the shadows of the world, and who yet must be fitted for the majestic duties of republican citizenship.

In conclusion I beg to assure you that in all of your efforts to advance the cause of popular education in North Carolina, the influences that go out from its walls will be quick to serve you with brain and heart and soul.

Yours very truly,

EDWIN ANDERSON ALDERMAN,

President.

RESOLUTIONS OF THE FACULTY OF THE NORMAL AND INDUSTRIAL COLLEGE.

NOTE.—These resolutions should have been placed with similar resolutions in another part of this Report, but were not received in time—hence they appear here.

In compliance with the request of the State Superintendent of Public Instruction for an expression of their views on public education, the Faculty of the State Normal and Industrial College, at their regular meeting on November 14, 1898, unanimously adopted the following resolutions:

Resolved 1. That, collectively and individually, we hereby declare our advocacy of the most liberal system of public education, not only as a means of intellectual and moral culture, but also as an absolute necessity to the material prosperity of any people.

2. That, believing that the cause of public education would be greatly promoted thereby, we earnestly advocate the general adoption of local taxation for the public schools of the State.

3. That, realizing that thorough supervision is absolutely necessary for the success and protection of the public schools, we heartily favor a complete and effective system of school supervision.

FACULTY OF BINGHAM SCHOOL, MEBANE, N. C.

REPORT OF THE STATE NORMAL AND INDUSTRIAL COLLEGE.

REPORT OF THE DIRECTORS.

To His Excellency Governor Daniel L. Russell:

In compliance with the requirement of Section 3, Chapter 139, Laws of 1891, creating The State Normal and Industrial College, the Board of Directors begs to submit its biennial report of the operation, progress and work of this Institution for the two years beginning October 1, 1896, and ending September 30, 1898, being the fifth and sixth years of the existence of said Institution.

By reference to the act creating the Institution it will appear, from the fifth section thereof, that The State Normal and Industrial College was established for the following purposes: (1) "To give to young women such education as shall fit them for teaching; (2) to give instruction to young women in drawing, telegraphy, typewriting, stenography, and such other industrial arts as may be suitable to their sex and conducive to their support and usefulness."

In the management and development of this Institution, the Board of Directors has endeavored to keep constantly in view this purpose, and to observe, as far as possible, the legislative intent in establishing the College.

We transmit herewith as part of this report, the report of the Executive Committee, the report of President McIver, and the financial report of E. J. Forney, Treasurer and Bursar.

The report and accounts of the Treasurer and Bursar of the College were carefully examined in every detail by the Executive Committee of this Board and reported correct. For further information in regard to the Treasurer's report, we refer you to the Executive Committee's report published herewith.

The Board of Directors begs to call your Ecellency's attention to the scope and character of the work accomplished by The State Normal and Industrial College as shown by the comprehensive report of the President, and to the patronage of the Instituion, so representative in its character, ninety-four counties in the State having shared and enjoyed its privileges and benefits. During the scholastic year 1895-'96, there were in attendance upon the Institution, exclusive of the Practice and Observation School, 412 young women, and during the year 1897-'98, 437.

On account of lack of dormitory room, the Institution has never been able to accommodate all the applicants for admission.

The Board of Directors most heartily appreciates the generous aid given from time to time by the Trustees of the Peabody Education Fund through their General Agent, the Honorable J. L. M. Curry.

Dr. Curry has rendered much valuable personal aid and encouragement, as well as official support, for which we desire to express the thanks of the people of the State.

The Board of Directors desires to call the attention of your Excellency to the recommendations of President McIver, looking to the further development and usefulness of the Institution, which recommendations are endorsed by the Executive Committee and by the Board of Directors.

Two years ago the Board of Directors announced as the most urgent needs of the College:

1. Increased facilities for a Practice and Observation School.
2. Enlarged library room and increased number of books.
3. Department of Horticulture.
4. New Gymnasium.
5. Steam Laundry.
6. Kitchen.
7. Literary Society Halls.
8. Extension of Heating System.

The Board is gratified to be able to state that the increased appropriation given by the last General Assembly has made it possible to secure four of these improvements, as is indicated in the reports of the Executive Committee and the President of the Institution.

Moreover, it gives the Board peculiar pleasure to find that the students of the College, appreciating the very great need for literary society halls, have begun to raise, by private subscription, first among themselves, and then among their friends, $10,000 to erect a suitable building for the society halls and a hall and reading-room for the Young Women's Christian Association and for other similar purposes. About $2,500 of the amount has been subscribed by the faculty and students now at the Institution.

The following resolution is quoted from the Minutes of the Board:

Resolved, That the Board of Directors of The State Normal and Industrial College desires to express its earnest appreciation of the efforts of the students of the Institution, led by the committees of the Adelphian and Cornelian Literary Societies, to raise the requisite funds to erect a building suitable for society halls, reading-rooms, etc.

Two years ago the Board, in its report to the Governor and the General Assembly, called attention to the lack of literary society halls, as one of the eight most urgent needs of the Institution. It regrets that for the lack of sufficient means it has been unable to provide these halls, though the Board has never abandoned the idea of doing so as soon as practicable. Seeing the impossibility of taking such action at a very early date, and realizing the immediate good which will accrue to the Institution by the action of the students and their friends, the Board is peculiarly gratified at the spirit and enterprise manifested in this most worthy undertaking.

Resolved, That a copy of these resolutions be sent to the Cornelian and Adelphian Literary Societies.

We trust that the Legislature of the State, which assembles January next, will honor us by the appointment of a committee to visit the College, examine its work and progress, and acquaint themselves with the needs of the Institution, and recommend such appropriations as in their opinion will enable it to fill the full measure of its usefulness.

In concluding this report, we desire to express our appreciation of the interest shown by your Excellency in the work of the College, and to assure you that you will always be a welcome visitor to the Institution.

Very respectfully,

C. H. MEBANE,
President of the Board of Directors.

J. M. SPAINHOUR,
Secretary of the Board of Directors.

Greensboro, Dec. 2, 1898.

REPORT OF THE EXECUTIVE COMMITTEE.

GREENSBORO, N. C., Dec. 1st, 1898.

To the Board of Directors of The State Normal and Industrial College.

GENTLEMEN:—The Executive Committee of the Board beg leave to report that they have examined the books of E. J. Forney, Bursar and Treasurer of the Institution, and find that the books are neatly and accurately kept, and that he has accounted for all receipts and moneys and disbursed same upon proper vouchers. For details of receipts and expenditures we refer you to his report, which we have thoroughly examined and approved.

Since the meeting of the Board of Directors in May last the improvements and additions authorized by the Board have been made in accordance with the spirit and authority therein granted and in keeping with the financial conditions of the Institution. These improvements are embodied in the report of President McIver, and consist principally of the building of a steam laundry and equipping it with the necessary machinery, the erection of a power-house with sufficient room for the present and prospective needs of the Institution, the construction of a commodious and modern kitchen, and the extension of the heating system to all the buildings of the Institution, the warm air and fan system being used in the College building, the steam heat for the main dormitory, hot-water heating for the wooden dormitory and the President's residence, the warm air system having been previously introduced in the Infirmary.

There are certain other improvements necessary to meet the present demands of the Institution suggested in the President's report, which your Committee endorses, and it urges upon the Board the necessity of securing an appropriation by the Legislature for the same as soon as practicable.

We are specially impressed with the immediate necessity of securing a building for the Practice and Observation School, a modern gymnasium, and additional library and class room.

Your committee visited the various recitation rooms both in the College proper and in the Practice and Observation School. We were greatly pleased with the thoroughness and effectiveness of the work done in every department. We are profoundly impressed with the great good this Institution is accomplishing.

The State is to be congratulated, not only upon its large patronage representing every section of the State and every class of our citizenship, but especially upon the earnestness and dignity of the student body, evident even to the casual visitor.

Very respectfully,

[Signed.] W. D. TURNER, Ch'm.,
R. D. GILMER,
Executive Committee.

PRESIDENT'S REPORT.

November 30, 1898.

To the Board of Directors:

GENTLEMEN:—I beg to submit herewith my third biennial report.

In October The State Normal and Industrial College commenced the seventh year of its work.

I think it not out of place in this report to give a brief history of the establishment and growth of the Institution.

HISTORY OF ITS ESTABLISHMENT.

By act of the General Assembly of 1891, the North Carolina State Normal and Industrial College was established. Its charter name was "The Normal and Industrial School," but the General Assembly of 1897 changed it to "The State Normal and Industrial College."

In 1886, the Teachers' Assembly, then in session at Black Mountain, passed unanimous resolutions asking for the establishment of a Normal College, and appointed a committee to memorialize the General Assembly on the subject. Each succeeding Teacher's Assembly, up to 1891, passed similar resolutions and appointed similar commit, tees to present the matter to the Legislature. In his biennial reports to the General Assembly, Hon. S. M. Finger-State Superintendent of Public Instruction, repeatedly urged the importance of establishing such an institution.

But it was not until the session of 1889 that the question really came before the General Assembly for serious consideration. At that session the bill presented by the committee from the Teachers' Assembly passed the Senate by a large majority, and failed in the House by only a few votes.

By the time the next General Assembly had met in January, 1891, the late Governor Fowle had, in his message, urged the establishment of the Institution. In the meantime, the King's Daughters had petitioned the Legislature to establish an Industrial School for girls. The North Carolina Farmers' Alliance, in 1890, at its annual meeting in Asheville, passed resolutions asking the State to aid in the higher education of girls and women. Hon. J. L. M. Curry, agent of the Peabody Fund, appeared before the General Assembly and made an earnest and powerful plea for a Normal College, and, through him, the Peabody Fund gives substantial aid to the Institution.

The committee from the Teachers' Assembly suggested the establishment of a Normal College with industrial features, whereupon the act establishing The Normal and Industrial College was passed and an annual appropriation made for its maintenance. The mangement of the Institution was placed in the hands of a Board of Directors, consisting of one member from each of the nine Congressional Districts, the first Board being elected by the General Assembly of 1891. The State Superintendent of Public Instruction is, *ex-officio*, an additional member of the Board, and its President.

The act establishing the Institution required that it should be located "at some suitable place where the citizens thereof will furnish the necessary buildings, or money sufficient to erect them."

The Board of Directors decided to accept Greensboro's offer, which was $30,000 in money, voted by the town, and a beautiful ten acre site, located in the corporate limits of Greensboro, and donated by Messrs. R. S. Pullen, R. T. Gray and others.

Since the original donation the Directors have purchased about 116 acres of land, adjoining the original site.

The first Board of Directors, appointed by the General Assembly of 1891, was composed of Hon. S. M. Finger, ex-officio President, W. P. Shaw, Esq., Dr. R. H. Stancell, B. F. Aycock, Esq., Prof. E. McK. Goodwin, Hugh Chatham, Esq., Supt. M. C. S. Noble, Col. A. C. McAlister, Dr. J. M. Spainhour, R. D. Gilmer, Esq.

In 1893, Hon. John C. Scarborough became ex-officio President of the Board, displacing Hon. S. M. Finger. Almost immediately Hon. S. M. Finger again became a member of the Board, representing the Seventh District, the appointment from which became vacant at the expiration of Col. McAlister's term of office. Randolph county having been changed from the Seventh to the Fourth District, Col. McAlister was not eligible to re-election. Soon thereafter, however, Supt. E. McK. Goodwin moved from Raleigh to Morganton, and thus created a vacancy in the Fourth District, which was filled by placing Col. McAlister again upon the Board.

These were the only changes in the membership of the Board until March 1st., 1896, when Dr. R. H. Stancell, B. F. Aycock, Esq., and Dr. J. M. Spainhour were succeeded respectively by Prof. John Graham, Hon. John E. Fowler, and Dr. J. O. Wilcox.

In 1897 Hon. C. H. Mebane became ex-officio President of the Board.

In 1898 Col. McAlister was succeeded by J. A. Blair, Esq., as the representative of the Fourth District.

In December, 1896, a vacancy in the Seventh District, caused by the death of Hon. S. M. Finger, was filled by the election of W. D. Turner, Esq., and a similar vacancy in the Eighth District, caused by the death of Dr. J. O. Wilcox during the present year, has been filled by the election of A. E. Holton, Esq.

The present Board of Directors is composed of Hon. C. H. Mebane, ex-officio President; W. P. Shaw, Esq , Prof. John Graham, Hon. J. E. Fowler, J. A. Blair, Esq., Hugh Chatham, Esq , Prof. M. C. S. Noble, W. D. Turner, Esq., A. E. Holton, Esq., R. D. Gilmer, Esq.

APPROPRIATIONS, EXPENDITURES AND GROWTH.

The General Assembly of 1891 established The State Normal and Industrial College with an annual appropriation of $10,000.

STATE AGRICULTURAL AND MECHANICAL COLLEGE RALEIGH N.C.
BUILDING
CARPENTER WORK
AT THE BARN

In 1893 the General Assembly increased the annual appropriation to $12,500, and made a special appropriation of $4 500 a year for two years, to pay indebtedness incurred for general equipment.

The General Assembly of 1895, in addition to the annual appropriation of $12,500, appropriated $5,000 a year for two years, for maintenance and general improvements.

The General Assembly of 1897 made the annual appropriation for maintenance, improvements, and equipment, $25,000 without any special appropriation.

Many difficulties and expenses attend the inauguration and development of such an Institution as The State Normal and Industrial College, which do not embarrass an older Institution. Moreover, the crowded condition of the dormitory and recitation rooms, which have never been adequate to our needs, has added to the ordinary difficulties of a new Institution. The limitation in our charter requiring board "to be furnished at actual cost not to exceed $8.00 per month" calls for the most careful management and watchfulness both in collections and expenditures. The purchase of equipment for the College and furniture for the dormitories, providing lights, water, bathing arrangements, a sewerage system and heat for the various buildings, and the general improvement of the grounds and the care of the buildings and furniture, constitute necessarily large items of expense.

Beginning in 1892, with dormitory capacity for less than 150 boarders, with only fifteen recitation rooms in the College building, including chapel, President's office, and Physician's office; with a teaching force of fifteen, including assistants, and with an enrollment of 223 students, the Institution has steadily developed until, at the end of its sixth year, it had dormitory accommodations for about 350 boarders, 25 rooms in the main building, a teaching force of thirty, and an enrollment of 437 regular students, besides 188 pupils in the Practice and Observation School,

14 non-resident students in Stenography, and 44 specials in cooking—making a total of 683 people receiving instruction from the faculty of the College.

Moreover, the following substantial improvements and additions have been made:

1. A good brick building, used as an Infirmary.

2. A sewerage system and baths with conveniences of hot and cold water.

3. A dining-room, connected with the main dormitory, which will seat nearly 400 people.

4. Nine rooms in the wooden dormitory used temporarily for a Practice and Observation School, in which about 200 children of the community are taught by the most advanced students in the Department of Pedagogics, under the supervision of expert teachers.

5. The lighting of all the buildings with gas and Welsbach burners instead of with kerosene lamps

6. The purchase of 112 acres of land adjoining the 14 acres already occupied by the College, thereby affording room for the expansion of the Institution on the only side not already occupied by residences, and providing a private park for the students, admirably adapted for outdoor exercise, an outlet for a sewerage system on our own premises, and ample facilities for a Department of Horticulture.

7. A Horticultural Department has been inaugurated.

8. A modern barn and a dairy have been erected.

9. A steam laundry has been built and equipped.

10. Steam heat has been provided for the main dormitory.

A complete system of hot water heating for the smaller dormitory;.

Warm air with the fan system, providing heat and ventilation for the College building, and the warm air system of heating for the Infirmary.

11. A large and comodious kitchen has been built.

12. A cold storage room is provided, though not yet equipped.

13. A number of minor additions have been made to complete the main dormitory according to the original plans.

14. Besides planting flowers, trees, grasses, and making roads and bridges, considerable work has been done upon the grounds in the way of drainage and preparation of the soil for horticultural work and small farm operations.

I desire to call attention to the fact that the last eight improvements mentioned in this list have been undertaken since the meeting of the General Assembly two years ago.

Some of these improvements are not quite completed, and some of the bills for the improvements have not yet fallen due. It is believed that by rigid economy the present appropriation will enable the Board of Directors to complete these improvements and pay all indebtedness therefor within the next two years, but, without a special appropriation, the Board will not be able to inaugurate any of the several very much needed improvements mentioned below.

IMMEDIATE NEEDS.

The Institution is still in urgent need of the following improvements:

1. A Practice and Observation School building.

2. A modern gymnasium.

3. Library room and more literature. The former is a more serious need than the latter, as we have now more books than can be placed in our library room.

4. More recitation and dormitory room.

5. Hall for the two Literary Societies and the Young Women's Christian Association. I am glad to say that the students themselves have begun to solicit a subscription of $10,000 for this purpose, and are meeting with much encouragement.

6. Considerable expenditure in fencing the park and improving it so as to afford the proper opportunities for exercise and recreation.

7. An auditorium.

PATRONAGE.

The following statistics obtained from the registration cards, indicate the scope and character of the patronage of the Institution during its first six years:

	'92–3.	'93–4.	'94–5.	'95–6.	'96–7.	'97–8.
Number of regular students enrolled	223	391	405	444	412	437
Average age of students	$19\frac{2}{3}$	$19\frac{2}{3}$	$19\frac{3}{4}$	$19\frac{3}{4}$	$18\frac{3}{4}$	$18\frac{3}{4}$
Number of counties represented	70	77	83	89	81	83
Number of graduates of other Institutions	14	24	27	12	6	13
Number who had taught	80	104	103	107	79	87
Number who defrayed their own expenses	95	127	128	131	113	132
Number whose fathers were not living	53	97	109	93	89	101
Number whose fathers were farmers	83	153	146	161	139	140
Number whose fathers were merchants	16	26	31	46	48	39
Number whose fathers were book-keepers	9	7	1	6	------	19
Number whose fathers were clergymen	8	7	7	10	10	17
Number whose fathers were physicians	8	16	9	20	18	17
Number whose fathers were teachers	5	6	4	7	9	9
Number whose fathers were lawyers	5	11	13	9	18	15
Number whose fathers were lumber dealers	------	8	5	8	5	5
Number whose fathers were liverymen	------	1	1	2	------	------
Number whose fathers were drummers	2	5	5	5	6	7
Number whose fathers were auctioneers	------	1	1	1	------	------
Number whose fathers were manufacturers	4	7	4	12	11	9
Number whose fathers were mechanics	4	5	9	7	7	8
Number whose fathers were engineers	2	3	2	3	------	------
Number whose fathers were railroad agents	2	7	8	8	6	10
Number whose fathers were hotel proprietors	2	3	2	4	2	------
Number whose fathers were insurance agents	2	4	6	5	3	2
Number whose fathers had retired from bustness	2	6	15	15	7	5

	'92-3.	'93-4.	'94-5.	'95-6.	'96-7.	'97-8.
Number whose fathers were engaged in miscellaneous business	15	17	27	17	29	33
Number educated partially or entirely in the public schools	------	317	326	368	329	362
Number who, according to their own statement, would not have attended any North Carolina College if they had not become students of The State Normal and Industrial College	------	246	271	314	278	263
Number who graduated at this Institution	10	8	28	23	22	27
Number of counties represented during the six years	------	------	------	------	------	94
Number of matriculates during the six years	------	------	------	------	------	1354
Total number receiving instruction from the Institution, including pupils of the Practice and Observation School, workers in special departments, and correspondence students	223	401	420	541	538	683

The records show:

1. That during the six years about 31 per cent. of the regular students defrayed their own expenses without help from parents.

2. That 66 per cent. would not have attended any other North Carolina college.

3. That about 81 per cent. received their previous training partially or entirely in the public schools.

4. That including the enrollment of new students this scholastic year, the total number of matriculates will be about 1,600.

The patronage of the Institutiou has been what its best friends desired for it. Confined to no class as to wealth, locality, social position, or previous educational opportunity, it has been thoroughly representative of our good old State. To the efforts of the students the success of the institution is largely due. They have suffered many inconveniences during these first years, and have borne them with cheerfulness because they knew that the Board of Directors was providing for their comfort and their education as liberally as its means would justify.

CHARTER REQUIREMENTS AND COURSES OF STUDY.

In Section 41 of the Constitution of 1776, adopted at Halifax, the State acknowledges its obligation to provide educational facilities for the "instruction of youth" "at low prices," and the section closes with the words, "and all useful learning shall be encouraged in one or more universities."

This mandate had been only partially obeyed. The State University for young men began its career of usefulness very soon after the adoption of the Constitution. A few years ago the Agricultural and Mechanical College, also for young men, was established under State auspices and by the aid of the State and the general government.

But it took the State more than a century to come to a practical realization of the fact that "youth" means young women as well as young men. From one-half to nine-tenths of the money used to employ instructors in higher education for young men is paid by State and Federal annual appropriations, or by the income from college endowment funds. It was largely in response to the just sentiment that, if the State proposes to pay for nearly all the expense of a young man's higher education, it ought to do at least as much for his sister that The State Normal and Industrial College was established. It is not exclusively for people who feel unable to go elsewhere, any more than are those institutions for young men where the faculties are paid by State appropriations, or by incomes from endowment funds.

The State wants this Institution to be good enough for any of its citizens, and the expenses low enough for all.

The purpose for which the Institution was created is clearly stated in Section 5 of the act establishing it. It is as follows:

"SECTION 5. *The objects of this Institution shall be (1) to give to young women such education as shall fit them for teaching; (2) to give instruction to young women in drawing, telegraphy, typewriting, stenography and such other industrial arts as may be suitable to their sex and conducive to their support and usefulness. Tuition shall be free to those who signify their intention to teach, upon such conditions as may be prescribed by the Board of Directors.*"

It is the general purpose of the Institution to give such education as will add to the efficiency of the average woman's work, whatever may be her field of labor. To that end there are three distinct departments in the course of study. But the value of the training received in either department will be greatly enhanced by a mastery of the work in the other two. The course of study has been arranged with a view to meeting the needs of the young women of North Carolina, and it embraces:

1. The Normal Department.
2. The Commercial Department.
3. The Domestic Science Department.

It is the special province of The State Normal and Industrial College to emphasize the useful and practical rather than the ornamental, though it does not mean to depreciate, nor will it neglect, the æsthetic features of education.

While the entire course of study has been arranged with a special view to preparing young women to teach, it is doubtful whether any young woman who wants a good general education could pursue a more profitable course of study than one of the four regular, prescribed courses.

For admission to the Freshman Class, examinations must be passed in the following subjects, all of which are taught in the public schools of the State—

Arithmetic.

United States History.

North Carolina History.

English Grammar and Composition.

Hygiene.

For a student who enters the Freshman Class, four years will be required to complete either of the following courses, whereupon she will receive a diploma, which is a life-license to teach in North Carolina.

No student will be allowed to take more than twenty-four recitations a week, including Physical Culture.

REGULAR COURSES OF STUDY.

These courses of study are of equal rank. The diploma of the college will be awarded for the completion of any one of them.

All students who take the pledge to become teachers are required to pursue one of these regular courses, and, as a rule, others are advised to do so. When it seems advisable, however, special courses will be arranged for students who are not under contract to teach.

COURSE I.

FRESHMAN.	Hrs.	SOPHOMORE.	Hrs.	JUNIOR.	Hrs.	SENIOR.	Hrs.
Algebra	4	Geometry	4	Trigonometry		English	3
English	4	English	3	or	3	Latin	
Latin		Latin		History		French or	3
French or	5	French or	4	English	3	German	
German		German		Latin		Review	2
Physical Geogra-		Chemistry	5	French or	4	Pedagogics, with	
phy and	3	General History	2	German		practice	7
Botany		Reading	1	Physics or		Geology	
English History	2	Vocal Music	1	Architectural	5	Zoology	
Drawing	2	Drawing	2	Drawing		Mathematics or	4
Vocal Music	2	Physical Culture	2	Psychology	3	Architectural	
Physical Culture	2			Civics 3		Drawing	
				Elocution 2	3	Elocution	1
				Music 1		Physiology	3

COURSE II.

Allowing special attention to the Department of Domestic Science.

FRESHMAN.	Hrs.	SOPHOMORE.	Hrs.	JUNIOR.	Hrs.	SENIOR.	Hrs.
Algebra	4	Geometry	4	Psychology	3	Pedagogics, with	
English	4	English	3	English	3	practice	7
Latin		Latin		Latin		English	3
French or	5	French or	4	French or	4	Latin	
German		German		German		French or	3
Physical Geogra-		Chemistry	5	Physics	5	German	
phy and	3	Reading	1	Civics 3		Physiology	3
Botany		General History	2	and	2½	Elocution	1
English History	2	Sewing	2	Elocution 2		Review	2
Drawing	2	Physical Culture	2	Cutting and		Dressmaking 4	
Vocal Music	2			Fitting 3	3½	Household Eco-	4
Physical Culture	2			Cooking 4		nomics 2	

NORMAL COLLEGIATE INSTITUTE, ASHEVILLE, N. C.

COURSE III.

Allowing special attention to the Commercial Department.

FRESHMAN.		SOPHOMORE.		JUNIOR.		SENIOR.	
Algebra	4	Geometry	4	English	3	English	3
English	4	English	3	Latin		Latin	
Latin		Latin		French or	4	French or	3
French or	5	French or	4	German		German	
German		German		Civics 3		Pedagogics, with	
Physical Geogra-		Chemistry	5	Elocution 2	3	practice	7
phy and	3	General History	2	Music 1		Review	2
Botany		Reading	1	Pschology	3	Elocution	1
English History	2	Drawing	2	Shorthand		Shorthand	
Drawing	2	Vocal Music	1	and	8	and	7
Vocal Music	2	Physical Culture	2	Typewriting		Bookkeeping	
Physical Culture	2						

COURSE IV.

Allowing special attention to the Languages. Two Languages are required in this course. Four years of Latin and three of a modern language, or four years of French or German, and three years of Spanish, French or German.

FRESHMAN.		SOPHOMORE.		JUNIOR.		SENIOR.	
Algebra	4	Geometry	4	English	3	English	3
English	4	English	3	Civics 3		Latin	
English History	2	General History	2	and	2½	French or	3
Latin		Latin		Elocution 2		German	
French or	5	French or	4	Latin		Elocution	1
German		German		French or	4	Physiology 3	
Physical Geogra-		Chemistry	5	German		Geology or	4
phy and	3	French		Physics	5	Zoology 4	
Botany		German or	4	French		French	
Drawing	2	Spanish		German or	4	German or	4
Vocal Music	2			Spanish		Spanish	
Physical Culture	2			Psychology	3	Pedagogics, with	
				Physical Culture	2	practice	7
						Review	2

SOME DISTINCTIVE FEATURES OF THE COLLEGE.

In any course of study intending "to give to young women such education as shall fit them for teaching" there must be much that is similiar to courses of study in all colleges. There are several features, however, of The State Normal and Industrial College which are not common to all colleges for women. Among them may be mentioned:

1. All Students before receiving the diploma of the Institution must, for a year, spend a part of each day in teaching under the supervision and kindly criticism of expert

teachers. This teaching is done in the Practice and Observation School connected with the College.

2. Before receiving a diploma a student must study Psychology and Pedagogics for at least two years.

3. All candidates for the teaching profession are required to take free-hand drawing and vocal music.

4. All candidates for the teaching profession are required to take a course in civil government, in order that they may be better fitted to teach in the schools of the State the duties, rights, and burdens of citizenship.

5. The regular courses of study require at least two years, and allow four years, of thorough work in science with laboratories.

6. Latin, French, German, and Spanish are offered.

7. There are no extras, and the charter of the college requires board to be furnished "at actual cost not to exceed $8 a month."

8. Instrumental music is not a part of the course of study. Wherever it is desired, a private teacher may be secured.

9. Physiology and hygiene are taught by the resident physician, who is a woman. The resident physician also has general supervision of the physical culture work.

10. Under no circumstances can any student receive free tuition without taking the pledge to become a teacher for at least two years after leaving the College.

11. Of the 118 young women who have received the College diploma during the past six years, all except six have taught since their graduation.

12. About 100 graduates of other colleges have been among the students of The State Normal and Industrial College. These students usually come for special work in the Normal Department or in some Industrial Department.

13. There is no section of the State and no kind of educational institution requiring women teachers with ordi-

nary professional training, from the country public school to our best colleges, where students trained at The State Normal and Industrial College have not been employed. Of course, the largest class of teachers trained by the Institution have gone to the country public and private schools, and these can be numbered by the hundred.

It is a notable fact, however, that every city public school system in the State, from Asheville to Wilmington, has given employment to our students. More than sixty have been employed within the past five years in the public schools of Asheville, Shelby, Statesville, Charlotte, Salisbury, High Point, Greensboro, Mt. Airy, Winston, Reidsville, Durham, Raleigh, Goldsboro, Wilson, Tarboro, and Wilmington.

Four of the six orphanages in this State and several prominent colleges for women, also number among their faculties ex-students of The State Normal and Industrial College.

14. A large number of young women trained in the Commercial Department have been enabled to earn salaries ranging from $250 to $1,200 a year as stenographers, bookkeepers, and in kindred employment. Some have secured lucrative government positions by competitive civil service examinations.

For the past four or five years the proceedings of the North Carolina Medical Convention, the State Firemen's Association, and the North Carolina Teachers' Assembly have been reported by stenographers trained at The State Normal and Industrial College.

15. About twenty students each year earn their board and laundry by caring for the dining-room. No servants do any work in that room. Ten students care for it in the forenoon and ten in the afternoon. They all do their college work when not engaged in the dining-room.

16. A student who shows good ability or special merit is rarely allowed to discontinue her course for want of

means. The two Literary Societies, the Alumnæ Association, the Woman's Education Club, and a few friends of the institution, who have established small loan funds, lend money without interest for a reasonable length of time to as many as possible of the worthy applicants for aid. In each of the last five graduating classes students were so aided.

17. Of the 118 graduates, twenty have pursued special courses of study at the institution since their graduation.

18. In addition to the work done by the Faculty at the College, considerable work, especially in Pedagogics and in the Commercial course, is done by correspondence. Forty-four people received instruction in this manner during the past year. Moreover, certain members of the Faculty conduct Teachers' Institutes in counties in every part of the State during the summer vacation, receiving no extra compensation for this labor.

19. The State Normal and Industrial College stands for a public educational system that will educate all the people. It teaches its students and urges them to teach others the doctrine of universal education. The authorities of the Institution regard the College as a part of the public school system of the State, and believe that it has a duty to discharge, not only to those who study within its walls, but to that great body of people who, for one reason or another, will not enter this or any other school or college. The greatest amount of educational opportunity to the greatest number of people, is its motto and its aim. Without reservation, members of its faculty stand for local taxation for public schools and for every movement which tends to secure to the State effective teaching for every child, preparing him for productive labor and intelligent citizenship.

20. This Institution undertakes to emphasize in every legitimate way that any system of education which refuses to recognize the equal educational rights of women is un-

just, unwise, and permanently hurtful. It is the privilege and duty of your Board to lead the educational thought of North Carolina in this direction.

I respectfully submit that there is no part of North Carolina's public educational system from which she can expect more in proportion to what she has expended than she may reasonably hope to reap from the work of this College. As you know, it is the only college in North Carolina for women of the white race which has an appro-appropriation from the State, and no woman college has a large endowment fund.

One-third of North Carolina's population is composed of women and girls of the white race, and the opportunities given to this class of our population will determine North Carolina's destiny. The chief factors of any civilization are its homes and its primary schools. Homes and primary schools are made by women rather than by men. No State which will once educate its mothers need have any fear about future illiteracy. An educated man may be the father of illiterate children, but the children of educated women are never illiterate. Three-fourths ofall the educated women in North Carolina spend a part of each day educating their own children or the children of others, whereas, three-fourths of the educated men in the State spend a very short time daily with their own children, to say nothing of educating them.

Money invested in the education of a man is a good investment, but the dividend which it yields is frequently confined to one generation and is of the material kind. It strengthens his judgment, gives him foresight, and makes him a more productive laborer in any field of activity. It does the same thing for a woman, but her field of activity is usually in company with children, and, therefore, the money invested in the education of a woman yields a better *educational* dividend than that invested in the education of a man. My contention, therefore, is that the State, for the sake of its present and future educational interest, ought to decree that for every dollar spent by the government, State or Federal, in the training of men at least another dollar ought to be invested in the work of educating womankind.

If it be claimed that woman is weaker than man, then so much the more reason for giving her at least an equal educational opportunity with him. If it be admitted, as it must be, that she is by nature the chief educator of children, her proper training is the strategic point in the universal education of any race. If equality in culture be desirable, and if congeniality between husbands and wives after middle life be important, then a woman should have more educational opportunities in youth than a man; for a man's business relations bring him in contact with every element of society, and if he have fair native intelligence, he will continue to grow intellectually during the active period of his life; whereas, the confinements of home and the duties of motherhood allow little opportunity to a woman for any culture except that which comes from association with little children. This experience which comes from living with innocent children is a source of culture by no means to be despised, but how much better would it be for the mother and the father and the children, if the mother's education in her youth could always be such as will enable her in after life to secure that inspiration and solace and power which come from familiarity with the great books of the world, which are today a possible possession in every home.

In compliance with your request, I have endeavored in this statement to lay before you as briefly as practicable the general history of this College, its plan of work and the good it hopes to accomplish in North Carolina's educational vineyard.

I cannot close my report without placing upon record my high appreciation of the confidence and kindness, personal and official, shown to me by the Board of Directors, nor would I be true to my feelings if I should fail to make grateful acknowledgment of the work and support of the able Faculty and Official Corps you have associated with me in the management of the College. The responsibility for the daily work of 700 people would be too great a burden for any President of your Institution, if that burden were not lightened by the hearty co-operation of the students, faculty, officers and Board of Directors.

In conclusion, I beg to say that The State Normal and Industrial College has had no better friends than the State Superintendents of Public Instruction, Hon. S. M. Finger, Hon. John C. Scarborough and Hon. C. H. Mebane.

The hearty endorsement it has received from these State Superintendents and the cordial co-operation and support it has received from Hon. J. L. M. Curry, who, as General Agent of the Peabody Fnnd, can give endorsement and financial assistance only where, in his judgment, the greatest educational good to all the people will result, prove conclusively, if argument be needed, that The State Normal and Industrial College is a most important factor in the public educational development of North Carolina.

Very respectfully,

CHARLES D. MCIVER,
President.

REPORT OF TREASURER.

GREENSBORO, N. C., Dec. 2, 1898.

To The Board of Directors:

As Treasurer of the Board of Directors and Bursar of the Institution, I make the following financial statement of the moneys received and disbursed for the two fiscal years ending September 30, 1897, and 1898:

RECEIPTS.

1897.	Annual State Appropriation	$25,000 00	
1898.	Annual State Appropriation	25,000 00	
			$50,000 00
1897.	Peabody Fund	$ 2,800 00	
1898.	Peabody Fund	3,000 00	
			5,800 00
1897.	Tuition	$ 6,838 91	
1898.	Tuition	5,482 00	
			12,320 91
1897.	Received from rent of books and apparatus	$ 1,958 00	
1898.	Received trom rent of books and apparatus	2,066 00	
			4,024 00
1897.	Physician's, physical culture, registration, and incidental fee	$ 3,481 00	
1898.	Physician's, physical culture, registration, and incidental fee	3,673 00	
			7,154 00
1897.	Sundry Cash—single beds, piano rent, net profit on laundry, money received on open accounts, etc.	$ 2,413 64	
1898.	Sundry Cash—single beds, piano rent, net profit on laundry, money received on open accounts, etc.	2,328 30	
			4,741 94
1897.	City of Greensboro, graded school fund	$ 500 00	
1898.	City of Greensboro, graded school fund	500 00	
			1,000 00
1898.	*Sundry Cash—butter, milk, vegetables, hack fares, etc.		627 19
	Notes due at bank		3,500 00
	Total		$89,168 04
	Bank account overdrawn September 30, 1898		1,149 55
			$90,317 59

OXFORD FEMALE SEMINARY, OXFORD, N. C.

DISBURSEMENTS.

1897.	Bank account overdrawn Oct. 1, 1896	$ 1,758 77	$ 1,758 77
1897.	Salary of faculty	18,991 48	
1898.	Salary of faculty	21,781 19	
			40,772 67
1897.	Books for use of institution, text-books, and library	$ 1,636 86	
1898.	Books for use of institution, text-books, and library	1,495 71	
			3,132 57
1897.	General expenses—servants' hire, carpenter, printing, catalogues, postage, stationery, water rent, gas, repairing, expense incidental, to Board meetings, coal, interest at bank, rent of Teague building, etc.	$ 4,650 17	
1898.	General expenses—servants' hire, carpenter, printing, catalogues, postage, stationery, water rent, gas, repairing, expense incidental to Board meetings, coal, rent of Teague building, etc.	4,464 33	
			9,114 50
1897.	Advertising and announcements	$ 435 10	
1898.	Advertising and announcements	454 60	
			889 70
1897.	Permanent improvement of buildings and grounds	$ 246 50	
1898.	Work on new kitchen, laundry building, power-house, porches to dormitory, painting, etc.	3,961 71	
			4,208 21
1897.	Insurance	$ 75 00	
1898.	Insurance	304 03	
			379 03
1897.	Miscellaneous	$ 281 22	
1898.	Miscellaneous	85 78	
			367 00
1897.	Repairing, white-washing, and tinting all buildings		908 76
1897.	Equipment—furniture, pianos, chairs, desks, tables, and general school equipment	$ 1,664 38	
1898.	Equipment—furniture, pianos, chairs, tables, and general school equipment	2,202 78	
			3,867 16
1897. and 1898.	Greenhouse, farm buildings, pig-pens, dairy building, stables, sheds, fencing, etc.	$ 5,330 19	
	Horses, wagons, cows, hogs, etc.	1,571 44	
	*Labor on farm and grounds, feed, greenhouse stock, farm implements, lawn machinery, etc.,	3,793 59	
			10,695 22
1897.	Land	$ 1,650 00	
1898.	Land	1,574 00	
			3,224 00
	Notes		11,000 00
			$90,317 59

Dormitory and other expenses of students for the two years:

Amount received and disbursed for expenses of boarders in dormitory, for laundry, and for supplies bought and sold to students at actual cost (no income to the institution), $50,928.20.

*I will say that the total receipts from the farm and dairy amounted to $2,857.53, $1,907,84 being for milk and supplies furnished to the dormitories, $322.50 for hauling coal, sand, etc., and for other services, and $627.29 cash receipts for products sold on the general market. In the above statement the dormitory and general expense accounts debited with their respective amounts, and labor, feed, etc. credited.

OUTSTANDING OBLIGATIONS.

Bank account overdrawn $1,149 55; Sundry accounts, $1,250.

OPEN ACCOUNTS.

Money due to the institution, $647.34.

E. J. FORNEY,
Treasurer and Bursar.

THE NORTH CAROLINA COLLEGE OF AGRICULTURE AND MECHANIC ARTS.

HISTORY.

The Colleges of Agriculture and Mechanic Arts, now doing such useful work in the United States, were established by the States largely as a result of the liberality of the general government, which, in 1862, passed a law by which each State in the Union received public lands in proportion, equal to thirty thousand acres for each Senator and Representative in Congress "for the endowment, support, and maintenance of at least one college whose leading object shall be, without excluding other scientific and and classical studies, and including military tactics, to teach such branches of learning as are related to agriculture and the mechanic arts * * * in order to promote the liberal and practical education of the industrial classes in the several pursuits and professions of life."

In 1887 the Legislature of North Carolina decided that the funds arising from this act, should go to establish an Agricultural and Mechanical College for North Carolina, and ground for the institution having been given by the late R. S. Pullen, of Raleigh, the work of putting up a suitable building in the western suburbs of Raleigh was finished in 1889, and the College opened its doors in October of that year.

In 1890, what is known as the "Supplementary Morrill Bill," was passed by Congress. This bill makes a direct yearly appropriation from the United States Treasury to each State that maintains an Agricultural and Mechanical College.

From these two acts the College gets about two-thirds of its annual income—the other third is supplied by State appropriation. In 1889 the new institution began its work with five members in its faculty and with one building.

The intelligent citizens who contended successfully for the establishment of an Agricultural and Mechanical College in North Carolina did so for two reasons: first, that a stage in the agricultural life of the State had been reached in which men specially and specifically trained for the farm were necessary; second, that, as North Carolina was rapidly changing from its past condition as a purely agricultural State, and was engaging in manufacturing, milling, mining, and in various other mechanical and engineering pursuits, men from our own State should be specially trained to manage and assist in these pursuits. They further contended that in this day of sharp competition, complex processes, intricate and extensive machinery, only men of both broad and special education could measure up to the needs of the hour, and that such an institution could and would turn out such men as filled the needs of the State.

GRADUATES.

That the advocates of technical education were right is proved by the careers of the graduates of this institution. With few exceptions, they are adhering to their specialties and most of them are filling important and lucrative positions. Since its founding to 1897 it has had five graduating classes. These included seventy-seven young men. These seventy-seven are engaged as follows: Mechanical engineering, 22; civil engineering, 4; electrical engineering, 2; chemists, 7; architects, 3; farming and dairying, 16; army officers, 4; teachers in technical institutes, 5; teachers, 2; business, 9; medicine, 1.

GROWTH.

Since its foundation the growth of the institution has been steady and healthful. Each year almost has seen an increase in its number of buildings, in its equipment, in the number of professors in its faculty, and in the number of students.

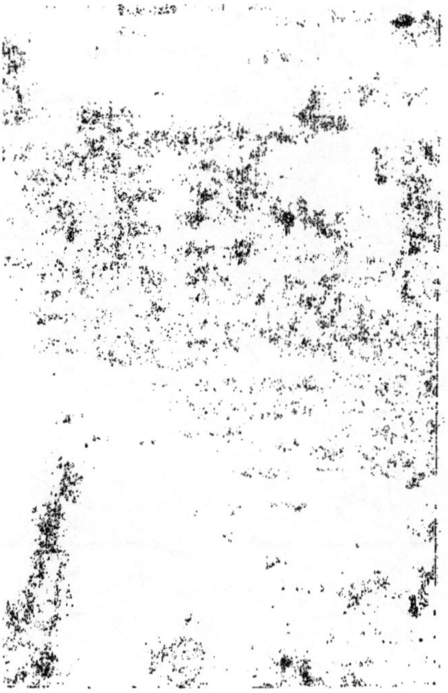

LATHE ROOM—N. C. COLLEGE OF AGRICULTURE AND MECHANIC ARTS, RALEIGH, N. C.

BUILDINGS.

The College now has twelve buildings in use. The central building is excellently adapted for its purpose of furnishing offices, lecture-room, and some laboratories. It is a three-story building with a basement. The machine shops occupy a separate building—a large two-story brick building that contains the mechanieal laboratory, three drawing-rooms, one lecture-room, and iron, wood and forge shops. The dynamo and its appurtenances are also provided for in this building. The Horticultural department has a separate building, comprising lecture-room, botanical laboratory, working rooms and three large hot-houses. The first floor of Watauga Hall, a brick building of three stories, is devoted to the dinning-room, kitchens, bakery, and store rooms. The upper floors are used for dormitories for the students. In addition to this dormitory room, there are four comfortable brick buildings used entirely for dormitories for the students. Last year, a beautiful and carefully planned infirmary building was finished. Every convenience for the sick is supplied by this building, which was constructed with especial attention to hygienic regulations. The Matron, who devotes her time to the care of the rooms and to any who may be sick, has her rooms in this building. The large barn and the dairy are equipped with all modern implements for practice and instruction in the agricultural department.

The College has its own light and heat plants, and all the buildings are lighted by electricity and heated by steam or hot water. The water supply comes from deep pipe wells and is both abundant and excellent.

LABORATORIES AND EQUIPMENT.

The whole theory of technical education rests on the bed rock that practical work must immediately follow, illustrate and clinch theoretical instruction in the lecture-room.

To attain this ideal end, this College is liberally supplied with well-equipped laboratories, draughting-rooms, apparatus, machinery and live stock.

The barn is supplied with hay carriers, silos, silo elevators, and ensilage cutter, engine, and all sorts of farm tools and machinery. The dairy, a three-roomed building, is equipped with a DeLaval Separator, Babcock tester, rectangular churn, butter works, etc. The students in this work take turn about in getting thoroughly familiar with all the processes of butter-making and dairy implements, and are also trained in preserving, packing and shipping dairy products.

The horticultural and botanical laboratories are furnished with the best compound microscopes, dissection lenses, and all supplies needed for histological work. The two chemical laboratories are supplied with fume closets, evaporating baths, drying chambers, blast lamps, and tile tables. Each working space is provided with gas, distilled water, reagents, and a sink. The Laboratory of Quantitative Analysis will accommodate thirty-two students; and the Laboratory of General Chemistry will accomodate fifty-six students. The Chemical Library has a carefully selected list of standard works of reference. The Physical and Electrical Laboratory occupies large basement apartments. The rooms are spacious, have brick piers for delicate instruments, and a dark room for optical work and photometric measurements. The laboratory is especially well supplied with up-to-date electrical instruments. In the rooms are one series, one shunt and one compound dynamo and two alternators. The laboratory is also connected with the electric light plant of the City of Ralegh for the sake of getting strong currents for advanced work. The mechanical laboratory and all the machine shops are in like manner supplied with improved and standard machinery and equipment, including everything necessary for boiler and engine tests, machines for testing belt friction, apparatus for making analyses of flue gases, ram, motors, friction brake, weirs, indicators, planimeters, etc., etc.

COURSES OF STUDY.

There are three general courses of study; the course in Agriculture; the course in Engineering, including Mechanical, Electrical and Civil Engineering; the course in Science. Each of these courses includes technical and general studies. The Agricultural course offers technical work in stock breeding, zoology, botany, entomology, inorganic, organic, agricultural and industrial chemistry, staple crops, veterinary science, dairying and dairy bacteriology, greenhouse propagation, palæobotany, landscape gardening, soil physics, meteorology, drawing, and practice work. In its general studies are included mathematics, book-keeping, history, composition, rhetoric, logic, American and English literature.

The courses in Engineering include in technical work architecture and architectural drawing, free-hand and mechanical drawing, kinematics, steam engine, gears, mechanics, graphic statics, surveying and field work, including land-surveying, topography, leveling, railroad surveying, platting, road-making, electricity and magnetism, industrial chemistry, machine designs, boiler designs, roofs, bridges, arches, dynamos, electrical machinery, and constant work in the shops and mechanical and electrical laboratories. The general courses include mathematics through calculus, history, logic, rhetoric, book-keeping, American and English literature.

The technical work of the course in Science embraces botany, forestry, histology, palæobotany, greenhouse propagation, live stock, feeding, zoology, inorganic, organic, industrial and agricultural chemistry, surveying, mechanics, electricity and magnetism, meteorology, soil physics, advanced quantitative analysis, agricultural economics, and constant laboratory and draughting work. The general course includes mathematics, English composition, history, rhetoric, logic, literature.

GOVERNMENT.

The College is governed by a Board of Trustees appointed by the Governor and confirmed by the Senate. This Board is constituted as follows: Messrs. J. C. L. Harris, J. R. Chamberlain, and J. W. Harden, Jr., of Raleigh, Jas J. Britt, of Bakersville, Matt Moore, of Warsaw; L. C. Edwards, of Oxford; J. Z. Waller, of Burlington; S. L. Crowder, of Ridgeway; H. E. Bonitz, of Wilmington; W. C. O'Berry, of Goldsboro, and the President of the College.

FACULTY.

The members of the Faculty and their subjects of instruction are as follows: Col. A, Q. Holladay, LL. D., President and History; W. G. Massey, C. E., Horticnltnre and Botany; W. A. Withers, A. M., Chemistry; D. H. Hill, A. M., English; W. C. Riddick, C. E., Mathematics and Civil Engineering; F. E. Emery, M. S., Agriculture; F. A. Weihe, Ph. D., Physics and Electrical Engineering; C. W. Scribner, M. E., Mechanical Engineering; Cooper Curtice, D. V. S.; E. G. Butler, Assistant Professor of English; C. M. Pritchett, M. E., Instructor in Drawing; C. B. Park, Superintendent Shops; B. S. Skinner, Superintendent of Farm; C. D. Francks, B. E.; T. L. Wright, B. S., Instructors in Mathematic; J. A. Bizzell, B. S.; H. W. Primrose, Instructors in Chemistry; C. W. Hyams, Instructor in Botany; J. M. Johnson, M. S., Instructor in Agriculture; N. R. Stansel, B. S., Instructor in Physics; J. W. Carroll, B. S., Instructor in Dairying; W. A. G. Clark, B. S., Instructor in Civil Engineering; J. L. Watson, Instructor in Mechanics; H. McM. Curran, Instructor in Horticulture; Mrs. S. C. Carroll, Matron; Dr. J. R. Rogers, Physician.

AGRICULTURAL AND MECHANICAL COLLEGE FOR THE COLORED RACE, GREENSBORO.

This College was established by an Act of the General Assembly of North Carolina, ratified March 9th, A. D., 1891. The leading object of the institution is declared by the Act to be instruction in practical agriculture, the mechanic arts, and such branches of learning as relate thereto.

The management and control of the College and the care and preservation of all its property is vested in a Board of Trustees, consisting of nine members, one from each Congressional District, who are elected by the General Assembly for a term of six years.

The Trustees by the act of the Legislature have power to prescribe rules for the management and preservation of good order and morals at the College; to elect the President, instructors and as many other officers and servants as they shall deem necessary; have charge of the disbursement of the funds, and have general and entire supervision of the establishment and maintenance of the College.

The Board is empowered to receive any donation of property, real or personal, which may be made to the College, and have power to receive from the United States the proportion of funds given to the institutions for agricultural and mechanical training.

FACULTY AND OFFICERS.

JAMES B. DUDLEY, A. M. (Livingstone College),
President, Professor of History and Civics.

C. H. MOORE, A. M. (Amherst College),
Professor of English.

JOHN THOMPSON, B. AGR. (University of Minnesota),
Professor of Agriculture.

JESSE HASKALL BOURNE, M. E. (Massachusetts Institute of Technology,
Professor of Mechanics and Mathematics.

JNO. H. M. BUTLER, A. M. (Livingstone College),
Principal of the Preparatory Department.

MISS S. M. PARKER, (St. Augustine School),
Domestic Science.

D. A. WILLISTON, B. S. A. (Cornell University),
Instructor in Agriculture.

MISS M. R. PERRY, (High School, Washington, D. C.)
Instructor in Preparatory Department.

C. H. EVANS, (Hampton Normal Institute),
Joinery and Wood Turning.

S. G. SNOW, (Massachusetts Normal Art School),
Architectural Drawing.

R. W. RICHARDSON, *Instructor in Music.*

MRS. A. V. WILLIAMS, *Matron.*

J. ROOKS, *Steward.*

The College curriculum comprises four departments, namely: Agricultural, Mechanical, English, and Domestic Science.

AGRICULTURE.

In the Freshman year the work of all the students is the same. At the beginning of the Sophomore year each student makes choice of the course of study best suited to his plans for the future.

The study of Agriculture is not confined to the lecture-room alone, but all class-room instruction will be supplemented with the practice of the principles thus laid down, either in the field, dairy, or with live stock, so far as equipment will permit.

The study of live stock and dairying has received much encouragement in the past year by adding to our equipment a well planned and well equipped dairy building, a model barn for the care and feeding of cattle, and a herd of Jersey cows selected from the famous Occoneechee farm.

MECHANICS AND PHYSICS.

"There are two most valuable possessions which no search warrant can take away, nor reverse of fortune destroy. They are what is put into the brain, knowledge, and into the hand, skill."

The work in this department is designed to give the student such a combination of knowledge and skill that he may be something more than an ordinary mechanic or an impracticable theorist.

From the begining of the Freshman year the time is divided between the lecture room, drafting rooms, and shops. Students are given an opportunity of visiting the various manufactories in and around Greensboro, and every lecture and exercise is illustrated as far as possible, and the practical applications pointed out.

The graduate of this department will be able to enter upon any special line of work, pertaining to mechanics that he may choose, and will have a good chance of excelling in his line.

It is recognized at the outset that a knowledge of how to make and read drawings is necessary to success in mechanical work, and further that both practical knowledge and mathematical science are necessary in preparing any reliable drawing or interpreting the same. The course, as laid down, is designed to make the student familiar with either machine shop practice, or building, design, and construction.

An important feature of the department is the mechanical training arranged for the students in the course in agriculture. It is intended to make the farmer largely independent of the tradesman to whom much of his profits annually go, and to enable him to operate modern farm machinery successfully.

EQUIPMENT.

This depart is well equipped for the work in hand and other machinery will be added from time to time as required.

ENGLISH AND MATHEMATICS.

The ability to write a clear and elegant English sentence is an accomplishment much to be desired; and it is a recognized fact that English forms an important branch in all well-rounded courses of study.

Therefore the course in this department extends through the entire four years. It is designed to acquaint the students with the essentials of English grammar, the stucture of sentences, and so make them thorough English scholars.

To excite and cultivate a taste for good literature, to acquaint the students with the thoughts and writings of the best authors and to form habits of correct expression, a diligent and critical study of standard works containing masterpieces in prose and poetry, is required of all students.

The College Library, containing some of the best works in English and American literature, affords splendid facilities for instruction in this department.

The course in mathematics has been laid out with great care and is strictly adhered to. The art of being rapid and accurate in computations, and also the analytical powers, are developed at the same time. The Mechanical and Agricultural departments give the student a fine field for practical problems.

HISTORY.

It is the purpose of this department to treat briefly, but as comprehensively as possible, in ancient and modern history, of the great events which indicate the main highway of man's progress and civilization; especial attention being given by lectures and otherwise to the subject of industrial evolution. By attentive study of those historical links—the causes and effects of leading events which mark great epochs, the chronological order of general history will be presented with the purpose of making impressions upon the student's mind that will excite interest and encourage independent reading and reflection.

As this College was established and is sustained by both State and National governments, it is under special obligations to train its students to become good and patriotic citizens, and since we must know that which we would love and to which we would be loyal, it will be deemed a special mission of the College to give the history of North Carolina and of the United States as thorough study as possible.

The course begins in the Preparatory Department with the history of North Carolina. After the student has acquired a knowledge of his own State he passes in the Freshman Class to the history of the United States. In the more advanced classes he takes up the study of European and Oriental civilization, Ancient and Modern history. Throughout the entire course the choice selections of historical works contained in the College Library will prove a valuable auxiliary to the instructor in awakening interest and stimulating desire for historical knowledge and students are encouraged to avail themselves of the facilities at hand.

DOMESTIC SCIENCE.

The national life depends almost entirely upon the individual homes, the home demands the exercise of woman's best powers broadly and carefully trained. This department was established in order to see that the girls are trained in the habits of neatness, thoroughness and gentleness, and to afford training and instruction in these special subjects, which must be considered in the daily administration of every home. Special attention is given to the study of food economy. There is a general demand for persons trained in the art of plain, wholesome cooking. The selection of food material, with regards to quality and cost, and the method of preparing, by appropriate apparatus, will receive careful attention.

OUR NORMAL WORK.

Quite a number of the students have to teach in order to sustain themselves in college. Besides, it is highly probable that not a few will find places in the school-room as soon as they have finished their courses of study. Such an end is kept in view and no pains are spared in securing proficiency in those subjects in the different departments which may be of use to them as teachers.

But our regular teachers are not the only ones who should be fitted for school-room work. Many of the teachers in the public school need to be instructed how to teach to an advantage the subjects of the common school.

The necessity for competent teachers early impressed the Board of Trustees, who required the instructors of the college to pursue, during the vacation, in high grade Summer Normals, courses pertaining to their work here. It was observed, from the beginning, that students from many parts of the State, although having covered in some cases much ground, were deficient in essential studies. In order to add to educational interest, to contribute its quota to the improvement of the schools and methods of instruction, the Board of Trustees, in 1897, decided to establish a Summer Normal. In connection with a part of the college faculty, leading teachers of both races were secured for this movement.

The Normal was a success from the beginning. One hundred and twelve teachers were enrolled at the last session. Besides, a number of persons, not representing any special educational work, were in attendance. The work of the Normal covers every phase of common and hig school education. Competent judges have asserted that they have seen nothing to equal it for colored teachers in the South.

The care and time spent in the study of English, the sciences and mathematics correllated in many practical ways, together with industrial training, peculiarly fit the youths to understand the purposes and possibilities of education, and prepares them to discharge the duties incumbent upon them as citizens and factors of society.

THE CORRESPONDENCE DEPARTMENT.

A Correspondence Department of Study has been established to meet the conditions of persons unable to attend the regular sessions of the institution. Instruction will be given in all of the subjects of a regular college course, including the classics and other branches of liberal culture.

The Aricultural and Mechanical College for the Colored Race is unsectarian, and is under the control of no particular denomination. Religious and moral training will receive the closest attention, and students will be required to attend churches of which they are members. Ministers of all denominations are invited to interest themselves in the religious welfare of the College.

The College, broad in its purposes, practical in its work, elevating in its influences, is intended to assist and strengthen the colored people in *all* their efforts for industrial and intellectual advancement. As such its peculiar mission must commend it to the intelligent colored men and women of the State, from whom the Trustees and Faculty confidently expect such sympathy and support as will enable them to make the College of inestimable value to the people for whom it was instituted, as well as the government by which it is fostered.

Correspondence solicited. Address the President, A. and M. College, Greensboro, N. C.

EDITORIAL SKETCH OF THE EDUCATION OF THE DEAF IN NORTH CAROLINA.

The question of the education of the Deaf in North Carolina dates back to 1843, during the administration of Governor Morehead, when he urged the establishment of such institution. On the 1st day of May, 1845, the institution for the Deaf and Dumb and the Blind (in Raleigh) was opened, with W. D. Cook, as Principal.

The deaf and the blind remained under the same management till 1894, when the white deaf pupils were removed to Morganton, and placed in the North Carolina School for the Deaf and Dumb.

The General Assembly of North Carolina passed a law, which was ratified March 7th, 1891, creating and establishing this school and at the same time elected a Board of Directors, consisting of N. B. Broughton, Martin Holt, M. L. Reed, S. McD. Tate, B. F. Aycock, R. A. Grier, and J. J. Long. After a very heated contest in the Legislature, Morganton was selected as the location; and the town made a donation of $5,000 in cash, and 100 acres of land as an inducement for its establishment. On the 23rd day of April, 1891, the Board of Directors met in Morganton, and among the very first acts was the election of E. McK. Goodwin, Advisory Superintendent. At this meeting the Board appointed a committee consisting of N. B. Broughton, Prof. M. H. Holt, B. F. Aycock and E. McK. Coodwin, Advisory Superintendent, to visit leading institutions to inspect buildings and equipments for such schools. The committee inspected the Columbia Institution, and Gauladet College at Washington City, the Pennsylvania Institution at Philadelphia, and the New York Institution for the Deaf. At these institutions our committee were accorded every opportunity to inspect and gain all information possible.

In November, 1891, plans and specifications for our main

building, prepared by Augustus G. Bauer, were selected, and on May the 16th, 1892, the first brick in the building was laid by Maggie LeGrand and Robert Miller, two deaf children from the Institution at Raleigh. This school opened its doors October the 2nd, 1894, and within a few days there were 102 pupils. The name of Siewers P. Angier is the first to appear on the roll.

There were then seven regular teachers, besides the teacher of art. As soon as our means would permit, we opened industrial departments, and to-day in these departments we can turn out handiwork that will compare favorably with any manufactory in the State. We teach shoemaking, carpentry, and printing, besides we produce a large quantity of various food products, which go a long way toward the support of the school.

From the printing office we issue the *Kelly Messenger*, a weekly paper. This paper and the Kelly Library take their names from John Kelly, of Orange county, who bequeathed $6,000 for the education of the Deaf in North Carolina. The interest only on this fund can be used.

The course of study in this school covers the common school course, as prescribled by law. In addition to this course about thirty-five to forty per cent. of the children are taught speech, by what is known in the profession as the "Oral Method."

The method in the school, as a whole, is known in the profession as a "Combined Method," that is, having both an Oral and a Manual Department. About eighty per cent. of all the schools for the Deaf in America come in this class. Both of these departments have the same object in view, from an educational standpoint—that is, to teach every child to read and write, as fluently as possible; and in the Oral Department to give speech to such as we think, after a fair test, can acquire it.

The General Assembly of 1897 appropriated $20,000 for the erection and equipment of a school building, which was begun April the 13th, of the present year, and which will be completed by January 1st. Our Biennial Report will show over 250 pupils. The census of the State shows over 400 white deaf children of school age—eight to twenty-three. When a child is too deaf to be instructed in the common schools he is eligible to this school, if "not of *confirmed immoral character, or imbecile or unsound in mind, or incapaciated by physical infirmity for useful instruction*." We earnestly request all school officers to report to the Superintendent of this school the names of deaf and dumb children in their communities. This school is intended to accomodate all white deaf children in the State, while the white blind, and negro deaf and blind attend school in Raleigh, in the North Carolina Institution for the Deaf and Dumb and Blind.

EDUCATIONAL DEPARTMENT.

SUPERINTENDENT.—Edward McK. Goodwin, M. A.

TEACHERS MANUAL DEPARTMENT.—E. G. Hurd, M. A., J. C. Miller, D. R. Tillinghast, Mrs. L. A. Winston, O. A. Betts, Z. W. Haynes, H. McP. Hofsteater, Miss D. W. Young, Miss O. B. Grimes, Mrs. O. M. Hofsteater.

TEACHERS ORAL DEPARTMENT.

CHIEF INSTRUCTOR.—Mrs. A. C. Hurd.

Miss Flora L. Dula, Miss Carrie Stinson, Miss Hesta Reed, Miss E. T. Welsh, Miss N. M. Fleming, Miss Mattie Simms.

TEACHER OF ART.

Mrs. O. A. Betts.

NORTH CAROLINA INSTITUTION FOR THE EDUCATION OF THE DEAF AND DUMB AND THE BLIND.

In 1843 the question of establishing a school for educatting the deaf and dumb was agitated. Mr. W. D. Cooke, of Virginia, came to the State the same year and went into several counties giving exhibitions of the manner of teaching the deaf and dumb.

Governor Morehead urged the establishment by the State of such an institution. On January 12, 1845, a bill entitled "An act to provide for the education and maintenance of poor and idigent deaf-mutes and blind persons in the State" was passed. The sum of $5,000 aunually was appropriated.

The act placed this fund under the supervision of the "President and Directors of the Library Board." The Board was composed of His Excellency, Governor Grahrm, *ex-officio*, President of the Board, and Weston R. Gales, David Stone, Charles Manley, and R. S. Myers.

The Board secured a building on Hillsboro street, and the school was organized by the appointment of Wm. D. Cooke, A. M., Principal. On the first day of May, 1845, the school opened with seven pupils, and during the session seventeen entered.

At the sesson of the General Assembly of North Carolina, in 1847, an act was passed to provide for the erection of a suitable building for the comfortable accommodations of deaf-mutes and blind persons in the State. The act appropriated only $5,000, but provided that the surplus out of the annual appropriations, amounting to ten thousand ($10,000), be placed in the hands of the Board.

On the 14th day of April, 1849, the corner-stone of the main building, on Caswell square, was laid by the Grand Lodge of Masons, under the direction of William F. Collins, M. W. G. M., after which an address was made by Rev. Samuel S. Bryan, of New Berne, N. C.

In 1851 Mr. John Kelley, of Orange County, N. C., bequeathed the sum of six thousand dollars to aid in the eduation of indigent deaf-mutes. The will provided that only the interest accruing on this fund should be used.

Mr. Cooke continued Principal until 1890, at which time he was succeeded by W. J. Palmer, who remained until 1869, when he went to Bellville, Canda, to assume the superintendency of the Institution for the Deaf and Dumb. The school was kept open during the entire time of the Civil war, though the means of maintenance were very limited. Mr. John Nichols, who had no professional experience with the education of the deaf, succeeded Mr. Palmer as Principal. In 1871 Mr. Nichols was succeeded by Mr. S. F. Tomlinson. He had no knowledge or experience in such work. But Mr. Tomlinson remained only about two years, being succeeded in 1873 by Mr. Nichols, whom he had so recently succeeded. These changes were made on political prounds.

It will be remembered that formerly our Institution owned and operated a well-equipped printing office and book-bindery. At one time the institution did the printing for the State Printer. The American Annals for the Deaf was printed in this office, and the Institution published a paper, *The Deaf-Mute Casket.* The office had costly appliances for printing raised type, and printed several works for the blind. But the printing appliances were sold and the building torn down.

In 1877 Mr. H. A. Gudger was elected principal, he having had no professional experience in the education of the deaf. But he devoted his energy and attention to the work and became conversant with the sign-language and methods of instruction. It was during Mr. Gudger's administration that the articulation department was introduced. Notwithstanding all these changes that the Institution

HORTICULTURAL DEPARTMENT—N. C. COLLEGE OF AGRICULTURE AND MECHANIC ARTS, RALEIGH, N. C.

underwent and the inexperience of the chief officers, it continued to grow in numbers.

Mr. Gudger remained as Superintendent till January, 1883, when he resigned and was succeeded by Mr. W. J. Young, who had been principal teacher in the blind department for more than twenty years. Mr. Young retired in June 1896, and Mr. F. R. Place, of New York State succeeded him. At the end of three months Mr. Place resigned and Mr. John E. Ray, who had taught ten years in this Institution, and who had since been Superintendent of the Colorado and the Kentucky Institutions, was induced to return to his native State and take charge of the old Institution, October 1st, 1896.

When Mr. Gudger resigned there were 193 pupils on his roll, and the number has steadily increased, till now our report shows 379.

The North Carolina Institution has furnished to the profession some prominent teachers, who have been honored in other States. Mr. W. J. Palmer was called to the responsible position of Principal of the Ontario Institution at Belleville, Canada, and Mr. Coleman also went to the same Institution as teacher, where he still remains in the profession. Mr. Grow, of the Maryland school, first "taught the young idea how to shoot" in North Carolina. Mr. D. C. Dudley spent his youth and young manhood in the North Carolina Institution, from whence he went to the Kentucky Institution, and afterwards filled so acceptably the Superintendency of the Colorado school for the Deaf and Blind. Mr. C. H. Hill, for several years Superintendent of the West Virginia Institution, gained his first experience in North Crrolina. Mr. John E. Ray, Superintendent of the Colorado Institution seven years and of the Kentucky Institution more than two years, spent ten years teaching the deaf in his native State. Mr. J. A. Tillinghast, Superintendent of the Belfast (Ireland) School and E. S. Tillinghast, Superintendent of the Montana Institution, are North Carolina boys, as is Superintendent F. D. Clarke, of the Michigan School.

The colored department has furnished teachers to the South Carolina, Georgia and Texas Institutions.

In 1868 the General Assembly made provisions for the education of the colored deaf and dumb and blind children of the State. North Carolina was the first State to provide an institution for the colored race. The colored department opened on the 4th of January, 1869, with 26 pupils. Mr. John J. Turner was in charge of this department for one session, when Mr. Z. W. Haynes was elected. He taught in this department for twenty years, and was removed to the white department in 1890. The Institution for the colored is a commodious, well arranged building, more suitable for its purpose than the buildings for the white department. The colored department is under the same general management as the white department, and enjoys the same care and privileges. This department has been under the immediate charge of W. F. Debnam, A. W. Pegues and Joseph Perry, respectively, ever since.

An act of the General Assembly of North Carolina creating and establishing the new North Carolina School for the Deaf and Dumb was passed and ratified March 7, 1891. The school is located at Morganton, in Burke county, and the white deaf children were removed there in 1893.

The General Assembly of 1897 appropriated $57,500 for buildings and improvements for the Institution. Out of this amount five buildings have been constructed, three at the colored department, embracing two dormitory buildings and a heating plant and industrial building, which have increased the capacity of the department about 50 per cent; and two large buildings at the white department, embracing a dormitory which will accommodate 150 boys, a very handsome auditorium and gymnasium, and a heating plant of most modern construction, together with an industrial building. Four of these five buildings are fire-proof.

Four new pianos have also been bought, and a fine set of geographical, physiological and anatomical apparatus. In these respects the Institution is in a better condition than it has ever been.

DENOMINATIONAL COLLEGES.

GENERAL INTRODUCTION TO THE CHRISTIAN COLLEGES OF NORTH CAROLINA.

BY DR. C. E. TAYLOR, PRESIDENT WAKE FOREST COLLEGE.

In the annals of several of the older States, the fourth decade of our century is notable as an era during which a number of colleges of a distinct type were founded. These institutions, as well as others like them, founded before and after this decade, variously known as Denominational Colleges, or Christian Colleges, were brought into existence to supply certain definite needs. The necessity for them became evident about the same time in many quarters and to the leaders of almost all the evangelical Christian denominations. At least three reasons may be presented which, to the minds of their founders, justified the projection of these colleges; 1st, The better training of the ministry; 2nd, College education for all classes at a lower cost than at already existing institutions; 3rd, The desire that scientific and literary training should be given to to the young under distinctively Christian influences.

About fifty years had elapsed since the American Colonies had gained their independence. These years had been spent by a somewhat sparse population in subduing and settling a comparatively new country. Tides of emigration were flowing from the older into the newer States. It was a period of unrest among the masses of the people. It was also a period of great activity among hundreds of Christian ministers, many of whom were as unlettered as they were full of zeal. As volunteer and, for the most part, unpaid evangelists, they proclaimed the gospel far and wide and organized numerous churches. To these humble,

LIVINGSTONE COLLEGE (COL.), SALISBURY, N. C.

but often able men, who labored with apostolic zeal and success, is due much that is best in the life and institutions of our people.

Before the year 1830, however, it had become evident that men of better education were needed even for this evangelistic work; and the greater success in training and developing the churches which had been attained by the educated ministers in the several denominations made it plain that in order to the highest usefulness a larger proportion of the ministry should be educated. To the minds of the leaders this need had become imperative. But large numbers of young men who were entering the ministry were unable to pay the cost of liberal education. Hence, at the same time and for the same purpose, colleges were established and Boards of Education were organized.

Again, the charges for education in the colleges already existing were prohibitive to large numbers of the people. It was the hope that the cost of liberal education could be lowered that induced many who were indifferent as to the education of the ministry to aid in founding these new colleges. It was generally believed that the manual labor plan would give a practical solution to this problem. Though this proved to be an ignis fatuus, it is not unlikely that several very important colleges would not have been founded if this plan had been known from the first not to be feasible.

The third reason is found in the fact that many Christian people were unwilling to commit their sons to the State colleges, as these were at the time. This unwillingness was, in many cases, not due to lack of means, but to the fact that these State colleges were believed to be unfriendly to religion and morality.

In Europe, until recently, almost all colleges and universities have been denominational institutions. And, State and Church being united, they have also been State institutions. During the colonial period in our own country the colleges were, for the most part, both denominational and State institutions, for here, also, at that time, State and church were united. In each of these some definite system of religious belief was taught as a part of the curriculum. After the Revolution, when Church and State were severed, these institutions either fell under the control of some religious denomination, or else became more or less corrupt as the result of the withdrawal of religious influences. The same came to pass also with those State colleges which were founded after the Revolution. It would be easy to quote from contemporary and other records abundant authority for these statements. In 1830 only one college student in four was a professing Christian. Fifty years later more than half of the college students in the United States were church members. In 1810 Bishop Meade, of Virginia, wrote, "Educated men are infidels." That such an assertion cannot be truly made now is largely due to the influence, direct and indirect, of the Christian colleges

There can be no question that one of the most potent reasons for the founding of the Christian colleges was the desire to educate the young under religious auspices rather than under the influences which prevailed in the State colleges in the early decades of this century. Of course, as everybody knows, vastly better conditions prevail in these State institutions now.

When we look back and scan in detail the earlier history of these Christsan colleges, both in North Carolina and in other States, we find them to be stories, in almost every case, of heroic struggle, sacrifice, and determination. A comparatively small band of devoted men, seeing larger and better things afar, with patience and inflexible purpose, battled against opposition and apathy.

Nor did these consecrated Christian leaders labor and sacrifice in vain. Many hundreds of ministers have been trained for more efficient work in many States and in foreign lands. Many thousands of youths, who otherwise would have been denied opportunity for higher education, have been fitted for usefulness in church and State, and for success in every profession and calling. The influence of these colleges, and of the great majority of the men educated in them, has been solidly and potently exerted in behalf of Christianity. And there can be little doubt that the great change for the better in the moral and religious condition of the State colleges is due, to a large extent, to the example and influence of the Christian colleges.

The life of a great institution of learning is to be measured, not by years, but by centuries. The Christian colleges of North Carolina are still in the infancy of their usefulness. More and more, as the generations come and go, will they be amply equipped, generously endowed, and largely patronized. But should they ever cease to inculate the teachings and illustrate the spirit of the New Testament, their mission and usefulness will have ended.

TRINITY COLLEGE, DURHAM, N. C.

TRUSTEES.

FACULTY.

JOHN C. KILGO, D. D., A. M.,
President and Professor of Avera School of Bible Study.

W. H. PEGRAM, A. M.,
Professor of Chemistry, Geology and Astronomy.

ROBT. L. FLOWERS, (U. S. N. A.,)
Professor of Pure and Applied Mathematics.

W. I. CRANFORD, PH. D.,
Professor of Philosophy and Greek.

JNO. S. BASSETT, PH. D.,
Professor of History and Political Science.

EDWIN MIMS, A. M.
Professor in English Language and Literature.

A. H. MERITT, A. B.,
Professor of Latin and German.

W. P. FEW, PH. D.,
Professor of English Language and Literature.

JEROME DOWD,
Professor of Political Economy and Sociology.

J. J. HAMAKER. PH. D.,
Professor of Physics and Biology.

S. O. THORNE,
Assistant in Latin.

W. H. ADAMS,
Assistant in Commercial Science.

W. K. BOYD, A. B.,
Assistant in History.

M. T. DICKINSON, A. B.,
Assistant in Greek.

GEO. B. PEGRAM, A. B.,
Librarian.

W. H. PEGRAM,
Secretary of Faculty.

THE HISTORY OF THE COLLEGE.

Trinity College has its origin in Union Institute, a school of academic grade, located in the northwest corner of Randolph county, North Carolina. It was opened to meet a local demand on the part of leading citizens for educational advantages for their children.

The late Rev. Dr. Brantley York was Principal of Union

Institute from 1838, the year of its foundation, to 1842. Rev. B. Craven, then elected Principal, remained in office from 1842 to 1851.

With the year 1851 this institution entered upon the second stage of its history. It was re-chartered then as Normal College, the leading purpose of which was the training of teachers for the public schools.

Before the end of this decade it had outgrown its distinctly normal purpose and considerably enlarged its curriculum. In 1859 it acquired, for the first time, the charter of a regular college. The North Carolina Conference of the Methodist Episcopal Church, South, then convening at Beaufort, accepted the transfer of the property and rechartered it under the name of Trinity College.

The first class graduated in 1853. From that date to the outbreak of the Civil war, the institution enjoyed an unusual degree of prosperity.

During the Civil War its prosperity was, of course, greatly reduced. In 1863, President Craven resigned, and Prof. W. T. Gannaway, then a member of the faculty, was placed in charge as acting President. He held the position till the close of the war in 1865, the work of instruction being interrupted only from the time of the encamping of troops on the college grounds in the spring of 1865, until the following January, an interval of about five scholastic months.

Dr. Craven was re-elected President, and the college resumed its work in the beginning of January, 1866. Following this, the history of the college is one of heroic endeavor to restore its fortunes and regain its former degree of success. The building of the college chapel was begun in 1873, and completed in 1875. About 1883 the first bequest was made by Dr. Siddle, of North Carolina, for the endowment fund. The death of its President, Dr. Craven, November 7, 1882, was a heavy loss to the progress of the institution. At once Prof. W. H. Pegram, then a member of the faculty, was made chairman, in which capacity he served till June, 1883, when the Rev. Dr. M. L. Wood was elected President of the College. In December, 1884, President Wood resigned, and Prof. J. F. Heitman was chosen chairman of the faculty. In June, 1887, John F. Crowell, A. B., (Yale) was elected to the presidency, which office he held till June, 1894.

In 1892 the College was moved from Randolph county to the city of Durham, N. C. Mr. W. Duke donated more than $100,000 for buildings, and Col. J. S. Carr donated the elegant park upon which the college is located. John C. Kilgo was elected to the presidency August 1, 1894.

TRINITY PARK AND BUILDINGS.

Trinity Park is located on the west side of the city of Durham, and consists of sixty-two and one-half acres of land. The Park is incorporated and is under municipal government. It has been laid out in drives and walks, and otherwise improved at a large outlay of money. The main entrance to the Park is from the south side, through an iron gate that spans the entire avenue leading to the Washington Duke Building. More than five hundred trees have been planted, representing nearly all the varieties of trees in North Carolina. There is a half mile of graded athletic track, and large space devoted to out-door athletics. The Park was donated to Trinity College by Col. J. S. Carr, of Durham, N. C.

The Washington Duke Building is located near the center of the Park, and is approached from the south by a wide avenue. It was named in honor of Mr. Washington Duke, of Durham, whose great benefaction has made it possible for Trinity College to project new life into the educational work of the South. It is a three-story brick building, covered with slate, lighted with electric lights, heated with warm air, and ventilated by the famous Ruttan Warming and Ventilating system—a widely approved system for supplying pure air, warm or cold, and removing vitiated atmosphere from a building. This is the system in use in over forty of the government school buildings in Washington, D. C.

It contains fifty-six dormitories on the second and third floors; twelve lecture rooms and offices; bathing apartments on every floor except the first; dry-closet system; underground drainage from the inside and from the surface about the building; a basement 208x50 feet, the size of the building, thus rendering the building proof against unsanitary conditions. It may be well said to be the "most complete college building in the State," in point of ventilation, architecture, comfort and modern conveniences.

The Crowell Science Building is a large brick building, three stories high. It was built through the benefaction of Dr. John Franklin Crowell, President of Trinity College, 1887–1894, in memory of his first wife, who died during his presidency of the College There are located in the building the schools of Chemistry, Physics, Biology and Economy. The entire second floor is devoted to schools of Physic and Biology; the third floor is occupied by the laboratory and class-rooms of the school of Chemistry. The dynamo-room is in the basement.

The Epworth Hall is a college building of extraordinary merit, both in architectual design and in point of utility. It contains 75 dormitories, two parlors, the college chapel, a dining-hall having a seating capacity of 250, and a waiting-room. It is heated by warm air and lighted by electricity. Its sanitary arrangements are complete, including bath-rooms on each floor. This building was a gift from Mr. W. Duke, and cost thirty thousand dollars.

WOMAN'S BUILDING.

The Woman's Building is located on the west side of the Park, and is used as a boarding hall for young women who are students of the College. It is in easy reach of the College library and all of the class-rooms, and contains

Y. M. C. A. HALL, DAVIDSON COLLEGE, N. C.

PHILANTHROPIC HALL, DAVIDSON COLLEGE, N. C.

eleven dormitories, besides parlor, dining-hall, bath-rooms, closets and linen rooms. The rooms, halls and verandas are lighted with electricity, and the rooms are heated by open grates. It is another gift of Mr. W. Duke to Trinity College, and is a monument to his sincere interest in the higher education of women.

The residences of the Faculty and Officers of the College are mostly on Faculty Avenue, in the College Park. They are furnished with bath-rooms, cold and hot water, are connected with the City Water Works, and lighted by electric lights. Nearly all of the buildings in the College Park are lighted with electricity, furnished by a 720 light dynamo installed by the General Electric Company of New York.

ADVANTAGES OF THE LOCATION.

Trinity College is the only male literary college in North Carolina located in a city. Our ancestors thought it would endanger the moral character of students if colleges were located in towns or cities, but the facts have long since refuted their ideas, and almost all of the large colleges and universities are located in towns and cities. The educational influences of such environments are necessary. Students enjoy advantages in a city not to be had elsewhere, and come in contact with the questions that are prominent in the minds of the nation. They enjoy the best social and religious influences. Any young man's education is crippled who is denied these advantages.

GOVERNMENT.

Trinity College was founded as a Christian College, and its policy and aims are shaped by the methods and aims of Christ. The highest product of education is character, and the truest principles of character are those set forth by Christ. In the government of the college, this end controls all methods. Military regulations are avoided, because force can never produce personal character. Students are trusted, and when it is found that they cannot respond to confidence, they are quietly advised to return home. No publicity is given to their misfortunes, and the best ideals are constantly presented to them. This makes the government simple, and experience has more than vindicated the wisdom of the method.

PRIVILEGED STUDENTS.

The sons of ministers and young men studying for the ministry are exempt from paying tuition. They are required to pay all other college fees. Worthy young men who cannot pay tuition, are allowed, in some instances, to give their notes for it, payable after they have finished their education. Candidates for the ministry, who are not the sons of preachers, are required to give their notes for tuition. If they enter the regular ministry within three years after leaving college, these notes are surrendered to them, otherwise they will be collected.

AID TO WORTHY YOUNG MEN.

There are many worthy young men who are desirous of a collegiate education, but who cannot immediately pay the entire expenses. It has always been the policy of Trinity College to render to such young men all proper assistance within the control of the college. For this reason expenses have been put at the lowest possible point, tuition being less than at any of the leading colleges in the State. Besides these special advantages, such young men are credited for their tuition fees, payable after they leave college. In such cases the student gives his note to the college. This plan is superior to the free scholarship plan, and more satisfactory in many respects. It is of equal advantage, in that it furnishes every worthy young man an opportunity, and no man should ask for more; it does not depend upon any favoritism by which, frequently, the most worthy are denied scholarships, while those able to pay tuition receive them; it does not leave in a young man the sense of having received something for nothing, but develops in him the highest sense of independence and self-help; it does not enslave the student in any sense to the institution. These are reasons of vital importance, and should appeal to noblest impulses of a young man. It is bad policy to constantly emphasize a young man's poverty, and any benevolence that gives it emphasis, tends to create class feeling on a monetary basis.

EXPENSES.

Expenses at college vary largely, according to the habits of the student. Every item of expense has been reduced to the very lowest possible amount for the advantages offered. All necessary college expenses can be met with $175 to $200.

Room rent and janitor's fee	$ 7.50 to	$12.50	per term.
Heat and electric light	8 00 to	10.50	per term.
Matriculation	5.00 to	5.00	per term.
Library fee	2.00 to	2.00	per term.
Tuition	25.00 to	55.00	per term.
Board	27.00 to	55.00	per term.
Washing	4.50 to	4.50	per term.
Books, etc.	7.50 to	10.00	per term.
	$83.50	$113.00	per term.

OUTLINE OF THE HISTORY OF WAKE FOREST COLLEGE.

Before the close of the third decade of our century it had become manifest to the more observant and thoughtful Baptists of North Carolina that the institutions of learning which then existed could not possibly do all that was necessary for the education of the ministry and the development of the churches. Out of this conviction was born Wake Forest College.

After much conference and correspondence among leading ministers and laymen, the Baptist State Convention formally committed itself, in August, 1832, to the establishment of an institution of higher learning. Within a few days after this action the committee appointed to choose a location purchased from Dr. Calvin Jones a fine farm of six hundred and fifteen acres. This was in a beautiful rolling country sixteen miles North of the capital of the State. "The Manual Labor System" was in much favor in those days, and it was proposed to use the labor of the students in the cultivation of the farm.

The first charter was procured with difficulty from a reluctant legislature. At last, however, the President of the Senate giving a casting vote, a charter was given to the Trustees of "Wake Forest Institute," allowing them to hold twenty thousand dollars of real and personal estate. This was limited to twenty years.

Rev. Samuel Wait, D. D., a great and godly man, was elected president May 10th, 1833. His colleagues were Profs. T. Meredith, John Armstrong and C. R. Merriam. The first session began in February, 1834.

The institution opened under bright and hopeful auspices. The first sessions were very successful. But the manual labor plan had been a mistake from the beginning. The farm did not pay. The Trustees found themselves in debt.

OAK RIDGE INSTITUTE

Patronage began to fall off. Meantime a large, costly building had been begun. A widespread financial panic hindered the collection of subscriptions. Disaster and defeat seemed imminent. At this juncture, Rev. J. S. Purefoy, Dr. Wait and Prof. Armstrong took the field as agents and saved the institution. A loan from the literary fund of the State gave temporary relief. This was a purely business transaction. Every cent of it was repaid with full interest.

The manual labor system was abandoned and the institution reorganized as Wake Forest College under a new charter (December 28th, 1838,) which allowed the Trustees to hold $250,000 in property and money for a new term of fifty years. The college at once entered upon a career of continually widening usefullness.

Rev. William Hooper was elected president in 1845. The two years of his administration are notable for the elevation of the standards of scholarship in all departments of the college.

Rev. J. B. White (1849–'52), and W. H. Owen (1852-'54), successfully presided over the college. The beginnings of the Endowment Fund were raised in 1850.

The fifth president Rev. W. M. Wingate, D. D.; (1854–1879), was one of the foremost men of his day as an educational leader. His administration was in every way a great success. By 1861 the Endowment had grown to $46,000. In 1865 this had been reduced, as a result of the Civil War, to about $12,000. Before Dr. Wingate's death nearly $40,000 were added to this amount.

After the close of the war the old curriculum system was abolished and the college was reorganized into independent "Schools." In 1879 the Heck-Williams Building was built by the two public-spirited cititizens of Raleigh whose name it bears.

Rev. T. H. Pritchard, D. D., (1879–1882), the sixth president, spent most of his time during his administration in travelling through the State, speaking in every section on educational matters. He was gifted as an orator and had the ear of the people. His campaign for education was one of the most potent causes for the interest now felt in popular education. It also increased the patronage of the college.

In 1880 the Wingate Memorial Hall was built by the gifts of large numbers of people.

After the resignation of Dr. Pritchard, Prof. W. B. Royall presided for a year over the College as Chairman of the Faculty. It was during this period that, mainly through the generosity of large numbers of the Baptists of the State, the Endowment was increased to the amount of $100,000.

In 1884 Rev. C. E. Taylor, D. D., was made president. He still occupies the position. In 1888, through the liberality of Mr. Sidney S. Lea, of Caswell county, the Lea Laboratory was erected.

In 1893 the Law Department was inaugurated. In 1896 the School of the Bible was organized. The Endowment is now a little more than $200,000. The number of professors last session was 14, and of students, 253.

A contrast of the earlier with the more recent catalogues of the college reveals great expansion and improvement, especially during the last few years, in every department of the institution. That thorough and successful work has been done from the first is proved by the position occupied by the alumni of Wake Forest in all the professions and in public life, both in North Carolina and in other States. And yet throughout all the earlier years the Faculty, though composed of able and faithful men, was inadequately small and the equipment was meager. This is no longer the case.

The college is organized into twelve "Schools;" each of which under the general supervision of the Faculty, is controlled by its own professor or professors. The "Schools" are as follows :

I. Latin Language and Literature.

II Greek Language and Literature.

III. English Language and Literature.—(I). Rhetoric, (2) History of English Literature, (3) Old and Middle English, (4) History of English Language.

IV. Modern Languages.—(1) French Language and Literature, (2) German Language and Literature, (3) Spanish Language and Literature.

V. Pure Mathematics—(1) Algebra and Geometry, (2) Trigonometry and Analytic Geometry, (3) Differential and Integral Calculus.

VI. Physics and Applied Mathematics.—(1) Physics, (2) Surveying, (3) Astronomy.

VII. Chemistry.—(1) General Chemistry (*a*) Inorganic Chemistry, (*b*) Organic Chemistry, (2) Applied Chemistry, (3) Mineralogy.

VIII. Biology.—(1) General Biology, (2) Botany, (3) Zoology, (4) Human Physiology, (5) Geology.

IX. Moral Philosophy.—(1) Psychology, (2) Logic, (3) Ethics, (4) History of Philosophy.

X. History and Political Science.—(1) History, (2) Political Economy, (3) Constitutional Law.

VI. Physics and Applied Mathematics.—(1) Physics, (2) Surveying, (3) Astronomy.

VII. Chemistry.—(1) General Chemistry—(*a*) Inorganic Chemistry, (*b*) Organic Chemistry, (2) Applied Chemistry, (3) Mineralogy.

VIII. Biology.—(1) General Biology, (2) Botany, (3) Zoology, (4) Human Physiology, (5) Geology.

IX. Moral Philosophy.—(1) Psychology, (2) Logic, (3) Ethics, (4) History of Philosophy.

X. History and Political Science.—(1) History (2) Political Economy, (3) Constitutional Law.

XI. Law.—(1) Common and Statute Law, (2) International Law, (3) Constitutional Law.

XII. The Bible.

In his recently published work on "The Church and Private Schools of North Carolina," Prof. Raper says: "The present faculty, consisting of twelve professors, two assistant professors, and three tutors, is very strong. * * There are, among them, students and graduates of the University of Virginia, Leipsic (Germany), Johns Hopkins, Washington and Lee, and Chicago University. At the last State Convention, held in Oxford, E. W. Sikes, M. A., Ph. D., was elected to the Chair of History. Before this, history had been under the charge of the President or a professor of some other department. From this new department very much may be expected."

All the best methods of instruction are in vogue. While text-books are used in all departments, lectures, formal or familiar, are delivered more frequently than formerly by the professors of most of the "Schools." In the several scientific departments, great stress is laid on laboratory work. The chemical and biological laboratories, especially, are equipped with the best and most modern apparatus. Students are expected to take at least fifteen recitations a week. Excessive work is discouraged. In order to carry the work required for as many as seventeen or nineteen recitations a week, the student must make an average gsade of 85 or 95 respectively. In order to become a proficient in any "school" of the college a student must obtain a grade of at least 75 in each study of the "school."

The degrees conferred by the College are Bachelor of Arts, Master of Arts and Bachelor of Law.

A little more than two-thirds of the work necessary for the Bachelor of Arts degree consists of prescribed studies. Nearly one-third consists of elective studies. Two of the latter, however, must be Senior classes.

The Master of Arts degree is conferred on students who have completed sufficiently a year's work of not less than fifteen hours a week in addition to the requirements for the B. A. degree.

WAKE FOREST COLLEGE, WAKE FOREST, N. C.

Students who complete successfully Junior and Senior Law, History, Political Economy and Constitutional Government, are entitled to the degree of Bachelor of Law.

All applicants for degrees are required to submit original theses or to deliver original addresses.

Among the potent educational forces of the College are the two Literary Societies, which will soon celebrate their sixty-second anniversary. Their halls, in the Heck-Williams Building, are probably unsurpassed by any others in the South. These societies have for many years been recognized as valuable factors in the cultivation of mind and the shaping of character. They help to impart a knowledge of parliamentary law, to cultivate and direct taste for reading, to form correct habits of public speaking, and to discipline into self-control. As one result of their training, one seldom meets an alumnus of Wake Forest who is not able to think upon his feet and express himself clearly and forcibly before an audience. Greek-Letter fraternities are not allowed by the Trustees to exist in the College.

The College library now contains nearly fifteen thousand volumes, besides a large number of pamphlets. New additions are constantly made. It would be difficult to over-estimate the value of this aid to culture, as well as of the reading-room, which contains the best reviews, magazines and newspapers. In August, 1897, the college received from Rev. Thos. E. Skinner, D. D., a generous donation of nearly two thousand volumes.

The discipline of the College is intended and adapted only for young men—not for boys—who are sufficiently mature to be able to exercise self-control. Students are expected to be faithful in work, to be prompt and regular in attendance upon their college duties, and to cultivate those amenities which are universally recognized among gentlemen. Every effort is made to develop the principles of true manliness and self-respect. In order to do this, there is no espionage, and students are trusted and treated as young gentlemen. Those who cannot or will not respond to this open and generous regime are not welcomed to the College or encouraged to remain.

A few years ago nearly two hundred friends of the college contributed a dollar each for the purchase, in the name of each giver, of a magnolia tree for the collage grounds. As these and other trees, evergreen and deciduous, attain larger growth, the campus becomes more and more beautitul every year. The four large buildings near its center are admirably adapted to the purposes for which they were originally designed. They are all built of brick, and will, in a few years, be entirely covered with ivy.

The next building to be erected will probably be a gymnasium, the Trustees having already authorized a special effort to secure funds with which to build and equip it. Although the gymnasium now in use is inadequate to present needs, physical culture is by no means neglected. The athletic grounds are ample. Since intercollegiate football was forbidden by the Trustees, there has been but little interest in this game at Wake Forest. There is, however, enthusiastic interest in base-ball.

The periodical publications of the college are *The Wake Forest Student*, which is issued monthly, under the auspicies of the litererary societies, and the *Bulletin*, which is published quarterly by the college authorities.

The Students' Christian Association has a large membership and is very efficient in accomplishing its objects. These objects, as given in the constitution are, "to promote grwth in grace and Christian fellowship among its members and aggressive Christian work, especially by and for students; to train them for Christian service, and to lead them to devote their lives to Jesus Christ, not only in distinctively religious calling, but also in secular pursuits."

Wake Forest publishes in the forefront of its annual catalogue that it is a Christian college.

So far from wishing to forget or disguise the ends for

which it was founded, the Trustees and the faculty desire to emphasize and exalt them. The men who, sixty years ago, toiled and made sacrifices to establish the college were impelled by a desire to afford the best possible education under Christian influences. Those who now control the college have, doubtless, wider conceptions as to the scope and methods of instruction; but, as the ultimate end, they can have no larger or higher ideal than existed in the minds of the founders. It is the desire of the Trustees and faculty, in hearty co-operation, to provide instruction as extended and as thorough as is given in a purely secular institution. And, likewise, it has ever been, and still is, their purpose to be loyal to the higher trust which they habe inherited. New buildings have beeu erected, the number of professors has been increased, courses of study have been improved and standards of graduation have been raised; but amid it all, the development of Christian character has been kept in view as the highest aim of the institution. Few facts in the history of the college are more gratifying than those which are related to its religious life.

DAVIDSON COLLEGE, DAVIDSON, N. C.

HISTORICAL SKETCH.

The United States Government has issued a History of Education in North Carolina, prepared by Charles Lee Smith, a member of the Baptist Church. It is a book which every Presbyterian may read with interest and pleasure because it appears much like a history of Presbyterianism, so intimate was the connection of that church with education. The large number of high schools and academies under Presbyterian management in the earlier half of this century, and the controlling influence of this denomination in the State University for seventy years show to what an extent higher education is indebted to Presbyterianism in North Carolina.

For a long time the church was satisfied with its connection with the State University, but in the progress of events the belief was strengthened that a loss of spiritual power and influence must come if the education of her sons was left entirely to public institutions. Acting under this belief, in 1835 the Presbyteries of Concord ond Morganton in North Carolina, and Bethel in South Carolina, undertook to found a college jointly. Drs. Morrison and Sparrow raised thirty thousand dollars ($30,000) in five months, and the school was put in operation in 1837, under the presidency of Rev. Robert Hall Morrisyn, D. D.

Davidson College was named in honor of Gen. William Davidson, a Revolutionary patriot, who fell fighting bravely at the battle of Cowan's Ford, and whose memory is still fragrant in Western North Carolina.

For the first three or four years, the expenses of the students of the new institution were met in part by a manual labor system which served a good purpose for a time, but soon passed away as elsewhere.

The college opened with sixty six students, Dr. Morrison President and Professor of Mental and Moral Philosophy, Rev. P. J. Sparrow, D. D., Professor of Ancient Language, and M. D. Johnson Tutor of Mathematics.

The first buildings were four rows of cottages, of which two remain; Oak Row and Elm Row, the Old Chapel, the Steward's Hall and "Tammany" for the Professor of Ancient Languages.

In 1840 Dr. Morrison retired from his office on account of ill health and moved to his farm in Lincoln county, N. C., where he lived to a great old age, beloved and honored. "A grateful people will not soon forget his eminent services."

Dr. Samuel Williamson was President from 1841 to 1854, assisted usually by two professors. These were the dark days of struggle and anxiety to which new institutions are seldom strangers. The financial embarrassment of the close of his administration was relieved for a season by the sale of scholarships on terms which were ruinous to the College, though neither buyers nor sellers ever intended it should be so. The most of these scholarships have been surrendered or compromised and cancelled. Four hundred scholarships thus sold gave new life to the College for a little season, but the result was to cut off the tuition fees and thus defeat the end to be accomplished. At this crisis in her history, in the Providence of God there was raised up a friend to whose munificence is due the ever increasing success of the college; Maxwell Chambers, Esq., a native of Winston, N. C., conducted a prosperous mercantile business in Charleston, S. C., and in later years removed to Salisbury, N. C., where he died in February, 1855. One-half of his estate of a half million of dollars he gave to his kindred and friends, and the other half to the Trustees of Davidson College for the furtherance of Christian education. This legacy enabled them to provide a magnificent building, at a cost of $85,000, cabinets, apparatus, etc., and also to employ a large corps of professors.

Rev. Drury Lacy, D. D., served as President for five years, and was succeeded in 1860 by Rev. J. L. Kirkpatrick, D. D., and he, in 1860, by Rev. J. W. McPhail, D. D., who died in office in 1871.

The exercises of the college were not entirely suspended during the war, but a large proportion of the endowment was lost by the failure of the banks and the depreciation of securities, and the funds of the college were reduced to about $70,000 as contrasted with the present endowment of $120,000. Under Dr. McPhail's administration the college was again restored to prosperity.

Prof. J. R. Blake served as Chairman of the Faculty from 1871 to 1877. Then Rev. A. D. Hepburn, D. D., LL. D., was made President, which office he filled till 1885. On his resignation, Rev. Luther McKinnon, D. D., was elected President. His initial career was one of great activity and promise, but stricken by disease, he was soon forced, in 1888, on account of continned ill health to resign his office.

Dr. McKinnon was succeeded by the present incumbent, Rey. J. B. Shearer, D. D. LL. D., who has just completed the tenth year of a successful administration. He is associated with a homogeneous faculty of vigorous and earnest men, whose untiring effort and faithful work have secured for the college a larger success in all directions than ever before in its history.

There were registered during the past year 191 students in all departments. The North Carolina Medical College, which is located here at Davidson, of which Dr. J. P. Munroe is the head, is in close relation to the college, and many of its students pursue scientific studies at Davidson College.

In 1875-76, the several Presbyterians of South Carolina, Georgia and Florida took part in the control of the college by electing Trustees. All the Presbyteries in North Carolina had, some years before, united in the management.

At the Commencement last June, Davidson College completed her sixty-first year, and a noble record is hers. In this period there have been eight presidents, forty-four professors, and a number of tutors. The total number of matriculates is 2,265, and the total number of graduates 780. She has educated nearly 300 ministers of the gospel, and in other professions she has a good number of sons. Many of her graduates have filled positions of honor in the State and country. Many occupy distinguished positions in schools and college work, in Universities and Theological Seminaries. Many have proven themselves brave in battle, prudent in counsel, and gallant defenders of truth, as they learned it in their college days. The high grade of scholarship at Davidson has long been recognized.

During the last decade many improvements have been made in the various departments of the Institution. This is most noticeable, of course, in the Scientific Departments. The best apparatus is secured and laboratory facilities supplied, so as to keep in the very front of modern progress in these things. Several new laboratories have been fitted up in the departments of Chemistry, Mineralogy, Physics and Electricity. A gas plant has been secured, which supplies the laboratories and lights the central hall of the main building. Recently new apparatus was bought for the Senior Chemistry Laboratory.

In the Electrical Department there are to be seen a complete Roentgen Ray outfit of the largest size, and a large collection of electrical apparatus. All the fraternity halls are lighted by electricity. Our Y. M. C. A. Building was the first of its kind upon a Southern college campus, and its parlors, reading rooms, gymnasium and other appointments are all indicative of the material progress of the college. It is confidently expected that a Science Hall will soon be added to the eight brick buildings which now occupy the spacious campus.

On nothing does the college more justly pride itself

than the Union Library formed some years ago by the consolidation of the libraries of the two Literary Societies with the college library. The total number of volumes is nearly 12,000. These embrace, besides a fine collection of dictionaries, encyclopedias and like books of reference of every kind, most of the standard works in literature, history and fiction, a large number of scientific writings, and complete sets of leading magazines and reviews. It is not likely that any college of similar grade can surpass, if it can equal Davidson, in the excellence of its library.

Three publications are issued from the college: 1st, a *Historical Quarterly*—Studies in History. This is under the control of the Historical Society, which, together with the Alumni, prepares papers in the line of original investigation for its pages.

2. *The Davidson College Magazine*, published monthly. This periodical has proven itself worthy of the cordial support of both students and friends of the college, very generally maintaining a high degree of literary excellence.

3d. The College Annual, under the name of *Quips and Cranks*. It has now reached its third year, and has thoroughly vindicated its right to exist.

Any review of the changes at Davidson in the last decade would be partial without special mention of the introduction of the three years Bible course. This department is assigned to the President, whose life-work has been to place the Bible on the pedestal in liberal education. The theory at Davidson is that a thorough and comprehensive knowledge of the English Bible is essential to all true education.

It will not be amiss to mention that steps have been taken to secure a large supply of pure water for sanitary purposes and fire protection. A half dozen wells have been bored down to the underlying granite, averaging over one hundred feet in depth, and a contract has been made for boring a well of ample dimensions several hundred feet into

WAKE FOREST COLLEGE, WAKE FOREST, N. C.

the granite for a yet more ample supply for all purposes.

A note on athletics is proper here. The authorities seldom permit the college teams to leave their own grounds to play, but the inter-class games both in football and baseball excite intense interest and great enthusiasm. The offer last fall of the Alumni Trophy Cup to the class winning most games in football resulted in bringing up the several teams to a high degree of proficiency and skill.

The work in the gymnasium, under a trained instructor, is thorough and systematic, and arouses the enthusiasm of the student body generally.

The bicycle track is in constant use. It is hoped that before another year the repairs on the dam at Lake Wiley will be completed, and that this large sheet of water, with its bath-houses, spring-boards, boats, and toboggan slides will again offer its attractions. Tennis courts are scattered over the college grounds and see active service.

The interest culminates on Athletic Day. A generous Alumnus has furnished a very handsome prize cup to be won by the class making the best record that day.

The social and religious influences in and around Davidson are of the best. The hospitable and Christian homes of the professors and villagers are ever open to the students, and receptions are given them frequently. It is difficult to see how a young man who has left his father's home could have thrown around him more potent influences for shielding and protecting his Christian character, or where he could find an atmosphere more distinctly moral and religious.

All but a small per eent. of the students are members of the church. A third or a fourth of these are caudidates for the ministry. The result is that the Christian work among the students under the auspices of a thoroughly organized Y. M. C. A. is a conspicuous feature of the college life. Sunday Bible classes, mission bands, Sunday-school mission work in the country and prayer meetings and other religious services, both in and out of college are all sustained with wonderful zeal and regularity.

Davidson College offers three degree courses, Bachelor of Arts, Bachelor of Science, and Master of Arts.

FACULTY (1897-8).

REV. J. B. SHEARER, D. D., LL. D., PRESIDENT,
Professor of Biblical Instruction and Moral Philosophy.

HENRY LOUIS SMITH, PH. D., VICE-PRESIDENT,
Professor of Natural Philosphy.

C. R. HARDING, PH. D.,
Professor of the Greek and German Languages.

WILLIAM R. GREY, PH. D.,
Professor of the Latin and French Languages.

THOMAS P. HARRISON, PH. D.,
Professor of English.

WILLIAM J. MARTIN, JR., M. D., PH. D.,
Chambers Professor of Chemistry.

JOHN L. DOUGLAS, A. M.,
Professor of Mathematics.

F. F. ROWE, A. M.,
Instructor.

H. S. MUNROE AND L. G. BEALL,
Laboratory Assistants.

REV. A. K. POOL,
Instructor in Music.

PROF. MARTIN, *Bursar.*
PROF. GREY, *Clerk.*
PROF. SMITH, *Supt. of Grounds and Buildings.*
PROF. MARTIN, *Treasurer of Societas Fratrum.*
PROF. HARRISON, *Chairman Library Committee.*
F. F. ROWE, *Librarian.*
DR. J. P. MUNROE, *College Physician.*
O. J. HUIE, *Gymnasium Director.*

COURSE OF STUDY.

I. The Classical Course, embracing the studies of the ordinary curriculum and elective studies. It occupies four years, and those who satisfactorily complete it receive the degree of A. B.

II. The Scientific Course, designed for such as wish to pursue English and scientific studies mainly. It occupies four years, and leads to the degree of B. S.

III. Eclectic Course.—Students who do not wish to complete either of the regular courses are permitted to select such branches of study as they may be qualified for, and to recite with the college classes, the number of their studies being subject to the direction of the faculty. Certificates of branches studied and of attainments made will be given, if desired, to such as have satisfactorily pursued sperial studies.

IV. Master's Course.—The degree of A. M. may be taken by a year's study in addition to the full A. B. or B. S. course, to be elected out of the remaining studies of the college or post-graduate studies. This is open to the graduates of all regular colleges. No tuition fee. This is a course for resident students.

V. Non-Resident Course.—The degree of A. M. is also conferred on those who have passed a prescribed course of study and stood an approved examination. No tuition fee. This is for non-resident graduates of Davidson College, and includes a full year's work in some given line of study.

SCHEME OF STUDIES FOR THE DEGREE OF A. B.

FRESHMAN CLASS.

1. *Latin.*—Select orations of Cicero; Livy Gildersleeve's Latin Grammar (1894); Gildersleeve's Exercise Book; Composition.
2. *Greek.*—Xenophon's Cyropædia; Lysias; Goodwin's Greek Grammar (revised edition); Winchell's Greek Syntax; Goodell's Greek in English.
3. *Mathematics.*—Bowser's College Algebra; Olney's University Algebra; Phillips & Fisher's Geometry.

4. *Physics.*—Gage's Elements of Physics.
5. *English.*—Genung's Outlines of Rhetoric; Strang's Exercises in English; Composition; English Classics.
6. *Biblical Instruction.*—A Reference Bible; Bible Course Syllabus (Shearer); a Bible Dictionary; Coleman's Historical Text-Book and Atlas of Biblical Geography.

SOPHOMORE CLASS.

1. *Latin.*—Cicero's Brutus; Horace (Chase and Start); Private Reading; Gildersleeve's Grammar; Composition.
2. *Greek.*—Herodotus; Homer's Odyssey (Perrin & Seymour); Goodwin's Grammar; Seeman's Mythology; Pennell's Ancient Greece; Composition.
3. *Mathematics.*—Phillips & Fisher's Geometry—finished; Jones' Drill Book in Trigonometry; Algebra—finished.
4. *Chemistry.*—Remsen's Briefer Course; Lectures.
5. *English.*—Genung's Practical Rhetoric, and Rhetorical Analysis; Poetics; Selections from English and American Authors; American Literature; Compositions twice a month.
6. *Biblical Instruction.*—Same Books as in the Freshman class, and Prideaux's Connection of Sacred and Profane History (Harper).

JUNIOR CLASS.

(STUDIES ELECTIVE. FIVE TO BE CHOSEN.)

1. *Latin.*—Plautus' Menaechmi, and Pseudolus; Tacitus' Annals; Private Reading; Gildersleeve's Grammar; Allen's History of Rome; Latin Composition.
2. *Greek.*—Demosthenes; Euripides; Greek Literature (Jebb); Greek Poets in English Verse; Goodwin's Grammar; Composition; Lectures.
3. *Mathematics.*—Hardy's Analytic Geometry; Venable's Notes on Solid Geometry; Hardy's Calculus.
4. *Physics.*—Cumming's Electricity Treated Experimentally; Houston and Kennelly's Alternating Currents; Lectures.
5. *Applied Mathematics.*—Church's Descriptive Geometry; Davis' Surveying; Henck's Field Book for Engineers.
6. *Chemistry.*—Remsen's Laboratory Manual; Venable's Qualitative Analysis (second edition); Lectures.
7. *English.*—Old English Language and Literature; Middle English Language and Literature; Lectures; Essays.
8. *History.*—Green's Short History of the English People; Myer's Mediæval and Modern History; Topical Investigation.
9. *French.*—Whitney's French Grammar; Erckman-Chatrian's Waterloo; Pettit Histoire du Peuple Francais (Lacombe); Private Reading.
10. *German.*—Joynes-Meissner's Grammar; Grimm, Andersen, Hauff, and other prose writers.

CARY HIGH SCHOOL, CARY, N. C.

11. *Biblical Instruction.*—Bible; "Syllabus;" Bible Dictionary; "Coleman; Robinson's English Harmony; Lectures; Evidences.

SENIOR CLASS.

(STUDIES ELECTIVE. FIVE TO BE CHOSEN.)

1. *Latin.*—Juvenal (Hardy); Phormio and Andria of Terence; Pliny's Letters; Private Reading; History of Roman Literature (Crutwell.)
2. *Greek.*—Thucydides; Sophocles; Æschyles; Aristophaneus; Lectures; Comparative Grammar; Gayley's Mythology.
3. *Mathematics.*—Byerly's Differential Calculus; Byerly's Integral Calculus; Lectures.
4. *Astronomy and Meteorology.*—Young's Astronomy; Waldo's Elementary Meteorology; Lectures.
5. *Mineralogy and Geology.*—Foy's Handbook of Mineralogy; Le Conte's Elements of Geology; Lectures.
6. *Chemistry.*—Thorpe's Quantitative Chemical Analysis; Remsen's Organic Chemistry.
7. *Logic.*—(First Term) —Davis' Element's of Logic (Deductive and Inductive.) *Political Economy.*—(Second Term).—Perry; Jevons; Wells.
8. *English.*—English Literature; Poetics; Shakspeare; Milton; Browning; Tennyson; Lectures; Essays.
9. *Mental and Moral Philosophy.*—Elements of Psychslogy (Davis); Haven's History of Philosophy; Dabney's Practical Philosophy; Lectures.
10. *French.*—Whitney's French Grammar; Selections from Erckman-Chatrian, Coneille, Racine, Moliere, and Victor Hugo; Private Reading; Composition.
11. *German.*—Joynes-Meissner's Grammar; Hosmer's German Literature; Composition; Lessing; Goethe; Schiller.
12. *Bookkeeping and Commercial Law.*—(To be taken as an extra or eclectic study.)—Text-books reserved.

SCHEME OF STUDIES FOR THE DEGREE OF B. S.

FRESHMAN CLASS.—One Modern Language is substituted for Greek in the A. B. Course.

SOPHOMORE CLASS.—The other Modern Language may be substituted for Latin, and any Junior study may be elected in the place of Greek.

JUNIOR AND SENIOR CLASSES.—Any five studies may be elected out of the A. B. Course in each class, at leuast two of which must be scientific or mathematical each year.

SCHEME OF STUDIES FOR THE RESIDENT A. M. COURSE.

Any five elections out of such Junior and Senior studies as were not in the A. B. or B. S. Course, or Post-Graduate work in special departments.

SCHEME OF STUDIES FOR NON-RERIDENT A. M. COURSE.

A full year's work in any department of study selected by the applicant and agreed on by the Faculty.

EXPENSES.

Total necessary college expenses vary from $125 to $235 per year.
The post-office is Davidson, Mecklenburg County, N. C.

GUILFORD COLLEGE.

Guilford College grew out of what was originally known as New Garden Boarding School, and was founded by North Carolina Yearly Meeting of Friends, and opened in 1837. Since that date the institution has been operated continuously

From the outset the same facilities were offered to both sexes, and the school was the pioneer of co-education in the South. In 1887 the demand for higher instruction than the academic course then pursued caused a careful consideration of the outlook for education in the South, and the great need of thorough preparation for the work of training young men and women for the duties of life. Friends of education in the South, and notably Francis T. King, of Baltimore, came forward with means to improve the equipment of the school by the addition of new buildings, increasing the number of instructors, extending the courses of study, and augmenting the endowment which had existed from an early period in the school's history.

In 1888, the institution was chartered under the name of Guilford College.

The name locates the college. The buildings stand on a well-cultivated farm of 300 acres, six miles west of Greensboro.

At this place the elevation above sea is about one thousand feet; and the locality has long been known as one of the healthiest in the Piedmont section of the State.

Great care was taken by the founders to select a neighborhood as fre as possible from immoral influences. Time has proven the wisdom of their choice—the freedom of the place from allurements to idleness and vice being proverbial, and the entire surroundings being healthful and invigorating to both body and mind.

By a wide range of small contributions made by Friends, both in America and in England, the sum of fifty thousand dollars has been raised and invested as a permanent endowment. As a further source of income, the large farm has for many years been operated in accordance with the most approved methods of agriculture; and the institution boarding the young men and women, the products of the dairy have a market on the farm.

The five brick buildings have, in their development, marked the history of the school and college.

In the outset, the substantial building known as Founders' Hall was erected, and served the purpose of the school for nearly fifty years, the operation of the institution not being suspended for a day during the four years of the Civil War. The large Yearly Meeting House, built early after the close of the war, and standing near Founders' Hall, was subsequently donated to the school, and after being so used for a short time was destroyed by fire. Immediately two brick buildings were erected—King Hall, named in honor of Francis T. King, and Archdale Hall, named for John Archdale, the Colonial Quaker Governor of the Carolinas, two hundred years ago. In 1891 the Y. M. C. A. Hall was built, and in 1897 Memorial Hall, the gift of Messrs N. B. and J. B. Duke, in honor of their sister, Mary Elizabeth Lyon. The last named is mainly devoted to science; and the rooms on the first floor were planned for Chemical and Physical Laboratories and for a Museum of Natural History.

The second floor is given entirely to an auditorium.

The Library has grown gradually with the Institution, until the collection of books, about 5,000 volumes, is a valuable part of the college equipment.

The Museum of Natural History has been formed through the efforts of a number of gentlemen interested in science, and the co-operation of the friends and pupils of

COLLEGE AND GROUNDS—N. C. COLLEGE OF AGRICULTURE AND MECHANIC ARTS, RALEIGH, N. C.

the school. Prof. Joseph Moore devoted much thought and care for four years to these collections. Mr. T. G. Pearson, for five years, bestowed much time and labor in adding to the collection of specimens, made from a wide range of travel and research.

The courses of instruction are: The Classical, the Scientific, and the Latin Scientific. The first-named leads to the degree of Bachelor of Arts, and embraces a three years' course, of four recitations a week, in the Greek Language the same amount in Latin, with two or more years of preparatory training, one year in German four hours a week, and three hours a week for a year in French.

All the courses embrace English Literature, Mathematics, History, Psychology, Logic, Political Economy, the Natural Sciences and Astronomy.

The degre of Bachelor of Science is awarded to those who complete the Scientific, or the Latin Scientific Course. No honorary degree has ever been conferred.

Valuable scholarships have been established for graduates of Guilford at Haverford and Bryn Mawr Colleges. The former grants annually to the best scholar of the young men of the graduating class of Guilford a scholarship of $300, and Bryn Mawr to the best scholar of the young women of the graduating class each year a scholarship of $400.

ST. MARY'S COLLEGE, BELMONT, N. C.

Catholic education received an impetus, when in 1846, Rev. Bonifaer Weimmer, O. S. B., arrived from Germany and laid the foundation of the first Benedictine monastery and college, in the broad land of North America.

With amazing rapidity this institution of Western Pennsylvania spread its influence, until, after no great period of time, it became a power in the religious life of the United States, and indomitable energy, zeal and perseverance, became synonymous with Benedictine. Soon the great tree began to put forth shoots, missions were established in various localities, and Arch Abbot Weimmer looked upon his labors as completed, when from North Carolina came the offer of a tract of land from the Vicar Apostolic, now His Eminence Cardinal Gibbons, with the proviso that an educational institution be erected thereon. These acres were the Caldwell Place, purchased at a bankrupt price by Rev. J. J. O'Connell, D. D.

Others had refused to consider the proposition, deterred by the onerous condition of affairs in that country, but Abbot Weimmer, nothing daunted by the unpleasant prospect, accepted the gift and transferred the first colony thither in 1876.

Every person, possessing even a meager knowledge of history, knows the power and greatness of the Benedictines. Fourteen hundred years ago Benedict, of a noble Italian family, founded the first monasteries of the West at Monte Cassino and Subiacco, compiling the rule, which has been preserved and obeyed with careful tenacity through centuries, and to-day governs the Oredr the world over. So great was the reputation and sanctity of the noble Benedict, that men of all conditions and ages enlisted under his standard. Emperors abandoned their empires,

Kings their thrones and received the humble habit of the monk to labor in the work of christianizing Europe.

Every country was predominated with their influence, their monasteries became the nucleus of towns, the land was tilled, the schools crowded.

The monks were the greatest inventors the world has known, and the grand evidences of their progressiveness have made the history of the eastern hemisphere. Failure was a word never whispered within the comfortless cells of an humble beginning. Stimulated by the heroic traditions of their religious ancestors, the pioneers of the Order set foot on the fruitful soil of the Old North State.

So lowly were their expectations, they were not overpowered at the absence of everything suggesting success.

To labor for Christ and their fellow-men was their vocation, and so St. Mary's College had its birth with only the pine forests to behold its nativity and the labors of a brave few to help it into being.

Rev. Herman Wolfe, an ex-Confederate officer, was the Superior and Rector. Right manfully did he meet and over come difficulties, and each year recorded some noteworthy advancement in the career of the infant institution. Under his successors, Rev. Stephen Lyon, O. S. B., Rev. Edward Pierson, O. S. B., and Rev. Julius Pohl, O. S. B., the school developed rapidly, the number and capacity of the buildings increasing to meet the demands of the larger body of students in attendance, and St. Mary's educational power was firmly established. Degrees were conferred and the high standard of the school qualified the graduates to fill any position with credit.

In 1885, through the benevolence of the Sovereign Pontiff, Leo XIII., St. Mary's was raised to the dignity of an Abbey, with Father Leo Haid, O. S. B., Chaplain, Secretary and Professor of graduating class at St. Vincent's, in Pennsylvania, as mitred Abbot.

Six able young Benedictines volunteered their services in the new field and from that year dates the permanent success of the college. The corner-stone of a handsome structure was laid, the new building being rapidly completed. This was followed some years later by the grand Cathedral, dedicated with pomp in 1894, not to mention other necessary, but less important, additions, all the while the teaching facilities broadening.

Eighteen hundred and eighty-eight witnessed the consecration of Abbot Haid as Vicar Apostolic of North Carolina. No regression, but a constant pushing forward, and to-day we behold the fruit of toil—the reputation of the institution widespread. Last year much attention was directed towards it as the base of the ceremonies commemorating the Silver Jubilee of Bishop Haid as a priest, and of three days continuance. At this session a new building was thrown open, the exact frontage of the main building now being 215 feet. Buildings all lighted by electricity.

The courses of study embrace the Commercial, Classical, Scientific, Philosophical and Theological, each characterized by the greatest thoroughness.

Nothing is lacking to make the instruction equal to that of larger colleges and universities.

The students, according to age, form three divisions, each of which has its own study-hall, and is under the control of Prefects.

The climate of Gaston County is proverbially healthy. The land undulates gently, forming a most beautiful succession of hills and valleys. The summer is long, but never over-warm; the coolness of the night ever invites to quiet rest. The winter lasts scarcely five or six weeks—even then the student is seldom obliged to spend one hour of his recreation in-doors.

Strict attention is paid to the moral and religious training of the students. In regard to their studies the most approved methods and the most efficient means are adopted to stimulate, test and develop natural talents and to insure the acquisition of a thorough training and education.

The college possesses a library for the promotion of good reading, a chemical and physical apparatus, a mineral cabinet, and a complete set of anatomical models, etc., for the use of advanced students.

Aware that physical training is also necessary to a thorough education, the faculty spare no pains to secure for the students all the advantages to be derived from approved modes of exercise. The extensive grounds are provided with ball fields, tennis courts, hand-ball alleys, and a large gymnasium, well-equipped with bowling alley and athletic apparatus. The shady alleys, which everywhere penetrate the charming pine forests, afford most delightful walks at all seasons of the year.

THE COMMERCIAL COURSE.

A thorough, practical business education is the prime object of the Commercial Course. Yet it also aims to prepare young men for educated society, supplying them with such useful knowledge as may fit them for entering a professional calling, should this be desired. A competent knowledge of the elements of English, Arithmetic, Geography, etc., is requisite for admission to this course. Students who pass a satisfactory examination in all the branches prescribed, may receive the Diploma, with the title of Master of Accounts. Three years are ordinarily required for graduation; more advanced students may, however, be admitted to the second or first-class on entering the college.

CLASSICAL AND SCIENTIFIC COURSE.

To this course belongs a thorough and systematic teaching of Latin, Greek, English and German, Oratory, Mathematics, Logic. Ethics and Metaphysics.

The latter all taugh in Latin. Also Natural Philosophy, Chemistry, Astronomy, Geology and Physiology. The course is intended to last five years, at the end of which time the degree of A. B. is conferred on such as are found deserving of the honor. Two years' application to further study or literary career, attended with success, will entitle to the degree of A. M.

Philosophical and Theological course comprises five years after the completion of the Classical course. Sacred Scriptures, Dogmatic and Moral Theology, Church History, Canon Law, Hebrew, Liturgy and Homiletics are the studies by which the candidate for the priesthood prepares himself for the arduous duties of his sacerdotal career.

At this college, as will be seen from the above, a young man can begin his classics and continue his studies till he graduates from the Theological Course. Few, if any colleges in the State of North Carolina, cover such an extended course.

The present officers: Rt. Rev. Leo Haid, D. D., O. S. B., President, and Rev. F. Bernard, O. S. B., Vice-President and Rector, assisted by fourteen energetic, able young teachers, warrant thoroughness in their respective departments.

GREENSBORO FEMALE COLLEGE.

FACULTY AND OFFICERS, 1898–99.

DRED PEACOCK,
President.

MRS. Z. A. LONG,
Lady Principal.

REV. T. A. SMOOT, A. B.,
Science and Philosophy.

MISS LILLIAN LONG,
History.

MRS. N. F. SHELTON,
English Language and Literature.

MISS MINNIE H. MOORE,
Mathematics.

MISS ANNIE M. PAGE,
French and German.

MISS AVA L. FLEMING,
Latin.

J. W. PARKER, Musical Director,
Piano and Voice Culture.

MISS MARY O. BLACK,
Piano and Voice Culture.

MISS ANNIE SNEED,
Piano.

MISS RACHEL SIMS,
Elocution and Physical Culture.

MISS CATHARINE F. HEISKELL,
Drawing and Painting.

MISS BETTIE ARMFIELD,
Business Department.

REV. J. H. WEAVER, D. D.,
Chaplain.

MISS MAIE CATHARINE CURRIE,
Librarian.

MISS FANNIE ARMFIELD,
Supervisor of Health.

MRS. C. E. HUNDLEY.
Matron.

MR. J. A. ODELL,
Treasurer.

MISS MAIE ALICE CARR,
Assistant Treasurer and Private Secretary to the President.

HISTORICAL SKETCH.

For several years before any direct efforts were made to establish a female college of high grade by the Methodists in North Carolina, the necessity of such an institution was felt by prominent ministers and intelligent laymen of the church. It was the subject of frequent discussion in Annual Conferences.

In the year 1837, the trustees of Greensboro Female School sent a petition on this subject to the Virginia Conference, which met in Petersburg, January 31st. At this time the North Carolina Conference began its separate existence. That petition was referred to a committee consisting of Rev. Moses Brock, Rev. Peter Doub and Rev. Samuel S. Bryant.

After setting forth the necessity of a female school of high grade for the education of women, under the auspices of the North Carolina Annual Conference, the committee reported the following resolutions, which were adopted:

"Resolved, 1. That the Conference will co-operate with

GUILFORD COLLEGE, GUILFORD COLLEGE, N. C.

the trustees of Greensboro Female School, provided that one-half the number of the board of trustees shall, at all times, be members of the North Carolina Conference.

"Resolved, 2. That the board thus constituted shall petition the Legislature of North Carolina for a proper charter for a seminary of learning, to be called the Greensboro Female College.

"Resolved, 3. That the Conference appoint Moses Brock, Hezekiah G. Leigh, William Compton, Peter Doub, John Hank, James Reid, Bennett T. Blake, William E. Pell and Samuel S. Bryant, trustees, to carry into effect the object contemplated by the previous resolutions.

"Resolved, 4. That the Bishop be requested to appoint an agent for the purpose of raising funds for this object.

"MOSES BROCK, Chairman."

In accordance with the foregoing resolutions, the ten ministers named in the third resolution, and ten laymen, constituting the Board of Trustees, secured from the Legislature a charter granting the rights and privileges usually bestowed upon colleges of high grade. This charter was ratified December 28th, 1838.—(T. M. Jones, in Centennial of Methodism in North Carolina.)

On account of the severe depression in all lines of business, it required several years of canvassing to raise sufficient funds to erect the building. For the accomplishment of this difficult task we are indebted to the untiring efforts of S. S. Bryant, Moses Brock, James Reid and Ira T. Wyche, who were agents for the college in those trying years. The corner-stone was laid in September, 1843. In 1846 the building was completed and ready for occupancy, but the trustees did not select a faculty until the following year.

In the fall of that year the classes were organized and went to work under the administration of Rev. Solomon Lea, who had the honor of having been the first President of the first chartered female college in North Carolina, and the second one south of the Potomac River.

Mr. Lea resigned in 1847, and was succeeded in the Presidency by Rev. A. M. Shipp, D. D., of South Carolina. For three years the college prospered under his wise administration, and twenty-six young women were graduated from the institution.

Rev. Charles F. Deems, D. D., who succeeded Dr. Shipp in 1850, grasped the situation and mastered it at once, and the patronage of the college was largely increased. It continued to flourish to the close of his administration in 1854. At that time Rev. Turner Myrick Jones, afterwards Rev. T. M. Jones, D. D., was a Professor in the college. The Board of Trustees recognized in him the qualifications needed in a man to render him suited for great enterprises. Fortunately for the college, he was elected President and held that position until his greatly lamented death in 1890. For thirty-six years Dr. Jones labored for the cause of female education as no other man in North Carolina ever labored. His valuable life was given to this work. While he was President, in 1863, the college building was destroyed by fire in the midst of its greatest prosperity. The Conference at once formulated plans to rebuild. In 1871 work on the present building was begun, and on the 27th day of August, 1873, the college was re-opened in the present commodious building.

Dr. B. F. Dixon was elected to succeed Dr. Jones. For three years the college enjoyed an unusually large patronage, and ninety-three young ladies were graduated during Dr. Dixon's administration. In April, 1893, Dr. Dixon resigned, and the board of directors elected Rev. Frank L. Reid, D. D., President of the Faculty. Dr. Reid came to the college in the prime of life, and his first year's work proved the wisdom of his election. The fall session of 1894 opened with most favorable prospects, but the honored President was not destined to see the fruition of his labors. On September the 24th, 1894, this gifted scholar and preacher was called from earth to Heaven, and left the college family in deep mourning for its beloved head. Dred Peacock, at that time a Professor in the college, was elected to succeed Dr. Reid, and is now the President of the Faculty.

Under the present administration the different departments have been thoroughly re-organized. The courses of study have been expanded and enlarged. This was rendered possible only by the addition of more appliances in the form of laboratories equipped with ample chemical and philosophical apparatus, mathematical instruments and figures, and new pianos. A well selected library, containing more than 5,000 volumes, besides pamphlets and general magazine and periodical literature, has enabled the student-body to do a grade of work unattainable in the average college for young women. The past four years have been unusually successful, both as regards numbers in attendance and the highly satisfactory quality of work acomplished.

A very large debt was incurred in erecting the present building, which the Conference tried for years to pay. Having failed to do this, the college was finally put up and sold at public auction for debt. At this juncture a syndicate of large-hearted, liberal men was formed to purchase it in order that it might be continued as a female college for the Methodist Church in North Carolina. These gentlmen still own and control the college. They have no desire or expectation of making any money out of the investment. Their expectations and highest desire will be met when the college is filled with pupils; and they stand ready to enlarge the buildings and make other improvements whenever the patronage of the college demands it. They offer first-class facilities for female education at what it costs to provide it, and all they ask is that large patronage of which the college is so eminently worthy.

THE BAPTIST FEMALE UNIVERSITY.

For several years the Baptist State Convention of North Carolina has been earnestly fostering a movement to afford for their young women an educational opportunity similar to that which they offer to their young men in Wake Forest College It is with great pleasure that it may be stated in this report that in the fall of the year 1899, they will open, at Raleigh, the institution into the establishing of which they have given themselves with such sacrifice and faith.

Located beautifully and conveniently in the heart of Raleigh, the magnificent building is now all but finished. Than it, there is no handsomer educational building in North Carolina. It will easily accommodate about 150 young women.

The plan of the Trustees is to have it endowed as rapidly as possible, to the end that the cost of education may be reduced to a minimum. It will be, in a little while, what its founders have purposed—a fit companion for their Wake Forest College.

In the near future its Faculty will be selected; and the Trustees are desirous of selecting the very ablest men and women that may be available.

Mr. W. C. Petty, of Carthage, is President of the Board of Trustees, and Rev. O. L. Stringfield, of Raleigh, is the Secretary and Public Representative.

SCHO…

PEACE INS…

This Ins…
It has been…
have been…
refitted and…
Everything…
Institute…
gives a m…
ments at m…
Its Music…
The foll…
of study and…
viz:
Mental…
Christianity…
Chemistry…
Criticism…
man, one…
and Vocal…
colors and…
Elocution…
Typewriting…
and Fitting…
From the…
pared a…
The F…
it is pre…
accom…
Cat…

PEACE INSTITUTE FOR YOUNG WOMEN, RALEIGH, N. C.

This Institute has had a continued existence of 61 years. It has been located at Raleigh since 1872. The buildings have been greatly enlarged in recent years and the whole refitted and refurnished.

Everything is in excellent order and up-to-date. The Institute stands in the forefront of female education, and gives a most thorough education with added accomplishments at most reasonable rates.

Its Music and Art Departments are unrivalled.

The following schedule will show the different branches of study and the number of teachers to each department, viz:

Mental and Moral Philosophy and Evidences of Christianity, one; Mathematics and Sciences, three; Chemistry and Physics, one; English Literature and Criticism, two; Latin and Greek, one; French and German, one; Music—Instrumental, Piano, Organ and Violin, and Vocal, six; Fine Arts, Drawing, Painting in Water colors and Oil, and Modeling, two; Physical Culture and Elocution, two; Bookkeeping, one; Stenography and Typewriting, one; Primary Department, and also Cutting and Fitting.

From the above it will be seen that young ladies are prepared also for the practical avocations of life.

The Faculty is an exceptionally strong one. In Music it is presided over by a Professor, assisted by five able and accomplished teachers.

Catalogue of the Principal, Jas. Dinwiddie.

PEACE INSTITUTE FOR YOUNG WOMEN, RALEIGH, N. C.

This school has stood for many years in the forefront of female education. It has perhaps done more for the thorough education of young women than any school in the South. Its high moral tone, its thorough instruction in all advanced departments of female education, its high standard and the culture and refinement of the families from which its pupils are drawn, speak volumes in commendation of the school. Its buildings are excellent and its grounds beautiful, but it does not rely on brick and mortar to draw patronage to its halls, but upon the brains of its Faculty, their earnest work, high attainments, earnest Christian charcter and loving service for the Master, and upon the careful and practical attention to the physical, intellectual and moral needs of its students. It is probably less expensive for the advantages offered than any school of its grade in the South, but it does not offer a finished education at less than the cost of good table board, as some profess to do. The school does not make servants of its pupils, nor occupy their time in household duties, to the neglect of their studies and of the culture and refienment of manners and personal habits, which should characterize young women in such schools. Our courses equal those of the colleges for young men, and our standards are as high. Its Faculty contains one M. A. of University of Virginia; a lady full graduate of Cornell University; a lady graduate and post-graduate in Mathematics, of Chapel Hill; a lady graduate in Science, of Cornell, and specialtists in every department of female education. Its musical faculty were educated at Vienna, Berlin, New York, Boston and Leipsic. Its numbers are limited to 75 boarders, and the aim is to have a select school, where there shall be a quiet home life with close and intimate association between teachers and pupils, and to avoid the demoralizing influences of great numbers, collected together, with no common bond of sympathy. In such a school as PEACE the advantages for the development of true character and habits, and the correction of individual defects of either, are very great. Compared with the so-called "cheap schools," the few dollars additional which are expended on a pupil during the two or three years of her school-life in PEACE are re-paid to her a thousand fold by her broader culture and increased usefulness during her whole life.

Illustrated catalogue free on application.

OXFORD SEMINARY FOR GIRLS, OXFORD, N. C.

HISTORY.

For over forty-eight years Baptists have had in Oxford a college for the education of girls. The first session was opened in 1850, with Rev. S. Wait, D. D., as President. In 1857 he was succeeded by Mr. J. H. Mills, who remained in charge till 1868. For several years it was continued, under different managements, till in 1880 the present President was called to take charge. The buildings were remodeled and enlargd at a cost of several thousand dollars.

BUILDINGS AND GROUNDS.

The buildings are imposing in appearance and conveniently arranged. They contain a chapel 30x80, a dining-hall 26x50, a studio 26x30, a reading-room 20x30, six large class-rooms, a large number of music-rooms, parlors, a suite of rooms for an infirmary, and thirty-five large and comfortable sleeping rooms.

The grounds, comprising several acres, are richly and tastefully decorated with shade trees, evergreens, flowering shrubs, etc., and are among the prettiest in the State.

COURSE OF STUDY

is distributed into the following schools:

1. English Language and Literature, four years.
2. Latin Language and Literature, four years.
3. Modern Languages, three years.
4. Mathematics, three years.
5. Natural Science, three years.
6. Moral Science ,two years.
7. History, three years.

Five teachers are engaged in teaching this course.

CONSERVATORY OF MUSIC AND ART.

Piano, organ violin, mandolin, voice harmony, history.

The outfit consists of ten pianos, one organ. Three teachers are engaged in music.

The course in Art embraces three years. In it are taught Crayon Drawing, Painting in Oil, Water Colors, Pastel, etc., Kensington Embroidery, Point and Battenburg Lace. Two teachers.

SCHOOL LIBRARY.

has 1,000 selected volumes.

CALLIOPEAN LITERARY SOCIETY,

of fifty members is a valuable auxiliary in Literature, Essay Writing, Music, etc.

The Maggie Mett Missionary Society has been in existence for a long period, and from the ranks of its members three missionaries to foreign lands have gone out. The spiritual tone of the school is helped by the society.

The number of students enrolled for the session of 1897 and 1898 is 120. One-half of these are boarding and one-half day pupils. The number of music pupils is about 70.

F. P. HOBGOOD, A. M.,
President.

CATAWBA COLLEGE.

Catawba College is the outgrowth of an educational movement that took its rise about the middle of this century in the growing demand for higher and broader education in Western North Carolina, and especially in the Reformed (German) Church. She was founded under a liberal charter granted by the Legislature of 1851, and was opened for the reception of students in the fall of that year. She was the first institution of the kind in this part of the State, except Davidson College, and was eminently popular and successful from the beginning. During these forty-seven years she has done an important part in training the youth of this section of the State, with many from other sections and other States, for the activity in the professions and in business that makes Western North Carolina so prosperous and so promising today. Of the 2,000 who have gone out from her fostering care many are in the front ranks of their various callings. Among these are two State Superintendents of Public Instruction.

The location, Newton, N. C., in one of the most prosperous counties in the State, is elevated, undulating and very healthful. The scenery is delightful, with many peaks of the Blue Ridge on the west and mountains of less elevation on the north and east. The town, without a barroom for forty-five years, but with her sterling population, manufacturing and business prosperity, railroad, telegraph and telephone connections, is an ideal village for an institution of learning.

With her large and beautiful shaded campus, on the quiet southern suburb of the town, her ample buildings for dormitory, recitation-rooms, boarding and society halls, libraries, cabinets and facilities for science, she is well equipped, and her Faculty of ten qualified and experienced teachers are doing thorough and practical work. With her curriculum in the Acadamic, Literary, Scientific and Collegiate courses on a parwith the best schools in the State, the expenses are exceedingly economical, the discipline firm but parental, and the opportunities for social, moral and religious improvement unsurpassed, perhaps, by any institution in the State. Music, Art and Business courses also receive due attention.

In all the departments study and excellence are stimulated by liberal prizes in beautiful medals and in gold awards. The President of the Faculty of the University of Virginia, Dr. Paul Barringer, has recently established a prize of $20 in gold, annually, for that member of the Senior Class making the highest scholarship during the year.

The William Wirt Roller scholarship of $500 has also been established recently by another friend of the college in Virginia.

The most valuable and helpful friend of the college in North Carolina is supporting a number of worthy students, paying all their expenses. Besides these valuable adjuncts and her valuable property in real estate, the college has an endowment of $34,000, with no debts, but many needs. With the inspiration of half a century of past history, the strong and fostering hands of her large host of alumni, a deep sense of the present and growing needs of higher education, and live sympathy with the work of the public schools of the State, and a spirit of hearty co-operation with her sister institutions, Catawba College is doing what she can to broaden and elevate the culture of the age and advance every noble effort to further the civilization, peace and happiness of our people and their highest spiritual interests.

NORTH CAROLINA COLLEGE.

North Carolina College is located at Mount Pleasant, Cabarrus County, nine miles east of Concord, in the midst of a most healthful and prosperous section of the country.

This institution was founded by the Evangelical Lutheran Synod of North Carolina, and has always been conducted under the auspices of that body. It was first opened in 1855, under the name of the Western Carolina Male Academy, and received a charter from the Legislature of the State January 21st, 1859, at which time the name was changed to North Carolina College. The school was kept up without interruption until the beginning of the war, during which the college was closed. A private school was carried on most of the time from 1861 to 1867; in the latter year the college was reopened, and has been in successful operation ever since.

Three handsome brick buildings occupy a beautiful site commanding the prospect of the town and surrounding country. The estimated value of the property is $15,000. The college is well provided with apparatus for illustrative purposes in the study of Chemistry and Physics. It possesses a library, which, together with those of the two Literary Societies, numbers about three thousand and five hundred volumes. There is also a reading-room, which is supplied with daily and weekly newspapers and with a number of the leading magazines.

Since 1871 fifty-nine young men have graduated from the institution, and have taken a good stand among the business and professional men of this and other States. The average annual attendance of students has been about seventy. Last session the total enrollment was seventy-five. During the history of the college over one thousand young men have been students within its halls; some for one, others for two or three years without completing the course. Many of these have become successful teachers in high schools and in the public schools of the State.

There are three courses of study offered, leading respectively to the degrees of A. B., B. S. and Ph. B. These courses include all the branches usually required for the same degrees, and the text-books are such as are in use in leading colleges of the country. Provision is made also for those who may wish to take a Commercial Course.

The Literary Societies, the Philalaethian and the Pi-Sigma-Phi., are active, and are a means of much improvement to the members.

Special attention is paid to the moral and religious culture of the students, and the local influences are of the most favorable.

The present faculty consists of the following: Rev. M. G. G. Scherer, A. M., President and Professor of Moral and Mental Science and History; Prof. H. T. J. Ludwig, A. M., Ph. D., Professor of Mathematics, Astronomy and Physics; Prof. Edgar Bowers, A. M., Professor of Ancient Languages and Literature, who also supplies the Chair of German and French; Prof. Geo. F. McAllister, A B., Principal of the Preparatory Department.

WEAVERVILLE COLLEGE.

Weaverville College, situated in the little town of Weaverville, in the northern part of Buncombe County, eight miles from the city of Asheville, is one of the oldest institutions in our State west of the Blue Ridge. For twenty-five years this institution has given instruction of a high order to the youth of both sexes. Its influence for good has been felt in hundreds of homes in Western North Carolina, and in parts of Tennessee. It numbers among its Alumni men of prominence in the pulpit, at home, and in foreign fields, at the bar (more than one Judge has received his college training at Weaverville), men of marked success in the mercantile world, and teachers and physicians of prominence.

The school was chartered by the Legislature of North Carolina in 1873. It is now under the full control of a board of trustees, twenty in number. The property belongs to the Western North Carolina Conference of the Methodist Episcopal Church, South, and is ultimately controlled by that body. It is now presided over by a member of this Conference, President George F. Kirby. Mr. Kirby is a young man, an Aluminus of Wofford College, of Spartanburg, S. C. He has with him a corps of five teachers, including music. The course is high, but not the highest. The following is the required course in Latin: Freshman year, Caesar, Sallust, Latin Prose, Composition, Grammar.

Sophomore year: Virgil, Cicero, Composition, Grammar.

Junior year: Horace, Livy, Juvenil, with Composition and Grammar.

The course is correspondingly high in all other branches.

The college has been remarkably successful during its whole history, enrolling more than two hundred preparatory and college students almost every year since its charter was granted. It is in a most healthful locality, "The Land of the Sky," and offers to all health, with education.

This institution has always been the friend and benefactor of the poor boy. Scores of them have been helped, and many have been educated without cost to themselves—such as ministers' sons and young ministers. To-day she offers peculiar advantages to those who must practice economy in the matter of education. All expenses may be reduced under one hundred dollars for the whole session of nine months.

For information, address the President, Rev. George F. Kirby, Weaverville, N. C.

CLAREMONT COLLEGE, HICKORY, N. C.

FACULTY.

STUART P. HATTON, A. M., PE. B., PRESIDENT,
(McGee College, Mo.; Mo. State University.)
English and Anglo-Saxon.

MRS. STUART P. HATTON, L. B., VICE-PRES.,
(Woodland Academy, Mo.; Mo. State University.)
Commercial Branches.

WM. C. CROSBY, A. M., L. I., DEAN OF NORMAL DEPT.,
(Grand River College. Mo.; Univ. of Nashville, Tenn.)
Latin and Greek.

LULA R. KAMMERER, A. B.,
(Western Female H. S. and Woman's College, Baltimore, Md.)
Science.

(To be supplied.)
German and French.

MOSES W. HATTON, A. M., PE. B.,
(McGee College, Mo.; Mo. State Univ.; Harvard Univ.)
Mathematics and Astronomy.

AGNES SHEARER,
(Huntersville High School; Claremont College, N. C.)
Assistant in Mathematics.

ANNIE L. PITTS, A. B.,
(Catawba H. S. and Claremont College, N. C.)
History.

ELIZABETH VAN WAGNEN,
(Omaha High School, Neb.; Bardstown Inst., Ky.)
Elocution and Physical Culture.

B. F. WHITESIDE, M. D.,
(University of Md.; Post-Graduate Medical School and Hospital, N. Y.)
College Physician; Lecturer on Physiology and Hygiene.

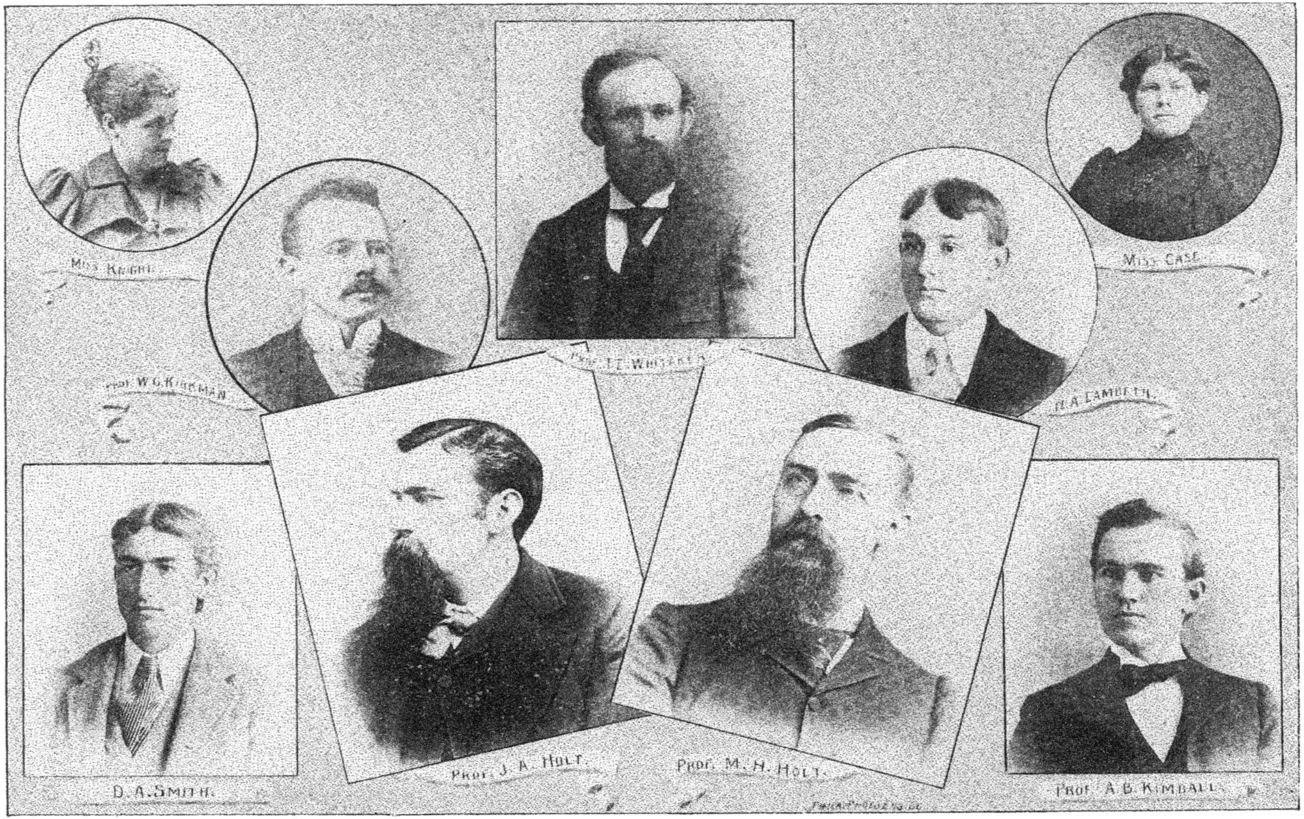
Miss Knight
Prof. W. G. Kirkman
H. A. Lambeth
Miss Case
D. A. Smith
Prof. J. A. Holt
Prof. M. H. Holt
Prof. A. B. Kimball

SCHOOL OF MUSIC AND ART.

JANIE E. PRICE, DIRECTOR,
(Johnson's Female College, W. Va.; Cincinnati Conservatory. Studied with Hugh A. Clark, Mus. Doc., Philadelphia.)
Piano, Harmony and History.

BURNIE DEARMOND,
(Huntersville High School, N. C.; Due West Female College, S. C.)
Piano.

LOIS SEAGLE,
(Claremont College, N. C.)
Piano.

EDWINA CHADWICK,
(Wellesly, Class of '80; studied with Mme. Edna Hall, Boston; Mme. Louise DuBarry, N. Y.; Mrs. Sumner Salter, N. Y.)
Voice.

ANTOINETTE EWING,
(Famous Mrs. Willard's Seminary, N. Y.)
Art.

ORGANIZATION.

Claremont College was organized as a college for the higehr education of young women in 1880. The same year it was chartered by the State Legislature and placed in the control of an independent board of trustees, who have since conducted it as a thoroughly Christian but non-sectarian school. It was the purpose of the founders to establish a college which would furnish the very best advantages for the higher education of women. This purpose has been kept constantly in view, and the institution, though it has had its struggles and varied success, has moved steadily forward until its permanent establishment among the leading colleges of the State and South.

THE BUILDINGS AND GROUNDS

Consist of a large three-story brick structure, situated in the middle of a beautiful campus of twenty acres. Also there are several out-buildings, such as barn, store-houses, bowling alley, etc., all conveniently arranged for the comfort of students.

THE AIM.

As stated in the charter, is to furnish the very best facilities for the higher education of women. To this end there are sustained ten courses of study: Classical (A. B.), Scientific (S. B.), Literary (L. B.), Normal (B. D.), Music, Art, Elocution, Shorthand and Typewriting, Business and Preparatory.

ADMINISTRATION.

During the eighteen years of our history six Presidents have served, in the following order: Rev. Vaughn, Mrs. A. G. Thurston, Mrs. E. C. Bonney, William Sanborne, Rev. J. L. Murphy and S. P. Hatton. At no time since its founding has the institution suspended work. The patronage and enrollment varied and even waned at times, but on the whole the institution moved steadily forward until it was permanently established and placed on a self-supporting basis. For a number of years the average attendance has been about 100. During the last administration this has been raised to 160, and the present enrollment (1898) promises a larger number. Last year there were in attendance students from every Southern State but four, also from Canada, and some of the Northern and Western States. The present faculty is composed of fourteen teachers from leading colleges, conservatories and universities. The school is looked upon as being permanently established, and has within the past few years entered upon a wonderful career of usefulness to the State.

Very respectfully,

S. P. HATTON, President.

Hickory, N. C., Sept. 28, 1898.

SALEM ACADEMY AND COLLEGE, SALEM, N. C.

FOUNDED 1802.

This institution is the oldest college for young women in the South, and was the third school for the higher education of young women established in the United States. It was originally planned to provide a school and home for the children of the many missionaries of the Moravian Church, and hence the plan of the school was much more homelike than is usually the case with schools. This strong combination of fine educational advantages, united with the special care given to the character and health of the pupils, has made the school a favorite one from the earliest times. It is very difficult, even in these days of many schools, to find an institution where the above points are guarded with the same care that is to be found in old Salem. Hence from the earliest times the patronage has been large, and the careful and painstaking training has fitted the pupils to fill some of the very highest positions in the land. In the White House, at Washington, in Governor's Mansions in the various States, in the homes of foreign representatives of our country, and in thousands of the homes in which order and the highest type of home is to be found, there you will find the former Salem pupils. The effort has always been to make the school a real home, and though much special effort is required, and also much extra expense, the school is well repaid in the large patronage it has always enjoyed, and the excellent results attained, to say nothing of the later love and friendship of the pupils.

The work done within the school at the present time consists of a four years' preporatory course, a four years' college course, and a post-graduate course. In addition to this there are first-class schools of Music, Art, Languages,

Elocution, Commercial and Industrial studies. All these departments are in the hands of specialists, and we may add that in the matter of music the institution has always stood very high, the number of pupils at times reaching three hundred or more in the study of music. There are thirty or more members of the faculty, and the attendance of pupils varies from three to four hundred, acording to the register of the past years. The situation is ideal for a school. The buildings are large and comfortable, the front is near the main street of the town, but just back of the buildings the school has a park of thirty acres that is one of the most romantic spots imaginable. The attendance is drawn from almost every State in the Union and many foreign countries, there being twenty-four States and foreign lands represented last year.

During the Civil War the school was a safe place of refuge for hundreds of girls, and, although both armies passed through the town, the most careful measures were taken to protect this large number of precious young lives.

It is the reproach of modern education in many cases that the work done is superficial. As it was the work of this, our oldest institution, to champion the higher education of the young women, when there was no education to be obtained elsewhere, so in our day when there is much that is not as it ought to be in some schools, this Moravian institution clings firmly to the thoroughness of its work, and a pupil who takes a course in the school is usually not only strong in mind and thoroughly trained in intellect, but she also has those beautiful graces of character which go to make up the happy home, and, we may add, the leadership in the community in which she lives. In addition to these things the health of the body has the most careful and interested attention.

In concluding this brief sketch we desire to call attention to the very high standard of womanhood that has

HOME INDUSTRIAL SCHOOL, ASHEVILLE, N. C.

always existed in the South. That the type of Southern women has challenged the world. When we remember the fact that the daughters of very many of the leading families of the entire South have been educated in this venerable institution, and that, too, for three, and even four generations, and when we remember furthermore that from ten to twelve thousand of the very ladies of the land have received their education in the midst of the surroundings described above, who can estimate the influence this school has had on the high standard of womanhood in the South, who can begin to say how far and wide the influence of the institution has gone, or how much the South owes to this venerable but stil active, energetic, and prosperous college.

JOHN H. CLEWELL, Principal.

ASHEVILLE NORMAL AND COLLEGIATE INSTITUTE.

This institution has been established by friends of higher education for young women, and is under the efficient control of the Woman's Board of the Northern Presbyterian Church.

Its admirable site of some thirty-three acres, which it shares with the Home Industrial School, under the same management, forms the most delightful suburb of the famous Mountain City. The imposing and spacious building which it occupies can easily be made to furnish accommodations for 225 pupils, in the construction and furnishing of which reference was constantly had to the health and comfort of the students. It is heated with steam, lighted with gas, furnished with hot and cold baths, and abundantly supplied with pure water from springs on the premises. No pains or expense has been spared to make the sanitary arrangements as perfect as possible.

The furniture is simple and substantial. The health and habits of the pupils are carefully guarded. Abundant space for out-door exercise is found within the grounds, and a well-arranged gymnasium has been fitted up within the building.

As in the case of the famous Mt. Holyoke, School, and Mr. Moody's, at Northfield, all pupils are expected to share in the domestic work of the household under the supervision of the Matron. This occupies ordinarily not more than one hour a day; the time so spent is found conducive to health, the developments of character, and is an admirable preparation for the duties of after life.

The aim of the institution is to furnish solid and thorough training, under teachers competent and qualified to use the best modern methods.

It has provided—

1. A Normal Department for the thorough training of teachers, under instructors from the best Normal Schools in the country, embracing careful instruction in the most improved methods of teaching with practice in the model school.

2. A Musical Department, in which class instruction in the theory and history of music, sight reading, chorus, and choir singing, is furnished, without extra charge, and single lessons in vocal and instrumental music are given at reasonable rates by thoroughly trained and experienced teachers.

3. A fully organized Commercial Department for the preparation of young women for office work, embracing Stenography, Typewriting, Bookkeeping (single and double entry), Penmanship, Commercial Arithmetic and Correspondence. The head of this department is an accomplished teacher with large experience.

4. A Department in Domestic Science, (a) in which the pupil is taught to draught, cut, fit, make garments and millinery; (b) to prepare a meal which shall be healthful, ecomomic and appetizing. The teachers in these departments are from Pratt Institute, Brooklyn, N. Y.

A specialty is made of health culture under one of the best teachers in the South.

By special enactment of the Legislature of North Carolina, graduates from the Normal Department are exempted from examination when applying for positions in the public schools of the State.

The cost of the pupil has been reduced to the lowest practicable limit, that the advantages offered may be within the reach of the largest number, especially those who may be desirous of becoming teachers, with all others who may find it impossible to avail themselves of like privileges in connection with more expensive institutions. Whilst aiming at the utmost thoroughness in every department of study, the management never loses sight of the fact that the Institute is pre-eminently a Christian school, and its paramount object the development of Christian character. The Bible is a text-book in every department, and its daily study is obligatory upon every pupil.

Since the opening of the school, in the fall of 1892, there has been a steady increase each year in the number of students. During the session of 1897-'98, 230 have been enrolled, about 200 of them being boarders.

The success of the Institute has far more than justified the expectations of its founders and it is fast being recognized as one of the most beneficent institutions of the State.

FACULTY.

REV. THOMAS LAWRENCE, D. D., PRESIDENT,
(Western University of Pennsylvania; Bonn University, Germany.)
Evidences of Christianity and Bible Study.

MRS. THOMAS LAWRENCE,
(Graves Seminary, New York.)
Principal and Treasurer.

MISS MARY L. MATTOON, ASSOCIATE PRINCIPAL,
(Elmira College, New York.)
Psychology, History and Physical Culture.

MISS MINNIE B. WOODWORTH,
(Syracuse, New York.)
Latin, Language and Literature.

MISS MABEL K. DIXON,
(State Normal School, Potsdam, N. Y.)
Mathematics and Normal Methods.

MISS MINNIE E. JOY,
(State Normal School, Potsdam, N. Y.)
Natural Sciences.

MISS ALICE N. WIGHTMAN,
(Oberlin University, Ohio.)
English.

CATAWBA COLLEGE, NEWTON, N. C.

MISS ETHELYN HARPER,
(State Normal School, Potsdam, N. Y.)
Preparatory Department.

MISS MAUDE MARY MORGAN,
(Crane Normal Institute of Music, Potsdam, N. Y.)
Instrumental and Vocal Music.

MISS ISABEL K. HUBBARD,
(Metropolitan College of Music, New York City.)
Instrumental Music and Drawing.

MISS KATHARINE J. MECHLING,
(Groves College, Pennsylvania.)
Stenography, Typewriting, Bookkeeping and Penmanship.

MISS ELLA HUBBARD,
(Pratt Institute, Brooklyn, N. Y.)
Sewing, Dressmaking and Millinery.

MISS ELLA BICKERSTAFF,
(Pratt Institute, Brooklyn, N. Y.)
Scientific Cooking.

MISS M. ELIZABETH GIST, MATRON.

MISS LYDA MECHLING, ASSISTANT MATRON.

SHAW UNIVERSITY.

Shaw University, named in honor of the late Elijah Shaw, of Wales, Mass., is situated in Raleigh, the capital city of North Carolina. It has a beautiful location, within the city limits, and is only a few minutes' walk from the Union station, the capitol, and the United States government building.

Although within the city limits, it has an entire square to itself, and is as quiet and secluded as if it were situated miles away in the country. This quiet and seclusion, together with a bountiful supply of pure water, perfect sanitation and sewerage and other city advantages, make Shaw well-nigh an ideal place for study. Its grounds are spacious and well kept, and its principal buildings large, imposing brick structures. Its buildings (eleven in number) and grounds are the most attractive feature in the southern part of the city.

A HUMBLE ORIGIN.

This institution was started in a very humble way in a negro cabin on the outskirts of the city, in the year 1865, by Rev. Henry Martin Tupper, an ex-Union soldier and a native of Monson, Mass. The enterprise grew on his hands and a larger building became necessary, but there was little money either for carrying on or extending the work. Accordingly, with a few faithful helpers, day after day he shouldered his axe and went out of the city into the woods, and together they felled huge yellow pines and hewed the logs into timber. After many weeks of struggling, and after receiving a little help from the North, the actual work of building began. A large two-story structure, to be used both for a church and a school, was finally erected on Blount street, a block north of the present location of the University.

The work continued to grow, and again larger quarters were required. At this juncture the mansion and grounds of the late General Barringer, ex-Minister to Spain, were for sale. This property, comprising several buildings and twelve acres of land, and occupying an entire square, was purchased, and then began the great expansion that has made the institution what it is to-day. Shaw was incorporated in 1875. At this time the work was more elementary than now, but such as was adapted to the needs of the people. The management, however, has kept pace constantly with the progress of the race and the demands of the times, until there are to-day, in addition to Normal, College, Missionary Training and Industrial departments, Schools of Law, Medicine and Pharmacy.

AN EDUCATED MINISTRY.

A goodly number of our young men, as has been the case from the founding of the institution, are studying for the ministry. Shaw has furnished nearly all the denominational leaders in North Carolina and many in other States. In the gospel ministry her greatest influence has been exerted, for her Theological Department has always been well attended, and the minister is still the influential factor in directing the life of the great mass of colored people in every community.

Nearly all the leading ministers of the denomination in the State were educated wholly or in part at Shaw. It is an interesting fact that a few months ago, when there was trouble in the eastern section of the city of Raleigh between some white United States soldiers and colored residents, the Mayor of the city, Hon. W. M. Russ, came down to Shaw and got Rev. A. W. Pegues, Ph. D., a colored man of culture and refinement, the Dean of our Theological Department, to go out to the scene of the trouble and assist in quieting the disturbance.

AN EDUCATED LAITY.

Many of her former students are thrifty farmers, successful business men, and occupy positions of honor and trust in their respective counties. The aim of the institution, from the very beginning, has been to turn out well-equipped Christian men and women, who shall be leaders in the best sense of the term, and thus, indirectly but effectually, reach the great masses of the people. This has been done with signal and gratifying success.

LAW, MEDICINE AND PHARMACY.

Graduates of our Law Department go into court and plead their cases with the same courteous treatment from judge and jury as is accorded to white members of the bar.

Success has also been won by the graduates in Medicine and Pharmacy, and they are found very generally throughout the Southland. A graduate in pharmacy, A. W. Benson, of Atlanta, Class of '95, was the first colored man to obtain a license from the Virginia Board of Examiners. His standing in examination was slightly in excess of 95 per cent. The first man of any race to receive 100 per cent. in an examination before the Virginia Board of Medical Examiners was C. R. Alexander, of Lynchburg, Class of 1891.

CO-EDUCATION.

Shaw believes in co-education. Men and women meet in the class-room, in the chapel and around the family board, on terms of equality. The women's department is known as Estey Seminary. Estey Hall, the gift of the late Deacon Estey, of Brattleboro, Vt., is said to be the first building ever erected for the education of colored women. It was predicted that co-education would be a dismal and disgusting failure, but it should be said to the great credit of the race that there never has been a scandal connected with the institution. It gives me much pleasure to state that, after nearly a quarter of a century spent in educational work among white young men and women, Indian young men and women, and colored young men and women, I have found it as easy to maintain good discipline and proper relations here between the sexes as I have in other fields with the other two races.

A WORLD-WIDE INFLUENCE.

The influence exerted by Shaw is well-nigh world-wide. At the present time she has students from the West Indies and Africa, and has enrolled them from Central and South America. Although a Home Mission School, her spirit reaches out to other lands. Missionary Hayes, the well-known African missionary, was a Shaw student. Dr. Lulu C. Fleming and four others from Shaw are in missionary work on the Congo.

CONSERVATION OF LAW AND ORDER.

It is worthy of note that Shaw men and women do not become criminals, and seldom, if ever, do educated colored young men and women belong to the criminal or lawless classes. Rather are they conservators of law and order and preservers of the peace. Our students and graduates are, as a rule, Christian men and women, of clean lives, and some of them are earnest workers in the cause of temperance and social purity. Deplorable, indeed, would be the condition of the freedmen and their descendants only a generation from actual slavery, were it not for these stalwart men and pure women now found in nearly every community, who, by their example and precept, show the possibilities of the race, and exert such a strong, controlling influence for good over ignorant and less favored members of the race.

LIVINGSTONE COLLEGE.

Among the evidences of negro ability to establish and control great institutions, we have no better example than Livingstone College. In a quiet, antiquated-looking town of historic connection with those stirring times of our American Revolution, and with those more than stirring times of our country's civil strife, in the town of Salisbury, N. C., is Livingstone College, the pride of a great church, an honor to the negro race. This institution stands as a towering monument to the heroes of that bloody struggle whose lives were lost for their country's sake and to make an enslaved people free.

The Ecumenical Conference of the Methodist Church was held in England in May, 1881. Bishop J. W. Hood, D. D., who was President of the Board of Trustees of what was then known as Zion Wesley Institute, and Rev. J. C. Price, with other representatives of the A. M. E. Zion Church, were in attendance.

Bishop Hood, recognizing the ability of Dr. Price, who was then a young man, just out of school, prevailed upon him to become an agent for the school and to remain in England after the close of the Conference.

During the Conference Dr. Price made himself famous among the delegates and visitors as an eloquent orator, and after its close had no trouble in getting before the English people, who welcomed him everywhere and responded to his appeals in a sum amounting to $9,100. This, of course, was great encouragement to the trustees and the church. The congregation of the Zion Church in Concord, where the school started in 1879, offered seven acres of land for a site to erect buildings and locate the school permanently. But the trustees of the Institute decided that Salisbury would be a more favorable place, and the school was located in that city.

It was in the spring of 1882 that Bishops Hood and Lomax, with $3,000 of the money raised by Professor Price in England and $1,000 donated by the business men of Salisbury, purchased the site now occupied by Livingstone College. There was on the place one two-story building, with ten rooms, including basement. The tract of land consisted of forty acres, and the total cost of the place amounted to $4,600.

The Board of Bishops, at the meeting in Chester, S. C., in September, 1882, adopted Zion Wesley Institute as a connectional school, electing a faculty with Rev. J. C. Price, President; Rev. C. R. Harris, Prof. C. R. Harris, Prof. E. Moore, instructors; Mrs. M. E. Harris as Matron. Up to this time it had been under the auspices of the North Carolina Conference.

October 9, 1882, the Institute was opened on its own premises in Salisbury. The name was soon changed to Zion Wesley College, and in 1886 or 1887 it became Livingstone College, in honor of the great African explorer, David Livingstone.

When the second session began, another teacher was added, this being necessary because the President was required to travel and solicit donations. Dr. W. H. Goler, a personal friend and college-mate of the President, was the teacher added. The institution was very much strengthened by this new addition, for, besides the literary advantages to the school, the business tact of Dr. Goler, as well as his practical knowledge along certain industrial lines, made the addition very valuable.

In the middle of the second session, when the number of students reached 120, the building for boys was taken for girls, and rented houses in the community were provided for the boys. This meant to the young men inconvenience and a sacrifice of comfortable quarters, but they were in full sympathy with the school and its struggles, and bore the hardships without a murmur. These days are often referred to as the "Dark Days" of Livingstone College for both teachers and students. Then it was that some of the teachers were laboring without knowing wnat they would receive for salary, and Dr. Goler often says "he never received a penny during his first year's work."

The faithful discharge of duty by Prof. Moore, Prof. Harris (now Bishop Harris), Mrs. Harris, as matron, and Prof. Goler, was of incalculable value to the President in these struggling years of the school for existence.

In 1884 an addition (42x56) was made to the original ten-room house, for a chapel, a dining-room and dormitories for girls. Mr. C. P. Huntington was the chief donor, and the building, "Huntington Hall," is named for him. The dimensions of the building are 91x38. It is four stories high, including basement.

In the fall of 1885 the necessity for more buildings caused Dr. Price to visit the Pacific coast. After lecturing about four months, he secured the donation of $5,000 from the late Senator Leland Stanford and $1,000 from Mrs. Mark Hopkins. The entire amount collected by Dr. Price on the coast was about $9,000. Only a little over $1,000 was needed to make up the sum of $20,000. The Hon. William E. Dodge, who had assisted Mr. Price through school, promised him a donation of $5,000 if he should raise that sum. Mr. Price lost no time in securing the residue and Mr. Dodge kept his word.

In 1887 Mr. Stephen Ballard, of New York, erected the Ballard Industrial Hall (60x39) and fitted it up with complete outfits for the departments of Carpentry, Shoemaking and Printing. The industrial feature has not been neglected, although recently the school has not been able to do as much as formerly. The reason for this has been the withdrawal of the Slater Fund. However, this department has been operating with such means as the officers have been able to obtain. The students in the carpentry shop make and repair all the furniture used in the school, such

AGRICULTURAL AND MECHANICAL COLLEGE (COLORED), GREENSBORO, N. C.

as bedsteads, chairs, tables, desks, washstands and dressers. The printing office is well-equipped, and much minute and pamphlet work has been done, besides publishing the College journal. The institution has been running but little over a decade. It boasts, however, of a prominence equal to any institution in the South founded and sustained by colored men. The character of its graduates and the showing they have made bespeak the thoroughness of its work. In fact, the officers of the institution, while recognizing the need and the cry for the industrial training of the negro, have stoutly maintained that industrial education should not supplant the higher development of the negro. The success of the 160 graduates since 1885 has been sufficient argument for them to hold this point.

The death of Dr. Price occurred October 25, 1893. To him directly is due the permanent establishment of the institution.

Dr. W. H. Goler, the new President, took charge with a vim that delighted all. His ability, his friendship for and acquaintance with Dr. Price, and his experience, give him a confidence that makes success doubly sure.

During the past five or six years the school has averaged an enrollment of over 200. The enrollment one year was about 300. Students representing New England, Michigan, Missouri, Kentucky, Illinois and all the States along the coast, from Massachusetts to Florida, as well as Alabama, Mississippi, Louisiana, Arkansas and Tennessee, have been enrolled. Besides these, representatives of Liberia, west coast of Africa and the West Indies are among the number.

The death of Dr. Price was a great blow to Livingstone. Its friends were thrown into a state of anxiety for its future. But many believed that Price's work was accomplished when he demonstrated to the world his practical production of his great lecture, "Negro Capabilities." When Livingstone started, the world had not learned that a college could be established and controlled entirely by negroes.

The school is the argument and the proof. Price is gone, but the school is going on, and it is doing nobly and well its part in swelling the stream of workers for God and humanity.

SCOTIA SEMINARY.

Some time during the year 1866 Rev. Dr. Logan, Secretary of the Freedmen's Committee of the Northern General Assembly, visited Concord ,and the conclusion reached was that this was a good place for a girls' school.

In January, 1867, Rev. Luke Dorland and his wife reached this place, and settled down to stay and grow old in their work. No one now can realize how much of moral courage and patience it took to lay these foundations in those times, when sectional feeling was so bitter. A few months previous a parochial school had been started in anticipation of their coming. Soon after this a church was organized. Probably the first building erected was that known as the Manse, then close by No. 1.

In 1870 letters-patent were issued by the Governor of the State and the parochial school became a seminary. The first seminary building was the aforesaid No. 1, a one-story building, 20x22 feet. During this year a two-story building, 24x40 feet, was put up, of which Dr. Dorland said: "I have handled nearly every stick of it myself."

In 1876 the first brick building was begun, the front of what we call the old building. It might well be called Morris Hall, in memory of Rev. Mr. Morris, of Pennsylvania, one of the most liberal friends the Seminary ever had, to whom also we are largely indebted for money to pay for the church erected in 1880 and 1881. The name "Scotia" was the choice of Matthew Scott, of Ohio, one of the first to come to the support of our cause. Having made a liberal gift, he was asked to find a name for the infant. He modestly preferred to have it bear the name of his native land, rather than his own.

In 1881 and 1882 the stem was added, completing the T, almost the entire expense being met by a gift of eight thousand dollars sent by E. A. Graves, Esq., of New Jersey, whose name is placed over the parlor, from the estate of his deceased brother, Augustus Graves, for whom the addition is named.

In 1885 the two-and-a-half-story frame building was erected for the use of the Industrial Department, which was since moved, and now serves the purpose of a music hall.

In the spring of 1890 Mrs. Satterfield visited Cincinnati, Ohio, and sopke before a meeting of the ladies there in the interest of the enlargement of the work. A committee was appointed soon afterward by the Home Missionary Society of the Presbytery of Cincinnati to raise funds for this purpose, of which Mrs. Sidney D. Maxwell was appointed president. Rev. Dr. J. J. Francis was requested to act as corresponding secretary. On Commencement Day, 1891, the corner-stone of the new building was laid by Mrs. Maxwell, who gave to it the name "Faith Hall." It was completed and ready by November 15, and by December 1 was full. The expense for the improvement—about $22,-000—was met without drawing anything from the treasury of the Board. About $16,000 was raised by the committee in Cincinnati.

The chapel was named in honor of Mr. Duncan Mackay, of Morristown, Ill., whose bequest of $2,000 came while we were building. The heating plant of the two buildings was paid for out of the bequest of Wm. F. Childs, of Niagara Falls, received August, 1888, amounting to $5,000.

When Dr. Dorland retired in 1886, he estimated the expense for land and improvements at $35,750. Not less than $25,000 have been added since.

In its first year the Seminary enrolled forty-five, twelve of whom were boarders in the little 20x22 house. The first class graduated in '76, a class of nine, in what was then the teacher's course, now the grammar school. The total enrollment to date is 2,078. The number having completed the grammar school course is 346, while 64 have taken a higher course. Of these graduates, some are teaching, some filling woman's highest sphere and doing her noblest work—home-making; some are in Heaven; some are helping Scotia by sending us their children; one has already completed a full course in the Missionary Training School in Chicago; one a course in kindergarten work in Philadelphia; two have taken the nurses' training in Boston; two have taken the full medical course in Philadelphia. And of nearly all it can be said without boasting, they are, in a quiet way, bringing the light into dark places and helping to make the world better, their associates happier, and to reflect honor on their Alma Mater and their Master.

In 1886 Rev. Dr. Dorland resigned. Since that time the Seminary has been under the care of Rev. D. J. Satterfield, D. D., and his wife. The present faculty consists of the President, Principal and thirteen associate teachers. The average enrollment is about 280.

HIGH SCHOOLS AND ACADEMIES.

THE BINGHAM SCHOOL—ITS PAST, ITS PRESENT, ITS FUTURE.

The Bingham School was founded in 1793 by the Rev. William Bingham, the grandfather of Robert Bingham, its present headmaster, and was temporarily located at six places in Eastern and Middle North Carolina before its permanent site, near Asheville, was secured and developed. It is the oldest school for boys in the Southern States, is older than any other Southern institution of learning of any grade south of Virginia, and is the only chartered institution of learning, of any grade in the United States, which has been handed down from grandfather to grandson during a period of more than a hundred (100) years with no break in its continuity of superintendence, methods, discipline, and instruction, never "removing the ancient landmarks" except for the acquisition of valuable territory, always preserving the old, when the old, like "the old wine" of the Scriptures, "was better," and always adopting the new when the new increased power or reduced friction.

THE REV. WILLIAM BINGHAM.

The Rev. William Bingham, a native of County Down, Ireland, and a Scotch-Irish Presbyterian, was the first headmaster of the Bingham School. He was a first honor graduate of the University of Glasgow and was regularly educated for the Church. But his family becoming involved in one of the many unsuccessful efforts for Irish independence, he, with several of his uncles, sought safety in America. All his uncles but one settled in the Northern States and became the progenitors of the Binghams of New York and Ohio. But before William Bingham left Ireland, he had made an engagement to take charge of a school in Wilmington, N. C., and this made New Hanover County the first location, and the Rev. William Bingham the first headmaster, of what was then Bingham's, and is now The Bingham School. After teaching in Wilmington for several years, he moved his school to Pittsboro', in Chatham County, and after a brief connection with the University as Professor of Ancient Languages, he resumed his work of administering a school for boys, first in Pittsboro', then in Hillsboro', in Orange County, and spent the last years of his life teaching boys at "Mt. Repose," a point in the country, ten miles northwest of Hillsboro', where, says Prof. C. L. Raper, of the Greensboro' Female College, in his History of the "Church and Private Schools of North Carolina," (1898), "he instructed the youth as few others have instructed them, and long before his death he had won a great name for himself as a scholar and as a teacher, and for his school as a place where true manhood was developed and cultured." He founded the school in 1793 and died in February, 1825, after having conducted it for thirty-two (32) years.

W. J. BINGHAM, THE SCHOOL'S SECOND HEAD-MASTER.

At the death of the Rev. William Bingham, in February, 1825, his eldest son, William J. Bingham, who was studying law with Judge Murphy, the most distinguished jurist of the State in his day, abandoned his legal studies, temporarily as he thought, and took charge of his father's school, expecting to complete only the unexpired session; but he was its headmaster for forty (40) years. After teaching for a short time at "Mt. Repose," he moved the school back to Hillsboro', where he made a reputation hardly equaled by that of any other master of a school in the

South before him, and hardly possible for any one after him. In those days teaching boys was a very unusual employment for a gentleman and a scholar, unless he was a preacher as well. The schoolmaster of literature was a Dominie Sampson or a Squeers, and the schoolmaster of fact was generally overworked and underpaid, and did much more for others than he did for himself. There were no public schools at that time. There were very few private schools, except of a merely local character, and W. J. Bingham occupied an almost unoccupied field and occupied it in such a way as often to have been called the "Napoleon of Schoolmasters." His reputation brought him boys from distant States at a time when a hundred miles was a three days' journey, and his success as a teacher and trainer of good boys, and as a conqueror of bad ones was phenominal. But after twenty (20) years of work with a hundred pupils a year in a town, he grew weary and sought the country, where he might enjoy his fondness for farming, and where, by reducing his number to thirty (30), he might pick his pupils. He accordingly moved his school, a second time, to "Oaks," a point in the country, twelve miles southwest of Hillsboro', where he conducted it till January, 1865. When he reduced his numbers, as a compensation he more than doubled his rates of tuition; and so great was the desire of parents of that day to get the benefit of his training for their sons that often places had to be engaged five years ahead, and for years he refused ten applicants for each of the thirty places in his school, conditions which can hardly occur again.

Prof. Charles L. Raper, in his book on The Church and Private Schools of North Carolina, already quoted, speaks of him as follows:

"William James Bingham was the second and the greatest of all the Principals (of the School). He lived at a time which gave remarkable opportunities in his line, and he added remarkable ability. When he began, teaching

was rather in disrepute; but he raised it to a high and honorable calling. He increased tuition fees from twenty ($20) to one hundred and fifty dollars ($150.) per year. After he moved to Oaks he limited his school to thirty (30) students and it had such a reputation all over the country that he had to refuse admission to three hundred applicants in a single year. Walter P. Williamson, editor of the Tarboro' Southerner, on page 372, of Vol 2, of Our Living and Our Dead, says: "His success was pre-eminent and his reputation, though less brilliant than that of some of his contemporaries, was more extensive than that of any of the men of his day; and while he was a stern and rigid disciplinarian, I may say truly, though upon the testimony of others, that his pupils loved him like a father and trusted him as a tender and sympathetic friend. I venture to say that he was the means of putting more teachers upon the rostrum, more professional men into the various professions, more preachers into the pulpit, and more missionaries into the field than any ten other men in the State. He died Febreuary 19th, 1865, and his death removed one of the most striking personalties and unique teachers this State has ever produced."

THE SCHOOL OF W. J. BINGHAM & SONS.

In 1857 W. J. Bingham associated his two sons William and Robert with him, they having graduated from the University with first distinction, and the business was conducted as W. J. Bingham and Sons' School.

Prof. Raper speaks of this period in his History of Schools already quoted, as follows: "They (that is, the new firm) increased their facilities to a large extent, and under them the number was limited to sixty (60). Their method of instruction was of the very highest grade. The father had the beginning classes and the sons did the upper and advanced work. Those were the days when this school stood unequaled in the State and in the whole South. For a good many years two-thirds of all the first honor graduates of the State University were prepared at Bingham's.

The first class that left them under the name of W. J. Bingham & Sons was composed of five. Of these, four took first honors at the University, and the fitth took second honors. There were more than eighty members of this class at the University ,and besides the four from Bingham but one took first honors, and he was from Horner's, whose founder was Jas. H. Horner, a pupil of W. J. Bingham."

Early in 1861 the military feature was introduced by the younger Binghams with the entire approval of their father, was administered by William Bingham till his death, with a high and constantly increasing estimate of its value on his part, and it has been a potent factor in the conduct of the school from 1861 to the present day.

Soon after the Civil War began, Robert Bingham raised a company and joined the Confederate army and was one of Gen. Lee's seven thousand five hundred armed men at Appomattox Court House; but by an agreement with the other partners, his place in the school was reserved for him as a partner in it during the whole period of this absence. Early in 1862 William Bingham Lynch, a nephew of the headmaster, resigned his position as Professor of Greek in Davidson College and became a partner in the school and remained with it till his withdrawel in 1879 to establish a school of his own at High Point, and later in Florida, where he occupies a very high position as a man and as an educator.

THE INCORPORATION OF THE SCHOOL.

In December, 1864, a thirty years' charter for a Military School was obtained from the State Legislature in the name of William Bingham, and those who might be associated with him, which took effect March 1st, 1865; and the other members of the corporation having died or withdrawn, the charter was renewed by Robert Bingham and those who might be associated with him, and took effect in February, 1895, by which renewal the legal continuity of the Bingham School, as a corporation, is perpetuated till 1925. Under the charter of 1865 the school of W. J. Bingham & Sons was merged into the Bingham School. The teachers were commissioned by the State, the Superintendent with the rank of Colonel, and the other teachers with the rank of Major, and were exempted from conscription as officers in the State militia. The cadets were armed by the State, and were exempted from conscription up to the age of 18; but teachers and pupils were subject to being called into active service by the Governor, and they were called out once in the spring of 1865 to assist in repelling Stoneman's raid. Under these circumstances William Bingham deemed it necessary that the Commandant of Cadets should have had military experience in actual service, and he urged Robert Bingham to resign his captaincy in Lee's army and accept the promotion as Major Commandant of the Bingham School Cadets. Robert Bingham declined, however, to leave the Army under any conditions while he could do duty at the front; but it was agreed by all the parties concerned that he should resume his work in the school if he should be disabled in the service, or in any case, after the war should end, which latter he accordingly did.

WILLIAM BINGHAM'S SUPERINTENDENCY.

In January, 1865, William Bingham moved the school from Oaks to its sixth temporary location, at Mebane, and opened it under its charter as a Military School, where he administered it till Feburary, 1872, when, his health failing, Robert Bingham took charge of it as Acting Superintendent, and became Superintendent at his brother's death in February, 1873. William Bingham's superintendency was the shortest in the history of the school, and he divided his energies more than any other headmaster of the school has ever done. He was a very gifted and a very versatile man. He showed talents of a high order as a teacher, as a disciplinarian and as an administrator of the school during the difficult period of the Civil War, when, though ably supported by W. B. Lynch, his fathers' failing health, and his brother's absence in the army greatly increased his responsibilities. He was disqualified for service at the front by the condition of his health; but he did efficient and often dangerous duty at home as Colonel in the State Militia and head of the local police force. In addition to these exacting duties, he spent much of his time during the war and in the difficult period immediately succeeding the war, on the preparation of his text books, through which he acquired a national reputation, while those who knew him best regarded his power as a speaker, which he was often called upon to exercise, on political, religious and literary subjects, as perhaps his chief talent. By his early death, before his sun had reached high noon, the teaching profession lost one of its greatest ornaments, the South one of its most successful authors, the Church one of its efficient leaders and the State one of its best and purest citizens.

Prof. Raper speaks of William Bingham as follows: "William Bingham, the third Principal, was born in 1835 and died in 1873. He took his A. B. from the University in 1856. He was of very delicate health and hence did not do active service in the field of war. He was equally great as a teacher, public speaker, and author of text books. His Latin texts have received the greatest praise. They at one time were used in every State in the Union, especially in the South and West. They were perhaps more extensively used than the works of any other Southern author. He was also the author of an English Grammar. The School was moved (in his hands) from Oaks to Mebane in 1865, where it remained till its removal to Asheville in 1891. It was placed under Military control about 1865 and has so remained. The Principal was given the title and rank of Colonel by the State.

ROBERT BINGHAM'S SUPERINTENDENCY, AND THE SCHOOL IN HIS HANDS.

At William Bingham's death in 1873, Robert Bingham, who had been connected with the School continuously since 1857, took charge of it and was soon thereafter commissioned by the State as Colonel and Superintendent, and since the withdrawal of W. B. Lynch in 1879 he has been its sole corporator and owner under its original and renewed charter. He has given his undivided time and attention to it, has expended more money on its equipment than all his predecessors combined, in his hands it has reached its greatest numerical, financial, territorial and educational expansion, and his income from it has been greater from about 1878 to the present time than that of any other headmaster of a private school in the South, as far as has been ascertained; and from being patronized from the Southern States only, it has attained a national repute and has had an occasional pupil from outside of the United States. The United States Government Bureau of Education in Washington, the highest authority in America on such a subject, speaks very clearly on this point, as follows on pages 131 and 132 of its official "History of Education in North Carolina," issued from the Government Printing Office in 1888, fifteen years after Robert Bingham's superintendency began:

"The Bingham School," says the United States Government's Report, referred to above, "stands pre-eminent among Southern schools for boys, and ranks with the best in the Unin. It is the oldest and the most successful male boarding school for secondary instruction in the South, and for the past five years it has been second to no institution of similar character in the area of patronage. The Bingham School has reached its greatest efficiency under the present Superintendent, Maj. Robert Bingham."

This is only as it should be. When Sir Isaac Newton was asked why he saw farther into the secrets of nature than other men, he replied: "Because I stand upon the shoulders of giants." Robert Bingham had the achievement of his distinguished predecessors behind him; and he has given his undivided energies to the work, maintaining what they had attained and of adding to it. When the School came into his hands in 1873, it had only about thirty-five (35) tuition fees, from seven (7) States, and it had attracted pupils from only about twelve (12) States in the eighty (80) years of its previous history. During the twenty five (25) years of Robert Bingham's superintendency its patronage has extended to thirty three (33) States in the Union, from New Hampshire, Wisconsin and California on the North, to Florida, Texas and Arizona on the South; it has had an occasional pupil from Mexico and Brazil in the Western Hemisphere, and from England, Scotland, Germany, Greece, Siam and Japan in the Eastern Hemisphere, and it is attracting more paying pupils to North Carolina from other States for education than all the other institutions of learning of all grades in the State for males combined.

THE DEPARTMENTS OF INSTRUCTION IN 1873 AND IN 1898.

To the departments of instruction existing in 1873 have been added the School of German, the School of French, the School of Chemistry, the School of Physics, the School of Gymnastic, the School of Military Science and Tactics, and English, which had not been much stressed anywhere up to 1873, has been expanded and placed on an equality with the other Schools of Instruction.

THE MILITARY WORK OF THE SCHOOL SINCE 1873.

When Robert Bingham took charge of the school in 1873, the cadets composed but one company, were armed with muzzle-loading guns and were dressed in round jackets. In Robert Bingham's hands the muzzle-loading guns were soon replaced by breech-loaders, the West Point uniform was adopted by permission of the Secretary of War, and the single company became a fine Battalion, which was spoken of (at one of its usual visits to the State Fair) in the Raleigh Observer of Oct. 19th, 1879, over his signature by Lieut. E. E. Gayle, U. S. Army, himself a graduate of West Point, as follows: "I was astonished at the manoeuvers of the Bingham School Battalion today. Their appearance was magnificent; their drill in the manual of arms, in the field movements, in the skirmish, was superb, and their volley firing was most excellent. I feel safe in saying that the West Point Cadets have never done better. Nothing can be said except in praise of the military excellence of this cadet corps in all respects, and their conduct and general bearing at all times while in the city indicate a high moral training which should be more gratifying to the teachers, and which is more valuable to the cadets, than even such unusual military skill."

(Signed) E. E. GAYLE, 2nd Lieut., 2nd Art. U. S. A.

When the act of Congress detailing army officers as Professors of Military Science and Tactics at Colleges and Schools was passed, the Bingham School was chosen as one of the original thirty in the Union to have a detailed officer. Since that time the military work has been done by the United States Government, and the Army Inspectors who visit the School yearly rank it as one of the best four or five among the hundred in the Union now having details. Gen. (then Col. and Inspector Gen.) W. H. Lawton reports as follows to the Secretary of War, after his official inspection in 1892, in the Annual Report of the Inspector General, U. S. Army, page 273. "Its (the Bingham School's) reputation is that of one of the best military schools in the South. The discipline is to be commended. The service in the mess hall is excellent; the Gymnasium is a model of all particulars. The inspection was most satisfactory in all particulars.

(Signed) W. H. LAWTON,
Lieut. Col. and Inspector Gen. U. S. Army.

And at the outbreak of the Spanish war, when 155 additional lieutenants were taken from civil life for the expanded U. S. Army, three (3) were selected from the graduates of the Bingham School, over more than 7,000 applicants for the appointments, while no other school with a detail got but one, and many got none, as far as has been ascertained after careful inquiry.

THE BUILDINGS OCCUPIED BY THE SCHOOL DURING THE TIME OF THE FIRST THREE HEAD-MASTERS.

One of the things most strongly taught by the history of the Bingham School from 1793 to 1873 is that the teacher and not the school-house is the SCHOOL. President Garfield said that the greatest school he ever knew anything of, was himself sitting on one end of a log and Mark Hopkins on the other. The Rev. Wm. Bingham owned no academic building or dormitories of any kind at the first three locations of his school, Wilmington, Pittsboro, and Hillsboro. At "Mt. Repose," he invested less than a hundred dollars in a log school-house, which remained till about 1890, and he accommodated his boarders in log cabins which did not cost more than two hundred and fifty dollars ($250), and which remained till about 1885. W. J. Bingham, the School's second headmaster, never made any investment in dormitories, as he never boarded any of his pupils during the forty (40) years of his administration. He made no investment in academic buildings at Hillsboro, and he occupied a building at Oaks from 1845 to 1860 which cost less than five hundred dollars ($500). In 1860 the firm of W. J. Bingham & Sons built an academy at Oaks in which the two younger Binghams were equally interested. This building was abandoned in 1865, revert-

ed to W. J. Bingham and was sold for more than it cost him. Wm. Bingham, the third headmaster of the School, made no investments at all in academic buildings during his administration of eight years, from 1865 to 1873, and his log dormitories at Mebane, four rooms of which the School rented from him as temporary class rooms, were torn down and hauled away within three years after his death. He did not regard the location at Mebane as permanent. The School was located on land bought from W. B. Lynch, and the conditions on which the land should revert to him in case of the removal of the School from Mebane were provided for by a written contract between the parties concerned. The forty thousand dollars ($40,000) buildings of the Hillsboro Military Academy, erected by Col. C. C. Tew about 1858, being unoccupied after the Civil War for several years, the Bingham School opened negotiations with Mrs. Tew for the purchase of them, and Wm. and Robert Bingham visited her, inspected the property, and pressed the sale of it upon her. It was, however, encumbered not only by debt, but also by the widow's dower; and as Mrs. Tew declined to relinquish her right of dower, or to cease to live in the buildings, the Superintendent's purpose to buy the property was reluctantly abandoned. And failing in this effort to secure suitable buildings, he often spoke of selecting a permanent location for the school among the mountains of Western North Carolina.

THE BUILDINGS ERECTED BY ROBERT BINGHAM FROM 1873 TO 1891.

As has been already stated, the first two Binghams invested less than six hundred dollars in academic buildings during the seventy two (72) years of their administrations, from 1793 to 1865, except the academy building of 1860 at Oaks, which brought more than it cost the headmaster. Wm. Bingham made no investment at all in academic buildings or appliances during his administration of eight years, from 1865 to 1873. But the time has passed when the School could any longer command the best class of patrons and the highest tuition fees without academic buildings and appliances, and it had declined to the danger point when its fourth headmaster took charge of it in 1873. Other private schools had costly buildings. The founder of the Hillsboro Military Academy had erected a forty thousand dollars ($40,000) building about 1858, and the building of the Charlotte Military Academy, erected a little earlier, cost about the same. Colleges and Universities were everywhere building more and better than in their past. The handsomest and most costly buildings in many of the cities and towns in the North and West were their public schools, and a little later Boston put seven hundred and fifty thousand dollars ($750,000) in one of her public school buildings. In view of this demand for better school buildings everywhere, Robert Bingham began his superintendency by investing seventy-five hundred dollars ($7,-500) in an academic building and appliances: and when this building became too small for the expanding school, he enlarged it by an additional outlay of fifteen hundred dollars ($1,500.) This nine thousand dollar ($9,000) building was burned in 1882, and the Superintendent made an eleven thousand dollar ($11,000) investment in academic buildings and appliances, including the first Gymnasium in a Southern school, the only steam-heated and gas lighted bath house in a Southern school, and a two thousand dollar ($2,000) gas plant. These improvements are spoken of as follows by the U. S. Government Bureau of Education in its official "History of Education in North Carolina," already quoted, page 132. (1888). "The log huts in which the cadets were quartered when the school was first removed to its present site (at Mebane) have been replaced by frame buildings, with increased accommodations. The lecture halls, society halls and barracks are excellently equipped for their specific puposes, and a gymnasium and bath house, with swimming baths, have been added to the school buildings. The buildings are provided with gas."

THE SECOND FIRE AND THE CONSEQUENT REMOVAL OF THE SCHOOL IN 1891 TO ITS SEVENTH AND PERMANENT LOCATION.

In December, 1890, the academic buildings were burned a second time; and a little later a section of the dormitories were destroyed by fire. Under these circumstances the owner of the School could not rebuild a third time at a place where misfortune had crippled him in the past and where the fear of it would disable him in the future. For this cause he determined to abandon his still costly equipment, which the fire had spared, and to rebuild in brick at a seventh and permanent location of his own choosing, which should furnish the ideal climate, and in a form where the ideal conditions for health, comfort, safety from fire, discipline and instruction could be provided for in buildings of his own planning. After having tried the complete isolation of a location ten miles in the country, the first act of Wm. Bingham, the third headmaster, was to abandon such isolation by moving the School from Oaks to the railroad village of Mebane, with its double daily trains, telegraph office, etc. Of late years proximity to a large town has been secured or is in contemplation by most institutions of learning everywhere, commanding more than a merely local patronage. After his personal experience of the location at Oaks, ten miles from a railroad, then at the railroad village of Mebane, and finally near, but not in Asheville, the fourth headmaster congratulates himself on the advantages gained by his change of location, advantages which he did not realize till he got the benefit of them. Some of these advantages are, access to medical experts and trained nurses in case of sickness or accident, access to churches and the supervision of pupils by pastors of their parents' preference; the stimulation of an audience for literary, athletic and militay exercises; access to hotels and boaring-houses by parents wishing to visit their sons; access to a good market; the opportunity of securing distinguished lecturers; and the legitimate sources of entertainment, instruction and social training off the School grounds and out of study hours, so that the pupil may be in the world, and yet not of it.

ASHEVILLE'S CLIMATE AND ITS LOCATION AS AN EDUCATIONAL CENTRE.

Asheville furnishes the ideal climate and all the other attractions which the School had lacked for a hundred years. It is visited by forty thousand (40,000) Southern people in the Summer, and by sixty thousand (60,000) Northern people in the winter, and is the most famous all-the-year-round-health-resort in America. It has been chosen by George W. Vanderbilt and several other multi-millionaries, with the world to chose from, as a place of residence. And its being chosen by the Northern Presbyterian Church as the location of a two hundred and twenty five thousand dollar ($225,000) investment in school property for their benevolent work among Southern boys and girls; by A. A. Jones, late of Lexington, Mo., for his seventy-fice thousand dollar ($75,000) investment in the Asheville College for Young Women, and by the Bingham School for a sixty thousand dollar ($60,000) investment on its permanent location, is giving it great prominence as an educational centre, for which its magnificent climate and its being in the geographical centre of a circle touching Lake Erie on the North, the Atlantic on the East, the Gulf on the South and the Mississippi on the West eminently fit it. And the School finds that Asheville's physicians, its churches, its hotels, and boarding-houses, its audiences, its market, its distinguished citizens and visitors from whom lecturers can be selected, and its sources of

BIRD'S-EYE VIEW OF LIVINGSTONE COLLEGE—BUILDINGS AND GROUNDS.

legitimate pleasure and amusement, are advantages of great value.

THE NEW BUILDINGS.

An ideal location having been secured, a million and a quarter of bricks were laid in the summer of 1891 to accommodate only 120 pupils, quality and not quantity being the object aimed at. The form of the buildings was the result of the study of school buildings in many States of the Union and abroad, with a view to utility and safety rather than to mere appearance and cheapness. Prof. Raper, the State Historian of North Carolina Schools already quoted, speaks as follows of Robert Bingham and his work: "At William Bingham's death in 1873, his brother Robert became the fourth principal; and still (in 1897) guides the institution.

"His administration of twenty-four (24) years has been wise and progressive. The School had its first destructive fire in 1882 and another in 1890. The principal, immediately after the second fire, began to look for a new location. The city of Asheville (the location chosen) has a world-wide reputation for healthfulness and natural beauty. On one of the finest spots near by, the School is located. The buildings have the best possible ventilation and sanitary arrangements; they were made for health and utility and not for show. Their arrangement for managing boys is excellent. They are built of brick, one story high, and one room deep. The floors are doubled, with building paper between; and beneath the floor is a course of cement and slate to prevent dampness from rising. The rooms are made practically fire-proof. The site is two hundred and fifty feet above the French Broad, and the drainage is perfect. The dormitories are in eight sections; and a class room, with quarters for a teacher behind, is placed in the centre of each of the sections. To move the School to a far away location and to house it in buildings so well adapted to good discipline and good health required much judgment and skill. However, the Principal was fully equal to the demand. He had had a personal experience of thirty (30) years and the traditional experience of the School for almost a hundred. To his great experience he added a careful study of the educational systems of the whole country. Since its removal to Asheville the School has extended its field of patronage as well as made its equipment far better. Its expenses are still higher than other Schools in the State, and it has been a financial success. In 1895, in spite of the hard times, more than six thousand dollars ($6,000) were made from the earnings above the regular expenses. And its course of study has been extended in order to meet the demands of such a location and the times in which it exists."

This favorable opinion of the State's historian of schools is affirmed by the judgment of many prominent men from all parts of the country, who have visited the school in its permanent location at Asheville, including officials of the United States Government, officers of the Army and Navy, the heads of the Executicve and Military Departments of the State Government, and one of the members of the Judicial Department, distinguished educational, medical and architectural experts and other prominent men, who unite in saying that the Bingham School is a great forward movement in the all-important matters of sanitation, ventilation, safety, comfort, discipline and instruction. Among many similar endorsements the following are quoted: Vice-President Stevenson speaks as follows in a letter to Hon. Josephus Daniels, which appeared by permission in the North Carolinian of March 29, 1894, the original of which has been framed and placed in the Superintendent's office:

Vice-President's Chamber, Washington, D. C.

Hon. Josephus Daniels,

My Dear Sir:—It was my good fortune, a few days ago, to visit the Bingham School at Asheville, N. C. It is impossible to speak too highly of this celebrated institution. Its location, buildings, sanitation and water supply are all that could be desired. It would indeed be difficult to find a school whose location possesses equal natural advantages. The corps of teachers, moreover, is excellent. Under Maj. Bingham, its present efficient Superintendent, this historic school has more than sustained its well earned reputation. I take pleasure in commending it most earnestly.

Yours truly,

A. E. STEVENSON.

Rev. Edward Rondthaler, D. D., Bishop of the Moravian Church and President of the Board of Trustees of Salem Academy, speaks as follows over his signature:

"When in Asheville recently I was very much impressed with the visit I paid the Bingham School. I was delighted with its splendid situation on the French Broad bluffs, overlooking the same general scene which has made Mr. Vanderbilt's Biltmore mansion famous throughout the land. With the exception of Robert College, Constantinople, I can recall no institution in the world which has so royal a position. The street of school buildings which compose the Bingham School is, I think, nowhere surpassed in sanitary equipment, safeguards against fire, arrangement for ventilation, and provision for the proper exercise of discipline. Every consideration bearing upon the physical, mental and moral development of young manhood has been thought out and applied with an admirable foresight and enthusiasm in educational work. When to these advantages come to be added what I know of the scholastic and Christian opportunities offered, I believe the Bingham School to be one of the finest instances of the application of educational science to be found in our country or any other.

(Signed) EDWARD RONDTHALER.

From Karl Von Ruck, B. S. M. D., Medical Director of Winyah Sanitarium, Asheville, N. C.:

"I take pleasure in reporting the results of my recent inspection of the buildings and environments of the Bingham School. I find that its sanitary appointments are exceptionlly perfect and MUCH BETTER THAN I HAVE EVER FOUND BEFORE in the numerous public institutions I have heretofore examined. I have not one single suggestion to make for improvement. On the contrary, I commend its appointments as a standard well worth study and imitation of every similar institution in the land. The favorable climate of the Asheville plateau, the natural advantages of the school's location, its perfect system of sewerage, and its water supply (which my chemical and bacteriological examination shows to be absolutely pure), as well as the liberal and wholesome diet furnished, are matters of such importance as to justify the unqualified recommendation of this school for the education of youths whose parents or guardians consider the physical development and good health of the student of equal importance with mental culture.

(Signed) EARL VON RUCK, M. D.

Member of the Am. Pub. Health Association, Am. Clima tological Association.

From Dr. S. C. McGilvra, of West Superior, Wisconsin.

Office of McGilvra & Straw, 1303 Tower Av.,
West Superior, Wis., April 16, 1894.

To Whom it May Concern:

On the 24th of March last I made a very careful and critical inspection of the Bingham School at Asheville, N. C., and I was astonished at its high excellence in every detail. The location, the quarters, the class rooms, the gymnasium, the equipment, and service of the mess hall and kitchen, the ventilation, the drainage and sanitation are much the best that I have seen anywhere North, or South, and must appeal very strongly to the smaller but higher class of parents who are satisfied with only the best for their sons.

(Signed) S. C. M'GILVRA, M. D.

From Dr. F. V. Van Artsdalen, of Philadelphia, in "Odd Fellows' Siftings."

The most distinguished among all the educational institutions in North Carolina is the Bingham School. It stands pre-eminent among Southern schools for boys and ranks with the best in the Union. For sanitation and the principles of hygiene, I look upon it as not being surpassed by any similar or other institution in the world.

(Signed) F. V. VAN ARTSDALEN, M. D.

From Col. J. S. Carr, President of the Durham Tobacco Company.

I am pleased to have enjoyed the opportunity of making a trip to the celebrated Bingham School, at Asheville, and of going carefully over the premises. I need say nothing with respect to the curriculum, for the well-known repute of the school is older than I. But of the location, sanitation, etc., I desire to speak more particularly. It is beautiful as to location. The French Broad sweeps past the base of a bold cliff, upon which the institution is situated. For miles down the river towards Paint Rock the view is charming. And towards the south rise Pisgah and the Blue Ridge; towards the east one sees the Black Mountain, the late home of Vance, and the burial place of Mitchell. Then there is Vanderbilt's glittering in the sheen of the setting sun. How can such a location, enshrined in the home of the health giving ozone, be otherwise than charmingly, delightful and remarkably healthful for the school. From the way the land lies the drainage is natural, and nature has done her work perfectly. The sewerage is most perfect and complete, and the ventilation and sanitation of the buildings is perfect. Neither pains nor expense have been spared to make the barracks the most perfect living rooms I ever saw. Health and disciplinary care is written in every feature of the institution, and those IN SEARCH OF THE BEST need go no further. I am proud that North Carolina can boast of Bingham and Bingham School.

(Signed) J. S. CARR, Durham, N. C.

THE COURSE OF STUDY.

The course of study for the current (106th) year includes eleven (11) schools or departments, as follows:

The School of Military Science and Tactics.
The School of Gymnastics.
The School of English.
The School of Mathematics.
The School of Latin.
Each covering four years.
The School of Greek, covering three years.
The School of German.
The School of French.
The School of Physics.
The School of Chemistry.
The School of Commercial Science.
Each covering two years.

Besides the work in the Military Department, which is obligatory during the Fall and Spring on every member of the school not physically disabled, and the work in Gymnastics, which is obligatory during the Winter, when outdoor military exercises are suspended, each pupil is required to recite at least three times a day—once in English and once in Mathematics—while his third recitation is left to the option of parent or pupil, or to discretion of the teachers; and he may take as many more classes than the required three as his ability and the schedule of recitations will admit of. Each pupil is classed in any department by his actual knowledge of the subject; so that no one is held back in one department because he is backward or deficient in another; nor is he dragged over studies in advance of his knowledge in any department in order that he may be in the same year or grade all round. And as under the school's system of grading each pupil by an absolute standard, rigidly adhered to, the upper classes are disproportionately small, each new pupil is put as high as possible, that the upper and lower classes may be equalized as nearly as may be.

The work in the MILITARY DEPARTMENT consists of out-door drill of the whole corps, and of class room instruction of the cadet officers in the United States Infantry and Artillery Drill Regulations and Manual of Guard Duty, and of lectures on military subjects by the United States Army officer, detailed as Professor of Military Science and Tactics.

The work in the Department of Gymnastics consists of setting-up exercises, as prescribed by the United States Army, of exercises in the gymnasium and of the study of some sutiable manual of gymnastics.

The work in the School of English includes, during the four years' course, Reading, Writing, Spelling, Grammar, Dictation, Composition, Declamation, Geography, Rhetoric, History, English, Literature.

In the School of Mathematics, the first year is given to Arithmetic; the second year to Algebra, the third to Algebra and Geometry, the fourth to Algebra, Geometry and Trigonometry.

In the school of Latin the first year is given to the Grammar, and Caesar is begun; the second to the Grammar and Caesar, and Sallust is begun; the third to the Grammar and Sallust and Cicero, and the fourth to the Grammar, Virgil, Lily and Cicero—equivalents being always accepted, and the course being varied from time to time.

Written exercises are used throughout the course, and Roman History is studied during the fourth year.

In the School of Greek, the first year is given to the Grammar, and Xenophon is begun; the second to the Grammar and Xenophon and Demosthenes, or some equivalent is taken up; the third year, to the Grammar and to extracts from Homor, Lycias, or some equivalent; written exercises are used throughout the course and the History of Greece is studied during the third year.

In the School of German, the first year is given to the Grammar, and the second to the Grammar and to extracts from German classics.

In the School of French the first year is given to the Grammar, and the second to the Grammar and to extracts from the French classics.

In the School of Physics, the first year is given to studies suited to beginners; the second to more advanced pupils, with some studies in Electricity.

In the School of Chemistry, the first year is given to studies suited to beginners; the second to more advanced pupils.

In the School of Commercial Science, the first year is given to studies suited to beginners in Bookkeeping, and the second to more advanced pupils.

THE CHARGES.

The Bingham School has never offered cheap education or desired to be classed as a "cheap school" in the ordinary acceptation of the term, having always preferred quality and net income to mere quantity. With this end in view W. J. Bingham, after 1844, limited his school to thirty (30); W. J. Bingham and Sons limited theirs to sixty (60); and Robert Bingham has limited the capacity of his buildings to one hundred and twenty (120). The patrons of the school have always belonged to the smaller but higher class of parents who choose what is best rather than what is cheapest; and through the continued support of such patrons, from its beginning hitherto it has commanded somewhat higher tuition fees than any other institution of learning of any grade. in the State, and has attracted many pupils from other States at rates higher than the schools nearer home command. But those who know most of it and its methods say that in consideration of what a boy gets for what he gives in time and money, the Bingham School is cheaper than schools whose rates are lower.

THE ALUMNI OF THE SCHOOL.

It is a source of regret to the friends of the School that no roll of its Alumni exists. The records were imperfectly kept before 1857, and the more carefully kept records since '57 were lost in the fires of '82 and '90. But enough is known to justify the statement that the School's Alumni have been leaders of thought and action at home and abroad, in church and in State, in war and in peace. An Alumnus of the School has been Vice-President of the United States. Its Alumni have been Cabinet Officers; they have been Senators and Representatives in Congress from many States; they have been Governors and Judges in many States; an Alumnus of the School, who was Chief Justice of his State, is one of the very few American Jurists whose decisions are freely quoted in England; and three of its Alumni have filled a Governor's chair for three successive terms, a distinction enjoyed, as far as has been ascertained, by no other private school in the Union.

THE FUTURE OF THE SCHOOL.

Mr. F. B. Arendell, staff correspondent of the Raleigh News and Observer, after an official visit to the School speaks in his report over his signature of its FUTURE as follows:

"It is no wonder that such a school, with such a past, with a greater present, and with a future greater than its past and its prssent combined, should attract pupils this year from eighteen States in the Union, extending from Ohio and Wisconsin on the North, to Florida and Texas on the South, from the U. S. Army, and should reach outside of the United States to Mexico; nor is it to be wondered at that it actually brings to North Carolina for education probably more young men from outside of the State than all the other colleges and private schools for boys combined. The only wonder is that under the pressure of calamity by fire and the consequent change of location, of persistent rumors of temporary and permanent suspensions, under the pressure, too, of the long continued financial troubles which have swamped so many business enterprises all over the country, the wonder is that under all these untoward circumstances, the Bingham School has risen, Phoenix like, so grandly from its ashes, and that it should have equipped itself so grandly for another century of pre-eminence among Southern schools. The general public outside of North Carolina has already given its most unqualified approval by sending eighty (80) pupils to the School from eighteen (18) States during the current year; and every North Carolinian who has inspected it is enthusiastic in his concurrence with this judgment of prominent people from Ohio and Wisconsin on the North, through Florida and Texas to Mexico on the South."

HORNER SCHOOL, OXFORD, N. C.

In numbers actually attending private schools, North Carolina stands fifth or sixth in the United States; but in percentage of total school population, she stands first. This condition of the educational affairs of the State is due largely to the strong character of the men who have been at the head of the work throughout the State. In some instances the mantle of father has fallen on son for two or three generations, and thus methods and experience have been handed down by men whose lives were given up to the training of boys.

Notably in this class of schools stands the Horner Military school at Oxford, North Carolina, founded by the late James Hunter Horner, M. A., LL. D., nearly a half century ago. Many men, who are now leaders in thought and action in all parts of the United States, remember the strong individuality, scholarly attainments, and wonderful ability for imparting knowledge possessed by this eminent instructor, whose name must now occupy no insignificant place in the history of education in the South. Many years before his death Dr. Horner associated with himself his two sons, the younger of whom has been elevated to the Bishopric of the Jurisdiction of Asheville. Mr. J. C. Horner after twenty-four years work in the school is eminently fitted to carry on the work successfully. For forty-eight years the Horner School has steadily grown in influence and in fame, until today it stands among the foremost Preparatory Schools of the country.

The school is located on an eminence in the suburbs of the little town Oxford, which is on the Southern Railway, forty-five miles north of Raleigh, and one hundred and twenty miles south of Richmond, Va. The location is an ideal one for a school. The climate is delightful, there being comparatively few days in winter when out-door exercises and sports cannot be engaged in with benefit to boys. The buildings are commodious and in excellent condition. The main structure was erected in 1891 and planned with a special view to the requirements of a school for boys. Recitation-rooms, society halls, parlors, reading-rooms, and bed-rooms are all located in this building. Every door opens into the central hall, so that exposure in inclement weather is never necessary. The bed-rooms are large, comfortable, homelike, attractive and invite to study. They are neatly furnished in oak, with stained floors covered with rugs, and are supplied with patent fire escapes. The method of heating and ventilating is the best known to modern science. The air in the whole building in the coldest weather can be changed by the large ventilating fan every thirty minutes, and yet maintain temperature at 65 to 70 degrees.

The grounds are extensive, containing nearly three hundred acres, forty of which are within the corporate limits of Oxford. The large dairy farm and vegetable garden supply the boarding department with fresh vegetables and the best milk and butter. Every member of the faculty and all the ladies of Mr. Horner's family eat at the same tables with the cadets, and thus good table manners are maintained. In front of the main building is a well graded quarter-mile track for running and bicycle riding, enclosing foot-ball and base-ball grounds, and outside the track are tennis courts. These advantages add greatly to the efficiency of a school in a climate that admits of out-door sports for the whole year. The Harvard system of anthropometry, gymnastics, field and track athletics is used.

The Faculty at this time is especially strong. Three members have the M. A. degree, representing Davidson College, Harvard, and the University of North Carolina. Bishop Horner's place has been supplied by an M. A. of Harvard, who has taught for 25 years and speaks fluently four languages. He was pronounced the most scholarly man teaching the secondary schools of the State that surpasses all other States of the Union in point of scholarship. The other members of the Faculty are very strong men of cholarly instincts and high moral character and experienced teachers. Maj. Shirley, of Virginia Military Institute, has charge of the military instruction and his influence is very strongly felt throughout the school. He is impartial, punctual and attentive to duty.

The most marked features of the school are: The broad, yet accurate scholarship it imparts—the firm yet reasonable discipline it maintains—and the strong emphasis it lays on character, thus successfully imparting a sense of personal responsibility. To these may be added, the attention paid to the physical well-being of the students. The curricula cover all the ground necessary for the foundation of a liberal education. The boys are carefully taught how to study, and trained to use their faculties to the best advantage. The result has been that graduates entering the Universities and Colleges have found themselves well equipped for work.

OAK RIDGE INSTITUTE.

Oak Ridge Institute was founded in the year 1852 by Dr. John Saunders, Jesse Benbow, Allen Lowrey, James B. Clark, Wyatt Bowman and other public spirited citizens of Oak Ridge. They erected a commodious house, supplied it with an excellent library and a fine set of philosophical apparatus, and at their own expense employed the best teachers obtainable.

John M. Davis, a graduate of Emory and Henry College, Va., and Rev. D. R. Bruton, of the M. E. Church, were in charge of the school for the first few years, both men of sterling worth, peculiarly fitted by nature and training to lay the foundations of a great school. Founded and nurtured under these favorable auspices, the institution had won an enviable and extended reputation within and even beyond State lines at the outbreak of the Civil War; but like all other enterprises in the South, it went down under the pressure of those four dark years, many of its students volunteering at the outbreak of hostilities. In 1866 the building itself was reduced to ashes, but the public spirit which reared the first was not slow to rear the second on the same spot. From this date till 1875 the school was under the successive charge of Prof. O. C. Hamilton, at present of Union County, Hon. Pendleton King now keeper of the archives of the State Department, Washington, D. C., Rev. G. D. Hines, now of California, and Prof. W. S. Crouse, now Principal of the St. Michael's public schools, Md., all of them men of unusual scholarship and intellectual ability, but it took no rank as a permanent institution.

At that time Prof. J. Allen Holt took charge of the Institution, and in 1878, Prof. Martin H. Holt formed a partnership with him, and the school has been under their joint management ever since. The capacity of the building was doubled in 1879, the property purchased by the principals in 1884, and the subsequent history of the institution has been one of marvelous growth and prosperity. Additions have been made to the facilities and equipments almost every year. The Chapel and Literary Society Halls building, a mammoth three story building of brick, was built in 1884, at a cost of nearly $15,000. This is one of the most imposing school buildings in the State. It belongs to the classic style of architecture, and was designed by the late Lyndon Swain, Esq., of Greensboro, a well known architect. The chapel is one of the most pleasant and beautiful in the State. The Literary Society Halls are surpassingly beautiful. They are furnished with upholstered opera chairs, handsome Brussells carpets, Lincrusta-Walton walls, and frescoed ceilings and are graced with handsome paintings and statuary.

Again in 1892, Holt Hall, an immense and exceedingly handsome building, Romanesque in architecture, was erected at a cost of nearly $20,000, Epps & Hackney, architects, Greensboro, N. C. It contains eighteen large rooms, including Library, Gymnasium, Y. M. C. A. Assembly Room and Parlor Museum, as well as several class rooms. The Library, with its natural wood furnishings, convenient and spacious arrangement, is one of the most attractive to be found in the State. It contains several thousand volumes of well selected books, the best in literature, as well as reference books, Encyclopaedias, etc., etc. The gymnasium is very large, measuring about 60 feet square, with high ceiling, and is equipped with hundreds of dollars worth of apparatus, dumb bells, Indian clubs, vaulting horse, parallel bars, chest weights, etc., etc. The Y. M. C. A. is cosily and comfortably fitted up and tastily furnished. The class rooms are all arranged on the north side of the building to protect eyes of students. The plant is very complete, and in beauty of grounds and situation is unsurpassed in the country by any similar school. Among the men who have been here as teachers at the head of various departments are R. O. Holt (Ph. B., U. N. C.), now at Washington, D. C.; H. H. Ransom, now of City Schools, Galveston, Texas; Geo. S. Wills, (A. M. Howard), now Professor of English at Western Maryland College; S. L. Davis, (Ph. B., U. N. C.); A. B. Kimball, (Ph. B., U. N. C.), now attorney at law in Greensboro, and R H. Wright (B. S., U. N. C.)

What we are: Oak Ridge Institute is strictly a high grade preparatory school, with a business college department. It prepares for college, for business, for life. Those who expect to go to college, find here ample perparation in body, mind and morals, for a pleasant and profitable college career. They can go from the classes here to the Sophmore classes at most colleges. The course of study is four years in Latin; two years in Greek; Arthmetic, Algebra, Geometry, and plain Trigonometry in Mathematics; a thorough prepartory course in English Language and Literature, and an elementary course in Botany, Physics, Physiology, Astronomy and Chemistry. Those who do not or cannot go to college, find this course well suited to their needs and get here a valuable fitting for life. The Business College course is equal in all respects to that of the leading business colleges in the country. It includes thorough instruction in all the principles of Bookkeeping, simple and double entry; Commercial Law, Commercial Arithmetic, Shorthand and Typewriting (Ben Pittman System of Remington Typewriter) and Telegraphy.

NON-DENOMINATIONAL.

Oak Ridge Institute is strictly non-denominational; it has never been under the control of any church. Among its Trustees and Faculty are members of the various denominations, and almost all creeds have been represented among its students. It appeals for patronage on its intrinsic merits alone. All denominations are welcome, and there are no favors extended to one to the exclusion of the others.

It does not undervalue Christian education, and the

LIVINGSTONE COLLEGE (COL.), SALISBURY, N. C.

best efforts of the school are always exercised to build up the moral manhood of those intrusted to its charge.

Where is Oak Ridge Institute? It is situated in the northwestern part of Guilford County, fifteen miles northwest of Greensboro, forty minutes from Kernersville on the Southern Railway, and the same distance from Summerfield on the C. F. & Y. V. R. R.

The elevation is more than 1,013 feet above sea level; no malaria; sickness almost unknown; excellent views of the Blue Ridge and its spurs, Pilot Saura Town; "beautiful for situation," pure, cold water and fruitful orchards; fertile agricultural section, noted for the high tone and culture of its citizenship; beautiful farms and farm houses on every hand; noted for the absence of the specious temptations to bays incident to town and city locations; Christian homes for the boys, with plenty of good, wholesome food, pure milk and butter, comfortable quarters; enough oversight to protect, and enough freedom to develop manliness; encouragement to all kinds of out-door athletics; champion State school in 1898 on track athletics, and in baseball and football has not been defeated by a secondary school in twenty years.

What it is doing: Growing, strengthening, doing its best to fit men—"men of thought and men of action"—to fight the world's battles. More than three thousand have gone out into the various walks of life from these walls to bless this and other States. It had last year an enrollment of 281, which establishes the claim of Oak Ridge Institute to being the largest private fitting school in the South. The enrollment this year promises to be 300. Several handsome and convenient boarding halls have been built this year. The motto of the institution has long been the one recently adopted by the State, "Esse quam videri," and it is striving harder, year by year, to prove in every way worthy of this ideal. Over 50,000 students have up to date been educated here.

WHITSETT INSTITUTE,

WHITSETT, GUILFORD COUNTY, NORTH CAROLINA.

FACULTY.

WM. THORNTON WHITSETT, A. M., PH. D., President:
(North Carolina College. University of North Carolina.)

J. HENRY JOYNER,
(Whitsett Institute. University of North Carolina.)

WALTER CLINTON BLAGG,
(Shenandoah Institute. Kee Mar Conservatory.)

DELOS E. HAMMER,
(Guilford College. Whitsett Institute.)

WM. M. MONTGOMERY,
(Whitsett Institute. Eastman Business College.)

MISS MINNIE BELL MONTGOMERY,
(Whitsett Institute.)

EDMUND T. BURGESS,
(Shiloh Academy. Whitsett Institute.)

MRS. ELIZABETH HARLLEE,
(New England Conservatory, Boston, Mass.)

CHARLES BARNHARDT, Physical Director,
(Whitsett Institute.)

G. E. JORDAN, M. D., Hygiene,
(Baltimore College of Physicians and Surgeons.)

HISTORY.

Whitesett Institute was established in 1884, and has had an honorable record in the educational world during all the years of its history. Year after year its facilities have been increased to meet an ever widening patronage, until to-day from almost every section of North Carolina, and even from distant States, it gathers annually a student body numbering more than two hundrend students. In the earlier years of the institution, here labored Rev. Brantley York, D. D., Hon. Chas. H. Mebane, now State Superintendent of Public Instruction, and others well known in the world of educators. The school is regularly incorporated by the Legislature of North Carolina, with an authorized capital of one hundred thousand dollars. The school buildings, boarding halls, and dormitories are located in a beautiful oak grove of twenty acres. This is one of the few Southern schools for which the government has established a postoffice upon the school campus. There are no licensed saloons within a radius of five miles of the institute.

COURSES OF STUDY.

The work of Whitsett Institute is classified under various departments of courses of study, as follows:

PREPARATORY DEPARTMENT.

This department is for those who are not sufficiently advanced to enter the regular courses.

REGULAR LITERARY DEPARTMENT.

This department gives a full course of preparation in Mathematics, the Sciences and the Languages, and students completing the full course are received at Wake Forest College, Davidson College, the University of North Carolina, and other leading institutions without examination.

BUSINESS COLLEGE DEPARTMENT.

This department offers a complete course of business training in Boookkeeping, Commercinl Law, Typewriting, Business Practice, etc.

TEACHERS' NORMAL DEPARTMENT.

In this course students are prepared to teach in the public and private schools. No one completing this course has ever failed to obtain a first grade certificate.

DEPARTMENT OF MUSIC.

Instruction is here offered upon the piano, guitar, Mandolin, organ, etc.

ART DEPARTMENT.

Instruction is offered in this course in Crayon Drawing, Pastel, Oil, Free-Hand Drawing, etc.

TELEGRAPHY.

A course, preparing for actual service on railroad lines, is taught and every detail of the work is given.

EXPENSES.

Board is furnished at $7 to $7.50 per month. This includes furnished room, lights, etc. Tuition is $20 per term of five months. This makes a student's total expenses for five months about $55 or $60.

The school publishes a handsome Register in June of each year, and an illustrated quarterly journal, The Whitsett Student.

Within the past few years students have attended Whitsett Institute from the following States: North Carolina, South Carolina, Georgia, Virginia, Alabama, Mississsppi, Tennessee, Massachusetts, New York, Indiana, etc., etc. Each term generally has representatives from about one-third to one-half of the counties in North Carolina.

DAVIDSON COLLEGE, N. C.

RALEIGH MALE ACADEMY.

HUGH MORSON (University of Virginia), PRINCIPAL.

Prominent among the private preparatory schools of North Carolina stands the Raleigh Male Academy, founded in 1878 by Hugh Morson and Capt. J. J. Fray, both graduates of the University of Virginia.

For the past twenty years this school has prepared large numbers of the young men of Raleigh and other sections of the State for the University and Denominational Colleges of North Carolina, where they have always taken a high stand in their classes.

The object kept steadily in view is to fit boys for the higher classes in such institutions of higher learning, or for the active business pursuits of life. There is no curiculum, or division of the whole body of students by the rather inflexible classification so often practiced in the secondary schools, often at the sacrifice of thoroughness and to the detriment of many of the backward; but each pupil is placed in such classes in his various studies as he may be prepared to join with benefit to himself, and thus more attention is given to the individual and better results secured. A prominent place is given to the study of ancient languages and mathematics, as those best calculated to promote sound and thorough intellectual training.

The character of a school may be best judged by the results accomplished, and as evidence of the thorough work done at the Raleigh Academy, it may be mentioned that five of the physicians of Raleigh, and eight members of her bar, were prepared at this institution, while members distinguished in both professions are located at other points in the State or elsewhere.

The school is, besides, represented by more than three hundred of the successful business men and mechanics of the city and other places in the State.

The Academy occupies a most excellent location in the Northeastern part of the city near the street railway. The grounds contain two acres, affording ample facilities for athetlic sports and games, on which stands a large, well ventilated, and comfortable building, fully adapted to the requirements of the school.

The Principal is ably assisted by competent and experienced instructors, and no efforts are spared to do thorough work and give full satisfaction.

References and catalogues containing full information sent upon application.

THE BINGHAM SCHOOL, ORANGE COUNTY, NEAR MEBANE, N. C.

The beautiful and healthful home of this famous school in Orange County, near Mebane, has been well-known for a century. It is in the Piedmont section of North Carolina, on the Southern Railway, in the country. The accompanying sketch shows its Faculty of nine specialists, eight of whom are college and university graduates. The school has a first grade business course, including Short-Hand, Typewriting, Bookkeeping and Telegraphy, and while strictly non-denominational, yet is distinctly Christian in its teachings and influence. It is probably the only High School in the Union which employs one Profesor to teach the Bible Course alone—Rev. E. C. Murray, A. B., B. D., D. D. The course in Physical Culture is also a specialty, being in charge of a skilled physical director, and also a gymnasium director. A good table, low terms and home influences keep the school up to its ancient standard of excellence, while wisely managed athletics, including baseball, football, tennis and bicycling, help to maintain its popularity with the students.

REV. WILLIAM BINGHAM, who came from Ireland in 1785, established the school in 1793. He was the great-grandfather of the present owners, and attained great excellence and eclat in its management.

In 1825, his son, WILLIAM J. BINGHAM, inherited the school and continued its conduct in ORANGE COUNTY for thirty-nine years—until 1864. In that year COL. WILLIAM BINGHAM, father of the present owners and author of "Bingham's Latin Grammar," "Reader," "Caesar," "English Grammar," etc., became Principal, and incorporated the school under the name of "The Bingham School," continuing its conduct in ORANGE COUNTY, and at the same point, near Mebane, where it now exists, for nine years, until 1873.

After his death, his brother and the heirs of Col William Bingham, carried on the school, still in Orange, and near Mebane, for eighteen years, until 1891, when Col. Bingham's brother removed from Orange.

The next session HERBERT BINGHAM, son of Col. William Bingham, taught in Orange, the school for the next five years being conducted under the name and auspices of the church, but supported financially and otherwise by Mrs. William Bingham. In 1896 Herbert Bingham died, after laying the foundation for a most successful career.

After his death, PRESTON LEWIS GRAY, B. L., on the ceasing of the church name and control, became Principal of the Bingham Schoool, which is now being administered by him on the old grounds in ORANGE COUNTY, near Mebane, N. C. He is the son-in-law of Col. William Bingham, and under his guidance the number of students has nearly doubled and the high standard, demanded by the great history and distinguished Alumni of the school is maintained and its reputation increased.

BUIE'S CREEK ACADEMY AND COMMERCIAL SCHOOL.

REV. J. A. CAMPBELL, PRINCIPAL, Poes, Harnett County, N. C.

It is probable that no school in North Carolina, if, indeed, anywhere, has had so striking a history as this school. Prof. Campbell, just out from Wake Forest College, commenced a school, twelve years ago, in what was then the backwoods of Harnett County. The students numbered sixteen, and were gathered from the homes immediately around the small public school building in which the school was taught. From this small beginning has grown the splendid institution of to-day, with its ample buildings, large, well equipped Faculty and host of students, male and female (for the institution is co-educational), gathered from twenty counties in North and South Carolina.

The institution now has a Faculty of eleven teachers, educated at such institutions as Wake Forest College, N. C.; Trinity College, Durham, N. C.; Bryant and Stratton's Business College, Baltimore; Oxford Female Seminary, and Woman's College, Richmond, Va. Besides the regular academic branches, there are departments of Music, Art and Business, including Bookkeeping, Shorthand, Typewriting and Telegraphy. The military feature is optional. The school buildings present a handsome appearance. The Tabernacle, used for commencement occasions, seats 2,000 people. The Music and Art Departments are separate from the main building. The principal building is a three-story structure, with a wing on the north side. It contains a hall for the Business Department, two Society halls, a room for the Library, and six recitation rooms.

An arrangement for a boarding club, a number of boarding houses and a hotel, supply board at from $4 to $7 per month.

The school is non-sectarian, various denominations being represented both in the Faculty and in the student body, but everywhere the Christian spirit is manifest.

The school starting twelve years ago in a small way, with no capital except a man with religion, brains, executive ability and boundless energy, has grown with the years until last session saw two hundred and fifty-seven students, gathered from twenty counties. It has transformed Harnett County, and its influence is widening and deepening as the years come and go.

CHAPEL HILL SCHOOL—ITS HISTORY, GROWTH AND WORK.

FACULTY.

JOHN WILLIAM CANADA, A. B., PRINCIPAL,
(University of North Carolina.)
Greek, English, German and History.

CHARLES STAFFORD CANADA,
(University of North Carolina.)
Latin, Mathematics and Science.

JAMES HERBERT COLE,
(Eastman Business College.)
Bookkeeping and Commercial Law.

MRS. SALLIE MAY WILSON,
(Albemarle Collegiate Institute, Charlottesville, Va.)
Higher Grades and French.

MISS MARY E. DAVIS,
(Virginia State Normal.)
Intermediate Grades.

MISS FANNIE V. ATWATER,
(State Normal and Industrial College.)
Primary Grades.

MISS SALLIE M. STOCKARD, A. B.,
(University of North Carolina.)
Assistant in Preparatory Department.

MISS EFFIE M. KESSELMORE,
(School of Music, Salem, Ohio; N. E. Conservatory, Boston, Mass.)
Music — Vocal and Instrumental.

MISS MARY HARRIS,
(Art Students' League, New York.)
Art and Drawing.

Recognizing the need for a school in Chapel, Hill and believing that with time and work, a good school, even a large one, might be built up in the place, the Principal of Chapel Hill School, assisted by two lady teachers, opened a school for boys and girls in September, 1896. There being no school house, a residence was fitted up as well as possible, and the school opened with 35 pupils, the number increasing to 70 by the close of the term.

For the next term the school was so fortunate as to secure the house it occupies at present. A Music Department was added also. The year closed with a total enrollment of 135 pupils.

Preparations were made for a large opening the next year. Two teachers were added to the Literary Department, and departments of Art and Business were added. The second year opened with an atendance of about 100, this number increasing to 125 by the close of the first term, and the enrollment for the entire year reaching 165. This year saw the first graduating class of the school, two young ladies and eight young men, all of whom, save one, are now in the University and colleges. A cut of this class appears elsewhere in this Report.

[NOTE.—The word *faculty* was placed under the cut instead of *class* by mistake.

The third year of the school opened August 30th, the attendance for the first month being about 120, and the fall term about 145. This number is increasing and the attendance for the entire year will exceed that of the past year. The school now has a large and constantly growing patronage other than local.

The building, a cut of which appears in this book, is one of the best private school buildings in the State. It is well arranged and fully equipped with new furniture, desks, blackboards, charts, pianos, everything necessary for effective school work.

The school is organized as a Graded and Preparatory School. It has in its scope the work of six years as done in the city schools, and three years' work as done in the preparatory and high schools. The lower grade pupils are

in charge of the grade teachers, and the higher work in charge of the Principal and his assistants, who have had special training for their work.

The teachers are all well qualified, college-trained teachers, who have had experience in the work they have in charge.

The aim of the school is to give a thorough preparation for the University and colleges, and for those who will not go to college, a sound, practical education for the affairs of life.

SALEM BOYS' HIGH SCHOOL, SALEM, N. C.

This school was founded in 1794, and was conducted for over a century in the same building, but the patronage having increased so largely, the present commodious school edifice was erected in 1896, and thoroughly equipped as a first-class up-to-date school building, at a cost of $10,000. The school is conducted under the auspices of the Moravian Church, in Salem. It is recognized by the University as an affiliated school, its graduates being received there without examination.

There are three courses of instruction; The English, the Classical, and the Business Course. Graduates in the English Course complete more than is required for entrance to the Freshman Class at the University, and some have entered the Sophomore Class at college. The Classical Course embraces, in addition to the work done in the English, thorough drill in the principles of Latin, Caesar, Virgil and Cicero. The Business Course offers unusual advantages, as good as are found at business colleges. The efficiency and thoroughness of this department are attested by the very satisfactory manner in which its graduates in Short-Hand, Bookkeeping and Typewriting are filling responsible positions with large manufacturing establishments, leading law firms, and others. Of the present enrollment of 96 pupils, 42 are connected with the Business Course.

JAS. F. BROWER, Headmaster.

HOME INDUSTRIAL SCHOOL.

The Home Industrial School is situated in the suburbs of Asheville, about one mile south of the business center of the town. It is surorunded by a plot of ground, consisting of thirty-three acres, which it occupies jointly with the Normal and Collegiate Institute. This is the property of the Board of Home Missions of the Presbyterian Church, which has its headquarters in New York City. All the school work of that board being under the auspices of the Woman's Board, the women have, from the first, appointed all teachers and supplemented all expense beyond what the students are able to pay.

The Home Industrial School was organized by Rev. L. M. Pease, in October, 1887, and, until April, 1893, he was Superintendent of the institution, when he resigned on account of failing health. The purpose of the school is to place within the reach of girls, who would otherwise be deprived of educational avantages, an opportunity to secure an education, such as will enable them to become useful, self-supporting women. The capacity of the house for boarders is 115, and for ten years it has been full during the school term. The charge made for board and tuition is $50 for the school year of nine months, the only expense beyond this being for book rent and for instrumental music lessons.

The name of the school indicates its scope of work. It is a Christian home where the Scriptures are read and studied daily. Each member of the family has some share in ministering to the family comfort, as all the work of the house is done by the girls, under the direction and personal supervision of the Matron, just as the daughters in a family of moderate means work under the mother's direction. All the necessary family sewing is superintended by the sewing teacher. The work thus carried on lessens the expense of the institution, and, at the same time, gives the students an opportunity to become proficient in all departments of housekeeping and sewing. The work periods include six week's time, and at the close of each period every girl is assigned to a different kind of work, and by this method each one, during the year, has practice in all departments of housework. The principles of housework and household economy are taught in kitchen-garden classes. The Sewing Department gives training in plain sewing, in drafting, cutting and fitting of dresses, and in fancy work and embroidery. Besides the cooking that must necessarily be done for the family, each student has the advantage of twenty-four lessons in the Cookery Class, where scientific instruction is given and the instruction applied in the practical work done by the class.

The course of study begins with the primary grade and covers six years' work. Those who complete the course are competent to secure first-class certificates from County Superintendents of Public Instruction, but they are not well equipped teachers until after completing the course in the Normal and Collegiate Institute, which requires four years' additional study.

That the State has need of schools of this character, and that they are appreciated by the people, is proven by the fact that we have every year hundreds of applicants, who, for want of room, cannot be received.

FLORENCE STEPHENSON, Principal.

SHALLOTTE ACADEMY.

Shallotte, N. C., Aug. 18th, 1898.

Hon. C. H. Mebane,

State Supt. Pub. Inst., Raleigh, N. C.:

Dear Sir: The Faculty is composed of the students. By charging low tuition, they willingly assist me, and I believe they learn more rapidly; and as the specialty of the school is to prepare young men and ladies to teach in the public schools, I teach them how, as well as what, to teach. I opened a private school here in 1855. The notice was, all children wose parents were not able to pay, were admitted free. During the Confederate war the same privilege, and also all children, whose father was in the army, were admitted free.

When the war ended there were many young men returned mained, all of whom were admitted free, some here now doing well by accepting the offer.

In 1879 we erected a school building in the suburbs, known as Eureka School. In the year 1892, the present building was completed and well furnished with desks, blackboarding, globes, charts, wall maps, etc. It will comfortably seat 150 or 200 pupils.

The school is known as Shallotte Preparatory School.

The first session opened September 5th, 1892. The enrollment for the past six years has varied from 73 to 113 pupils. We have prepared 96 for teachers—75 males, 21 females.

The difficulty with the female teachers is, they soon marry and have a little school of their own at home; but I do not consider that lost labor; the greater loss is, the males are forced to abandon teaching in self-defence; for $20, or even $25, as the price per month—as is now offered—and that for only two months in the year, cannot feed and clothe them, and keep them abreast with the times; so, the first opportunity, they accept other occupations, and the result is, that men with devilish religion, no Christian, not even gentlemen principles, come in, and the committee, being ignorant, employ them for $10 or $12 per month, and they, caring nothing for the welfare of the rising generation, get more meanness into the children than the best teacher can get out in several years, if ever.

The school is still run with all the foregoing privileges, and also young men preparing for the ministry, and all children of ministers in good standing of Christian denominations are admitted on half tuition.

You will please select from this such only as in your judgment will redound to the promotion of popular education.

With great respect,

I am sincerely yours,

GEO. LEONARD.

WOODLAND HIGH SCHOOL

Northampton County, N. C., was founded about the year 1875, being one of the first high schools in the county.

The object of the school was, from the first, and is now, to give boys and girls a better opportunity for fitting themselves for life's work than is offered by the public schools, and to prepare those for college who can go. About sixty pupils are enrolled each year. The school has done much good and its friends are standing by it yet.

The following gentlemen have been Principals: J. H. Picot, J. W. Fleetwood, C. J. D. Parker and N. W. Britton. The last named is Principal now.

WANCHESE HIGH SCHOOL.

REV. CHAS. R. TAYLOR, Principal; MRS. C. R. TAYLOR and MISS HATTIE S. TAYLOR, Assistants.

This institution was begun in 1895, at a cost of $1,800. Its establishment was due to the efforts of Misses Ophelia and Sophronia Langston, the accomplished daughters of Rev. G. D. Langston, of the North Carolina Conference. These ladies had the active encouragement of their father and Rev. R. B. John, and were supported in the enterprise by such progressive men as E. R. Daniels and S. C. Pugh.

The children, by arrangement of the School Board with the Principal, have the advantage, during the public school term, of receiving instruction in the branches required to be taught by law, free of charge. The enrollment for free school is 100, for entered school 70.

In addition to the simple English course, our pupils study Latin, Greek, French, Algebra, Geometry, Music and Art. Under the present management, pupils can prepare themselves to enter Trinity, the University or any other college in the State, male or female.

MOUNT MORIAH MALE AND FEMALE ACADEMY.

Mt. Moriah Male and Female Academy is located in the southern part of Wake County, one and a half miles from Auburn, N. C., ten miles southeast of Raleigh, and on the North Carolina Railroad. The building was erected in 1894, by thirteen stockholders.

The stockholders constitute the Board of Trustees. They have the general direction and management of the school—as employment of teachers, etc. By their written constitution, or agreement, it is stipulated that all stockholders shall share the losses and gains of the school in proportion to the amount of stock held by each; and that any stockholder who refuses to bear his proportional part of the losses forfeits his stock.

The Academy is chartered, and by provision of the charter all children of school age in Wake county living in any adjoining school district may attend the school and their proportional part of the school fund may be drawn by the teacers of said Academy. (In redistricting under the new school law a public school is to be taught there regularly.)

The school building is 24x40 feet, with separate music and recitation rooms, and is furnished with modern desks, blackboards, &c. It is situated on a high elevation and in the midst of a remarkably healthy locality, having pure water and pure air. The Mt. Moriah locality has long been known for the high, moral and Christian character of its people.

EXPENSES—TUITION, &c.

Primary	$ 1.00
Intermediate (including Mathematics)	1.50
Academic (including English Grammar)	2.00
Advanced (including Algebra)	2.50

Languages—Latin, Greek, French, each, ...	.50
Not taught the present year—Instrumental music..	3.00
Vocal music—special lessons	1.00
Incidental fee (per session)	.25
Board, per month—all included (lights, laundry, etc. $5.00 to	7.00

All expenses payable quarterly.

The school was presided over the first two years by J. E. Yates, the third year by L. C. McIntosh, the present year by J. P. Canaday. The enrollment for the past year was above 60.

The school continues ten months in the year.

Respectfully,

J. P. CANADAY

CARY HIGH SCHOOL—CARY, N. C.

E. L. MIDDLETON, Principal.

Cary has for twenty years been a quiet cultured village. Many men of distinction have shown an active interest in her school. During the summer of 1896, Rev. C. W. Blanchard purchased the school property and organized a stock company.

Many showed an active interest in the school. Rev. Jno. E. White, J. C. Angier, F. R. Gray, Rev. A. D. Hunter, and Rev. C. W. Blanchard were chosen directors. Four well equipped teachers were employed. The patronage was at first largely local, but by united effort the school has drawn patronage from fourteen counties and two States during the present year. The following things may be said regarding location, teachers, course of study, &c.:

No more desirable location can be found, since Cary is at the junction of the two leading railroads in the State.

The health record cannot be surpassed.

No village has a purer moral atmosphere.

The school is distinctly a Christian school.

The course of study is comprehensive and practical.

The teachers are well prepared by learning and experience and are enthusiastic and faithful in their work.

The work done is not for show but for thorough mental drill and a broad and practical knowledge of men and things.

The school building is convenient in arrangement, well equipped in all departments and neat in appearance.

The Clay Society for boys, and the Browning Society for girls, are a great aid in fitting pupils for the highest duties of life.

The lecture course is a delight and of great profit to the entire community.

The current history class sees public affairs—social, political, religious, etc.,—as they are, and not as they will appear on the pages of history in the future.

The course in English is not surpassed by any school in the State. The motto in this department is—"Read much—write much."

The work in the Music Department is of the highest order.

The charges for tuition and board are low considering the advantages offered.

THE CONCORD HIGH SCHOOL, CONCORD, N. C.

The Concord High School is a successor of a number of unsuccessful attempts to carry on a high school in Concord. The school, as at present constituted, was organized in 1895 by Holland Thompson, a graduate of the University of North Carolina, who has had charge ever since.

The school receives no primary pupils, but asks an age time of twelve, and advancement sufficient to allow the pupil to study Latin with profit. Large numbers are not desired, as the personal element in teaching is very much stressed in this institution. The results have been satisfactory. The pupils have usually taken a high stand in the different colleges which they have attended, and over ninety per cent. of the graduates do attend some institution of higher learning.

The first assistant was Walter R. Thompson. The assistant for the past two years has been Mr. Jay D. Lentz, also a graduate of the University.

Note.—This matter was not received in time to be put in with other city schools, hence it appears here.

STATESVILLE PUBLIC SCHOOLS, STATESVILLE, N. C.

The Statesville Public Schools were authorized in 1891, by act of the Legislature, and by vote of the citizens of the town. Messrs. Wm. M. Robbins, A. D. Cowles, J. H. Hill, L. Harrill, L. C. Caldwell and William Wallace were elected and constituted the first school board. Much is due these gentlmen for their untiring efforts in the establishment of these schools.

Prof. D. Matt. Thompson was elected the first Superintendent. He has been unanimously re-elected with each succeeding year, and under his management there has been very much less friction than usually come to new schools of this character. Superintendent Thompson has had an experience of more than twenty-five years as a successful manager of public and private schools.

The schools were first opened on the 23d of September, 1891, in five buildings, three for white and two for colored. New buildings were erected for both races during the year 1892. These buildings are commodious, comfortable and well-arranged. The building for the white school is particularly well suited for its purpose, having been planned and built under the direction of the Superintendent. It is heated by furnaces and contains class rooms, office, library and an excellent auditorium.

Since the organization of the schools there has been a steady growth, both in numbers and the kind of work done. The increase in attendance since the schools were established has been more than 30 per cent. greater than the increase in population since that time.

The course of study extends through eight grades, or years, in the white schools and six in the colored, and is broad, thorough and practical. English, Civil Government, Nature Work and History of North Carolina are especially emphasized. A certificate is granted to those that satisfactorily complete the course. There are now in college twelve pupils from the white schools. The results of these schools, directly and indirectly, have surpassed the most sanguine expectations of their most hopeful friends.

The Public Schools of Statesville are noted on all sides to be a grand success, and they are a monument to the foresight and generosity of her citizenship, and are justly the pride of the town. The schools are supported by a direct tax of three mills on property and ninety cents on the poll, and the pro rata portion of the Public School

INDEX.

PART ONE.

	PAGE.
Letter of Transmittal	3
Introduction	4
Recommendations to the General Assembly of North Carolina—	
State Board of Examiners	5
County Board of Education	6
Supervisors	9
School Committeemen	11
Township system	12
Duties of Township Committee	14
Colored Normal Schools	15
Text Books	17
Ohio Text Book Law	21
Text Books, Price in California	24
Text Books, How Adopted by the Different States	25
More Public School Money Attainable	34
Rates of Railroad Taxation for Schools in Different States	37
Local Taxation	42
School Attendance	46
Civil Government	47
Official Standing of this Office	48
Relation of this Office to Party Politics	48
Relation of this Office to Private Schools and Denominational Colleges	49
School Fund, Supervision of	50
Letters from County Supervisors—	
J. M. Loringood, Cherokee	53
R. W. Askew, Bertie	54
Plummer Stewart, Union	56
W. P. Jervis, Madison	57
R. B. Lineberry, Chatham	58
W. M. McIntosh, Yancey	59
L. H. Michael, Watauga	59
J. W. Jones, Ashe	59
J. R. Tingle, Pitt	59
W. H. Sellars, Columbus	60
H. S. Aviritt, Cumberland	61
L. M. Conyers, Nash	61
M. N. McIver, Richmond	61

Letters from County Supervisors— PAGE.
H. L. McGowan, Hyde 62
H. T. J. Ludwig, Cabarrus 63
J. H. Patterson, Yadkin 63
L. Bassnight, Dare 63
J. A. Anthony, Cleveland 64
Jno. W. Williams, Surry 64
R. B. Hunter, Mecklenburg 64
Francis Picard, Perquimans 65
Geo. L. Reynolds, Montgomery 66
Gaston Pool, Pasquotank 66
Augustus Masters, Mitchell 67
E. P. Ellington, Rockingham 67
David L. Ellis, Buncombe 68
Official Letters of Superintendent from Apr. 1897, to Nov. 1898 70–100
Address of Superintendent Before Teachers' Assembly at Morehead City, 1897 100
Expressions of Interest From Public Schools—
University of North Corolina 104
Trinity College 105
Wake Forest College 106
Davidson College 106
Catawba College 107
Guilford College 107
Claremont College 108
Oak Ridge Institute 109
Whitsett Institute 110
Bingham School 110
Peabody Education Fund, and Peabody Scholarships in Peabody Normal at Nashville, Tennessee 111
Peabody Fund, Disbursed 1897–1898 114
Peabody Scholarships for North Carolina 117
Apportionment of Public School Fund by State Board of Education 120
School Fund, Receipts and Disbursements, 1897–1898 123
Census of School Children from 6 to 21 years old, 1897–1898 123
Enrollment in Schools, 1897–1898 123
Percentage of School Children Enrolled, 1897–1898 124
Average Attendance, 1897–1898 124
Percentage of School Population in Average Attendance on Schools, 1897–1898 124
Percentage of Enrollment in Average Attendance, 1897–1898 124
Average Length of School Term 124
Average salary of Teachers 124
Value of Public School Property 124
Number of School Houses 125
Number of Public Schools Taught 125
Number of School Districts Reported 125

	PAGE.
Comparative Statistics, 1884 to 1898—	
Receipts	125
Census from 6 to 21 years	125
Enrollment	126
Average Attendance	126
Average Length School Term	127
Average Salary of Teachers	127
Value of Public School Property	127
Number of Public School Houses	129
Number of Public Schools Taught	129
Number of Districts Reported	130
Townships with Special Donations	132
Townships Voted Local Tax	134
Normal Department Cullowhee High School	135
Normal Schools of the Colored Race—	
Names of Local Boards of Managers and Principal	139
Report of State Normal, Winston	139
Relation of Slater Industrial Academy to the Normal School as Provided by Act of Legislature of 1895	143
Report of State Normal, Goldsboro	144
Report of State Normal, Salisbury	146
Report of State Normal, Fayetteville	150
Report of State Normal, Elizabeth City	153
Sketch of State Normal, Plymouth	159
Report of State Normal, Plymouth	162
Report of State Normal, Franklinton	165
State Board of Examiners	169
First Grade Life Certificates	170
Examinations for First Grade Life Certificates, 1897—	
History	172
Physics	173
Physiology and Hygiene	174
Algebra	175
School Law	176
Arithmetic	177
Geography	178
Civil Government	179
English Literature	180
Elementary Psychology	181
English Composition	182
Botany	183
English Grammar	184
Examination for Applicants for Life Certificates, 1898—	
History	185
Arithmetic	186
Civil Government	187
Physiology and Hygiene	188

	PAGE.
Examination for Applicants for Life Certificates, 1898—	
English Literature	189
School Law	190
Physics	191
English Grammar	192
Algebra	193
Botany	194
Psychology	195
Geography	196
Course of Study for Teachers in the Public Schools of North Carolina by State Board of Examiners, 1898	197
Reading	200
Phonic Method	201
Spelling	205
Writing	205
English	205
Lessons on the Sentence	206
Lessons on the Noun	207
Lessons on Kinds of Sentences	208
Lessons on Errors	209
English Literature	210
Teachers' Course	211
Geography	212
Analysis of North America	212
Teachers Course	214
History	214
Purpose of History Reading	214
How and When to Introduce	215
What to Teach Each Class	215
Snggestions to Teachers	215
Teachers' Course	216
Pedagogical Library	217
Civics—Brief Course	217
Outline of Work	218
Duties of Citizens	222
Arithmetic	222
Physiology and Hygiene	226
Botany	227
School Room Suggestions	228
Care of School Room	229
Recess	229
Punishment	229
School Museum	230
The Care of Eyes of School Children—by R. H. Lewis, M. D	230
The Care of The Teeth—by N C. State Board Dental Examiners	235

	PAGE.
Public School Law Explained—	
Formation of Districts	236
School Near Township Line.	236
Balance on Ledger	237
Old Contracts	237
Next Apportionment—How Made	237
Name of School Districts	238
How Schools are Graded	238
Salaries of Teachers and Length of Term	239
Taking the Census	240
Average of Sixty-five Pupils	240
Small Attendance	242
List of County Supervisors and Members of the County Board of Education	243
Proceedings of Meeting of Supervisors in House of Representattves December 30, 1897	255
Table I—1897—	
Showing School Fund Received by County Treasurer	278
Table II—1897—	
Showing School Fund Disbursed by County Treasurer.	282
Table III—1897—	
Showing Number of Children Between 6 and 21 Years old. Number Enrolled; Average Attennance; Institute Statistics of State During Year Ending June 30	286
Table IV—1897—	
Showing Number Public School Districts, School Honses, Schools Taught; Value of Public School Property; Average Length of Term; Average Monthly Salary for School Year Ending June 30, 1897.	290
Table V—1897—	
Showing Number of Teachers Examined and Approved—Race, Sex, Grade	294
Table VI—1897—	
Showing Number of Pupils of Different Ages. From 6 to 21 Years, Studying Different Branches	298
Table VII—1897—	
Showing Amount Apportioned to White and Colored; Assessed Value of Property of White and Colored; Insolvent Polls; Poll Tax Levied; Amount Applied to Schools	302
Table I—1898—	
Showing School Fund Received by County Treasurer.	306
Table II—1898—	
Showing School Fund Disbursed by County Treasurer	310
Table III—1898—	
Showing Number of Children Between 6 and 21 years; Nnmber Enrolled; Average Attendance; Institute Statistics	314

	PAGE.
Table IV—1898—	
Showing Number of Public School Districts; School Houses; Schools Taught; Value of Public School Property; Average Length of Terms; Average Monthly Salary of Teachers	318
Table V—1898—	
Showing Number of Teachers Examined and Approved—Race, Sex, Grade;	322
Table VI—1898—	
Showing Number of Pupils of Different Ages, from 6 to 21 Years, Studying Different Branches	326
Table VIII—1898—	
Showing Amount Apportioned to White and Colored; Assessed Value of Property of White and Colored; Insolvent Polls; Poll Tax Levied; Amount Applied to Schools	334
List of Teachers, by Counties	338
North Carolina Teachers Assembly	353
Association of Academies of North Carolina	358
County Institutes	360
County Institute Work—	
Report by P. P. Claxton	360
Report by J. Y. Joyner	363
Report by F. H. Curtis	365
City Public Schools—	
Greensboro Public Schools	369
Charlotte Public Schools	373
Wilmington Public Schools	376
Raleigh Public Schools	378
Wilson Public Schools	380
Asheville Public Schools	382
Durham Public Schools	384
Reidsville Public Schools	389
Mt. Airy Public Schools	391
High Point Public School	393
Goldsboro Public School	397
The Place of the Academy in our Educational System, by W. T. Whitsett	400
Historical Sketch of the Office of Superintendent of Public Instruction, by C. H. Mebane	410
Sketch of the History of Education in North Carolina, by C. H. Wiley	428
History of Public Schools, by Dr. Stephen B. Weeks	503
Sketches of Some Old or Extinct Schools in the Counties of North Carolina, by Kemp P. Battle, LL. D.	575
Schools in Tennessee When Part of North Carolina	579
Sporadic Educational Minutes	580
Attempt to Obtain Public School Failed	580

Sketches of Some Old or Extinct Schools, etc.— PAGE.
List of Authors 581
Alamance........ 584
Alexander 586
Alleghany........ 587
Anson 587
Ashe 589
Beaufort........ 589
Bertie 590
Bladen........ 593
Brunswick 594
Buncombe 595
Burke........ 598
Cabarrus........ 600
Caldwell........ 603
Camden........ 606
Carteret 606
Caswell........ 607
Catawba 609
Chatham 610
Cherokee........ 612
Clay........ 613
Chowan........ 613
Cleveland........ 616
Columbus........ 616
Craven 616
Cumberland 619
Currituck 622
Dare 623
Davidson........ 623
Davie 625
Duplin 627
Durham 629
Edgecombe........ 629
Forsythe........ 631
Franklin 632
Gaston 635
Gates........ 635
Graham........ 635
Granville........ 636
Greene........ 640
Guilford........ 640
Highpoint Public Schools 642
Halifax........ 645
Haywood 646
Henderson........ 646
Hertford 647

Sketches of Some Old or Extinct Schools, etc.— PAGE.
Hyde.... 649
Iredell.... 651
Jackson.... 655
Johnston.... 655
Jones.... 656
Lenoir.... 657
Lincoln.... 658
McDowell.... 659
Macon.... 659
Madison.... 660
Martin.... 661
Mecklenburg.... 662
Mitchell.... 666
Moore.... 666
Montgomery.... 668
Nash.... 668
New Hanover.... 670
Northampton.... 674
Onslow.... 675
Orange.... 675
Pamlico.... 684
Pasquotank.... 684
Perquimans.... 686
Pender.... 687
Person.... 687
Pitt.... 688
Polk.... 688
Randolph.... 689
Richmond.... 690
Robeson.... 690
Rockingham.... 692
Rowan.... 693
Rutherford.... 695
Sampson.... 696
Stanly.... 698
Stokes.... 698
Surry.... 698
Swain.... 700
Transylvania.... 700
Tyrrell.... 700
Union.... 702
Vance.... 702
Wake.... 703
Warren.... 710
Washington.... 716
Watauga.... 716

Sketches of Some Old or Extinct Schools, etc.— PAGE.
Wayne 717
Wilkes........ 718
Wilson 719
Yadkin 720
Yancey 721
Addenda 722
Early Legislation for Public Schools........ 725

PART TWO.

STATE COLLEGES AND INSTITUTIONS.

Introduction........ 3
University of North Carolina 6
Resolutions of the Faculty of the Normal and Industrial College 20
Report of State Normal and Industrial College........ 21
North Carolina College of A. & M. Arts........ 47
A. & M. College, Colored, Greensboro 53
Sketch of Education of Deaf in North Carolina........ 60
North Carolina Institution for Deaf and Dumb and Blind, Raleigh 63

DENOMINATIONAL COLLEGES.

General Introduction to the Christian Colleges of North Carolina 68
Trinity College 72
Outlines of History of Wake Forest College 80
Davidson College........ 83
Guilford College 99
St. Mary's College, Belmont 102
Greensboro Female College........ 107
Roper Female University........ 112
Peace Institute, Raleigh........ 113
Oxford Seminary........ 116
Catawba College........ 118
North Carolina College 120
Weaverville College 122
Claremont College. 124
Salem Academy and College 127
Asheville Normal and Collegiate Institute 130
Shaw University 134
Livingston College........ 138
Scotia Seminary........ 143
Bingham School, Asheville 146
Horner School 171
Oak Ridge Institute 174
Whitsett Institute 178
Raleigh Male Academy........ 181

HIGH SCHOOLS AND ACADEMIES.

	PAGE.
Bingham School, Mebane	183
Buies Creek Academy	185
Chapel Hill School	187
Salem Boys School	190
Home Industrial School, Asheville	191
Shallotte Academy	193
Woodland High School	195
Wauchese High School	196
Mt. Moriah Male and Female Academy	197
Cary High School	199
Concord High School	201
Statesville Public School	202

LIST OF ILLUSTRATIONS.

PART ONE.

PAGE.

C. H. Mebane, Superintendent Public Instruction 1
State Normal College, Greensboro 17
Claremont College, Hickory 32
Glimpse in Campus, University North Carolina. 49
Alumnus Hall Building, University North Carolina......... 64
A Campus View, University North Carolina 81
Main Building Chapel Hill School 96
Smith Hall Library, University North Carolina.. 113
Commons Hall, University North Carolina 128
Old East Building, University North Carolina.............. 145
Library, University North Carolina.... 160
Philanthropic Hall, University North Carolina 177
New East Building, University North Carolina 192
Faculty Chapel Hill School............ 209
Whitsett Institute, Whitsett, N. C 224
Trinity College, (Front) Durham 241
Trinity College Technological Building. 256
Trinity College, Epworth Hall 273
Trinity College, Washington Duke Building 288
A. & M. College, (Colored) Greensboro... 369
A. & M. College, (Colored) Greensboro 384
Lindsey St. Public School, Greensboro 403
Ashboro St. Public School, Greensboro 418
Geeensboro Female College......... 435
Scotia Seminary, Concord 450
Guilford College 467
Guilford College...... 482
Memorial Hall, Guilford College 499
Guilford College 514
Administration Building, Shaw University............. 531
Estey Hall, Shaw University.... 546
Salem Female Academy 563
St. Mary's College; General View. Belmont... 578
Missionary Training School, Shaw 595
Medical Dormitory, Shaw.... 610
Geo. H Crowell 627
High Point Public School.............................. 642
Industrial Building, (new) White D. & D. Institute, Raleigh .. 631
Auditorium, (new) D. & D. Institute, Raleigh 638
Industrial Building, (new) D. & D. Institute, Colored......... 647

PAGE.
Main Building, (New Wing) D. & D. Institute, Colored........ 654
Leonard Medical Building, Shaw........................... 659
Pharmacy Building, Shaw.................................. 674
Baptist Female University................................ 707

PART TWO.

Chapel, Shaw University.................................. 1
Bell St. Public School, Statesville...................... 5
Buies Creek Academy, Poes, N C........................... 12
Shaw Hall, Shaw University............................... 16
Faculty of Bingham School, Mebane........................ 21
State Agricultural and Mechanical College................ 28
Normal College Institute, Asheville...................... 37
Oxford Female Seminary................................... 44
Lathe Room, A. &. M. College............................. 49
Horticultural Department A. & M. College, Raleigh........ 64
Livingston College, (Colored) Sa isbury.................. 69
Y. M. C. A Hall, Davidson College........................ 76
Philanthropic Hall, Davidson College..................... 76
Oak Ridge Institute...................................... 81
Wake Forest College...................................... 85
Wake Forest College...................................... 92
Cary High School... 96
A. & M College and Grounds, Raleigh...................... 101
Y. M. C. A. Guilford College............................. 108
St. Mary's College, Main Building, Belmont............... 113
Dumbbell Exercise, Main Hall, Horner School, Oxford...... 117
Faculty Oak Ridge Institute.............................. 124
Home Industrial School, Asheville........................ 128
Catawba College, Newton, N. C............................ 133
A. & M. College (Colored) Greensboro..................... 140
Horner School, View from Barracks........................ 149
Horner School, View Towards Barracks..................... 156
Livingston College, Birds-Eye-View....................... 161
Livingston College....................................... 176
Davidson College... 181
Davidson College, Main Building.......................... 188

Lightning Source UK Ltd.
Milton Keynes UK
UKHW010614200119
335821UK00008B/663/P

9 780265 971017